W9-CEV-879

Peasants and Politics in Kampuchea, 1942–1981

WITHDRAWN

Ben Kiernan and Chanthou Boua

Dedication

for Boua Kim Meua
Chea Neat
Boua Chan Vuthy
Boua Chan Vuthea
Boua Chantha
Boua Visoth
Boua Vises
Boua Somnea
Boua Somealea

Born of tears, raised on hunger, possessing only poverty,
Waited on by suffering, through till death, destiny begins again,
A life as a slave of the leisure class, because of the royalist system,
And the selfish class that bloodily exploits the subject people who love their country.

Keng Vannsak
from *Khemara Niset*, Paris, no. 14, August 1952

Zed Press, 57 Caledonian Road, London N1 9DN

M.E.Sharpe Inc., 80 Business Park Drive, Armonk, New York 10504

Peasants and Politics in Kampuchea, 1942-1981, was first published in 1982 in the United Kingdom by Zed Press, 57 Caledonian Road, London N1 9DN and in North America by M.E.Sharpe Inc., 80 Business Park Drive, Armonk, New York 10504.

Copyright © Ben Kiernan and Chanthou Boua, 1982

Copyedited by Beverley Brown
Proofread by Penelope Fryxell
Cover design by Jacque Solomons
Printed by Redwood Burn, Trowbridge, Wiltshire.

All rights reserved

Burgess
DS
554.8
P4
1982
c.2

ISBN: Hb 0 905762 60 6 (UK)
Pb 0 905762 80 0 (UK)
Hb 0-87332-217-7 (USA)
Pb 0-87332-224-X (USA)

Library of Congress Cataloging in Publication Data
Main entry under title:

Peasants and politics in Kampuchea, 1942-81.

Contributions in English; some translated from the Khmer and French
Includes bibliographical references and index.
1. Cambodia – politics and government – Addresses, essays, lectures. 2. Peasantry – Cambodia – Addresses, essays, lectures.
I. Kiernan, Ben.
DS555.8.P4. 959.6'04 82-5451
ISBN 0-87332-217-7 AACR2
ISBN 0-87332-224-X (pbk.)

British Library Cataloguing in Publication Data

Peasants and politics in Kampuchea 1942-1981

1. Cambodia – History
I. Kiernan, Ben II. Boua, Chanthou
959.6'04 DS554.8

ISBN 0-905762-60-6
ISBN 0-905762-80-0 Pbk

Contents

Acknowledgements

We would particularly like to thank Michael Vickery for allowing us to publish "Looking Back at Cambodia, 1942-76", and the School of History, University of New South Wales for making possible the translation from Khmer of Hou Yuon's *The Cooperative Question.*

In preparing this book, we have also benefitted greatly from discussions and exchanges with Anthony Barnett, Wilfred Burchett, the late Malcolm Caldwell, Timothy Carney, David Chandler, the late Peggy Duff, Denis Gray, Prudhisan Jumbala, Muy Hong Lim, Tony Malcolm, David Marr, Gavan McCormack, Jacques Nepote, Val Noone, William Shawcross, Chalong Soontranavich, Julie Southwood, Keng Vannsak and over a hundred other Khmers – many of them refugees – who unfortunately cannot be named here.

We would also like to thank the peasants of Phluang village, with whom we lived for three months in 1979.

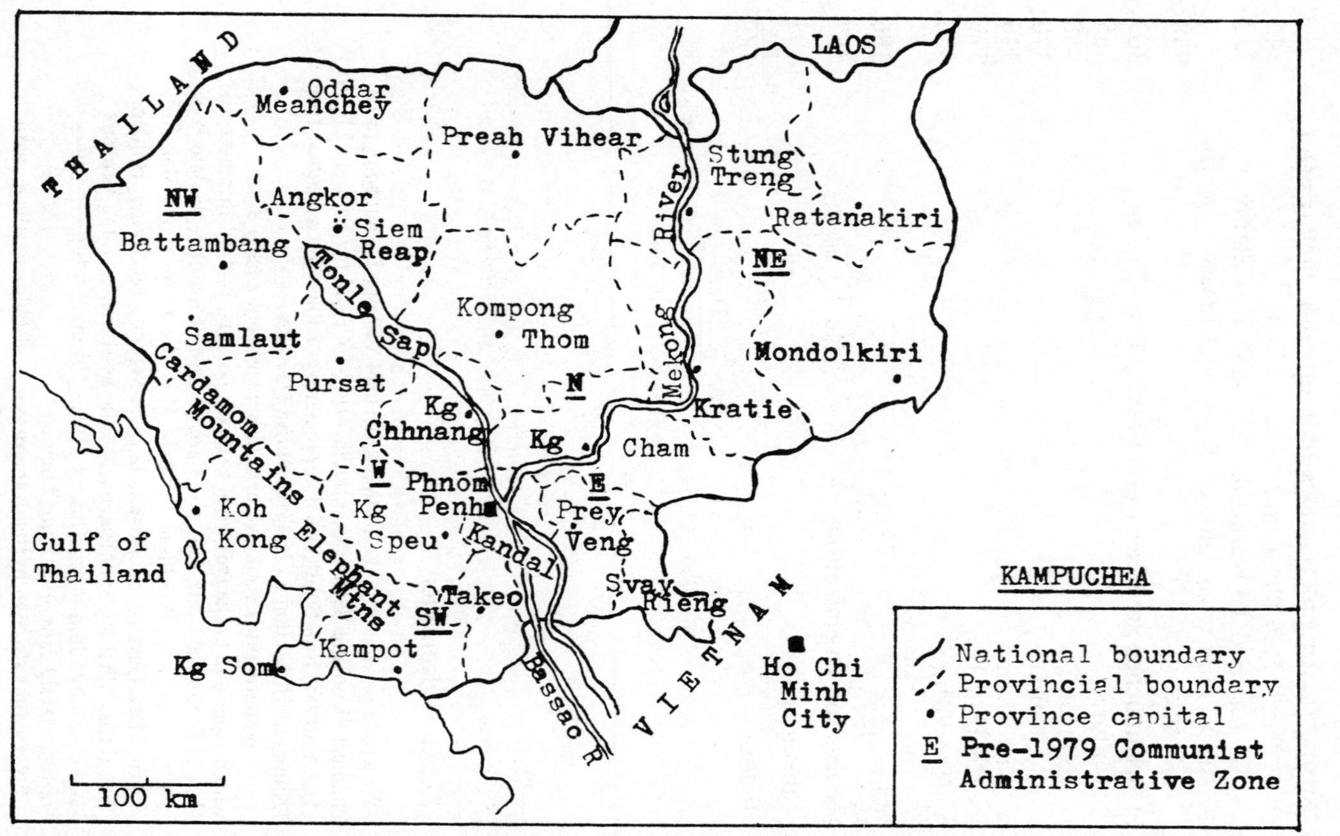
THAILAND
LAOS
Oddar Meanchey
Preah Vihear
Stung Treng
Ratanakiri
NW
Angkor
Siem Reap
Battambang
Tonle Sap
River
NE
Kompong Thom
Mekong
Samlaut
Mondolkiri
Cardamom Mountains
Pursat
N
Kratie
Kg Chhnang
Kg Cham
W
Phnom Penh
E
Koh Kong
Kg Speu
Prey Veng
Gulf of Thailand
Elephant Mtns
Kandal
Svay Rieng
Takeo
SW
VIETNAM
Kampot
Kg Som
Bassac R
Ho Chi Minh City
KAMPUCHEA
National boundary
Provincial boundary
Province capital
E Pre-1979 Communist Administrative Zone
100 km

Preface by Wilfred Burchett

Without prejudging the results and conclusions of the authors, they can only be congratulated on having undertaken expert and scholarly research into one of the most baffling and tragic political phenomena of our time. How could a structured revolutionary movement, enjoying great international support, having conducted what seemed to have been an exemplary national liberation struggle, turn against its own cadre which included veteran revolutionaries; its own people, its own culture and traditions, to set up what can be defined as a modern slave society? What precepts taught the physical extermination of so many of those who had acquired education, starting with the privileged who had studied abroad and acquired a foreign language and ending with the most humble who had acquired literacy in their own tongue?

My first contact with the authors symbolizes the catastrophe they try to explain. After a talk on Kampuchea, in the Grand Committee Rome of the House of Commons on 26 July 1979, a young woman stood up and asked in a rather trembly voice if I had any information about the fate of students who had returned to Kampuchea after the Khmer Rouge came to power on 17 April 1975. In an even more trembly voice I had to reply that I feared they had all been killed. My reply was based on what I had been able to discover on a visit to Phnom Penh two months earlier and an examination of some of the daily lists of those tortured to death in the Khmer Rouge extermination centre at the former Tuol Sleng Secondary School in Phnom Penh. The young woman presented herself after the meeting – she was Chanthou Boua, accompanied by her husband, Cambodia scholar Ben Kiernan, an Australian compatriot. I could only repeat the reasons for my reply, based on investigations as to the fate of some of my closest friends whom I came to know during the four years' residence of our family in Phnom Penh (1965-69), and the terrible daily statistics and identifications of those tortured and executed at the Tuol Sleng extermination centre.

Later Chanthou Boua received horrifying confirmation that what we feared was indeed so; also, that her whole family and the families of her closest friends had been exterminated under the most barbarous circumstances. Having regularly visited Kampuchea (Cambodia as we then called it) for a quarter of a century; having lived there for four years, during which my wife was professor at the University of Fine Arts and our three children studied at the Lycee Descartes; having visited the country three times since the overthrow of the Pol Pot regime, I am well aware – as are all other foreign observers who have been on the spot – of the enormity of the auto-genocidal crimes committed against the Kampuchean people, including the ethnic minorities there. As to the rationale for such horrors, opinions differ very widely. The authors are amongst those best qualified to answer the question: 'Why?' In so doing, they will render an immense service, especially to politically engaged people whose natural sympathies are with the 'underdogs' and those seeking new ways and methods of social progress.

My own awareness of Cambodia and its problems dates back to a few weeks before the opening of the 1954 Geneva Conference on Indochina. To my surprise – and in self-defence, to the surprise of many of my non-specialist colleagues, not to mention the general public – I discovered there was no such country as 'Indochina', but three separate countries, Vietnam, Laos and Cambodia, each with their distinct cultures, languages and differing variants of Buddhist religious philosophy. The only thing that united them was that they had been the object of cultural influences from India and China in ancient times, and in more modern times had been colonised by France and lumped together as the Associated States of Indochina. More pertinent to contemporary history were the armed struggles waged by the three peoples – unco-ordinated at first, co-ordinated later – to free themselves from French colonialist occupiers. All this was first explained to me by Ho Chi Minh at his jungle headquarters in North Vietnam at the beginning of the historic battle of Dien Bien Phu and the eve of the 1954 Geneva Conference on Indochina. When later I began to read about the 'traditional hostility' between the Kampuchean and Vietnamese peoples as an explanation for Khmer Rouge-Vietnam armed struggle, I realized that Ho Chi Minh, the internationalist, had been talking of solidarity generated during common resistance to foreign invaders, whereas Pol Pot and his apologists had turned the clock back to feudal times when rival monarchies waxed and waned and secured as much as possible of each other's territories. Yet these historical rivalries of contending feudal states were presented in colours of irrevocable hatred between peoples.[1]

During my four visits to the Liberated Zones of South Vietnam between the end of 1963 and mid-1966, it was at first the militant solidarity between Cambodian and Vietnamese revolutionary forces which lent comparative security to the frontier crossings. Later, I could make them legally, because of the open support of the Cambodian Head of State, Prince Norodom Sihanouk, for the resistance forces in South Vietnam. In those days, unbeknown to most 'outsiders', including myself, there were two factions contending for power within the Khmer Communist Party. One, headed by Nuon Chea,[2] advocated critical support for Sihanouk's policy of neutrality, his opposition to U.S. imperialism in the area and his covert material support for the National Liberation Front in South Vietnam. This faction saw the main struggle of the day as across the border between the N.L.F. and U.S. imperialism, the outcome of which would be decisive for the future of Cambodia's own revolutionary forces.

The other faction, headed by Saloth Sar (Pol Pot), insisted that the main task for Cambodian Communists was to push on with their own revolution and seek the overthrow of the Sihanouk regime by armed struggle, regardless of external factors. Thus, when Pol Pot was away in Peking – often, from 1965 onwards – it was the 'Support Sihanouk and the Vietnam struggle' line that predominated in Cambodia. When he was back, it was the 'Overthrow Sihanouk regardless' line. The Pol Pot faction was reinforced by China's attempt to export the 'Great Proletarian Cultural Revolution' to Cambodia (by means of the large and influential Chinese community and Pol Pot-type local 'Maoists') and Sihanouk's repressive counter-measures, Sihanouk's natural tendency to suppress 'dissidence' was fertilized by the activities of the Pol Pot faction of the Khmer Communist Party, which Sihanouk began to call the 'Khmer Rouge' (Red Khmers).

To my great consternation, in late 1966 or early 1967, I was approached – on the basis of my consistent support for national liberation movements – by Pok Deuksoma, whom I then knew only as assistant manager of Phnom Penh's main foreign exchange bank, to lend my support to an armed 'national liberation movement' about to be launched against Sihanouk. That the conversation took place in the bank manager's office added to the fantasy element of the proposal. To my objection that elements of 'national liberation' were lacking due to the absence of any foreign occupier and that, in view of Sihanouk's increasingly open support of the struggle on the other side of the frontier, this would be equivalent to stabbing the Vietnamese resistance forces in the back, Pok Deuksoma replied in effect: 'You cannot demand that the revolutionary forces in one country retard their revolution because it is not in the interests of another country's struggle.' My argument that the future of the whole area, and even areas far removed from the former states of Indochina, would be decisively affected by the outcome of the struggle in Vietnam was of no avail. 'There are no avenues of legal struggle left to us, so we have to take to arms' were the final words of Pok Deuksema. He had the courage of his convictions and disappeared on the day following our conversation. His name appeared briefly in the news a few years later, as Deputy Foreign Minister of the GRUNK (Khmer Royal Government of National Union) and subsequently, as far as could be learned, he was among the many Khmer Rouge adherents to be executed by Pol Pot because of their 'bourgeois backgrounds.'

Arguments for and against the merits of the Khmer Rouge armed struggle against Sihanouk's regime and the role this played in Sihanouk's overthrow by Lon Nol will doubtless be continued by historians for years to come. The research of Ben Kiernan and Chantoua Boua throws much light on the background to the armed struggle, especially the peasants' uprising in the Samlaut district of Battambang Province which started in April 1967. The Vietnamese leadership, as I was well aware through discussions at the time, was seriously embarrassed. On the one hand, they had neither the inclination nor the right to dictate policy to the Khmer Communist Party, on the other, they could not betray Sihanouk who was proving to be an increasingly important loyal friend in the hour of Vietnam's greatest need. Also they believed that despite Sihanouk's suppression of the political Left, there was not the level of popular discontent essential to support armed struggle. When the Khmer Rouge were on the run, they could find sanctuary in N.L.F. bases on the South Vietnamese side of the border, but were refused arms. That policy continued until Lon Nol's coup in March 1970 and the formation of a resistance front (FUNK: Khmer National United Front) under Sihanouk's leadership, of which the Khmer Rouge were an important component. One of their leaders, Khieu Samphan, was appointed by Sihanouk as head of the resistance forces – Minister of Defence and Commander-in-Chief.

At the time of Sihanouk's overthrow, Pol Pot was on one of his periodic visits to Peking. At the request of Sihanouk, who arrived in Peking from Moscow on the day following his overthrow, the Vietnamese Premier Pham Van Dong flew to Peking and played a key role in effecting a reconciliation between the Khmer Rouge and Sihanouk and in encouraging Sihanouk in his determination to launch a resistance struggle against the U.S.-installed puppet regime of Lon Nol. One of Sihanouk's first requests to Pham Van Dong was for Vietnamese instructors to train Cambodian resistance forces.

With Pol Pot in Peking, his deputy Nuon Chea – by then in a sanctuary inside South Vietnam – asked for Vietnamese help to clear Lon Nol troops out of an area sufficiently large to serve as a base for the future resistance struggle. This was done and virtually all of the eastern province adjoining the Vietnamese frontier were cleared of Lon Nol forces. Rarely did a national liberation movement have such excellent take-off conditions! It was in this large base area that the nucleus of the anti-Lon Nol forces were recruited, trained by Vietnamese instructors and equipped from arms stockpiled in the frontier areas. By the time Pol Pot returned from Peking, the resistance war was off to a good start. He asked the Vietnamese forces to withdraw – which they promptly did. This established a pattern to be repeated on a number of decisive occasions when the Cambodian P.N.L.A.F. (People's National Liberation Armed Forces) were in military difficulties.

At the Summit Conference of the Peoples of Indochina, held in Canton on 24-25 April 1970, at Sihanouk's initiative, it had been agreed that a co-ordinated struggle would be waged by the forces of the two halves of Vietnam, Laos and Kampuchea until victory over the United States and their local puppets was achieved. The armed forces of one country could operate in the territory of its neighbours at the express request of the country concerned. Such requests were made by the Kampuchea resistance forces during the invasion of Saigon by the U.S. (starting 30 April 1970), during Lon Nol's two major offensives (Chenla 1 in September 1970 and Chenla 2, from August to December 1972) and in the decisive battle for Phnom Penh (January to 17 April 1975). Sihanouk gives due credit to Vietnamese aid in his book, *Chroniques de Guerre et d'Espoir.*[3]

Deriding the claims of Pol Pot, Ieng Sary and Khieu Samphan to have defeated the Lon Nol military machine by their own forces, Sihanouk writes:

> Certainly it is good to be patriotic, but to deliberately adopt a chauvinistic attitude and one of bad faith in order to deny to the North Vienamese allies and comrades-in-arms the preponderant role – to say the least – that they played in first stopping the American and Saigon invalders, then in rolling them back in 1970, 1971 and 1972, is not only to insult them, but to insult history itself. It is something that adds little to the stature of the authors of such claims.[4]

At the time he was writing, Sihanouk was certainly no great friend of Hanoi. He considered that, having overthrown the Pol Pot regime, Vietnam should have immediately withdrawn its troops again. But he had some sense of proportion when he commented on the Khmer Rouge leadership's habit of claiming the Vietnamese victories over Lon Nol as their own: 'Unfortunately, Pol Pot allowed his head to be turned somewhat too soon about "his" victories to the point of comparing himself with the great conquerors of the past – Alexander of Macedonia, Rome's Caesar, the Corsican [Napoleon], and the Nazi, Hitler . . . .'[5]

Sihanouk relates his astonishment, on visiting 'liberated' Kampuchea in September 1975, to hear the Khmer Rouge leaders 'with broad smiles and a very satisfied air' talk about recovering areas of South Vietnam and Thailand that had belonged centuries earlier to the Khmer Empire. 'According to Son Sen, then deputy Defence Minister, his glorious "Kampuchean Revolutionary Army" reckoned that Giap's Army represented only a "mouthful" for them and the miserable army of Kukrit Pramoj and Kriangsak Chamond [Thailand] even less! . . . .'[6]

It is in the light of the spirit of wild delusion that one must interpret the Khmer Rouge attacks on Vietnamese territory (Phu Cuoc Island, for instance) almost immediately after both countries' victories in their respective national liberation struggles. 'Dizzy with success' would be a mild term to describe what Sihanouk referred to as Pol Pot's 'megalomania which exceeds in its madness even that of Hitler.'[7] Efforts of the Hanoi leadership to conceal what was happening along the frontiers from 1975 to the end of 1977, on the grounds a) that these were, as the Khmer Rouge leadership explained, isolated incidents due to 'enemies within the ranks'; b) that they could be settled by negotiations, and c) that they did not want to comfort the enemies of socialism by drawing attention to the spectacle of armed conflict within their ranks, were taken by Pol Pot as proof of Vietnamese weakness, tiredness after 30 years of war. He was encouraged in this belief by Peking.

Hanoi maintained this 'cover-up' posture far too long for its own interests and against the advice of some high-ranking cadres who were later promoted to leadership positions precisely because they had fought for greater frankness in revealing problems with Kampuchea and also on the home front. In late April 1977, having learned from on-the-spot sources of serious Khmer Rouge incursions, in depth and on a large front, in the southern areas of Vietnam, I was officially informed: 'There are no problems between us and Kampuchea. However, the Kampuchean comrades are following internal policies which we think are contrary to objective laws of economic and social development. We regret this for their sake, but that is their affair.'

Even after serious attacks from April to September 1977, in which several Khmer Rouge divisions were used from the southernmost point of the Vietnam-Kampuchean land frontier in Ha Tien Province to the northernmost point in Gia Lai-Kontum and after which Vietnamese forces struck back, expelling the invaders to the east bank of the Mekong River, then withdrawing to their own territory, it was left to the Khmer Rouge leaders to give their version of events first. Lack of frankness in Hanoi gave Pol Pot and Ieng Sary an important initiative in denouncing the Vietnamese as 'aggressors'.

But, as the United States had so often done in their aggression against Vietnam, the Khmer Rouge leadership took the Vietnamese restraint – withdrawal of their forces and offer of negotiations at summit level – as a 'last gasp' gesture of weakness. Claiming that 29,000 Vietnamese troops had been killed for a cost of only 470 of their own troops, the Khmer Rouge leadership argued that Kampuchea could wipe out the entire population of Vietnam and still have six million survivors. In his book, Sihanouk comments on a Phnom Penh radio broadcast in early 1978, as follows:

> The Khmer Rouge leaders, in all seriousness, ordered their troops and people to kill Vietnamese in the ratio of 30 Viets for one Kampuchean . . . basing themselves on the calculation that 'by sacrificing only two million Kampucheans, we can wipe out up to 60 million Vietnamese and there will still be 6 million Kampucheans left to build up and defend our country'.[8]

Many Khmer teenagers, guns behind to cut them down if they hesitated, rushed to their death in increasing numbers, especially in 1978, indiscriminately and barbarously slaughtering Vietnamese of all ages. They had been indoctrinated to the effect that they were liberating Kampuchea Krom (South Kampuchea), part of which has long been in South Vietnam, and the former 17th-Century Cambodian fishing village of Prey Nokor (today's Ho Chi Minh City and yesterday's Saigon). This was to be part of an 'easy push-over' attempt to restore the territorial confines of the former Khmer Empire. Peking encouraged this aspect of what will surely be known as the 'great Khmer Rouge madness'. China not only sent in many thousands of military advisers from April 1975, to make possible the rapid expansion of the 'Kampuchean Revolutionary Army' (from two to 23 divisions), but apparently also assured the Khmer Rouge leadership that an invasion of Vietnam would be supported by demobilized officers and troops of the former Saigon army and by the 700,000 Hoa (Vietnamese of Chinese origin) residing mainly in Saigon-Cholon. Also, that at a certain stage of the 'easy pushover' it would be supported by a Chinese invasion from the North.

In visiting Vietnam's Tay Ninh Province in December 1978, I was amazed to encounter convoys of bewildered-looking Vietnamese peasants, ox-carts piled high with freshly-reaped sheaves of rice and household belongings, moving back into the interior. As I passed them, driving in the opposite direction along Highway 22, distant booms turned into whines, sharp cracks and pillars of black smoke on the road ahead – from shells fired from the Kampuchean side of the frontier. Our vehicle was forced to turn back. At Tay Ninh's provincial capital I learned that 1,181 civilians had been killed in frontier shellings and commando raids since September 1977, and that the sad-faced people with the ox-cart convoys represented part of the 70,000 peasants evacuated from frontier villages. The N.L.F. bases which I had known 15 years earlier were now in the hands of Khmer Rouge commandos who launched almost nightly forays against the frontier villages. In addition to settling the 70,000 evacuees, the provincial authorities explained they had to look after 30,000 refugees, survivors of the gauntlet of Khmer Rouge security forces, who killed on sight anyone attempting to escape, and murderous minefields laid by them on both sides of the frontier. It was from these refugees, Khmer, Chinese, Vietnamese and Chams, that I was able to piece together the same almost unbelievable picture of what had been going on in the Kampuchea of the Khmer Rouge, that Ben Kiernan and Chanthoua Boua found in their independent investigations among refugees in Thailand and elsewhere.

Shortly after visiting Tay Ninh, I was in the Mekong Delta province of Dong Thap. There were the same familiar explosions of 130 mm shells from Chinese artillery pieces zeroing in from the Kampuchean side of the frontier; the same horrifying accounts of Vietnamese refugees who had made it to safety, leaving hundreds of their compatriots dead along the perilous escape route. On the day of my arrival, two Khmer Rouge regiments drove five miles deep across the frontier where defences had been weakened by the unprecedented autumn floods. By then, according to the military maps I was shown, 19 of Pol Pot's 23 China-equipped divisions were stationed along – or inside – Kampuchea's frontier with Vietnam.

It is by shedding some well-researched light as to how such a situation could have arisen between supposed 'comrades-in-arms' in the greatest anti-imperialist struggle of our times that the work of Ben Kiernan and Chantou Boua will be most appreciated by today's political activists and tomorrow's political historians.

Wilfred Burchett
Phnom Penh
May 1980

References

1. As an example of the racist outlook of the Khmer Rouge leadership, it is sufficient to cite the reason given for referring to the Vietnamese as *'yuon'* in their official publications. Thus, in the English edition of the *Black Paper: Facts and Evidences of the Acts of Aggression and Annexation of Vietnam Against Kampuchea,* (published by the Department of Press and Information of the Ministry of Foreign Affairs of Democratic Kampuchea: September 1978), one reads: *'Yuon* is the name given by the Kampuchea's people to the Vietnamese since the epoch of Angkor and it means "savage". The word "Vietnam" and "Vietnamese" are very recent and not often used by the Kampuchea's people.' In fact, the term 'Vietnam' was suppressed in school textbooks by the French colonialists because of Vietnam's historic struggles against Chinese, Mongol and other foreign invaders.
2. Nuon Chea had been a member of the Cambodian element of the Communist Party of Indochina, set up at Ho Chi Minh's initiative in 1930 and formed as a separate Cambodian Communist Party in 1951 – also at the initiative of Ho Chi Minh. Pol Pot, Ieng Sary, Khieu Samphan, Hou Youn, Hu Nim and others belonged to what are known as the 'Paris Group' of students who – with the exception of Pol Pot – returned to Cambodia after the anti-French resistance war had ended. Pol Pot returned a few months before the end, but played no part in the armed resistance struggle.
3. Norodom Sihanouk, *Chroniques de Guerre et d'Espoir* (Paris, Hachette-Stock, 1979).
4. Ibid, pp.64-65.
5. Ibid., p.79.
6. Ibid.
7. Ibid., p.147.
8. Ibid., p.110.

Introduction by Ben Kiernan

Chantaburi, Thailand, May 1885:

> Officials in charge of the border post arrested two Vietnamese who said they had escaped from Kampot, where 300 Khmers had attacked the French who were selling opium there. The French and the Vietnamese had to flee the town. The Khmers moved in to occupy the river estuary, and recruited local residents to ship in rocks to block the waterway. The French sent two steamships and two Vietnamese ships to bombard the Khmer rebels, many of whom were injured and the rest scattered. Later the French sent their troops to attack the Khmer rebels who had to abandon the town. The French then moved in and burned down the town.[1]

Although Kampuchea had become a French protectorate in 1863, extended contact between most Kampucheans and the West did not begin until the 1885-8 anti-colonial uprising, when French forces (including Vietnamese auxiliaries) – their area of control reduced to Phnom Penh, the other small towns, the river banks and the coast of an overwhelmingly rural country– took the war to the villages. According to one French source, the number of people living within the then borders of the 'protectorate' was reduced by 195,000, or one-fifth of the total, during those two short years.'

A century of Western attempts to dominate Kampuchea had begun in earnest. It was an era, however, both preceded and followed by similar (if less mechanized) attempts by neighbouring Asian powers. Thus Kampuchea's place in the world of the 1970s, at the heart of one international crisis after another, could even be said to be a 200-year-old phenomenon, dating from the final decay of the powerful Angkor Empire and the seizure, by Thailand and Vietnam, of areas inhabited by large numbers of Khmers. The major task of this book, however, will be to examine modern Kampuchea, not just so as to throw light on one variable in international equations, but also for its own sake, from the point of view of the internal dynamic of Kampuchean society and politics.

Colonial Background

The early 19th Century was marked by Thai and Vietnamese invasions as well as several internal rebellions.[3] The country was laid waste and massive numbers of Khmers moved to Thailand, either to escape the turmoil or herded along by retreating armies. Relative peace in the 1850s was followed in the next decade by three rebellions, two of them explicitly anti-French as well as anti-monarchical, led by the messianic figures of Pou Kombo (Achar Leak) and Achar Sva.

Pou Kombo, a member of the Kouy tribe from Kompong Thom Province, recruited actively across Indochina's ethnic and national boundaries. In 1866, according to French historian Jean Moura, his forces numbered 1,000 Khmers, 300 Vietnamese, and 100 Chams and tribal Stiengs. He even recruited some Tagal deserters from the King's personal units brought from the Philippines. Thai intelligence at the time reported that Pou Kombo was telling villagers in Kompong Thom that he planned to go to Vietnam 'and kill all the French at Hue', and would then do the same at the Khmer royal capital of Udong. Though mobilized by such leaders' claims to the Kampuchean throne, these were peasants already sceptical of King Norodom's insistence that French protection was necessary to save the country from Thai and Vietnamese invaders. In October 1866, Pou Kombo personally led 5,000 troops, including 700-800 Vietnamese, against the King's forces and won the day. At his peak, the rebel is said to have commanded an army of 10,000. Only with French military assistance did the King finally defeat and then execute Pou Kombo in 1867. Moura commented: 'With Pou Kombo's death this immense revolution came to an end. It had lasted eighteen months and had turned the tiny Khmer kingdom upside down.' Even then, one of Pou Kombo's lieutenants escaped, to return to the fray in 1872 with an army of '400 men of every race in Indochina'.[4]

A comparable rebellion in 1876-7, led by Prince Si Votha, was similarly put down; but Votha escaped to take a leading role in the unsuccessful 1885-86 revolt and his forces were not subdued until 1889. He again escaped capture and died a natural death in 1892, in a remote jungle base that the French had been unable to penetrate – an inability that was symptomatic of the French failure ever to communicate fruitfully with the Kampuchean peasantry. A colonial official in Kratie Province summed up 1925-26, during which 400 of the local inhabitants had died of cholera, in the following way:

> On the whole, impoverished by bad harvests, deranged by their customs and decimated by disease, there was nothing in the past year for which the population could congratulate themselves. Nevertheless they have maintained their sound good sense and judgement, and their attitude of loyal confidence in the aims of the Administration . . . .
>
> . . . Under these conditions one might be forgiven for asking if this invariable calm manifested by the population of this region even in a

> bad year is not an external impression disguising some vague feelings, probably not disloyal, but which we can't really perceive.[5]

The lack of communication was to continue. In 1976, David Chandler wrote that in Kampuchea peasants 'have been "outside history" for many years'. 'We know very little, in quantitative or political terms, about the mass of Cambodian society, many of whom, for most of their history, appear to have been slaves of one sort or another.' French colonists preferred 'to reconstruct Cambodia's ancient temples, nurture a small elite, and modernize the economy to provide surpluses of rice and rubber'.[6] The powerful presence of the French, although it could not eliminate endemic rural banditry, did preserve peace with Kampuchea's neighbours (until the Second World War) and bring a stability to the countryside that fostered a tremendous extension in land under cultivation and rice production. This potential for improving the material conditions of most peasants' lives, is discussed in detail by Hou Yuon in Part I. On the whole, in bad years hunger and disease still plagued the countryside, but there was little starvation, and the population-land ratio was still low: the first half of the 20th century was later described as the years of 'colonial calm'.[7]

Perhaps for this reason, French control of Kampuchea was secure, although not unchallenged. In 1916, demonstrations against unjust treatment by minor colonial officials involved 100,000 peasants,[8] and led to 20,000 arrests.[9] Interestingly, this affair also had its 'international' connections: it parallelled demonstrations and uprisings in the same period in South Vietnam, organized from a headquarters in Chaudoc near the Kampuchean border.[10] According to a French official in Kampuchea's Prey Veng Province at the time:

> The recent events [in South Vietnam] quickly became known here, and the Cambodians immediately seized the opportunity to spread the rumour among the population that the Vietnamese were rising up in order to come to their aid. So the mood of the population is still very uneasy, and under these conditions it will be necessary to maintain for a little while longer the police forces which have now been put at the disposition of the [local] authorities.[11]

The apparatus of colonial repression became ever more sophisticated. 1923 brought the first aerial bombing of an Indochinese village, following the assassination of a Khmer colonial official and his party by 'unsubdued' tribespeople near Kratie on the Vietnamese border. The village of Pou-than, comprising 12 hamlets, was, in the words of a French Governor of the time, 'effectively bombarded' by a military aircraft.[12]

The rubber plantations of eastern Kampuchea were established by the French in the 1920s. The workers were press-ganged, impoverished Vietnamese from the Red River Delta, as well as local peasants and tribespeople and other Kampucheans 'in an irregular situation because of the taxes, who find temporary refuge in the plantations'.[13] The conditions there were harsh. In April 1927, a French official noted: 'Already 450 coolies have fled. Most of them have been recaptured and sent back to [the rubber plantation at] Mimot, and have undergone punishment that should frighten the rest.'[14]

Socio-Economic Structure, 1930-70

Landowners

In the 20th Century most of the Kampuchean peasantry did not have a landowning aristocracy pressing down on them. The landlord class that did emerge as the century progressed was of limited scale, developing within a context of small family properties, and competing with a very successful Chinese moneylending class for the position of the most powerful social overlords of the Kampuchean peasantry.

But unequal distribution of land *amongst the peasantry* was nevertheless significant. Those 80% of Kampuchean landowners who in 1930 each owned less than five hectares of land accounted for only 44% of the land cultivated; more than half of the land was owned by the wealthiest 20% of the farmers. By 1950, while the *ratio* was still the same, four-fifths of the rural population were now subsisting on less than *two* hectares. This amount is crucial, since *one* hectare of rice land on average supplied the rice needs of a family of three or four people.[15] (In the 1960s the average family size was five.) Thus, for food and everyday expenses a family would require two (occasionally even three)[16] hectares of rice land, or about half a hectare of river-bank land.

As a result, during the period 1950-70 there was a marked increase in the proportion of tenants and sharecroppers – smallholdings became too small and farmers were forced to sell out and work for a landlord. In 1950, this section represented only 4% of farming families, but in 1962 they were 6%, and in 1970 20%.[17] A wider definition of landlessness, to include very small landowners and agricultural labourers, gives a figure of about 20% of the rural workforce even in the 1950s. Not included in this are ruined peasants incapable of any re-absorption into rural life. The numbers of people migrating to the cities increased dramatically in the 1960s, as Hu Nim shows in Part I.

In 1964, Hou Yuon wrote about the landless:

> Where is this class of people? What is their life like? Their feet are off the ground [they own no land]; some of them have to live by sharecropping or working on rented land; some have to transform their lives by becoming rural labourers in their areas. Others have to leave their villages and look for jobs in the towns, as lower class workers (pedicab drivers, sellers of water and bread, porters) or medium class workers (construction workers, repair workers) or higher class workers (factory workers and company employees). The rest of them who do not know where to go subsist from day to day by doing small jobs for other people, catching fish or fetching vegetables to exchange for rice or for money, or by making and selling cakes, biscuits, fried bananas, etc . . . .[18]

More important, perhaps, was the proportion of part-time tenancies held by peasants whose lands were too small for family subsistence. Although this category rarely shows up in the records and is usually difficult to quantify, their numbers may well have been substantial because many did have inadequate properties. In the 1962 Census these farmers were estimated at 7% of the rural workforce.[19]

While holdings were shrinking at the bottom end of the social scale, an opposite but related trend was developing at the top. Landlordism increased significantly, especially after 1954, as urban classes enriched by foreign capital bought up land, usually near the towns, from ruined peasants. But the trend was evident before this. The number of landlowners with more than 10 hectares increased from 4,500 in 1930 to 10,491 in 1950; those with more than 20 hectares numbered 1,191 in 1956 and 5,020 in 1962.

A well-placed source has revealed that in 1965 over 400 bodies were found in a cave in the forest of Kompong Speu Province; they were peasants who had been massacred resisting forcible seizure of their land by military officials. In 1967 in Samlaut District of Battambang Province, and in 1968 in Rattanakiri, similar land seizures by officials and military officers provoked further organized peasant resistance which was also ruthlessly repressed. But this extension of landlordism, however rapid and violent, was not, as will be shown, a predominant factor in the Kampuchean rural social structure.

What was more significant was the unequal distribution of holdings among the peasants themselves, and it was not merely restricted to rice land. In sugar palm cultivation, Fontanel writes, a 'typical exploitation comprises 25 palms in owner-cultivation and three in tenancy, for a family . . .'. However, he then points out 'that only 60% of the families actually work the sugar palms and that these are in general the poorer families. The rich peasants prefer to rent out their palms.'[20] (In the light of this it is likely that the owner-cultivation mode of exploitation was not a 'typical' social reality but simply a statistical mean.) For a hamlet in the same area west of Phnom Penh, Ebihara's data shows that the four richest of 32 farmers owned 60% of the 400 sugar palms, as well as one-third of the hamlet's rice land. The poorest 20 peasant families, on the other hand, owned only 18% of the sugar palms, and one-third of the rice land.[21] The table 1.1. is compiled from the landholding statistics cited by Hou Yuon for 1929-30, by Delvert for 1956 and Hu Nim for 1962.

Several trends are apparent from Table 1.1. In the first place, as Hu Nim points out, there is the increase (from 6 to 14%) in the proportion of rich peasants (those with over 5 hectares) and landlords (with over 10 hectares). It is also significant that the percentage of the total land owned by these groups increased from 31 to 46%. Interestingly, however, developments at the other end of the social scale are not quite symmetrical. Between 1930 and 1956, the ranks of the poorest proportion of the rural population (those with less than 1 hectare) swelled from 43 to 55%; the proportion of 'middle peasants' (with 1–5 hectares) decreased by 14%, and the small number of landlords, etc., increased slightly. Unfortunately, it is hard to examine this period more closely without detailed statistics on the increase in the area of cultivated land.

Landownership and Cultivation Trends, 1929-62

	1929-30		*1956*		*1962*	
Owners of	*% of the Rural Population*	*Their % of Cultivated Land*	*% of the Rural Population*	*Their % of Cultivated Land*	*% of the Rural Population*	*Their % of Cultivated Land*
Less than 1 hectare	43	25	55	25	31	5
1-5 hectares	51	44	37	40	55	49
Over 5 hectares	6	31	8	35	14	46

Between 1956 and 1962 the opposite trend emerges. Possibly because of the energetic opening up of new lands after the insecurity of the 1946-54 anti-French war, nearly half of the 55% who had owned less than one hectare in 1956 had more than one by 1962. But this does not account for the much greater degree of expansion in cultivation: whereas the rural population increased by 15% from 1956 to 1962, the area of land under cultivation increased by 53%.[22] A reasonable explanation is that the rapid increase in the proportion of landlords and rich peasants (from 8 to 14%) was accompanied by a rapid increase in land cleared and rented out *by each landlord* (on average). This land would have been rented out in particular to those among the 31% still owning less than one hectare who were rice farmers and, if not indeed landless, needed to farm additional land for their subsistence.

Although Kampuchea's rice lands were divided into tiny plots farmed individually by hundreds of thousands of peasant households, contrary to general belief, this did not rule out landlordism. Hou Yuon in 1955 had already raised the possibility that 'big property is divided up . . . disguised, somehow hiding behind small family farms'. In 1965, Hu Nim noted that '*fragmented* land is concentrated more and more' in the hands of a relatively small number of landowners.

Perhaps more significantly, though, there was now a considerable number of *upper* middle peasants' (with 2-5 hectares). Their proportion had increased from 12%, owning 18% of the cultivated land, to 33% with 38% of the land, over the six-year period from 1956 to 1962. It appears that a significant polarisation had taken place *within the peasant population,* quite apart from the growth of landlordism.

The political ramifications of the fairly even socio-economic divisions within the Kampuchean peasant community are far from clear; but it is obvious that, alongside a landowning and (in that respect) more independent middle peasant group, there was also a class of rootless, destitute rural dwellers *with very few ties to the land.* It is this group that Hou Youn termed the 'semi-proletariat'. They were not a majority, but by the late 1960s their position was desperate enough for them to have nothing at all to lose in any kind of social revolution.

Money-lenders

For the majority of rural Kampuchean families, who were 'middle peasants', land tenure was not the major problem. In 1959, Khieu Samphan pointed out the relative strength of this middle peasant class:

> In this respect, Kampuchea differs from its neighbour Vietnam. In that country, big landlords own the overwhelming majority of lands while poor peasants, numerically the most important, share out only a tiny portion of the cultivated land area. In Kampuchea, middle peasants own their own agricultural implements as well as their own work animals.[23]

But, he went on:

> Most often, they lack operating capital. This they obtain from village usurers who are also large landowners or traders. They get away with nothing in dealing with these people. Much to the contrary, property ownership is no more than the appearance of ownership for a substantial number of middle peasants. Interest rates attaining 200% to 300% per annum amount in practice to cheating them out of all their labour product just as if they were working the land of usurers. The belief in 'ownership' exists only as a result of the fact that they shelter on the land as best they can under the most difficult circumstances while waiting for 'better times'. Usurers, landlords and traders have every interest in perpetuating this belief and do not feel the need to go ahead with expropriations for reasons of insolvency.
>
> The situation is evidently even more serious for smallholder/share-croppers who must pay rent in addition to interest . . .

It is clear that although ethnic Chinese money-lenders were legally barred from owning land, this did not reduce their economic power over the peasants.

In the 1930s, Virginia Thompson wrote that Kampuchea was 'eaten up by usury'.[24] Though the colonial regime attempted to wrest the peasants from the clutches of the Chinese by means of an agricultural bank, it's credit terms, according to a contemporary newspaper, 'supported the unfortunate farmer like the rope that supports the man being hung'. The paper pointed out that a peasant who borrowed 100 piastres, at the 'truly prohibitive' prevailing interest rate of 12%, received only 88 piastres because the interest was deducted in advance – and another 12 were deducted for 'expenses'. 'He has 76 piastres, and he owes 100 piastres on it'.[25]

In 1938, the only newspaper then published in the Khmer language launched an attack on Chinese usurers, who it alleged forced peasants to repay 10 times the amount they had borrowed.[26]

In 1939, a French official described the plight of the Khmer peasant:

> . . . the blows of chance catch him disarmed; sickness, death and calamities make him prey to the Chinese usurers. From then on he struggles hard, working more and more land in the vain hope of wiping out a debt that usury is ceaselessly swelling. His harvests are automatically confiscated from him, his family goes into slavery, beginning with the youngest and the females, and the day comes when in spite of all his sacrifices he is brutally dispossessed of his property by his creditors. There is nothing left for him to do but go and live off a relative whom luck has made better off, or enter religious life.[27]

Jean Delvert, who carried out his major geographical study of the Kampuchean peasantry in the 1950s, found that Chinese shopkeepers would sell to peasants on credit at 10% interest per month (in some cases it was even 20%) a staggering annual rate of 240%. Money-lending itself was usually at a rate of 12% per month.

> When he cannot pay his debts, the peasant can be obliged to sell his land, but not to the lender who is usually Chinese and could not acquire it. He can also repay his debt by working for the creditor himself or having a member of his family do so (the daughter, very often). But debt slavery no longer exists, at least in theory (we knew one example which was not far from it).

If a peasant borrowed 2,000 riels at 5% interest, Delvert noted that one form of repayment was for the peasant's daughter to work as a servant for the creditor for 14 months.[28]

The colonial Credit Office found in a survey in 1952 that 75% of peasants in Kampuchea were in significant debt, but it was ineffective in remedying the situation. Delvert's own surveys, one detailed and one cursory, of the extent of debt in a number of communities, yielded average figures of 50% and 33% respectively. He pointed out that in the rural areas near the capital, peasants were able to get seasonal work in the city and thus pay off their debts. 'This region is one of the most populous in the kingdom, and one of the poorest, [but] indebtedness there is much rarer than elsewhere.'[29]

Anthropologist May Ebihara studied a small village in this area during the year 1959. She adds to Delvert's findings: . . .'it does happen that most or all of an unfortunate household's crop is carted away immediately after harvest by creditors . . . two or three families [out of 32] are caught in a seemingly unbreakable cycle of annual debt because of grossly inadequate holdings.'[30] Ebihara agreed that 'large-scale indebtedness was not widespread' in the village; but the reason was that 'most can pay off their debts in a year or so, but to do this have to sell most of their crop and so will need to borrow again and work extremely hard the next year, or sell an ox'.[31] In a nearby village several years later, Jean Fontanel found a similar cycle of seasonal endebtedness disguising an underlying recurrent poverty.

> An inquiry made by the expert of the Bureau for the Development of Agricultural Production, covering 104 farms, [found that] for a family of five people . . . when debts and credits are balanced, there remains a net surplus of 1,094 riels . . . [However], the preceding year the prices for palm sugar were lower and a summary inquiry revealed . . . a total deficit of 2,000 riels per family . . . in effect, at the end of the palm sugar season, the peasant manages to repay his debts, but, when the rice is planted, the debts reappear to enable food, seeds, and various equipment to be bought. The total profit for the family is therefore practically nil.[32]

Again, within this area where endebtedness was 'much rarer' than on average, a survey of 420 farmers in 14 villages of Kandal Province in 1966 found that 80% had contracted large debts during the year and 67% had not repaid them.[33] Hou Yuon summed up the social mechanics of usury in 1964:

> Actually, interest rates vary from 3% to 20%. CAPITAL is shaped like a cone *[sachi]* – big at the bottom and rising to a small point at the top. For rich people, the interest on money borrowed from the bank is 5% or 8% per year, that is 0.4% or 0.6% per month. Outside the bank, interest rates vary from 3% up to 10% or 20% per month, depending on one's wealth. The poorer the borrower, the higher the interest rate; it's his fault if he is poor! So people who borrow for luxuries pay low interest rates, but those who borrow for luxuries pay low interest rates, but those who borrow out of necessity pay high interest rates! *Human lives are all the same, but their value varies so much!*

If, after 1954, landlords became a significant though secondary force in rural Kampuchea, village usurers, nearly always the ethnic Chinese shopkeeper or trader, multiplied their activities even more quickly. In the rural centre of Slap Leng, studied by a Kampuchean writer in 1974:

> The interviewees recall that around 1950 there were already about 30 Chinese or Sino-Kampuchean shops. In 1960, there were more than 100 . . . Overall, the Chinese and the Sino-Kampucheans make up 70% to 80% of the total population of Slap Leng.
>
> It is noteworthy that the Chinese or Sino-Kampucheans who established their shops in Slap Leng were people who amassed rather

> large fortunes from their activities while living in surrounding Kampuchean villages for about ten years. However, the settlement and development of the Chinese in the Slap Leng region can only be understood in the general context of the Chinese push into the Kampuchean countryside.[34]

With the widespread need to borrow and the exorbitant interest rates, it seems likely that debt repayments took up a similar proportion of a landowning peasant's crop as if the land had been leased from a landlord. There is a curious irony here. The fact that large numbers of Khmer peasants owned smallholdings gave their land very little scarcity value, and, as Khieu Samphan put it, 'only strengthened the economic position of large estates [10-50 hectares] in spite of their small number'.[35] Land was not accepted as collateral on loans. The interest rate would be halved if the borrower possessed capital, but peasants rarely did. Landholding peasants, because of their large numbers, still had to compete with one another for the services of moneylenders and were perhaps as economically dominated by this small privileged group as tenants by landlords. Though clearly not the guarantee against oppression it was often taken to be, the fact that a majority of Khmer peasants owned some land did give them important ties with their land and their village society. In this important respect they differed from the less numerous but still numerically significant dispossessed 'semi-proletariat'.

Merchants

In 1955 Hou Yuon described how the merchants would trick the peasants by altering standard quality measures, depending on whether they were buying or selling rice.[36] In their later works, Hou Yuon and Hu Nim showed how the low rice prices paid to the peasants were maintained. The merchants grip over the peasants was so strong that once, in the 1950s, even after a very bad harvest when rice was scarce, the price of rice actually fell by 30%. The peasants' position was so weakened that they were simply desperate to sell what little surplus they had.[37] In 1964 Hou Yuon wrote:

> How do the peasants sell their produce? At ploughing and transplanting season, the peasants worry whether their work will be productive or not, whether they will be lucky or not, whether they will have enough to eat or not, or whether they will produce enough to pay their land rent or not . . . At harvesting and threshing time, the peasants have other worries – whether there are merchants to buy their produce or not, whether market fluctuations will be up or down, whether merchants will pay them for their produce or not. These problems arise from worry, irregularity, and *uncertainty about the future.* The peasants' concern arises from the experience that they have suffered several times before, without knowing when their plight would come to an end!
>
> During the colonial period, the market fluctuated without control.

> The peasants, the producers and owners of rice, corn, and beans, had no power at all to control prices. Actually, whether the price was 'high or low' did not matter so much; the crucial problem was whether there would be a buyer or not – this was a life and death problem. The majority of the peasants sell their produce as soon as a buyer comes along – they never have time to delay or hold back. The need for money is something that must be satisfied immediately. Even if they can delay, their prospects are uncertain. They are alone in the darkness. Power is not vested in the people who have produce to sell; power is with the buyer.
>
> Why is this so? The production system is different from that of commerce. *Peasants do not organize themselves.* Each one produces separately from the others, striving on his own. They compete to sell their produce, they try to persuade merchants to buy their produce, they rush to sell it before the others do, to get a higher price. Their absolute need gives rise to this sort of attitude and behaviour. Naturally, the merchants become very arrogant, and they have every effective way of maintaining their superior position. Confronting the peasants who are not organized, who are 'individualistic' and 'independent-minded', are the merchants who have their institutions and leaders. They have their contacts everywhere from low to high levels, based on agreements. It is this strong institutional backing that allows the merchants to be so 'arrogant' and to become the controllers of 'market fluctuations'. The peasant, the seller, depends on the price offerd by the buyer! *The peasants are masters neither of the sky nor of the price of their goods!* In the market gardens, as in the market place, all power is vested in the *Chinese.*

Although much work remains to be done in this field of research, it seems that the unusually privileged position enjoyed by merchants and money-lenders (most of whom were ethnic Chinese) in the Kampuchean countryside accounts for the fact that '41% of the Chinese in Cambodia are rural; that is, they live outside the three or four major towns in each province'.[38] Rural Chinese in Kampuchea were in 'a substantially higher proportion than in most other South East Asian countries'.[39]

How did all these factors affect the living standards of the peasants? Delvert offers a detailed study of five families.[40] Two of these, possessing two hectares and three hectares of rice land, had annual deficits. Another family was able to break even with two hectares, and another, with 12 hectares, made a comfortable profit, as did the fifth, with one and a half hectares of river-bank land. It is highly significant that *all* of these families owned well above the average amount of land – Delvert found that 55% of landowners owned less than one hectare of rice land and another 25% owned from one to two; on the river-banks the average landholding was one hectare or less.[41]

In a study of a Khmer village in Siemreap Province in 1960-61,[42] Gabrielle Martel concluded a section on the economic situation of the peasants with the following categorization: 1) 36% of the farming families in the village either had an annual surplus of rice which they sold for cash, or had enough to 'broadly cover their family needs'; 2) 32% of the families had 'hardly enough rice' for family consumption. Their situation was 'very precarious' and they were often in debt; 3) 23% of the families 'quickly register a very big deficit' for the year, 'sometimes leading to penury a few months after the main harvest'; 4) 6% harvest enough rice for their needs but have to part with it because they have been obliged to borrow on credit or have had to sell their crop in advance.

As we have seen, it is true that Kampuchea's class of landowning middle peasants was large. (For this reason Delvert described the country in 1960 as an 'agrarian democracy, rare in Asia'.)[43] On the other hand, studies of Khmer villages carried out in the 1950s and 1960s indicate a high level of rural debt among landowning peasants, and detailed statistics from both 1956 and 1962 reveal a significant if slightly smaller class of poor peasants with *less than half* the two hectares of rice land required on average to feed a family (there was also another sizeable group with between one and two hectares).

Town and Countryside

Finally, it is important to note that the Kampuchean economy as a whole remained overwhelmingly rural throughout this period. In 1970, the number of workers employed in industry (as distinct from less productive service sectors) was still tiny. And since in Phnom Penh, for instance, ethnic Chinese and Vietnamese populations were numerically predominant, the number of Khmer industrial workers was smaller still. Perhaps more than any other South East Asian country, and despite a rapidly growing urban population, Kampuchea was a peasant economy. But the cities did play a role in the system. Hou Yuon summed up the balance of social forces in Kampuchea in 1964:

> We can compare the establishment of commercial organizations in the colonial period to a large spider's web covering all of Kampuchea. If we consider the peasants and consumers as flies or mosquitoes which get trapped in the web, we can see that the peasants and consumers are prey to the merchants, the spider which spins the web. The commercial system, the selling and exchanging of agricultural production in our country *suppresses production, and squeezes the rural areas dry and tasteless, permanently maintaining them in their poverty.* What we habitually call 'cities' or 'market towns' are *pumps* which drain away the vitality of the rural areas. Any type of goods that the cities and market towns provide for the rural areas is just bait. The large rural areas feed the cities and market towns. *The cities – the market towns with their fresh and up-to-date appearance – live at the expense of the miserable rural areas.* The cities *do not support the rural areas – they ride on their shoulders.*

On the basis of a table indicating the distribution of the benefits from the national product among various social classes, Hou Yuon concluded in his 1955 thesis (part of which is translated in Part I):

> Those who work the land, ploughing, harvesting, enduring the entire burden of nature, under the sun and in the rain, getting gnarled fingers and cracked skin on their hands, and feet, receive only 26% as their share, that is, about one-quarter. Whereas the others, who work in the shade, using nothing but their money, receive a share of up to 74%, that is, three-quarters . . . The rural areas are poor, skinny and miserable because of the activities of the commercial system which oppresses them.
>
> The tree grows in the rural areas, but the fruit goes to the towns.

The general problems of usury and unfavourable trade prices, seriously affecting nearly all landowning Kampuchean peasants by the 1960s, pointed to the need for significant social change. But there was no such change under the Sihanouk regime – in fact pressure on the peasants increased – and it was not surprising that by the late 1960s and early 1970s the appeals of socialist revolutionaries found an audience in many Kampuchean villages.

Beyond this, however, loomed the problem of a politically significant minority within the peasant community who were in increasing numbers being torn from their land, and their social setting, by powerful forces well beyond their control. This dispossessed 'semi-proletariat' would have very little to lose from a quite different revolution, a rapid and total social upheaval, even if it eventually brought few material benefits to the rural population as a whole.

By 1970, the social basis had been laid in Kampuchea for the possible development of *two* very different social transformations. And after 1970, the ranks of those torn from their land and village community were to swell greatly.

The Early Communist Movement

In 1929, a member of the French *Surete* network wrote:

> In fact the Cambodians, in spite of the proximity of the Vietnamese and Chinese, have not yet learnt to organize meetings, to hatch conspiracies. They only know how to gather together on pagoda feast-days and for funeral ceremonies, which are not very suitable for intrigues.[44]

The first Khmer known to have become involved in Communist activities was Ben Krahom, a 24-year-old coolie at the Phnom Penh electricity works.

Also involved were two other young Khmers from a Phnom Penh monastery and two young Vietnamese from the prestigious College Sisowath, as well as Krahom's Vietnamese wife, with whom he lived in Phnom Penh's Catholic village. On 31 July 1930, the six distributed in Phnom Penh an 'important' number of Vietnamese-language leaflets advancing, among other causes, the struggle of the proletariat against imperialism. They also hung three red banners 'with Soviet emblems' from trees, bearing slogans, in Vietnamese, calling on the population to establish a 'workers' government'. Krahom, along with two of the others, was arrested and sentenced to 18 months' jail. He and his wife said they had been given some of the leaflets by a guard at the electricity works and others by a travelling hairdresser, confessions which do not seem consistent with their explanation that they thought they were distributing cinema programmes.[45]

Conscious or not, Krahom's Communist connections were rare enough for a Khmer at that time: revolutionary activity in Kampuchea was restricted almost exclusively to the ethnic Vietnamese community – particularly the rubber plantation workers but also officials and skilled urban workers in the French colonial apparatus. The vast majority of the Khmer remained rural and, as far as the colonialists were concerned, 'outside history'. The French official was undoubtedly right when he wrote in 1934 that: 'On January 14, the anniversary of the deaths of Liebknecht, Rosa Luxembourg and Lenin, there were no demonstrations or leaflets distributed in Cambodia.'[46]

But there were growing nationalist sentiments among Khmer Buddhist monks linked with other signs of change. In 1932, a 28-year-old ethnic Khmer from Vietnam, who was working as a fisherman on Kampuchea's Great Lake, joined Ho Chi Minh's Indochina Communist Party (ICP). Under the name of Thach Choeun, he carried out a political 'mission' in Kampuchea until 1936, when he briefly took a job in Mekong Delta printworks. The next year he returned to Kampuchea and became a Buddhist monk in Takeo; in 1939, he left the monastery to become chief of the ICP for Svay Rieng Province.[47]

After the outbreak of the 2nd World War and the arrival of Japanese troops in Kampuchea, Choeun is said to have fled to Thailand where Ho Chi Minh had established contacts. His activities over the next few years are unclear. According to Vietnamese sources, Choeun 'took a leading part' in the anti-French demonstration of July 1942[48] (see Part II) in Phnom Penh. From 1943 until June 1945 he lived in another monastery, apparently Wat Yeay Tep in Kompong Chhnang Province. Re-entering lay life again at the end of the war, he took part, according to French intelligence, 'in the insurrectional movement at the side of Son Ngoc Thanh',[50] the anti-colonial nationalist leader. When the French re-established their control in late 1945, Choeun fled across the Vietnamese border to Rach Gia, as did other nationalist figures such as Pach Chhoeun. He was later to adopt the name Son Ngoc Minh and become Chairman of Kampuchea's first Communist Party.

Norodom Sihanouk

1945 is the year from which Michael Vickery takes up the story of modern Kampuchean political history in Part II. Vickery's discussion of politics in the 1945-54 period and of Prince Sihanouk's regime (1954-70) throws much light on the aftermath of the *coup d'etat* that led first to Lon Nol's Khmer Republic (1970-75), during which period American B-52s dropped half a million tonnes of bombs on Kampuchean populated areas (compared to 160,000 tonnes dropped on Japan in the Second World War), and then, from 1975 to 79, the radical and violent Communism of Pol Pot's Democratic Kampuchea regime (see Part III). But first, an examination of some of the issues that arose during the 1946-54 independence war throws some light on the changes and continuities in the years that followed.

King Sihanouk was crowned in 1941 at the age of 18. The 1952 Vietnamese Communist description of him, in a Khmer-language broadcast, as 'the fascist novice',[51] was not entirely inaccurate: he had been selected by the (Vichy) Governor-General of French Indochina, at that time an ally of the Japanese. As Part II shows, in the 1940s and early 1950s, Sihanouk was quite clearly an important asset to Western colonialism, and in no way favoured Kampuchean civil or religious progressives. In 1951, the Communists put it like this: 'King Sihanouk, already gone to fat, who shamelessly makes use of sensuous perfumes . . . must not rule.'[52]

When they failed to have their way, however, the Communists began a reassessment after the end of the war in 1954. Sihanouk abdicated the throne in 1955 and, standing for election in that year, robbed the leftist Democratic and Communist Pracheachon parties not only of victory but also of their foreign policy platform of neutrality.[53] Vicious in his repression of the Left, the Prince's internal position in Kampuchea was impregnable in the short term; but at the same time, at the height of the Cold War, he was, like it or not, advancing the cause of anti-imperialism.

The socialist bloc considered that on balance he could prove to be an asset. At the beginning of 1956, Chinese Premier Chou En-Lai visited Phnom Penh. Around the same time, the Pracheachon Party called for a united anti-imperialist front between Sihanouk's Sangkum Party and the Democratic and Pracheachon Parties. The scene was set for 20 years of sporadic but at times mutually fruitful collaboration between Indochinese Communists and Prince Sihanouk.

For the Communists this relationship had disadvantages, particularly for any possibility of a Kampuchean revolution in the short term. But it also bore its fruit: in the mid-1960s, Sihanouk broke completely with the United States, permitting supplies to go through to the revolutionary bases in South Vietnam and Vietnamese Communist 'sanctuaries' to remain in the border areas of Kampuchea.

To underline the ambiguity of the relationship, one need only take the experience of one Kampuchean Communist, Hou Yuon. In 1953, as a left-wing student and chairperson of the General Union of Khmer Students in Paris, he had sent a telegram to King Sihanouk in Phnom Penh, stating among other things that 'the suffering existing in the Khmer land is the fault of the monarchy', and that 'the King is trying to destroy the freedom of the Khmer people'.[54] This was the first known conscious, frontal attack on the monarchy in Kampuchean history. Completing his doctoral thesis two years later, Hou Yuon refused to follow the accepted practice, even among left-wing students, dedicating his thesis to the King. (Khieu Samphan, for instance, did so in his 1959 thesis.)

On his return to Kampuchea in 1956, however, Hou Yuon seems to have seen the need for a more flexible political approach. He became involved in the legal struggle for a neutral foreign policy and for rural co-operatives to serve the peasants. He later even joined the Prince's Sangkum Party and held a number of Cabinet positions; in 1964, he published a book calling for a United Front between the Communists and the Sihanouk regime in order to defeat the greatest enemy, American imperialism. Yet in 1967, hounded by the regime's police, he fled to the countryside where he took a leading role in an anti-Government guerrilla movement. Then, with Sihanouk's overthrow in 1970, he again called for a United Front with the Prince, becoming Minister of the Interior in the revolutionary government headed nominally by Sihanouk, which eventually came to power in 1975. Disappearing from public view almost immediately, however (even before Sihanouk himself was put under house arrest), Hou Youn apparently died in a Pol Pot prison.

What is the explanation for what seems an unusual Communist tolerance for royalty? It goes beyond the need of Hanoi and the N.L.F. for a neutral or favourable regime on their western flank as they struggled with the might of the U.S. military. For a combination of reasons – personal flair, a quasi-religious royal legitimacy, a spirited defence of his country's independence and a dose of genuine if haphazard populism, especially in his education policies – Norodom Sihanouk, at the height of his career, was an impressive figure to most Kampuchean peasants. Outright confrontation with his regime might well have meant courting political disaster. And a Sihanouk totally committed to the U.S. anti-Communist cause would have been much more dangerous for all the revolutionaries of Indochina than South Vietnam's Thieu or Prince Souvanna Phouma of Laos. In fact, Sihanouk's role, in what was a key country (especially after 1970), as an ally of the Communist forces, played an important part in their triple victory in Indochina in 1975.

Even the anti-Vietnamese Kampuchean Communists led by Pol Pot realized this, opting for a formal and public alliance with the Prince after 1970, while nevertheless persecuting his followers (who included many peasants) who had been encouraged to join Pol Pot precisely by that very alliance. This policy was to deprive Pol Pot of political communication with the majority of the Kampuchean people. It certainly contributed to the 1975 evacuation of Phnom Penh, a war-weary and disillusioned city where many looked forward to the Prince's return. Yet after the evacuation the Pol Pot group still maintained the Prince for another year as titular head of state.

Sihanouk posed, perhaps more clearly than ever before, the question of internationalism in the Communist movement. Did his fierce repression of socialists and other dissidents mean that Kampuchean revolutionaries should go into armed offensive against his regime? And if they did, what would be their chances of success, once the offensive had driven the Prince and his followers much closer to the U.S., thus putting the Americans in a better position to weaken the overall prospects of social revolution in Indochina?

On the other hand, as the Vietnam War dragged on through the 1960s and there seemed no light at the end of the dark tunnel in which the Kampuchean revolution found itself, was there ever to be any pay-off to an endless and debilitating alliance (or, as in the case of Hou Yuon, defenceless restraint)? Might it not just end in a U.S. victory or stalemate in Vietnam, and a still unchallenged Sihanouk in Kampuchea? Wouldn't it be preferable to try to defeat U.S. imperialism in one country?

Faced with this dilemma, it is little wonder that the Kampuchean Communist movement split. What is more difficult to understand (and is discussed in Part III) is why the movement did not find unity once again with the departure of the main divisive factor – the desperate situation caused by the hammer blows of the U.S. machine throughout Indochina.

It may be appropriate at this point to round off this historical picture with the case of another Kampuchean Communist, Keo Chenda who was involved in the anti-French struggle as early as 1949, at a time when Sihanouk had 'proved he is a traitor to his people, a slave of the French colonialists [and] must be beaten in the work he is undertaking'. After spending the next 30 years in the jungle, in Hanoi, in the anti-Lon Nol resistance and then in the forces which overthrew Pol Pot's Democratic Kampuchea, Chenda became in 1979 a leader of the People's Republic of Kampuchea in Phnom Penh and Minister of Information in the pro-Vietnamese government (see Part III). When Chenda broke with the 'Pol Pot-Vorn Vet clique' in 1973, he maintained that Kampuchean revolutionaries should march against the U.S.' with Prince Sihanouk'. But by 1979, his government proclaimed that Prince Sihanouk was 'objectively a traitor' because of his close association with Pol Pot's backers in Peking and had 'no role to play' in Kampuchea's future. The revolution's attitude to the Prince had come full circle.

The Vietnamese Connection before 1954

The second Kampuchean political issue that arose in the pre-1954 period was the relations between Vietnamese and Kampuchean revolutionaries and between the two populations. That they also had their ambiguities can be seen in the accounts of 1942 demonstrator Bunchan Mul and Krot Theam, a former member of the Khmer Issarak (a generic term for the 1946-54 anti-French armed resistance) (see Part II). Cultural and racial differences created important problems. Perhaps political ones did too: a 1934 'letter to comrades in Cambodia' from the ICP leadership stressed that 'there can be no question of a separate Cambodian revolution' because of the French hold throughout Indochina.[55] The early impact in Kampuchea of such a strategy, which incidentally was also adopted by nationalist forces of the period in other colonial transnational agglomerations such as Indonesia and India, is not documented. But it raised the question of whether co-ordination of the anti-colonial strategy in the three countries of Indochina would necessarily lead to the creation of a single post-colonial state dominated by the much more numerous Vietnamese. This question was addressed in 1940 by the Eighth Plenum of the Central Committee of the I.C.P., which resolved 'to settle the national question within the framework of each of the three countries of Vietnam, Laos and Cambodia, and . . . to create favourable conditions for the Cambodian and Lao peoples to develop the spirit of independence and sovereignty'.[56]

However this issue was viewed by 1953, the Vietnamese Communists did achieve political successes in Kampuchea, winning the sympathy of significant numbers of Kampucheans, including people with impeccable nationalist credentials, some of whem were very influential in their country. French intelligence sources described an important Issarak leader named Neang (Mme.) Muon as 'pro-Viet Minh', adding: 'Intelligent, very energetic, an experienced horserider, Neang Muon enjoys great prestige in Siemreap and Battambang and must be considered as a dangerous rebel element'.[57] And Leav Keo Moni, head of the important 'National Liberation Central Committee' based in Battambang, was described as: 'An ardent nationalist, he enjoys great popularity among the Khmer Issarak of the north-west. Crafty and greedy, he is nevertheless renowned for his honesty and integrity'.[58] After the 1954 Geneva Conference, Leav Keo Moni withdrew to Hanoi with 2,000 or so other Kampuchean revolutionaries.[59] Then there were the seven minor Khmer officials who, in August 1945, stormed into King Sihanouk's palace in an attempt to force his abdication and impose an independent government before the return of the French. Five of these young nationalists later worked very closely with the Vietnamese Communists. One, Neth Laing Say, became political commissar in a joint Vietnamese/Khmer command set up in Battambang in June 1946. Another, Mam Koun, was arrested by the French in 1952 'for supplying secret information to the Viet Minh'. A third, Mey Pho, after escaping from jail in late 1945, became an Issarak leader in the north-west of Kampuchea. From January to April 1951, Pho travelled with Hong Chhun and Neang Muon through Viet Minh-held areas of the Mekong Delta on behalf of the National Liberation Central Committee. Like the other two delegates, Pho returned to Kampuchea 'a partisan of collaboration' with the Vietnamese Communists.[60]

Son Ngoc Thanh, the best known non-Communist nationalist of the pre-independence period, took to the *maquis* in 1952. Although he kept his distance from the Viet Minh and their Kampuchean allies, as they kept theirs from him, both sides saw the logic of a united anti-colonial front in Indochina. French intelligence sources noted that before his departure for the *maquis*, Son Ngoc Thanh had been in contact with the Viet Minh. A captured Viet Minh document even gave the Viet Minh the credit for persuading him to leave Phnom Penh, through the intermediary of Neang Muon and 'the National Liberation Central Committee. The French reported that from his base in a north-western guerrilla zone, Thanh 'praised collaboration with the Viet Minh' and promised listeners to his clandestine radio broadcasts that military aid was coming from 'these allies . . . thanks to which the French will soon be swept from Cambodia'. The French, in fact, believed that Thanh was in 'regular' communication with Kampuchean Communist leader Son Ngoc Minh. They knew that two autonomous Kampuchean rebel leaders had been invited by Thanh to unite forces with other rebels, specifically including the Viet Minh, 'to bring peace to Cambodia again'. Another had been urged by the Viet Minh to join forces with Son Ngoc Thanh.[61]

It was, therefore, not without precedent, when, in 1970-73, and again in 1979, Vietnamese Communist troops found relatively few Kampuchean villages hostile, and often managed to establish good relations with the peasants there.[62] The Western colonial strategy, as expressed by the Vietnamese in 1951, 'to keep the Cambodians out of the Issarak movement and make the Cambodians hate the Vietnamese',[63] had at least partially failed. Although the Vietnamese claim, in the following year, that racial hatred between the two peoples 'was caused and maintained by the French colonialists and the U.S. imperialists', was a half-truth,[64] a contemporary statement put it another way: 'What is the use of dwelling on facts a thousand years old?[65]

It is certainly true that the behaviour of Vietnamese Communist armies in Kampuchea has been notably different to the cruelty and pillage, not to say cultural domination, displayed by traditional Vietnamese invaders, as well as by troops of the U.S.-backed Saigon regime from 1970-72.[66] The political strategy of attempting to form an alliance with an extremely broad section of current Kampuchean opinion (including, for instance, Son Ngoc Thanh in the 1950s and Prince Sihanouk in the 1970s), was also unlike that of other Vietnamese armies.

One of the earliest Viet Minh documents captured in Kampuchea provides a useful insight into both the motivation and the style of Vietnamese Communist operations there. Dated 30 April 1949, the statutes of the League for National Salvation of Vietnamese Residents in Cambodia point out that Kampuchean and Vietnamese revolutionary organizations.

> must live side by side to help one another, to exchange initiatives and lessons drawn from experience, to help the two peoples to understand one another, to realize in deeds Khmer-Vietnamese friendship, to conclude on the basis of equality an alliance between the two peoples in the struggle against the reactionary French colonialists, invaders of

> Cambodia and of Vietnam.

The same document then goes on to show how revolutionary power should be allocated in Kampuchea.

> Following the agreement of 16.1.48 of the [revolutionary] Government of the Southeast of Cambodia
>
> Following the agreement of 23.4.49 of the representative of the Government of the Southwest, M. Meas Svam
>
> a) In the localities inhabited entirely by Vietnamese, the latter may take part in the Government of their localities.
>
> b) In the localities populated by Cambodians and Vietnamese where the Cambodian element forms the majority of the population the Vietnamese may occupy auxiliary posts in the Government of their localities to aid the Cambodian authorities and conciliate the interests of the Vietnamese with those of the Cambodians.
>
> c) The internal administration is entirely the province of the Cambodian Government and is assured by the Cambodians.[67]

In the Communist Party itself, at least in the early period of its political formation, the Vietnamese role was much more significant. In 1951, the I.C.P. split into separate Vietnamese, Kampuchean and Lao parties, but the Vietnamese body evidently claimed at that stage a continuing 'right to supervise the activities of its brother parties in Cambodia and Laos'.[68] It began a large-scale programme to train Khmer cadres. A fragment of a Viet Minh document captured by the French, dating from late 1951, noted that the Vietnamese Party was 'responsible for a major part' of the training of Kampuchean Communists, although liaisons between the two parties should 'observe the principles of secrecy'.[69] According to French intelligence, until August 1951, the Cambodians admitted into [the I.C.P.] were few in number. From that date, a larger place was made available to them',[70] including some Khmers who were sent to study in liberated areas of South Vietnam. Despite difficulties such as, according to the same source, 'candidates who at once proved to be lacking in understanding, nonchalant and undisciplined', significant results were recorded. According to the captured fragment (which was marked 'to be burnt after reading'), in 1950 the Communist movement in Kampuchea had 1,300 members, of whom only 40 were Khmer. Within one year, the document continued, these figures had risen to 4,000 and 1,000 respectively.[71]

By what methods were these people trained? A conference organized in June 1952 by Son Ngoc Minh and the leader of the Viet Minh troops in Kampuchea decided to set up, in each of Kampuchea's four military zones, a political-military school

> led by the Vietnamese but teaching in the Cambodian language, following a plan established by the [Communist South Vietnamese]

> Command. The Vietnamese cadres, put at the disposition of the Issarak groups, must know the Khmer language which will be the sole language used in the ranks of the Cambodian resistance.[72]

It is not surprising to read, in a history written by officials of the Communist Party of Kampuchea in 1973, that Marxism-Leninism had been 'injected into our revolutionary movement by the international Communist movement and by the Vietnamese Communists'. In this internal document, produced when the Party was 'at the age of a man in his prime, capable of directing the revolution by itself, with satisfactory support', there are no traces of resentment on the part of Kampuchean Communists of the close supervision exercised by the Vietnamese during the early period of their Party's political formation.[73]

Outside the Communist Party, the number of Khmers who worked with or fought alongside the Viet Minh before 1954 remains difficult to estimate. French intelligence sources in 1952 appeared unwilling to name a figure for the strength of the Communist-led Issaraks. They did point out, though, that the movement was in the process of forming a main force unit of Khmer fighters in Takeo and the south of Kompong Speu Province, and that a similar armed force already existed in Prey Veng.[74] Krot Theam's account in 'Resisting the French' in Part II shows the strength of these Khmer revolutionary forces in Battambang, suggesting that the 5,000 figure usually quoted for armed guerrillas in the country by 1954 is an underestimate.

The Viet Minh and 2,000 or so of their Khmer allies withdrew to Vietnam after the Geneva Conference, while elections were held in Kampuchea in which Sihanouk's Sangkum Party took all the seats. The repressive conditions in which these elections were held are discussed by Michael Vickery in Part II. But in some cases the former Communist-led Issaraks, campaigning under the banner of their Pracheachon Party, still managed to win large numbers of votes. Men Suon, for instance, a Pracheachon candidate in Kompong Speu, was one of two leftists shot dead by local authorities a month after the poll; according to the International Commission for Supervision and Control, 'the motive appeared to be Men Suon's success in the elections'.[75]

Still, in some provinces, the Vietnamese and their allies encountered a good deal of peasant apathy towards the nationalist cause (as did the non-Communist Issaraks). For, despite the fact that 'the poor' were specifically exempted from membership dues in the communist-organized Issarak Front,[76] it was nationalism and not social change that the Front regarded as the major issue during this period. The Communists also found many peasants still reluctant, from traditional racial feeling, to work with the foreigners. But by far their biggest failure was among the relatively few (but, perhaps, politically significant) city-based Khmers. While a single agent of the Viet Minh Committee for Phnom Penh managed to recruit, in 1951, 150 ethnic Vietnamese workers and 50 officials and students, results among urban Khmers were not so spectacular. The Committee complained, in a document captured by the French and dated 11 September 1951:

> Contrary to what they promised us, the monks have not yet presented any Cambodian candidates. We have addressed a letter to R.L., a progressive element in the city, but we have received no reply . . . Of our plan to create the Issarak movement [in Phnom Penh], we are able to achieve only one aspect: propaganda.[77]

Apart from this failure in the Kampuchean capital, it might be said in conclusion that the Communists did succeed in making political inroads in rural areas, recruiting a substantial peasant following, and attracting the support of many leading Kampuchean nationalists and forming a more temporary alliance with some others. King Sihanouk had recognized this when he said in 1951 that 'these disruptive foreign elements, by pressure or lying propaganda, have managed to win to their cause a great number of our compatriots'.[78] In October 1959, Son Ngoc Thanh, who had broken his working agreement with the Communists some years before and aligned himself with the U.S., wrote that Sihanouk 'is certainly not unaware of the Cambodian students, high school and normal school pupils, porters and dockers who have moved to North Vietnam to join up with the Khmer Communist army at Hoa Binh'.[79] It is important to note, too, that despite the vast cultural differences between Vietnamese and Khmers, the Communist-led Issaraks included many former Buddhist monks (or *achar*). The two most prominent examples are Son Ngoc Minh and his deputy in the Communist Party, Tou Samouth, who had studied at the Pali School of Higher Learning in Phnom Penh. 'Facts a thousand years old' had not been shown to be irrelevant, but they were at least losing some of their significance in Kampuchea.

But not in Paris.

Pol Pot

In 1950, a small group of Kampuchean students in France has formed a 'Marxist circle'. One of them, Saloth Sar, signed his contributions to a 1952 Khmer student magazine as the 'Original Khmer'.[80] These writings included fierce attacks on King Sihanouk and on the monarchy, not an attitude one would have expected given his own background. Another, Ieng Sary, admired Josef Stalin for his tactic of controlling the organizational structure of a Communist Party by 'holding the dossiers', but also took a great interest in Stalin's treatment of the question of 'National Minorities'.

Saloth Sar was born in 1928 in a village of 100 families in Kompong Thom Province, a part of Kampuchea whose inhabitants had been described by a French official in 1929 as 'the most deeply Cambodian and the least susceptible to our influence'.[81] According to a former local resident, his father was a well-known landowner who had a herd of 30-40 buffaloes, employed about 40 labourers at harvest time and often sponsored village festivals. Saloth Sar's cousin, Luk Khun Meak, had been one of the prominent wives of King Monivong (Sihanouk's predecessor) and his sister, Neak Moneang Roeung, also held a title as one of the King's concubines. At one point in the 1930s, King Monivong had visited Saloth Sar's family in their house in the village. Sar's elder brother Suong, with whom he lived in Phnom Penh before his departure for France in 1949, worked in the royal palace.[82]

Saloth Sar, Ieng Sary and the other dozen members of this small group of left-wing Khmer students in Paris were to go many different ways over the next 20 or more years – already in discussion groups Saloth Sar found himself in disagreement with Hou Yuon.[83] Returning home in 1953, Sar spent the last year of the independence war in the jungle, with the Communist-led Issaraks. His own role in Communist politics at that time was later revealed in the *Black Book*, published in 1978 by the regime he headed (see Part III). According to this, the party, which had been formed in 1951, was 'secretly organized' by the Vietnamese 'without the knowledge of the revolutionaries of Kampuchea'; and it was only in 1957 that 'some revolutionaries' learned about its leading organs. During the 1955 elections, Saloth Sar carried out liaison work between the Democratic Party and the Communist Pracheachon group. According to a former close associate, it was at this time that Sar 'really learned about politics'. Although a relative late-comer to the Communist struggle, it was not long before the 'original Khmer', later under the name of Pol Pot, was to make his mark.

References

1. *Chotmaihet Phraratkitraiwan Phraratniphon nai Phrabat Somdet Phrachulachomklaochaoyuhua* ('Diary of King Rama V'), Part 19 (Bangkok, 1970), entries for 4 and 10 May 1885, reports from the Governors of Chanthaburi and Pacchangirikhet. I am grateful to Chalong Soontranavich for providing me with the translation from Thai.
2. Armand Rousseau, *Le protectorat francais du Cambodge – Organisation politique, administrative et financiere* (Dijon, Pillu Roand Imprimiere, 1904), pp. 169-70.
3. See the Ph.D. thesis by David P. Chandler, *Cambodia Before the French: Politics in a Tributary Kingdom* (University of Michigan, University Microfilms, 1 April 1977).
4. The preceding information about Pou Kombo's rebellion comes from Jean Moura, *Le Royaume du Cambodge* (Paris, Ernest Leroux, 1887) pp. 159-61, 170, 172, and from Milton Osborne, *The French Presence in Cochinchina and Cambodia, 1858-1905: Rule and Response* (Cornell University Press, 1969), p. 187. I am also grateful to Chalong Soontranavich for providing me with the contemporary Thai intelligence reports.
5. Archives d'Outre-Mer, Aix-en-Provence, France. Fonds de la Residence Superieure du Cambodge, 3E 7 (6), Kratie Province, *Rapports Annuals*, 1925-6. I am grateful to David Chandler for drawing these archives to my attention.
6. 'Transformation in Cambodia' (Commonweal, 1976).

7. See Milton Osborne, *Politics and Power in Cambodia* (Melbourne, Longmans, 1973).
8. See Milton Osborne, 'Peasant Politics in Cambodia: The 1916 Affair', *Modern Asian Studies* No 12, 1978, pp. 217-43.
9. Archives d'Outre-Mer, Cambodge, 3E 4 (3), Kompong Cham Province, 1st trimestre, 1916.
10. Georges Coulet, *Societes Secretes au Terre d'Annam* (Saigon, C. Ardin, 1926).
11. Archives d' Outre-Mer, Cambodge 3E 8 (2), Prey Veng Province, 1st trimestre, 1916.
12. Ibid., 3E 7 (4), Kratie Province, 1st trimestre, 1924.
13. Ibid., 3E 4 (4), Kompong Cham Province, 1st trimestre, 1927, dated 15 April 1927.
14. Ibid.
15. Jean Delvert, *Le Paysan Cambodgien*, (Paris, Mouton, 1960), p. 370, note 283.
16. Ibid, pp. 267, 346, 360. See also Khieu Samphan's Ph.D. thesis, *Cambodia's Economy and Industrial Development*, University of Paris, 1959; English translation by Laura Summers as Data Paper No. 111, Southeast Asia Program, Cornell University, 1979).
17. Hou Yuon, *The Peasantry of Kampuchea*, (1955) (see Part I); Remy Prudhomme, *l'Economie du Cambodge* (Paris, 1969), p.70; International Bank for Reconstruction and Development, *Report of Economic Mission to Cambodia–1969*, Vol. 1, 'The Main Report', 12 October, 1970, p.12.
18. *Pahnyaha sahakor* ('The Cooperative Question') (Phnom Penh, 1964), Chapter 1. Further quotations from this chapter, which does not appear in Part II, can be found below.
19. Prudhomme, op. cit., p. 70.
20. J. Fontanel, 'Un Example de Modernisation Rurale au Cambodge: le centre pilote de Chhak Chhoeu Neang', *Revue de geographie alpine*, Vol LV, No. 1, 1967, 341-69.
21. May Ebihara, *Svay: A Khmer Village in Cambodia*, (Ph.D. thesis, (Columbia, 1968), pp. 680-1.
22. For the 1956 figures, see Delvert, op. cit., pp. 322, 371, 495. For 1962, see Hu Nim, *Land Tenure and Social Structure in Kampuchea* (see Part I).
23. Khieu Samphan, op. cit. By coincidence, Samphan was in fact referring to 1930-31 statistics from Battambang, Prey Veng and Svay Rieng Provinces, which had higher than average proportions of medium holdings, due to the fact that local rice cultivation techniques require greater land areas. He estimated the middle peasants ('2 to 7 hectares') as 'numerically the largest group (60%), with the major share of cultivated land (40%)', estunates which were well above the national average in 1931 but closer to the 1962 figures.
24. Virginia Thompson, *French Indochina*, New York, Octagon, 1968

reprint), p. 356.

25. *Le Khmer,* Phnom Penh, 4 April 1936.
26. *Nokor Wat,* 29 January 1938. This newspaper was run by Son Ngoc Thanh and Pach Chhoeun (see Part II).
27. *Monographie de la Province de Kompong Cham* (Saigon, 1939), p. 144-5.
28. Delvert, op. cit., Ch. 17.
29. Ibid., p. 552.
30. Ebihara, op. cit., pp. 275, 333-4.
31. Ibid.
32. Fontanel, op. cit., p. 350.
33. Prudhomme, op. cit., p. 83.
34. Oum Sakun, 'Le Centre Rural de Slap Leng: un exemple de l'exploitation des paysans cambodgiens par les Chinois' (Phnom Penh, June 1974), reproduced in Roland Thomas, *l'Evolution Economique du Cambodge, 1900-1940* (these de 3e cycle, University of Paris, 1976), pp. 157-64.
35. Samphan, op. cit.
36. For corroboration, see Oum Sakun, op. cit, for example.
37. Delvert, op. cit., p. 361.
38. W.E. Wilmott, *The Chinese in Cambodia* (1967), p. 17.
39. W.E. Willmott, *The Political Structure of the Chinese in Cambodia* (1970), p. 6.
40. Delvert, op. cit., pp. 524-31.
41. Ibid., pp. 495, 492.
42. Gabrielle Martel, *Lovea: Village des environs d'Angkor* (Ecole Francaise de l'Extreme-Orient, Paris, Vol. XCVIII, pp. 143-4.
43. Delvert, op. cit., pp. 652-3.
44. Archives d'Outre-Mer, Cambodge, 7F 15 C (7), *Surete Report,* 1928-9.
45. Ibid., 7F 15, 'Direction de la Surete', *Rapport annuel,* 1930-31, pp. 9-12.
46. Ibid., 7F 14 (1), 'Notes mensuelles', January 1934.
47. Ibid., 7F 29 (2), *Note sur l'Organisation Politique et Administrative Viet-Minh au Cambodge*, Direction des services de securite du H.C. en Indochine, December 1952, p. 23.
48. *Vietnam Information*, issued by Vietnam News Service, in English, Rangoon. No. 365, 23 December 1950, p.7.
49. 'Biography of Chandara Mohaphtey' (former Khmer Issarak Minister of the Interior), by himself; unpublished, English translation, p. 7. Archives d'Outre-Mer, *Note sur l'Organisation,* op. cit., p. 23, gives the name of the monastery as 'Wat Pao I (?)'. According to Charles Meyer, in *Derriere le Sourire Khmer* (Paris, Plon, 1971), it was Wat Unnalom in Phnom Penh.
50. Archives d'Outre-Mer, *Note sur l'Organisation,* op. cit.
51. U.S. C.I.A., Foreign Broadcast Information Service (E.B.I.S.); Viet-

Minh Radio Voice of Nam Bo, in Khmer to South Vietnam, 30 June 1952.

52. F.B.I.S. 27 April 1951, CCC 4; Voice of Nam Bo, 19 April 1951.
53. See the discussion of the 1955 elections in Michael Vickery's contribution to Part II of this volume.
54. *Khemara Nisit* (Paris), No. 14, August 1952, in Khmer.
55. The letter went on: 'There is only one Indochinese revolution. As Indochina is under the domination of a single imperialist government, all the revolutionary forces must be unified, and brought under the direction of a single party: the I.C.P . . . Cambodia has no right to have a distinct communist Party.' Quoted in Pierre Rousset, *Communism et Nationalisme Vietnamien* (Paris, Galilee, 1978), pp. 200-2.
56. *History of the August Revolution* (Hanoi, Foreign Languages Publishing House, 1972), pp. 28-9. In 1935, an I.C.P. document captured by the French dealt with the smaller nationalities in Indochina as follows: 'After the eviction of the French imperialists from Indochina, these minorities will have the right to run their own affairs, up to and including the right to separate and form an independent State and adopt the political regime of their choice. The worker, peasant and military soviet government of Indochina undertakes not to interfere in their internal affairs.' Rousset, op. cit., p. 201.
57. Archives d'Outre-Mer, Cambodge, 7F 29 (7). *Etude sur les Mouvements Rebelles au Cambodge, 1942-52*, Index, p. 24.
58. Ibid., Index, p. 26
59. Meyer, op. cit.; Meyer also says that Leav Keo Moni spent the next 15 years working with the Pathet Lao revolutionaries in Laos and is said to have been in charge of liaison with the Thai Patriotic Front. He then returned to the revolutionary movement in Kampuchea in 1970, when he 'reappeared in Stung Treng', pp. 188, 389.
60. Archives d'Outre-Mer, *Etude,* op. cit., Index, p. 10.
61. Ibid., pp. 40, 50, 62, 59.
62. See Part III. Prince Sihanouk wrote in 1979 that in 1970-73, 'the Vietnamese know that in their later operations at least 50% of the Khmers would not fail to welcome them as "liberators" and . . . as old friends!' *Chroniques de Guerre et d'Espoir* (Paris, Hachette-Stock, 1979), pp. 149-50.
63. F.B.I.S., 2 March 1951, Khmer-language broadcast to South Vietnam.
64. F.B.I.S., 15 April 1952, CCC 4; Voice of Nam Bo in Cochinchinese to South Vietnam, 12 April 1952. There is no doubt that it was half true. French intelligence noted that it was 'comforting' to see that the Khmer people were 'rather reticent' towards the Communists, 'except in the regions where the Viet Minh are solidly implanted'. 'This state of mind should doubtless be attributed to their centuries-old hatred of the Vietnamese'. Archives d'Outre Mer, *Note sur l'Organisation,* op. cit., p.22.
65. F.B.I.S., 2 March 1951, op. cit.
66. In 1840, Vietnamese Emperor Minh Mang reacted to a rebellion in Kampuchea as follows: 'Sometimes the Cambodians are loyal; at other

times they betray us. We helped them when they were suffering, and lifted them out of the mud . . . Now they are rebellious: I am so angry that my hair stands upright . . . Hundreds of knives should be used against them, to chop them up, to dismember them . . .' Elsewhere he ordered that they be 'crushed to powder'. Chandler op. cit. On the behaviour of the Saigon army in Kampuchea in the early 1970s, see for instance William Shawcross, *Sideshow; Kissinger, Nixon and the Destruction of Cambodia* (London, Andre Deutsch, 1979), pp.151, 174-5, 185, 222-3, 249.

67. Archives d'Outre, *Note sur l'Organisation,* op. cit. Annexe 3, 'Statuts de la Ligue des Vietnamiens emigres au Cambodge pour le Salut National', section 6, 'Independance entre les pouvoirs revolutionnaires du Cambodge et la Ligue d'Emigres Vietnamiens'.

68. 'Remarks on the Official Appearance of the Vietnam Workers' Party', in *U.S. Operation Mission Vietnam Captured Documents Series,* No. 2, quoted in Stephen Heder, 'Kampuchea's Armed Struggle: The Origins of an Independent Revolution', *Bulletin of Concerned Asian Scholars,* Vol. 11, No. 1, 1979, p.1.

69. Archives d'Outre-Mer, *Note sur l'Organisation,* op. cit. Annexe 3, 'Traduction d'un fragment de document redige en langue vietnamienne' Chapter 6, 'Consolidation du Parti Cambodgien'; undated, probably late 1951.

70. Ibid., p.21,

71. Ibid., Annexe 3, Chapter 6.

72. Ibid., p. 21.

73. *Summary of Annotated Party History,* 'copy of the original text, by the Eastern Region Military Political Service', translated captured document, Echols Collection, Cornell University Olin Library.

74. Archives de l'Outre-Mer, op. cit., p. 98.

75. Reports of the I.C.S.C., Command Papers, *Cambodia No. 1, 1957, Cmnd 253,* p.34.

76. Archives de l'Outre-Mer, *Note sur l'Organisation,* op. cit., Annexe 2, Samakhum Khmer Issarak, 'Sommaire du statut de l'association et du front d'union nationale', 15 November 1950, issued by the Political-Military and Administrative Committee of Kompong Chhnang and north Kompong Speu.

77. Ibid., pp.16-7. 'R.L.' is almost certainly Ray Lomuth, editor of a Khmer newspaper which, according to French intelligence, was suspended two months previously, following 'its violent anti-French campaigns'. This may be part of the reason why in the general elections of 9 September 1951 (two days before the Viet Minh Committee for Phnom Penh wrote the letter), Lomuth's 'Three Stars' political party gained no seats. At any rate, French intelligence described Lomuth as 'a shifty character, not very intelligent, with no serious political culture'. Archives de d'Outre-Mer, *Etude,* op. cit., Index, p.17.

78. *Cambodge,* 26 July 1951, p.1.

79. 'Manifeste du Mouvement Khmer Serei', in *Documents et ecrits se rapportant au 'Khmer Serei'*, copy in the Wason Collection, Cornell University Olin Library.
80. *Khemara Nisit*, No. 14, August 1952.
81. Archives d'Outre-Mer, Cambodge 3E 6 (2), report from Kompong Thom, 1929.
82. The information about Saloth Sar's family comes from Laau Thouk, who spent his boyhood in the village of Kompong Rotes, next to Saloth Sar's native village of Prek Sbauv; interview in Paris, 9 February 80. Sar's very close family connections with the palace are independently confirmed by other Khmer sources, two elderly princesses interviewed in Paris with the assistance of Mme. Saksi Sbong, for which I am grateful. The names they gave for various relatives of Saloth Sar were the same as the names given by Laau Thuok.
83. Francois Debre, *Cambodge: La Revolution de la Foret* (Paris, 1976), p.86.

PART I

Introductory Note by Ben Kiernan

Extracts of two studies of the Kampuchean peasantry are presented here in translations from the French original. These academic works by active socialists, Hou Yuon (1955) and Hu Nim (1965), provide perhaps the most detailed and penetrating analysis of the Kampuchean rural socio-economic structure available.

The two works are extremely helpful in identifying the major factors affecting the living standards of the Khmer peasantry. These were: poor natural conditions and a low level of agricultural technology, the fragmentation of rural property into small family farms and the development of both a large class of 'middle peasant' smallholders *and* a slightly less numerous class of landless or land-poor labourers and farmers (a development connected to the phenomenon of limited but increasing landlordism), the burden of usury, and low prices received from merchants for their rice.

A survey of paddy soils in all the countries of tropical Asia revealed that Kampuchean soils are the poorest in four of 14 soil qualities and second or third poorest in seven others. In none of these qualities were Kampuchean soils found to be above the tropical Asian average, making them the least fertile of all. A selection of soils in nearby Thailand, for instance, were found to be poorer than the Kampuchean in four of the soil qualities, but richer in nine others.[1] Kampuchean farmers were concentrated in the country's poorest soil regions, and remained so even while the population quadrupled in the period 1900-50. Kampuchean yields, according to economist Remy Prud'homme, 'have hardly increased beyond one tonne per hectare in the last half century. They are among the lowest in the world.'[2]

Not only were Kampuchean farmers working with poor soils, but their access to equipment was extremely limited. Hu Nim's table (Table 2.8) showing the farm tools and stock owned by the average rice farmer (i.e. four-fifths of Kampuchean peasants) in the various provinces, indicates that: 1) In Takeo, Kandal and Kompong Cham (the three most densely populated rice-growing provinces) the *average* rice-growing household possessed just over the necessary two oxen or buffalo. It is likely that many households did not possess adequate draft animals; 2) In four provinces (Kandal, Takeo, Kampot and Kompong Speu) there were not enough ploughs to go around, and in 13 provinces not enough ox-carts, even if they had been evenly distributed among rice-growing households. The same applied to almost all other farm tools.

This scarcity of equipment was reflected in the high prices of farm tools and stock, much higher than the price of land. In his 1964 work, *The Co-operative Question* (see Part II), Hou Yuon noted that, all other things being average, one hectare of Kampuchean farmland 'equals .302 of a plough, .278 of a rake, .212 of an ox-cart, .620 of an ox, .203 of a buffalo'.[3] And these scarce implements, according to geographer Jean Delvert, were inferior in efficiency to the tools used by French peasants during the Middle Ages.[4]

But the greatest value of Hou Yuon's and Hu Nim's work is in their discussion of Kampuchean social problems. They describe in detail the exploitation of the peasant's labour by other social groups, and attempt to quantify the varying rate of exploitation. They provide a wealth of data not easily available in the West.

They also deal with the highly political question of Khmer peasant 'individualism', important because of the prevalence of small family farms throughout most of the countryside. Youn and Nim both reject the widely-held view that such individualism is an integral part of Khmer society, stemming from racial characteristics or cultural influences such as the Theravada Buddhist religion. On the contrary, Nim considers that just as private property and 'inheritance of equal shares by all children is dominant in many countries influenced by the Napoleonic code or by Roman law', so the land-holding system in Kampuchea was 'also inherited from the colonial era'. For his part, Youn wrote (in 1964) that 'individualism in the minds' of the peasants was 'simply the ideological influence of the capitalist system': 'Individualism is definitely not a "disease" of the masses and the workers, who are all increasing production together. Production has long been a common task . . .' The last sentence is true only in the limited sense of mutual aid in harvesting and transplanting rice.

In fact, a third explanation for 'individualism' among Khmer peasants might be the fragmented nature of the rural economy. Peasant households were generally quite autonomous, not linked, for instance, by any communally-owned land (unlike Vietnam). Even village organizations such as watch committees or occupational associations were almost unknown in Kampuchea. Moreover, most crafts were underdeveloped and nearly everyone was involved in subsistence rice-farming. (Hou Yuon seems to be referring to this social phenomenon when in 1955 he showed how capitalist farming was unable to establish a foothold in the Kampuchean countryside; he attributed this to 'the natural and semi-natural character of the Kampuchean peasant economy', as well as to 'the low level of agricultural technology'.) There was little of that specialization and division of labour whose interdependence characterizes commodity exchange and gives rise to generalized social conflicts whose solution might involve community organizations. The Khmer village, or *phum* (which means simply 'inhabited place' and has no organizational connotations) 'is only a grouping of houses in particular geographical conditions'. The author of these words, Jean Delvert, goes so far as to say: 'One fact seems certain. The absence of a rural community.'[5] Perhaps the words 'organized community' would be more accurate.

The situation was therefore open for a movement like that of Pol Pot to overturn completely a society barely cemented together by its fragile social organization.

References

1. K. Kawaguchi and K. Kyuma, *Paddy Soils in Tropical Asia,* (University of Hawaii Press, 1977).
2. Remy Prud'homme, *L'Economie du Cambodge* (Paris, 1969), p.75.
3. *Pahnyaha sahakor* (Phnom Penh, 1964), Ch. 1. Chapters 2 and 3 of this work can be found in translation in Part II of this volume.
4. Jean Delvert, *Le Paysan Cambodgien* (Paris, Mouton, 1960), p.235.
5. Ibid., pp.213, 218.

1. The Peasantry of Kampuchea: Colonialism and Modernization by Hou Yuon

Landowning in Kampuchea

Do Big Property-owners Exist in Kampuchea?

This is a question that is often asked and which it is unfortunately impossible to answer with a yes or a no. Widely held opinion tends to deny the existence of big property in Kampuchea, and at first glance this seems to be confirmed by a number of known facts.

Table 1.1
Landownership Classification, 1929-30

Type of Land	*Provinces*	*Small Landowners (%)*		*Medium Land-owners (%)*	*Big Landowners (%)*	
		(0-1 hectares	*(1-5 hectares*	*(5-10 hectares*	*(10-50 hectares*	*(more than 50 hectares*
Rice-fields	Battambang	18.5	57.8	18.3	5.3	0.12
	Svay Rieng	12.9	67.4	16.5	3.0	0.22
	Prey Veng	28.3	58.7	10.5	2.4	0.14
	Kg. Cham	48.6	48.2	2.8	0.4	–
	Kandal	64.1	34.9	0.9	0.1	0.002
River-bank land	Kg. Cham	88.0	11.8	0.2	0.01	–
	Kandal	81.0	18.1	0.7	0.1	–

*Extracts from *La paysannerie du Cambodge et ses projets de modernization,* doctoral thesis, University of Paris, 1955.(Translated from the French by Ben Kiernan.)

Source: Yves Henry, *L'Economie Agricole de l'Indochine.*

Table 1.2
The Kampuchean Land Survey Situation 1950.

Provinces	*Landowners*	*Surveyed Plots*	*Declared Plots*
Battambang	3,082	7,360	108,152
Kandal	118,238	310,143	175,333
Kampot	30,400	220,081	41,571
Kg. Cham	183,016	273,350	224,769
Kg. Chhnang		211	229,537
Kg. Speu	19,876	71,655	179,204
Kg. Thom	9,532	150	180,149
Kratie		432	37,336
Pursath		259	85,010
Prey Veng	22,617	85,436	291,944
Stung Treng		223	4,657
Svay Rieng	8,830	27,740	188,634
Siemreap		1,095	126,891
Takeo	38,147	118,529	275,412
Sub-Total	435,744	1,116,934	2,040,599
Phnom Penh City	2,144	3,387	
Total	437,888	1,120,321	2,040,599

Kampuchean land is very parcellized. The rice-fields are generally small, bounded by high or low dykes. The *chamcar* [garden farmlands, usually on the river-banks] also take the shape of long, narrow strips. This observation is confirmed by Table 1.2 which gives the land survey situation of the provinces of Kampuchea in 1950. It shows that 437,883 landowners possessed 3,168,920 surveyed or declared plots. It is important to understand that often these small plots do not form single holdings, but are scattered, especially in the countryside, far from the owner's dwelling-place. The Kampuchean countryside is made up of small and medium-sized family farms. One cannot find large, capitalist-type operations, employing a lot of labour. Everywhere one notices that the peasant works the land himself, that he cannot own more than his working capacity permits.

But these facts, though true, need to be looked at more closely. Social and economic complexities can hide many important facts which need to be revealed if the evolution of our rural areas is to be traced.

The parcellization of the land does not imply the absence of big property. We have seen that the small and medium-size properties do not always correspond to one rice-field, to one field, to one surveyed or declared plot;

there can be rice-fields, paddocks, parcels of a few ares, just as there can be ones of a few hectares. By the same token, large holdings are not held in one rice-field, one paddock or one plot and encompass several rice-fields, several fields or several plots, not necessarily in a single holding. Our peasants use the word *khtung* to refer to a continuous series of rice-fields; *sen* to refer to a big *chamcar*. When the rice-fields or the *chamcar* are dispersed in several places, they are known by the name of the locality. Table 1.2. shows us that 437,888 landowners possess 3,168,920 plots, that is, excluding the town of Phnom Penh, 3,157,533 plots for 435,744 landowners, i.e. still 7.22 plots for one landowner.

In the same way, the predominance of small and medium-size farms does not preclude the existence of large holdings. It does not mean that the small and middle peasants cultivate their own land. It is often the case that the land they work belongs to others, and they are only tenants or sharecroppers. For their part the large landowners do not cultivate all their land themselves, cultivating only the best part, and leasing or renting out the rest. The large holdings are thus divided up into several small farms. And the big capitalist-type farms contain several small properties. This is the way that rich peasant-tenants proceed when they rent several plots belonging to several small landowners and farm along capitalist lines. The general point is that big property is thus disguised, somehow hiding behind small family farms. This is true in the first place of the pre-capitalist forms of the relations of production in our country. The existence of big 'absentee' landlords, i.e. those who do not manage their property along capitalist lines, is characteristic of this period of economic development.

Apanages [feudal landholdings] were officially abolished from 1905. But their mark remains. How could one suggest that our princes, mandarins and high officials of all categories would so casually divest themselves of what they, at the time, considered was the best basis for fortune and honour! It is very probable that they kept some domains for themselves. It is not uncommon to see the peasants going into town, not on holidays, but loaded with presents (rice, vegetables, fruit, firewood, etc.) for the big landlowners from whom they rent their land. One can also be certain that our princes, former mandarins, etc . . . do not just live on their former fortunes of silver and gold, on their retirement pensions or on the salary from their new position. They must have other sources of income. What has been said about *apanages* is also valid for the royal donations. In principle, these were personal and revocable, but in fact, they could be transferred and alienated; these donations were numerous.

One can also look at the problem in terms of the evolution of Khmer society, from the point of view of the development of the Kampuchean peasantry. We know that in the feudal period everyone could acquire land by tilling it. Certainly, this liberty was still restricted and theoretical, given the archaic state of the means of production, but by its nature it favoured the establishment and consolidation of individual properties. Among the mass of the people, there are advanced elements who, without carving out a fief for themselves, were nevertheless able to establish an important domain for themselves. When Doudart de Lagree said 'that there is no middle class in Kampuchea', that did not mean that the Kampuchean peasant mass was absolutely homogeneous. It was these advanced elements of the urban and rural centres who embodied, so to speak, the latent seeds of capitalism. They were to become a new social strata, the origin of the bourgeoisie.

The 'constitution of property' [by the colonial Administration] which gave 139,559 hectares in 8,532 land grants to settlers, to a certain extent created favourable conditions for the development of this new strata, for it signified a kind of land redistribution. Those who already had some sought to consolidate and expand it; those who had none naturally strove for some; and there was speculation. From this viewpoint, 'constitution of property', and the system of rural concessions which was its main expression, gave rise to two economic and social consequences. First, it consolidated the economic and social position of the former mandarins and feudal officials, who were able to add to the property they had inherited from the old regime. Through it, the new colonial authorities who were seeking their collaboration offered them an opportunity to satisfy their ambitions. We know that the notables and administrators, including the interpreters, to whom the Administration gave extensive powers, acted like real petty tyrants. And secondly, it facilitated the ascendancy of the advanced elements. Because of the 'normal mode' of alienation of rural land, by public auction to the highest bidder, and the many complicated formalities, 'the rural or urban concessions turned out in fact to be restricted to the rather advanced elements of the population, in particular inhabitants of the urban or rural centres where land was valuable'.[2]

As for the huge mass of peasants who know nothing of administrative affairs and speculation, they contented themselves with transforming their precarious ownership achieved by the plough 'into full and definitive property by the process of administrative sanction and prolonged occupation'.

Out of these circumstances, large holdings tended to expand at the expense of the small. In the semi-feudal and semi-colonial society of Kampuchea land concentration took on a particular form – not through the extension of large capitalist enterprises to absorb small family farms, but through the practice of usury linked to commercial and money-lending capital. Widespread usury, which diverts funds from production and continuously accentuates the inequality of wealth, has retarded the progress of Kampuchean agriculture. Those who lend cannot help but enrich themselves and those who borrow can never escape. The poor and middle peasants are deprived of their lands without intending it: 'The owner who sells his land deprives himself of it knowingly: he who borrows too often ends up in the same position without having wanted to.'[3]

Two forms of usurious loans which end up dispossessing the heavily endebted small peasant are: 1) sale subject to vendor's right to repurchase, and 2) borrowing money by pawning land. In the former, the land is sold, a suitable price paid, but the seller retains the right of repurchase. When an (often verbally) agreed period of time has elapsed the seller again becomes its owner if he pays back the sum received. Obviously this seems preferable to a definitive sale, for it offers hopes of re-purchase – a hope frequently dashed. The usual result is that the big property owner or usurer gains the land and at a very low price compared to the normal level. The second form of loan, borrowing money by pawning land, usually ends up with the same result. As guarantee for the loan, the borrower hands over to the lender an extract from the Land Book – or other equivalent title – showing the plot. While continuing to own the pawned plot, paying the tax on it and keeping its produce, the owner is also responsible for the high rate of interest (10–20% per month). Thus the acknowledged initial debt is not just the original loan, but that sum plus all the interest accumulated by the end of the loan period. At that time, either the borrower pays off the principal and interest or, failing this, asks for a supplementary extension. All too willing to consent, the lender then demands as further guarantee a larger area of land and the acknowledgement of a greater debt; the sum at the date of payment increases up to the expiry of the new agreed period. Thus, credit snowballs. Finally, the poor peasant cannot pay back principal and interest. He hands over his land. In this case, either he goes elsewhere or he continues to work the land which is no longer his. He is transformed into a tenant or a sharecropper.

With economic development, the feudal forms of land appropriation necessarily make way for more modern, capitalist, forms of monopoly. In effect, the Kampuchean economy is evolving towards capitalism – given time, that is. But modern means of agricultural production are incompatible with the maintenance of parcellized property. Capitalist development demands large estates to permit the utilization of modern means of production and the required concentration of property is manifested in the disappearance and elimination of the small farms, with the small and middle peasants transformed into tenants, sharecroppers and agricultural workers. Thus the separation between the means of production and labour, between capital and labour, takes place, giving birth to a new social stratum in the countryside: the agricultural proletariat.

From what has been said, however, we must not conclude that latifundia exist in Kampuchea, nor that large property holdings predominate. The large, capitalist-type farms run by settlers form isolated islands surrounded by small family farms. The great feudal farms, because of their precapitalist character, are disguised as small and medium-size farms, in the form of tenancies and share-farms, and materially are indistinguishable from other small and medium-size farms. But economically and socially speaking, the position of the landed proprietors makes them a class apart from the peasantry: the landlord class.[4]

Kampuchea is a country of small peasant farms, but the social relations of production are those of feudalism and semi-feudalism . . .

Material and Social Conditions of the Peasant Classes

Under the feudal system, the economy was largely turned in on itself, and the Kampuchean peasantry were relatively homogeneous. We use the word 'relatively' because the absence of the middle class noted by Doudart de Lagree did not rule out the existence of advanced elements of the peasantry. Khmer society did not involve commercial production, but its seeds were already there. The artisans who were also farmers, the free and independent peasants, and the merchants all engaged in commercial exchanges. Certainly, these relations were as yet very weak, limited to irregular and insignificant barter, since the food, textile and other industries still were of a purely household kind – but they were developing day by day. Feudal Kampuchea did not lack for buying and selling, but they were not the bases of its existence, as in modern society.

The introduction of the capitalist mode of production, exchange and property accelerated the process of economic and social transformation. Medieval forms of ownership and social relations of production were modified, making the social structure of the peasantry more complex. Under the pressure of commercial production, social differentiation gave rise to new social strata.

Social Relations

We have seen that after the 'constitution of property', the Kampuchean peasants nearly all owned some land, leaving few tenants, sharecroppers and agricultural workers, at least in the 'Western' sense of these terms. But it seems to us more precise to group the Kampuchean peasants into four main categories according to their mode of farming: 1) landowning peasants, i.e. those who have a lot of land that they do not cultivate themselves or that they only cultivate in part, renting out the rest; 2) landowning peasants who rent additional land, i.e., partial tenants; 3) peasant-tenants, i.e., those who have no land of their own or have so little that they can only live by renting land; 4) tenants who are also agricultural workers, i.e., tenant-agricultural workers.

Tenancy and Sharecropping: These take various forms.

Tenancy is the renting of land in return for a payment fixed in advance in money or in kind. The landowner, in need of labour, rents out or leases an area of several hectares to several peasants.

Sharecropping is the sharing of the harvest by the farmers and the landowner according to defined proportions. For example, the landowner asks his farmers to cultivate for themselves one-third of each hectare for the five hectares leased. This is the mode adopted by the French landowners, in Kampuchea. Another form is an association between the landowners and the farmers to put the land into production, each taking half of the profits. The owner provides half the expenses, gives the necessary advances in kind and in money which the farmer repays, principal and interest.

In a tenancy the owner pays the land tax and receives the rent, while the tenant provides the livestock and farming equipment, running expenses, seed, manure and all the work on the land. If the owner advances money or livestock, that forms part of a special contract and is paid for in supplementary rent. The tenant manages the farm in his own way, plants and harvest when he wishes, and carries the entire burden of a bad harvest.

In sharecropping, on the other hand, the owner has a direct interest in the harvest. He alone provides the land, livestock and agricultural instruments, and the sharecropper is obliged to return the animals or the farm equipment in good condition. The owner can dictate what crops to grow, and the date of their planting. He demands that the land be suitably worked and maintained.

Tenancy and sharecropping contracts are usually verbal, but can be by a written agreement signed by the tenant and the landowner and countersigned by the subdistrict authorities.

Tenancies can be found in certain *Khand* (districts), usually near townships and on rice-fields where sowing is by broadcasting, particularly on the large estates, where the landowners live in the town or cultivate their fields and orchards on the river-banks. Rice-fields are the most common form of tenancy, the area cultivated by a tenant varying from two to four hectares of transplanted paddy fields, and from five to six hectares of floating rice fields (Battambang, Kompong Thom, Prey Veng, Takeo).

Sharecropping in the strict sense is rarer than tenancies. However, one can find examples of it in Battambang, Svay Rieng, Prey Veng and Takeo, especially in new rice-fields of uncertain yield. The big landlords often do the clearing to put the newly-acquired land into cultivation, then the peasants who work on it are exempted from rent for one or two years. In such cases the owners only ask the peasants to put their land into cultivation in order to be better able to rent it out later. However, if the definition of sharecropping is broadened to include the small landowners who do not have enough land and ask the landlords to give them some to work, dividing the produce in half, then one can say that sharecropping is more common than tenancy, which is found notably in the regions of commercial production. The sharecropping contracts vary a lot. The percentage of rent paid also varies from half to a third of the harvest, depending on whether the owner provides just the land, or livestock or agricultural equipment as well; it also varies according to one's relations and friends.

In Kampuchea are found all the forms of rent that history has known; rent in labour, rent in kind, and rent in money.

Rent in kind, or in produce, is linked to the economic structure of feudalism, to the natural subsistence economy. In the modern period of semi-feudal and semi-colonial Kampuchea, the dominant form of land rent remains rent in kind.

Rent in labour can be seen as the main complement to rent in kind. Besides paying the land rent in kind, the peasant must provide various services *(prestations)* on the owner's farm.

Rent in money only appears when rent in produce has attained a sufficient level of development. With the development of commercial relations in the countryside, and of foreign trade, several changes occur in the forms of land rent. Rent in money develops notably in the regions of commercial production of the river-banks and the [European] concessions. Territorially, rent in money has developed in a very unequal fashion, being relatively widespread only in the regions where the commercial economy has been more advanced.

Tenancy on river-bank land is nearly always paid for in kind, the rate varying with the quality of the land. For tobacco and vegetable cropland, it is 30 to 40 piastres per hectare (1930), for cotton-bearing land, 25 to 30 piastres, for corn or peanuts cropland and the heavily flooded inland, 10 piastres.

Tenancy of rice fields is nearly always paid for in produce, that is to say in paddy, varying according to the quality of the rice fields. In Battambang, in the low-lying zone, it is 25 to 31 thang per hectare, on high rice fields, 12 to 21 thang per hectare. Elsewhere, it is 20 to 25 thang for good rice fields, 15 to 20 thang for mediocre. This amount varies from a third to half of the harvest, or even more, in real value representing 25-40% of the value of the land. In Battambang and in the regions near urban centres the proportion is larger, 30-50%, because the price of land there is relatively higher.

Tenants also frequently have to pay the owners the rent on buffaloes or oxen for the crop season. This rent reaches a very high price because of the dearth of draft animals and the risks run from frequent epizootic disease. In Battambang the cost of renting a pair of buffaloes is 50 to 60 thang for a season, and 30 to 50 thang for a pair of oxen.

In the sharecropping contract, the owner generally provides buffaloes and advances seed at the rate of 100% interest per season, often paddy needed to feed the family of the sharecropper as well, and a complementary sum of money at the rate of 140-200% interest for upkeep. For his part, the sharecropper builds his house, brings tools and provides his labour and that of his family. At the harvest the owner is first repaid for his seed, his interest and his loan; the rest is divided in half. Crédit is regulated so that for 16 piastres or a Nen (the nominal value of a silver bar) the interest is 10 thang per year. If the buffaloes belong to the sharecropper, the sharing is three thang for the sharecropper and two thang for the owner. In this case rent takes up 40% of the total harvest. There is a great variety of forms of sharecropping according to the quality of the rice fields, whether the owner lives in the area, whether the owner or the sharecropper pays the land tax.

In practice, rent in kind is completed by rent in labour, that is to say, by *corvees:* days of ploughing, harvest, domestic tasks such as the water *corvee*, the rice-milling *corvee*, bleaching the rice etc., for the owner

The co-existence of three forms of rent in the Kampuchean agrarian economy stems from the existence of three economic and social formations.

The prevalence of rent in kind is determined by the whole structure of the economy, by the character of peasant production and exchange.

Rent in kind is the index of the low level of productive capital, the index of the semi-feudal and semi-colonial character of the economy. The tendency of the economic development of our country is to transform rent in produce into rent in cash. Already, as we have pointed out, in the export crop farms, especially in the river-bank regions, rent in cash of the capitalist kind exists. But in a semi-feudal and pre-capitalist society this rent still occupies a very small place. On the other hand, in certain conditions it can resume the form of rent in kind. During the years of economic and monetary instability and of inflation, which caused the capitalists to seek refuge in land acquisition, the landowners demanded payment in kind. However, outside these exceptional circumstances, there is a strong tendency to transform rent in kind into rent in cash. The peasant is forced to adapt himself to the monetary economy of the market. This necessity has been imposed on him by the State, which now demands duties, taxes and rights of all kinds in cash, and by the feudalists and landlords, who increasingly demand their rents in cash. It has been noted that, subjected to this social and economic pressure, the peasant must either produce more or go and sell his labour power elsewhere.

Direct Family Farms: The small and medium landowners cultivate their land themselves. However, in certain regions they sometimes call upon some wage labour for certain urgent tasks.

From the economic point of view, a small property of one to five hectares, cultivated by family labour, is hardly enough rice land for a family to live on and, in a normal year, yields a very small surplus, with which to pay for taxes and small purchases.

The small landowners often own their land, their agricultural equipment and also their draught animals, but they possess no working capital. In general, they can only get this from the village usurers, who are also big landowners. Obliged to sell their paddy at the start of the season to pay the taxes, repay debts and buy cloth to clothe their family, they often lack paddy for food and seed for the next crop. The only way out is to borrow. One thang of paddy loaned at the start of the season is repaid by two thang at the harvest (rate 100%). If the peasant cannot get clear at the harvest, his debt is carried over to the following harvest as four thang (rate 200%). If he needs oxen or buffaloes, he also approaches his neighbours and pays them, usually in days of labour, the same number of days for which he borrowed the team. Sometimes he will also borrow draft animals for the whole season at the same rate as tenants and sharecroppers. Another method of regulating debts is to repay 40 thang of paddy for 16 piastres borrowed that season. Very often the debt snowballs.

The medium landowners, like the small, nearly always cultivate their own land. If they do not own all the land they cultivate, only a small part will be rented. In general, they possess the necessary means of production for their tasks, and can rent some out, notably to small landowners. Their situation is better than the latter.

While the small landowners only have exceptional recourse to wage labour, the medium landowners often call upon it. At transplanting and harvest time the small landowners mutually exchange unpaid days of labour; they only use paid labour in an emergency, when, for example, flooding threatens a low-lying rice field before the harvest or low-lying lands on the river-banks.

Tenant-Agricultural Workers: there are not many agricultural workers in Kampuchea. However, they are an important index of the degree of development of agrarian capitalism, and they are especially found in the regions of commercial production on the river-banks and in the paddy-exporting provinces where there is medium and big landownership (Battambang, Svay Rieng, Prey Veng). One can distinguish the seasonal labourers from day labourers and year-round labourers, and those hired to pay off debts.

Day labourers, recruited among poor people in the village itself or in neighbouring villages, are needy tenants or small landholders who have finished their tasks after working with their family for landlords or rich peasants. This is complicated by the fact that many small landowners or small tenants pay off debts by providing days of work to their creditor.

The employment of day wage labourers is not widespread, especially in the countryside. The predominant practice is mutual aid at the time of hard work and reciprocal provision of days of labour. The river-bank crops demand rather a large amount of labour. There the use of day labourers is more common than in the interior. But often seasonal or annual workers are preferred.

Average daily wages vary a lot, depending upon supply and demand, the price of paddy, age, sex and the region. However, we can get an idea by considering the daily wages current in the years 1929-30. General hands, in the slack season, earned 0$50 plus food (three meals) [$ denotes a piastre]; the woman doing transplanting or harvesting 0$40 plus food (one meal); the reaper 0$40 plus food (one meal); the contract harvester 0$50 per 100 buckets; on the river-bank farmland a general hand earned 0$40 per day plus food.

Seasonal and annual workers are not only recruited from poor local families, but also from those who have come from the interior of the country to find work in the *'Srok Tonle',* that is, the river country. These workers are taken on for the year or for the season, from ploughing to harvesting, that is to say, for 10 months, from March to January, on rice-fields, or for the dry season and rainy season crop on river-bank land. They are employed to perform all the jobs in the rice fields or *chamcar* as well as domestic tasks. They are paid after the harvest. They are fed, lodged and given two sets of clothes per year. Mostly, at the time of hiring the landowner must take care of their tax card or advance them the small sum necessary, generally without interest.

In Battambang, one source of labour is found among the ruined Kampucheans from Cochinchina [the Meking Delta region of Vietnam]. On their arrival, they are hired for a year or two and then to try to settle down by becoming tenants or agricultural workers. There are also migrations from regions of drought or flood. Thus, for example, Battambang attracted agricultural workers from Prey Veng after the big flood of September 1929.

The wage level of seasonal or annual labourers not only varies with age, sex, region, the quality of the crops and demand, but is also affected by climate and by the length of time required to do the work for which they have been hired. In general their wage is hardly enough for their upkeep, and they must live from day to day.

In the past Kampuchean laws recognised debt bondage. We do not know if the laws still obtain, but the practice remains as a social fact. Any insolvent debtor, at the time when the total interest owed equals the principal, falls into the hands of his creditor to whom he can be allocated by a judicial ruling. Sometimes, acknowledgement of the debt stipulates (in advance) committal of a designated member of the family in case of non-repayment, or the whole family for large sums. Entry into bondage halts the interest accruing but still leaves intact the debt, consisting of the principal plus the interest accumulated at the time of entering bondage.

The master provides food and upkeep, the bondsman his work. The bondsman is freed either by payment of the debt, or by being charitably released. He can also change masters if he finds someone who will buy him out. The bondsmen form part of the household, working under the master's orders.

This social practice is often mixed in the countryside with simple committal for debt where, by mutual agreement, the two parties decide that in the case of non-repayment the debtor will owe either a certain number of days' work to the creditor during the period of heavy work, or a continuous commitment for several months or years.

With this system the large landlords can exploit their land using labour which, in the case of bondage, costs only the price of upkeep and in the case of simple commitment costs virtually nothing. In the towns and in the countryside, the feudalists, the great bourgeois and the big landowners surround themselves with numerous servants, entire families, in fact, of poor and ruined peasants. Debt bondage is one of the the vestiges of feudalism.

Table 1.3
Land Appropriation and Modes of Exploitation

Province	*Direct Cultivation (%)*	*Cultivation by Sharecroppers (%)*	*Cultivation by Tenants (%)*
Owners of Rice Fields:			
Battambang	93.6	5.0 (Khand)	9.0 (Khand)
Svay Rieng	95.1	3.5	1.4
Prey Veng	97.0	1.6	1.3
Kg. Cham	93.9	2.9	3.2
Kandal	96.8	0.6	1.6

Table 1.3 continued:

Province	*Direct Cultivation (%)*	*Cultivation by Sharecroppers (%)*	*Cultivation by Tenants (%)*
Owners of Chamcar			
Kampong Cham	98.1	0.2	1.7
Kandal	99.3	0.1	0.6

Table 1.3 refers to peasant-tenants and peasant-sharecroppers who have no land or only a very small portion, so can only live by being tenants or sharecroppers. They can thus properly be termed tenants and sharecroppers. But the table does not represent peasants who, without being reduced to living solely as tenants or sharecroppers, still rent some additional land. They can be termed partial tenants in the sense that they are essentially landowners and are only partly tenants. Nor has the table taken into account the situation of tenants who are at the same time agricultural workers. In brief, if we take account of the many forms of tenancy and sharecropping, they will be seen to involve a very much greater proportion than the table indicates, for there are many 'mitigated' forms of sharecropping and tenancy.

The progressive trend towards land concentration only leads to the development of even more exploitation by tenancy and sharecropping. This development will have as its counterpart the disappearance and ruin of the small family farms of the poor peasants, which at present, as we have noted, predominate, especially in the *chamcar* lands.

Social Classes among the Peasantry

The determination of class membership in the countryside is a very delicate and difficult problem. Difficult because there has been no study of this problem in Kampuchea, and delicate because of the way Kampuchean agriculture is entangled in a dense network of feudal and pre-capitalist relations. Besides the structure of property, it is also necessary to take account of the nature of these relations. The classification that we present here is based on the economic, social and political position of each category of the peasant strata. This definitively leads to a consideration of the relations of each with the land, in its productive function. There are five social categories in the countryside: the landlords, the rich peasants, the middle peasants, the poor peasants and the semi-proletariat.

Landlords: We call a landlord someone who possesses land (from 10 to over 50 hectares) but does not work himself or is occupied with work that constitutes only an auxiliary source of income. Therefore he lives on income from renting or sharecropping or from both. In addition, the landlords also gain supplementary income by practising usury, by exploiting wage labourers and from commercial undertakings. But the main form of their income is still rent. For landlords very rarely employ wage labour. Their mode of exploitation remains fundamentally that of renting out, sharecropping, or, sometimes, the employment of debt bondsmen.

Landlords are not numerous in Kampuchea – we estimate their number at less than 10% of the total number of landowners – but their influence is very great. Through their powerful economic and social position they are directly linked to the big merchants, to the compradors, to the high officials of the Administration. Politically and socially they are part of the feudal class. They have public office and honorific titles. Under the colonial regime, the village notables were recruited from this social category.

The landlords make up a sort of tyrant caste. Big landlords, big money-lenders, notables or administrators, they make the peasants suffer from burdens and exactions of all kinds. Wishing to please their superiors and attract their good graces, they deliver the taxes very early, and then use them as an instrument of exploitation. They pay the taxes with their own money, on the understanding that they will be repaid by the penniless taxpayers later. In this way they achieve two ends. On the one hand, they gain the approval of their superiors and on the other, they create for themselves a vast clientele of debtors and debt bondsmen. Advances are often reimbursed in days of labour. The landlords also establish themselves as village lawyers, a role which seems to come naturally to them, by virtue of their strong economic and social position, their liaison with the members of the Administration and their public power.

From the political point of view, they are powerful rural supporters of the feudal monarchy. Their political representatives are the 'Popular Socialist Community' Party of ex-King Norodom Sihanouk and the liberals of the Liberal Party of Prince Norindeth [See Part II].

Rich Peasants: These, as a general rule, are landowners. Nevertheless, some of them only own part of the land they farm and rent the rest. Their position is then two-sided. To the extent that they own land which they rent out, wholly or partly, they can be considered as powerful landlords, which brings them close to the landlord class. Some of them are bourgeois from the towns who have acquired property in the countryside, but are not primarily concerned with agriculture. On the other hand, the rich peasants who rent more land to work from big landlords are to a certain extent dependent on the latter. Some rich peasants have no land of their own and rent all the land that they farm. These are rich tenants.

The rich peasants, as a general rule, have fairly substantial agricultural equipment and working capital. They take part personally in working the land, but nevertheless, since they often use wage labour (agricultural workers) a part of their income still comes from such exploitation. They also use the labour of servants, debtors and debt bondsmen, which brings them in significant income. Otherwise, they rent out some of their land and are repaid in rents, or they practise usury, or they even own commercial enterprises. Still, the main source of their income remains the labour of agricultural workers of all categories.

The rich peasants, as distinct from the big landlords, play a very important role in economic revitalization, but their social influence is still weak. But 'as soon as they emerge they set about distinguishing themselves by immediately refusing to farm themselves. They turn over their land to tenants in exactly the same way as the big notables whose bad qualities they keenly adopt.' The consequence of this attitude is absenteeism – their hallmark, although to a lesser extent than landlords. However, it is noteworthy that the rich peasants are increasingly oriented towards the adoption of the capitalist mode of production.

The rich peasants belong to the national bourgeoisie class, which is comprised of the national capitalists, the merchants, the well-off artisans, the administrative officials, the purveyors, the members of the liberal professions and the higher levels of the intellectuals. Their political representatives are the Democrats of the Democratic Party, the party of the national bourgeoisie and the petty bourgeoisie.

Middle Peasants: A large section of the middle peasants own land of their own (from 5 to 10 hectares), while some own only part of the land they farm and rent the rest. Because of this, their position is also two-sided. To the extent that they own their own land, they can be considered as rich peasants, close to the class of the national bourgeoisie. On the other hand, to the extent that they rent a large part of the land they farm, they are dependent on big landowners or rich peasants to whom they pay their rent. Some middle peasants own nothing, renting all the land they cultivate. They are well-off tenants.

Middle peasants own adequate agricultural equipment, and provide for their existence exclusively or principally by their own personal labour. Very seldom exploiting the labour of others, they frequently engage in mutual aid. Many of them are themselves partly exploited, whether by paying for the land they rent, or by paying interest on the loans they have had to contract. Nevertheless, they do not usually sell their labour power. A certain section, notably the well-off middle peasants, do make use of a small amount of wage labour, but that is not their essential source of income.

The middle peasant class belongs to the class of the petty bourgeoisie, like the salaried workers, the small businessmen, the artisans, the students at high school and college, the shopkeepers, the local lawyers, the lower levels of the intellectuals, the schoolteachers in primary and technical schools, and the lower clergy.

Poor Peasants: This class is the most numerous and complex and includes about 80% of the rural population. Almost all the poor peasants are owners of 0.1 hectares. But none have enough land or farm tools. They are the small and very small landowners.

Some poor peasants own some of the land they farm, but have inadequate agricultural equipment, while others have no land and inadequate equipment. As a general rule, they are obliged to rent land, livestock and farm equipment in order to work. They undergo exploitation by paying their rent and the interest on loans they have had to take out and, to some extent, by selling their labour power, as day or seasonal labourers.

Semi-Proletariat: By this we mean both the permanent agricultural workers and those who work by the day, month, season or year. These agricultural workers either have no land, no tools and no financial means, or have only a little plot of land with or without limited farm equipment. They can subsist only by selling their labour power.

The agricultural semi-proletariat comprises peasants who are partial tenants, poor peasants, landless peasants and debt bondsmen from needy peasant families who have been completely ruined – all those who are more or less destitute through exploitation or by usury.

Their position is not like agricultural workers in the capitalist countries. It is between that of agricultural workers properly so-called and that of small and very small landowners. Obliged to sell their labour power to subsist, the Kampuchean agricultural workers cherish a secret hope of becoming land-owning peasants once again. This will not happen; instead, they will inevitably become real agricultural workers.

Travellers to Kampuchea can see groups of beggars, men and women, young and old – entire families driven out of their village by misery and hunger – scouring the towns and villages in search of alms. These people, who are called 'vagabonds, unknowns and wanderers' or 'thieves, gamblers, vagrants, infamous individuals', are ruined and impoverished peasants. Under the colonial regime, they were used for *corvee* work by the administrators and the notables, handed over to the Government as soldiers, or sent to the wars in the military colonies. Kampuchean agriculture, because of its archaic technology, cannot absorb this mass of impoverished small producers. Unable to use their labour power as wage labourers in agriculture, they look to the towns for escape from the famine which ravages them in the countryside. But as industry is relatively weak, it cannot absorb the 'excess' population which is driven out of agriculture.

This situation leads to the formation of a sub-proletariat of unskilled and insecure people – the last to be hired and the first to be fired. The sub-proletariat also comprises the great mass of the unemployed, called 'common labour'. Recently arrived in the towns, they will do whatever they can – street porters, pedicab drivers, builder's labourers, workers on roads, bridges and naval work-sites, hawkers, jumble sellers, shoe-shiners, bicycle repairers along the footpaths, water-carriers, cake-sellers, female servants, cooks, childminders, domestics, etc.

The mass of Kampuchean workers, both in the towns and the countryside, live under extremely hard conditions. Nothing, either in custom or in law, stands in the way of the arbitrary employers. There is no protection for the workers, neither as far as security is concerned, nor in terms of hours of work. There is no union organization or social security. Family endowment as well as unemployment allowances are unknown in Kampuchea.

The material living conditions of the masses of the people become harder and harder further down the social scale. Between the lifestyle of the landlords and the agricultural workers and poor peasants, there is a great divide.

The material situation in each social category corresponds to its economic situation. Poverty increases as a function of the relationship of the various categories with the land.

Under the feudal system, in the words of Doudart de Lagree, the masses of the people were 'exploited to the utmost'. Although not to be taken literally, it is true that the masses of the people lived very miserably – and we know why. The archaic means of production could only provide for a low level of production, yet charges of all kinds were very heavy. All the peasants had to pay the Royal tithe, fixed at one-tenth of the rice harvest, which went to the King, Master of Life, land and water, to feed him and his family, harem, mandarins, guards, pages, workers, slaves, serfs and entourage. Other princely dignitaries enjoyed an income from the provinces of their own respective Houses.

The peasants also owed further accessory dues, some fixed, others proportional, such as the share (one-twentieth) for the chiefs of the Brahmins, the compensation in advance for losses and waste in the stores, the expenses of transporting the Royal tithe to the capital where the King's rice stores were located (law of circulation of grain inside the kingdom), and a tenth on rice exported.

They were also subject to all sorts of exactions, to the performance of many personal services owed to the mandarins and to the officials, to *corvees* which could take up 90 days per year.

And how were all these taxes and charges collected? Aymonier explains it to us in these terms: 'Besides the territorial apanages reserved for the high princely dignitaries, the taxes from a region were generally endowed to the profit of favourites, high officials, governors of provinces who were charged with ensuring their collection and offering to the King his fixed share.' There is no better way to describe the living conditions of the masses of the people under the fedual system than to repeat here the sacred formula and say that they were 'subject to tax and *corvee* at will' *(corveables et taillables a merci)*.

What of the material conditions of the Kampuchean peasants under the colonial system? Has there been an improvement, or further accentuation of the misery? It is not easy to answer this without studying and comparing living standards under the two systems. Unable to do this, we must be content with a few findings.

It is generally estimated that a person needs 600-800 grammes of rice daily to be adequately fed. The average Kampuchean does not consume more than 350 grammes. The poor and middle peasants, in particular, have to supplement their diet with a large proportion of other cereals (corn, sorghum), tubers (potatoes, taro, yam, *kdouch*) or vegetables (soya beans, etc).

It is true that in Kampuchea people do not die of hunger, but they live miserably from day to day. One could describe the middle peasant's budget as follows: nothing for agricultural expenditure, nothing for technical purchases, nothing for housing and comfort, only what is strictly necessary for clothing and very little, although this is nearly everything he spends, for food.

However, national production has increased and so has the national wealth. Where does this wealth, created by the labour of the masses of the people, go to? Who profits from the 'peace maintained by the French, from the roads and railways created by their science and their capital'? 'Although an "increase" [in production] has been noted since fifteen years ago [the daily ration was formerly 265 grammes] the peasant remains underfed and financially destitute', writes A. Chevalier, who goes on to explain:

> From 1935 to 1939 Indochina exported on average 1,553,000 tonnes of rice, paddy and related products per year, equivalent to 2,060,000 tonnes of paddy. The highest figure for exports was attained in 1936 with 1,763,000 tonnes of rice, paddy and related products, a tonnage only once surpassed, in 1928 with 1,798,000 tonnes. The exportable surplus comes from the difference between production and internal consumption . . .[5]

In our opinion it would be more correct to say that the exportable surplus comes not from the difference between production and internal consumption; but from that between production and solvent internal demand. For how else can both the undernourishment of the masses of the people and the existence of a large export quantity be explained? The latter is only possible because the peasants remain 'under-fed and financially destitute'. Rather than describing the various aspects and consequences of undernourishment and financial destitution instead we will show how this misery is perpetuated and why, in spite of the increase in the national wealth, there is no improvement in the living conditions of the broad peasant masses.

Forms of Oppression of the Masses of the People

> It is the implacable progression of duties which for eight or nine years has dominated the whole financial policy of Indochina . . . the tax receipts have become the basic preoccupation and any other problems pale in comparison. Even in France, the work of the governors is judged by their budget surpluses . . . .

In these terms Colonel Bernard had characterized 'The Work of Doumer'.
[Doumer was Governor-General of French Indochina, 1897- 1902.]
One of the preoccupations of the colonial Administration was the co-ordination of a proper general budget for the whole of Indochina, supplemented by a policy of building roads and railways in the interests of 'Indochinese Unity', the 'pacification' of the country and 'opening up' its land. The resultant taxes, customs and excise, and the great *corvee* comprised the three great forms of oppression which directly hit the broad masses of the people, i.e. the peasants.

Taxes
Taxes strike the same terror in the heart of the peasant as plague or cholera. For this tax is not a function of income; it is totally unrelated to the peasant's actual income. The tax has its political content, as described by Delaisi: 'By the tax, the natives are obliged to bring to the market a still larger quantity of local products, and by borrowing, many more European products penetrate foreign countries than their normal purchasing power allows them to absorb. The foreign markets are in virtual euphoria. Imports and exports are thus artificially stimulated.'[6]

Examination of the expenditure and income sections of the General Budget of Indochina entirely confirms this opinion (see Table 1.4). To cover all these expenses, which increase from year to year, Government income is necessary. Where does it come from? The answer is to be found in Table 1.5

All these receipts go into the General Budget which only marginally subsidizes the local budgets. The local budgets depend on the personal taxes of the Europeans and Asians, and on various taxes on junks and craft, on weights and measures, on cattle and buffaloes, on fishing nets, pots, ferries, etc. Thus the interest of the communes (sub-districts) is sacrificed in the general interest of the Union.

What is interesting about the income of the local budget is the personal or head tax, based on the number of inhabitants. This contrasts with the form of levy on the Europeans; their taxes are based on their income. For the 'natives', the tax burden is shared out by the communal authorities who also add on all the communal charges. Their personal taxes are based on the collective responsibility of the villages, of the commune, who are made responsible for regular payment of the taxes even though they have no say in their use. The commune also has the task of recruiting soldiers and replacing deserters; responsibility for damage to timber and forests; responsibility for fines and damages for fraud concerning alcohol, salt, opium, tobacco, etc. The commune is directly dependent on the Administration, yet it is not consulted, neither on the nature of the taxes to be established, nor on the amounts, the basis and the mode of collection. It brings in the taxes only to relinquish them without retaining a treasury. The principal role of the commune is just to get the taxes in within the prescribed periods.

The operation called 'bringing in the taxes' is an epidemic for the masses of the people. During this period their main worry is where to find the money and how to do so. Here are two extracts from a text describing this operation which appeared in the Indochinese newspaper *L'Epoque:*

> The Administration had given the order to collect the tax very quickly. Eight days after the distribution of the tax map, Prefects and Sub-Prefects scoured their respective districts commune by commune. For every hundred piastres which were not yet levied by the Mayor and his Assistants, blows with a cane were meted out, one-

quarter to the Mayor and the remainder in equal shares to the other notables.

The taxes are in and without difficulty. This does not mean that all the peasants have paid, far from it. It is said that certain Mayors and notables advanced the money, recouping on the village property that they have controlled for many years and at an absurdly low rate . . . . The collection of the taxes has also been an excellent business for the Chinese; they have lent money at a phenomenal rate.

Table 1.4
Categories of Expenditure in the Ordinary General Budget, 1931-38
(in thousands of piastres)

	1931	*%*	*1935*	*%*	*1938*	*%*
Servicing of loans	3,335	3.5	14,022	26.7	15,616	19.2
Amount sent to the metropole*	11,517	12.2	3,941	7.0	4,327	5.7
Administration	54,234	57.0	26,625	47.6	38,860	48.0
& public works	15,158	15.0	4,545	7.6	9,841	12.2
Subsidy to local budgets	10,762	11.4	6,316	11.1	22,537	15.5
Total	*96,006*		*55,445*		*80,881*	

*The Finance Law of 13 April 1900 established the principle of the financial autonomy of Indochina in relation to the metropole. However, certain expenses incurred by the metropole for the military defence of Indochina are reimbursed by means of an annual amount transferred outright from the general budget to the French budget.

Table 1.5
Income of the Ordinary General Budget, 1931-38

	1931	*%*	*1935*	*%*	*1938*	*%*
Customs and Excise	42,097	82.3	42,255	82.1	65,525	79.6
Registration	5,363	10.4	5,467	10.6	11,181	13.5
Industrial exploitation	3,773	7.3	3,700	7.3	5,747	6.9

Coercion was widely used to ensure payment of the taxes. The provincial chiefs were accompanied by their militia. During the crisis of 1929-30, when a deficit of 16 million piastres was registered, the tax payable was hardly modified, even though productive resources had diminished by three-quarters.[7]

To get an idea of the heavy tax burden one need only compare the following percentages: in Indochina taxation absorbs 18% of the income of each inhabitant, while it takes 25% in France, 20% in England and 10% in the USA.[8] There is no doubt that this burden is more overwhelming since peasant production is very low, given the backward state of the instruments of production. We have seen that the peasant, short of money, obtains it from a usurer, from a boss who hires him. Money-lenders or usurers thenceforth have at their disposition 'a priority right to the services' of those whom they have obliged. The tax burden thus aggravates the misery of the population and there have been many uprisings against taxes. (For example, the 1926 insurrection in which Achar So led the people of Kompong Chhang in the struggle against the taxes. The Resident Bardez and his assistants were killed in the course of this uprising which later spread through the whole country.)

Customs and Excise

Customs and excise each year provide more than 82% of the income of the General Budget, and monopolize 'three beasts of burden': alcohol, salt and opium.

Many testimonies confirm that the colonial Administration had obliged the 'native' populations to consume alcohol and opium. In the French National Assembly on 16 November 1908 Deputy Aynard declared:

> To avert this disastrous fiscal situation, increases in the sale of monopoly alcohol have been stimulated by all means. The Residents, official instruments of the Monopoly Administration, wanted to stimulate consumption. What did they do then? They fixed consumption quotas per province and per locality and arrived at a sort of coefficient of personal consumption.

In a letter addressed to the provincial Residents, the Director of Customs of Cambodia wrote:

> I have the honour to beg you to give your support to the efforts of my service to achieve new retail sales of alcohol. To this end I permit myself to convey to you a list of sales to be achieved in the various villages mentioned, most of which are totally deprived of alcohol depots . . . . Through the intermediary of the Cambodian Governors your prevailing influence would happily convince certain small native merchants of the interest they would have in taking advantage of the extra trade, since retail alcohol licences are free . . . . Only by full understanding between your Administration and ours will we obtain the best results for the great good of the Treasury's

interests.

And here is a third testimony:

> The Administration has decided that as from today (8 September 1934) each conscript must consume 7 litres of alcohol per year. Each village which has not bought the quantity fixed by the Administration will be considered as involved in contraband and its notables will be punished. The sum owed from the quantity of alcohol delivered, whether it is all sold or not, must be paid in full.[9]

Under these conditions, it is no exaggeration to say that the alcohol and opium policy, for fiscal reasons, has 'forced the Natives to consume these poisons as if it was desirable to stupefy them in order to better subjugate them'.

As far as salt is concerned, an order of 23 June 1903 acknowledged the Administration's right to restrict individual sales to personal consumption. Thus the Administration has the right to ration the people, to measure out to it an indispensable product, to create a salt shortage. This greatly affects the masses of the people for, as is well known, the Kampuchean people consume a lot of salt, notably in the preparation of fermented and salted fish. Gourou tells us, 'It is not uncommon to see a tearful fisherman abandon the product of a day's work on the shore having failed to save enough money to buy this condiment, with its high duty, which he can see is in abundance several hundred metres from his junk, in the prohibited area of the salt marshes'. While Colonel Bernard adds that, 'From 1889 to 1906 the price of salt quintupled, but receipts hardly doubled, in other words the continual price rises were far from compensating for the lower consumption which was their consequence, and from that can be judged the frightful misery of a people which has come to be deprived of an indispensable commodity'.

Obviously such measures require a surveillance network, and agents of Customs and Duties on land and water are armed with almost unlimited powers. They can carry out continuous searches, visit homes by day and by night, confiscate and sentence people to fines or imprisonment. Enormous rewards – and large shares of the takings – draw numbers of agents, interpreters and informers, whose zeal does not hesitate at denunciations. Even without sworn agents, any indigenous official (mayors, notables, etc.) can claim illegalities, seize merchandise, arrest alleged criminals and subject the natives to searches. Any exaction or personal vengeance is permitted. And these 'social outcasts', assured of impunity, do not stop short of this sort of conduct.

General retailers with concessions to sell opium must contract to move the quantity fixed by the Administration, to increase retail sales, and to co-operate in the repression of frauds.

'The Great Corvee'
The construction of roads, bridges and railways, in the interests of consolidating 'Indochinese Unity', administrative centralization, and 'opening up' of the country, demanded a lot of labour. The colonial Administration established the 'Great *Corvee*', a system of recruitment calculated on the basis of the head tax, the quota system.

The poor peasants – it is always them – are torn from their rice fields and paddocks, abandoning their animals and their ploughs. They are picked out in their villages and sent to the labour camps in the unhealthy swamp and bush regions. Public Works, Jean Ajalbert tells us in *Au Retour d'un Voyage*,

> can requisition coolies. Requisition becomes disguised deportation ... and takes no account of farm work, festivals, of any obligations; Public Works drains entire communities on to the worksites from which only a few will return. How many villages, suddenly deserted on the approach of a traveller, are quickly repopulated when it is learnt that the passer-by is undoubtedly not from Customs or Public Works.

In these conditions it is not surprising that there are frequent revolts on the worksites (for example, the revolts of January-February 1906 in connection with the road construction works in the provinces of Ksach-Kandal, Muk-Kampoul, Kompong Siem . . .).

The peasant pays the taxes, the peasant provides the cheap labour, the peasant becomes a soldier, the peasant organizes welcomes for official personalities – for it must not be forgotten that at each official gathering, at each welcome for local personages, the peasant pays a contribution in money, in kind, or in labour. After all that, the peasant should see his condition progressively improve in proportion to his labour. But alas! The peasant takes pains for others. And he continues to live and grovel in misery.

Forms of Exploitation of the Masses of the People

The Cambodian peasants are not victims only of the whims of their 'land spirits', but of the exploitation of landlords, usurers, big merchants and businessmen as well.

Exploitation of the Peasant Masses by Landlords, Rich Peasants and Usurers
There follow several examples taken among the *chamcar* and rice farms and summarized in Table 1.6.

Although the data we are discussing are incomplete and subject to question, we can still make some remarks about the findings. These are:

Expenditure on the means of production is very low: It varies very little from one farm to another, even though areas cultivated vary by as much as 100%. Buildings and fertilizer do not figure in the expenditure on the means of production. In general the buildings are not only used for farm work, while dwellings of various values are also used for farm work. Cow-yards either do not exist or are lumped together with pens for buffalo or cattle built on the spot and of no estimable value, although certainly demanding significant materials and labour. Usually, there are no granaries or sheds: the paddy is kept in a living room, tools under the house. However, in *chamcar* cultivation, where the land is on an island, a long way from the dwelling place, solid constructions are needed especially for tobacco and corn farming. As far as fertilizers are concerned, they are hardly used. Domestic manures are not included in these calculations of production expenses.

The percentage of expenditure on the means of production is low, and progressively diminished down the social scale, from peasant-landowner to tenant-labourer, as does expenditure on labour. The insignificance of expenditure on the means of production reflects the natural and semi-natural character of the Kampuchean peasant economy, with its low level of agricultural technology.

Expenditure on the means of subsistence is very high in relation to that on the means of production. Expenditure on the means of subsistence varies considerably from one farm to another, as well as from one category to another. The percentage of expenditure per family member increases with poverty; in other words, that part of the income that is spent on consumption increases as the total income decreases. The percentage of expenditure on the means of subsistence in relation to total expenditure varies from 70% for peasant-landowners to 85-90% for tenant-labourers.

The high expenditure on the means of subsistence does not mean that it is possible to increase the quantity of surplus output. The peasants cultivate the land with primitive tools and can only achieve a small quantity of surplus output. And although this small quantity is the result of the labour of all the members of the family, it cannot guarantee them a 'vital minimum'. The closer to the most oppressed strata of the peasantry, the lower the expenditure on the family's means of subsistence and the further this is below the vital minimum.

The rate of surplus output is low: Despite what Table 1.6 indicates, the rate of surplus output cannot be reasonably estimated at more than 50% in the best cases (dry season rice fields, floating rice fields, certain river-bank land). The general average rate of surplus output is about 20%. This corresponds to economic and social realities. As we have seen in the course of this study, the tools of production are archaic, there is no use of fertilizer, cultivation risks are high and yields are mediocre. On the other hand, since living standards are very low, one must take account of the fact that expenditure on the means of subsistence for the family is below the vital minimum, limited to basic necessities (paddy, cloth, fish, and certain condiments), and sometimes completely inadequate for the survival of a family.

Table 1.6
Five Examples of Peasant Exploitation in Kampuchea, 1930.

Example No.	1	2	3	4	5
Farm size (hectares)	3	3	2	5	1.2
Annual expenditure (piastres)	104.20	67.70	94.20	103.75	231.00
on means of production	29.20	20.30	23.20	42.00	31.00
on means of subsistence	75.00	47.40	73.00	61.75	200.00
Annual Income (Piastres)	225.00	100.00	160.00	225.00	338.00
Surplus output (income-expenditure)	120.80	32.30	63.80	121.25	107.00
Charges	58.25	5.00	40.00	63.00	44.46
Tax on yield	11.25	5.00	8.00	15.00	12.96
Interest on loans	47.00	–	32.00	48.00	–
Rent	–	–	–	–	31.50
Rate of surplus output (surplus output/expenditure on means of subsistence) (%)	160	68.14	87.4	183.41	53.5
Real rate of exploitation (charges/surplus output) (% of surplus output)	48	15.47	63	52	41.55

Example 1: owner-cultivated by family labour, wet season ricefield, transplanted once, moderately fertile soil.
Example 2: owner-cultivated plus supplementary labour, wet season rice-fields, transplanted once, high climatic risks, high density of sugar palms.
Example 3: owner-cultivated by family labour, dry and wet season ricefield.
Example 4: owner-cultivated with supplementary labour, floating rice fields.
Example 5: Intensive river-bank cultivation (*chamcar*), with supplementary labour.
Source: Y. Henry, *l'Economie Agricole de l'Indochine, 1932.*

Consider that a peasant family of five people needs 80 to 100 thang annually for food, that is 80 to 100 piastres simply to buy necessary paddy, in relation to the 40 or 50 thang for food cited for the examples in Table 1.6. Finally, rice accounts for 50-60% of the budget of the Kampuchean peasant family, while bread represents oly 5-6% of the expenditure of a French family. The peasant's rate of surplus output can thus only be very low, hardly enough to pay the total rent, usurious interest and State taxes.

The real rate of exploitation is high: According to the findings of our study, the real rate of exploitation is of the order of 50% of the surplus output, not at all insignificant, especially when production is low and the rate of surplus output very low. But the real rate of exploitation can be, and indeed is, much higher. It can reach 100%, 150% and even more, of the surplus output, so much that it can eventually absorb all the surplus output plus a part of the necessary output. This is why there are more and more impoverished and ruined peasants and debt bondsmen.

We have seen that the various taxes are very heavy. The land taxes are particularly severe because they are calculated on the basis of presumed productive capacity rather than real effective production. This leaves a broad and arbitrary margin in the evaluation of the quantity produced.

Payment for sharecropping is normally 50% of the total harvest. Out of this the sharecropper must also pay the land taxes, repay borrowed seed at a rate of 100%, repay loans at interest rates of 20% per month, as well as paying in days of work, or in kind, or in products, for borrowed plough-teams or working equipment.

For tenancy, land rent is usually:
65% of the harvest for the best land
50% of the harvest for average quality land
25% of the harvest for poor quality land.
In other words, the rate of land rent (principal dues) is directly proportional to the size of the harvest.

This is still not all that the peasant has to pay. Part of the supposed income drawn from agriculture can in fact be lost to the peasant on the market, for example, by sale at low prices and purchase at high prices, or, through necessity taking out loans against the next harvest, which is called 'selling on your feet'.

To all this, one must add the exactions, complementary taxes, traditional gifts, small voluntary *corvees*, thievery with weights and measures, trickery . . .

In these conditions the real rate of exploitation can only be very high, while the rate of surplus output is very low, making the real gap between the two enormous, and depriving the peasant not only of all his surplus output, but also of a significant part of his necessary output. But this real rate of exploitation is not the manifestation of capitalist land rent, which is the excess above an average profit, but of feudal rent. This great burden for the peasants explains the quasi-stationary character of the Kampuchean economy, whose development on the basis of simple reproduction is difficult.

The high rate of exploitation is a fetter not only on the development of agriculture but also on the free development of the whole national economy, including industry: In these conditions of very high rates of exploitation, 'how can money be earned for anything beyond food'. For the peasants it is neither possible nor desirable to improve or enlarge their farms. But neither do the landlords, or, to a certain extent, the rich peasants wish to change the traditional state of affairs or adopt the modern mode of production. It is not in their interest, at least at the present stage of agricultural technology. In Example 5, for $31.00 spent on the means of production, expenditure on supplementary labour is as high as $150.00. On the other hand, the example of the hypothetical case of a capitalist farm with all labour paid shows that for $17.50 spent on the means of production, expenditure on wage labour is as high as $246.40.

As long as modern production technology does not manage to bring them greater advantages, landlords will maintain the feudal mode of production and the feudal social relations which provide them with substantial incomes in the form of principal dues, usurious interest, very cheap labour and various gifts and services in the form of secondary dues already mentioned.

Thus the very high real rate of exploitation fetters the progress of agricultural technology. To liberate the peasant from this subjection and permit rapid technical progress in agriculture, in our opinion requires an end to feudalism and semi-feudalism. The tiller must own his own field and be master of the produce of his labour, so that the system of agrarian relations is completely free of feudal remnants.

Exploitation by Usury and Commercial Capital

The market in Kampuchea is such that the peasant is robbed when he sells his agricultural produce and held to ransom when he buys the products he needs. All the country's trade is in the hands of foreign monopolies, and there are middlemen at every level of the organization and distribution of merchandise and credit. The role of the middleman in the import and export trade has been compared to the circulation of blood in the human body. Here is a rather picturesque description of it:

> . . . there is, in effect, a two-way circulation, one of imports which flows from the great Cholon business houses and branches out into the whole country, first to the small wholesale houses which comprise the secondary arteries, then the merchants of the big towns, the small arteries, and the small retailers, whose thatch shops may even be established at the corner of two ricefield embankments, completing the arterial network.
>
> These arteries are common to both circulation systems; they convey imported products out to the most remote parts of the countryside, but they also drain away all the paddy which remains in the hands of the peasants and smallholders, and deliver it first to the merchant who collects the paddy, who then sends it on to the small wholesale merchant in the provincial centre, and finally, thanks to the transport network, connects the entire wholesale rice trade to the shops of the big Cholon importers where the paddy is delivered for export, ending the circulation and closing the trade cycle . . . .
>
> Now all these Chinese houses make up a body, each element of which depends on the preceding one and controls the following one, from the viewpoint of the circulation of goods as well as that of credit, since this credit, descending in a cascade through to the smallest

> arteries, constitutes the fundamental point of the Chinese organization.
>
> The wholesaler importer extends credit to the small wholesale merchant in the provincial centre, who delivers goods also on credit to the small shopkeeper in his hut, who extends credit to his clients, the peasants and smallholders, for the whole year and is only repaid at harvest time, not in cash but generally in paddy.
>
> On the other hand, the Chinese exporter or wholesaler in Cholon gives advances to the small paddy wholesalers in the provincial centres, who in turn give advances to their appointed collectors.[10]

The industrialists, the merchants and the French and foreign businessmen make wide use of this 'Chinese organization', finding that the tendency of the Chinese 'to mingle with the natives' makes them an indispensable intermediary. But the Chinese are also formidable competitors. 'There is no speculation that the Chinese does not throw himself into . . . . Credit facilities have accustomed him to audacity in business which often gives him the advantage over his European competitor; there is no Chinese in business who has not committed higher sums than a European with the same amount of capital'.[11]

The business houses attach themselves to a Chinese comprador who will advise them about the ways of Chinese business, on the solvency of the Asian clientele, even on the need to guarantee this solvency for the sake of security. On the other hand, the comprador for the banks is the controller of credit to the Asian clientele, no credit can be advanced without his signature, nor discount given without his guarantee. Then there is the comprador for an export house who buys export merchandise from the native producer on behalf of his house, and the comprador for the import house who supplies foreign products to merchants who are his compatriots. These services are paid for by a fixed salary plus commission. But these are not all the comprador's profits: the client always pays out funds without the knowledge of his boss, for which he secures another commission of 10-15%. On the other hand, the comprador often gets involved in underhand deals.

The Chinese permeates the economic and social life of the country. He is the grocer, the retailer, the agent or the informer who penetrates the smallest hamlet. He is the collector, the pedlar; he is the manager of the junks in the river fleet which circulates on the waterways of Kampuchea and of the road transport companies. Here he levies taxes on the markets, there he feeds the prisoners, elsewhere he farms the salt marshes and rents the fisheries on the Great Lake, usually in order to sublet them. He is even assigned the right to exploit gambling houses, ferries, markets, etc. The heart of this organization of trade and credit is Cholon, where the big buyers, the millers, the exporters and importers co-operate directly, their interests inextricably intertwined.

What becomes of the isolated, individual peasant in the context of this powerful organization of trade and credit? He could be compared to an insect trapped in a spider's web. From all sides, he is oppressed and exploited, both as a producer and as a consumer.

The prices of the agricultural products are determined on the market by the monopoly position of the big foreign businessmen, with the laws of supply and demand playing an insignificant role. The peasant is totally disarmed because he does not decide the prices, which are fixed in Cholon by the big businessmen, the capitalists of industry and trade.

Agricultural products can always be arbitrarily depreciated or rejected by the merchants. The peasant, totally ignorant of the state of the market, is always trying to get hold of ready cash, and worried about 'what no one will buy'; consequently he agrees to sell at any price at all. The producer's major concern is not to let his harvest 'perish'.

Now we come to the thousand ways of falsifying weights and measures. We will only mention the use of the thang here. There are two types of thang in Kampuchea, and this difference is put to advantage by the merchants and usurers. Thus, when they sell or lend their stock of paddy during the hungry period ('the period of the gap'), they use the popular thang, 20 kilograms, but when they buy or are being repaid, they demand the royal thang of 30 kilograms. The manipulation of weights and measures by merchants and usurers constitutes a real swindle.

The producers often deliver their agricultural produce on credit, to be paid for their produce only when it has been loaded and is on the way to Cholon. Between the time of purchase and shipment the price of paddy can fall drastically, with disastrous consequences for the producers. No law, no social measure protects the peasant producers from a rapid fall in prices, linked to the operations of thoughtless speculators.

An individual producer and isolated seller, the peasant is absolutely tied to the village merchants, who use all sorts of links – advances, loans, credit – to create a clientele of faithful suppliers. Finally, trade and business are combined, in an extremely skilful way, with usury.

A few figures will eloquently demonstrate how much of the product of the producer's labour is taken by the various intermediaries. Consider the distribution of the product of the sale of rice exported from Saigon:

To the producer – 26%
To the intermediaries – 33.6%
To the transporters – 21%
To the millers – 5%
In taxes – 14.4%.

The part which returns to the producer hardly represents a quarter of the total product. Thus usury, commercial capital and the State appropriate three-quarters of the output of the producer.

The peasant is not robbed only when he sells. He is again held to ransom when he buys. In order to live a peasant family must buy commodities and food products of all kinds: salt, cloth, groceries, sugar, lard, oil, areca nuts, betel . . . . To work the land, the peasant needs ploughshares, sickles, nails, rakes, picks, hoes. For all these small purchases he must pay dear to the capitalists, the wholesalers and retailers.

> The prices paid by the Indochinese citizen for the products heavily protected by the Customs regulations are on average 15% higher than prices elsewhere. If this coefficient is applied to the total French imports, one can deduce that the Indochinese citizen annually pays the metropolitan importers a tithe of 12 million piastres for the single purpose of offering them a privileged place on his market. This is an indirect tax which weighs on the population and has come to be added to the existing taxes.[12]

Who profits from these imports on which the citizen pays an annual tithe of 12 million piastres? If we study the distribution of products imported in 1931, by class of the population, there are four types of products:

Products of no direct interest to the consumer: This is notably true of charcoal, asphalt, heavy oils, railway lines and carriages, steamrollers, heavy machinery, cleaning equipment, weapons, steel boats, etc .... These imports represented 9% of the total value of Indochinese imports.

Products designed for the Europeans, the feudal class and the bourgeoisie: These are conserves, flour, fruits, confectionary, perfumes, beauty products, opium, drinks (champagne, cognac), glassware, porcelain products, wool and silk cloth, books, electric lights, bicycles, cars, furniture, umbrellas, packets and tins of cigarettes, cigars, hats, fish, shellfish, swallow's nests, onions, shallots, dried vegetables, raisins, starches, preserved fruits and vegetables, shark fins, tourist cars, petrol ... These represent 49% of the total value of imports, for less than 10% of the total population.

Products consumed by the masses of the people who constitute 90% of the population: These are notably crude cotton thread or cloth, sugar, kerosene, tools, petards, *papier de culte,* incense sticks, candles, household articles, areca-nuts, garlic, various condiments .... These represent 42% of total imports, for 90% of the population.[13]

From what we have said, it is difficult to see how living conditions, the standard of living of the masses of the people, have improved since the beginning of French colonization. The national wealth has undoubtedly increased as a result of works of economic interest. But it is clear that the wealth created is very unfairly distributed, so that in spite of higher production, 'the peasant remains underfed and financially destitute'.

The formation of monetary relations, with capitalism developing in a feudal pocket, is not of the kind that creates more favourable conditions for peasant farming, already limited by the difficult natural environment. By raising the price of land, commercial production constantly increases land rent, since the rise in land prices does not proceed from development of productive capital and significant increases in the cultivated area, but from land speculation, from the buying up of land by landlords and rich peasants. Although the development of monetary and capitalist relations favours the rise in agricultural prices, at the same time the speculators – landowners, merchants, officials – are investing their capital in land, purchasing land not to take up agriculture but because land speculation brings them big profits. They are essentially taking a gamble on rising prices of agricultural products. Further, the more land one has, the more land rent one makes the peasants pay, and the greater the profits from usury and commerce.

We have tried to describe objectively the technical, economic and social conditions of peasant production. At the same time, we have posed a certain number of related problems, which can be solved only by establishing a rational system of agrarian relations to pave the way for the development of capitalism and create the necessary foundations for the industrialization of our country. The improvement and raising of the material and cultural levels of the masses of the people can only be achieved by equipping and modernizing the rural areas and by the rational organization of labour with a view to the development of national production.

The Persistence of Usury

At every point the peasant needs money, to pay debts, pay taxes, buy seed, rent land, farm equipment and stock, . . . and maintain his family through the difficult periods to keep them going until the next harvest, etc . . . . He always finds money-lenders who are benevolent, sympathetic and eager to provide their services. According to one author, usury 'prospers wondrously' at the expense of the miserable mass of the people.

The French Administration in Indochina has long realized the severity of this social scourge, and thus introduced European credit methods, founded on the provision of real guarantees: pawning, securities, mortgages. But they have not succeeded in wiping out usury. The Bank of Indochina was established in 1875, and granted a monopoly over all the territory of the 'Indochinese Union'. To allay Indochinese suspicions of European bankers and encourage them to use the services of the new network, the system of compradors was adopted, which we have already mentioned. As a result credit became a weapon to eliminate business competitors, and the compradors became the arbiters of credit distribution. Further, the compradors to some extent financed the big usurers, who in turn maintained the big landlords and rice merchants associated with them.

In 1927, *Credit Populaire Agricole* (Popular Agricultural Credit) was established, inspired by the Dutch system in Java. The Bank of Indochina was called upon to finance loans that would be drawn up by *Credit Populaire,* with the Governor-General of Indochina's guarantee. Finally in 1942, the Office of Popular Credit was formed, with five sections, for rural credit, craft credit, maritime credit, small industries credit and rural settlement. The Office set itself the aim of

> assisting and encouraging rural production, native crafts, maritime fishing and its industries. It is especially responsible for ensuring the management and distribution amongst applicants [co-operatives' coffers] of the capital and discount credit put at its disposal by government measure, as well as to co-ordinate and control the process of these applications.

The Office of Popular Credit was run by an Administrative Council presided over by the Councillor at the level of the High Commissariat and comprising: five Indochinese notables representing the various affiliated companies, a representative of French affiliates, three high officials of the French Administration (Agriculture, Finance, Treasury) and an Office Director. The Office was directed by a High Commission for Popular Credit flanking the High Commissariat and was composed of four representatives of the Indochinese companies, one representative of the French companies and five High Officials of the French Administration (Planning, Finance, Public Works, Agriculture and Treasury). In each country of the Indochinese Union a local Committee of Popular Credit was also established, presided over by the head of the local Administration and composed of four representatives of the local administration, two delegates of the Indochinese companies, one representative of the Chamber of Agriculture and two representatives of the Chamber of Commerce.

We have nothing to say against the aim of the Office of Popular Credit, which in principle is excellent. But as for the composition of the Administrative Council and of the High Commission, as well as that of the local Administrative Committee, we believe that they do not accord with the aim. There is no representative of the masses of the peasants, artisans and fishermen in the Administration, unless a member of the French or Indochinese companies is supposed to be the masses' representative. But we come to the main point if we look at Table 1.7. This shows that:

Table 1.7
Distribution of Agricultural Credit by Province, 1950-51

	Agricultural Credit	
	(31.12.50)	*(31.12.51)*
Province	*(thousands of piastres)*	
Kandal	3,512	4,564
Kompong Cham	3,111	4,866
Prey Veng	792	1,404
Kompong Thom	1,007	1,369
Siemreap	11	76
Battambang	161	789
Svay Rieng	518	118
Total	*9,112*	*13,186*

Table 1.7 shows that:

1) There are only seven Popular Credit banks for the whole of Kampuchea, where more than 90% of the population are peasants and the whole economy is based on agriculture, i.e., one-half of a Popular Credit bank for each of the 14 provinces with more than 200,000 inhabitants; 2) The credit provided by the seven banks is quite inadequate for the real needs of production in agriculture, crafts, fishing, and small native industry. But this sum is not insignificant in servicing the operations of commercial speculation in agricultural products, i.e., in the last analysis, usury; 3) The advances were mainly distributed, not in the productive rice-growing regions (Battambang, Prey Veng and Svay Rieng) but in regions of significant active commercial operations (Kompong Cham, Kandal and Kompong Thom). Loans advanced by Popular Credit are used for commercial speculation rather than for productive investment.

Who gets the loans from the coffers of *Credit Agricole Mutuel?*[14] A look at the following Table 1.8 will answer this question.

Table 1.8
Distribution of Agricultural Credit through Banks, 1950-51

Banks	*No. of Loans*	*Amount (thousands of piastres) (31.12.1950)*	*Average*	*No. of Loans*	*Amount (thousands of piastres) (31.12.1951)*	*Average*
Kandal	5,976	3,653	611	6,198	5,636	910
Kompong Cham	2,603	1,493	574	2,981	2,527	847
Prey Veng	1,861	666	358	2,710	1,077	510
Svay Rieng	1,211	348	287	1,309	466	356
Kompong Thom	1,272	666	524	1,287	776	603
Siemreap	—	—	—	—	—	—
Battambang	636	92	144	539	439	815
Total	*13,559*	*6,918*	*510*	*14,424*	*10,921*	*757*

It shows that: 1) The number of loans advanced by the seven agricultural banks in Kampuchea is tiny in comparison to the number of loans advanced from individual to individual in the many forms of usury, not only from one social class to another but even within the same class, including the working class in the towns and fields, 2) The loans from the agricultural banks go to the merchants, to small industrialists and to landlords. In effect, the size of the average loan (510 piastres in 1950 and 757 piastres in 1951) leaves no doubt about its destination. Can one imagine a Kampuchean peasant borrowing an average of 600 piastres per loan?[15] The peasant certainly has a pressing need for money but he does not need much. A few dozen piastres would be enough. For this moderate sum he does not travel hundreds of kilometres from home, entailing lost time and expenses of all sorts not only through his trip but through administrative formalities.[16] Thus the peasant with his urgent needs prefers to approach the village usurer, who agrees to the loan quickly and with hardly any formalities. The peasant only has to hand over the title to his property; the usurer can then go privately to the bank and borrow money on the strength of this. With the peasant's property title he obtains money from the bank to lend out at double or triple the bank rate.

The Office of Popular Credit thus becomes little more than an official tool in the service of the merchant or landlord usurer, since the loans reach the masses of the people only through intermediary usurers. Nor are the loans used for production; they are basically subsistence loans to all needy farmers through the critical hungry period. A look at the table of the monthly advances by the Office of Popular Credit (Table 1.9) reveals that all this credit has been deflected towards usurious ends, and has essentially served those ends.

Table 1.9
Monthly Advances by the Office of Popular Credit, 1950-51

Month	*Advances (in thousands of piastres)*	
	1950	*1951*
January	53	57
February	114	174
March	172	205
April	61	1,052
May	60	534
June	23	882
July	8	589
August	441	548
September	1,081	1,715
October	614	1,276
November	294	709
December	526	349
Total	*3,447*	*8,090*

It emerges from Table 1.9 that:
The important loans are carried out during two specific periods of the year:
1) The hungry period, extremely severe for the peasants, extends over the three long months (August, September and October) between sowing (May, June, July) and harvesting (November, December, January). Just to 'hold on' until the next harvest, the peasants are obliged to borrow in kind (a quantity of paddy) or in cash (a few dozen piastres) at usurious rates, to request advances on the harvest, to 'place' their children with usurers as security on a loan – whether a voluntary one or simply one to ward off death by starvation. All this is multi-faceted and rampant usury. Creditors

and usurers of all kinds create for themselves a sort of faithful clientele and prosper at their expense. They top up their landholdings by demanding land as security, they surround themselves with servants and debt bondsmen. Every year, the end of this period is marked by accumulated ruin, misery and the dislocation of poor families; 2) the period of speculation in grain covers the three months (February, March and April) after the harvest. Good or bad, the harvest always gives rise to speculation, to collection and hoarding of paddy and of stocks intended for dispatch to Cholon or sale during the hungry period.

The advances made by the Office of Popular Credit are smallest during the season of heavy work which demands major investment. This period covers the three months (May, June and July) when ploughing, sowing and transplanting take place. There is no investment of funds. Modern capitalists deliberately shun productivity in favour of more secure and lucrative commercial speculation and usury. The controllers of wealth have no interest in investing in agriculture, which stagnates as it smothers its base by simple reproduction.

Here is how and why credit from the rural treasury tends to be continually channelled towards usury. The practice of usury simply makes a mockery of the idea of lending money or equipment to all strata of society and for all the purposes of human activity. Usurers of all kinds subject the working masses to obligations of all kinds. Operating under such conditions, the Office of Popular Credit by no means demonstrates the advantages of the role of credit in production. What lessons can we draw from this short study of the role and function of the Office of Popular Credit? We believe that an institution which simply proposed to open up credit facilities to agriculture with no distinction between the various peasant classes has ended up: 1) reinforcing and extending the position of the creditors, usurers and underhand bankers who make the institutions of agricultural credit their own more or less official usury establishments; 2) directly facilitating the buying up of land to the profit of the usurers and creditors who are at the same time landlords; 2) thus facilitating the perpetuation of the usurious credit system of which the broad masses of the people are the victims.

Taking account of these lessons, we shall advocate a truly popular credit system, in the interest of the peasant masses who are the real creators of the nation's wealth.

References

1. The French word 'Cambodge' has been translated here as 'Kampuchea'— [Eds.]
2. R. Kleinpeter, *Le probleme Foncier au Cambodge* (Paris, 1937), p.212.
3. A. Boudillon, *Regime de la Propriete Privee en Indochine* (Paris, 1915).

4. For further discussion, and some qualifications, of this picture of land-holding, see the extract from Hu Nim, which follows. The qualifications parallel similar passages in Hou Yuon not translated here.
5. A. Chevalier, *Le Riz,* (Presses Universitaire de France, Paris, Que sais-je? series 1948), pp.71-2.
6. Cited by Paul Bernard in *Le probleme Economique Indochinois* (Nouvelles Editions Latines, 1934).
7. Rice prices fell from $13.10 a quintal in April 1930 to $3.20 in November 1933. The fall was 72%. But personal taxes and land taxes remained the same as in 1929 (Bernard, op. cit., p.124).
8. Bernard, op. cit., p.45.
9. *L'Aurore Indochinoise,* 8-9 September 1934.
10. Cited by Bernard, op. cit., p.29.
11. Bard, 'Les Chinois chez eux', cited by Rene Dubreuil in *De la condition des Chinois et de leur Role Economique en Indochine* (thesis, Paris, 1910).
12. Bernard, op. cit., pp.38-9.
13. Ibid., pp.32ff.
14. Presumably Hou Yuon is referring here to the Office of Popular Credit– [Eds.]
15. A statistical error by Hou Yuon has been corrected here, without affecting the author's argument– [Eds.]
16. The difficulties of the actual borrowing process, which involves formalities and expenses that are too high for small loans, mean that the peasant misses the advantage of credit. See Yves Henry, *L'Economie Agricole de l'Indochine* (1932), p.662.

2. Land Tenure and Social Structure in Kampuchea by Hu Nim

The Agrarian Structure

The Serious Drawbacks of a Parcellized Structure

It is a commonly held belief that Agrarian problems are problems of large landholdings, the big concentrations of land found in most of the old countries of Europe, indeed, the countries of latifundia. According to writers on agricultural economics such as Louis Baudiny and Andre Garrigou-Lagrange,[2] the precise scientific definition of latifundia designates big property under-cultivated by default of the owner. The Romans used the term to describe the huge private domains established for the benefit of a small number of mostly patrician families from the 3rd Century B.C. onwards in Italy, particularly in Latium. These estates arose as much from ancient usurpations of the *ager publicus* as from expropriations of endebted small and medium landowners.

However, the latifundium in the classical sense, is only one aspect of an agrarian problem. Rural economics teaches us that there are two opposite agrarian phenomena. Concentration means that a minority of landlords possess almost all the land. Fragmentation is the opposite phenomenon: a majority of small landowners each possess a small plot of land. Thus the actual dispersal or scattered location of the parcels is only a consequence of fragmentation.

Concentration is accompanied by very harsh exploitation: the small landowners, poor peasants and agricultural labourers work for the prosperity of the big landlords. There are plenty of examples of this throughout the world and this was the target of the agrarian revolution in Eastern Europe which swept away the landlords and overthrew the system of exploitation.

Historically, fragmentation is linked to the antiquity of agricultural use, combined with demographic expansion and consequent high population density. Each individual wants his share of land: the more individuals there are the smaller each one's share. But this process is itself facilitated and con-

*Extracts from *Les services publics economiques du Cambodge*, doctoral thesis, University of Phnom Penh, 1965. Translated from the French by Ben Kiernan.

solidated by juridical factors – the system of private property and the inheritance of equal shares by all the children is dominant in many countries influenced by the Napoleonic Code or by Roman Law.

While there is general agreement that concentration is a problem, there is more hesitancy in recognizing that fragmentation is also a problem. However, the major writers on rural economics, including Pierre Fromont,[3] have come to see that agrarian parcellization presents many serious drawbacks. These are of two kinds: lower productivity and hindrance to innovation.

Lower productivity is brought about by the interplay of two factors: reduced production and increased costs. Reduced production occurs when a piece of land becomes under-cultivated as a direct corollary of parcellization. Thus boundaries between individual plots – divisions between farm strips, contact zones, embankments – will not be cultivated, while generations of subdivision finally produce parcels of land too small or too distant to cultivate at all. According to Pierre Fromont, divisions between strips account for a loss to production of 200,000 to 400,000 hectares of land out of a cultivated area of 20 million hectares. Accepting this ratio, divisions between plots in Kampuchea, with its cultivated area of 2 million hectares, would result in a loss as high as over 40,000 hectares. Contact zones and plough headlands, also very inadequately worked, make up about 1-4% of the total area.

The second factor in low productivity is increased costs due to time lost in various ways, for instance, travelling, turning machinery around at the end of the strip, and getting started again. All this lost time adds up. The amount of productive labour necessary for a given crop can thus vary with the size of the plots, as research undertaken in France in 1951[4] shows (see Table 2.1). Thus, on the whole, as the average size of the plot falls from 2.5 to 0.25 hectares, labour time increases by 50%. As a result, there are parallel developments in production costs.

Table 2.1.
Productive Labour and Plot Size

Size of Plot (hectares)	*Cereal Crops Hoed in Rows*		*Potatoes for Consumption*	
	Average Area	*Hours per Hectare*	*Average Area*	*Hours per Hectare*
Less than 0.5 hectares	0.27	173.4	0.30	977.8
0.5-1 hectares	0.65	138.3	0.87	749.8
1-2 hectares	1.29	139.6	1.30	704.8
2-5 hectares	2.55	135.5	1.50	644.5
More than 5 hectares	9.11	111.6	–	–

The use of machinery provides little encouragement to remove the root cause of these productivity losses. It is true that below a certain threshold area, the output due to machinery falls drastically, but, on the other hand, above that threshold output increases only slightly as the cultivated land area increases.

So if each cultivator could spread his risks by having several plots, a property of eight hectares could be made up of four plots of two hectares each – economical use of machinery and small cultivation would go together.

Parcellization also constitutes a hindrance to innovation. The introduction of updated production historically has been one of the most lucrative forms of agricultural progress. But modern innovation depends for its success upon conditions which are naturally absent from a parcellized landholding system. Agricultural innovation demands collective maintenance, irrigation and drainage works, for example, which cannot be achieved in a parcellized system. As Pierre Fromont puts it, 'parcellization ensures the triumph of the routine, and bars the way to any initiative'. In other words, parcellization is an obstacle to the development of agriculture and the raising of the peasants' standard of living.

Parcellization is not only an agrarian problem as serious as concentration: at a given stage of economic development, especially in countries with semi-capitalist, semi-undeveloped structures, the two phenomenon *combine together.* Concentration increases and develops alongside parcellization. The smaller and more fragmented the peasants' land becomes, the more yields and production are reduced, the poorer the peasant gets. To subsist from day to day the poor peasant takes out loans at very high interest, usually involving collateral. Thus the poor peasant mortgages the title to his land and contracts to pay the rich man the principal with interest. When the poor peasant does not manage to pay the very high interest rates, the rich man appropriates the land, the title of which is already in his hands. Thus, fragmented land is concentrated more and more in the hands of the rich landlords or merchant usurers, while the number of poor and landless peasants is constantly rising.

The agrarian structure in Kampuchea is mixed, both fragmented *and* tending towards concentration. Parcellization is prevalent in all the river-bank land and the fertile rice-growing regions, but for over a dozen years there has been a marked tendency towards concentration, not only in the newly-opened areas, but also, to a still limited extent, in the fragmented regions themselves.

The Evolution of the Agrarian Structure since 1930

A preliminary remark must be made about the difference between European and Kampuchean landholding classification. In Europe and elsewhere, less than 10 hectares count as 'small property', with between 10 and 50 hectares regarded as 'medium property' and more than 50 hectares as 'big property'. This classification of properties dos not correspond to the agrarian and social systems in Kampuchea, where as little as 10 hectares provides a comfortable rental income. Such a landowner is therefore regarded as a landlord in Kampuchean society. The landholding classification given by economic realities in Kampuchea would place less than 5 hectares as 'small property', between 5 and 10 hectares as 'medium property', and over 10 hectares as 'big property'. This study is based on this classification.

The Situation in 1930: According to M. Yves Henry's study in 1930, property in the rice lands of the five provinces of Battambang, Svay Rieng, Prey Veng, Kompong Cham and Kandal was on average distributed as in Table 2.2, which also shows the distribution of river-bank land (for Kompong Cham and Kandal, the two main provinces watered by the Mekong River). This makes it clear that river-bank land is more fragmented than the rice land. Owners of more than 50 hectares are non-existent there. As for the

Table 2.2
Distribution of Land, 1930

Size of Plot	*Families (%)*	
	Rice Fields	*River-Bank Land*
Less than 5 hectares	87.88	99.50
5-10 hectares	9.80	0.45
10-50 hectares	2.24	0.05
More than 50 hectares	0.07	0.00

ricelands, the degree of parcellization still varies from province to province. In Battambang, Svay Rieng and Prey Veng, owners of more than 50 hectares can be found, with Battambang Province claiming the lowest proportion of properties of less than 5 hectares, as confirmed in Table 2.3.

Table 2.3
Distribution of Rice Field Ownership in 5 Provinces, 1930[5]

	Families (%)				
Size of Plot	*Battambang*	*Prey Veng*	*Svay Rieng*	*Kompong Cham*	*Kandal*
Less than 5 hectares	76.3	80.3	87.0	96.8	99.0
5-10 hectares	18.3	16.5	10.5	2.8	0.9
10-50 hectares	5.3	3.0	2.4	0.4	0.1
More than 50 hectares	0.12	0.12	0.14	–	–

Approximately and on average, these figures lead one to say that in 1930 property was distributed across Kampuchea as follows:

Less than 5 hectares – 93.70%
5-10 hectares – 5.12%
More than 10 hectares – 1.18%

The Situation in 1956: According to M. Jean Delvert[6], in 1956 there were 733,491 landowners, including:

Less than 1 hectare – 402,000 or 55%
1-2 hectares – 183,000 or 25%
2-5 hectares – 90,000 or 12%
5-10 hectares – 48,000 or 7%
10-20 hectares – 9,300 or 1%
More than 20 hectares – 1,191

When we adopt the Kampuchean agrarian classification, we find property distributed across Kampuchea in 1956 as follows:

Less than 5 hectares – 92%
5-10 hectares – 7%
More than 10 hectares – 1%

The Situation in 1962: The Kampuchean agrarian structure, from the latest statistics to hand, was as follows: 2,446,750 hectares of land belonging to 835,540 farming families.

Table 2.4
Agrarian Structure in 1962

Size of Plot	*Families* *Number*	*(%)*		*Land* *Amount*	*% of Total*
Less than 1 hectare	256,000	30.7	on	126,800 hectares	5.18
1-2 hectares	186,410	22.3	on	260,280 hectares	10.65
2-5 hectares	272,500	32.6	on	926,600 hectares	37.90
5-10 hectares	86,930	10.4	on	608,510 hectares	24.82
10-20 hectares	28,420	3.4	on	386,510 hectares	15.80
More than 20 hectares	5,020	0.6	on	138,050 hectares	5.65
Total	*835,540*			*2,446,750*	

This distribution clearly shows that there is an agrarian problem in Kampuchea. In effect, more than 256,200 families, or 30.7% of all farming households, possess only a total of 126,800 hectares of land, representing only 5.18% of the total cultivated area (in 1962). As each Kampuchean family includes at least five members, then this section of the peasantry possesses only a very small plot of land, or 10 ares per person.

At the same time, if we consider the category of 'less than 2 hectares', 53% of families possess only a total of 15.83% of the cultivated land, while 4% of landowners (with more than 10 hectares) have at their disposition 21.45% of the land. Is this not a serious problem? Regrouping the categories (small, medium and big), in 1962 the distribution of property was as follows:

Less than 5 hectares – 85.60%
5-10 hectares – 10.40%
More than 10 hectares – 4.00%

By comparing the structure in the three periods (1930, 1956 and 1962), it can be clearly seen that a tendency towards concentration has become more and more noticeable.

Table 2.5
Evolution of the Agrarian Structure, 1930-62

Size of Plot	*1930 (%)*	*1956 (%)*	*1962 (%)*
Less than 5 hectares	93.70	92.00	85.60
5-10 hectares	5.12	7.00	10.40
More than 10 hectares	1.18	1.00	4.00

We can see that the proportion of owners of less than 5 hectares has evolved in the opposite direction to that of owners of 5 to 10 hectares and more than 10 hectares. In other words, the number[7] of small landowners is decreasing, while that of medium and large landowners is increasing. The first, over 32 years, fell by about 8.1% (from 93.7% to 85.6%). The second moved from 5.12% to 10.4% and the third from 1.18% to 4%. In 1956, the number of big landowners slightly diminished due to the departure of certain French rice-growing landlords after Independence. But from 1956, landowners with more than 10 hectares have progressively increased. This is because on the one hand, the Administration gave more and more land concessions to private persons, and, on the other, certain landowners actively concentrated land in their hands. In 1956, there were only 1,191 landowners with more than 20 hectares, but in 1962 this number had risen to 5,020, that is, almost a fivefold increase over six years. The greater the increase in the number of big landlords, the greater the increase in the number of poor and landless peasants.

The fact that the percentage of small properties (less than five hectares) has progressively diminished shows that some farmers have been deprived of their land (8% over 32 years).

The 1962 plot distribution shows that more than 30% of agricultural households possessed less than one hectare of land and in all only 5.18% of the total cultivated area. As each agricultural household is composed of at least five members (some bear even heavier burdens, without mentioning social and political obligations) and as on average these 30% of households only have a half-hectare each, improvement of the lives of this category of farmers is difficult.

From this analysis we can conclude that both the parcellized structure and the trend towards concentration present problems. Concentration, if it is not speculative, can play a role in increasing production, providing the opportunity to apply scientific and technical progress. But because of the weak development of capitalism in Kampuchea, this tendency exists only for speculation (in the sale of land, tenancy, sharecropping, etc. This agrarian structure still varies from one region to another. If concentration is in progress in certain rice-growing provinces like Battambang, fragmentation and dispersion of holdings is increasing in the river-bank regions, and these are the most fertile regions with the highest population density.

Regional Variation in Agrarian Structures

Landholdings of less than two hectares are the rule in nearly all of central Kampuchea, which has two geographically and economically (both densely populated) different regions: the central rice lands and the Mekong river-bank areas. The central rice lands can be located between a line along the Bassac-Tonle Sap Rivers and the Elephant Mountains chain, from South Vietnam up to Kompong Chhnang. Here the average property is as low as 0.4 hectares; basic subsistence is obtained by sugar palm cultivation or rural crafts. In the river-bank regions of the Mekong, the Tonle Sap, the Bassac and the Tonle Tauch, the average property is around one hectare, but even this level is not attained in certain *Khums,* whose population reaches 150 to 300 inhabitants per square kilometre.

Property from two to three hectares in the eastern rice lands (Svay Rieng and Prey Veng)[5] regions of moderate population density, about 80 inhabitants per square kilometre; in the southern confines of Kampuchea (Koh Thom, Kirivong); north-east of the Lakes plain (density of 30 to 40 inhabitants per square kilometre; and west of the Lakes plain (Bakan, Maung-Russey, Sisophon).

Property averaging over three hectares is found especially in the infertile regions inland from the river banks and the more or less arid or unsuitable regions. Geographically these are located east of the plain of the Four-Arms (at Svay Teap and Kompong Trabek where floating rice is cultivated); south of the plain of the Four-Arms (where floating rice is also cultivated and some parts are uncultivated); north-east of the Lakes plain (at Kompong Svay, Staung and Chikreng where some areas are flooded); and west of the Lakes plain (at Sangker, Battambang and Mongkolborrey) where rice is planted by broadcasting[8].

Overall, land-holding in nearly all the poor and arid land averages three hectares per family with the exception of the western part of the Lakes plain where the land is still fertile. As for the fertile regions, here the Kampuchean peasants engage in disputes over land from which to earn a living. These are the extremely fragmented river-bank regions. The harder life becomes, the more the poor peasants are deprived of their land as they take out loans at high interest rates in order to feed their large families. Unable to repay their debts, they are obliged to hand over their land to landlords or merchant-usurers. They come, in constantly increasing numbers, into town to push a pedicab or work as hired coolies, while others head for the plantations.

(According to the census taken by M. Jean Delvert, for example, 345 out of 816 workers in the Pean-Cheang plantation, that is about 50%, were landless peasants.) In Phnom Penh, the number of pedicab drivers has increased constantly in recent years. There are about 20,000,in particular people from the countryside. Thus the town of Phnom Penh in the 12 months from 15 April 1958 registered an effective population increase of 20,000 people, 10,000 of whom came from the countryside. Meanwhile, the people of the poorest provinces emigrated to other regions, producing a negative migratory flow for the provinces of Takeo, Svay Rieng and Kompong Speu, of the order of 6,000, 4,000 and 2,000 respectively. Kompong Cham and Kandal – the most fragmented river-bank regions – also had a negative migratory flow of the order of 4,000 and 12,000 people respectively.

The increase in the number of landless peasants is mainly a result of the extremely parcellized agrarian structure and of the agrarian social structure with its exploitation by merchant capital, usury and very high land rent. This increase is reflected in the high rural exodus, demonstrated in Table 2.6.

Table 2.6
Population Movement in Kampuchea, 15 April 1958-15 April 1959

Province	*Births*	*Deaths*	*Migratory Flow*	*Net Increase*
Phnom Penh City	16,000	6,000	+ 10,000	20,000
Kandal	28,000	12,000	– 12,000	15,000
Kompong Cham	25,000	13,000	– 4,000	8,000
Battambang	19,000	9,000	+ 1,000	11,000
Prey Veng	18,000	8,000	–	10,000
Takeo	15,000	9,000	– 6,000	–
Kampot	11,000	4,000	– 1,000	6,000
Kompong Speu	11,000	6,000	– 2,000	3,000
Kompong Thom	10,000	5,000	–	5,000
Svay Rieng	12,000	6,000	– 4,000	2,000
Siemreap	11,000	5,000	+ 1,000	7,000
Kompong Chhnang	9,000	3,000	–	6,000
Pursat	6,000	4,000	+ 3,000	5,000
Kratie	5,000	3,000	+ 3,000	5,000
Koh Kong	2,000	1,000	–	1,000
Ratanakiri	1,000	500	–	500
Stung Treng	1,000	500	–	500

Source: *Annuaire Statistique Retrospectif du Cambodge,* 1958-60.

A serious census is necessary to ascertain the exact number of landless peasants. One can maintain, however, that the property categories approximately correspond to the different social categories of the peasants in Kampuchean society.

This short study of the agrarian structure of Kampuchea enables us to see its serious problems. The parcellized structure constitutes an obstacle to the development of production and of innovation and renders any modernization of the means of production impossible. The use of tractors is only lucrative on areas of 15 hectares and over, and in Kampuchea properties of more than 10 hectares only represent about 21.45% of the land, belonging to a mere 4% of families. Secondly the trend towards concentration is already taking place in such a way that, unless some intervention is made, the life of a large section of the peasants will become more and more difficult and the number of rural labourers will increase. Moreover, the nature of the agrarian structure combines with the social structure of rural life to aggravate the lives of the peasants and compound the obstacles to modernization and the development of agriculture.

The Social Structure

The peasants are not only victims of natural calamities resulting from serious climatic defects and of the agrarian system inherited from the colonial era, but also of exploitation by landlords, usurers, merchants and comprador businessmen. Commercial capital, usury and land rent comprise an outdated system exploiting the masses of the peasantry. Thus, before we look at the social differentiations of the Khmer peasantry, we must outline the characteristics of the system of exploitation.

Commercial and Usury Capital

Before the 1963 reforms, general opinion had it that 'the nature of the market is such that the peasant is robbed when he sells his products and held to ransom when he buys the goods that he needs'. This was because he was exploited by merchants, comprador businessmen and usurers. According to the 1962 census, 100,400 people, or 4.2% of the active population in the rural areas, were engaged in commerce or real estate business.

The merchant in the countryside effectively plays a double role; he provides the peasant with his essential purchases and, with a view to sale or export, collects his agricultural produce. As over 70% of peasants are more or less poor, purchases and sales are not carried out under normal conditions: generally, products for consumption are not actually sold to the peasants but advanced to them against the harvest. When the peasants need commodities, they approach the merchants or shopkeepers and then pay them back at the harvest in paddy, corn, tobacco, etc. Certainly, 'sale of a green crop on credit' is subject to very high rates of usury. We will examine further the efforts of OROC (The Royal Co-operative Office) in the struggle against usury. For the majority of the peasants, these sorts of loans are for the purpose of daily consumption, to bridge the food gap or even to celebrate religious festivals or family occasions. The loans are difficult to repay, and the debts accumulate so much that one day the peasant is obliged to abandon his plot of land to the merchants, which further explains the increased number of landless peasants and debt bondsmen.

At each sale of agricultural produce, a multitude of middlemen from the bottom to the top – shopkeeper, individual collector, miller, transporter, small wholesaler, wholesaler, exporter – take out exorbitant profits so that a very tiny portion of the sale value at the last exchange gets back to the peasan

The reorganization of foreign trade in 1964 enabled the State to put an end to speculation by importers and exporters and to realize a profit of 11 thousand 336 million riels in the balance of payments. However, towards the beginning of 1964, because of bad weather, the Government was unable to set up immediately its service for the collection and purchase of agricultural produce; then the wholesalers (former exporters) profited from the opportunity for gain on the backs of the peasants. So the price of paddy dropped considerably at the beginning of 1964; in certain provinces the price per picul (68 kilograms) of paddy fell to 80 or 90 riels, while the general average for the first two quarters was established at 117 and 126 riels.[10] The average price of a picul of paddy was therefore of the order of 120 riels during the first half of 1964.

At this price, the peasant is selling his paddy at below production cost, selling at a loss. Because of the low per hectare yields, the cost price of a picul of paddy, according to the estimates of the *Direction de la Statistique Agricole,* was 150.28 riels (February 1964). Taking into account the number of days worked by the peasant in a season which varies from four to nine months, the *Direction de la Statistique Agricole* estimates that the producers must be attributed a minimum profit margin of about 25%, which brings the production cost of a picul of paddy to 187.85 riels.[11] Now during the first half of 1964, the producer could only sell his paddy at a lower price, 120 riels on average. On this basis, let us try to calculate the share that the producer gets back, and the percentage of the latter in 100 riels of export value or value on transaction in Phnom Penh.

In effect, SONEXIM[12] has fixed the purchase price of rice in Phnom Penh (sold in Phnom Penh shops) at 480 riels per 100 kilogram of number 1 rice 25% broken (without bag). To obtain this 100 kilogram of rice, according to the calculations of people in the industry, requires 2.3 piculs at 68 kilograms of paddy each (156 kilogram, in other words an amount equivalent to: 58 kilograms of no. 1 rice, 25% broken, 30 kilograms of ½ broken rice, 12 kilograms of ¾ broken rice, and 7 kilograms of bran. At 120 riels per picul on average, the rice producers therefore retain about 276 riels (120 x 2.3).

According to information provided by the *Direction Generale des Impots,* the Phnom Penh wholesalers bought 100 kilograms of this quality rice from the millers or the provincial wholesalers for only 380 riels. After simple repackaging and storage, these wholesalers (former exporters) sold it to SONEXIM at the price fixed by the latter, 480 riels. On this 100 kilogram of rice equivalent to 2.3 piculs of paddy, the Phnom Penh wholesaler makes 100 riels (480 less 380). The amount which must go to the collectors, millers and transporters to Phnom Penh would therefore be 104 riels: 480 – (276 + 100). And the amount which would go to each social group is: 276 riels to the producer, 104 riels to the semi-middleman, and 100 riels to the wholesaler.

However, this distribution is fictitious, because the producer carries another significant loss by selling below the cost of production. For basic subsistence the producer must in fact sell 2.3 piculs of paddy for 187.85 x 2.3 = 432 riels (approximately). Therefore, by selling at 120 riels per picul, he must be losing 432-276 = 156 riels. As a consequence, to calculate the effective share of each social group we need to deduct from this 276 riels the loss that the producer has suffered (156 riels) to ascertain the producer's effective share, and add 156 riels to the final price of 480 riels fixed by SONEXIM to find the total value of the shares. Thus: 276-156 = 120 riels for the producer, which means that he produces 2.3 piculs but only receives the fruits of his labour on a single picul. Finally, 480 + 156 = 636 riels, the effective value of 100 kilograms of rice sold in Phnom Penh.

The effective share for each social group would be as follows: 19% to the producer (that is 120 riels),[13] 81% to all the intermediaries from the point of production to that of export (collectors, millers, small wholesalers, transporters, wholesalers, not counting the usurers), SONEXIM and taxation (that is 516 riels). It is in order to resolve this serious problem that the Government has set up a company to collect and package agricultural produce.

Sharecropping and Tenancy

If exploitation by commercial and usury capital is at the expense of the entire peasantry, land rent drawn from sharecroppers and tenants is the direct exploitation by landlords and rich peasants of the poorest strata of the peasants.

Sharecropping: Generally, in the regions of high population density where fragmentation is the most advanced, sharecropping is very widespread . . . . In the river-bank regions, the rich peasants with more than three hectares, as well as elderly rich peasants or widows, and in the rice lands those who have more than five hectares, generally rent out their land to poor peasants.

Such sharecropping varies with the region. It is the mode of exploitation most frequently used by the big concessionaires (Kampuchean and foreign) in Svay Rieng and Battambang Provinces where big property is dominant. It is also found in certain *srok* (districts) of Kompong Cham, Prey Veng, Kompong Thom and Siemreap. The form of sharecropping has scarcely changed since Yves Henry wrote *L'Economie Agricole de l'Indochine* in 1932:

> The landowner generally provides buffalo and advances the seed, often the paddy necessary for food for the family as well and a complementary sum for maintenance. The sharecropper builds his house, makes his tools, provides his labour and that of his family. At harvest time, the landowner is first repaid for his seed and the remainder is divided in

half. The advances are repaid thus: for 16 Nen (nominal value of a silver bar), the interest is 10 *thang* per year. If the buffaloes belong to the sharecropper, the division is made on the basis of 3 thang to the sharecropper and 2 for the landowner (Battambang).

Tenancy: Tenancy is a lease on the land for an amount fixed in advance in money or in kind. This mode of exploitation is significant in the rice lands of Battambang (Sangker, Battambang, Mongkolborrey districts) and in certain river-bank regions (Koh Sautin and Kang Meas in Kompong Cham Province, and some parts of Kandal). The rent is generally paid in kind (paddy). The rates vary: low in Battambang where labour is scarce, high in Prey Krabas (30 thang, i.e. 660 kilograms per hectare at Kampeng for a yield of 1200-1500 kilograms) and in Chikreng (40 thang or 880 kilograms at Kampong Kdey for a yield of 1,200 kilograms). Rent in cash is exceptional: rent is 200 to 300 riels per hectare at Phsar-Krom (Pursat), 150 riels at Tonleap (Kirivong).

As for the proportion of sharecroppers and tenants, in 1930, according to Henry, on average the five provinces of Battambang, Svay Rieng, Prey Veng, Kompong Cham and Kandal had 2.7% landowners employing sharecroppers and 3.3% landowners employing tenants. The situation according to the 1962 Census is shown in Table 2.7.

Table 2.7
Professions in the Rural Areas, 1962

Profession (Household Head)	*Owner-Cultivation*	*Tenants or Share-croppers*	*Prospective Tenants or Share-croppers*	*Unspecified Cultivation*	*Non-Cultivating Household*	*Un-Declared*
Farmers, fishers, hunters, foresters, and associated workers (834,500)	673,800	48,100	53,600	24,600	33,100	1,300
Other professions (151,500)	30,000	2,400	400	1,200	116,100	1,300
Total (986,000)	*703,900*	*50,500*	*54,000*	*25,800*	*149,200*	*2,600*

By 1962 the number of tenants and sharecroppers was nearly three times that of 1930. Even so, the 1962 figure does not reflect the real situation, since it gives the number of all owners regardless of the amount of land they possess. At least half of the 30.7% who are 'small landowners' possess less than one hectare of land,[14] and cannot subsist without renting land from others or even selling their labour power. In our opinion, the percentage of tenants and sharecroppers would now be even higher than 25%.

The Rate of Exploitation of the Peasant

Whether by commercial capital, usury or land rent, the exploitation of the peasants is very harsh. In the first case, we have seen that for 100 riels of value (exported, or as transacted in Phnom Penh), the peasant only receives 19 riels. If we add the necessary processing expenses, that is for transportation (which could not be more than 20 or 25 riels), to the share that the peasant gets, and deduct the total from 100 riels, we find an approximate rate of exploitation of the peasant, namely 61%. In the second case, the rate is higher. A debt of 100 riels in cash, or 10 thang of paddy in kind, requires a repayment of 200 riels in cash or 20 thang in kind, that is a rate of 100%. In the third case (land rents for sharecropping or tenancy), the rate is about 50%, for at least half the harvest must be paid to the landlords and rich peasants by the poor peasants. From the above, we can say that the real rate of exploitation of the peasants would be of the order of more than 50% of their surplus output *[surtravail]*.

The Different Social Strata of the Peasantry: Landlords

In modern Kampuchean society, it is difficult to distinguish the landlords from the rich peasants, since these two social classes are intimately linked. The criteria we will use to classify them is that of the size of their lands in relation to the fertility of the region.

Generally, all of those who possess over five hectares of land are either landlords (if they only exploit peasants) or rich peasants (if they work themselves but employ labour). According to the 1962 Census about 14.4% of the landowning families are in this category.

However, to this percentage must be added some of the landowners in the river-bank regions or the fertile rice-growing regions (Battambang, for example), who only possess four to five hectares, but who can live on income from land without working themselves. We would argue that one-tenth of the landowners possessing between two and five hectares (32.6%) fall into one of these categories, either rich peasants or even landlords. The percentage for these two social categories would therefore be 17.66% (14.4 + 3.26), of whom from 4% to 7% are landlords.

There are landlords in Kampuchea then. Here are some figures for landlords spread throughout the river-bank regions and the rice lands. *River-bank regions:* In 1956, the existence of landlords[15] was noted in the following regions and provinces: In Kompong Cham Province—27 at Roang, 21 at Koki Thom, 12 at Rokakoy, 6 at Koh Samrong, 5 at Koh

Sautin, 5 in srok Saang, 5 in srok Srey Santhor, 5 at Kang Meas (farms of 30 hectares) and 1 at Pongro; in Kandal Province – 78 in srok Lovea Em, 91 in srok Kien Svay; at Loeuk Dek and Peam Chor – 351 and 356 respectively were counted.

Rice lands: In the rice lands of central Kampuchea, landlords possessing more than 10 hectares are rare except at Trapeang Krassang (Bati, Takeo) where one owner of 75 hectares was found, and another of 20 hectares in srok Kandal Stung. In the rice lands of the North-East, 5 big landlords were noted at Roluos (Siemreap), and in the east, 11 at srok Romduol, 6 at Baphnom, 1 at Kamchay Meas, 5 at Peareang, 3 at Sithor Kandal and 2 at Romeas Hek. However, one finds significant numbers in several districts: 53 landlords in srok Svay Rieng, 8 of whom own more than 20 hectares, including 2 with 100 hectares in Chambak out of about 680 landowners; 60 at Svayteap; 263 at Kompong Trabek, notably in the south, including 51 with more than 20 hectares at Banteay Chakrey.

Though insignificant at the national level, this number is nonetheless important at the regional level: about 11 in the province of Battambang including at Kauk Khmum, 30 with from 20 to 50 hectares, 8 with from 50 to 100 hectares and 1 with 132 hectares (for this region alone, this makes 2,037 hectares or 23% of the land area).

Apart from a few noble families – 41 hectares at Anlong Romiet, 24 hectares at Phsar Dek in Ponhea Lu, and 52 hectares at Lovea in Prey Chhor,[16] as well as a few pagodas – landlords are either merchant-usurers or former officials. Commercial origins are particularly important in the establishment and development of big property. Outside the river-bank regions, where land is acquired by exploitation (tenancy, usury), the rice lands are farmed by landowners as concessionaires – there are 40 Khmer concessionaires with 630 hectares in the province of Svay Rieng and 22 with 2,488 hectares in Battambang.

There are also foreign landowners in Kampuchea.[17] Firstly, the rubber plantation companies. All the companies (La Compagnie du Cambodge, La Compagnie des Caoutchoucs du Mekong or Camekong, La Societe des Plantations Reunies de Memot or SPRM, La Societe de Caoutchoucs de Kompong Thom or SCKT, La Societe des Plantations de Kratie or SPK . . .) have 75,000 hectares of red-earth land, of which 48,898 hectares were planted in 1963-64, as against 2,686 hectares of State plantations and 6,900 hectares of Kampuchean family plantations.

As well as the planters, before 1953 the missions owned rather extensive lands at Rokar Koy and Chhlong, etc. and rice farming concessionaires mainly in Svay Rieng and Battambang Provinces. In the former, in particular at Svayteap, there are 101 foreign concessionaires and 13 in the latter, especially French (Societè Rizicole de Battambang). Certain concessions have already returned to the public domain and there now remain only about 6,000 hectares of land in the hands of foreign owners. It should be noted that since 1955, many concessions have been accorded to Kampuchean landowners. The 6,900 hectares of family plantations belong to a few owners who are either big merchants or high officials (civil or non-civil).

Middle Peasants, Poor Peasants and Agricultural Labourers

These three social classes of the Kampuchean peasantry represent the vast majority of the rural population of Kampuchea, 82.34%. If the agricultural labourers sell their labour power in order to subsist, the middle peasants and poor peasants are no less exploited by the merchants, the usurers, the landlords and rich peasants.

We can also give an approximation of the proportions for each of the three social classes, based on the information we have gathered from the preceding study. For example, as far as middle peasants are concerned, they form 90% of the group of landowners with between two and five hectares, that is 29.34%. The remaining 53% (of the total) are poor peasants and agricultural workers. According to the 1962 Census, 156,700 people, or 6.6% of the work force, are agricultural workers. In our opinion, to this figure must be added a percentage representing some of the poor peasants, that is some of the 'small landowners' who possess less than one hectare of land: at least one-third of this group (30.7%) are agricultural workers, because with an average of 20 ares per head, they cannot live without selling their labour power. Therefore, to the 6.6% must be added a percentage of around 10.23%, which gives a total of about 16.83%.

Therefore we can give the outline of the approximate distribution of rural Kampuchea into different social groups:

Landlords and rich peasants – 17.66%
Middle peasants – 29.34%
Poor peasants – 36.17%) 53%
Agricultural workers 16.83%)

Thus, more than half of the agricultural population of Kampuchea are in an economically weak position.

Looking at the recent findings of the census survey of tools and livestock owned by each household in each province (see Table 2.8), we can see that the above distribution is close to the truth. For, in all Kampuchea, households possess an average of one ox-cart 'unit' in only two provinces (Battambang and Kratie). These are generally only rich peasants or, in certain cases, a family of middle peasants with an ox-cart. The poor peasants, the agricultural workers and even a large section of the middle peasants could never obtain an ox-cart. Without even mentioning difficult natural conditions – one or two years of drought is enough for a serious enough crisis to break out – the present outdated agrarian social structure poses difficult problems: 16.83% of peasants possess nothing, while 36.70% possess a small plot of land and lack farm tools, and 29.34% possess a little land but still live in difficult circumstances. Nearly two-thirds of the arable land still remains uncultivated and all forms of exploitation still exist in the countryside.

This is the structure – serious climatic disadvantages, more or less arid land, irregular rainfall, floods or droughts, a heavily parcellized agrarian structure marked by a stronger and stronger trend towards concentration of

Table 2.8
Equipment and Livestock per Rice-growing Household, 1964

Province					*Equipment per household*							
	Tractor (total)	*Plough*	*Harrow*	*Roller*	*Winnower*	*Mortar*	*Noria*	*Cart*	*Loom*	*Hoe*	*Sickle*	*Other*
Battambang	375	1.375	1.283	–	.039	.491	1.015	1.046	.083	.848	8.940	.319
Kampot	15	918	895	–	.006	.842	–	.606	.085	.488	2.606	–
Kandal	4	.705	.693	.008	.021	.193	.105	.373	.012	.113	1;697	.252
Kompong Cham	111	1.009	.961	.002	.136	.672	.009	.886	.081	.412	1.581	.396
Kompong Chhnang	3	1.006	.936	–	.018	.253	.043	.888	.024	.296	2.666	.907
Kompong Speu	–	0.929	.811	–	.017	.166	–	.662	.082	.916	1.258	6.469
Kompong Thom	40	1.142	1.025	–	–	:271	–	.943	.017	–	.077	–
Kratie	10	1.083	.083	–	–	–	–	1.000	–	–	.000	–
Prey Veng	1	1.034	.985	.004	.004	.804	.157	.742	.002	–	.057	.081
Pursat	18	1.054	1.054	–	.054	.619	–	.782	–	1.054	1.576	5.173
Siemreap	30	1.087	.850	–	–	,637	–	.856	–	.937	1.256	2.912
Stung Treng	–	1.000	1.000	–	.375	1.000	–	.250	,250	1.500	4.500	–
Svay Rieng	–	1.225	1.245	.005	.051	1.257	.002	.637	.005	.362	.100	9.580
Takeo	11	.934	.710	–	.019	.122	.122	.453	.309	.947	1.921	4.361
Koh Kong	–	1.500	1.500	–	–	–	.125	.875	–	–	–	–
Average per province	619 (total)	1.067	.935	.001	.049	.488	.172	.733	.063	.524	1.900	2.030
General average per hectare	–	.302	.278	.000	.009	.162	.013	.212	.021	.149	.781	.620

. . . continued overleaf

Table 2.8 continued
Equipment and Livestock per Rice-growing Household, 1964

Province	*Livestock per Household*					
	Oxen	*Buffalo*	*Horses*	*Sheep*	*Pigs*	*Poultry*
Battambang	3.084	.493	.007	.100	.473	5.879
Kampot	2.393	.363	.003	–	.849	7.632
Kandal	2.008	.008	–	–	.352	1.546
Kompong Cham	1.227	1.110	.003	–	.737	4.964
Kompong Chhnang	3.125	.370	.012	–	.228	3.641
Kompong Speu	2.276	.302	.004	–	.692	3.109
Kompong Thom	2.349	.758	.004	–	.655	3.780
Kratie	.625	2.583	–	–	.166	10.916
Prey Veng	1.514	1.240	.008	.004	.871	5.524
Pursat	2.304	1.347	.021	–	.500	3.891
Siemreap	3.412	.700	.012	–	.912	7.156
Stung Treng	.250	3.500	–	–	.750	8.125
Svay Rieng	1.788	1.971	–	–	1.385	16.862
Takeo	2.148	.061	.006	–	.838	3.490
Koh Kong	2.000	3.750	–	–	.625	11.875
Average per province	2.033	1.237	.005	.007	.669	6.559
General average per hectare	.620	.203	.000	.006	.200	1.673

Source: Survey in 1963-4, *Bulletin de la Statistique et des Etudes Agricoles*, No. 4, 1964.

land, undeveloped productive forces as a result of exploitation – which stands in the way of the rapid development of agriculture.

References

1. *La Reforme Agraire en 1932 en Andalousie.*
2. *Production agricole* (1950), p.142.
3. Professor at the Faculte de Droit et des Sciences Economiques, Paris; *Economie Rurale*, p.144 ff. [Fromont was Hou Yuon's supervisor when he wrote his 1955 thesis, partly reproduced here in translation – Eds.]
4. Fromont, *op. cit.*, p.147.
5. [For further discussion of this table, see Hou Yuon's 1955 thesis, partly reproduced in translation above, at chapter 3. Eds.]
6. Jean Delvert. *Le Paysan Cambodgien* (Paris, 1960), p.495.
7. [Timothy Carney has correctly pointed out that this word should really be 'proportion'. However, this does not undermine Hu Nim's point about increasing concentration of land. The proportion of small landowners was decreasing. See Carney's valuable book *Communist Party Power in Kampuchea (Cambodia)*, Cornell University Southeast Asia Program Data Paper No. 106, January 1977, p.15 – Eds.]

8. [The information on agrarian structures is a summary of pp.493-4 of Jean Delvert, op. cit. – Eds.]
9. [This expression is similar to one used by Hou Yuon on p.192 of his 1955 thesis. The '1963 reforms' nationalized the import-export trade as well as banking and insurance – Eds.]
10. *Bulletin de la Statistique et des Etudes Agricoles,* Nos. 4, 5, 1964.
11. 'Rapport de la Direction de la Statistique et des Etudes Agricoles', published in the daily *La Depeche du Cambodge,* 19 February 1964.
12. [The State Import-Export Company – Eds.]
13. [Hu Nim's 1964 calculation is significantly lower than Hou Yuon's in 1955 (26%). Commercial pressure on the peasants may well have been increasing – Eds.]
14. [In fact, according to Hu Nim's summary of the findings of the 1962 Census, *all* of this 30.7%, who were 'small landowners', owned less than one hectare – Eds.]
15. [i.e. owners of more than 10 hectares of farmland – Eds.]
16. [Lovea formed part of Hu Nim's electoral district of Chrey Vien, which he was elected to represent in the National Assembly in 1962; again, in 1966, Nim received 52% of the vote, to his closest rival's 14%; in Lovea, he received 63% of the local vote – Eds.]
17. [Most of the landholding statistics here are taken from Ch. 16 of Delvert, op. cit. – Eds.]

PART II

3. Looking Back at Cambodia, 1942–76 by Michael Vickery

It rarely happens that a historian can look back over the recent past of any contemporary society with the feeling that a curtain has been rung down on the play and that what happened up to that time may be studied without regard to what is going on at present or what may happen in the future. Such is the way Cambodia appears. The appearance is misleading, of course, as the development of other revolutionary countries over the past 30 years clearly shows; but there is no doubt that the end of the 1970-75 War marked for Cambodia the end of an entire way of life – something which was dramatically confirmed by the unexpectedly rapid removal of Sihanouk from even a figurehead role. A black-out on information was imposed by the new government; what the refugees, the only first-hand source of news, say is contradictory; and contributions from other sources, principally the Cambodian community in Paris, alternate between the trivial and the absurd.[2]

Revolutions have occurred elsewhere, but seldom within such an absolute void of information, or in a manner so contrary to all predictions. For all wise old Indochina hands believed that after the War had been won by the revolutionary forces – and there was no doubt by 1972, at the latest, that they would win – it would be the Vietnamese who would engage in the most radical and brutal break with the past. In Cambodia it was expected that both sides, except for a few of the most notorious leaders, would be reconciled and some sort of mild, tolerant socialism instituted. Certainly most of the Phnom Penh elite expected this, even imagining that the new socialism would drift back into something resembling the old Sihanoukism, which is why so many of them stayed on until the end. Among the Indochina countries only Laos has come out of the War true to form, while Vietnam and Cambodia have behaved in ways nearly the opposite of what had been expected.

What this means first of all, of course, is that the Vietnamese and Cambodians were misunderstood and that the facets of their culture and history, which might have revealed an unexpected capacity for tolerance in the one and vindictiveness in the other, were missed. In the case of Cambodia much more was missed – that the position of the royalty, headed by Sihanouk was not after all so solidly rooted; that, in spite of its heady atmosphere as the last exotic Asian paradise, Cambodia was rent by political, economic and class conflicts; that the War did not begin suddenly in 1970; and that the conflict which seemed to explode at that time proceeded naturally from trends in the country's political history over the preceding 25 years, a period characterized by intense efforts of the traditional elite to frustrate any moves towards political, economic or social modernization which would threaten its position.

The Struggle for Independence and the Democratic Party

The raising of the curtain on the scene which ended in 1975 began, I would say, on 9 March 1945, when, after over three years of co-operation, the Japanese suddenly interned the French colonial forces and soon after encouraged the Indochina countries to declare independence. The Cambodian Government, under Sihanouk, duly followed this suggestion, and existing treaties with the French were abrogated.

On the whole, up to that time, the Second World War had not been a very traumatic experience for Cambodia. The Japanese occupation was cushioned by the French administration which remained in place, there was no leftist or anti-fascist resistance to stir up trouble, and the only nationalist movement of any importance, although anti-French, had co-existed comfortably with the Japanese.

The last was a group of fairly prosperous urban Khmer, with French education and a commercial orientation, organized around Son Ngoc Thanh, a Cambodian from Southern Vietnam. In 1936 they had founded the first Khmer-language newspaper and through it advocated very moderate reforms – more Cambodian participation in commerce, greater educational opportunities, equal treatment for Cambodians and French – developments which probably worried the traditional Cambodian elite more than the French, since their realization would have meant bringing more new men into positions of wealth and power and thereby undermining the old oligarchy.

During the first years of the War, under the tolerant eye of the Japanese, they organized propaganda activities to undermine support for the French among Cambodian soldiers and monks. The French broke this up in 1942; most of the leaders were arrested and the newspaper was closed down, but

Son Ngoc Thanh himself escaped to Japan. Although little-known outside the country, these men were considered thereafter as heroes of the first Cambodian independence movement, and Sihanouk seriously misjudged the mood of his people when he attacked them in later years as traitors for attempting to subvert their, and his, colonial masters.

When the Japanese took over all authority from the French in March 1945, Son Ngoc Thanh was brought back and imposed on the government as Foreign Minister, and in August, after a palace coup by his followers, was made Prime Minister. Thus the first independence may have been, for the traditional elite, the most traumatic moment of the whole War period, since it meant the emergence into leadership of their most dangerous local opponent; and the return of the French was probably welcomed. Indeed, oral tradition of the time, which cannot be proved wrong by any published records, affirms that Son Ngoc Thanh was betrayed to the French by Sihanouk and the ministers loyal to him.

This occurred in October 1945, less than a year after Cambodia's first independence had been proclaimed. Thanh was carried off to exile in France, becoming the first martyr for what, at the time, was termed the Cambodian 'Left', and for the next 25 years he remained, for much of the educated youth, a hero, a man under whom things might have been different. Such confidence was probably misplaced. Thanh's own principles appear never to have developed beyond his position of the 1930s, and his ultimate espousal of the American cause may have kept a lot of his followers in Phnom Penh after 1970, at a time when they might otherwise have moved elsewhere. But any study of Cambodian politics in the 1940s and 1950s must keep in mind that he was a hero for an important section of the progressive forces who had been betrayed by Sihanouk and the conservative elite.

Although the French returned easily in 1945, this did not mean a simple restoration of the pre-war situation. Due to decisions taken by the Free French during the War, Cambodia became an autonomous state within the French union and acquired some of the trappings of independence. Among these was a Constitution to be 'granted' by the King, and a National Assembly. The first election was held on 1 September 1946 for the purpose of choosing a Constituent Assembly to discuss and vote on the Draft Constitution which had been drawn up by a joint Franco-Khmer committee.

Three parties plus a number of independent candidates contested this election. The Democratic Party, headed by Prince Sisowath Youtevong and other young men who had recently returned from university studies in France, took 50 of the 67 seats in the Assembly. Their goal was the achievement of a European-type parliamentary system with a maximum of democratic rights. It was well known that they intended to work for full independence, and they made little secret of their admiration for Son Ngoc Thanh. Many people also thought, perhaps correctly, that the Democrats were secret, anti-monarchists who dreamed of establishing a republic. In the election results, they were followed by the Liberal Party whose candidates won 14 seats. Strongly pro-royalist, and led by another prince, it was favoured by many of the Phnom Penh bourgeoisie and considered by its opponents to be pro-French. The third organized party, was a small, conservative group of old-fashioned bureaucrats, the personal friends and clientele of its leader, also a prince. Its programme was very vague and urged moderation on all questions. It won no seats, and the remaining three were taken by independent candidates.

After lengthy, often stormy, discussion of the Draft Constitution, which the Democrats considered insufficiently democratic, the Assembly produced a revised text which was accepted by the King in July 1947 and, with a few minor changes, became the country's first basic law. Although stating that 'all power emanates from the King' and that the Constitution had been 'granted' by him, it nevertheless contained the proviso that the King 'must use his power in conformity to the Constitution', and in fact set up a system of government in which the National Assembly was dominant.

Since the work of the Constituent Assembly had been limited to drawing up a Constitution, it was dissolved and elections were held in December 1947 for the first National Assembly. The same three parties were still contestants, but by this time ideological and interest lines had been more sharply drawn and two new parties appeared on the scene, one of them being Lon Nol's 'Khmer Renovation'. Drawing members both from among the independents and from the older parties, these two new groups were strongly pro-monarchist, traditionalist and authoritarian, although, in contrast to the Liberals, probably as strong on independence as the Democrats. Their leaders were men of the traditional elite who had already achieved positions of authority before the War and within the colonial system and who were probably unhappy with the rapid rise of the relative newcomers among the Democrats.

The election results were much as before, Democrats 54, Liberals 21, with the new parties completely out in the cold, and the new National Assembly was convoked in January 1948. The parliamentary game, however, proved hard to play. The Democrats' leader, Prince Youtevong, had died in July 1947, and the party in any case contained too many disparate elements. Ever since the appearance of their first newspaper in the late 1930s, the ideology of Cambodian nationalists had never gone much beyond the advocacy of Cambodians going into business in order to take control of the country's economic life from the French, Chinese and Vietnamese, and for a number of prominent Democrats parliamentary and eventual independent government were simply extended means to this end. Some of these people considered ministerial power to be a green light for self-enrichment; a number of scandals came to light. The Democrats also continued to make a hero of Son Ngoc Thanh, and hardly concealed their sympathy for the Issaraks, anti-French *maquis* cum bandits who controlled much of the countryside and in some cases probably had contact with the Viet Minh. This naturally displeased the French, who still had ultimate power in Cambodia and were trying to put all rebels into the Communist basket; and it angered the King and local conservatives who preferred to put law and order before either parliamentary government or independence.

The inevitable conflicts resulted in the dissolution of the Assembly in September 1949, occasioned by the Democratic Party's attitude towards the Issaraks. A new government, responsible only to the King, was formed around a group of conservative Democrats who split off to form their own party under Yem Sambaur (who was to become prominent again in 1970 as a non Nol supporter). Even with the Assembly out of the way, ministerial stability proved as elusive as before, and six Cabinets followed one another until the date of the next elections in September 1951.

In the interim, the country's political life had been embittered by the assassination of the Democrats' new leader in January 1950, an attempt on the life of another, and an effort by the King to push a revision of the Constitution through the Council of the Kingdom, the parliamentary upper house which had continued to remain in session.

As time for the elections approached there was a good deal of manoeuvring, in which the King came out clearly in favour of the conservatives, to prevent the Democrats from repeating their earlier victories. Insecurity due to rebel activity was a major problem throughout the country. At a meeting of the King and leaders of the by now seven political parties in October 1950, four of the parties, including the Democrats, declared that elections could not be held because of the lack of security. About a month later, when party leaders met again to discuss proposals submitted to them by the King as alternatives for the country's political life in the immediate future, two of the parties, including Lon Nol's Renovation, reversed their policy and voted to have elections. The Democratic Party newspaper of the time suggested that their strategy was based on the belief that the Democrats would not take part in the elections and the field would be clear for the other groups.

As alternatives to holding elections the King had also proposed: 1) temporary suspension of the Constitution, which would have meant the end of party activity and government by Cabinets responsible only to the King, and 2) re-establishment of the old National Assembly.

For obvious reasons the Democrats supported the latter, and the Government, led by the King's uncle and dominated by non-Democrats, favoured the former. Interestingly, the only party which found the first proposal acceptable was the Khmer Renovation, since its leaders obviously knew they would be the beneficiaries of dictatorial government.

Since the holding of elections on time was the only proposal to receive the support of a majority of the parties, it was adopted and an 'election government' was formed under the leader of one of the conservative parties. The task of this government was primarily to prepare for the elections and, to ensure that the preparations were fair, it was supposed to include ministers from all political parties. However, the Democrats, because of their conviction that security was too threatened, refused to take a seat in the Cabinet and announced that they would take no responsibility for incidents which might occur during the campaign. They nevertheless participated in the elections and won handily against the seven other parties which were now on the scene, even though voter turn-out was very low and they received less than half the total vote. The composition of the Assembly showed little change from 1947, with 55 Democrats and 17 Liberals. In addition, four seats went to the party of Dap Chhuon, a former Issarak who had rallied to the Government at the end of 1949, and Lon Nol's Renovation finally got into the Assembly with two seats.

The election results did not give a true picture of the balance of forces, however. In the voting itself the six parties of the far Right polled a total of 100,477 to the Democrats' 144, 728, with the Liberals getting over 72,000 and independent candidates, mostly conservatives, over 8,000. It was already clear that any movement which could unify the Right could immediately cut the ground from under the Democrats.

The Democrats had also gradually been losing ground in other ways. At the end of 1949, after the Democratic National Assembly had been dissolved, Dap Chhuon, the most powerful of the Issarak leaders, rallied to the King and was left in control of his territory, which included Siemreap and parts of Battambang and Kompong Thom – in all a large portion of northern Cambodia. Soon afterward one of his men formed the 'Victorious Northeast' political party, which found its place as one of the group of small parties opposing the Democrats. This coup alone assured that a large piece of territory would not again be under the effective control of a Democrat government and gave the Right the support of an experienced military force with a proven leader.

Thus the Democrats, in spite of controlling the Cabinet, were really on the defensive. They were trying to negotiate with the French for independence, but the latter accused them of aiding the Issaraks and thereby the Viet Minh. In effect, the Democrats refused to take strong action against the Cambodian Issaraks, considering them to be genuine, if somewhat misguided patriots, but also drew a distinction, which their opponents refused to accept, between the Issaraks and the Viet Minh. The internal opposition took up the accusation, and added to it the charge that the Democrats were striving for absolute power in the manner of Mussolini and Hitler. Lon Nol's newspaper was particularly voluble on the latter subject, but there seem to have been no real grounds for the charges, for the Democrats tolerated strong criticism from their opponents and never harassed opposition newspapers in the manner of the Cambodian Right after it won power.

The return of Son Ngoc Thanh in the Autumn of 1951 did nothing to calm the situation. He began publishing a newspaper, *Khmer Awake,* which pushed strongly for independence, and in the spring of 1952 suddenly left Phnom Penh to form a new Issarak group on the Northern Khmer-Thai border. The Democrats were accused of aiding him – a charge which they did not take great pains to deny.

In June 1952 the trouble came to a head. An army jeep drove around Phnom Penh scattering leaflets signed by Dap Chhuon and calling for the King and the people to take action against the Government. The latter, evidently assuming that the other right-wing parties were also involved, sent police to search the houses of their leaders, including Lon Nol and Yem Sambaur, and some of them were taken to Police Headquarters for questioning. The searches, in fact, turned up nothing incriminating. Lon Nol had permits for the three machine-guns and three cases of hand-grenades found at his house, which says something about the supposedly totalitarian regime imposed by the Democrats on other parties. The arrested men were released after questioning and the whole procedure, as the Democrats emphasized, and as their opponents could never deny, was carried out with scrupulous legality.

Nevertheless, the incident provided the opposition with a chance to pillory the Democrats for their allegedly dictatorial methods and to charge them with attempting to destroy all other political parties. Again it should be emphasized that the opposition newspapers were not harassed and their charges were answered in the Democrats' own party organ.

King Sihanouk then entered the fray with a message true to the type of logic he was to use against political opponents in the future. He charged that the Democrats had refused to work against criminals (read Issaraks), alleging constitutional guarantees against search without warrant and indiscriminate arrest, but now it was clear that the Democrats only observed these rights for their own people. Since it was clear, according to Sihanouk, that the Democrats intended to use power indiscriminately against present and future opponents, contrary to the Constitution which 'I gave to the people', he asked the Government to resign. In this speech Sihanouk placed himself squarely on the side of the right-wing parties and let the Democrats know that those parties' leaders were not to be treated as run-of-the-mill citizens.

Sihanouk himself headed the new Government and asked the Assembly to grant him full powers to rule personally for three years, within which time he promised to achieve full independence. The Assembly refused on constitutional grounds, which refusal the King apparently accepted for the time being, and the body continued to meet. The Democratic Party, however, suspended political activity and closed down its newspaper at the end of July 1952.

Another crisis came in January 1953 when the King asked the Assembly for a special law declaring the nation in danger, and when this was refused by the Assembly, both it and the Council of the Kingdom were dissolved. Then the King proclaimed the special law and he and his right-wing supporters finally ruled alone with such powers as indiscriminate right of arrest, the right to forbid publications and meetings and the right to censor mail. Many Democratic Party members and members of the Assembly were arrested because, according to Lon Nol's newspaper, 'there was clear proof that they were following the orders of Son Ngoc Thanh and Ea Sichau who are certainly communist and who are allied with the Viet Minh'. This line was repeated in February by Sihanouk in an interview with foreign journalists. He also added that there was 'documentary proof' that Son Ngoc Thanh and Ea Sichau were working with Ho Chi Mnih and Mao Tse-Tung.[3]

Their highhanded methods in internal politics notwithstanding, Sihanouk and his supporters made good their boasts about independence. Obviously the French preferred to grant it to the Cambodian Right, and by the autumn of 1953 the major attributes of independence had been transferred.

It was also in this period that Lon Nol established himself solidly as a power figure. In 1952 the important rice-growing region of north-western Cambodia, Battambang Province, was reorganized as the 'Battambang Autonomous Region', French military forces withdrew from there, and military responsibility was transferred to the Cambodian army. Lon Nol switched from civil service to the military and assumed command of the region with the rank of colonel. After this he was never to be far from the top of the military establishment. During the next two years this area was the scene of operations by the Government forces against Issaraks and Viet Minh, characterized by gratuitous brutality. A participant told me how they would move into villages, kill the men and women who had not already fled and then engage in individual tests of strength which consisted of grasping infants by the legs and pulling them apart. These events had probably not been forgotten by those of that area who survived to become the Khmer Rouge troops occupying Battambang in 1975 and whose reported actions have stirred up so much comment abroad (see *Time Magazine*, 26 April 1976).

The 1955 Election

With independence achieved and the Democratic Party apparently destroyed, power seemed to be securely in the hands of the King and his supporters. But the Geneva Conference of 1954 added a new dimension to the Cambodian political scene. At the Conference Cambodia had guaranteed that general elections would be held in 1955 and that all political groups, including the former pro-Viet Minh *maquis*, would be allowed to participate. Moreover, the International Control Commission was to be present to supervise the fairness of the electoral process.

In the meantime, a new generation of university graduates began to return from France and enter the political scene with an entirely different outlook from the founders of the Democratic Party. Whereas the latter had specialized in politically neutral subjects (Youtevong was a mathematician, another had a degree in literature) and had been in France during the last pre-war years and the Vichy period, the new group was made up of lawyers and political economists and had seen Paris student life during the radical ferment of the early post-war days.

Several of them soon achieved prominence by getting themselves elected to the Executive Committee of the Democratic Party, which in the post-Geneva political freedom was able to resume activity. The new Secretary-General of the Party was Norodom Phurissara (who joined FUNK in 1972 and emerged after the 1970-75 War as Minister of Justice), and among his colleagues was Thiounn Mum, who also opted for the anti-Lon Nol forces from 1970. In reaction to this new leadership some of the older Democrats resigned, and one, Sim Var, denounced the new group as Communist.

Another group to take advantage of the 1954-55 situation was the Khmers, who had fought along with the Viet Minh against the French right up to the end of the War. They formed a party, the Pracheachon, 'citizens', and began publishing a newspaper. A third group which benefited from Geneva were the members of the non-Viet Minh *maquis*, Son Ngoc Thanh's followers, who also came out of the woods. Some of them formed a political party, the Khmer Independence Party, whose very name was a challenge to Sihanouk, and published a series of newspapers which, like those of the Democrats and Pracheachon, were generally critical of the Government.

The other political parties on the scene after Geneva were the old Liberal Party and the small right-wing groups which had been present for previous elections. It appeared that a revived Democratic Party would repeat its previous victories, especially with electoral freedom guaranteed by Geneva and the International Control Commission.

The Right was determined not to let this happen. In October, four of the small parties, including the important groups of Lon Nol, Yem Sambaur, and Dap Chhuon, formed an alliance and published a newspaper which announced that they were rightist, monarchist, traditionalist and in principal opposed to party politics. In February 1955, this alliance broke up and most of its members joined another political formation which appeared in the same month and was to have a much longer life. This was the Sangkum Reastr Niyum, or Popular Socialist Community, as it was usually translated. Its supreme counsellor was Sihanouk and among its prominent members were leaders of the old right-wing parties. Within the first few months of 1955 all of these groups, except Yem Sambaur's, dissolved in favour of the Sangkum. As Hou Yuon, one of the important FUNK leaders between 1970 and 1975, wrote in his doctoral thesis in 1955, 'the Popular Socialist Community of ex-king Norodom Sihanouk and . . . the Liberal party of Prince Norindeth' are 'the political representatives' of the large landowners, who made up less than 10% of the population but whose influence was very great.[4]

The unification of the Right was nearly complete and from the beginning the Sangkum made its conservative ideology clear. In the first issues of its newspaper, which began publication in June, it set forth an authoritarian philosophy according to which natural leaders should rule and those less fortunate should not envy them. The natural leaders were the rich and powerful who enjoyed such a situation in the present because of virtuous conduct in previous lives (a common belief in South East Asian Buddhism). The poor and unfortunate should accept their lot and try for an improved situation in the next life through virtuous conduct in the present. The Sangkum was also strongly anti-Communist, desired close relations with the United States and American military aid, and felt that Cambodia should not really be bound by the Geneva Accords because she had achieved independence before the

Conference.

The Sangkum's main opposition, the radicalized Democrats, the Pracheachon and the Thanhists, held closely related positions on major issues. They emphasized the importance of the Geneva Conference in securing Cambodia's independence, the undesirability of American military aid (an agreement was signed on 16 May 1955), the dangerous situation in Vietnam and imperialist, i.e. American, responsibility for it (in the light of the 1970s their analyses seem extremely prescient), and the necessity for free elections as guaranteed by Geneva and according to the Constitution of 1947.

Once the Democratic Party had reorganized, it asked for a Cabinet post, since the Cabinet was an 'election government', supposed to contain representatives of each party in order to assure the fairness of the election. This was refused because of the suspicion of Communism cast on them by Sim Var, a former Democrat who had become prominent in the Sangkum. Naturally, this attitude also meant that there was no chance of a Cabinet post for anyone from the Pracheachon.

Thus, as the 1955 elections approached, all Government power was concentrated in the hands of the pro-Sangkum Right, formed of parties which had never been able to achieve any success in the generally free elections held previously.

The election had at first been set for April, but at that date it was almost certain that the Democrats would win. Then delegations from the provinces began turning up at the palace with petitions asking for an end to elections and parliamentary rule and for Sihanouk to rule the country personally. Sihanouk claimed that these petitions represented the will of the people exasperated by the abuses of party government. Of course, with the International Control Commission present, outright abolition of parties and Parliament was impossible, but Sihanouk tried to get around this obstacle with a constitutional reform which would have taken power from the National Assembly and, under the guise of returning it to the people, given it to the Right. The reform would also have prevented the ex-*maquisards* from participating in the election. The ICC disapproved and the subject was dropped. The election was then postponed until September, which was still within the limits set at Geneva and gave the Right more time to prepare.

From then on the 'local news' columns of the anti-Sangkum newspapers were filled with accounts of campaign irregularities. The Sangkum had the administration in its hands and was making full use of it. Villagers were threatened with punishment, including death, if they did not vote for the Sangkum. People were coerced into taking out Sangkum membership cards, and then told that if they voted for any other party they would face punishment. Another technique was to force villagers to take an oath to supernatural powers that they would vote for the Sangkum, after which they would not dare to do otherwise.

Are these accounts all true, or simply dishonest left-wing election propaganda? The answer is based on indirect evidence. The left-wing papers were constantly harassed throughout the summer of 1955. One Thanhist paper was suspended in February. In May another, representing a group which had just come from the Thanh *maquis,* was closed. Still another paper in the same camp opened on 7 June and was shut down after its second issue on 10 June. Its energetic editor immediately started another paper on 17 June, but it only lasted for a few issues. The Pracheachon paper published its first number on 1 April and was suspended after number 19 on 10 June. Its place was taken by a successor on 24 June and it lasted for 39 issues, until 25 October, and thus covered the election. It devoted a good deal of space to the incarceration of three editors whose papers had been closed down.[5] When they were finally brought to trial they were sentenced, on 6 August, to three months each for 1)claiming that independence had been obtained at Geneva through the efforts of the whole population; 2) *lese-majeste;* and 3) false statements about United States military aid. Thus the reports of election irregularities did not figure in the charges and it may be inferred that the Government did not consider it expedient to make an issue of them. Moreover, the Democratic Party paper, which was somewhat more moderate on the above subjects, was able to survive the election campaign, although it too chronicled the election abuses. Harassment of candidates was also common. Three Pracheachon candidates spent most of the campaign period in jail, as did two Democrats, and others were arrested for brief periods or brutalized.

The results of this election are well known. The Sangkum took all the seats with the Democrats coming in a very poor second. The Pracheachon did surprisingly well with five of their candidates getting over 25% of the vote in their districts, including one who had spent the entire campaign period in prison. The I.C.C. certified the election as 'correct', which only shows how little such inspection may mean.

The Sangkum victory was the victory of the traditionalist Cambodian Right, chiefly the Renovation group. Lon Nol entered the Government as Minister of National Defence, and from then on, except for brief periods, retained control of the military establishment in one post or another.

The Sangkum System

After this election the Sangkum never again had any real challengers. The Democratic Party dissolved itself in 1957 after its leaders had been called to the palace for a friendly conference with Sihanouk and then were beaten up on departure by Lon Nol's soldiers. They later asked for admission to the Sangkum, as did anyone whose future lay in public life or administrative work. The elections of 1958 and 1962 were rubber-stamp affairs with candidates hand-picked by Sihanouk. Only the Pracheachon feebly contested the 1958 elections, and before the 1962 contest its leaders were arrested on charges which may or may not have been true. The timing is suspect, and it looks as though even this negligible opposition was more than Sihanouk could tolerate. His true feelings about electoral opposition bubbled up in the heat of a speech in 1965 in which he berated his adversaries of 1955 for unfair tactics – using the question of American military aid and SEATO to discredit the Sangkum – and, because of this, '16% of the voters, normally attached to me, voted against the Sangkum'.[6]

Power throughout these years remained solidly in the hands of the old Right, although a number of young intellectuals were allowed into the National Assembly in 1958 and 1962. This has given rise to the illusion among Sihanouk apologists that 'the politicians of the extreme right were progressively confined to strictly honorific posts', where they waited in 'hibernation' for their hour, the coup of 1970, to come.[7] Nothing could be further from the truth. Throughout the 15 years from 1955 to 1970 the same old names recur constantly in the key government posts: Lon Nol, Nhiek Tioulong, Penn Nouth, Kou Roun, Huot Sambath, Sirik Matak, Tep Phan, Son Sann, to name only a few of the more prominent. As for the new intellectuals, Sihanouk clearly wished to make use of their abilities if they were willing to offer him absolute loyalty. He recognized that they were of much greater value than the conservative rank and file which had cluttered the Assembly after 1955. Co-operation between them and the old guard proved impossible though and, when the chips were down, Sihanouk always opted for the latter; members of the new intellectual elite were never allowed to hold one job long enough to work effectively or develop power positions.

Thus, for example, Hou Yuon was in the Ministry of Commerce and Industry from April to July 1958, in the Budget Office from July 1958 to February 1959, in the Planning Ministry from February to June 1959, then in the Ministry of Public Health from June 1959 to April 1960. He was again in Finance from August to October 1962, and in Planning from October 1962 to February 1963, at which time unexpected events made possible a nearly permanent and complete exclusion of 'leftists' from the Government.

Chau Seng, whom many foreign observers in the 1960s considered the *eminence rouge* behind Sihanouk, is a special case, which perhaps proves the rule. He was on the Left, although distrusted by those who eventually went into the *maquis*, but was able to ingratiate himself with Sihanouk in a way the others either would not or could not do, and remained prominent in the Government throughout the 1960s.

Another case which shows where the road to power really lay is that of Mau Say. Of the same generation and academic attainment as Hou Yuon or Khieu Samphan, he threw in his lot from the very beginning with the extreme Right, and held important posts, mainly connected with financial affairs, in numerous Sangkum cabinets up to 1967, at which time his involvement in financial scandals forced his resignation. Sihanouk then rewarded his loyal servant with appointment to the *Haut Conseil du Trone,* one of the kingdom's highest honorific positions.

In contrast, but to prove the same point that Sihanouk's Sangkum favoured the worst elements of traditional Cambodian society – there is the case of Douc Rasy, one of the same generation of French-educated intellectuals, born into an elite family and trained as a lawyer. Choosing his position on what could be called in the Cambodian context the 'progressive right', he favoured the development of a capitalist economic system and Western-style parliamentary democracy, but insisted on the necessity for honesty in public life and strict adherance to legality in the exercise of power. This would not do in Sangkum Cambodia, and Douc Rasy, although probably never in physical danger, due to his personal situation, was the object of nearly as much Sihanoukian invective as Hou Yuon.

Once the Sangkum had given the Right a vehicle with which to rule absolutely and with Sihanouk as permanent Chief of State after 1960, constitutional reform was no longer a major issue, and in its essential provisions, such as assembly government with regular elections, the Constitution of 1947 remained in effect.

The style and ideology of internal politics remained the same throughout the Sangkum years, although it was never again expressed so frankly as in the early numbers of the Sangkum newspaper. Power was to remain in the hands of the traditional elite with new blood accepted into the system as long as they did not attempt to introduce any significant changes. The interest groups which had organized earlier as political parties became cliques within the Sangkum, and meaningful political activity lay in inciting Sihanouk against one's enemies. Thus, proposals for policy were not discussed so much in terms of specific goals related to Cambodia's gover-
that their rivals were hatching treasonable plots.

The rewards in this type of political life were what they had always been in traditional Cambodia – personal wealth and power for those who found favour with the sovereign. Before the French Protectorate, officials were rewarded, not with regular salaries, but with a cut of the fees or taxes they collected for the crown. The provinces into which the country was divided were distributed in *apanage* to certain members of the royal family, each of whom headed a chain of officials extending down from the palace to the district level. Although this system formally ended over 70 years ago, the mentality which went with it persisted, and all state employment, which was the only employment with prestige value, was ranked on a scale of desirability according to the possibility it provided for private profit, now termed graft. The Cambodians even found that socialism could be integrated into this system. The value of the term in modern international relations had soon been apparent and the official translation of the party name Sangkum Reastr Niyum was Popular Socialist Community. Of course, it was not to be Marxist socialism, but rather a 'Royal Buddhist socialism' – without class conflict, which was declared non-existent in Cambodia – and dependent on the 'ancient' Cambodian practice of the sovereign always providing for the welfare of its people. Since the sovereign, by definition, always did provide, any kind of criticism was seen as subversive and anti-monarchist.

The State industries and nationalized enterprises became in effect *apanages* for Sihanouk's mandarins, who grew wealthy while the accounts were in the red. Periodic scandals served to spread the wealth around, placing some individuals in temporary eclipse, while others took their turn at the trough. Never was any high official forced to repay or attempt to repay what he had taken from the State till.

Within such a context 'progressive' or 'radical' meant not only the Left as it is usually understood, but any position seeking to rationalize and depersonalize the economic and administrative systems. This explains why the group around Douc Rasy, whom I have termed progressive rightists, came in for almost as much criticism as the Marxists, and why Sihanouk in his more excited moments accused the Thanhists of working both for the CIA and the Viet Cong.

Sceptics might ask why did the system not break down, since those in power were continually taking wealth out of the public purse without doing anything in return? In fact, it did break down, and that is why Cambodia passed through a war and revolution. Breakdowns occurred even in pre-modern times, although a good deal of wealth was redistributed then through conspicuous consumption within the economy and by the support of the large clientele which every wealthy and powerful figure collected. In those days a breakdown resulted in a palace coup or replacement of the royal family by a new dynasty.

As a mid-20th century operation, such a system is much more fragile, and, without special props, unlikely to last more than a few years. The conspicuous consumption indulged in by the elite is no longer chiefly within the economy, but involves expensive foreign products, frequent trips abroad, and hard currency bank accounts; and the large clientele which in former times resulted in the redistribution of much wealth is no longer necessary. Besides what is spent abroad, perhaps even more serious for a country like Cambodia is the way in which the consumption patterns of the richest foreign societies become norms to which everyone aspires. The elite insist on living like their counterparts in Paris or New York, stores are filled with consumer goods which are of doubtful value anywhere and sheer waste in a country with a level of income such as Cambodia's; everyone tries by hook or by crook to obtain the status symbols he feels are his due and which, on the whole, the country cannot afford.

Certain special features of the Cambodian situation, which represented non-material returns to the general welfare, prevented the breakdown from coming even earlier. First, there was the character of Sihanouk himself. For most of the Cambodian peasantry a monarch was essential to the well-being of the country and even for the maintenance of Buddhism. Any king properly enthroned and who maintained the traditional rituals would serve the purpose (indeed a major error in 1970 may have been the failure of Lon Nol to immediately proclaim another king), but Sihanouk went beyond this and attempted to become a popular sovereign, for in spite of his 1955 abdication, for the people, he was still a king. With frequent trips to the countryside and entertaining speeches in popular idiom he largely succeeded and, as a result, the mass of the population, who feared and detested the administration, felt that if only they could get to Sihanouk he would solve their problems.

Another return from the system was a few years of complete peace and internal security, something which the country had not known within living memory. Throughout the 19th Century Cambodia had been plagued by warfare, and the colonial period had seen whole regions ridden by endemic large-scale banditry, that is, outlaw bands who would raid, rob and burn entire villages with impunity. In the years following the Second World War, these bands turned themselves into 'Issaraks', and fought for independence against the French and the last of this activity wasn't ended until 1958-59. By 1960, when I first arrived, one could travel anywhere without danger from outlaws or hindrance from the authorities, and the Sangkum Government, in the eyes of the people, received credit for this.

Even the wasteful expenditures of the elite had certain psychic returns peculiar to Cambodian beliefs and attitudes. Since a feature of Buddhist belief is that one's situation in future existences is conditioned by behaviour in the past and present, wealth and power are the results of virtuous conduct in previous lives, and even their misuse in the present need not be too severely criticized, for punishment will be sure to follow later. Moreover, the opulent living of a Phnom Penh functionary served as an example of what the poor peasant might hope to attain in the future if he was virtuous in the present.

These beliefs matched, or perhaps conditioned, the general Cambodian attitude towards what modernization really meant. For all but a tiny minority who had truly absorbed European intellectual values, modernization meant the type of growth exemplified by Bangkok and Saigon – lots of chrome and concrete, streets clogged by cars, a plethora of luxurious bars and everyone dressed in Western clothes. Countless times I heard Cambodians comment favourably on the progress of Bangkok 'because it has so many bars and hotels', and one of the main objections to Sihanouk's 1963 rupture with the United States was that he was depriving Phnom Penh of 'development' equivalent to Saigon. At least Cambodian concern with external show resulted in Phnom Penh becoming one of the most attractive, and certainly the neatest, of Asian cities, and although the money spent on it was irrelevant to economic development, most Cambodians observed it with pride and gave the credit to Sihanouk and his Sangkum.

However, without props, the Sangkum could not have survived as long as it did, and the props were in the form of foreign aid. American military aid began in the early 1940s and was then distributed through the French. After Independence, in 1955, a Khmer-American military aid agreement was signed and made the U.S. the chief supplier of the Cambodian army. This agreement was bitterly opposed at the time by the Sangkum's opponents, the Democratic Party, the former Son Ngoc Thanh *maquis* and the Communists. At the time Sihanouk and the Sangkum sought U.S. support and had to defend themselves at home against charges of selling out to the imperialists.

Very intelligently Sihanouk set out to improve Cambodia's image and normal diplomatic relations were established with the socialist countries, including China, between 1956 and 1958. Diplomatic relations were accompanied by aid – China, for example, building factories and the Soviet Union a hospital. Neutrality was to be Cambodia's foreign policy and Sihanoukian rhetoric, for foreign consumption, at least, was full of 'socialism'. All of this was very disturbing to U.S. officials, still in the grip of Dullesian hysteria and hopeful of drawing Cambodia into SEATO. American embassy personnel in Phnom Penh spoke darkly of the red prince and his Communistic policies, although it should not have been so difficult to distinguish rhetoric from substance. Within the country anti-Communism was still the rule. In his speeches to the populace Sihanouk made it abundantly clear that Russia and China were good friends, but their economic systems were not for Cambodia. He emphasized the point that Communists were against religion, something sure to carry weight with his listeners.

The whole point of the manoeuvre was to obtain the maximum possible aid from competing foreign countries without allowing Cambodian society to be influenced either by modernizing capitalists or revolutionary socialists, both of whom were equally subversive to the Cambodian system. Thus the U.S. was to be frightened just enough by talk of socialism to keep the aid coming, while the socialist countries were to be convinced that their aid might bring Cambodia closer to them. The aid itself was the cushion which permitted the Cambodian elite to extract more from the country than they redistributed and to avoid any of the basic reforms which must be undertaken by a developing country relying mainly on its own resources.

Strains on the system began with the recrudescence of the Vietnam War in 1958-59. There was pressure from South Vietnam and the U.S. for Cambodian support, which even the Cambodian right-wing wished to refuse, for in spite of their anti-Communist stance they had no sympathy for Diem or any of his successors, who were feared for their territorial demands on Cambodia and detested for their alleged oppression of the Cambodian minority in South Vietnam. Ultimately, Saigon and the U.S. accused Cambodia of providing refuge for Communist troops, and frequent raids across the Cambodian border caused many casualties.

At the same time, the Cambodian Left urged support for the N.L.F. and closer ties with the socialist world, and accused Sihanouk and his clique of secretly selling out to the U.S. Sihanouk's policy, from 1958 to 1962, of using talented intellectuals in the Government gave some of them, for example, Hou Yuon and Khieu Samphan, prestigious platforms for promoting their ideas, and the general diplomatic rapprochement with the socialist countries often made it appear that they were only following Sangkum policy. The Right, of course, reacted vigorously, probably assuming that with foreign policy oriented towards the socialist camp, there would be no objection from that side to suppression of the domestic Left. The Pracheachon leadership (Non Suon and 12 others) was arrested just before the 1962 elections, and, in the beginning of 1963, as a result of student demonstration in Siemreap which was allowed to grow into a mini-rebellion, for which they were blamed, the left-wing ministers were forced to resign. Thus, after early 1963, with the exception of Chau Seng, important left-wing participation in Sangkum ministries came to an end. These events also convinced some of the Left that gradualist efforts within the system would not succeed, for in the early summer of 1963 Ieng Sary, Saloth Sar (Pol Pot) and Son Sen disappeared from their jobs and, as we now know, fled into the *maquis.*

With respect to Vietnam, the basic policy of the Sangkum leadership was to calculate the likely outcome of the war, and by 1963 they had apparently become convinced that the U.S. would give up and the N.L.F. would win. A propaganda campaign against the U.S. and its aid missions was begun, which sometimes looked like an effort at blackmail to get even more aid, but with less control by the donor over its ultimate disposition. If it was blackmail it failed, and at the end of 1963 American aid in all forms was rejected.

This break cannot be put down to left-wing agitation, as many Americans seemed to think. The grass-roots leftist leaders of the Pracheachon had been jailed or driven underground in 1962, the intellectual elite were cut out of all power in early 1963 and during the entire period of what was seen as the Sangkum socialist era, from 1963 to 1969, the Government was solidly in the hands of Sihanouk and his supporters of the traditional elite.

The end of American aid was accompanied by much rhetoric about Cambodia preferring to aid itself and the necessity of a policy of austerity, accompanied by the development of local industries to avoid importing foreign products. Austerity, however, was not for the Cambodian elite. Cars and other luxuries continued to be imported at an ever increasing rate and luxury construction in Phnom Penh showed no signs of slowing down. In fact, the number of bars and elite restaurants doubled and it could no longer be said that they were for the entertainment of American aid personnel and diplomats. Among the most conspicuous clientele were Cambodian army officers who were obviously not living on their salaries – the U.S. accusation of collusion with the N.L.F. was finally coming true, and it is now estimated that it became a large enterprise around 1965. Besides being diplomatically expedient, it provided one of the props needed for the Sangkum system after American aid had ended.

In itself it was not enough, though, or perhaps the problem was that it benefited chiefly the military rather than the groups who had profited most from American aid. Thus at the same time, in the years immediately following the end of U.S. aid, attempts were made to squeeze more out of the countryside by buying up the rice crops at artificially low prices and selling them through State outlets to retain the profits for the budget, or at least for those in charge of the government agencies through which the transactions passed.

As could be expected, discontent in the countryside increased, although it was directed towards the local administration rather than Sihanouk. Discontent also spread among teachers and urban intellectuals, who knew where to place the ultimate blame. The discontent was accompanied by repression; the secret police were omnipresent, people mysteriously disappeared and by 1966 Cambodia, though still smiling and pleasant for the casual visitor, was a country in which everyone lived in fear.[8]

If the elections of that year showed rifts in the Sangkum system, it was because it was failing, not because of plots organized by its enemies, either external or internal, but simply because Sihanouk and his closest advisers refused to face any of the basic problems. They had established a system which required constant infusions of external aid in order to exist, had lost some of the aid through greed and then tried to make up for it by squeezing the country harder.

Sihanouk tried a new tactic in the 1966 elections, the purpose of which is not entirely clear. Instead of choosing single Sangkum candidates for each seat, as in 1958 and 1962, he threw the election open, allowing all Sangkum members to stand in districts of their choice; and in some districts as many as 10 candidates competed. At the same time, the official Sangkum newspaper began publishing attacks on a number of young representatives who had incurred Sihanouk's ire, such as Hou Yuon, Hu Nim and Khieu Samphan on the Left and Douc Rasy of the progressive Right. In earlier years this would have resulted in 'spontaneous' demonstrations or petitions against these men, to force their withdrawal from, or defeat in, the election. Surprisingly, nothing happened – one of the first indications that Sihanouk was losing his magic – and when the votes were in these enemies of Sihanouk were among the few who won with large majorities in an election distinguished by the enormous number of narrow pluralities and contests whose legality was later questioned. The victories of the three leftists, two of them in rural areas which were among the first to go to the anti-Phnom Penh forces in 1970, are clear-cut cases of popular support in the face of official opposition.

Otherwise, the characteristic feature of the new Assembly was the reappearance of some of the riff-raff of the Renovation Party, who had been absent from the political scene since the 1950s. Six seats were won by Sangkum conservatives of 1955, who had been passed over in the elections of 1958 and 1962, while 13 others had last been seen in the 1951 elections, mostly as candidates of right-wing splinter parties. The re-emergence of these reactionaries, however, in no way affected the balance of power, since the Sangkum had always been the vehicle for the Right, chiefly the Renovation.

Sihanouk apologists have tended to portray this election as a sort of unexpected coup by the Right which opened the way to the real coup of 1970. Jean Lacouture quotes Sihanouk himself as saying that he had opened up the elections against the advice of the 'best leaders of the youth' and that, instead of an Assembly which 'up to then [was] in majority young men, I let them elect the most corrupt and reactionary Chamber I was ever subjected to'.[9]

Corrupt and reactionary the Assembly certainly was, but the evidence of the contemporary press shows that Sihanouk had cut himself off from the advice of 'the best leaders of the youth' and hoped for nothing so much as their defeat. Since his major anxiety in internal affairs, since 1963 at least, had been the influence of, first, the intellectual Left in Phnom Penh, and later, leftist exploitation of peasant discontent in the countryside, a better explanation is that Sihanouk had decided that salvation lay with the extreme Right and by allowing them to win through their own devices he could later, should it prove necessary, avoid the onus of having delivered the country over to them.

When certain statistics of all the elections are examined closely it almost seems as though Sihanouk and his Sangkum advisers had been planning this as far back as 1958. The early Sangkum had been frankly reactionary, but such a posture was dangerous both at home and abroad. Therefore, in the 1958 elections, in order to answer criticism that he discriminated against younger men, for the 62 available seats Sihanouk chose 33 candidates who were under 40, including 11 aged 30 or under, and favoured those with university degrees. Although this would seem to be a progressive measure, real power remained concentrated in the hands of the same conservative coterie who held most of the important Cabinet and advisory posts. The conflict between Assembly and Government which resulted allowed the conservatives to say that in spite of their degrees the younger men were incapable of solving the country's practical problems.

In the 1962 elections only 25 of the deputies were maintained as candidates, and although this group included the most notable of the leftists it was heavily weighted with proven supporters of the Right. Thus the 1962 Assembly was planned to be both older and more conservative than its predecessor, and by 1963 the younger Left had been shorn of all power and influence.

The election of 1966 is then nothing but the logical culmination of Sangkum politics and Sihanouk must bear full responsibility for it.

Breakdown, War and Revolution

As the American build-up in Vietnam became more massive, an N.L.F. victory became less certain, and the Cambodian leaders must have begun a painful reassessment of their situation. Perhaps it seemed that they had been betting on the wrong horse. After 1967 even Sihanouk's public declarations became more nuanced. He several times mentioned the need for a stabilizing American presence in South East Asia, and, for domestic consumption at least, asserted that Cambodia's chief enemies would always be the Vietnamese, of whatever stripe, and that U.S. military activity in Vietnam was good since it got rid of so many of these hereditary enemies. Some Khmer-language newspapers devoted most of their space to anti-'Viet Cong' news and articles, and the desirability of resuming relations with the U.S. was reconsidered.

In domestic affairs the years after 1966 saw a steady decline economically and politically. Prices rose, corruption increased and finally, in an effort to squeeze more out of the population, a State gambling casino was established in Phnom Penh. The first large peasant revolt broke out at Samlaut in Battambang Province in the Spring of 1967 and was suppressed with bloodshed reminiscent of the 1950s and prefiguring that of 1975. The military tried to link the Phnom Penh intellectual Left to it and soon afterwards two of the most important of this group, Hou Yuon and Khieu Samphan, disappeared and were presumed to have been murdered by the police or military. In the autumn a third, Hu Nim, also disappeared.

There were more revolts in 1968, and more disappearances, and by 1969 one of Sihanouk's own French-language publications was devoting a large amount of space to details, with maps, of 'Red' and 'Khmer-Viet Minh' activities in different parts of the country. In some cases blame was placed directly on the N.L.F. or North Vietnamese, who were charged with attempting to take over certain border areas. Finally, official contacts were resumed in July 1969. Cambodia seemed to be swinging back, not just to its position of the middle Sangkum years, but even to that of the early, pro-Western Sangkum of 1955. Why, then, the Lon Nol coup that overthrew Sihanouk on 18 March 1970? Since Sihanouk was already moving towards the U.S., it is unlikely that it was directly inspired from that direction. Indirectly, of course, it means that the U.S. Government was promising, or at least suggesting, to Asian allies and potential allies that it intended to win in Vietnam, no matter what methods were required. There is also the fact that although both Sihanouk's supporters and those who overthrew him were rather close ideologically, they represented different economic cliques within the country. The so-called 'socializing' reforms of 1963 had in fact turned over the direction of the economy to a group personally close to Sihanouk at the expense of another right-wing faction who would have preferred a more rational, modern, capitalist-type of economic organization, and this latter group was one of the important elements behind the coup. There is also the possibility that some of the moves were unplanned and that no one expected Sihanouk to react as he did. In any case, it must be emphasized that the leaders who emerged were by no means new men, fascist opponents of the Sangkum or disgruntled nonentities who had been in 'hibernation'. Lon Nol, Sirik Matak, Yem Sambaur and Sim Var had always been among the big guns of the Cambodian Right who had sabotaged democracy, opposed the Geneva Accords, organized the Sangkum and helped maintain Sihanouk's absolute rule from 1955. Lon Nol had been the military strong man, Yem Sambaur had managed Sihanouk's campaign to break the Democrat-led National Assembly in 1949 and Sim Var switched noisily to the Sangkum from the Democratic Party when the latter became so radical as to denounce a Khmer-American military aid agreement, foresee the development of a dangerous situation in Vietnam and insist on the observance of the Geneva

Accords.

Although Son Ngoc Thanh, who also returned after the coup, had been an old opponent of Sihanouk and the Sangkum, their enmity had originated at a time when Thanh was considered a left-wing radical, and if his later drift to the Right led to his rehabilitation with the Sangkum conservatives, he was not completely trusted. His well-trained troops were much desired in the fighting, but they were split up under different commands. Thanh himself was kept out of political power as long as possible, and his debacle as Prime Minister in 1972 was partly because of lack of support from his old enemies among the Phnom Penh leadership.

Of the main Cambodian parties to the 1970-75 War, Sihanouk, the *maquis*, the population on the government side and the Phnom Penh leadership, the role of the last is easiest to assess. To a large extent it lost out of sheer greed and incompetence. With an army larger than its opponent's and continually replenished by volunteers (full conscription was never instituted, and could not have been enforced), adequate food (if it had been equitably distributed) and superior military equipment supplied by the United States, the Lon Nol Government nevertheless succeeded in demoralizing its army and civilian population and losing the War largely by default.

As for Sihanouk, in retrospect, it looks as though his moves throughout the War were calculated to bring him back eventually as a hero who could confound his enemies both of the Left and Right.

When he arrived in Peking and issued his declaration establishing the anti-Phnom Penh resistance movement, FUNK, in March 1970, he probably had no very clear idea of how it would be received, what the organization of the *maquis* was, possibly not even which of the vanished leaders were still alive. It is, however, clear where his sympathies lay with respect to the men whom he believed, or knew, to be among the insurgents, and his declaration must be understood as an attempt to divide them. Thus he spoke of Khieu Samphan, Hou Yuon and Hu Nim as leaders of the forces within the country, and the response from the *maquis* appeared over the names of those three. The group which had disappeared in 1963 – Ieng Sary, Saloth Sar (Pol Pot) and Son Sen – was not included, and did not appear until Ieng Sary journeyed to Peking in 1971 as the representative of the FUNK forces.

It is possible that Sihanouk may not have known the situation of the 1963 group, but his later relations with Ieng Sary show more animosity than towards the 1967 defectors;[10] and the latter had made a show of co-operation with the Sangkum, while the former, possibly more intransigent, had written the Sangkum off just when Sihanouk was trying to give it a socialist facade. Among the FUNK leaders themselves, the late public appearance of the 1963 group may have indicated less the internal split, which we now know existed, than consideration for the feelings of Sihanouk, whom they still needed for his international contacts, and who, as they well know, was capable of making his own arrangements with Phnom Penh and the United States if he became disillusioned with leftist objectives. As a result, the real importance of Ieng

Sary, Saloth Sar and Son Sen was not clear to the outside world until after the War, and their apparently sudden elevation to prominence prompted misplaced speculation about their supposed role as agents for the Vietnamese.

Among the politically-conscious part of the population on the Phnom Penh side, the new alignment of 1970 produced a good deal of confusion. There was a brief period of euphoria occasioned by the disappearance of Sihanouk and several of his most hated henchmen plus the return of freedom of speech and press. In a general liberation of political prisoners even the Pracheachon leaders were released, but they, having no doubts about what was what, took off for the *maquis* soon after their speeches of thanks to Lon Nol.

For the less doctrinaire, Sihanouk's switch from head of the reactionary government of Phnom Penh to leader of a progressive government in exile was extremely disconcerting. Had he remained in Phnom Penh as head of a government allied with the United States against rebel forces led by Hou Yuon and Khieu Samphan, masses of the dissatisfied youths who remained under Lon Nol would have defected to the *maquis,* and Sihanouk's move at first rallied support to Lon Nol which the latter had no right to expect.

The euphoria quickly gave way to disillusionment. At first the Government was the old Renovation-Sangkum group of the 1950s, whose policy turned out to be Sihanoukism without Sihanouk. When it proved incompetent, Son Ngoc Thanh was finally brought back as Prime Minister early in 1972, and this was the moment of truth for all those who had considered Sihanouk and Lon Nol as equivalent evils and who imagined there could be a progressive solution without the ideological Left. When Thanh also proved incompetent disillusion was complete, and by mid-1972 nearly everyone was convinced that without a thoroughgoing reformation of the Phnom Penh Government, the other side would win.

It was also clear by this time that the opposing forces, rather than the Vietnamese invaders depicted in government propaganda, were Khmer, and that some, at least, of the missing leftist intellectuals were leading them; and the demoralization which increasingly gripped those on the Phnom Penh side was probably compounded by guilt over supporting one's declared enemies against one's erstwhile friends. Although a considerable number of well-known figures left Phnom Penh for the other side in 1972 and later, thousands of others remained to work for, half-heartedly, and by their actions support, more or less, a regime which they made no secret of hating.

The hope of such people, who probably made up a majority of the population on the Government side, was that Lon Nol would be overthrown by someone who would arrange an end to the War and a moderate socialist coalition with the other side – a solution which would save them from the difficult choice of remaining under a regime with which they had little sympathy or engaging in the dangerous career of a guerrilla fighter. Their position was made even more uncomfortable by the fact that FUNK offered no encouragement towards this solution, and made little effort to explain its position to the urban population or offer them any particular incentive to overthrow the Government. It almost seemed as though FUNK had already written off the urban areas, seeing them as hopelessly corrupt and enjoying the luxury brought in by U.S. aid and the sense of adventure offered by an anarchic city given over to the pursuit of pleasure.

The FUNK leaders must also have observed that colonial reflexes were being reinforced by the War. Increasingly people were convinced that Cambodia could only exist as the client of a more powerful state, and common opinion held that it was better to be a slave of the United States than of the Vietnamese. Particularly during the severe U.S. bombing which lasted throughout the first eight months of 1973, and which produced no reaction in Phnom Penh other than relief, it must have seemed to FUNK that their urban compatriots were quite willing to see the entire countryside destroyed and plastered over with concrete so long as they could enjoy a parasitical existence as U.S. clients.

It is certain that FUNK policy became much harsher after the bombing. Whereas in 1971-72 they made considerable efforts at conciliation and, in general, Cambodian villagers did not fear them, from 1973-74, with all allowance for government propaganda, there are authentic accounts of brutal imposition of new policies without adequate ideological preparation of the population.

A major mystery over the last two years of the War was what U.S. goals were in Cambodia. In spite of repeated protests by their own subordinates and by responsible Cambodians, the American leadership insisted on preserving Lon Nol, even when it was certain that a change of regime offered some possibility of renewing morale and turning the War around. Of course, the latter could only have meant a temporary advantage, and perhaps a position strong enough to force the other side to compromise, for any leadership capable of rallying strong support would have seen that the ultimate solution lay in a coalition between the best elements of Phnom Penh and FUNK and the establishment of a moderate socialist regime.

This was probably the last thing the U.S. Government wanted. Recently some publicity has been given to the 'Sonnenfeldt Doctrine', named after a Kissinger protege in the State Department, and according to which pluralistic and libertarian Communist regimes will breed leftist ferment in the West.[11] Thus, for these people, it was a good thing that the Prague uprising was crushed and, I would say, when it became clear that they could not win in Cambodia, they preferred to do everything possible to ensure that the post-war revolutionary government be extremely brutal, doctrinaire and frightening to its neighbours, rather than a moderate socialism to which the Thai, for example, might look with envy. The success of this policy may perhaps be seen in the 1976 Thai Election, in which the defeat of the socialist parties has been attributed in large measure to fear of a regime like that of Cambodia.

It would be unfair to conclude without some remarks about the chances for success that the post-1975 Cambodian society enjoyed.[12] First, the Phnom

Penh Government had been unpopular for so long, and the population had become so demoralized, that the final defeat must have come as a relief, and eyewitnesses reported the massive, spontaneous welcome which the first FUNK troops received in Phnom Penh in April 1975. Probably few revolutionary governments have taken over amid so much goodwill. Opinion abroad, however, always held that the new government, by its gratuitous brutality, destroyed this goodwill and ruled only through terror. The first such allegations, throughout 1975 and 1976, were often dishonest and nearly always exaggerated, although it now seems that the worst predictions eventually came true; and for a full understanding of what happened we require careful, honest analysis of the increasing amount of first-hand information which is becoming available.

The basic policies of the new regime seemed clear enough, though, and they may be usefully compared with the recommendations of a 'Blueprint for the Future' prepared by an anonymous group of Western and Thai social scientists and published in the conservative *Bangkok Post* in February 1976. For Thailand to avoid a breakdown of its society and a revolution, they suggested that people should be taken out of the cities and put back on the land, decentralization should give more power to local authorities, much more investment should go into agriculture and the old elite should lose some of its wealth and political power. This is precisely what Cambodia did from 1975, though of course on a much more massive scale than envisaged by the 'Blueprint', but it illustrates that the basic policies are considered by 'bourgeois' economists and political scientists to be rational and practicable for a country with problems similar to those of Cambodia.

In short, there was nothing in the early actions of the revolutionary regime which argued against ultimate success. Even the rigid exclusion of nearly all foreign contacts and the 'hermit republic' stance could have become an acceptable norm for Cambodians, for, in spite of the generally open attitude towards strangers which characterized pre-1970 society, there was agreement among all classes and factions that Cambodian affairs were of no legitimate concern to foreigners and the country would be better off if they all went away. The post-1975 leadership would certainly have had no trouble teaching their people that Cambodian suffering was mainly due to foreign intervention, and although one may legitimately ask whether the new egalitarian society could not have been established with less deliberate destruction of the old, there are ample reasons why that leadership might answer in the negat

References

1. A French translation of this article was prepared and was to have appeared in a special Indochina issue of *Les Temps Modernes* (January 1980), but the editorial board of that journal became uneasy about the article for reasons that were never made clear, but were probably political, and decided to reject it at the last minute.

2. For example, see Edith Lenart's reports in the *Far Eastern Economic Review,* 7 May 1976, pp.22-3, and 28 May 1976, p.14. I take for granted that such sensationalist treatments as Francois Ponchaud's *Cambodge Annee Zero* are not acceptable as serious analysis; see the discussion of Ponchaud in Noam Chomsky and Edward Herman, *The Political Economy of Human Rights,* (Boston, South End Press, 1979) Vol 2: *After the Cataclysm: Postwar Indochina and the Reconstruction of Imperial Ideology.*
3. Ea Sichau was perhaps the first genuine Cambodian leftist of unequivocal identity to have become prominent in national politics. Description of his character and intellectual qualities by former acquaintances reminds one of Khieu Samphan. He died in the 1950s.
4. Hou Yuon's thesis, *Le Paysannerie du Cambodge et ses projets de modernisation* (Paris, 1955). [Part of this thesis appears in translation in Part I of this book.]
5. One of them was Saloth Chhay, of *Samakki,* supposedly a brother of Saloth Sar (Pol Pot).
6. Speech to the 14th National Congress, 31 December 1965.
7. Charles Meyer, *Derriere le Sourire Khmer* (Paris, Plon, 1971), pp.136-7; although Meyer himself should not be classified as a 'Sihanouk apologist'.
8. Ibid., p.149, speaks of the 'terreur sacree' which was never far behind the smile.
9. Jean Lacouture, *L'Indochine vue de Pekin,* p.82.
10. Some details of Ieng Sary's relationship with Sihanouk may be found in Milton Osborne, Norodom Sihanouk: A Leader of the Left? in Joseph J. Zasloff and MacAlister Brown (eds.), *Communism in Indochina: New Perspectives* (Massachusetts, 1976).
11. *Time,* 12 April 1976.
12. This was written before the overthrow of the Pol Pot government; but unless the new leadership wish to reintroduce bourgeois institutions, which seems unlikely, there is very little they can do to alter the path set by their predecessors.

4. The Umbrella War of 1942 by Bunchan Mul

Introductory Note

What follows are extracts from Kuk Niyobay (Political Prison) by Bunchan Mul (Phnom Penh 1971). Mul was Minister of Cults and Religion in the Lon Nol regime (1970-75) in the early years of its struggle against Khmer and Vietnamese revolutionaries. In this context, some of his comments about the Vietnamese political prisoners, and their relations with Khmer prisoners, on the French Indochina prison island of Tralach (Con Son) from 1942-45, are revealing. This account is in fact a record of some of the very first contacts Khmer nationalists had with political developments in the outside world.

Their relative lack of political sophistication is honestly outlined by Bunchan Mul. (At the 20 July 1942 demonstration in Phnom Penh, he describes how he himself 'automatically and without thinking threw a bicycle at the police, and had my photo taken by them'.) It is also evident from the easy arrest by the French of the most prominent leader of the 1942 'revolution', Achar Hem Chieu. (An achar *is a Buddhist monk or learned man residing in a* wat *or temple.) Although even Chum Moung, the Secretary of the Minister of the Interior, was an agent of the revolutionaries, he 'panicked' when given the order to summon Chieu, and the* achar *duly presented himself for arrest. From a section of the text not translated here, it appears that Moung was afraid that the affair would 'spread all over me'; he did not dare ask what was happening but simply went to fetch Chieu. On the way back he told Chieu that 'he did not know what was behind the order', but apparently did not say that he suspected Chieu would be arrested. The* achar *replied, rather hopelessly: 'If they ask anything about our activities, just say we don't know.'*

It is also apparent that many of the nationalists did not suspect possible manipulation by the Japanese, whose activities, although it may not have been clear in Kampuchea at that time, had imperialist goals and were carefully planned long in advance. Son Ngoc Thanh, in particular, is shown here to have associated himself closely with Japanese imperialism. He escaped arrest after the demonstration and, while Pach Chhoeun, Hem Chieu and Bunchan Mul were in prison, he spent the next three years in Japan.

In the 1950s, Thanh became involved with the C.I.A.; he emerged as leader of the main Khmer from Kampuchea Krom (K.K.K.) movement, which the C.I.A. sponsored in its guerrilla attacks against neutral Kampuchea from South Viêtnam and Thailand during the 1950s and 1960s. The original K.K.K. were seen by Bunchan Mul on Con Son island in 1945. (Son Ngoc Thanh died in Vietnam in 1976, Pach Chhoeun in Phnom Penh in 1971.)

There are other notable points about the 1942 'revolution'. The first is the very important role played by Buddhist monks in nationalist politics in that period. Communist sources later claimed, probably exaggerating, that 4,000 monks had taken part in the demonstration. Indeed, the movement's cadres certainly seem to have been drawn almost exclusively from monks and Phnom Penh dwellers, although Bunchan Mul's account makes it clear that independence from the French was a goal that also appealed to many peasants. Secondly, the strategy adopted by Son Ngoc Thanh, namely, to win over the Khmer troops in the French colonial army and force the French out by provoking a mutiny amongst their own forces, is reminiscent of the abortive Yen Bay revolt led by the Vietnam Nationalist Party in the north of Vietnam 12 years earlier (in 1930). Such a strategy was almost certainly doomed to failure.

According to historian David Chandler, writing in the Journal of the Siam Society *in January 1972, Bunchan Mul's book 'could not have been published before 18 March 1970, because it successfully corrects the myth that Sihanouk alone was responsible for Cambodia's independence. In its own right, the book is a valuable addition to the historical record.'*

The translation is by Chanthou Boua.

One Group of Khmer Nationalists' Struggle for Freedom, 1936-42

During the period of French colonialism, the French controlled and oppressed our land and our people. Khmer people underwent such great sorrows and sufferings that everyone's eyeballs almost jumped out of their sockets; it was very painful, we all had it up to our necks living under their iron yoke; we couldn't move or shake off the yoke except to shed tears, not knowing what to think. The Khmer people had no rights or liberty at all; they took away our rights and we could not protest. Heavier and heavier taxes were imposed so that it was almost unbearable.

When the Second World War started, communications by sea were cut off because of the extensive and strict control of the sea. Transportation of goods by sea was stopped and so our country became poorer and poorer; we hardly had enough clothing to cover ourselves. In some households of two or three members, there was only enough clothing for one person. If they wanted to go out (to the market or to festivals) they had to take turns because of insufficient clothing. The ones that stayed home dared not go outside, because they had only an old piece of cloth or rags, or a piece of mosquito-net or matting, just enough to cover their genitals; some even went naked. If friends or relatives came asking for them, they would reply from the inside of the house and did not dare to come out to greet guests. This only applied to the poor. As for the rich, they were not that badly off, for they had money to buy enough clothing. Since clothing was hard to find, people from the province of Svay Rieng had this bright idea of making shorts, using the special grass for making mats and selling them.

During that time, because there were no imports and exports, the French collected all the products of the country so that they could trade; that is, all the products in the country, anything at all, had to be sold to them cheaply; then, they put their trade mark on those products and retailed them back to the public at high prices. If they saw us carrying goods, like one kilogram of dried fish or smoked fish, a jar of fish fat or even a bowl of beeswax, they would confiscate them and punish the owner as well. We could neither grow cotton nor weave our own clothes. Some people fearfully tried to weave their own clothes, behind clumps of banana trees or in the forest, only so that they could have sufficient clothes to wear. Since the French came to our country, Khmer women, who used to be very good at weaving, gave up this art almost completely, because the French imported foreign fabrics, which were of better quality than those locally made, to sell to us.

During that period, salt was very hard to get because none was on sale. People who lived near the sea-shore tried to boil brine to get salt, but they did it in secret, not letting the French know about it because they feared punishment. As for the poor who lived far away from the sea, they had to do without, which made them suffer from salt depletion. Some marinated their fish in water mixed with ashes so as to get the salty taste.

This was the policy of the oppressor; the French were the same as the British in India. But the rich were not that hard up; they bought a sufficient amount of clothing and salt and stored them for their own family's needs.

A good opportunity came for our people when the French were busy fighting their war with Germany, and later on with the Thais. This prevented them transporting all the weapons and military equipment that could have been used to suppress us. (In our country, the French had used only old-fashioned weapons since 1914.) They confiscated carts and buses from the people to transport their troops and armaments back and forth, to show that the French were very strong and to frighten the Khmers from considering resistance.

But the struggle had first started in 1936, by means of a newspaper called *Nokor Wat.* It was Son Ngoc Thanh's idea to found a newspaper at that time . . . When *Nokor Wat* came out, the majority of its readers were poor people and workers who could not read the French-language newspapers. As for the officials, they did not condescend to. They looked down on and detested the national script, especially those high officials who could not even read Khmer but learnt French because French was very valuable – at that time

Khmer was very inferior, below zero. Why? Because the French stood on our country. Those who spoke French considered themselves very civilized, as if they had descended from heaven . . . . French literature and culture ran had so much influence on the Khmer that our literature and culture ran and hid in the pagoda. It is only thanks to the Khmer monks, who preserved, supported and kept it intact till today, that our literature did not disappear from Kampuchea. From 1942, Khmer writing was prohibited by the French and was not used officially. The French invented a romanized script *(quoc ngu Khmer)* to write Khmer words in French, and this was in use from the high governmental to the district offices. . . .

When the newspaper *Nokor Wat* had been out for a while the Khmer people, who used to be fast asleep and deadly scared of the French, started to open their eyes, to wake up, to like their nation, to help and to defend one another in time of danger, to dare to protest to the French over injustice or oppression . . . . The revolutionary group, i.e. the newspaper personnel, was very popular among monks, peasants, workers and government officials, and this popularity increased all the time. Wherever they went, Pach Chhoeun, Son Ngoc Thanh, Sim Var, etc. always attempted to explain things, to enlighten the people about the country's politics, besides publicizing them in the newspaper. That's why everywhere they went – to a pagoda, to a small or large village or to a government office – they were always well received and welcomed happily by the people. Men and women, government officials and monks, waited to listen to the descriptions and explanations of the national politics and they also prepared them meals.

However, apart from Pach Chhoeun, they did not go out to other provinces much, because they were busy working for the government. Pach Chhoeun visited many more places than the others. That's why people knew him, recognized him more easily and liked him more than the others. There were some places he could not get to, but the people came and carried him to the agreed meeting place. At that time Pach Chhoeun was the most prominent character of all.

. . . At that time the black-boot and red-boot armies were constantly feuding with one another in different factions. So the French asked the Khmer monks to preach to them and discipline them at the barracks once a month, in order to educate them to acquire wisdom and good behaviour. The red-boot army were the [French-sponsored] fighting soldiers with red bands around their stomach and legs and with red berets. The black-boot army had black bands and black berets. Their task was to look after the country like police.

The allocation of Buddhist monks to go out and preach or to call a conference in order to educate the soldiers according to Buddhist religion was the duty of the Buddhist Institute. Sometimes monks were assigned to go and preach and educate Khmer Krom [lower Kamuchean] soldiers in Moat Chrouk [Chaudoc in Vietnam], for example. At that time, Son Ngoc Thanh was working at the Buddhist Institute, so he had the opportunity of picking only those monks who were strongly nationalist, good talkers and who were skilled in explaining and convincing the soldiers, using the Buddhist style of enlightenment, to love their country, to prepare to struggle, etc.

The most nationalistic monks were Achar Hem Chieu (a teacher of Pali) Achar Pang Kat (a teacher of Sanskrit), Achar So Haiy, Achar Uk Chea and Achar Khieu Chum. After every conference each monk had to write a report for the General-Secretary of the Buddhist Institute about the results of his preaching, and also report to Son Ngoc Thanh about the results of the close contact he had made with the soldiers after the preaching. When there were soldiers who they hoped would participate in the revolutionary struggle to chase out the French, Son Ngoc Thanh would assign Chum Moung to contact them to give them further details of the plan . . . .

As for myself, Bunchan Mul and Nuon Duong, we were assigned to make contact with and win over the people, and also to spy on and investigate the exact number of soldiers and weapons in, and the locations of, the French army barracks . . . .

In 1940, when we were planning our policy, the Japanese troops, who were fighting a war with their enemies (Americans, English, French, etc.) entered Indochina under a secret agreement with the Governor-General in Hanoi, who reluctantly agreed to let them in because he knew that the French forces could not resist the Japanese.

The Japanese troops moved into Kampuchea before King Sihanouk's [April 1941] coronation. Taking this opportunity, Son Ngoc Thanh secretly contacted a Japanese commander, through the owner of a store called Dainang Kousi opposite the old market in Phnom Penh to ask for military intervention in case the French uncovered the plans for the revolution. The owner of Dainang Kousi, who had opened his department store a few years before the Second World War, was there to spy on the French troops: the number of soldiers and their equipment. He knew how many Khmer nationalists there were, and he agreed to help us and keep contact because he was also an army intelligence commander. He also contacted his superior, the military chief. So the contacts between Son Ngoc Thanh and the Japanese army went on while I worked as an agent to deliver secret messages to the Japanese.

Son Ngoc Thanh told the revolutionaries to work very carefully, so that there would be no leaks, because the French would make arrests if they found out. If by any chance there were any mistakes, they should urgently enter the Japanese headquarters (police station), there they would be protected from arrest by the French.

As for Achar Hem Chieu (and other monks) in every province he went, on the job or when asked to preach, he always attempted to teach and convince the people to become nationalists, to be courageous in the revolutionary struggle for independence from the French. He did this with great success . . . .

At that time there were very few French soldiers in Kampuchea. In each barracks there were many Khmer soldiers, all under the orders of a few French soldiers. Many French soldiers died during the 1940-41 war between the French and the Thai. And many were sent to fight in France. The French civilians were also conscripted to serve in the army in France. In some provinces there were only one or two Frenchmen left; others had four or five. In Kompong Speu Province there were none; the provincial Governor was in charge as Resident there. So the revolutionary project was not very constricted; it could work. But you will see the difficulties we had.

The Secret Explodes

The revolutionaries proceeded with their work, but because they were new to politics and lacking in experience, the plan got out of control and the French found out about it. Among the soldiers who had contact with Achar Hem Chieu and Nuon Duong, there were some who liked the French and stuck fast to them like moss to rocks. These people told them that Achar Hem Chieu and Nuon Duong were leading the soldiers towards rebellion against the French. Fifteen Khmer soldiers were arrested, secretly, so as to avoid forewarning the revolutionaries.

On 17 July 1942, a French inspector and two Khmer secretaries with bundles of letters went to see Ung Y, the Prime Minister, and Tea San, the Minister of the Interior and of Cults and Religion, and other ministers. Tea San then ordered Chum Moung, who at that time was Tea San's secretary, to invite Achar Hem Chieu to the office. Chum Moung, who was one of our group, panicked; he went to Wat Unnalom to invite Achar Hem Chieu, who came straight away with him . . . .

When Achar Hem Chieu arrived, Tea San asked a worker to buy a pair of trousers and a shirt for Achar Hem Chieu to wear; they took off his saffron robe, and the French immediately took him away in a car; he did not have time to tell anyone. They defrocked him without a word!

The arrest of Achar Hem Chieu led to chaos among student monks at the Higher Institute of Pali Language and at every pagoda in Phnom Penh, who were all friends and students of his.

At the same time, Nuon Duong was also arrested by a French inspector, at his home.

The revolutionaries, with help from the monks, were spreading the news to every pagoda in the city and in other provinces, some nearby and some far from the city, using all possible means. The order went out from Son Ngoc Thanh to organize a demonstration on 20 July 1942 in front of the office of the Resident-Superior, calling for the release of Achar Hem Chieu and Nuon Duong. . . .

At that time my duty was to pass information to the monks in every pagoda in Phnom Penh. I used a bicycle to carry out this task.

After Achar Hem Chieu and Nuon Duong were arrested, Son Ngoc Thanh took refuge in the Japanese police headquarters to avoid being arrested by the French. However, he continued to lead the revolution, and contact between him and myself continued through a little boy living at his place, who brought him food every day. On the night of 19 July, Son Ngoc Thanh asked me to get a gun from his house and deliver it to him at the Japanese police office. There I met Son Ngoc Thanh and a Japanese army captain. They told me again and again that the next day's demonstration had to be carried out exactly as follows:

> Tomorrow morning all demonstrators, monks and lay people, must eat before 6 a.m., then walk to meet together on Boulevard Doudart de Lagree, right behind the western entrance to the palace. After meeting one another they must parade peacefully, i.e. empty-handed and with no weapons, in an orderly, quiet fashion, without talking, with a banner up the front saying: 'We are calling for the release of Achar Hem Chieu and Nuon Duong'. The parade should then stop in front of the office of the Resident-Superior. If the police chase or hit them, they must resist passively, not fight back or do anything; they must stay calm. But if they wait till 12 midday and the French still have not fulfilled what is asked for, then the demonstration must parade back and stop right in front of the office of the Japanese police. They must then read the proclamation to the Japanese police relating the events, and ask the Japanese to intervene with the French government to release the two persons whom they had arrested. The Japanese can intervene or contact the French government only if the demonstrators follow these steps as ordered.

When I got back I delivered this message to the monks in every *wat* in Phnom Penh, such as Wat Langka, and to lay people and also to Pach Chhoeun.

The First Demonstration to Awaken the Khmer Conscience (20 July 1942)

On the 20 July 1942 at 6 a.m., after meeting at the agreed place, the demonstrators, monks and lay people, so many of them that they were all over Phnom Penh, paraded from that place to the office of the Resident-Superior. That is, people came out of Wat Langka, Unnalom, etc., to meet each other behind the palace with Pach Chhoeun as leader, courageously striding in front. The demonstrators paraded bravely, with no illusions. French, Khmer and Vietnamese spies walked alongside, but they were pale and scared of the demonstrators. (The French spy called Sambraige was more careful than the others.) Everyone walked towards the office of the Resident-Superior.

When the demonstrators got there they stopped; there were people everywhere to the west of Wat Phnom, opposite the Hotel Royal, with a banner in front of them. First of all, Pach Chhoeun came out to describe the events to some French officials who were waiting for us on the steps. Pach Chhoeun asked to see the Resident-Superior. The French said: 'Not many can go in, you must choose only three or four representatives to meet the Resident-Superior! Hearing that, the demonstrators screamed out, 'We can't send just two or three, they will arrest them again.' They all pushed one another further up to the front. Because of the pressure from the back, those in the front, who were monks and lay people, Pach Chhoeun for example, were driven into that big building.

The French saw this. They closed the front door so that the rest of the group could not get in; then they arrested Pach Chhoeun alone. They took him inside, out through the back door and into a car which took him away. The police prevented the demonstrators from going inside, which caused a big fight and chaos all over. Some demonstrators were wounded by police batons. Police were also wounded by the monks' umbrella handles, sticks, stones and *kaun tang*. [A *kaun tang* is made from a large rivet tied to a long elastic lead. When thrown, the elastic stretches; once it hits something it bounces back to the thrower's hand. Some *kaun tang* are made from lead.] When they met one another later, after their escape to Battambang, a demonstrator called Rous told Chum Moung that during the demonstration he had thrown a *kaun tang* and hit four or five Frenchmen. According to some information, many people were using this special weapon at the demonstration. A bald French security commander called Brocheton was hit on the skull by a *kaun tang,* which made his head bleed and his shirt all red . . . .

Some demonstrators who struck security officers were arrested on the spot. (Other demonstrators were later searched out and arrested on the basis of photos taken by security men during the fight.) Some demonstrators, who had not fought with the police, were still scared of being arrested by the French. Achar Pang Kat withdrew from the scene. However, although the leaders of the monks tried to escape and hide, the French knew them by sight. As for myself, at that time I automatically and without thinking threw a bicycle at the police, and had my photo taken by them. It is very difficult to describe correctly the chaotic events of that day, because from what I remember even the monks' umbrellas were also used as weapons to bash people, leading to many injuries.

Later, when I was an Issarak [anti-French independence fighter] with the Vietnamese Viet Minh in the Dang Rek mountains, they included this story in their discussion lessons. They wrote in their newspaper *Rumdoh* (Liberation) that even monks, novices with no ambitions who were very tolerant people, could not put up with the oppression of the colonialists. They stood up to protest to the French and even used the handles of their umbrellas to hit and wound the heads of many Frenchmen. The Vietnamese described this struggle of our monks as 'The Umbrella War of 1942'.

. . . The security officers arrested many demonstrators and took them away in cars, but I could not make out who was who because everyone was scared and also because there were just so many people that even I could not recognise everyone's face or know everyone's name. There were many hundreds of armed French red-boot soldiers at the scene to intimidate and frighten the demonstrators.

At the point when the demonstration was in chaos, the Japanese army sent two truckloads of soldiers who stopped nearby. But how could they possibly make any intervention with the French government? The plan was carried out wrongly, different from how they had been told, so they stayed still.

. . . The revolution was unsuccessful, and the demonstration was also unsuccessful, because it was our first try and also because we Khmer nationalists were at that period very young in national politics. Because we had only opened our eyes a few years before . . . For nearly one century we had never thought of wanting to free ourselves from being slaves of the French. We know and have heard from old people, who passed on the story from one generation to another, how the French had already arrested many nationalists, those who led the earlier revolutions, such as Pu Kombo, Moeun Peang, Achar Sva, Kralahom Kong, Oknhya Pisnulok Chhuk, and left many of them to die on Tralach Island. Those who were traitors did not care about their nation, they pleased the French to secure high positions and privilege for their own family clan. These included members of the palace group such as Sihanouk who, if he was upset with a Khmer, got a Frenchman to replace him. He abused the monks, calling them 'the shaven-headed ones' *(A-Trangoul).*

. . . This was the first revolution ever to occur in our country. However, even though it was unsuccessful, it was at least a model, an outline for the descendants and youth of later generations to follow with appropriate corrections . . . . It is only those who never do anything but lie back and scratch their belly, mere onlookers, who are always correct and never wrong.

. . . From the day of the demonstration the French security officers pursued their task of arresting demonstrators all over Phnom Penh and in other provinces. Most of the demonstrators were from Wat Unnalom and Wat Langka. That is why many monks and lay people who were known to have been involved with the revolution or in the demonstration panicked and ran away to hide in other provinces. Some crossed over to Battambang, which was then a Thai province. Achar Uk Chea, a teacher at the Buddhist school at Wat Langka, escaped to Bangkok. In Pursat, Chum Moung saw French security officers arrest two or three demonstrators, monks who had thought of escaping to Thailand, and send them back to Phnom Penh . . . .

After I got back from the demonstration, I came home and carried on trading as usual at my house in Signek market. On 25 July at about 8 o'clock, while I was selling noodle soup and coffee, a security officer called upon me; he told me that they would detain me.

. . . In the big prison, I met four or five friends who were being punished for the same matter. They were Mom Lon, who lived in front of Wat Langka to the south, Pouk Ny, who lived to the west of Wat Langka, Mr Im from Takeo Province, Mr Prey Eam from Prek Loung village, Khsach Kandal district (Kandal Province), and two others whose names I do not remember . . . . I stayed there for 18 days, then was taken to Prey

Nokor [Ho Chi Minh City] Prison in a boat. On the boat I met Achar Pang Kat and seven or eight red-boot soldiers who were brought from other detention centres along with Pach Chhoeun.

. . . Conditions in Prey Nokor Prison were much better than in Phnom Penh. Achar Hem Chieu was there, and still preaching; he was the best, the number one preacher among the preacher monks.

. . . The Vietnamese prisoners living in the same hall were not like the Khmers; they had been politically educated for a long time. They treated one another like brothers. In Prey Nokor Prison, the Vietnamese political prisoners kept teaching one another to struggle hard to free their nation. Achar Hem Chieu and Nuon Duong were lucky enough to be put with them and were able to learn much from them. They were with the most important prisoners.

. . . . Capital punishment was usually carried out at 5 a.m. They would call out farewell to their compatriot friends: 'Dear friends of common blood! We are going off to die, all you friends please remember to continue the struggle until it is successful.' At that time, their friends in every hall would stand up and sing songs to send their friends off to die bravely and courageously. They would shout: 'Long Live Ho Chi Minh, long live Ho Chi Minh . . . .' And those who were not yet killed would shout back: 'We won't forget your last testament, friends, we'll struggle, struggle . . . until we succeed.' Then they would stand to attention in respect for the souls of the heroes who were going to die.

Friends, did you know that only in 1942 were there any Khmer political prisoners serving sentences in Prey Nokor jail? There were none before then. That's why the Vietnamese political prisoners were hospitable to the Khmer political prisoners. They gave everyone food and snacks. They got food from their friends, relatives or people in their group who were outside the prison and had the right to send in food every Saturday. The Vietnamese political prisoners were happy to see us serving sentences in that year of 1942. They said that when we all united to bash the French on the head, the French could not bring 'our Khmer brothers and sisters' to bash them. The Vietnamese understood the idea of rebellion with a common interest before we did. I'm writing about this here not to praise the Vietnamese, but to awaken the conscience of all of our compatriots to unite and strongly defend our country.

The Vietnamese political prisoners, at that time, looked after Achar Hem Chieu, Nuon Duong and Pach Chhoeun very well. Why? Because it added to their strength and was in their interest too . . . .

After two months in Prey Nokor we were all sent to Tralach [Con Son] Island . . . . I noticed that among the prisoners on Tralach Island, some rested after work, some chatted or joked with one another, some played chess or *raek* [Khmer chess] . However, there was an unusual set of prisoners, split into groups of five or six people, who attempted to learn English, French or Russian, for example. They used white lime as chalk to write on the cement floor where they slept. I noticed that the majority of them were Vietnamese, belonging to a political group called the Viet Minh. They were always teaching one another about politics, i.e. to do whatever possible to keep themselves aware and struggling psychologically. They also made efforts to teach the common law prisoners (who were not political prisoners) about their ideology, their understanding, and encouraged them along the right path towards progress. However, there were many prisoners who were determined not to absorb their good advice. These were left to play non-political roles, for example, if the political prisoners were moved by the French police, to go and live with the common law prisoners, they would ask these others to look after their people. As for the common law criminals, they acknowledged and accepted the other group as political strugglers to liberate their country from the French yoke; they did not oppose them, which left the politicians in peace and equipped with courage to pursue the political struggle without hesitation.

This is the truth which I saw with my own eyes.

During the midday break they studied together for one hour; at night they studied from 6 pm for another three or four hours before they went to sleep. This is the truth. They said that struggle is the duty of the Vietnamese people, men and women, young and old, in order to help liberate the country from the French yoke, however long it takes. It is essential, they said, to unite without fail in the interest of helping their descendants to gain freedom and peace in the future. They forbade one another to talk about fear of death, about flinching or turning back: 'If we are scared to die, no one knows when we will become free men. And how our descendants will abuse us, the earlier generation! So we Vietnamese must establish our unity, attempt to struggle without fear of death until our goal is achieved'. This was the Vietnamese ideology . . . .

At the end of 1943, Achar Hem Chieu died at the age of 46. He died in the lap of Nuon Duong, who was also sick; he said to Nuon Duong before he died: 'I'm not scared of death, but still I am very sorry not to see Kampuchea independent'. . . .

I was waiting for the outcome of the Second World War, which was burning strongly nearly all over Asia. I understood that if the Japanese won the War I would probably be back home before completing the sentence passed down in Prey Nokor, which was 'five years in jail on forced labour and 15 years deportation from Kampuchea'. On the other hand, if the Japanese lost the war and the French were still the colonial masters of the Indochina states, I would never get home before that sentence was completed . . . .

In 1944 [in fact, 9 March 1945 – Eds.], the Japanese won the war against the French in Indochina. All over Tralach Island the French were completely disarmed by the Japanese and had no more power. But not for very long: the Allies (Americans) helped the French in February 1945. On 8 February, Tralach Island underwent Allied bombing which created chaos. Phnom Penh also underwent bombing on the same day . . . .

A week after the bombing a group of Japanese soldiers delivered a telegram from Phnom Penh, which contained orders to take four political prisoners, Achar Hem Chieu, Nuon Duong, Pach Chhoeun and myself, back to Phnom Penh . . . .

At about 6 p.m., they took the three of us who had survived aboard a Japanese Second World War patrol boat, Boarding the ship behind me were a group of K.K.K. [Khmer from Kampuchea Krom] soldiers, about 100 of them with their wives and children, whom the Japanese helped to get back to Prey Nokor. These were soldiers whom the French had brought to Tralach Island to work.

We got to Prey Nokor at 8 a.m. the next morning. Half an hour later a Japanese soldier led us from the ship to a place the Japanese Government had set up for big Vietnamese leaders of political groups such as the Cao Dai, Hoa Hao and Binh Xuyen . . . . I got to know these groups. They took us to stay with the Cao Dai group, who welcomed us warmly. But no one in this group ate any food with fatty meat in it . . . . The Cao Dai, Hoa Hao and Binh Xuyen were religious groups of rebels who wanted to liberate their nation from the French yoke. They collected money from their people in order to buy weapons to struggle against the French. I saw members of these groups carrying bags of money to their leaders many times. There were committee members (I saw many of them) who sat down and counted this money. These groups collected many millions of riels. The Cao Dai collected the most.

At 9 a.m. one morning, two weeks later, the three of us left Prey Nokor in a Japanese army van, for Kampuchea! When we got to the ferry at Neak Leung we met Achar Pang Kat, Chum Moung and other friends. We hugged one another happily! After we had finished talking and asking about each other, our friends let us continue our trip to Phnom Penh while they continued on to Prey Veng and Svay Rieng, to help with propaganda with the Japanese troops in order to lead the people in those regions.

After I had been back in Phnom Penh for four months, I heard that other Khmer political prisoners from Tralach Island had got back home alive too. I met many of them and asked them about their trip back home. I found out that after the Japanese had helped transport Khmer political prisoners home, the Viet Minh group quickly took the opportunity created by the Japanese defeat of the French, and sent 15 to 20 boats to pick up their friends imprisoned on Tralach Island, and take them back to their country. And Khmer political prisoners were allowed to go with them. About 4,500 Vietnamese political prisoners came back at that time.

When they arrived at Prey Nokor, those political prisoners were welcomed by the Vietnamese there very enthusiastically, with national flags and platforms and food . . . . As for our political prisoners, after thanking them for the lift, they hurriedly said goodbye and came home. The rest of their trip home was quite tough, because they did not have any money . . . .

Please note that all the political prisoners, including myself, were jobless and had no friends when we got back home. Nuon Duong, who was sick from

Tralach Island jail, died in Preah Ket Mealea Hospital. Those of us who were alive did not have jobs, partly because the group who were slaves to the French still hated us, and partly because Sihanouk was at that time pleasing the French, since he saw that they now had the Allies to help them defeat the Japanese; he did not care, think about or assist us or raise our esteem in any way at all. He even oppressed us further . . . .

In the year of 1946 I joined the Issarak group in the Battambang region. Then, in 1951 I volunteered to be a representative in Parliament, but unfortunately that Parliament was dissolved by Sihanouk on 13 January 1953, and I was arrested with another friend and jailed for another eight months and 20 days.

5. Resisting the French 1946–54: The Khmer Issarak by Ben Kiernan

Introductory Note

The following story is compiled from five hours of recorded conversations with Krot Theam, a Kampuchean now living in Australia. The interviews took place at St Kilda and Hanging Rock, Victoria, on 2 and 30 December 1976, and were conducted by Muy Hong Lim and Ben Kiernan. Theam's story of his revolutionary activities from 1949-52 is of value because of the light it casts on the little-known movement of revolutionary nationalists called the Khmer Issarak ('Independent Khmers') in the First Indochina War.

Events in Kampuchea between 1945 and 1955 were overshadowed by those in Vietnam. As a result, the independence of action, the numbers and the influence of members of the Khmer Issarak have all been underestimated. So much becomes apparent in Theam's narrative, which suggests that the early revolutionary nationalist movement was strongly rooted in Kampuchean history. This is despite the fact that, unlike some other smaller groups also known as Issaraks, the movement was closely aligned with the Vietnamese Communists.

Krot Theam

Krot Theam was born in 1934 in the village of Kranhoung, in the Samlaut district of north-west Kampuchea. The 1930s ended the relatively peaceful period of French colonial rule; in 1941, the entire north and north-west of Kampuchea (Battambang, Siemreap and Preah Vihear Provinces) were seized from France by Thailand, with Japanese backing. Thai influence was now strong and in 1944, Theam's cousin, a Buddhist monk, took him to live in the town of Trat in eastern Thailand. Theam was only 10 at the time, but he says he discovered later that armed groups of nationalists were being established in Kampuchea that same year, including some in his own district. We know from other sources that one such nationalist who began his activities in the north-west in 1944 was a man called Sieu Heng.[1]

In 1949, Theam returned to Samlaut for a few days to see his family, and was arrested by a group of Khmer nationalist rebels. They had close connections with Ho Chi Minh's Viet Minh and in spite of (or perhaps because of) five years of Thai occupation of the area (1941-46), they were decidedly anti-Thai. Theam was charged by this Issarak band with being a 'Thai spy', and his parents were accused of supporting espionage by not reporting Theam's movement to Thailand five years before. Fortunately for all three, Theam's Uncle Yot was the Khmer Issarak mayor *(mekhum)* of their home village of Kranhoung. Yot gave Theam the chance to prove his innocence, and in July 1949 Theam found himself in an Issarak military unit and taking part in attacks on colonial forces.

When asked if this was a typical case of Issarak recruitment, Theam replied that usually two or three armed Issarak leaders would enter a village seeking out recruits. Some peasants, he said, joined the nationalist movement voluntarily, but there were others like him who initially were forced to enlist.

The political and ethnic make-up of the movement gave Theam some of his very first impressions. Just prior to Theam's joining, Sieu Heng, who was the local Issarak leader, had handed over the administration of the Pailin area to a Vietnamese revolutionary, and had gone to the Issarak headquarters 'to study'. For the next two years, until Heng's return, this Vietnamese official showed considerable cruelty to people whom he considered to be 'spies for the French'. While Theam does not remember the name of the Vietnamese, he does recall him burning some people alive.

Theam says his Issarak band received no aid from Thailand, although they did raise funds by engaging in border trade, especially in cardamom (a plant after which Kampuchea's western hills are named). Theam emphasized that Khmer nationalists of another kind such as Son Ngoc Thanh, were, as far as he was concerned, 'on the other side'. Leaders of his revolutionary nationalist movement whom Theam recalls from the 1949-52 period were Son Ngoc Minh, Leav Keo Moni and Chan Samay.[2] All three were later reported to have gone to Hanoi in 1954-55.[3] Theam noted that the ethnic Vietnamese in the Issarak forces were obviously not long-time residents of Kampuchea because they had 'black teeth', a sign, according to popular Khmer belief, of someone from Vietnam proper.

Theam began his military career in 'Brigade 140', but because of his age (he was then only 15), he joined the *senachon,* or youth brigade, in September 1949. He thus became a member of the first intake of Khmers aged 15-21 at a revolutionary training centre in the forest. The centre, which Theam refers to as the Anlong Phiem 'fortress', was quite close to his home village. Surrounded on one side by tall trees and on the other by a stream, it consisted of longhouses in rows 300 metres long. 2,700 people lived and studied there, 50 of whom were Vietnamese ('mainly cooks', according to Theam). The commander of the camp was a Khmer political commissar named Kun; Theam also described him as a 'professor'. Vietnamese teachers were often called upon to give lessons in guerrilla warfare and politics, but always in conjunction with a Khmer instructor, and they would always leave the camp immediately afterwards, returning to their posts in Brigades 140 or 180.

Theam's memory of this year-long training course is not always clear, but some of the details that he does remember merit attention. The day began with the raising of the Issarak flag, which as far as he recalls consisted of a blue five-towered temple on a red field. The whole camp would stand by and salute, three shots would be fired and then an anthem sung.

The main component of the lessons was a textbook, mimeographed locally, which was over an inch thick. Theam does not remember the name of the author, but says it had been written in the hand of a man called Lim Pat, and had been corrected by Achar Pres. Among other things, the book contained rules and regulations for revolutionary conduct (injunctions against theft, consumption of alcohol, adultery) and exhortations to help the local inhabitants by working with them in the fields, an important part of the practical side of the year's course. 'People liked the Khmer Issarak because we helped them a lot on their farms', Theam says.

Another section of the book was devoted to the art of guerrilla warfare – Theam took part in many military training exercises – and he proudly recounts its effectiveness. The Khmer Issarak controlled the jungle and the outlying areas, leaving 'only the roads' to the French. Theam estimates that if the colonial administration had not been handed over to King Sihanouk by the Geneva Conference of 1954, the monarch would have been in serious military trouble within two years. Achar Chum, a colleague of the nationalist monk Hem Chieu, was cited as the great military tactician of the Khmer revolution.[4]

As far as politics were concerned, lessons in the book dealt with French colonialism, and its economic oppression, and Khmer nationalism. Hem Chieu was much praised for his 'spirit of freedom',[5] while a 19th-Century figure, Pou Kombo (or Achar Leak), was honoured as Kampuchea's first nationalist hero for rebelling against the French and King Norodom in the 1860s.

Two teachers whom Theam recalls vividly were Achar Leak, a dark-skinned revolutionary who had adopted Pou Kombo's religious title,[6] and Achar Pres, also named after a 19th-Century rebel leader.[7] Pres, Theam recalls, was very light in complexion; neither was of local origin – both spoke with a Phnom Penh accent. In fact, Achar Pres had participated in the July 1942 demonstration against the French, calling for the release of Hem Chieu. Theam remembers Pres saying that it was the repression following this demonstration which made him realize that 'the peaceful road to independence had failed', and so he had taken to the rural areas to 'wake up' the people and lead them in the armed struggle against the French invaders. Although Pres referred to himself as a 'socialist' rather than a 'Communist', Theam remembers him as 'very red'. His teachings often referred to the 'abolition of exploitation' and to 'the creation of a classless society', as well as to anti-colonialism. Both Pres and Leak worked closely with Vietnamese revolutionaries, Theam says.

While Leak and Pres were religious men – according to Theam they were very learned in Buddhist philosophy, they always wore the *achar's* black trousers and white shirt, they were not adorned with magical tattoos or pendants and they harboured none of the local superstitions of monks from isolated areas – they were also strongly opposed to wealthy merchants and middlemen, to the money-lenders who charged the peasants '300-400%' interest rates and to the capitalist class. According to Theam, few people of status cared as much as they did about alleviating the plight of the poor and the peasants. Theam notes that nearly all the people in the area were poor peasants, apart from a small number of traders and money-lenders.

At the end of his course, Theam re-entered Brigade 140, which (with apparent exaggeration) he says was a 'shock troop' of over 2,000 Issarak soldiers, 300-400 of whom were Vietnamese. The Brigade's task was to come to the assistance of local troops in action against colonial forces in any part of Battambang Province. Brigade 140 was named after Achar Chum. It was commanded by a Khmer named Chey Samreth, with a Vietnamese called Yeih as second-in-command. Other Issarak 'brigades' were 127 (named after Pou Kombo) and 180, which were attached to other provincial headquarters, and 516, the district-level militia in Battambang.

The troops in 'brigades', 140 and 516, when combined with the *senachon,* may have brought Khmer Issarak strength in the northwest alone to about 5,000, a figure close to the generally accepted Western estimates of the revolutionary forces *throughout Kampuchea* at this time. Charles Meyer, for instance, gives a figure of 'a minimum of 5,000'.[8] Francois Ponchaud gives the same figure. Laura Summers says that in January 1953 there were '8,000 Issaraks, divided into several tendencies',[9] of which the Communist-led movement in which Theam participated was only one.

A new look at the Khmer Issarak also seems necessary in view of Theam's assertion that around 1950-51, the Vietnamese and Kampuchean soldiers began to form into separate units. 'The Vietnamese lost influence', and 'didn't eat in the same mess any more', Theam says. In 1951, Sieu Heng returned from his period of study (which we know from other sources included some time in Vietnam) to take over control of all Issarak operations in Battambang Province. Sieu Heng was 'capable', according to Theam, and the Vietnamese 'cooled down' and 'stopped showing off'.

Sieu Heng's organization consisted of three branches – the *military* brigades under Moul Sambath, *economics* (logistics and food supply) under Long Reth, and *politics* (administration, education and propaganda) under Achar Bun Kasem. Theam remembers Kasem as an orator. One of his speeches dealt with the French demand that Kampucheans buy and carry identification cards:

> You have to pay 25 riels for your I.D. cards, but what good do they do you? Your great-grandfather never needed one, but your grandfather was jailed if he didn't have one. You wait for years for them to do you some good, but they never do. Why?

> And what about these roads that the French make us build? They are no good to us either. They are only used by the French, and by the people who have cars . . . .

One of the most dramatic episodes in Theam's career as an Issarak was the French bombing of the fortress at Anlong Phiem. In 1951, near the end of the second intake of Khmer Issarak youth, word was received through spies in the French forces of an impending bombing raid. Right at the end of an afternoon lesson, a frantic evacuation began. The shock troops gave their assistance. Everything portable, including the electricity generators, was carried during the night on ox-carts 20 kilometres through the jungle, to an even larger fortress to the south-west, in the Ta Sanh-Kranhoung area. The bombing began at 8 a.m. the next morning and lasted six hours. The Issarak troops suffered no casualties, although a number of local villagers were killed.

One thing that stays in Theam's mind is that Lon Nol, then a colonel in the French colonial army, took part in the bombing operation. Another is that the Issarak agents in the colonial forces were later identified and executed.

In July 1952, Theam applied to leave the Issarak movement to become a Buddhist monk. He was somewhat disillusioned, especially with the 'jealousy' that he says often existed between members. He believes that people were sometimes wrongly executed as 'spies', simply because of this jealousy. (In another context, Theam explained that 'mistakes' and 'crimes' were as a rule dealt with by political re-education for the first and second offences, while a third would mean execution.) It took another three months, and the intercession of the Chief Monk of Thvak Pagoda, before Theam received permission to leave. Issarak leaders tried to discourage him from joining a monastery, which they said would be 'useless'. But Theam persisted, pointing out that all young Khmer men customarily spent three months at least in a pagoda. He also mentioned that he saw the pagoda as a means of educating himself, and of paying his moral debt to his parents. Theam also notes that he wanted to clear his name as a 'rebel'; whether he regretted his three years in the revolutionary movement, or whether he feared reprisal by the administration, is not clear.

Late in 1952, Theam entered the pagoda at Thvak, not far from Samlaut, and remained there for 17 years.

Norodom Sihanouk

Theam's impressions of Sihanouk, possibly atypical because of the extent of his political training, are interesting. While he claims that the Issaraks would have won the war if the Geneva Conference had not taken place, he attributes this to their training. On the other hand, he says, their 'psychological policies' were not as effective as those of Sihanouk. Although people in the Samlaut area, heavily influenced by the revolutionaries, considered the monarch a 'puppet' of the French, Theam concedes that there were many others who thought of him as their 'god-king', and who had become emotionally attached to him. Theam used a Khmer expression, 'they could only see as far as the tip of their nose', to describe what he considers to be the political ignorance of such people. He continued: 'If you watch him and listen to him speak, you grow to be fond of him; but if you think harder about what he says, you realize that what he says is good, but what he actually does is not so good. . . Sihanouk is sometimes good and sometimes bad.'

On the other hand, Theam admits that by the end of 1955, when Sihanouk had obtained considerable power, many people changed their minds about him because he was 'doing something for the country'. But some of the local people in Samlaut continued to support the revolutionary movement nonetheless, and this is confirmed by the events of the elections of late 1955. The International Commission for Supervision and Control reported that Suon Seng, a campaign officer for the Communist Pracheachon, had disappeared during the elections after being shot at by government troops in Battambang Province. However, despite such repression of his party, the Pracheachon candidate in southern Battambang, Mel Van, received 2,900 of the 7,000 votes cast.

References

1. Personal communication from Andrew Antippus, who interviewed Sieu Heng in late 1970.
2. Theam also said he remembered the name Pol Pot from his Issarak days; he held to this under questioning, insisting that April 1976, when a man called Pol Pot became Prime Minister of Democratic Kampuchea, was not the first time he had heard that name. However, it seems impossible that Saloth Sar, who only in 1976-77 publicly became known as Pol Pot, could have been known to Theam in the early 1950s. Saloth Sar returned to Kampuchea from France in January 1953. He did not hold an important position in the anti-French resistance. There is a slight possibility, however, that there was *another* Pol Pot (see Part III).
3. Charles Meyer, *Derriere le Sourire Khmer* (Paris, Plon, 1971), p.186.
4. Theam pointed out that Achar Chum was not the same man as Khieu Chum, a monk who also took part in the 1942 demonstration and later became associated with the Lon Nol regime.
5. On 11 June 1950, the Issarak revolutionary leadership formally opened the 'Achar Hem Chieu Political School' in a liberated area of south-west Kampuchea. 140 students from all over the country made up the first intake. Lessons included 'the place of the Khmer revolution in the Indochinese revolution'. By March 1951, the fifth intake of students in this school had begun.

6. French historian Jean Moura says Pou Kombo 'was called Achar Leak by the people', *Le Royaume du Cambodge* (Paris, Ernest Leroux, 1887, p.159.

7. In 1866 Achar Pres, a native of Kompong Svay in Kompong Thom Province, worked with other Kampuchean rebel leaders Snang Sor and Achar Prak to recruit 100 followers in Nang Rong, a Khmer district of modern Thailand, south of Korat. They then began an unsuccessful march on Thai-held Siemreap and Angkor Wat. We are grateful to Chalong Soontranavich for this information from official Thai-language documents.

   Other Communist-led Issarak forces in eastern Kampuchea at this time adopted the names Si Votha (a mixed Khmer-Vietnamese unit, which in May 1952 numbered over 200 troops, on both sides of the Mekong in Kompong Cham Province). Achar Chieu (over 100 soldiers in Prey Veng) and Ang Phim. There was also unit 127 in eastern Kompong Cham named after Pou Kombo. Archives d'Outre-Mer, Cambodge 7F 29 (7), *Etude sur les Mouvements Rebelles au Cambodge, 1942-52,* map.

8. Meyer, op. cit., p.187.

9. Cited in Noam Chomsky and Edward S. Herman, *The Political Economy of Human Rights,* Vol. 2, *After the Cataclysm: Postwar Indochina and the Reconstruction of Imperial Ideology,* (Boston, South End Press, 1979), p.365, note 211.

6. Solving Rural Problems: A Socialist programme to Safeguard the Nation by Hou Yuon

Introductory Note

In 1970, Sihanouk's former adviser, Charles Meyer wrote that 'no serious work of history, politics, economics or literature has been written and published in the Khmer language over the last fifteen years'.[1] *Hou Yuon's* The Co-operative Question, *published in Phnom Penh in late 1964, is one of the rare exceptions. The greater part of two of its three chapters are reproduced here in translation by Chanthou Boua.*

A secret Communist Party member and the country's leading leftist, Huo Yuon was largely outlining a blueprint for socailist transformation in Kampuchea, at least as far as this could be done in a climate of widespread political and cultural suppression. Perhaps more significantly, though, the book was also a blueprint for a 'United Front' between Communists and anti-imperialists, including the Sihanouk regime, against the United States. In that sense, then, the book was a proposal to the Government, by a former Minister of the Economy who was still an elected member of the National Assembly. Hou Yuon was attempting to combine the class struggle with the Sihanouk-led national anti-imperialist struggle. In his conclusion he wrote that Sihanouk's 'Popular Socialist Community movement has provided our peasants with a very efficient and sharp weapon. That weapon is the co-operative . . . The people cannot savour the idea of 'social priorities for the little people alone' without employing the co-operative set-up.' To achieve this, he argued, co-operatives should become 'a basic mass organisation to extract the wonderful taste of the best ideology of the Popular Socialist Community', so that 'the little people can hold their heads high and open their mouths freely [as] masters of the co-operatives for their own benefit, [through] very hard and intense struggle based largely on their class consciousness. As a result, the peasants will believe that 'their era has come!' '

Hou Yuon considered that Sihanouk's extensive nationalizations and rejection of U.S. aid in late 1963 created 'the possible means to build up the national economy in the interests of the people'; and he hoped – in vain, as was clear in three years' time showed – that this potential would be developed. His book may also be seen as a reply to the anti-Sihanouk activities of Communists like Pol Pot and Ieng Sary, who had gone underground in July 1963: 'We must understand that class conflict should be resolved by a method that will not damage the unity of the nation against the American imperialists'.

However, the book is also aimed at the rural population. Much of the imagery springs from the life style of those who 'live on land, as fish live in water'. Human labour is described by the use of the term kamlang bae, *'the strength that comes from rice'; co-operatives are said to be, in literal translation, 'seed-beds for sowing and nourishing co-operative consciousness'. The author is clearly concerned that his argument is understandable to people not versed in political discourse. There is occasional repetition and slow logical progress, as in the following passage:*

> *Labour power or work is an instrument of the productive forces. When we say a person is working for someone else, we mean that that person is selling their labour power to someone else. Someone who is working is expending their labour power. Work is the expenditure of labour power, the transmission of energy. That is why people get tired, and are forced to rest.*

Even this astonishing tautology is seen as necessary, presumably for emphasis: 'The masses of the people are an absolute majority in our national society'.

Although Yuon 'stands by' the peasantry in vigorously dismissing critics who blame them for their own poverty, he does not see the issue as primarily a moral one arising from the 'faults' of individuals or groups. Rather, it is a social struggle that arises out of material conditions. 'The poor lower class is the class which represents truth and faithfulness, because *this class have their own experiences, they actively engage in productive work . . . . practice is the basis of truth'. Elsewhere he continues:*

> *The words used to insult the poor are: 'You are poor because you are lazy and worthless.'* Whether these insulting words are true or not is another question, *but oppression through high land rents and interest rates, which crushes tenants and debtors, has left no hope for its victims.*

In his 1955 thesis, Yuon writes: 'The low level of labour productivity of our peasants is a result of the primitive and archaic state of the tools and techniques of their labour, rather than of their clumsiness, their inbred habits, or their laziness so much'. Or, he might have added, of simply the lack of a 'correct and clear-sighted leadership' over the past 1,000 years. Quite possibly a distinction between Hou Yuon's socio-economic and materialistic perspective and what might be called the 'moral' standpoint of psychological rebirth, political tactics and military force, independent of material circumstances, that seems to have dominated the ideology of the Pol Pot regime (see Part III), *is perceptible here.*

Hou Yuon also stresses that 'economic progress must be built on the foundation of modern technology', a statement with which Pol Pot after 1975 is unlikely to have agreed. Yuon lamented the fact that 'low quality productive forces and outdated tools require intense human labour . . . hard work. No matter how hard one tries, production is low and disproportionate to the labour input'.

Not only the materialism and the pro-technology aspects of his position, but also the cautious, step-by-step approach to rural social change advocated in this book differs from that later adopted by the Pol Pot regime. Yuon points out that 'common property co-operatives . . . need a high degree of awareness among the peasants . . . This process is slow, it takes a long time, and cannot be achieved immediately'. Labour pools and production co-operatives, however, 'are very suitable for the present situation, which is not too advanced; our people can understand and participate in them. We understand that the plans should not be too advanced'.

Yuon also places great emphasis on the need for democratic processes in the organization of co-operatives. Even allowing for the vast difference between 'the present situation' of 1964 and the circumstances prevailing after the 1970-75 War, it seems clear that the rural co-operatives of the Pol Pot period were not those envisaged by Hou Yuon 10 years before. Even the 'higher-stage co-operatives' which he described as 'the concept of the future' differ from organizations of the same name established by Pol Pot's regime. While Yuon envisaged communalization of the means of production, he saw the crop being shared among members according to workdays performed – not as rations doled out more or less arbitrarily according to one's perceived social or political or geographical background, and not in institutionalized communal meal sittings. Yuon also outlined legal autonomy for co-operatives vis-a-vis the state, with relationships based on cash transactions and contracts between various government and popular organizations.

Introduction

The economic and financial reforms of Samdech Sahachivin,[2] President of the Sangkum Reastr Niyum and the leader of the Khmer people, have made important changes to the structure of our economy and have brought three advantages for the advancement of the national economy, independence and progress: 1) The complete rejection of the poisonous aid of the American imperialists, with the royal form of nationalization of the banking industry, insurance industry and foreign trade, has given the Royal Government the possible means to build up the national economy in the interests of the people. 2) The economic and financial reforms have given a new lease of life for national capitalism to progress cleanly in the interests of the nation and the people. The imperialism of international capital has to a large degree been reduced, and it does not exploit the national economy as it did before. 3) The economic and financial reforms have brought bright new changes for the farmers and the workers in general.

Because of the three above advantages, the nation's independent spirit in struggling against American imperialism and its lackeys has been further strengthened, on the road to political independence, peace and neutrality, and an independent, progressive economy . . . .

Our country at present is confronting voracious and inhumane aggression from the American imperialists and their lackeys. At present, the main contradiction is the one between the whole Khmer nation and the American imperialists. This is the conflict between the Khmer people and their enemy, the final stage of the evolution of our country.

The unity of the Khmer people at present is the unity of all those Khmers who consider the American imperialists to be the most dangerous enemy of the Khmer people. Other people who find advantages in the conflict with the American imperialists may also join. The unifying force within the United Front against the American imperialists and their lackeys is the safeguarding of independence, peace, neutrality, territorial integrity and development.

In order to strengthen the bonds of unity against the imperialists, we also have a programme to resolve the internal conflicts among the people as well. The internal conflict is quite different in character from the conflict with the enemy, such as that between our people and imperialism. So the method of resolving this conflict is different too. The conflict between the people and the American imperialists must be resolved by confrontation, or possibly armed confrontation. The internal conflict can be resolved by reconciling one another's interests, finding justice for one another based on democracy, equality and fraternity, and avoiding greedy exploitation of one class by another.

The middleman, the landowner, the poor peasant and the workers in general all have something to gain from the struggle against imperialism in order to 'safeguard independence, neutrality and peace'. But among these classes there is also conflict. We must understand that class conflict should be resolved by a method that will not damage the unity of the nation against the American imperialists and their lackeys. We must understand that: 1) If the internal conflict is correctly resolved in the framework of the conscious unity of the nation, the Front which strives against the imperialists will be much stronger and fiercer. 2) If the internal conflict is not correctly resolved in the framework of the conscious unity of the nation (or is not resolved at all), then the consequences will be bad for the Front in its struggle against imperialism, which will destroy its unity or weaken its ability to confront imperialism.

If one considers that the 1963 reforms are anti-imperialist in character and that they contribute to the construction of the national economy along the nationalist path, one can also consider the reforms a favourable opportunity to resolve the class conflict which exists among the people.

The struggle against imperialism, which is the enemy of the people, will only have full significance both politically and economically if the problem of oppression of a weak class by a strong one is correctly resolved.

Co-operatives are not born anywhere at any time. Sometimes they are created but are not successful. Why? The reason is that co-operatives are born out of a governmental, political, economic or cultural system. Another reason is that they are a sign of the struggle between classes which have opposing interests. If the governmental system does not allow co-operatives to come into being and progress, they cannot exist or prosper.

In the capitalist system where there is plenty of 'freedom', the co-operatives can exist indefinitely; there are laws about co-operatives, but no matter how large they are, they are unable to escape from oppression by the capitalist system. Capitalists are never worried by workers' co-operatives. This is because the capitalists still retain ownership of the industries, the banks, the companies, commerce and finance. They still control the economy. So in the 'free system' they allow the workers to compete freely with them! Sooner or later they will squeeze the workers' co-operatives, and change them into instruments to serve their own interests! This lack of concern on the part of the capitalists can be considered a signal which calls for immediate deep reflection about co-operative consciousness!

In the socialist system, co-operatives have progressed amid tremendous activity. This is because the socialist system takes the co-operative political road. Co-operatives are a method to build up the national economy of the socialist regime. Any systematic programme which is opposed to them or does not foster them must change into one which is in line with co-operatives and fosters them devotedly.

Our country, just like any other in the world, must advance. Economic progress must be built on the foundation of modern technology. Given our country's qualities, how can we introduce modern technology to increase production? The problem of co-operatives in our context is the problem of transforming an economy subject to nature into a progressive economy based on modern technology. The problem of transforming the rural economy is not just one of expertise, but also a political and social problem, where technology is only a means to increase production. The problem of co-operatives is the same. The co-operative problem is a political problem, a social problem, a technological problem, all in one. But if the basic political problem is not solved, there will be no hint of a solution to the other problems.

Co-operative Methods

There are two sorts of rural problems:

1) *The problem of building up the productive forces, to expand and modernize them.* What is it that keeps the productive forces weak? We can

enumerate as follows. Technology and work techniques are still very old and outdated and demand a lot of hard work, while production is slow. The landholding system is irrational and prevents the full use of technology and organization for the modernization of agriculture – *commercial* capital and *usury* capital are oppressive, tying down the rural economy, preventing it from rapidly progressing. This is one rural problem which has technological ramifications. It is also an important problem, and can only be solved if the rural problem, which is a social problem, is also solved.

2) *The problem of liberating the peasantry from the hold of 'commercial capital' and 'usury capital' and preventing their descent into slavery.* Peasants are held in the grasp of commercial capital and usury. Commercial organizations are like a large spider-web trapping them. On the other hand, a number of peasants have fallen into the class of citizens of humble rank. This tendency increases all the time. The evolution of the rural areas will continue in this way so long as the means of earning a living through agriculture remain unchanged.

How can the two rural problems be solved in the peasants' interests? We must emphasize that they must *be solved in the peasants' interests,* because to solve them without benefiting the peasants would solve nothing at all.[3] We must not forget that the rural problem as described above is two-sided, that is, it has both technological and social aspects.

Our country, like any other, cannot ignore modern technology, which must be applied in one way or another in agriculture. This is because modern technology is much more efficient than the old methods. We will now discuss the methods which technology can introduce to further our two goals, that is, increasing production by increasing the forces of production, and solving the problems relating to human beings (social problems).

In a number of non-socialist countries, the exploitation of farm land has been assisted by modern methods; agricultural production has increased tremendously because agricultural machinery and science have challenged the power of nature. But a number of peasants have descended into the ranks of agricultural labourers, living by selling their labour. The introduction of modern technology seems to place a heavy burden on the necks of the workers.

Co-operative methods can solve both these aspects of the rural problem in the interests of the peasants by full use of scientific and technological methods, and also by increasing the standard of living of the workers. Workers thus need not become *servants or coolies* of the capitalists, living in low status by selling their labour to them. Co-operatives support the workers so that they become the masters of their lives, their possessions and their work. If the co-operative concept is correct, the rural problems can be solved while supporting the peasants and raising them to their deserved status.

Taking up the questions we have raised above concerning the elements of the rural problem, we would like to describe and analyse four types of co-operatives, with the aim of solving the problem in the interest of the peasants . . . .

Labour Pools: [4]

Labour power or work is an instrument of the productive forces. When we say a person is working for someone else, we mean that that person is selling his labour power to someone else. Someone who is working is expending their labour power. Work is the expenditure of labour power, the transmission of energy. That is why people get tired, and are forced to rest.

Each person can work alone, doing his work separately without co-operating with others. But people can also work together; they have an interest in 'accumulating their labour power' in order to get a job done. 'The accumulation of labour power' increases 'the productive forces'. For example, one person can plough one plot per day, two people working separately can plough two plots per day, but two people mustering their strength can plough three plots per day. *The productive forces are thus increased by the accumulation of their labour power.*

In our country a good practice called 'mutual help' *(yok dai khnia)* or 'helping in turns' *(yok vei khnia)* merits attention. Our peasants have known and practised this custom up to the present day. Labour pools should support this worthwhile custom, maintain this positive attitude and establish it permanently using their reasoning power.

This type of 'co-operative' does not interfere with any rights or interests of the peasants. Each peasant has every right to choose the sort of crop he cultivates according to his own preference. 'They can grow corn, tobacco, beans, rice . . according to their desires, nobody orders them to grow anything else'. Also, they can choose the times when they want to work . . . . They are masters of their possessions, land, tools, beasts of burden and of their produce.

The only difference is that they 'accumulate their labour power'. They work on the land together, they accumulate their working strength, they co-operate with one another. But even though the co-operatives only reach this stage, the productive forces are greatly increased . . . .

If this type of co-operation is instituted with an organization, then its effect will be increased and the productive forces will be greater. An organization with leaders and some regulations has the following advantages:

1) Haphazardly and sporadically organized *(royik royauk)* co-operation becomes a permanent organization. This permanence is very important in organizing all sorts of tasks, such as allocating the numbers of people for jobs, allocating times and days, the division of labour, mustering labour power, and also methods of confronting crises, such as floods, fires, etc.

A permanent organization facilitates the satisfactory solution of problems, such as 'repaying by turns' (*song ven)* and the question of the price of reciprocal assistance. Present-day practice determines this by reference to the number of days worked. Repayment is calculated on the basis of the number of days of work owed. But there is a difficulty, when the number of days required differ. Some have small farms, and others have larger ones. So those who have less land can cease working in the 'mutual help' scheme when their needs have been fulfilled. Those who have more land then have to work on alone. This sort of thing breaks up co-operation, and makes it less efficient. The problem can be solved by fixing repayment in terms of *money or goods.* For example, one day's work equals a certain number of riels, or a certain number of thang of rice. This way people would be working together in co-operation from beginning to end; the work is finally completed without interruption. Such co-operation would be strong.

2) Such an organization can expand its activities. In the windy season (December-February), co-operation would not be disbanded. The co-operative organization can plan further programmes for its members. It can create supplementary employment in the windy season, such as forays into the jungle for firewood, making sugar palm juice, raising livestock, transporting goods, weaving grass mats or baskets, etc. Or the co-operative organization can muster labour to raise dykes, dig canals, lakes and ponds, level the land, build and repair roads for the transportation of produce, make fertilizer in various ways, etc. Or people can work together to clean up the village according to health regulations, or to organize local cultural activities, etc. . . .[5]

As described above, labour pools fall into two categories:

1) Labour pools that are seasonal, or occasional. Our peasants are familiar with this type of co-operation, and used to participate in them. If they are unqualified to become labour pools of the second type, this method can be preserved but should be re-arranged, corrected and shaped to make the system work better. For example, the repayment by turns *(song ven)* system, organizational methods, expansion of their activities, etc. And with that there should be a definite programme for gradual change into a group of the second type.

2) Labour pools that exist permanently in the sense described above. If they are sufficiently qualified, the second stage of co-operation can be created straight away without passing through the first stage. But normally the second type is a development of the first. Also, the second type can develop its qualities into those of a more advanced stage of co-operative. Development from the first to the second type depends on several factors, such as geography (depending on the region, the nature of the land), society, culture, economics and politics.

Talking in terms of co-operatives, groups which accumulate the productive forces are seed-beds for implanting and fostering co-operative consciousness. Co-operatives cannot be created if there is no co-operative consciousness and a sense of common interest. Labour pools are the first step in establishing production co-operatives. We believe the more advanced production co-operatives must go through this process; labour pools are the first basic step which must be taken. If this stage is consolidated, the advanced production co-operatives will also be strong . . . .

Production Co-operatives

This type of co-operative is more advanced than the simple labour pools. The establishment of this type of co-operative has a deeper impact. It accumulates the labour force like the co-operatives described above, but it includes the material forces as well, and in particular a stronger and more solid organization is established.

In these production co-operatives, each member is willing to pool their land, ox, buffalo, rake, plough and other working tools to utilize their combined forces. But each person is still the owner of his or her property – it is not communalized.

The other particular quality is the establishment of an organization which is properly run by a committee. This committee has to control the project of increasing all production, and in particular looks after and controls the equipment which is pooled, draws up programmes and plans activities so that the equipment is used with the best possible results. Individual ownership, but common control; common usage for common interests.

The division of the produce obtained by common effort must be on the basis of the continuing ownership rights. Produce can be divided into three portions:

1) The first portion must be divided amongst the members of the co-operatives taking into account two factors. Firstly, their property (land, ox, buffalo . . .). Each member receives more or less, according to whether they have more or less property. Secondly, the amount of workdays each has put in for the co-operative. Those who work fewer days receive a greater portion [sic] . So, with this method, we take into account both property owned and work performed. It is true that a method must be found for correctly evaluating the property which is pooled, so that injustice is prevented. All these procedures must be worked out democratically.

2) The second portion of the produce is for the co-operative to retain, that is, in the interests of all the members. Co-operatives are communal organizations which must develop progressively in order to serve the members. They must increase the productive forces using all possible means, such as building a workshop to make and repair tools, making natural fertilizers, buying machinery, buying chemical fertilizers . . . buying high-quality seed, conducting experiments, enlarging the cultivated area, etc. Co-operatives must have their own funds in order to increase their activities in the interests of all their members.

3) The third portion is for the social and cultural activities, such as a first-aid post, a school, facilities to train technicians, etc., of the co-operative, for which there must be a budget . . . .

Usually the produce would be divided into these three portions, between the members, for the co-operative's productive forces, for the co-operative's social activities, but this depends on a decision satisfactory to the members of the co-operative. Also, the allocation of a percentage for each portion must take into account what the members need to live, to progress, and also how to keep the co-operative alive and moving forward.

This type of production co-operative can bring the following advantages: First, the co-operative is of sufficient quality to utilize modern technology. Large areas of cultivated land mean that crops can be chosen that are suitable to the type of land (this plot grows this crop, that plot grows that crop), crops can be rotated (this year this crop, next year another crop, or leave the land fallow for a period), agricultural machinery and scientific techniques can be used as needed, and planning against drought or flood or pests is to a great extent facilitated.

Secondly, the co-operative's own extensive funds facilitate the running of social, economic and cultural affairs.

Thirdly, the co-operative, with defined organization and leadership, is a good basis for common success and decision-making that allow for planning of production and of other activities.

The co-operative has another new possibility, that of liaison with the government on technological, financial and administrative matters. Production co-operatives may be created using lanour pools of the second type as their base, or they can be built on brand new foundations. According to this evolution, labour pools of the second type must change slowly into the production co-operative stage. But if they are of sufficient quality, production co-operatives can be built on brand new foundations, for example, on newly cleared land distributed to the people. However, in order to establish production co-operatives, economic, social and cultural and political standards must be all sufficiently high.

The labour pools and production co-operatives are widely applicable in our country. In our opinion, we should give careful consideration to these two forms, and draw up plans to put them into practice, because the masses have hundreds of years of experience with labour pools and also because production co-operatives can solve production problems which the masses face. We know that the peasants would understand and would be willing to support strongly plans that the Royal Government implements along these lines.

The two above aspects of co-operation [labour pools and production co-operatives] are very suitable for the present situation, which is not too advanced; our people can understand and participate in them. We understand that the plans should not be too advanced. Although production co-operatives of this type do not yet lead to complete and efficient achievement of increased productive forces, nevertheless, we know that the results from that degree of co-operation would be good enough if it could be implemented.

Higher stage co-operatives, as described below, give us some indication of the concept of the future.

Common Property Co-operatives

This type of co-operative makes for closer co-operation and more efficient control and leadership, that is, its quality is sufficient to boost the level of production. Common property co-operatives are a higher stage than labour pools and production co-operatives. Members overwhelmingly agree to pool their wealth for common prosperity. Each member no longer has any rights to his wealth, which has been pooled. Land, oxen, buffaloes, all tools *now become common property, for the use of the common organization.*

It is true that pooling of property must be done by a method that ensures that property owners do not come off badly (such as selling their property to the co-operative, or receiving in return for their property a share in terms of goods . . .). This depends on the joint decision of the members of the co-operative.

When the co-operative comes into being, no member has any special privileges for himself within it. All the property which is pooled co-operatively becomes common property and belongs to every member. Members can own personal property which is not pooled co-operatively – this property can be owned individually and each member can use it as he wishes.

The common property must be under common control and direction, led by a group leadership established democratically by all the members of the co-operative. This directing organization has the right to act on behalf of the members. Every year (for example) members participate in a general meeting in order to examine closely the work of the directing organization and to choose members to become new leaders. After discussion of the activities of the directing organization, the general meeting sets up the plans or tasks for it to fulfil in the future.

How is the produce to be divided among the members? Because they are no longer owners of private property, the produce is divided only on the basis of the number of work days each performs. All the members are the owners of the co-operative's property; all the co-operative's produce is the property of the members. Members get a greater or lesser share depending on the number of work days they put in for the co-operative. There are no other factors to be taken into account.

So, are members of the co-operative in a similar position to that of workers who work for capitalists in return for money? No, they are not. The capitalists are the sole owners of property; they can administer it however they want; they can tell people what to do and how to do it; it is all up to them. They can limit wages to whatever they want to. Workers who need a living sell their labour to them. They are willing to sell their labour and do whatever they are told, they have no right to disagree or question their position. Whether profit or loss is made depends on the property owner. Workers must be careful in case they get sacked or get their wages reduced or get penalized for negligence, daydreaming or lateness! Members of co-operatives are joint owners and have common ownership rights over their property; they set themselves up and are their own masters; they are responsible for the good or bad results they get. They set their own tasks, and the benefits are divided according to the methods and regulations they set up themselves. Although no member is in direct control, each can express his ideas by voting to choose the members of the committee. The co-operative's regulations preserve full rights for the members . . . .

In the capitalist system, workers are servants, selling their labour to the capitalists. The capitalists prosper by living off the workers. Workers are goods, like fish sauce or monosodium glutamate, which the capitalists buy at the market known as the 'labour market'. The value of the workers' 'labour power' is the same as the value of any other commodity – that is, if there is more available, the value goes down; if there is less, the value goes up. If there is no demand, they are discarded. Co-operatives preserve the dignity and the value of the people. A lot of people combine their labour power, their enthusiasm, their wealth, and work co-operatively on the basis of strict equality, helping each other to maintain their dignity and value. They develop common happiness as 'free men' *(neak chea).* Co-operation is a system where 'people aid people to become equal in terms of rights and in terms of their standard of living'.

1) Common property co-operatives have sufficient capacity to utilize modern technology. This type of organization has increased productive forces, both financial and material. Co-operatives can accumulate lots of money (by direct saving or borrowing from various financial institutions) and so can easily expand their activities. Co-operatives with large enough land areas can use machinery, modern equipment and other scientific methods without any difficulty. One reason is that the area of land is large enough for the capacity of machinery; another is that crops can be introduced that are suitable to the soil type, and rotated, or the land can be left fallow for a period (to preserve the fertility of the soil). Besides these advantages, the soil can be improved where necessary, dykes can be raised, roads built, lakes and water channels dug, depending on needs and in the interest of production, because the obstacles that private property raises no longer exist. The private property system is a very narrow framework – it prevents these methods being used. Some clear examples can be shown: water is needed, but dykes and canals cannot be dug for one person, because his plot of land is so small, too narrow to allow one person to develop such projects. Every year, the production potential of our peasants is largely dissipated because of the narrow framework they work in. This problem is critical in the rural areas and has not yet been resolved. For instance: the problem of roads, dykes, canals. Every year our peasants worry a lot about these problems, which cannot be solved to everybody's satisfaction. This situation leads to disputes between peasants, who become divided. This is not in their interest because they all suffer from it. It raises the problems of land rent, of foreign property holdings, of buying land to raise dykes, dig channels, store water, etc.

A small narrow plot of land, held as private property, works against the use of modern technology. Whether we want it to or not, our country must develop; modern technology forces its use on us. We must resolve this problem. Our peasants should look for ways to do this, in their own interest; otherwise the problem will be solved in the peasants' ignorance, or in fact by a method which is detrimental to their interests. Our peasants should not wait until *machinery runs them off their land* . . . .

Small and destitute property holders cannot plan like the capitalists. They raise dykes to store water, but then the water floods half their crop! When this happens how can they drain it away? Through whose land can they dig canals to carry it away? When worms destroy cotton crops, science recommends that the cotton plants be dug up and burnt, to prevent the worm from spreading to neighbouring land. If this is done, what is left over? It's all gone! Small and destitute property holders become smaller and more destitute! . . .

2) If the common property co-operatives come into being and firmly hold on to this philosophy, members will have a new consciousness, that is, a sense of common interest, a sense of common property. It is true that common property co-operatives must first be built on the foundations of a 'common consciousness' before they come into being. When they do, this consciousness develops, and takes on a better and purer quality; their power helps them spread to neighbouring areas by revealing their actual advantages.

3) Common property co-operatives need many qualities, especially political ones, and a high degree of awareness among the peasants. In order to reach this stage, there must be a change from a 'philosophy of private ownership' to one of 'common ownership'. This process is slow; it takes a long time, and cannot be achieved immediately.

In the development of co-operation, common property co-operatives are an advanced stage of production co-operatives. Production co-operatives develop into common property co-operatives. The plans necessary to increase production push development to this stage.

Besides this development, common property co-operatives can also come into being where poor peasants without land establish a new life and start to carry out their agricultural pursuits on new land. Instead of dividing the land into private holdings, the new land can be held as common property from the beginning.[6] If its political road is similar to that described above, and various projects are put under way to support the system, we think that, in the interest of the poor landless peasants who have no means of production or capital to back them up, this project can be attempted.

We have described 'co-operative production' of three types. We could work out other systems or give this one other names – the 'form' or 'name' is not important. The 'form', as we describe it, is concerned with the characteristics of co-operation itself. Fragmented co-operatives are not very advanced, because co-operative consciousness and a sense of common interest are still low. Political awareness is still at a low level. Unity, strong and close co-operation with a strong organization built on the foundation of a sense of common interest and a high level of political awareness, gives rise to an advanced type of co-operative. Between the early stages and the advanced stages, there are several intermediate types of co-operatives, depending on the levels of consciousness of the peasants.

There are several of these types of co-operatives because of the need to suit different circumstances and standards, such as geography, economics, society and culture, and politics as well. Where these circumstances are different, different types of co-operative should be worked out, in order to ensure their suitability. It is true that we should not depend completely on the existing situation, that qualities should be developed in full; but this creation must conform to the actual existing situation. If care is not taken on this point, the future of the co-operatives will not be bright.

Co-operative production of all types can be established. Our purpose in this book is to *transform and develop the rural economy, based on establishing the peasant as the key to the organization of production.* We see it this way because the organization of peasants into co-operatives is very important. *Unless they are organized, the peasants have no power, and do not have complete capacity to defend their standard of living. With an organization. the peasants have power, and the capacity and the opportunity to defend and build their standard of living to one of happiness and dignity.*

Co-operatives that Provide Means of Production and Sell Produce

Besides the usual consumption goods, the peasant needs another type of goods to increase production. These goods, like any others, are always sold to the peasants *at high prices.* Although the means of production do not satisfy the hunger of human beings, they are very important in productive work. It is these means of production that increase and develop production. Without strong productive forces, production will never increase. So a plan should be worked out to provide the means of production directly to the peasants, to prevent unreasonable profiteering. When the means of production for some reason are too expensive, production will progress slowly, or will stay at a very low level.

In our country, there is as yet no industry to produce the instruments of production. We have to import even relatively ancient means of production, even axes, harrows and spades, let alone machinery, chemical fertilizer, insecticides, etc, which we cannot produce ourselves. Usually, imported goods are very expensive, so any additional unreasonable profiteering should be avoided. At the beginning of this section we said that the majority of the peasants have no opportunity to buy tractors or other machinery and have shown that the problem can only be solved by establishing co-operatives. But each peasant can afford to buy and use normal everyday tools. These are the tools we will discuss in this section . . . .

In this case, the peasants can unite to create *'an organization for common use'*. They put their money together to buy tractors or other machinery to be retained as common property over which everybody exercises control. The utilization of these machines must fit in with the timetable that has been drawn up and agreed upon. *'Groups for common use'* are a method that can be used to help solve financial problems of utilizing and repairing agricultural machinery.

Co-operatives that provide the means of production can fulfil another similar task, that is to handle the members' produce. We have said that 'the peasants sell cheaply'. In order to avoid price fixing at a low level, for the profit of the middleman, the co-operatives agree to sell the members' produce directly. They transport and sell directly (to government agencies or private organizations) independent of the middleman.

We cannot only make a profit this way, but also understand commercial methods, such as the quality of the product (good, bad, as ordered, on time or late), the situation on the domestic and international markets, the demand etc. Knowledge gained from direct experience is of great advantage in planning to counter insufficiencies, and to select the crop (what crop to produce) to meet the demands of the constantly changing market. With this method, increases in production become scientific and no longer a matter of guesswork . . . .

On the commercial system which exists in our country, here we can point to two characteristics:

1) Trade is a type of manoeuvre for the maximization of profit; it is robbery to 'buy cheaply and sell expensively'.

2) The city market lives off the rural areas: 'the tree grows in the rural areas, but the fruit goes to the towns'.

Consumer Goods Co-operatives

The role of 'selling co-operatives' and 'consumer goods co-operatives' is to solve the problems of peasants 'selling cheaply' and 'buying expensively'. This means that these two types of co-operatives *must have the capacity to withstand the destructive power of the present commercial system over the production and living standards of the peasants.*

In order to carry out these tasks successfully, a correct co-operative concept is essential. According to our assessment, the correct concept is the concept of the *co-operative system.* This means that co-operatives must establish a trading system of 'doing commerce through co-operatives' to replace the present commercial system. Unless we have a well-designed concept, the co-operatives will not have the capacity to liberate the rural areas from the grasp of commercial capital. A concept of *isolated co-operatives* will not be able to carry out this role. Since the power of the present commercial system is so strong as to squeeze the rural areas dry, a 'haphazard co-operative concept' is useless and will only dampen the strong aspirations of the people. The concept that co-operatives are 'just to sell goods, as people usually do, by trying to sell cheaper than others', and the concept that 'co-operatives must hold to the rules of 'the woman of all virtue' *(setrei krupleak)*' – who never stares at anybody, who never trips anybody up though they stare at her or trip her – are incorrect. They just sap the will of the people and make them lose their direction, their aims and their beliefs; they just frustrate and disappoint the people's hopes. The reason is that these concepts are unable to stand up to the power of the present commercial system. The correct concept is the 'concept of the co-operative system', which aims to replace the present commercial system with 'co-operative commerce'. This gives people a definite direction through regular and dynamic planning, in order to move forward step by step until the new system replaces the old one. Only this concept enables us to form a co-operative movement . . . .

Co-operatives to Provide Capital

. . . In the National Congress,[7] a request was made to close down the pawn-brokers' shops, and to defend debtors by not recognizing debts that accrue without a formal contract and to abolish *tong tin.*[8] What was the people's reaction to these plans? In general, the people did not express support for them. On the contrary, they expressed concern. Why was this so? Because the usury system, the system of borrowing from each other and from pawn-brokers, has become the system that 'sustains' their livelihood. It is this system which they value; it helps them 'solve problems' now and again. 'The oppression of these people and their low value' is very real. But if that system is abolished, is there any other system or organization to replace it?

The duty of the 'co-operatives to provide capital' rests here – *they must replace all usury and pawnbroking systems.* That is why we suggest that a 'co-operative system concept' is more suitable than an 'isolated co-operative concept'. If the correct concept is adopted and adhered to steadfastly, the co-operatives will definitely be able to carry out their functions in every sphere. A 'haphazard co-operative concept' would not be able to carry out the role of *substitution.*

'Co-operatives to provide capital' must solve the three following important problems: the problem of raising credit for the peasants to draw on; the problem of ensuring that the peasant is entitled to draw credit; and the problem of utilizing the money that is borrowed for the purpose of production . . . .

The co-operative has some capital to enable it to operate. This fund comes from the members' shares, and from the government. *The government lends money at very low rates of interest, for which the peasant organization acts as a guarantor.* In this process, the authorities have the right to follow and maintain an interest in the co-operative's activities. The authorities are also responsible for the development of the co-operative, helping solve all the problems which the co-operative cannot correctly resolve on its own. The authorities help the co-operatives and will not abandon them; they lend them money and also help them to achieve their goals. This is in the interest of the government and also of the co-operatives. Without this philosophy, the co-operatives cannot borrow money, or if they can borrow it is uncertain whether the money can be used effectively to achieve its purpose.

The co-operative must also have the same duty to its members. The co-operative lends at very low interest rates, and must not demand members' property as security for these loans, because the members would then have no possibility of borrowing money. *For security, the co-operative must depend on the work and co-operative consciousness of each member.* The leaders of the co-operative have a duty to foster and consolidate co-operative consciousness, and, most important, to stimulate the members to engage in productive work. The leaders must help find methods of all kinds to assist the members to solve the problems that they face, especially in production. When production is satisfactory, the problem of security does not arise. Money in the bank or in financial institutions is for the rich to borrow. Money in the co-operatives to provide capital is for the poor peasants to borrow. This can be done only if the government and the leaders of the co-operatives have a different philosophy from that of capitalist financial institutions.[9]

People in charge of distributing seed and of providing capital to the peasants usually complain: 'They eat all the seed that is distributed to them, and they spend all the money we lend them, instead of producing'. It's like pouring water on a duck's head! Anything we give them, they consume. How can there be progress? As we have already described, the leaders of the co-operative must have plans to solve the following problems:

Firstly, to develop and expand and give value to co-operative consciousness, a consciousness of common interest, and a consciousness of changing their life style by using their own ideas and their own resources. The members of the co-operative must be politically aware.

Secondly, to work hard to lay the foundations for a new and dignified way of living, by relying on themselves through co-operation. They must have responsibility for their lives, as well as for the progress of the co-operative as a whole. They encourage savings, give value to a consciousness of organization, organizing themselves rationally in the interests of the co-operative.

Thirdly, to be fully concerned with production, encouraging members to work hard, setting up effective plans to increase the speed of production.

The Co-Operative Concept

In this section are raised some fundamental problems in order to clarify the co-operative philosophy in action. Co-operatives are the weapons of the people; they serve to defend their interests. This must be correctly implemented, all the time, so that the co-operatives will never become 'hybrids'.

Co-operatives Are the People's Organisations, to Serve the People's Interests

. . . To serve the interests of the people purely is hard. For one thing, people don't want to abandon their old customs readily, so long as there is no actual evidence to show that such a break is possible and will lead to better results. For another, it is hard to work out what the interests of the people are. Elements which are not in the people's interests can be compared to duckweed on water, which, when parted, always drifts back. Merchant capital and usury capital and the economic, social, cultural and political structure are like duckweed, oppressing the people everywhere, drifting back each time it is parted.

Our understanding is that we must establish a plan to part the duckweed and so allow the interests of the people to emerge. More correctly, we must dare to toss aside the duckweed or uproot the reeds, because if we only part it, the duckweed always drifts back; and if we only cut the reeds, they always grow back to damage the interests of the people again. Forming the workers into co-operatives is a method of struggle against natural forces in order to increase the productive forces, and then of struggle against the oppressive activities of merchant capital and usury capital, as well as against any profit made by the middleman and against any forces which actively suppress the interests of the people.

Co-operatives are organizations of the masses to enable them to struggle to achieve the above-mentioned purposes. In this struggle the masses are the rank and file and the leaders are the front commanders. The masses definitely need the commanders. *The masses need both administration and leadership.* The commanders represent the masses; they are the members who have woken up and who consciously struggle for the interests of the people. It is they whom the masses trust and regard as their teachers and leaders.

The co-operative leaders should educate the masses in both theory and practice. Theoretical education is aimed at the 'reflexes' of the masses, because these reflexes are very important influences with power to stir the masses into motion. The leaders must dare to provoke the consciousness of the masses continuously and nourish the ideology of the masses until the necessary point is attained where the duckweed is tossed aside and the reeds uprooted. Practical education must demonstrate all methods of struggle, varying with conditions and circumstances. In order to fulfil these duties, the leaders must abandon their own interests and stand for those of the people honestly and sincerely.

Co-operatives are organizations of struggle for the interests of the poor people. How can we struggle if we do not even dare to analyse clearly who, how and in what context are the enemies of the people? On which pattern should we struggle; what means or methods should we use? The peasants themselves need to know and want to understand these questions profoundly, in theory, in political direction and in practice. If the leaders hold firmly to these standpoints and reflect deeply upon them, the co-operatives then will be able to build up the struggling power of the masses, maintain indefinitely the struggling leap of the masses, obtain the proper methods of struggle to fit strategies and show the bright objective purposes of the struggle. When their consciousness is profoundly developed, the masses will have the strength to struggle fiercely, without easily becoming fed up with the idea or running away (with nothing to do) from the co-operative at the first setback.

Co-Operatives Must Definitely Place Common Interest Higher than Self-Interest

The co-operative process only advances smoothly when co-operative consciousness is growing and widening. This consciousness does not grow by itself. We must regularly and constantly teach and cultivate it. Co-operation is not a strange thing among our people; in practice, they very often co-operate among themselves. But institutionalized co-operation is a new method which our people do not often understand. So we should seriously cultivate this new way of thinking.

The economy in the rural areas is divided into small sections distinct from one another; this is the basis of the self-centred mentality of the peasants. It is usually noted that peasants are 'independent-minded' and believe strongly in 'individualism', think only of their own work, oppose rules and regulations and institutions, detest any strong, regular co-operative measures, etc . . . . We have already shown that merchant capital and usury capital are able actively to oppress the peasants because there are no institutions among the peasants. The inadequacy on this point stems from the basis of the peasant economy; it does not stem from hereditary attitudes. *It is their way of life that shapes the ideas of human beings.* Because of this, the peasants' individualism can be shed. Our understanding is that peasants will benefit from shedding the ideas that others describe as an 'independent and individualistic conception of themselves'. These ideas are at present their enemies; they tie the peasants down, maintaining them in a weak position indefinitely. Those who are the enemies of the peasants are not reluctant to propagate and praise the peasants' 'independent and individualistic conception of themselves', because if the peasants believe their propaganda and flattery, then they will be able to continue their oppression of the peasants. In order to confront this unfortunate propaganda the peasants must know and understand their class well, and develop their class consciousness. The co-operative is a new way to build a new economic foundation. This new foundation will develop and spread new ideas, the ideas of co-operation between peasants in co-operative organizations . . . .

A meeting chooses the leaders. *These positions must only be given to people who have brave and firm attitudes on serving the people, who do absolutely anything for the people, who place the interests of the people above their own interests and who have sufficient political awareness.* It is usually said that the duty of the leader is to educate and teach members. This is correct, but it is usually forgotten that the masses, the members, also have a duty to educate and teach their leaders. If the masses have the consciousness to support the leaders, then the quality of the leaders will improve all the time. A good leader, loved and trusted by the masses, is the leader who lowers himself to learn from the people, listens to the opinions of the people and carefully reflects on the experiences of the people well. In this way, a new category of people, who will be the leaders in the future, will emerge from among the masses.

Cliquism and nepotism, the inclination to create privileges for oneself or one's own group, are tendencies which usually exist in any established organization and in the minds of those who hold power. These two tendencies are disastrous for the organization and for co-operative consciousness. When these two tendencies exist and spread, the organization no longer stands on unity and the leaders no longer represent the interests of the masses . . . .

The leaders must live with the people, among the people, must educate and lead the people, understand the people, talk and discuss with the people, try consistently to make the people understand their common interests as well as everything about politics and the plans of the leading organization. When the people understand, believe and have no more doubts, they will work and apply the plans enthusiastically, with definite success. Bureaucratism is the attitude that only one person 'knows how to give orders and dispatch messages'; a person who doesn't know how to explain things and cannot be questioned, does not know how to discuss things to find out what is correct and incorrect, is arrogant in character, and considers proposals, queries or discussion contemptible or insubordinate! Acting like a *balat,*[10] on the presumption of 'being a boss in order to give orders', is in complete opposition to the democratic methods which must be practised in the co-operative. Co-operatives are democratic organizations which resist the acts of *balats. The peasants' organization can survive, if it is democratic.* The constitution of the co-operative must spell out the wide-ranging use of democracy . . . .

Co-Operatives Must Regard Long-term Interests as More Important than Immediate Interests

. . . Like any other organizations, co-operatives have expenses. The need for profit to meet expenditure is normal. The problem we are concerned with is: in what terms does the co-operative make profit?

In our co-operatives there are strong tendencies towards making profit in terms of money, just like the capitalist philosophy. Selling anyhow, anyway at all, even to the Chinese, as long as profit is made in terms of *money.* The leaders need the cash profit, and the members also claim profit dividends. In the co-operative movement in our country, there is even a tendency to claim dividends according to shares held, which completely opposes the co-operatives' rules. These tendencies show that capitalist ideology is crippling the co-operatives, spreading its influence into the co-operative movement . . . .

What is the proper philosophy? The proper philosophy is *to serve willingly rather than seek profit.* Co-operatives are organizations to serve the interests of the people. It is definitely not the co-operative philosophy to regard the search for profit as more important than willingness to serve.

Co-operatives serve willingly, but also do not disdain profit. *Increasing the capacity to assure the needs of the masses as much as possible is serving the people, and makes profit for them.* The fact that we make the people feel secure by providing them with a few advantages, in a stable environment, at reasonable prices, will definitely provide them with a 'profit': profit in putting an end to their fear and uncertainty, profit in benefiting from stable and reasonable prices, profit in having new types of communication in co-operation to raise their dignity as human beings, profit in having a new way of life, profit in having a new kind of administration, profit in having a bright future for the masses. As we have said, the masses obtain 'profit' both moral and material. There is also the possibility that the masses can obtain profit in terms of money if the co-operative is sufficiently healthy and strong.

We know that co-operatives must make profit to meet operational expenditure, such as salaries for personnel, material costs, interest and various other expenses, and in order to expand its activities. Our understanding is that profit must be used in two ways. Firstly, co-operatives must spend money operating the organization; without such expenditure we cannot see how it could operate. It is true that this expenditure must be handled carefully. Another expense is the growth of the activities of the co-operative, such as expanding production, expanding commercial activities so that the masses are provided with everything they need, increasing the amount of money available for members to borrow in order to defend them effectively against oppression by usury, etc. Co-operatives must put forward an explicit plan in order to succeed along the above lines. A general meeting must decide upon this, according to the wishes of the members, who always push for their immediate interests, and according to the long-term interests of the co-operative as well. This problem demands a fair and reasonable decision; we cannot completely dismiss either immediate interests or long-term interests. The two problems must complement and match each other for the co-operative to fulfil its role. However, immediate interests are not to be understood as principally making profit to divide amongst ourselves. Immediate interest in this context means serving and bolstering the people's standard of living, based on reasonable and stable prices for goods. Selling goods expensively makes more profit, but the members might find the hard way of life difficult to cope with; and if this line is implemented for a certain period without considering the people's standard of living, because of the desire to make quick profits, members might lose interest and no longer believe in the co-operative since they can see no long-term future advantages. On the other hand, selling cheaply and making little profit makes the members happy and favourable towards true co-operation. Primarily pursuing immediate interests is a course which will make the co-operative shrink, and set it back, with no capacity to assure the future standard of living of members. Co-operatives' leaders must be able to solve all these very complex problems; leaders must not be too soft and agree to everything members ask for, but also not so firm so as to become unbearable, with the result that members lose hope and withdraw from the co-operative.

A correct profit philosophy can bring good results for the co-operative and the nation. Initially, co-operatives need aid from the government in one way or another, but they must not depend on this aid forever, nor must they eat up all the aid they get. *Co-operatives must regard relying on their own strength as the most important line.* A co-operative must develop itself, using its own ideas and its own means. This is the only correct line, because it is faithful to the members and the nation. In the first stages, co-operatives need assistance from the government; co-operatives must pay the government back, and must help the government.

Co-Operatives Must Receive Strong and Regular Assistance from the Government

For the co-operative movement to progress consistently and in a lively manner, it must have the substance of a mass movement, and a spirit of awakening among the masses. But this spirit of awakening needs some assets to contribute to its development. The duty of the government is to create these assets, outlining and opening the way for the co-operative movement to develop consistently and in a lively manner.

The Government Shows the Way for the Co-Operatives: Co-operatives are the mass movement to change the economic and social system which oppress the masses' interests. Also co-operation is organization of the masses. Arising from these two characteristics, a co-operative has the elements of a democratic movement, so *a democratic and free system is an important condition of the co-operative.* In capitalist countries they give full rights (freedom) to the 'people'. Co-operatives and all types of organizations have been established, spread throughout every field of activity. Co-operatives are established according to the dictates of the law; there are laws to 'help' and support the co-operatives but, no matter how strong or rich they are, these co-operatives are all still in a subordinate position, colonized by the capitalist system. The bosses have no headaches nor do they feel insecure in the face of these co-operative activities, because they are masters of the factories, masters of finance and masters of the economy. The capitalist concept of the democratic free system has no real meaning or savour for the masses!

In order for the masses to relish a democratic free system, that system must have an economic foundation. It must also comprise democracy both in speech, inviting everybody to attend meetings, and in the economy, way of life and society – equality in standards of living. For the co-operative movement in our country, the masses need a deep-seated and tasty democratic free system . . . Our people need 'firm rights' with real meaning; they do not want 'hollow rights'. 'Firm rights' will always keep the co-operative movement moving spiritedly, while 'flimsy rights' make co-operation sluggish.

There should be a plan to guarantee the complete implementation of the democratic free system, which the Popular Socialist Community has given to the poor people, both in the general co-operative movement and in the internal affairs of the co-operatives. If there is a 'firm' philosophy of democracy and a successful application of democracy to build up the people's strength, then cliquism, nepotism and individualism will vanish. There must be strong measures to *enable a leap forward in strength, for the leadership of the co-operatives to be truly in the hands of the people, and working in the people's interests.*

It can be said that the co-operative problem is the problem of grabbing hold of the peasants or 'liberating' them from the power of old conservative traditions, from the power of the individualist philosophy, from the encircling and oppressive activities of merchant and usury capital, from the peasant way of life. This seizure cannot be successful unless the government's *co-operative leadership is decisive, constant and firm.* This leadership must give a clear direction to the peasants, ensuring that they understand the advantages and the bright, favourable future. Along with this *there must be a genuine and very detailed education programme* to inform fully and demonstrate how to implement the leadership's policy, the means to be used and obstacles which may be met during the operation, as well as methods to be used to overcome or avoid those obstacles. The policy of everyday encouragement by the co-operative leadership must be quite firm, since it brings two advantages. Firstly, it strengthens the co-operative consciousness and faith of the peasants, grasping their hopes and wishes so they will not dissolve away or diminish. Secondly, strength helps to reduce the activities of capitalists and kill their hopes completely. In the people's opinion and understanding, 'when the capitalists do not dare move their heads, then we know that the co-operatives are truly in good health'!

A few other political measures can help push the co-operative movement along the way already outlined. In our opinion the necessary measures are:

Firstly, abolish all the old debts hanging around the necks of the peasants, who are unable to repay them. The peasants' produce will not go into the co-operative storehouse as long as these debts are not abolished, produce will still stubbornly make its way into the Chinese house, and the peasants' money will not enter the co-operative's coffer; it will go straight to the money-lender's house, and the productive forces cannot accelerate.

Secondly, reduce land rents in cash or kind to 20 or 30% of the land's produce. This helps increase the productive forces and also eases the burdens in the peasant's life.

Thirdly, reduce interest rates which, as already described, have been so high that debtors can never escape from debt.

Fourthly, arrange for proper laws concerning renting and sharecropping by providing full guarantees to tenants and sharecroppers. This can be done by limiting the right of the landowners wilfully to withdraw use of the land whenever they like, or to put up the rent as they wish. Only by having this type of legislation can the poor peasants, who rent or sharecrop land, obtain a fair and reasonable return from their labour and have their living standards assured . . . .

Our understanding is that a *peasants' association* must be created in order to grasp the above-mentioned measures and successfully implement them. Those poor peasants who are deeply in debt are faithful to these political measures; they are the ones who have an interest in struggling to liberate themselves from the oppressive system which has imposed itself on them. When the peasants fully free themselves, they will have new working strength as well as new ideas. We understand that giving help and support to *peasants' associations*, which we have already described, is one of the government's very important duties.

The Government Must Assist the Co-Operatives Financially and Technically: The government shows the way for the co-operatives and also must assist in every possible way to develop their activities.

1) The financial policy for the co-operative sector of the national economy has three basic characteristics: The first is that of helping *members* of the co-operatives before those outside the co-operatives, so as to attract the peasants to join the co-operatives and also to limit and reduce private capitalist activities. According to our concept, the stingy capitalist and stingy landowner may not join the co-operatives with the poor peasants; otherwise, the interests of the poor peasants will be eliminated and the co-operatives transformed into instruments of the 'big important people'.

Secondly, lending money at the lowest possible interest rates as well as allowing a long time for repayment. This has two aims: it both enables the co-operative to borrow and the co-operative members to borrow again and also to repay, and also acts as a stimulant to the co-operatives in the struggle against usury.

Thirdly, the co-operative organization must be taken as security. Co-operatives have no wealth to mortgage in order to borrow money. The government must take the co-operative organization and its work as guarantees, and the co-operative must take the work of each member as a guarantee. This brings advantages to the co-operative as a whole. The government becomes responsible for the 'life' of the co-operative, and the co-operative organization is responsible for the 'life' of its members. From top to bottom there is only one saying: 'When the co-operatives prosper the government prospers because of the co-operatives.'

2) Technical assistance aims at fulfilling two important purposes. The training of leading personnel is advantageous to the co-operative movement. The co-operative can be said to be moving and developing well, in line with the peasants' interests, if its leading personnel are of good quality. As we have already said, the leaders must possess three most important qualities. Firstly, they must be brimming with politics, so as to understand well the role of the leadership of the co-operative, and they must have the ability to resolve any obstacle or problem which may be met in its operations. They must know how to compete to grab hold of the masses, to maintain and broaden co-operative consciousness, etc.

Secondly, personnel must possess technical knowledge. Production technology and accounting techniques are the duties of the technicians; but the leaders must have some technical knowledge and know how to use technology and understand technical problems, so as to avoid smothering technology with politics, causing it to shrink and pale in a political mould, unable to fulfil its role. On the other hand, technology should not be considered superior to politics, as this will erode co-operative development.

According to our discussion so far, politics and technology must be combined for sound co-operative development. *There should be a plan to diffuse widely technical knowledge throughout the people's environment.* There are two ways to educate the peasant in technical knowledge – by widely publicizing technical knowledge, according to the needs of the co-operative, and by showing them proof in their own province, district, subdistrict, hamlet or region. They can organize exhibitions of all their achievements to demonstrate the victory of co-operative leadership and technical methods; they can create model stations and model co-operatives; they can arrange to make exchange visits between co-operatives or arrange meetings in order to exchange one another's experiences, etc.

The third important quality for the leaders involves ideas and consciousness. Leading personnel are commanders; they must have a determined awareness, they must be persevering, forgiving and enduring, struggling against any obstacles and hardship in serving the people by the co-operative method. The leading personnel of the co-operatives and the peasants' associations must be well and thoroughly informed about the theory of 'serving the people', the theory of the people. Without these, there is no ability, no faith, no courage to serve the people . . . .

The Government Must Educate the Peasants in Politics and Ideology: Political education should explain and thoroughly demonstrate co-operative leadership, and should be diffused systematically throughout the peasants' environment, paying attention to:

Firstly, analysis and demonstration of the correct cause and the fairness of co-operative leadership. Any policy which truly serves the people is the correct and just policy because the masses are the majority of the population.

Secondly, analysis and demonstration to the peasants that co-operative leadership is the only leadership which can provide them with a high standard of living, happiness and dignity.

Thirdly, developing the masses' belief and hope for the definitive success of co-operative leadership, etc.

We have also discussed some of the qualities of psychological leadership. Psychological and ideological education is very important. The ideology of the masses is the accelerator pedal of the co-operative movement. The ideology of the masses is the co-operative ideology; there is no other class with more interest in consolidating a co-operative than the workers and the poor peasant class. There is no problem, no question as to whether the masses like the co-operatives or not. They like them and frequently depend on them. On the other hand, the question which arises is whether the co-operatives truly serve the interests of the masses or not. Can they leave their future in the co-operatives' hands or not?

The components of power (the ruling system) and the quality of the leaders in their programme to serve the people provide the answer to the first problem. Education of the masses in ideological concepts provides the answer to the second problem as well as the first.

The little people, the lowly and poor class is the most faithful and generous class. Since it is the lowest stratum in the national society, its members cannot 'oppress' themselves or any other class. This class is replete with morality and excellent personal behaviour. Nor does it profit from deception, because its members have committed no crime, no injustice or inhuman deeds which need to be covered up. Neither do they need to lie or obscure the truth, but represent it. Because of their own experiences, they actively engage in productive work, increase production and struggle directly against nature. Practice is the basis of truth.

This class is always honest; its members are starving and their hopes and wishes are pure; there is no reason for them to hide the hardship of their productive work, their exhausting way of life, the oppression and scorn they receive from other classes, etc. They live off their own labour power; all they want is not to be oppressed!

Truth, justice and faithfulness are pedals to promote and push the co-operative movement forward. But if these lovely ideas become 'numb' or rusty, lacking in bounding energy, it is because an outside ideology is enveloping them. Psychological and ideological education of the peasants is the way to brighten up their psychology of class consciousness, imbuing it with leaping energy to lead and promote the co-operative movement.

The peasants should be encouraged and educated to reject influences that are by nature opposed to their interests – harmful influences such as those ill-omened traditional habits, individualism and the attitude: 'What can we do about it? It's our destiny, determined in our past lives'. The fact that our peasants still strongly adhere to these unfortunate habits is a major obstacle to changes in their standard of living. Even though this behaviour is not entirely the peasant's fault on an individual level, our peasants must be consciously awake and try to unite forces with the government's plans in order to reject all those habits.

The people of every nation have their own customs and habits and our people are no exception. But the evolution of the country has divided customs and habits into two types – the good and the bad. The former are those whose characteristics are suited to the evolution of the country, and which help it progress and develop towards finding happiness for the masses, help the peasants to escape from all types of oppression and obstacles that hold back progress, and help the peasants to enlightenment, brightening up their minds again and making their ideas clearer and clearer.

We have discussed individualism to some extent. Individualism is definitely not a 'disease' of the masses and the workers, who are all increasing production together. Production has long been a common task, with a social character. In the task of increasing production, people are always working together. It is the weapon with which they confront nature; nobody can exist and produce in isolation. Everybody in the nation preserves the tradition of common work, for example, in reciprocal work agreements. Individualism is not the workers' theory; it is definitely a theory of the capitalist system. Individualism in the workers' minds is simply the ideological influence of the capitalist system. The ideology of this system is 'individualism, selfishness, freedom, self-seeking' and so on; it gives self-interest and private property the main role, as the key to the leadership and direction of the human nation. 'The individual' is seen as the framework for the decoration and adornment of the human nation, whose future is left to heroes, regarded as commanders of history! The broad masses seem to have no role, to be of no help in rowing the national boat. Only the capitalists and their capital, generals and first-class politicians, seem to have a role.

Therefore, education of the masses must be aimed at sweeping away and rejecting the ill-omened power of capitalist ideology, raising esteem for the masses' role as builders and decorators of the world. It must give high priority to the common task of increasing production, to the common work of the masses. Truly, the masses are the heroes who build and decorate the human nation, which is the framework of human history.

The masses should be educated to appreciate exactly their energetic capacities. They are the force which creates all sorts of wealth in this world. The work of constructing the mass movement is what builds and adorns the human nation. We say that 'the masses make history, the masses are the masters of history'. This enables them to appreciate their own strength, to believe in their own energetic capacities. This is the aim of such education.

If the masses reject the unfortunate power of capitalist ideology, appreciate their own energetic capacities, and also believe strongly in their ability to build their own happiness, they will then become a force to support the co-operative movement and be deeply involved in the co-operatives, struggling against all obstacles until final success is achieved.

The Elements in the Economy and How to Resolve Them

Under the leadership of the Popular Socialist movement, the elements of our country's economic structure have been altered little by little. The Royal Socialist Government has designed a two-year plan, is now applying its first five-year plan, in the years ahead will design a second five-year plan, and so on. This means that the economy of our country has slowly 'withdrawn' from the mould of a purely capitalist economic framework, and is building up *the basis for another kind of capitalist economy which is to a certain extent dependent on state direction.* The theory of 'freedom', which takes private interests as the most important factor in directing the national economy, has been somewhat 'diluted'.

The reform of the financial economy at the end of 1963 has increased the possibility of state direction. In the new structure, the state economy consists of organizations interwoven and connected to one another from top to bottom. The Royal Government possesses new and favourable characteristics allowing it to 'serve the little people' more seriously than before.

The national economy has a dull lustre since it has been changing slowly and continuously, up to the recent wide-ranging reforms, and is now made up of four sectors. The first is the state sector, comprising state industries, state agricultural enterprises, the state bank, the state insurance company, the state construction office, etc. The Royal Government lends itself money, directing and controlling this sector by itself, with plenty of freedom to apply its policy of serving the people.

Then there is the mixed economy. This sector comprises mixed industrial, agricultural and trading companies, etc. The state owns shares in these, as does private capital. State and private interests together own, control and direct the mixed companies. The state has the responsibility *to encourage private interests and protect the people's interests.*

We have already discussed the third sector – the co-operative economy. Its sphere is very large, comprising, for example, the field of production (industry, agriculture, crafts), the commercial field and the field of credit. So long as one wants to use co-operative methods, there is always work to do in the interests of the whole people.

The fourth and largest sector is the private economy, which has deep roots in our economic system. Even though we have plans progressively to build up the national economy, the theory of 'freedom' retains the main role in directing this and other sectors of the economy.

These four sectors of the economy *co-exist* within the national economic framework. How should they co-exist? In a system of equality like a syndicate, or in a competitive system where everyone tries hard to defeat the others? This choice cannot be avoided in orienting the economy.

The most important matter in resolving this problem remains the issue of *leadership.* The idea of *the state directing the economy in the interests of the nation and people* always pushes the leadership to build up the state economy as the directing system. This means that the state economy, combined with the mixed and co-operative economy, must become a more powerful economic system than the private economy. It also means that *the state must grasp the economy in its hands, and have the liberty and the opportunity to direct it according to the interests of the nation and people.*

At the present time, the spirit of competition between the state and the private economy is haphazard and unclear. But what is clear is the fact that the private economy directs and steers the helm of the state economy in production and commerce, even putting prices on state goods and profiting on the back of the state's policy to serve the little people! There is no real competition. And if this is so, for whose benefit is the idea of 'the state economy kindly and justly competing with the private economy', and whose interests does it serve?

Our conception is that of the state economy arranging and directing the national economy in order to serve the nation and people. According to this, the state economy, combined with the mixed and the co-operative economy, must build itself into a *system with all the characteristics of leadership.* Not until then can the private economy compete in the interests of the nation and of the masses.

Within the interwoven threads of the state and the mixed economy, co-operatives are the most important sector for serving the poor and the little people. Co-operatives are the transmission belt to draw up the standard of living of the masses both materially and spiritually, so that it will advance and develop along the political path of the Popular Socialist Community movement. When the co-operatives work well, then the ideals of the poor and the little people will have been fulfilled. The Royal Co-operative Office is the transmission belt between the state economic organizations and the people.

State economic organizations		*People constituted in co-operatives*
State bank)	Royal	(Co-operative citizens
Industry, state and mixed)	Co-op-	(Production co-operatives
Agriculture, state and mixed)	erative	(Consumer goods co-operatives
Commerce, state and mixed)	Office	(Co-operatives to provide capital.

The Royal Co-Operative Office and the State and Mixed Economic Organizations: We have said that the financial policy of the Royal Government's state bank towards the Royal Co-operative Office is to loan money to farmers who are in the organization in preference to those who are outside it; to loan money at the lowest possible interest rates; and to loan money allowing long periods for repayment, etc.

The Royal Co-operative Office has the responsibility to the state bank to apply this financial policy fully as follows: to use credit properly to achieve this goal; to run the co-operatives carefully, so as to enable them to pay off their debts as well as to develop, progress and expand; and to draw up methods for the co-operatives to adopt savings plans which make it possible for them to fulfil their obligations to the state and also have money in the state bank, etc.

The state and mixed enterprises have the following responsibilities to the Royal Co-operative Office: to provide the co-operatives with all sorts of consumer and production goods; to buy primary produce from the co-operatives, and to provide the co-operatives with information about industry's needs for primary produce (the kind of produce needed, quality, quantity, price . . .) etc.

The Royal Co-operative Office has the following responsibilities to the state and mixed enterprises: to sell industrial and craft products through commercial co-operatives (consumer co-operatives, and co-operatives to provide the means of production . . .); and to provide industries and crafts with primary produce through the co-operatives to sell agricultural produce . . . etc.

The Import-Export Company (SONEXIM) has the following responsibilities to the Royal Co-operative Office to provide it with consumer goods and means of production; to purchase co-operatives' produce for export to foreign countries; and to provide the Royal Co-operative Office, directly or through the Ministry of Commerce or Agriculture, with all sorts of information about the quality of our produce, the conditions on the world market (prices, market demand), etc.

The Royal Co-operative Office has the following responsibilities to SONEXIM: to sell goods for which SONEXIM has a monopoly on importing from overseas through consumer co-operatives and co-operatives to provide the means of production; to collect, select and refine agricultural and craft produce to match samples of other countries' needs, in order to sell them to SONEXIM; and to inform SONEXIM, directly or through the Ministry of Commerce or Agriculture, about the production situation in our country, together with all sorts of information about the preferences and needs of the people . . . etc.

The Royal Co-operative Office also has responsibilities to its member co-operatives. It must direct its activities within the political framework of building up the economy to serve the people. It must be imbued with this policy and be clearly aware of its responsibilities to the state and mixed economic organizations. Beyond this, the Royal Co-operative Office has the following responsibilities: it must fix its policy and direction on political success in building up the economy to serve the people. Member co-operatives must clearly understand the orientation of the Royal Co-operative Office (co-operatives are base organizations for the implementation of the state plans). It must establish detailed programmes and methods, fix concrete responsibilities for itself and for the member co-operatives. Member co-operatives must be fully imbued with all these programmes and methods . . . etc.

Member co-operatives have the following responsibilities to the Royal Co-operative Office: to fix their own policy and direction towards achievement of the programme of the Royal Co-operative Office; to establish detailed programmes and methods, fix concrete responsibilities for themselves in order to achieve their own programmes; and to establish definite and regular programmes and methods in order to educate their members about politics, ideas and ideology, technology, social tasks, culture, etc . . . .

In order clearly to establish responsibilities within these relationships and also to facilitate tasks, the relationships should be organized in the form of mutually binding contracts. For example, the Royal Co-operative Office signs a contract to buy goods from SONEXIM, giving details of the goods – the kind, their quality, the price and the date. SONEXIM signs a contract to buy agricultural produce from the Royal Co-operative Office, fixing the quality and price of each product along with the day and month of delivery. This type of contractual relationship could also be arranged between other organizations.

This new system of relationships will create a new atmosphere. In the cities, sellers will no longer see buyers as 'people to be cheated', and buyers will no longer see sellers as 'helpful thieves'. In the countryside, sellers will no longer see buyers as 'helpful thieves', and buyers will no longer see sellers as 'people to be cheated'. Production and commerce will co-operate with one another, help and rescue one another. Neither party will squeeze or swindle the other. The relationship between buyers and sellers, between producers and traders, will be based on equality and esteem, as they help one another in the process of building up the livelihood of the nation and the people.

City and countryside, industry and agriculture, will co-operate and help one another, the cities providing the rural areas with all sorts of industrial products and the rural areas providing the cities with all sorts of agricultural and primary produce for industry.

The relationship between all sectors of the economy and between the various economic enterprises will no longer be characterized by oppression or bloodsucking, but by mutual assistance, protection and salvation, towards increasingly streamlined economic activity. Through this kind of relationship, that is a contractual relationship, state economic organizations and established people's organizations can control, examine and prod one another and competition will be based on precise, regular and correct implementation of the contract. Mutual criticism, exchange of opinions and experiences, co-ordinated resolution of problems will certainly be in the interests of all the organizations and of the national economy as a whole.

References

1. Charles Meyer, *Derriere le Sourire Khmer* (Paris, Plon, 1971), p.181.
2. [Or 'Prince Companion'; members of the Sangkum were known as 'Companion' – Eds].
3. International experience adequately demonstrates the following situations: 1) Agricultural machinery *expels middle peasants and poor peasants from their own land*. Independent peasants become agricultural labourers, with a lower standard of living than before. This situation exists in some Arab countries; 2) In some Latin American countries, the government distributed land to the people, but four or five years later the land reverted back to the landlords. The peasant who received land through governmental reform thus could not maintain possession of the land and became landless again. This situation was allowed to come into being because not all facets of the rural problem were resolved.
4. [Literally, 'groups for the accumulation of labour power' – Eds].
5. To utilize the productive forces to their full capacity is a big problem for weak countries. In India, 30 million peasants each work only five days per month, 40 million work 10 days, another 50 million work less than 15 days. In general, we can say that each peasant works 181-

219 days per year. In other Asian countries *apart from the People's Republic of China*, each peasant works 100-200 days per year. Because of land reform and the establishment of peasant groups, associations and co-operatives, each Chinese peasant in 1955 worked from 55 to 220 days, depending on the region. But by 1962, this figure had increased to 300 days per year. In weak countries, two-thirds of the population have to do agricultural work in order to feed the country's entire population. In developed countries, one-fifth or one-tenth of the population can produce enough to feed the whole country and still export a considerable amount.

6. [This, in fact, took place in some areas under the control of the revolution during the 1970-75 War – Eds.]

7. [This gathering, which met at least once every six months, involved Sangkum members, urban dwellers, 'selected provincials' and, in theory, the electorate in general. Its decisions were legally binding on the Government. Michael Leifer has described it as a 'populist tool' to reinforce Sihanouk's political dominance (see 'The Failure of Political Institutionalization in Cambodia', *Modern Asian Studies*, April 1968, p.130.) However, on some occasions, especially in the earlier years of Sihanouk's rule, the meetings were more than rubber stamp affairs. The Fourth National Congress on 12 January 1957, which adopted the foreign policy platform of neutrality, at one stage attracted a crowd of 15,000. Hou Yuon, incidentally, addressed the meeting and spoke in favour of neutrality–Eds.]

8. [Rotating credit associations – Eds.]

9. As long as security remains the prerequisite for borrowing money, the national credit system and Royal Co-operative Office will not be able to reach the people or the co-operatives, as is needed. The poor peasants or poor co-operatives cannot borrow, or can only borrow too little to operate, or not enough even to pay for the trip to the bank. Lending money on security can only serve the rich; the national organizations take money from the people and lend it to the rich; the rich borrow the money and lend it to the people at very high interest rates . . . . Because the national organizations are loyal to the rich, they do not help to free the poor peasants, and they even aid usury to continue tightening its grip on the peasants. If the government organizations cannot trust the poor, the peasant organizations, we believe that they cannot fulfil their function. Why do they always think that the poor peasants will cheat them?

10. [The title *balat* is that of a traditional official – Eds.]

7. The Samlaut Rebellion, 1967–68 by Ben Kiernan

The Samlaut Rebellion took place at a time when the N.L.F. in Vietnam, faced with half a million U.S. troops as well as other foreign armies, was especially vulnerable to American rearguard moves via Kampuchea. Sihanouk however, was not submitting to the tremendous U.S. pressure. In 1965 he had broken off diplomatic relations with the U.S. and sponsored an anti-imperialist Indochinese People's Conference in Phnom Penh, involving the N.L.F. and the Communist Pathet Lao. Kampuchea was the first country to recognize the N.L.F's Provisional Revolutionary Government (P.R.G.) when it was formed in June 1969; it was also, the following month, the first country to be visited by the P.R.G's Prime Minister, Huynh Tan Phat. Sihanouk was also the only foreign Head of state to visit Hanoi for Ho Chi Minh's funeral in September 1969. The supplies purchased in or transported through Kampuchea, and the 'sanctuaries' on the border, were extremely important to the Vietnamese Communists' efforts in their most momentous struggle. The contradictions between the Prince's foreign and internal policies were becoming more acute than ever.

The rebellion, which first erupted at Samlaut in north-western Kampuchea in 1967, was the most extensive outbreak of violence since the 1946-54 uprising against the French.[1] In June 1967, over 4,000 villagers fled their homes in southern Battambang Province for over a month. By 1968, the unrest had spread to many other provinces, where another 5,000 or more people took to the forest. Over 4,000 were arrested and at least 400 imprisoned. Prince Sihanouk said of this civil war, which lasted until 1970, 'I have read somewhere that the fighting resulted in ten thousand deaths'.[2] (Even during the Second World War and the First Indochina War of 1946-54, casualties in Kampuchea were nowhere near this level.) According to Douc Rasy, Sihanouk claimed in August 1968 that he had put to death 1,500 Khmer Rouge during the rebellion in 1967-68.[3]

The Samlaut rebellion was the baptism of fire for the small but steadily growing Kampuchean revolutionary movement. As Donald Kirk says, it was 'a prelude, in a microcosm, of the conflict that would sweep across the country three years later'.[4] It was an important manifestation of the deep political divisions within Kampuchean society.

After demonstrating against the Government and burning down a government farm, bands of rebels numbering in the hundreds, attacked and killed soldiers and village chiefs in the Samlaut area of southern Battambang, and stole their rifles. Armed attacks on villages, army posts and patrols multiplied, and the rebellion grew more serious as it spread to neighbouring districts. In the face of a political crisis, Prime Minister Lon Nol resigned. Sihanouk formed an emergency government to deal with the rebellion. This emergency government remained in office until January 1968, although the Assembly continued to be dominated by the Right. Although officially over in June 1967, the revolt continued into August, and flared up again early in 1968 in Battambang. Other provinces, particularly Kompong Speu, Kampot and Kompong Chhnang, were soon seriously affected.

Local grievances, particularly economic ones, played an important part in these uprisings, but the organization and leadership, provided in part by cells of former Viet Minh sympathizers and in part by younger revolutionaries from the towns and other provinces, was also essential. Working closely together by March 1967, the rebels had made extensive preparations for the revolt, especially for the second outbreak in January 1968, when they achieved far more widespread success than in 1967. That groups of left-wing Khmer Issarak had been in Battambang and elsewhere for a long time gave revolutionaries some standing with the inhabitants of the rebellious areas, and, combined with harsh economic conditions, provided a large and active local following for the rebels.

At the same time, another revolt broke out in the north-east, in the tribal areas of Ratanakiri and Mondolkiri. The armed resistance of these '*Khmer Loeu*' or 'highland Khmer', equipped by N.L.F. cadres, was sparked off by what they felt was racist domination from Phnom Penh, and by the settlement, for instance at Labansiek, of colonies of retired soldiers and refugees in their region.[5]

Discontent among the elite was also mobilized, in the National Assembly and by Lon Nol and the military, and the Right strengthened its position in the Government and in the towns. The Left was increasingly driven underground and into the *maquis*, where peasant unrest was increasing. By the time of Sihanouk's departure in 1970, rural dissidence was apparent in nearly all of Kampuchea's provinces, and some remote areas of considerable size were beyond Government control.[6] The growing conflict between Left and Right, with Sihanouk more a spectator than a participant, had set the stage for the overthrow of the Prince and a full-scale civil war.

The First Uprising

After the first Indochina War, revolutionary activity in Kampuchea had remained at a low level for many years, but then, according to Ieng Sary (speaking in 1971):

> In 1966 everything changed. The non-endorsement of election candidates by Sihanouk opened the door to the guns of Lon Nol and the intrigue of the C.I.A., with the blessing of the extreme right-wing Assembly. Then, an actual civil war was begun against us. We had to answer their guns with our guns.[7]

As the newly elected right-wing Government asserted its control over Kampuchea's provinces, penetrating to village level and supported by the army, it bore down heavily on many peasants, and forced the Left on to the defensive. Although armed resistance did not begin until April 1967, the Left had been in preparation for perhaps six or seven months. In February 1966, Sihanouk had imprisoned several Pracheachon party members, and his announcement of non-endorsement for the September elections convinced many that he was moving to the Right. From October onwards younger left-wing groups from the towns, including schoolteachers and ex-students, stepped up their liaison with previously dormant cells of Communist sympathizers in remote areas like southern Battambang, while others joined the *maquis.* The Left gradually co-ordinated its activities, holding demonstrations in the towns, attacking the Government in the National Assembly and doing intense propaganda work in parts of the countryside, especially where local grievances were severe. By March 1967, its lines of communication had been set up effectively and, as the right-wing Government increased its military and economic pressure, it was only a matter of time before the civil war began.

Earlier on 6 January 1967, Sihanouk left for two months' medical treatment in France, as he had done several times in the past. This left General Lon Nol freer to put his economic policies into practice. He was seriously concerned about the sale of large proportions of the rice crop to the N.L.F. or on the Saigon black market, clandestine sales apparently handled by local Chinese middlemen who had found friends, according to Gerard Brisse, among certain *'personnalites princieres'*[8] and worked in conjunction with cells of former Viet Minh sympathizers acting on behalf of the N.L.F. In 1966, Kampuchea exported an estimated 300,000 tons of rice, of which only 170,000 tons was sold legally – the official agencies collected only one-third of the crop.[9] Dependent on its heavy taxation of rice exports, the Government was running short of legitimate sources of income. The following year, in January 1967, the Mekong River rose higher than usual, considerably reducing the rice harvest. The army came to the aid of the peasants and set up special organizations to help collect the rice. Brisse says that Lon Nol was thus able to set up his own parallel chain of command: the 'temporary' military machinery became institionalized, with Lon Nol's troops taking over from the civil agencies.[10] An efficient *ramassage du paddy* was established to buy and collect from the peasants as much of the crop as possible through government channels. To symbolize his interest, Lon Nol set up his personal headquarters in Battambang City, with Mau Say as his deputy.[11] Government ministers were each assigned a province, for instance, Douc Rasy was made responsible for the *ramassage* in Kompong Chhnang.

This campaign was backed by local army units, and co-ordinated its activities with those of OROC (Royal Co-operative Office), whose function included the formation and administration of peasant co-operatives.[12] Many villagers resented this interference, especially as the prices offered by the Government were as low as one-third of black market prices.[13]

By the end of January 1967, leaflets written and distributed by Leftists began to appear in southern Battambang and the Chriev district of Kompong Chhnang. Propaganda was also intense in Kompong Cham, where in the Damber district, north-east of the rubber plantations at Chup, the Pracheachon allegedly organized secret meetings in the forest.[14] In *srok* Prey Chhor, Hu Nim's supporters distributed leaflets and formed propaganda teams. Finally, in *srok* Baray, on the border of Kompong Thom, a clandestine organization was set up for propaganda work, exploiting local discontent with the *ramassage.* Led by a 'President' (Mak Sean) and a 'Vice-president' (Net Pon), it included at least 19 others. Their leaflets claimed that OROC had been 'created to deceive the people', and that Sihanouk and Lon Nol were 'men of straw' who had 'sold out their country to the United States'. They appealed to villagers to join their struggle, allegedly promising them important administrative positions and an end to all state taxation when final victory was achieved.[15] The revolution was mustering its forces.

In southern Battambang, there had been a few isolated attacks on military units collecting rice, possibly by late January or February 1967, but the main form of rebel activity was still propaganda work. At night, rebels distributed tracts in the villages, accusing the Lon Nol government of 'selling the country to the United States', accusing the troops of having 'trampled underfoot and assassinated' the local people, and demanding the withdrawal of the army.[16] Rebels composed songs and performed traditional folk theatre for the villagers which depicted Lon Nol (and apparently Sihanouk) as inviting the U.S. to conquer Kampuchea, with the rebels staunchly defending the country from the invader.[17] One leaflet even claimed that land was being cleared at the government settlement at Stung Kranhoung for landing U.S. air force convoys.[18]

In Kompong Chhnang, near a 7,000-acre mechanized farm being developed by the army at Chriev, the Left was also active. Several hundred families, including retired soldiers and 80 Khmer families from South Vietnam, had settled there since early 1966.[19] The local *ramassage,* under Douc Rasy, seems to have run into trouble. Khmer Rouge distributed leaflets in February and March, claiming that Sihanouk wanted to live 'the good life' in France at the people's expense, and that they were going to get rid of him.[20]

On 10 March, the day after his return from France, Sihanouk made a major policy speech emphasizing the disunity in the socialist camp where each country, he claimed, had evolved its own nationalist form of socialism. He added:

> You see, companions, the revolutions have reached complete deadlock . if we made revolution where shall we go with such a revolution as the one which you have prepared here – for example, the one prepared by the Khmer Rouge in Kompong Cham and Pailin? As for me, I am not a reactionary, and I do not wish to move backwards, but I prefer evolution . . . . I want to stress one point. Although I do not support the leftist citizens we must evolve towards the Left, from Right to Left, but not towards Communism.[21]

However, the Khmer Rouge decided to pursue their initiative. On 11 March, 'a major demonstration'[22] took place in Phnom Penh outside the offices of Lon Nol's counter-government. Organized by Khieu Samphan and the left wing of the Sangkum, it demanded, along with the lowering of prices, the Government's resignation, singling out Lon Nol, Nhiek Tioulong and Douc Rasy. The crowd also demanded new elections and, in particular, the withdrawal of troops from the Pailin district of southern Battambang,[23] indicating that the left-wing leaders in Phnom Penh were aware of the developing situation in Battambang and co-ordinating with the *maquis.*

Sihanouk's reaction was to convene a Special National Congress on the following day, to which the demonstrators were invited, to 'discuss the problem with the people'. At this Congress, the Left complained that not enough rifles were being distributed to the population, especially to 'the Vietnamese in frontier regions such as Bathu' to enable them to defend themselves against U.S.-Saigon incursions,[24] and a general discussion ensued about village self-defence organizations. Among the delegates from Battambang Province, some denied that the army was mistreating people in the Pailin district, and stated that they were opposed to the previous day's demonstration, pledging full support for the Lon Nol Government. They returned home to find their houses burnt down.[25]

The next day, in a speech to the people of Saang, in Khieu Samphan's electorate, Sihanouk said that the Khmer Rouge 'only attack Companion Lon Nol in their demonstrations, but I believe that I myself am a target of their "clandestine" activity . . . . It's still the Sangkum and especially Sihanouk that give them nightmares. I am for them nothing less than Enemy No. 1.'[26] Then, in a typical display of his political style, at a press conference on 23 March, he charged that two high-ranking army officers and three government members who were alluded to but not named, as well as other senior members of the army, the National Assembly, the Cabinet and the Staff of the Royal Palace, were conspiring 'at C.I.A. instigation' to overthrow him. Soon afterwards, members of the Assembly, Cabinet and most members of the Government took an oath of loyalty to the Prince.[27]

This revelation apparently sparked off more activity from the Left for, on 29 March, we find Sihanouk accusing Khieu Samphan, Hou Yuon and

Hou Nim of encouraging, by their critical attitudes, the developments in Battambang.[28] The next day, the National Assembly passed a censure motion against two leading ministers, Mau Say and Douc Rasy, forcing their resignations.[29] A major victory for the Left, some considered this a censure of the Government as a whole, but, contrary to their expectations, Lon Nol refused to resign.[30] Within four days, the Samlaut rebellion, centred in southern Battambang, was in full swing.

On the morning of 2 April, villagers in the Samlaut area, enraged at their mistreatment by a military party collecting rice, murdered two of them and stole several rifles. Then, at 1.30 p.m., bearing bayonets, daggers and sticks, and carrying banners denouncing the Lon Nol Government and U.S. imperialism, 200 people marched on the nearby youth agricultural settlement at Stung Kranhoung.[31] After attacking the local provincial guards and stealing two rifles, they put the young colonists to flight and set the buildings on fire.[32] By nightfall, rebels had defeated guards from two other posts, Sre Ponlu and Ta Sanh, seized seven more rifles, executed the local mayor, Pen Ly, and unsuccessfully attacked an important army position, defended by 'many' provincial guards, at Sre Sdao, on the road to Battambang. That day they stole 13 rifles, and 'a number of provincial guards' disappeared.[33] During the next four days, the Khmer Rouge rebels burnt two bridges recently constructed by the army on the road to Samlaut, at Krachap and Chranieng Krom, and ambushed five more guards and some village officials from Ta Sanh, killing one of them. They also burnt down 'several houses' in the new agricultural settlements at Beng Khtum and Chamlang Kuoy.

A platoon of paratroopers had to be sent to Kompong Kou to 'protect the population'. The army discovered a rebel hide-out, consisting of five ration depots and three huts in the forest near Sre Ponlu, and killed one rebel there.[34] They also recovered seven of the stolen rifles, along with 25 locally-made rifles and, in different engagements, captured 73 rebels in all. Some of the captive rebels allegedly confessed to taking orders from 'big chiefs' in Phnom Penh, and Sihanouk was thus able to accuse, by implication, Khieu Samphan, Hou Yuon and Hu Nim of instigating the rebellion. Supporters of these three deputies then met openly in Kompong Cham to defend them, and attacked Sihanouk. Next day he actually named the three as responsible for the outbreak and on 10 April he went to Prey Totung, in Hu Nim's electorate, to defend not only the army's activities in Battambang, but also Lon Nol and himself against charges of selling out the country to the U.S. He offered the local 'Reds', but not the ringleaders, a complete pardon: 'As for the trouble-makers in Battambang, that is a more serious question. *But the rebels who are actually in the maquis* still have the chance of being amnestied by the Head of State if they submit to our military or civil authorities' (emphasis added).[35] However, police seized 'subversive' documents a few days later at Prey Totung,[36] and in Kompong Chhnang, rebels, in Sihanouk's words: 'burnt [army] vehicles, attacked merchants and even teachers, [took] justice into their own hands, and distributed tracts to insult me.'[37] The Prince later described the settlement at Chriev in Kompong Chhnang as a 'complete failure'.[38]

In Battambang the pace of events was quickening. On 20 April, troops arrested another 93 rebels, capturing seven Enfield rifles and 25 locally-made ones. In three weeks of fighting, nearly 200 rebels had been captured and 19 killed, but the situation for the government forces was deteriorating. Rebel operations now covered an area 29 kilometres square, south of the main Battambang-Pailin road. Military reports indicated that the rebels, including 500 men, 100 of them armed, and commanded by a man called A-Kouy, probably a local figure, had already killed at least four soldiers and wounded another four.

On 22 April, Sihanouk charged five deputies, Khieu Samphan, Hou Youn, Hu Nim, Chau Seng (ex-Minister of Education) and So Nem – with responsibility for the rebellion – (the last two, he said, were less blameworthy than the others). However, he refused to 'make martyrs of them by having them shot', as some right-wingers were demanding. They would simply appear before a military tribunal.

Two days later, Khieu Samphan and Hou Yuon vanished from their closely-watched homes to join the *maquis* and lead the rebellion. The Right unsuccessfully attempted in the Assembly to have Hu Nim's parliamentary immunity withdrawn, while rumours that the secret police had killed his two associates on Lon Nol or Sihanouk's orders, spread quickly, raising a storm of protest.[39] Faced with a political crisis in Phnom Penh and revolt in Battambang, Lon Nol resigned as Prime Minister, ostensibly to undergo medical treatment.

Next day, 15,000 students from Phnom Penh and Kandal Province, angered by what they presumed to be the murder of Khieu Samphan and Hou Yuon, attended meetings that had been organized by Phouk Chhay's General Association of Khmer Students in various schools and monasteries to celebrate May Day. They condemned imperialism and the Kampuchean reactionaries and demanded the release of all the 'workers, peasants, youths, students, professors and intellectuals' recently imprisoned.[40] Supporters of Khieu Samphan from Saang went to the National Assembly and, 'in the name of the people', demanded that the Government hand over the two deputies, 'living or dead'.[41] Four days later, students from Choeung Chnok College, in Hu Nim's electorate attacked and chased away three of their teachers. On 5 May, workers from the Kompong Cham textile factory, as well as its Director,[42] and students from Kompong Cham University staged a demonstration with banners and loudspeakers, blaming the Lon Nol Government for the disappearance and suspected execution of Khieu Samphan and Hou Youn.[43]

Confronted by the Left, Sihanouk himself formed an 'Exceptional Government of National Safety', expected to be in office for three months only, to deal with the Battambang affair. Consisting mainly of his own supporters such as Penn Nouth, it also included three members of Lon Nol's Government and three left-wingers, Chau Seng, So Nem and

Keat Chhon. On 1 May, the Prince replaced the military commander of Battambang region, accusing him of being 'too severe'; he also accused Yem Monirath, the Provincial Governor, of corruption, and replaced him with In Tam.

When Sihanouk visited Samlaut with the new Governor, some 3,000 people came to hear him speak.[44] Sihanouk explained to the people of Samlaut that land taxes were necessary in all societies where private ownership of land existed.[45] He distributed food, clothing and other gifts, provided for the building of a new road, a school and a medical centre, and offered an amnesty for local rebels and the release of prisoners held in Battambang and Phnom Penh. These terms reflect Sihanouk's clear perception of the duality of the rebellion – an alliance between a persecuted urban Left and a disaffected rural community. It is a measure of the strength of this alliance that the amnesty offered to the local rebels – a tactic to divide the active movement – was at least twice rejected.

The next day, despite Sihanouk's conciliatory gestures, a sergeant and a soldier were killed in Samlaut and rebels attacked more military posts. Total army strength in the district now amounted to 2,000 troops, one-sixteenth of FARK (Royal Khmer Armed Forces). But the rebellion had by now spread to other districts to the north and to the east, and on 8 May, 22 families from Chisang on the main highway fled their homes and disappeared into the forest with the rebels. On 10 May, two entire villages, Snalmone and Russey Preas, were abandoned as their inhabitants fled an advancing army battalion. Two days later, about 20 rebels, attempting to make off with two vehicles belonging to the army, clashed with paratroopers in the empty village of Snalmone.

In late May and June, the military became even more brutal, especially after Sihanouk announced on 18 June, that the trouble was officially over. Aircraft bombed and strafed villages and jungle hide-outs; some villages, such as Beng Khtum, Thvak[46] and Russey Preas were burnt to the ground; others were surrounded by the army and the peasants massacred. Bounties were paid for the heads of rebels, probably not scrupulously identified. According to Sihanouk, 'thousands of families' (a more precise figure of 4,000 people is given by most sources) left their homes, accompanied by monks, and hid in the jungle and foothills of the nearby Cardamomes.[47]

According to Milton Osborne, Sihanouk's Government used 'the greatest possible force. Lon Nol had been implacable and retribution had ranged from summary execution to the burning of villages. Ghoulish details were provided of trucks filled with severed heads that were sent from Battambang to Phnom Penh so that Lon Nol would be assured that his programme was being followed'.[48] On his visit to Samlaut on 4 May, Sihanouk blamed the unrest on Thai 'foreigners, who can easily infiltrate across the hills and whose only aim will be to lead you into error'.[49] A month later, however, his explanation veered back to accusing Kampuchean Communists. He 'clearly proclaimed that the local rebellion at Pailin was a strictly internal affair, and received no foreign support or encouragement'.[50] Although he rarely said so, the Prince now believed that Khieu Samphan, Hou Yuon and Hu Nim were the instigators of the resistance and, correctly, that the first two were now actively taking part in it.

The local leaders of the rebellion are more difficult to identify. Kouy the commander of 500 rebels in the Samlaut area, was only mentioned once in official reports[51], which would probably play down the local base of the rebellion. But, according to local resident Krot Theam (see Chapter Seven), an important revolutionary network had recently been reactivated in the area. Theam says that after the Geneva Conference of 1954, local Khmer Issarak leaders had laid low; for instance, Moul Sambath, former Issarak military commander for Battambang, had a farm plot with some of his followers, not far from the Thvak pagoda where Theam was a monk. Theam heard that Sambath's group was still 'talking politics'. Theam's older cousin, a veteran Issarak named Sieu Samreth, took a job looking after the electricity generator in the famous pagoda of Ratanaksophan, in Pailin. Ten years later, in 1965 according to Theam, these people disappeared into the forest. For some, like Moul Sambath, this was not easy. Harassed by troops of the Governor of Battambang, he moved from village to village – 'to Kranhoung, Thvak, Chamlang Koùy, Chamcar Stung, and finally back to Kranhoung' – where he managed to elude the soldiers and meet up with his old colleague, Long Reth (later known as Nuon Chea), former 'economics' cadre of the north-western Issarak movement. They immediately began to reorganize their followers and to engage in recruiting and propaganda. Also working with them was Bung Phoeuk, a man of Khmer-Lao parentage whom Theam had known well when they did an Issarak training course together in 1950. By 1967, Phoeuk, described as 'well known' in the area, had a price of 300,000 riels (U.S. $10,000) on his head because of his activities as a 'Khmer Rouge chief'. At about the same time, Theam learned that his former Issarak instructor, Achar Pres, had become politically active again, in the neighbouring province of Pursat.

In the Assembly meanwhile (May 1967), Hu Nim was staving off attacks from the Right, and defending his constituents at Prey Totung and Prey Chhor from Lon Nol, Nhiek Tioulong and Dy Bellong, who were calling them 'reds' and accusing them of 'disseminating leaflets to discredit the Prince'.[52] Hu Nim pledged his loyalty to the Sangkum and to Sihanouk and, in turn, accused the Right of attempting to divorce the Prince from the people of Prey Totung, Samlaut and Stung Kranhoung. Increasing 'red' activities in Chinese and other schools brought complaints from Sihanouk, however, who sarcastically invited Hu Nim and the left-wing principals of Chamroeun Vichea and Kambuboth private schools to form a government.

It was not until August that 'some' of the rebels in southern Battambang finally returned to their villages. The chief monk of Battambang Temple, Samdech Iv Tuot, negotiated an amnesty and 200 men and women from the Samlaut region visited the Prince in his Palace of Chamcar Mon on 15 August. They were lavishly entertained, and then toured Sihanoukville, Kampot and Angkor before returning home, where houses and villages, some in new locations, had been rebuilt for them by the army.[53] Seemingly, the Samlaut affair was over.

The Samlaut Area: Local Conditions

A significant proportion of the population of southern Battambang were colonists from Kampuchea Krom or 'Lower Kampuchea', i.e. the Mekong Delta area of South Vietnam.[54] (Formerly part of Kampuchea, the Mekong Delta was gradually taken over by the Vietnamese in the 17th and 18th Centuries. A population of some half a million ethnic Kampucheans, called Khmer Krom, still remain in South Vietnam, with perhaps another 500,000 of mixed parentage.)

The first Khmer Krom settlers came to Battambang around 1926 and a trickle of two or three families per year continued into the 1960s.[55] Some of the villages they formed in the 1940s, now small towns, were important centres of unrest during the Samlaut uprising, for example, Reang Kessey and Baydamran, birthplace of rebel leader Sar Chamroeun[56] and later celebrated by the Pol Pot regime as the site of the 1968 foundation of the 'Revolutionary Army of Kampuchea'. Many of the colonists, who found no land available and were forced to work as farm hands for large landowners, settled along the banks of the Sangker River and in Maung district.

With the escalation of the war in South Vietnam in 1965, the colonization of Battambang entered a new phase. Thousands of Khmer Krom families began to pour across the border. By the end of 1966, 12,815 Khmer Krom had taken refuge in Kampot, Takeo and the settlements established for them by the Government, especially in Battambang; 1,546 of them were monks and, surprisingly, at least a quarter of the other men (948 of 4,087) seem to have been unaccompanied. In February 1967, 346 Khmer Krom, including 87 monks, crossed the border into Kampuchea and in March, there were 813 more. Between 1 September 1967 and 31 March 1968, a further 1,874 arrived, bringing the total since 1965 to 17,147.[57]

The main government settlements were established in Kampot, Kirirom, Kompong Chhnang (Chriev), and Ratanakiri, and by far the largest in Battambang. One village established at Beng Khtum, 15 kilometres east of Samlaut, just north of Stung Kranhoung, provided a home and land for at least 600 Khmer Krom by February 1967, and another 200 settled by Svay Daun Keo on Route 5, near several villages which had been established by other Khmer Krom settlers in the 1940s. Generosity towards these refugees by the Government was a potential source of grievance to the local inhabitants, many of whom did not even own their land.[58]

Not all the Khmer Krom refugees, however, settled in colonies. Many took up their lives with relatives, or wherever they could find work.

Some planned to stay permanently in Kampuchea, while others hoped to return to South Vietnam when the war ended.[59] In southern Battambang, because of the development of industries such as jute and cotton, and the increasing number of fruit plantations, jobs were numerous but poorly paid. Of the dramatic population increase in the area in the middle and late 1960s, Khmer Krom accounted for 13% (about 2,000 in Andoeuk Hep alone).

The village of Beng Khtum in southern Battambang was burnt to the ground by the army at the height of the repression of the Samlaut revolt in June 1967. Since its intake of large numbers of Khmer Krom refugees from 1966 onwards may have had an unsettling influence upon the already disaffected local inhabitants, the burning of the village of Beng Khtum may also reflect the army's attitude to these newcomers.

But the army did not, of course, restrict themselves to attacking the Khmer Krom. The re-drawing of administrative boundaries and the creation of new districts *(sroks)* under the direct control of the provincial capital was one method used by Lon Nol to bring the inhabitants of outlying areas, especially in southern Battambang, under close supervision. For instance, a military man, Lieutenant Chau Ken, was appointed on 20 February as head of the new district of Samlaut,[60] and later, the new *srok* of Kirirath, which included the areas of Samlaut and Stung Kranhoung, was detached from the *srok* of Ratanak Mondol, to the immediate north. At least one new subdistrict chief was appointed,[61] and probably several village chiefs as well.

The official account of the first 45 days of the *ramassage,* up until 16 February, singles out for its success 'the scale and deployment of the means put at the disposal of the buyers'.[62] This probably refers not only to financial but military backing for the campaign. Lon Nol's presence in Battambang, with its obvious repercussions down the chain of command, no doubt considerably increased efficiency, partly by paying late or underpaying the peasants for their rice. *Le Monde*[63] mentions the unpopularity of the local police and army units who often made off with food belonging to the villagers. The army was also involved, on behalf of OROC, in forming co-operatives. Peasant resentment of these interventions arose partly because they were forced to regroup, and partly because co-operative members were obliged to pay subscriptions to finance loans – which were then whittled away through the corruption of local officials. In return they received such 'benefits' as insecticides often of mediocre quality or even false substitutes.[64]

Army units also built roads in the area. One ran from Snoeng to Roung and Kompong Kol; another, running south to Samlaut from the highway at Pang Rolim, was the northernmost section of an important road, both economically and strategically, which was being pushed south-east, parallel to the Thai border, across the Cardamom mountains, to join the Phnom Penh-Sihanoukville highway near Kirirom. By October 1968, the army had built landing grounds along this route for use by Dakota aircraft, as well as runways for light planes on liaison missions. Such military incursions into the mountain sanctuaries of the former resistance fighters and isolated villages of the Left, base areas during the rebellion, stirred a small 'hornet's nest' and further conflict. The reaction of the rebels was violent, especially since the Left believed that certain elements of the army had connections with the U.S. and Saigon.

It is likely that the troops forced peasants to help build these roads, although Sihanouk denied this in 1968, saying that earth-moving machinery was in use.[65] In 1967, however, on his visit to Samlaut in May, he had offered the villagers a wide, new road connecting Samlaut with Pang Rolim, and the use of graders and bulldozers.[66] As this road was already planned and even under construction, this concession to the villagers seems more like an exemption from forced labour.

According to Osborne, army officers benefited greatly from smuggling in the border regions.[67] In March 1968, at Battambang, Sihanouk mentioned that disputes over contraband had occurred between customs officers and troops, some of whom may have been supplying the rebels with uniforms and supplies bought from the Thai border police.[68] Generally speaking, the activities of the army in Battambang prior to the revolt were heavy-handed and often brutal,[69] alienating and enraging the inhabitants.

Official corruption also contributed significantly to the plight of the peasantry. On 30 April 1967, Sihanouk announced that not only the Khmer Rouge, but 'the ordinary people' in Battambang were 'very displeased' with the provincial authorities headed by Governor Yem Monirath.[70]

> These authorities have also supported the capitalists, allowing them to oppress the people, by, for example, granting them a monopoly or unrestricted rights to transport fish and other goods in Andoeuk Hep and Pailin. There is also the affair of the distribution of lands of certain high personages. *These rich men have transformed their lands into concessions* to the prejudice of the livelihood of the poor people residing in this area . . . . In Maung Russei, there is also trouble between the Chief of the Region and the common people because the latter have suffered injustice . . . . In fact, complete anarchy and agitation reign in Battambang. I must inform you that I shall remove immediately the responsible men in Battambang Province.[71] (emphasis added)

One district where the problem of land distribution was significant was Pailin, a gem-mining town near the Thai border. In 1964-67, its population doubled to 11,500, reflecting both mass immigration and the refugee resettlement programme. The increase was especially dramatic in the sphere of mining – 6% of the gem miners had arrived since 1964.[72] Location is very important for this mining, requiring access to water courses and canals. However, certain groups, especially the Burmese who had found the gem deposits, monopolized the land along the canals. Some 10% of the properties, owned by Burmese, covered 50% of the best gem land. These property owners, and others, demanded rent of up to a quarter of the value of the stones mined, in return for access to water. The majority of the miners, especially the new arrivals, were seriously disadvantaged.

As a result, 'spontaneous occupations' of large properties by the miners occurred on several occasions in 1967-68.[73] This kind of action, perhaps not surprising under the circumstances, may well have been encouraged by some of the many dissatisfied high school diploma-holders, forced by the lack of suitable employment to work as hired labourers in the mines.[74] They came from all over the Province and some were even university graduates. These ex-students were prime material for the rebellion.

As the population of the Pailin District continued to increase, exploitation by landowners became more acute and peasants were also affected. The best land was bought from the villagers and converted into plantations for the expanding fruit industry, dominated by the Chinese and Burmese. The Khmer peasants either had to work for them as coolies or were pushed more and more into the back woods.[75]

In the Andoeuk Hep District, between Battambang and Pailin, many peasants were also living under harsh conditions. Raymond Blanadet has noted, as one of the most startling features of this district, the continual mobility of its 14,000 people,[76] particularly those, the majority, engaged in the cotton industry. Because of the high cost, in labour and materials, of intensive cotton cultivation, the peasants cultivated large areas of land with low yields per hectare. These became increasingly vulnerable to encroaching weeds and insects, resulting in lower and lower yields. After four or five years' cultivation, the peasants were forced to move on to new fields or, since most could no longer afford this, to work as coolies on the fruit plantations.

Colonization of the area, based on the cotton industry, began in 1963. In 1964-66, the population of Andoeuk Hep almost doubled, from 5,000 to 9,300. However, the area of land under cultivation also increased from 530 hectares to 2,450 – a huge rise compared to the number of cultivators. If Blanadet is correct in allowing a cotton field four or five years' productivity, the rise in hectarage under cultivation since 1963 came to a head in 1967-68, with far too much land sown with cotton and far too low a yield per hectare. This, along with an insect plague and bad weather, accounts for the low yield in 1966, one-third less than that of 1965.

By 1967-68, the amount of land under cultivation in Andoeuk Hep had increased far beyond the population's capacity to care for it, and large areas of land had virtually lost their value. 42% of the peasants in such areas were in debt for more than 500 riels (U.S. $15) and 70% of these peasants owed more than 2,000 riels (U.S. $60). Among the first targets of the rebels in April 1967 were the provincial guard post at Sdau and the bridge at Lower Chranieng; both were in areas with very poor cotton harvests in 1966 and had been colonized about four years before.

In general, the areas around Andoeuk Hep and near Beng Khtum were the most seriously affected. By 1967, 48% of the farmers in these areas had abandoned cotton growing. By 1967, despite Government incentives such as moderate interest rates (1% per month) and credit for necessities such as insect spray. As we have already seen, the co-operative body, OROC, seems to have been very inefficient, if not blatantly corrupt; a much needed financial reorganization in 1968-69 was still unable to solve the problem of the basic indebtedness of many of the peasants.

With the 1966 crop failure and large population increases, in early 1967 many farmers sought to take up new land on the edge of the forest, leaving behind much of the cultivated land. This process mainly involved newly-arrived migrants, but there were also large numbers of settlers of up to six years' standing who were now landless and bankrupt. Some 20% of farmers, because of low productivity and high rents, also found it necessary to cultivate a second plot on the edge of the forest.

Another cause of peasant discontent was the growing domination by the Chinese and other landowners, including Government officials. The continual buying and selling of land, due to failed crops, produced increasing impoverishment and a class conflict that, although limited to southern Battambang, was nevertheless intense. Centred on the rapidly growing fruit plantations, it was a conflict between 'a rich and enterprising Chinese bourgeoisie which has taken possession of the land, and the alienated, endebted, and already semi-dependent village communities'.[77] For instance, 10 out of 22 plantations in the Tuk Pous area were owned by Chinese, and another six by officials. A 'rural proletariat' developed in these fruit orchards, especially in Tuk Pous, Chak Tir and Tuk Vieng, while other members of this emergent class were employed at the sugar mill at Kompong Kol, or in the new cotton-ginning factory on the highway near Treng. Completed in 1965, this factory employed 157 workers, producing 4,000 tons of cotton per year, and a town of nearly 1,000 people soon sprang up around it. This socio-economic environment would have provided fertile ground for the development of a rural 'working-class' movement led by revolutionaries.

However, the rebels in fact chose the J.S.R.K. (Royal Khmer Socialist Youth) settlement at Stung Kranhoung, the most obvious symbol of government presence in the area, as the target for their first organized display of force on 2 April 1967. This farm symbolized the grievances of the villagers in many ways and it was a particular example of official mistreatment. Among other things, local families must have resented having to purchase or make uniforms for the J.S.R.K. members at the farm.[78]

Founded in 1965, with 80 youths and three agricultural advisers, the settlement was part of a two-pronged government policy of opening up remote frontier areas, while at the same time assisting and encouraging young city-bred people to return to the soil. The youths at Stung Kranhoung came from Takeo, Kampot, Kandal and Kompong Speu, and from Phnom Penh. Working in competitive teams, they cleared the forest and planted cash crops such as jute, garlic and cotton, as well as rice. The black soil in the area is very fertile and the rice yield was as much as three tonnes per hectare.

The settlement was less successful, however, in achieving its social aims. Twenty of the youths dropped out by November 1966, and only 20 of those remaining were city-bred, children of civil servants. In February 1967, most of those who had stayed took up individual holdings, that may have once belonged to the local inhabitants. They cleared the land, built simple houses and put their newly-acquired knowledge of agriculture into practice. Only 51 new colonists came to replace them, when they left in February.

Moreover, the communal farm at Stung Kranhoung was only the centre of a much more extensive government project involving the redistribution of land in the district. In 1965, the Government formed a committee to establish the farm and to survey the surrounding land. In late 1966, after the election of the Lon Nol Government, the committee distributed titles to new landlords, who included 'high officers in the army and police and senior civil servants' as well as retired soldiers. According to Caldwell and Tan, several thousand peasant families were thus dispossessed and forced to pay rent for land they regarded as their own. Two delegates were apparently elected and sent to bring this grievance to Sihanouk's attention, but were intercepted and 'liquidated' by agents of Lon Nol.[79] The peasants in areas such as Samlaut and Suon were also impoverished by the land speculation that preceded and accompanied the project.

It is clear, then, that corruption, the misuse of military and other authority, and increasing impoverishment, in the Samlaut, Pailin and Andoeuk Hep districts, for example, created a vast reservoir of peasant unrest that lacked only a reasonably sophisticated leadership. By early 1967, that leadership had begun to take shape and it provided, as well as a sympathetic and purposeful ideology, the guidance to enable an already disaffected peasantry to carry out a serious and effective rebellion.

Urban Dissent and Repression

On 28 June 1967, youths and students sacked the offices of the newspaper *Khmer Ekareach,* which was directed by the right-wing Sin Var, tearing down a portrait of Sihanouk on the wall. As the Cultural Revolution in China neared its peak, there were similar signs of unrest in many Kampuchean schools, especially private ones, two-thirds of which were Chinese. The *Little Red Book* was in evidence and attacks on the Government by university students were frequent. When a telegram to the Khmer-Chinese Friendship Society arrived from Peking in early September, indirectly accusing the Government of 'reaction',[80] Sihanouk indeed reacted violently. He suspended all foreign friendship associations, the national student union, led by Phouk Chhay, and all private newspapers, and sacked two recently appointed left-wing ministers – So Nem, Minister of Public Health,[81] and Chau Seng, Minister of National Economy. This excluded the Left from participation in the Government. (The Prince also arrested Phung Ton, Rector of Phnom Penh University and an associate of Hou Youn, and in 1968, Keng Vannsak, a prominent French-educated radical professor[82] and confined them at Kirirom.) This was the time when he put the Marxist-Deputy Hu Nim, whom he had accused, along with Khieu Samphan and Hou Youn, of instigating the Samlaut outbreak, under even closer police surveillance, and began to make increasingly frequent attacks on China.

On 30 September, Sihanouk called a meeting in Hu Nim's electorate of Chrey Vien, in Kompong Cham, to investigate a petition from the local inhabitants, apparently protesting the dissolution of the Khmer-Chinese Friendship Society. Sihanouk said:

> At present I find that China has made a serious change because she has given up peaceful co-existence and the five principles. China has changed her policy since the Cultural Revolution. There have been a number of Khmer sho aid China. Phouk Chhay is the fiercest amongst this small handful of people who aid China. The most dissolute and dishonest is Hu Nim.

Then, addressing himself to Hu Nim, he advised him 'to go over to the other side, as Khieu Samphan and Hou Yuon had done'.[83] At a press conference on 5 October, he launched another attack on Hu Nim and Phouk Chhay: 'In front of the people I told [them] I would prepare two files . . . . I warned them that if they did not go to China, and if they continued their [activities], I would produce these files and they would have to face the military tribunal.'[84]

In the light of these threats, Hu Nim's disappearance four days later, into the *maquis* in Kompong Cham,[85] caused many to believe that he, too, had been secretly executed. Sihanouk 'ordered a much stricter watch to be kept on Phouk Chhay' who was soon after arrested and condemned to death for subversion.[86] During the next few months, So Nem was arrested, Chau Seng fled to exile in Paris,[87] and seven schoolteachers from Phnom Penh, accused of being 'red', were executed by the police at Trapeang Kraloeng in Kompong Speu Province.

Dozens of others on the left, fearing death or imprisonment, followed Hu Nim to the *maquis* in October and November. On 27 November alone, six 'intellectuals' fled their homes.[88] But it was not just prominent figures, fleeing for their own safety, who joined the rebels in the *maquis.* The Samlaut rebellion and subsequent unrest showed not only that popular disenchantment was growing, but also that it could be mobilized against the right-wing Government. The revolution was on the way. With or without their families, at least 100 teachers, students, professors and workers[89] left their urban positions to join the mushrooming resistance. According to Caldwell and Tan, some even managed to 'escape' from gaol.[90] Revolutionaries in Phnom Penh, acting on behalf of the *maquisards,* recruited 'a substantial number' of intellectuals, from private schools especially, and persuaded them to join the resistance.[91] By December 1967, word had been passed around that the Samlaut rebellion was about to enter another phase.

The 1968 Revolts

Meanwhile, in Vietnam, American escalation of the war was at its peak. On 8 January 1968, the U.S. Ambassador to India, Chester Bowles, arrived in Phnom Penh to discuss with Sihanouk the resumption of diplomatic relations. Later in the month, Marshal Tito of Yugoslavia visited Kampuchea. The Khmer Rouge, many of whom were Maoist, reacted by 'disseminating leaflets, from scooters and even cars' criticizing Tito. According to Sihanouk, 'they distributed cases of grenades to assassinate Tito and myself when we met together, and they claimed that Tito was meeting with Sihanouk to discuss a sell-out of Cambodia to the Americans.'[92] He ridiculed this charge, but admitted the necessity for contact with the U.S. 'We have no choice. When the U.S. threat of invasion and war appeared imminent, I had to defuse the bomb . . . which was about to explode on the heads of my compatriots and people . . . . This however, was not for a reconciliation with America.'[93] Whatever Sihanouk's explanation for these visits, and whatever discontent they may have provoked in Phnom Penh, it was too late to convince Kampuchea's outlawed, dissident Left to reverse its revolutionary plans for Kampuchea's countryside.

In mid-January, several wooden bridges near Samlaut in southern Battambang were burnt by the Khmer Rouge. On 18 January, a rebel ambush took the lives of three provincial guards, and after a successful attack on the important army post at Banan, rebels stole 32 rifles.[94] That same day, a Khmer Rouge from Kang Hat surrendered to the authorities, telling of a fortified rebel camp near Saing Raing. After several clashes in the next few days, troops discovered the underground hide-out of a band of about 40 Khmer Rouge. Only one kilometre from the large Saing Raing army post garrisoned by 40 soldiers, it was defended by traps made of bamboo spikes, and contained grenades, medical supplies, documents, sacks of leaflets and a roneo machine. In the vicinity, the Khmer Rouge had buried provisions in the forest. For example, five kilometres to the south, troops discovered four well-camouflaged underground caches, containing no less than 70 sacks of rice. Twenty-five people were arrested, five of whom were identified by military intelligence as 'known Khmer Rouge'. Unknown to the army, however, only 10 kilometres to the south-east, in the same expanse of thick forest, near Snalmone, a similar rebel camp had been established by another band of about 50 Khmer Rouge.[95] By this time, yet another group of 40 rebels were active in the Prey Thom area, some 40 kilometres to the north-west. There were at least 13 other rebel camps in this part of Battambang,[96] carefully provisioned and defended.

Severe local economic conditions had remained largely unremedied since early 1967 and continued to contribute to discontent in southern Battambang. However, it soon became evident to both Sihanouk and Lon

Nol that the new outbreak of dissidence in early 1968 had been well-prepared, giving evidence of leadership of a sophistication unprecedented in the history of Khmer rural movements. It was this leadership, brought by men like Khieu Samphan, Hou Yuon and Hu Nim to the disaffected rebellious peasantry, that was to make their revolt even more serious and much more widespread than the first outbreak at Samlaut in April 1967.

On the night of 25 January, rebels killed several guards at the provincial guardpost at Thvak and stole 50 more rifles. It was their most successful attack to date. They then 'succeeded in rounding up' about 500 families from Thvak, Chisang, Beng Khtum and Samlaut, who followed them into the forest.[97] The commander of the Battambang rebels was alleged to be former 'Viet Minh' cadre Achar Pres, a defrocked Buddhist monk.[98]

At this time, the first signs of tribal unrest also appeared in the north-east provinces, particularly Ratanakiri. Sihanouk's concern grew. As before, he attempted to place the blame, indiscriminately, on foreigners:

> The Khmer Rouge have previously got armaments from Thailand or Cochinchina, but it is not yet quite sure that they have obtained these arms from Thailand. But what is certain is that there have been Thai armaments, Thai uniforms and Thai medicines . . . . It is not known which party in Thailand – the pro-U.S. Thai Government or Communist Thailand – aids them . . .[99]

And: 'They are backed from Siam, and from it they get everything . . . . They even have . . . the same uniforms as the Thai police, that is, olive drab coloured, and they even have Mao Tsetung's books printed in China.'[100]

He also claimed that the Khmer Rouge were now collaborating with the right-wing Khmer Serei, 2,000 of whom, 'well-armed and ready to fight us', were drawn up along Kampuchea's northern border with Thailand.[101] Phnom Penh radio announced: 'People are increasingly aware that the Khmer Serei and the Khmer Rouge have co-ordinated their *anti-Sangkum* activities with the view of bringing about the collapse of this regime.'[102] That Sihanouk could consider this unlikely prospect throws an interesting light on his view of Kampuchea at the time. Basically, he saw the kingdom in terms of the Sangkum: in speeches during these years he frequently divided Khmers into those who were pro-Sangkum ('99%') and therefore patriotic, and those who were anti-Sangkum and thus 'agents' of other countries, who wished to sell Kampuchea to their 'foreign masters' ('1%').[103] Theoretically, there was no room for Left and Right in his interpretation of Kampuchean politics, and revolutionaries and reactionaries alike were indistinguishable.[104] For the Prince, the Sangkum was a circle, not a straight line, so it was relevant only whether one was on the 'inside' or the 'outside'. As the Sihanouk era drew to a close and the stability of the Sangkum and of Kampuchea itself threatened to dissolve in the wake of Left-Right antagonisms and rural unrest, the 'inside' grew smaller and smaller, both in terms of ideology and adherents. The centrifugal political whirlwind gathered speed, throwing more and more people out of the Sangkum, and Sihanouk felt the independence of his Kampuchea seriously threatened. He increasingly laid the blame on 'anti-Sangkum', i.e. 'foreign' factors, and so was able to avoid the crucial issue of the viability of his own regime. His internal crackdowns on Communist activities were represented as counter-attacks on China: 'I wish to remain very good friends with China, but after all, matters are as they are: this is not a mild chat, it is a war which has been imposed on us from outside.'[105]

To mend the tattered credibility of the Sangkum and save face he produced 'evidence' of collusion between the Khmer Serei and the Khmer Rouge; they 'no longer differ because both have the same objective, to overthrow the Sangkum, and because both serve only foreign interests'.[106]

For instance, he attributed[107] an attack on a car of travellers on 29 July 1968, at Veal Snong Preus in Koh Kong, to the leadership of two Sino-Thai revolutionaries taking their orders from the Khmer Serei leader Son Ngoc Thanh, and using Chinese weapons! The official weekly, *Realities Cambodgiennes*, even claimed that U.S. helicopters, based in Thailand and co-ordinated by the Khmer Serei, were parachuting supplies by night into bases in the Cardamom mountains, for the use of the Khmer Rouge.[108] This lumping together of the extreme Right and the extreme Left was partly to discredit each by association with the other, but also acted as an indispensable mechanism of defence.

On 27 January 1968, Sihanouk replaced In Tam, Governor of Battambang since May 1966, with Tim Nguon, who had held the position in the 1950s. At the same time, he replaced Meach Kon, the Director-General of OROC.[109] The timing underlines the connections between the Government *ramassages,* then in progress, and peasant unrest. In an attempt to stem the tide of rural revolt, the Prince also brought back Lon Nol, who had resigned as Prime Minister in April 1967 in the face of the Battambang uprising, into the Cabinet as Minister of Defence and Inspector-General of the Armed Forces.

In Battambang, the Khmer Rouge continued to seize rifles, seeking to equip as large a force as possible. Hundreds of them were not armed, and they used big groups to ambush small army units. One band of 50 rebels[110] for example, attacked four soldiers near Svay Sor on 6 February and, losing two dead, killed two of the soldiers and stole their rifles. The next day, 40 families from nearly Chisang took to the forest and, the day after, 20 rebels from the same group attempted to persuade the villagers of Chea Montrei to follow them, but were driven away by troops from the army post at Treng. Two days later another band of Khmer Rouge staged a daring raid on the provincial guard post at Beng Run, only six kilometres from Battambang City, but were repulsed. Still another group burnt down the barracks at Spoung Chreou which had been abandoned by retreating government forces.[111] Sihanouk announced on the radio on 9 February that the army in Battambang 'has been soundly beaten by the rebels'.[112]

Villagers often assisted the Khmer Rouge in their activities. Sihanouk complained of this later, when discussing the amnesty of August 1967:

'Some of [the rebellious villagers] did come over and were freed. We gave them money and clothes so that they could make their own living. We also took them to Sihanoukville and to restaurants in Phnom Penh as well. When everything was settled they went back to the Khmer Rouge again'[113] and on 8 February, in a speech at Kep, in Kampot, he said: 'On hearing that the children [at Samlaut, Beng Khtum and Thvak] were running short of supplies, I sent them supplies immediately, but they later gave them to the traitors in the bush.'[114] After a visit to Battambang in early February, Veng Eng, a reporter for *Realites Cambodgiennes,* wrote that 15 youths had joined the rebels from two small hamlets near Saing Raing, and that their families, who remained in their homes, 'probably supply their sons with provisions'. Veng Eng added that 'the Khmer Rouge sometimes benefit from the support of peasants who were once followers of the Viet Minh.'[115] (See Chapter Seven of this volume.)

The rebel attack on Prey Thom, on 27 January, and the execution of Chhe Phuong, the chief of the village defence committee,[116] were carried out, according to Phnom Penh radio, 'with the complicity of some villagers';[117] some of the peasants then joined the rebels in the forest, followed soon after by 42 families from nearby Damrei.[118] The population also reportedly participated in a subsequent ambush of 11 soldiers at Sre Khlong, near Kirirom in Kompong Speu.[119]

The popular support for the Khmer Rouge in Battambang was partly due to the local roots of some of the rebel leaders, identified by military intelligence. *Le Monde* reported that the Battambang rebellion was led by two 'red chiefs' known in the area since 1953.[120] One of these was Bung Phoeuk, 'well known' in the district of Chan Meanchey. In 1967, the army put a price of 300,000 riels (nearly US $ 10,000) on his head, so he was obviously considered very important, Bung Phoeuk's wife and three children accompanied him in the *maquis.*[121] The other rebel chief was Achar Pres, probably locally respected for his years in a monastery, and, as a former Khmer Issarak fighter, for the role he had played, along with many other monks and ex-monks, in Kampuchea's independence struggle. Most accounts mention that when whole villages took to the forest in May and June 1967, they were accompanied, sometimes led, by local monks; also, it was only through the intercession of the Chief Monk of Battambang Temple that many of the villagers finally returned to their homes in August. This may be, in part, a reflection of the influence of Achar Pres.

As well as the resumption of the *ramassage* campaigns in late December, another important reason for peasant support for the revolutionaries was the Government's decision to appoint village headmen and officials directly.[122] Before 1968, headmen were elected by the villagers, although the provincial authorities usually selected the candidates. Central Government intervention represented a significant development in rural administrative repression by Phnom Penh, no doubt resented by many peasants who cherished, for sound enough reasons, the traditional autonomy of village affairs. Local corruption and increased administrative domination now threatened to add to the other long-standing, peasant grievances.

In January 1968, the Battambang rebels were in touch with others in Kompong Chhnang (Amleang district),[123] and almost certainly in Kompot as well. Many of the rebels involved in the fighting in Battambang were younger radicals who had left the towns to join the *maquis*. For example, an unnamed teacher from Kompong Chhnang left his job in October 1966 (the month that Lon Nol became Prime Minister) and was captured by troops near O Beng Svay in February 1968.[124] According to Sihanouk, on 8 February certain teachers, followers of So Nem and Chau Seng, had 'recently' taken to the bush. One of them, a 'pro-Red teacher', was killed by soldiers in Battambang. The rate of these disappearances from the towns, already high in late 1967, increased as rural revolt flared up in early 1968. In January, 15 teachers and professors from Phnom Penh and other towns,[125] and in the first three weeks of February, three professors and a teacher,[126] vanished from their jobs, presumably to take to the *maquis*.

By early February, rebel activities had spread to several other provinces, In Amleang district of Kompong Chhnang, Sihanouk claimed that the 'majority of people' approached by the rebels 'sought the protection of our authorities in Thnal',[127] presumably some did not. On 3 February provincial guards from the post of Speu in Kompong Cham arrested two Khmer Rouge, 'one of whom was recognized as a chief propagandist', and seized a number of documents.[128]

Unrest in Kong Piseu district of Kompong Speu elicited a visit by Sihanouk on 10 February. He told the inhabitants of the world-wide support for Kampuchea's independence, and of the impending visits planned, that year, of four heads of state including the President of the U.S.S.R. 'Kosygin, Chairman of the Council of Ministers of the U.S.S.R.– the first Power in the World . . . announced jointly with the Indian Government that he formally supported *our Cambodia* and would defend it strongly against any countries which might attack it . . . . Russia has proposed to give us new military aid so that we can defend *our nation* in 1968.'[129]

With many of the Left in hiding or dead and still others in gaol, there were few to blame for the new outbreak of rebellion. His accusation on 8 February that 'the partisans of So Nem and Chau Seng' were the instigators of the revolt,[130] indicates that he still had no idea of the whereabouts of Khieu Samphan, Hou Yuon and Hu Nim. Unlike most people who believed that the three had been secretly executed, Sihanouk must have known that they were alive, most probably somewhere in Kampuchea and planning his overthrow or even assassination, playing leading roles in the rebellion. Such educated leadership of what many considered a mere *jacquerie* gave it an entirely different character, which Sihanouk well appreciated. But the Prince was in a double bind. Well aware of the popular following commanded by the three missing deputies in Phnom Penh, he was reluctant to mention their names or reveal that they had *not* been executed, since the admission that they were still pursuing their revolutionary ends would only add to their prestige and encourage others to join them. And if their activities did become widely known, while Sihanouk was still unable to apprehend or even locate them, his own standing would suffer considerably. But an official 'report' of their execution would make martyrs of them, and so, in a different way, fan the flames of revolt.

Sihanouk therefore decided not to upset the widespread belief in the executions, though occasionally and half-heartedly 'complaining' that the three were still alive. However, as the rebellion grew more serious and no intelligence reports materialized as to the whereabouts of its leaders, he became more confused and alarmed at the growing prospect of a Communist-led peasant revolution. Floundering in this public search for a solution, for a scapegoat, he announced, 'you have to choose between having war with the Americans or having war with us. You have to choose. That is what the Maoist camp told us. I do not mean the Peking Government but the camp of the Maoists. I do not know which of them either. You may guess. Anyhow, that is that. They are driving us into a corner.'[131]

Then, on 10 February, Sihanouk made some unusual and sweeping accusations. He claimed to have documents proving that the rebels were in contact with the Thai Patriotic Front, who were 'stationed in northern, southern and western Thailand', i.e. all areas far from Kampuchea, which borders on eastern Thailand. Interestingly, the seat of Thai Patriotic Front operations at that stage was in fact in north-east Thailand. Sihanouk also claimed that the Khmer Rouge were 'massed' four kilometres from the Thai frontier. The Pathet Lao, he said, were stationed near the Kampuchean frontier at Stung Treng, and the 'Viet Minh' were 'reactivating their former cells' in Kompong Speu, Kampot, Takeo and Prey Veng. He said that this proved, contrary to allegations made in *Le Monde* on 2 February[132] that 'the cause of the rebellion was not the Khmer people's discontent but the instigation of pro-Viet Minh Khmers'.[133] To Sihanouk, the two possibilities were mutually exclusive. By blaming foreign intrigue, he glossed over local disaffection and violence that had already reached an unprecedented scale.

The opening of new fronts in other provinces did not seem to diminish rebel operations in Battambang, where at least 15 ambushes, attacks on provincial guard posts and clashes with government troops occurred in the first three weeks of Feburary. Bitter fighting took place in the thick forests covering and surrounding Phnom Veay Chap[134] which, although dwarfed by the nearby Cardamomes, still towered 429 metres above the villages round about, such as Thvak and Beng Khtum. Over 10 kilometres from the nearest road or track, it had once sheltered a Viet Minh cell, and was now presumably the site of rebel headquarters in the north-west.[135] In three skirmishes at its foot, including a two-and-a-half hour battle with 'about one hundred Khmer Rouge',[136] government troops killed a total of 53 rebels. The Government admitted losing only seven wounded, but this figure is probably low. According to official sources, at this stage Khmer Rouge in the area numbered about 500, and 200 of them were well-armed.[137]

On 25 February 1968, the Khmer Rouge launched their most widespread and most successful campaign yet.[138] Sihanouk later described it as 'a concerted operation against our isolated troops; the same movements, the same tactics',[139] he said, were employed in Battambang, Pursat, Takeo, Kampot, Koh Kong, Kompong Chhnang and Kirirom. To the Prince, this meant that 'the blow of 25 February' was 'an operation ordered and co-ordinated by the Khmer Rouge command, which is exercised by a few intellectuals'. However, still worried by the absence of information on these people, he gave but little indication of their identity.[140] Claiming that former Communist cells now reactivated, 'rose up', he significantly qualified his claim of only two weeks before that the rebellion was a foreign conspiracy. 'I do not say they are Viet Minh; they are like the Viet Minh'.[141]

In Battambang, on 25 February, rebels made fierce attacks on provincial guards and soldiers at Kompong Kol, where at least 36 families (87 people) joined the *maquis,* and at Samlaut. In Kirirom rebels 'set up a team to steal weapons' and kidnapped local officials from Chambak, near a settlement for Khmer Krom refugees. Not very far away, some of the 50 or so rebels in the Sre Khlong sector, led by Van Nan, attacked 'two or three villages' and burnt down a government farm.[142] And in Koh Kong, rebels went into all the villages in the province, and executed seven village chiefs and some deputy chiefs, in front of their inhabitants.[143] In a single day, 50 rifles were stolen throughout the country, and rebels even seized some machine guns 'in certain areas'.[144] Hurried official reassessments of the Khmer Rouge forces now estimated them to number more than 1,000 armed guerrillas, more than half of them well-equipped.[145] During the next fortnight, according to Sihanouk, rebels 'fell "gloriously" upon provincial guards who were thinly spread out',[146] in areas of Kompot, Kirirom, Koh Kong, Kompong Chhnang, Battambang and Pursat.

Altogether, more than 10,000 villagers throughout Kampuchea took to the forest at the initiative of the rebels,[147] including at least 2,800 in southern Battambang,[148] while in the Kouk Banteay district of Kompong Chhnang, about 1,300 people left their villages[149] to follow a band of armed rebels led by a four-man cell comprising a leader called Oulum, Em Sophal, his political commissar, and two propaganda agents.[150]

Perhaps the rebels' greatest successes during the 25 Feburary offensive, however, were achieved in Kompot, where several years' patient work in the Chhouk district came to fruition. Militarily, the results were modest: rebels stole 36 rifles, two machine guns and some cases of ammunition from the guard posts they overran, and a few bridges were destroyed, including four in the Lboeuk area alone.[151] But, more important, the Khmer Rouge did demonstrate the power of their propaganda work, and the extent of their local following. Nearly 3,000 people left their villages and refused to co-operate with the authorities. The entire populations of Kaunsat (207 people),[152] Trapeang Reang, Sre Khnong[153] and Thkeam

Romeas,[154] along with 100 families from Chhouk[155] and '800 men and women' from Wat Ang Chak,[156] left their homes to follow the rebels into the forests and hills. This was achieved by less than 100 armed rebels – the largest group in the area mentioned in official sources comprised only 14 men with eight rifles[157] – at the cost of one of their number arrested at Kaunsat.

Coming on top of other events in late February, this mass exodus in Kampot and Kompong Chhnang was of profound significance for the revolutionary movement, and for Kampuchea, as Sihanouk, Lon Nol and the Government no doubt realized. Unlike southern Battambang, there is no evidence that peculiar *local* grievances played an important part in rebellion in these central and south-western provinces. The impetus for revolt in Kampot and Kompong Chhnang seems rather to have come from peasant discontent with the hardships resulting from the low fixed rice prices of the nation-wide *ramassage*, as well as such perennial grievances as debt, perhaps aggravated by military pressure and cruelty: Significantly, the irate peasants were politicized and capably led by a sophisticated cadre of left-wingers from the towns. In other words, by March 1968, *general* conditions that prevailed almost everywhere in rural Kampuchea were shown to be not unsuitable for the development of a mass-based revolutionary insurrection, among at least sections of what was ostensibly an easy-going Buddhist society, mainly of individual cultivators. Far from the idyllic 'property-owning democracy' presented to the outside world by Prince Sihanouk in Phnom Penh, traditional Khmer rural society was already undergoing the first of a series of convulsions whose full effects were to remain unnoticed to foreigners and even to many urban Kampucheans for years to come.

On 28 February, only three days after the Khmer Rouge offensive began, Sihanouk announced: 'Civil war has these days extended to other provinces such as Kompong Speu, Kirirom, Chambak and Kampot . . .'[158] He repeated his claim that the Khmer Rouge were collaborating with the Khmer Serei but, he said, only in Koh Kong province and in the Thai border area near Pailin; he also admitted that the Khmer Rouge, unlike the Khmer Serei, were able to start a civil war because they were 'rooted in the country'.[159] This is a statement that Sihanouk would not make lightly. Forced to admit, then, the seriousness of the internal situation, he said later, after outlining the activities of the Khmer Rouge, 'And so you see, it is total war . . . .'[160]

He replaced the Provincial Governors of Kampot and Pursat with high-ranking military officials, Brigadier-General Khlaut Bouth and Commander Deng Layom. And, as he had done in May 1967, Lon Nol again called in the air force to help repress the Khmer Rouge. Planes bombed jungle targets and rebel camps in the Cardamoms, and even Kong Pisei district of Kompong Speu, less than 40 kilometres from Phnom Penh itself.[161]

As hostilities continued, Sihanouk found it necessary to visit Battambang. On 4 March, in a speech to some wounded provincial guards in Battambang hospital, Sihanouk claimed that recently in that province six agents of Khieu Samphan had been captured, propagandists trained by the former deputy in his native village of Saang, in Kandal, before his disappearance. Some of them, he said, had also been trained as cadres in Hanoi, and one was an ethnic Vietnamese sapper called Nguon.[162] The latter claim would indicate that some of the Khmer Issarak who fought with the Viet Minh and then went to Hanoi for training in 1954 or after, had by now come home and were taking part in clandestine activity. But Sihanouk offered no direct evidence of this. He said that these captured agents were 'Not just ordinary people but ideologically dedicated people, wearing the insignia of Khieu Samphan and carrying cases full of documents. It was their job to transport the documents prepared by Khieu Samphan and distribute them in Battambang.'[163] There was, he said, 'no doubt about them because they had documents in their hands, because they were not natives of Battambang but came from Kandal, and because our police records showed that they had formerly acted as Viet Minh propagandists'.[164] Consequently he ordered the six to be shot without trial. Perhaps another reason for this decision was their evident refusal to disclose the whereabouts of their leaders, much to Sihanouk's frustration. He claimed that Khieu Samphan was in Saang, but quickly passed over the subject,[165] and at no stage did he publicly mention the name of Communist Party secretary Saloth Sar (Pol Pot).

Continuing his tour of southern Battambang, he arrived in the village of Thvak, not far from Phnom Veay Chap. There, on 6 March, he was presented with Khmer Rouge leaflets proposing an end to hostilities. They demanded in return that Sihanouk grant an amnesty to the rebels, and 'withdraw soldiers and police from all villages and precincts where the Khmer Rouge are located'.[166] This was an offensive rather than a conciliatory demand, and it reads almost like a claim for the spoils of victory. Reiterating the demands made by the demonstration in Phnom Penh a year before, it asks for the withdrawal of troops from the nearby Pailin district of Battambang.

Why was the Khmer Rouge leadership willing to negotiate a peace on these terms? Obscuring the seriousness of the situation, Sihanouk attempted to make the demands of the rebels appear conciliatory: 'They will leave the forests *to stay in cities and towns* if I withdraw police and troops from the local regions'.[167] (emphasis added). While it is possible that the leaflet was a response to military repression and cruelty to the local inhabitants, it is nevertheless highly unlikely that the Khmer Rouge intended to renounce the influence they had gained in the rural areas by retiring voluntarily to the 'cities and towns'. What they probably had in mind was the creation of a 'liberated zone' under the exclusive control and administration of the resistance, in which it could work and grow unmolested, and which would serve as a springboard for further activity. Realizing this, Sihanouk next day rejected the rebels' terms outright, in a speech in Mongkolborrey district of Battambang: 'This is not good. I will never agree to divide our country'.[168]

That same day, 7 March, Khieu Samphan was sighted in the Chhouk district, and military intelligence reported that he had established his 'headquarters' there. Sihanouk flew straight from Battambang to Kampot, and visited the town of Chhouk itself. Returning to Phnom Penh that night, he made a major statement to the press:

> Khieu Samphan is still alive, ha ha ha . . . . We have not yet located Hou Youn [and] Hu Nim . . . . Khieu Samphan is in Kampot Province, in the Chhouk area. But he may have been able to relocate his headquarters . . . . The messengers sent by Khieu Samphan [to Battambang] were trained by him at Saang when he was deputy there. He took them with him to his headquarters at Chhouk . . . . So they have a command, they have a plan; it is an extremely well co-ordinated movement . . . .

Again he played down the local causes of the revolt: ' . . . Cambodia is now being invited to participate in the struggle between Communism and the free world . . . the struggle between the Communist Viet Minh and the U.S.A. for the hegemony of Asia.'[169]

Throughout March the rebellion intensified, and at least 25 clashes occurred in several provinces. However, the Khmer Rouge were suffering heavier losses than in the previous weeks when they had first seized the initiative. Slowly, the army began to make up lost ground, after abandoning all isolated vulnerable positions in the affected areas, and with the help of the air force. Bombing destroyed three 'rebel camps' in Battambang and Koh Kong and, in conjunction with ground troops, a ration depot not far south of Phnom Penh, at Trapeang Rokur. The depot belonged to a band of about 50 rebels, led by Prom Leng, which was operating in the Kong Pisei district of Kompong Speu. During March, the army killed at least 106 rebels, and captured at least 108, compared to corresponding figures of 76 and 12 for February. A fortified camp at the foot of Phnom Veay Chap was destroyed.[170]

Sihanouk's mobilization of large numbers of townspeople in the campaign against the Khmer Rouge not only provided a demonstration of loyalty to the throne and the Sangkum but also prejudiced the military operations of the rebels. This tactic of exploiting the widening political chasm between city and country people was seen by Charles Meyer as 'shameful in the extreme'; ' . . . the officials and the urban population of Battambang were also mobilized against the 'reds' in the rural areas, and armed with sabres, clubs and a few firearms, were obliged to set out in pursuit of the unfortunate peasants'.[171]

No doubt the authorities hoped to capitalize on the revolutionary movement's relative weakness in the towns, due to the crackdown of the right-wing regime. But finally this merely served to increase the rural population's isolation from and resentment of the elitist, served basically urban political administration, thus strengthening peasant support for the revolutionaries. On 22 March, *Realites Cambodgiennes* claimed that 14,400 urban dwellers from Battambang City had 'participated actively' in the 'struggle' in the preceding six days.[172] But when Sihanouk, that same night, announced the replacement of civilian Tim Nguon, after less than a month as Governor of Battambang, by yet another military man, Colonel Sek Sam Iet,[173] it was clear that the rebels in the countryside were not yet defeated.

At the end of March, the Khmer Rouge on Phnom Veay Chap were still holding out in the face of army forays involving hundreds of troops at a time, and they continued to ambush small patrols and steal rifles. But by 29 March, their casualties had been heavy[174] and 2,042 villagers who had followed them into the forest had surrendered to the authorities. Then on 8 April, at least 1,000 troops, including two battalions of FARK and 100 commandos, took Phnom Veay Chap by storm. They destroyed 'an important Khmer Rouge network', two large fortified hide-outs, and 'important installations' including a rifle factory.[175] 89 rebels were killed and 32 captured. Over 700 local people, who had been hiding with the rebels in what must have been quite a large resistance base,[176] surrendered. Official reports put government losses at five killed and 31 wounded, probably an underestimate.

Two days later, on 10 April, the commandos withdrew from Phnom Veay Chap, leaving the two FARK battalions to pacify the region in a series of 'important operations'. By late April, no fewer than 494 teachers, under the direction of primary inspector and former deputy from Takeo, Thuy Bounso, were 'voluntarily participating' in the 'second phase of Operation Stantiheap' in the area.[177] The need for such intense propaganda work by the Government among the population indicates a continuing strong base of support for the rebels in the area.

In an interview with me in Paris in June 1980, Thuy Bounso recalled that the local peasantry had been seriously alienated by large-scale land-grabbing (in particular at Pailin and Thmar Kaul) on the part of high officials, some of whom were even members of Sihanouk's entourage. Bounso also said that military regroupment of the populations of 'over 100' villages and 'widespread' aerial bombardment throughout western Kampuchea in 1967-68 caused further resentment. As a result, when his dozen or more teams of about 50 propagandists accompanied by soldiers entered the villages of southern Battambang to put the government's case, the reaction was hostility and suspicion: 'The population just smiled and seemed to be saying to us: "We know that is what you say, but you are lying". We had no success at all in winning over the people of the Samlaut, Stung Kranhoung and Pailin areas.'

However, the destruction of the Khmer Rouge base at Phnom Veay Chap brought to an end, at least for the moment, rebel attempts to establish a liberated zone in southern Battambang. Soon after, military intelligence reported that a group of 44 rebels from Phnom Veay Chap, were moving south-east in teams of six to eight men, allegedly armed with explosives, and attempting to link up with the Khmer Rouge in Pursat, Kompong Chhnang and Kompong Speu.[178]

Samlaut and After

Although most of the 10,000 or so peasants involved in the February 1968 exodus to the *maquis* returned to their villages (many of them for the second time) by April and May, the Khmer Rouge still benefited from a degree of popular support and protection. By mid-1968, the rebels had established a network of bases, cells and lines of communication throughout Kampuchea.

Meanwhile, the revolt had spread to the north-east of the country. According to Pol Pot, speaking in 1977: 'In the north-east, we rose up on 30 March 1968. Only four or five guns were seized from the enemy. Coupled with the four or five guns we had for the protection of our Central Committee headquarters, we were armed with less than 10 guns with which to face the enemy in the north-east.'[179] In a radio speech Sihanouk complained about the activities of tribal highlanders in north-eastern Rattanakiri Province: ' . . . in the majority of villages, these Khmer Loeu have put down poisonous roots in the village school in order to have the schoolmaster killed.' In May 1968 Sihanouk travelled to Rattanakiri and complained of Khmer Rouge influence over the north-eastern population: ' . . . they gave rifles to the Khmer Loeu and ordered them to fire on the national forces.'[180]

It would appear that the Khmer Rouge had now managed to obtain more arms, probably from N.L.F. forces in local 'sanctuaries' or just across the border in areas of Vietnam inhabited by related tribes.

However, the developing situation placed the Vietnamese in a difficult position. The 1968-70 period was precisely that in which Sihanouk's neutrality – in 1969 he recognized the N.L.F.'s Provisional Revolutionary Government *and* resumed diplomatic relations with the U.S.A. – was of most assistance to the Vietnamese. It was also the time when their ability to obtain supplies in and through Kampuchea was of the greatest importance. Supporting the Khmer Rouge would have meant running the risk of disrupting this foreign policy, either causing the Prince himself to react by swinging towards the U.S.A. or being overthrown by a pro-American regime. As a result of this fear, according to Wilfred Burchett:

> Once the 'Khmers Rouges' had gone over to armed resistance in 1967 they were in fact something of an embarrassment to the N.L.F. The latter could not appeal to them to call off their own struggle in the higher interests of aiding the N.L.F. to defeat U.S. imperialism . . . . To the best of my knowledge the only help given the Cambodian resistance fighters was occasionally when a group was hard-pressed by Lon Nol's troops in the frontier areas and they would be allowed to slip through N.L.F. positions . . . .[181]

Not that Hanoi had abandoned the Kampuchean Communists. Its aid was more of a long-range project. According to Timothy Carney:

> A defector from the North Vietnamese Central Office for South Vietnam's research section reported in 1973 that seven years earlier, in 1966, the Vietnamese had organized a unit, designated 'P-36', to support the Communist Party of Kampuchea . . . . It aimed to help develop C.P.K. cadre, exploit propaganda themes, and give other assistance to the Cambodian party. Before Sihanouk's overthrow P-36 trained Khmer or ethnic Vietnamese born in Cambodia. Most returned to Cambodia in 1970 at C.P.K. request as advisors.[182]

And according to a 1971 U.S. intelligence study:

> Among the most important steps the Vietnamese Communists have taken to implement their long-range plans to bring Cambodia into the Communist fold has been the recruitment of ethnic Cambodians from South Vietnam and Cambodia for training in North Vietnam. An ex-Viet Cong commo-liaison cadre recently reported that he intermittently saw small groups of these recruits moving to and from North Vietnam during the period 1962-70. Between January 1968 and April 1970, the rate of returnees was said to be about 11 to 12 daily.[183]

It is not clear that any of these cadres returned to *Kampuchea* (rather than to South Vietnam) before 1970, however; and in the context of the development of the revolution there Vietnamese direct aid was limited, in the eyes of many Kampuchean Communists. The gap between their immediate interests and those of Vietnam widened.

Even in Hanoi, according to one of the 2,000-3,000 Khmer training there at the time, the issue was hotly debated. One of those involved was Keo Meas, a former Issarak and Pracheachon Party leader who had fled Sihanouk's Kampuchea in 1958:

> Concerned over Sihanouk's pogram against the Khmer Rouge in the late 1960s, Keo Meas tried to convince the party and the North Vietnamese to send the northern-trained Khmer south to do battle. When refused, Keo Meas was infuriated and accused Son Ngoc Minh of 'becoming fat in safety while the party faithful were being liquidated'. Keo Meas returned to Cambodia . . .[184]

In October 1968, Sihanouk's Government claimed that the 'Revolutionary Front of the Khmer People' was operating in Svay Rieng from bases in N.L.F. zones of Vietnam's Tay Ninh Province.[185] By 1969, there were at least 200 Kampuchean guerrillas in this area.[186] One of their leaders was reportedly So Phim,[187] former Issarak chief of Svay Rieng province and very high-ranking Communist Party leader, with connections with the

Vietnamese revolutionaries. One of his comrades recalled to me in 1980 that Phim 'never forgot' the Vietnamese refusal to supply his forces with guns in this period. Still, in March 1968, Sihanouk announced the capture, near an offshore island, of a motorized junk from South Vietnam, carrying arms for the Khmer Rouge in Kampuchea's south-west. On board, he said were three Vietnamese and two Khmer Krom. Whether these smugglers were Communists or not, the Prince's reaction became fiercer and fiercer. In his May speech about the situation in the north-east, he described what happened to some captured Vietnamese Communists. 'I . . . had them roasted. When you roast a duck you normally eat it. But when we roasted these fellows, we had to feed them to the vultures. We had to do so to ensure our society'.[188] As for the activity of the Khmer revolutionaries, the Prince said:

> I could not tolerate this and took stringent measures which resulted in the annihilation of 180 and the capture of 30 ringleaders, who were shot subsequently . . . I do not care if I am sent to hell . . . and I will submit the pertinent documents to the devil himself . . . I will have them shot . . . I will order the execution of those against whom we have evidence.[189]

The violence mounted. During 1968 in Kompong Cham, the Provincial Governor Nhiem Thien organized witch-hunts for suspected Communists. According to a witness, provincial officials were ordered to take part in beating innocent peasants to death. According to another witness, in Prey Totoeng (a village in Hu Nim's former electoral district) two young children accused of being messengers for the guerrillas had their heads sawn off with palm fronds. Also in 1968, 40 schoolteachers accused of subversive activities were, on Sihanouk's orders, bound hand and foot and thrown from a cliff at Bokor in Kampot.

From July to September 1968 the unrest spread to Phnom Penh itself. A wave of arrests took place and there were even shoot-outs in the street. Among those arrested was Phieuv Hak, 'one of the big bosses of the Khmer Rouge', who, incidentally, has not been heard of since.

In August 1968, the 'surrender' of Khmer Rouge chief Bung Phoeuk in Battambang, along with his wife and three children, was officially announced. Krot Theam reports, however, that in fact Phoeuk and his wife and son were captured and killed by troops.

In 1968-69, there was still a low level of guerrilla warfare throughout the country, but no indication from government sources as to its organizers. Occasionally, provincial guerrilla leaders were mentioned, including men called 'A Min'[190] and 'A Hay' in the south-western provinces of Kampot, Koh Kong and Kompong Speu; two ethnic Thais, Nava and Prachda, specifically in Koh Kong; Prom Leng in Kompong Speu with 50,000 riels (U.S. $1,600) on his head; Mam Pich in Kampot with 70,000 riels on his; Sou Yim in Kompong Chhnang and Peng Cheng in Pursat; the last four were all reported killed by the army in 1968-69.[191]

Perhaps it is significant, however, that the clandestine Communist Party of Kampuchea was publicly recognized in the world Communist movement, in an unprecedented reference in the organ of the East German Communist Party on 22 March 1968.[192]

At any rate, by the end of 1968, 'insecurity' was reported in 11 of Kampuchea's 18 provinces. In mid-1969, rebels felt sufficiently assured of local support to execute publicly centrally-appointed officials in five villages in different parts of the country. Army intelligence estimated the rebel numbers at 5,000-10,000 armed guerrillas, an estimate accepted by the C.I.A.[193] Prince Sihanouk openly admitted his fears at this time that the Kampuchean revolutionary movement might demand a role in negotiations for a settlement of the Vietnam War and 'lay claim to certain zones over which it already exercises its authority'.[194]

By early 1970, the Khmer Rouge had reached a point where they frustrated and occupied a large section of the nation's armed forces, but they did not yet constitute a major military threat to the Phnom Penh Government.[195] Still, the politicization of significant numbers of Kampuchean peasants – Charles Meyer has written that after 1967 Khmer Rouge armed propaganda teams 'circulated in nearly all the villages' of Kampuchea's densely-populated flat regions[196] – was itself a revolution in the countryside. Neither Sihanouk nor Lon Nol could afford to ignore it.

References

1. See Chapter Seven. Also my 'Origins of Khmer Communism', *Southeast Asian Affairs,* Institute of Southeast Asian Studies, Singapore, 1981. pp.161-80.
2. J. Lacouture, *L'Indochine vue de Pekin,* p.90.
3. Douc Rasy, *Khmer Representation at the United Nations,* p.53. I have been unable to find vertification of this report, but the figure may well be true. On the other hand, Sihanouk said in 1972 that in the three years of clashes, ambushes and mopping-up operations from 1967 to 1970, only 'a hundred or so' Khmer Rouge were killed in direct armed struggle 'against the legal authority'. See J. Lacouture, op. cit, p.92. My tallies of figures from published reports put this figure at 200-300 but these are mostly military reports and would perhaps overstate the number of armed rebels killed in clashes – they omit civilian casualties altogether. Douc Rasy's figure of 1,500, if authentic, certainly included a great majority of civilians who co-operated with the rebels, or simply got in the army's way. All sources agree that the army did engage in cruel and often unprovoked repression, especially in June 1967 in Battambang; and Charles Meyer, *Derriere le Sourire Khmer* (Paris, Plon, 1971) says (p.192) that the initial repression occurred without Sihanouk's knowledge.
4. Donald Kirk, *Wider War* (New York, Praeger, 1971), p.78.

5. This revolt in the north-eastern provinces was an important facet of rural dissidence in Kampuchea from 1967 to 1970. For instance, according to Meyer, these Khmer Loeu rebels played a part in the capture of the provincial capital of Kratie from the Phnom Penh Government in May 1970 (op. cit., p.197).
6. See *Le Sangkum,* October 1969, p.97.
7. Quoted by Sihanouk in Lacouture, op. cit., p.118.
8. Gerard Brisee in *L'Annee Politique et Economique* (Paris, July 1970), p.251.
9. Including legal sales to the N.L.F. See R. Prudhomme, *L'Economie du Cambodge* (Paris, 1969), p.255, Table 12, note *a.* See also *Phnom Penh Presse,* 23 February 1967, p.3.
10. *L'Annee Politique et Economique* (Paris, 1971), p.193.
11. *Phnom Penh Presse,* 1 February 1967, Lon Nol had been Governor of Battambang from 1946 to 1953 and during that time was involved in various 'mopping-up' operations against the resistance; he was probably aware that leftist influence still existed there and he may well have considered Battambang to be the N.L.F's main source of Kampuchean rice. He is said to have expressed the wish at the time to carry out the *ramassage* in southern Battambang personally. See M. Caldwell and Tan, *Cambodia in the South East Asian War,* (New York, Monthly Review Press) p.158.
12. For a general discussion of Kampuchean society and government during the 1960s, see Milton Osborne, *Politics and Power in Cambodia,* (Melbourne, Longmans, 1973).
13. J.F. Sonolet, *Realites Cambodgiennes,* 5 November 1971, p.15.
14. Damber was later described in a FUNK publication, as 'un haut-lieu de la resistance cambodgienne', Ieng Sary, *Cambodge 1972,* p.8.
15. *Phnom Penh Presse,* 12 April 1967, p.15.
16. *Les paroles de Norodom Sihanouk,* (Phnom Penh, Ministry of Information) 13 March 1967, speech at Saang.
17. *B.B.C. Summary of World Broadcasts,* FE/2434/A3/9. At this time, Sihanouk commonly claimed that the rebels were attacking him along with Lon Nol, partly as a means to discredit them, on the strength of his own popularity, and partly to defend Lon Nol by association with himself. Although undoubtedly some rebel leaflets attacked Sihanouk, it is likely that most limited their attacks to Lon Nol and his right-wing Government.
18. *Phnom Penh Presse,* 12 April 1967, p.1.
19. Don O. Noel, Jr. 'Cambodia: Up by the Bootstraps', Alicia Patterson Fund, New York, November 1966, p.12.
20. *La Nouvelle Depeche,* 12 April 1967, p.23.
21. *B.B.C. Summary of World Broadcasts,* FE/2425/A2/3.
22. Osborne, op. cit., 1973; p.101.
23. M. Leifer, 'Rebellion or Subversion in Cambodia', *Current History,*

February 1969, p.89.

24. *Les paroles de Norodom Sihanouk,* 13 March 1967, speech at Saang.
25. *B.B.C. Summary of World Broadcasts,* FE/2434/A3/7.
26. *Les paroles de Norodom Sihanouk,* 13 March 1967.
27. *Chronology of Developments Affecting Cambodia,* Despatch (1969), compiled by Frank Tatu, U.S. Foreign Service (unpublished), p.19.
28. Osborne, op. cit., 1973, p.100.
29. Neither the subject of this censure motion nor the voting figures are known. Interestingly, though, peasant uprisings against the *'ramassage'* broke out in the provinces for which Mau Say and Douc Rasy were responsible, namely Battambang (Samlaut) and Kompong Chhnang (Chriev); significantly, perhaps, both men were simultaneously right-wing and efficient.
30. Tatu, op. cit., p.18.
31. *Le Monde,* 14 April 1967.
32. Caldwell and Tan, op. cit., indicate that the camp may have actually been burnt by its committee head (Yim Dith), a top personality in the Lon Nol administration, in order to cover up his misuse of funds (p.158).
33. *B.B.C. Summary of World Broadcasts,* FE/2434/A3/8.
34. Ibid., FE/2438/A3/6.
35. *La Nouvelle Depeche,* 12 April 1967, p.23.
36. *Realites Cambodgiennes,* 19 April 1967, p.10.
37. *Les paroles de Norodom Sihanouk,* 8 May 1967, speech at Thpong.
38. *La Nouvelle Depeche,* 6 July 1967, p.3.
39. This view enjoyed widespread credence until 1970. According to *Realites Cambodgiennes* (12 May 1967, p.17), Hou Yuon's wife did not announce the disappearance of her husband until 29 April, five days later, the morning after she attended a banquet at which the Chinese Ambassador, Chen Shuliang, was also present. *Le Monde* (2 February 1968) reported that 700,000 riels was found in the house of one of the missing deputies – an enormous sum for men who lived simply.
40. *Realites Cambodgiennes,* 19 May 1967, p.3.
41. Ibid., 11 August 1967, p.4.
42. On 19 August 1968, Sihanouk announced that copies of the *Little Red Book* and photos of Mao had been found in a search of this man's home, *B.B.C. Summary of World Broadcasts,* FE/2854/A3/4.
43. *Realites Cambodgiennes,* 19 May 1967, p.3.
44. Including many soldiers stationed there. There were about 5,000 peasants living in the district at the time.
45. *Phnom Penh Presse,* 10 May 1967, p.1.
46. *B.B.C. Summary of World Broadcasts,* FE/2702/A3/6. For a discussion of the destruction of the village of Beng Khtum, see below (p.143).

47. *Phnom Penh Presse,* 27 June 1967, p.2. See also Meyer, op. cit., p.192, and Pomonti and Thion, *La Crise Cambodgienne: des courtesans aux partisans* (Paris, Gallimard 1971), p.112.
48. Milton Osborne, *Before Kampuchea: Prelude to Tragedy,* (London, Oxford University Press, 1979).
49. *Phnom Penh Presse,* 10 May 1967.
50. *Etudes Cambodgiennes,* Vol. 10, April-June 1967, p.4.
51. *B.B.C. Summary of World Broadcasts,* FE/2438/A3/6.
52. Ibid., FE/2480/A3/6.
53. *Kambuja,* September 1967.
54. Especially the three former Khmer provinces of Soctrang, Travinh and Rach Gia.
55. This flow was interrupted during the Second World War. See Jean Delvert, *Le Paysan Cambodgien* (Paris, Mouton, 1960), p.637.
56. He took part in the attack on nearby Banan military post on 19 January 1968, in which the rebels stole 32 rifles. Sar Chamroeun was in touch with leftists in the town of Pursat, and was later captured there. See *Realites Cambodgiennes,* 20 December 1968. I have been unable to find out whether these Khmer Krom settlers played a similar role in unrest in Kampuchea during the 1940s and 1950s.
57. Khmer Krom Refugees in Kampuchea, 1966-68

Date	*Men*	*Women*	*Children*	*Monks*	*Total*
31 December 1966	4,087	3,139	4,043	1,546	*12,815*
31 March 1968	5,294	4,975	4,534	2,344	*17,147*

A similar number of refugees were Vietnamese, Laotians and also some ethnic Khmers from Thailand, mainly former 'Khmer Serei' who surrendered to Kampuchean troops.

58. Beng Khtum was set up in 1966 to accommodate 75 families of Khmer Krom; in February 1967, another 105 refugee families (330 people) settled there. The army helped to clear land for the colonists and in March 1967, tractors and machinery arrived to facilitate this work. The Government allotted 2.5 hectares to each family and encouraged them to grow beans and cotton. Likewise, at Svay Daun Keo in Maung district, the army cleared 2,000 hectares for 58 Khmer Krom families, who each received a house and five hectares for rice cultivation. Schools, medical clinics and access roads were built for both colonies.
59. At Beng Khtum on 5 March 1968, a group of Khmer Krom asked Sihanouk for permission to return to their homeland after the war, but the Prince advised against this. 'Let them settle here instead, in this oasis of peace and liberty that I have preserved for you . . . .' *Realites Cambodgiennes.*
60. *Realites Cambodgiennes,* 12 May 1967, p.5.
61. Pen Ly at Ta Sanh. He was the first official victim of the Samlaut uprising.

62. *Phnom Penh Presse,* 23 February 1967, p.3.
63. Ibid, 2 February 1968.
64. *Realites Cambodgiennes,* 2 June 1967. p.10. After the rebellion broke out, some local co-operatives were dissolved, and the director of one co-operative even committed suicide at Pursat. See Brisse, op. cit., p.251.
65. He similarly denied the army units were quartered in any of the local villages before the uprising began. *Realites Cambodgiennes*, February 1968.
66. *Phnom Penh Presse,* 12 May 1967, p.3.
67. Osborne, op.cit., 1973, p.105.
68. *Realites Cambodgiennes,* 5 March 1968, p.18.
69. See *Le Monde,* 20 November 1969, p.7.
70. And his secretary, a naturalized ethnic Vietnamese. Under the protection of his patron, he is alleged to have perpetrated 'all sorts of abuses towards the common people'.
71. *B.B.C. Summary of World Broadcasts,* FE/2461/B/24.
72. See R Blanadet, in *Les Cahiers d'Outre-Mer* (l'Institut de Geographie de la Faculte des Lettres de Bordeaux, Vols. 22-3, 1970), pp.353-78, for a close study of the Pailin region, from which much of the following information is taken.
73. Ibid., p.369. Later in 1967, as a result of agitation and much violence, renting of land with access to water was abolished, and several large canals, formerly owned by established Burmese families, became public property.
74. Milton Osborne, personal communication.
75. Blanadet, op.cit., p.374.
76. Raymond Blanadet, article on the Andoeuk Hep district, in *Les Cahiers d'Outre-Mer*, Vols. 24-25, 1971, p.185-208.
77. Ibid., p.192.
78. J.F. Sonolet in *Realites Cambodgiennes,* 5 November 1971.
79. Caldwell and Tan, op. cit., pp.157-8. Several sources mention that at this point 'mass demonstrations' against the authorities took place in Battambang City. See Wilfred Burchett, *The Second Indochina War,* (1970, New York, Lorrimer), p.44. No further information is available.
80. *La Nouvelle Depeche,* 9 September 1967, p.2.
81. He was also the President of the Khmer-Chinese Friendship Society. Phouk Chhay was Secretary-General, and Hu Nim one of its Vice-Presidents.
82. As a young man during the 1955 election campaign, Keng Vannsak had published articles criticizing Sihanouk, and was an activist on the left wing of the Democratic Party. He was shot at during the 1955 campaign, and temporarily gaoled after it.
83. *B.B.C. Summary of World Broadcasts,* FE/2600/A3/3.
84. Ibid.

85. According to J.L.S. Girling, he 'is believed to have made his way to Hanoi, in 'The Resistance in Cambodia', *Asian Survey,* Vol 12, No 7, p. 562, July 1972, p.562.

86. His sentence was commuted and he was detained at Kirirom. In May 1970, Lon Nol released 486 political prisoners, Phouk Chhay among them. He soon joined the *maquis.*

87. On 27 January 1968 'speaking of Chau Seng [Sihanouk] said he should prepare to flee, because if he did not and Sihanouk himself took to flight, Chau Seng would not last a day'. See *B.B.C. Summary of World Broadcasts,* FE/2682/A3/10.

88. Caldwell and Tan, op.cit., p.168.

89. By the end of 1967, 40 disappearances had been reported by the official press, but only 28 of them were 'definitely' identified, and many more cases went unnoticed or unreported by the authorities. *Le Monde* (20 November 1969) reported another 40 disappearances by November 1969, making an official total of at least 80 since October 1967.

90. Caldwell and Tan, op.cit., p.168.

91. Apparently, however, it was not always an easy matter for individuals to establish contact with the *maquis.* One man, whom Sihanouk had singled out for a bitter public attack in 1966, went into hiding with relatives in late 1967, and then waited nearly two years before he was sure that he would be welcomed by the *maquisards.* Milton Osborne, personal communication.

92. *B.B.C. Summary of World Broadcasts,* FE/2702/A3/6.

93. Ibid, FE/2682/A3/12.

94. Le Monde, 2 February 1968, *Realites Cambodgiennes,* 20 December 1968. This attack was later claimed by Pol Pot and Noun Chea as the inauguration of the 'Revolutionary Army of Kampuchea'.

95. *B.B.C. Summary of World Broadcasts,* FE/2707/A3/4; *Realites Cambodgiennes*, 9 February 1968, p.23.

96. This figure is based on various reports, over several months, in *Realites Cambodgiennes,* and on Phnom Penh Radio.

97. *B.B.C. Summary of World Broadcasts*, FE/2682/A3/10.

98. Ibid., FE/2690/A3/18. The transcription of the radio broadcast actually reads 'Achar Kres'. For information on Achar Pres see Chapter Five of this volume.

99. *B.B.C. Summary of World Broadcasts,* FE/2682/A3/10.

100. Ibid., FE/2702/A3/6. Sihanouk alleged that the *Little Red Book,* printed in Thai, was being translated into Khmer by the Khmer Rouge, for distribution to the people of Samlaut region.

101. Ibid., FE/2682/A3/10. The 'Khmer Serei' or 'Free Khmers' were armed units of ethnic Kampucheans from South Vietnam and Thailand. They were formed in 1956 by Son Ngoc Thanh, an old enemy of Sihanouk from the pre-Independence years. However, after 1964 when the N.L.F. over-ran their main base in south Vietnam, the Khmer Serei, trained and

equipped by U.S. Special Forces, took part in sabotage and subversion missions into Kampuchea from Thailand. Thai troops and, on at least one occasion, four U.S. Special Forces men took part in such missions inside Kampuchea with the Khmer Serei. Repeated attacks on villages and outposts and sabotage of the Sisophon-Poipet rail section in the 1960s worried most politically-inclined Kampucheans, especially in the light of perennial Thai designs on Kampuchea's western provinces.

102. Ibid., FE/2690/A3/17 (emphasis added).

103. For instance, see his speech at Samlaut in May 1967 when he explained how, in 1955, 'I made the decision to abdicate the throne, to become a simple citizen, to gather together all Khmers who loved peace, justice and progress, and that is how our National Movement, the Sangkum Reastr Niyum, was born'. *Phnom Penh Presse,* 10 May 1967, p.1.

104. In 1967, at least three captured Khmer Serei leaders were executed – Chau Bory, Matura, and Sau Ngoy, who was sentenced on 8 April. *B.B.C. Summary of World Broadcasts,* FE/2445/B/24.

105. Ibid., FE/2682/A3/12.

106. Ibid., FE/2719/A3/11.

107. See *Realites Cambodgiennes*, 20 September 1968, p.23 and 4 October 1968, p.14, and *B.B.C. Summary of World Broadcasts*, FE/3018/A3/3.

108. *Realites Cambodgiennes,* 2 August 1968, p.24.

109. *B.B.C. Summary of World Broadcasts,* FE/2682/A3/10. Meach Kon was replaced by Hou Hong.

110. *Realites Cambodgiennes,* 16 February 1968, p.25.

111. Ibid, 22 March 1968, p.28.

112. *B.B.C. Summary of World Broadcasts*, FE/2706/A3/12.

113. Ibid., FE/2716/A3/11. Evidently this brief glimpse of high society in Kampuchea's towns had not endeared these 200 or so peasants to a government representing the interests of the urban elite. See *Kambuja,* 15 September 1967.

114. *B.B.C. Summary of World Broadcasts,* FE/2702/A3/6.

115. *Realites Cambodgiennes*, 16 February 1968, p.19.

116. By this time the army had organized the inhabitants of some villages into 'self-defence corps'.

117. *B.B.C. Summary of World Broadcasts,* FE/2690/A3/18.

118. *Realites Cambodgiennes,* 16 February 1968.

119. *Le Monde,* 20 November 1969.

120. Ibid., 2 February 1968 and 20 November 1968.

121. *Realites Cambodgiennes,* 23 August 1968.

122. Meyer, op.cit., p.140, note 1.

123. *B.B.C. Summary of World Broadcasts,* FE/2690/A3/18.

124. *Realites Cambodgiennes,* 1 March 1968, p.32.

125. *Le Monde,* 2 February 1968.

126. *Realites Cambodgiennes,* 23 February 1968, p.28.
127. *B.B.C. Summary of World Broadcasts,* FE/2690/A3/18.
128. Ibid., FE/2704/A3/4.
129. Ibid., FE/2707/A3/1 (emphasis added). Apart from an expression of his displeasure with China, this statement represents a retreat from Sihanouk's position of April 1967, when he had declared: 'I dare not . . . ask Russia and China [who] are Red . . . for ammunition and rifles to fight the Khmer Reds.' *B.B.C. Summary of World Broadcasts,* FE/2434/A3/10. Obviously he did not take this new outbreak of the rebellion lightly.
130. Ibid., FE/2702/A3/6.
131. Ibid., FE/2682/A3/13.
132. In an article by Jacques Decornoy, referring to student discontent and rural unrest.
133. *B.B.C. Summary of World Broadcasts,* FE/2707/A3/2.
134. In Khmer, *phnom* means 'hill', or 'mountain'.
135. *Realites Cambodgiennes,* 16 February 1968, p.19.
136. Ibid., 1 March 1968, p. 32
137. Ibid, 16 February 1968, p.19. Some had old English MK7 rifles, some had modern Chinese rifles stolen from provincial guards and a few even had machine pistols.
138. Interestingly, the N.L.F's much larger scale Tet Offensive had just taken place in South Vietnam.
139. *B.B.C. Summary of World Broadcasts,* FE/2719/A3/10.
140. Ibid., FE/2719/A3/8.
141. Ibid.
142. Ibid., FE/2719/A3/9: *Realites Cambodgiennes,* 1 March 1968, p.32.
143. *B.B.C. Summary of World Broadcasts,* FE/2715/A3/10, FE/2719/A3/9.
144. Ibid., FE/2715/A3/11, FE/2719/A3/8.
145. *Realites Cambodgiennes,* 8 March 1968, p.3.
146. *B.B.C. Summary of World Broadcasts,* FE/2719/A3/9.
147. This figure is based on compilations from various reports in *Realites Cambodgiennes* and on Phnom Penh radio.
148. *Realites Cambodgiennes,* 26 April 1968, p.22.
149. Ibid., 31 May 1968, p.19.
150. *B.B.C. Summary of World Broadcasts,* FE/2804/A3/6. In early 1952, a French military train on the Phnom Penh-Battambang railroad near Kouk Banteay district was attacked and destroyed by the Khmer Issarak and over 100 French soldiers were killed. According to Sihanouk current rebel activities in this district were due to the 'same cell which has been come back'. *B.B.C. Summary of World Broadcasts,* FE/2719/A3/10.
151. *Realites Cambodgiennes,* 6 April 1968, p.35.

152. Ibid, 8 March 1968, p.25.
153. *B.B.C. Summary of World Broadcasts,* FE/2724/A3/7.
154. *Realites Cambodgiennes,* 15 March 1968, p.35.
155. *B.B.C. Summary of World Broadcasts,* FE/2719/A3/8.
156. *Realites Cambodgiennes,* 15 March 1968, p.35.
157. Ibid., 22 March 1968, p. 24.
158. *B.B.C. Summary of World Broadcasts,* FE/2709/A3/13.
159. Ibid., FE/2709/A3/12.
160. Ibid., FE/2719/A3/9.
161. *Realites Cambodgiennes,* 22 March 1968, p.25.
162. *B.B.C. Summary of World Broadcasts,* FE/2715/A3/10.
163. Ibid., FE/2719/A3/8.
164. Ibid., FE/2715/A3/10.
165. Ibid.
166. Ibid., FE/2716/A3/11. At least seven battalions of troops were operating in Battambang province alone. R. Shaplen, *Time Out of Hand,* p.319.
167. Ibid.
168. Ibid.
169. *B.B.C. Summary of World Broadcasts,* FE/2719/A3/8, 10.
170. *Realites Cambodgiennes,* 6 April 1968, p.35.
171. Meyer, op. cit., p.193.
172. *Realites Cambodgiennes,* 22 March 1968, p.35.
173. Ibid., March 1968, p.21.
174. 23 were killed in a single clash at Phnom Veay Chap on 23 March. *Realites Cambodgiennes*, 6 April 1968, p.35.
175. Troops had captured at least 74 rifles over the preceding 12 months which had been manufactured at Phnom Veay Chap. It is likely that many more were never captured.
176. See *Realites Cambodgiennes*, 26 April 1968, p.22. After a search of the rebel hideouts, troops discovered 73 rifles, two grenades and various stocks of ammunition, as well as food, medical equipment and documents, several granaries, 50 kilos of saltpetre, 20 kilos of powder, 1 stove, 2 bullock carts and as many as 163 sacks of rice.
177. *Realites Cambodgiennes,* 18 May 1968, p.20.
178. Ibid, 12 April 1968, p.43.
179. Phnom Penh Radio, 28 September 1977, U.S. C.I.A. F.B.I.S. 4 October 1977, pp. H20-21. See also 'Discours Prononce par le Camarade Pol Pot', distributed by the Kampuchean Embassy in Peking, dated 27 September 1977.
180. Phnom Penh Radio, 19 May 1968; F.B.I.S., 20 May 1968, pp.HI-2.
181. Wilfred Burchett, *Second Indochina War* (London, Lorrimer, 1970) p.54.

182. Timothy Carney, 'Cambodia: The Unexpected Victory', forthcoming
183. *Communist Infrastructure in Cambodia,* D.I.A. Intelligence Appraisal, 8 July 1971, p.3.
184. 'Khmer Rouge Rallier Keoum Kun', Airgram, U.S. Department of State,Phnom Penh Embassy, 13 January 1972.
185. *Le Monde,* 20 November 1969.
186. Sangkum, October 1969, p.97.
187. *New York Times,* 19 April 1970, gives Phim's alais So Vanna
188. Phnom Penh Radio, 19 May 1968; F.B.I.S., 20 May 1968.
189. Ibid, and Phnom Penh Radio, 4 June 1968, F.B.I.S. 6 June 1968, pp.H2-3.
190. *Realites Cambodgiennes,* 7 July 1969 and 1 August 1969.
191. Ibid, 3 October 1969 and 10 October 1969, 22 March 1968, 2 August 1968.
192. *Neues Deutschland,* quoted in *Yearbook on International Communist Affairs* (1969), p.100. The Kampuchean party was referred to as 'one of several' Marxist-Leninist parties born since 1960' which should be invited to take part in preparations for a world Communist meeting.'
193. Samuel Adams' congressional testimony in *US Policies and Programs in Cambodia (1973),* pp. 92-3.
194. *Yearbook on International Communist Affairs* (1970), p.533, quotation in original.
195. For a different view, see Stephen Heder, 'Kampuchea's Armed Struggle', *Bulletin of Concerned Asian Scholars,* Vol. 11, No. 1, 1979, pp.2-23, Heder considers that 'the C.P.K's armed forces' may have then numbered as many as 50,000 and that by the late 1960s they 'represented a major threat to the Sihanouk regime's army' (p.14).
196. Meyer, op.cit., See pp.197-8 for more details.

8. The 1970 Peasant Uprisings Against Lon Nol by Ben Kiernan

On 18 March 1970, Prince Norodom Sihanouk of Kampuchea was overthrown by the National Assembly led by General Lon Nol. The unrest that soon broke out in parts of the east, south-east and south-west of the country was generally seen at the time as an indication of unswerving loyalty among the peasantry to their 'god-king'. I suggest that these events were more complex. While the Prince was a popular figure, other factors were also important in motivating the peasant demonstrations, in particular the existence of a strong revolutionary movement in the main sites of unrest, Kompong Cham and Takeo-Kampot.

The first sign of rural discontent with the Lon Nol regime seems to have come on 25 March, a week after the overthrow of Sihanouk. Fifteen hundred people from the village of Kompong Reap demonstrated outside the local district headquarters at Tuol Svay Chrum, 10 kilometres south of Kompong Cham City. They asked for the return of Prince Sihanouk 'to have it out with the Government', and for the dissolution of the National Assembly.[1] The Provincial Governor promised to pass on their request to the Phnom Penh authorities, and the crowd dispersed peacefully. Two extra army battalions, from units of Khmer Krom trained by the C.I.A. in South Vietnam, were moved to Kompong Cham.

Next day, another peasant demonstration led by the same people took place close to Kompong Cham. The Provincial Governor wrote:

> At the end of an hour and a half of negotiations, we were completely outflanked by the demonstrators who were moving towards the centre of town. . . . I had noticed old people, and above all women and children, among the demonstrators. For that reason I insisted that the armed forces not use guns.

He is said to have estimated the crowd at 25,000.[2] According to Laura Summers, this demonstration once again 'ended peacefully, but while the Governor was telephoning this news to Phnom Penh, other groups of demonstrators from Tonle Bet, Chamcar Loeu and Choeung Prey were sacking the provincial courthouse and the Governor's mansion'.[3]

They seem to have come from nearby rural areas, in particular the electoral districts of Saukong, Chrey Vien and Speu (Chamcar Loeu) on the right bank of the Mekong, and Mohaleap and Chup on the left. For instance, one eyewitness reported a meeting of 400-600 people from the villages of Peam Chikang, Rokar Koy and Angkor Ban, organized by local associates of Hou Yuon who had been the representative of Saukong in the National Assembly. While local officials laid low, the demonstrators travelled in five large buses from Peam Chikang towards Kompong Cham, but seven kilometres west of the town they were fired on by troops and forced to disperse.[4] In several other villages, 'the officials fled, while in others they were massacred'.[5]

Early on the afternoon of the 26th an official delegation from Phnom Penh arrived in Kompong Cham, saw the extent of the damage and immediately returned to the capital. Laura Summers concludes that 'the situation had passed the point of discussion. During this time, crowds were spreading all across the town. The Governor's mansion was sacked a second time.' The sign in front of the court of justice was altered to read 'injustice'.

The Government responded to these events by attributing them to Vietnamese-inspiration. Phnom Penh Radio announced: 'It is certain that this demonstration was instigated by the Vietcong, who are very skilful at this sort of thing. This provocation by people with a Vietcong mentality is most regrettable.'[6] At 6 p.m., two National Assembly representatives, Sos Saoun and Kim Phon, arrived unexpectedly. The peasant demonstrators accosted them and took them to the local textile factory, where they were killed and their livers eaten, a traditional means of drawing strength from enemies.[7] Meanwhile, in Tonle Bet, a crowd attacked and killed Lon Nill, a policeman and brother of Lon Nol. And further out in the countryside, a few kilometres south of Kompong Cham, 1,500 demonstrators took over the administrative post at Au Raeng O Raeng Au and hung up a portrait of Prince Sihanouk inside.[8] A supporter of the Lon Nol regime was cut to pieces while trying to speak to the rally.

Towards evening, the demonstrators in Kompong Cham began to seize trucks to take them to Phnom Penh. Between 20 and 50 trucks set out, followed by about 10,000 marchers. This was one of three columns to head for Phnom Penh from widely dispersed parts of the country. Evidently, they planned to meet up at the stadium in the capital.

Two columns of trucks, one apparently from Siem Reap in the northwest of the country and the one from Kompong Cham, met up north of Phnom Penh, but were halted not far from the capital at the Chrui Changwar Bridge on the morning of 27 March. Government soldiers opened fire, killing a truck driver called Kai Nam and wounding others, and forced the crowd to turn back. 'Military sources reported that more than a thousand demonstrators were arrested.'[9]

However, the most serious incident reported took place a little later at Skoun, on the road from Kompong Cham to Phnom Penh. Marchers had 'spread out along the road, stopping cars and painting "Vive Sihanouk" on the doors', and handing out pictures of Sihanouk to the drivers. When they arrived at Skoun, demonstrators and locals massed in the streets and were addressed by leaders with loudspeakers. They broke into the Government offices at Skoun, and burnt records. The air-force and Khmer Krom troops opened fire, and between 40 and 60 people were killed or wounded.[10] According to Pomonti and Thion, 'there was no indication of the brutality of the army's reaction . . . the repression turned into a manhunt. The army used anti-aircraft batteries . . . and tanks to repress a crowd of peasants, the vast majority of whom were unarmed.'[11]

In the elections of 1955, the province of Kompong Cham was one of the few areas in which the newly-radicalized Democratic Party and the socialist Pracheachon Party were able to gain sizeable proportions of the vote under the difficult campaign conditions.[12] In Mohaleap, for instance, which includes Kompong Reap and Au Raeng Au, the two parties received a combined vote of 44%.[13] This pattern was repeated in the next contested general elections, in 1966. Left-wing candidates gained a total of 53% of the vote in three electoral districts on the right bank: one revolutionary, Hou Yuon, gained 78% in Saukong; next door in Chrey Vien, Hu Nim gained 52% against his closest rival's 14%; and in neighbouring Speu, left-wing candidate Monh Moeung received 25% of the vote.[14]

The 1966 elections were important because they were contested. Previously, in 1958 and 1962, Prince Sihanouk's Sangkum Party had nominated the only candidate in each electoral district. But in 1966, the Prince was prevailed upon, and 425 candidates were nominated for the 82 seats. Sihanouk's withdrawal from the campaign in most electoral districts meant that local issues and in particular local interests played a crucial role. Only 42 incumbents were confident enough of their local strength to seek re-election, and only 27 of these were successful. One-third of the 55 incoming representatives had actually been absent from the political scene since at least 1955. They were all known as men of the traditional elite who had already achieved positions of authority before the War within the French colonial system (13 were members of Lon Nol's Renovation Party in the early 1950s).[15] These leaders of the landowning and official class, and similar younger men, were able to turn their political and economic grip on peasants in the localities to good electoral advantage. However, within a given electoral district such local interests were geographically diverse, and the 1966 vote in most districts was evenly divided among a number of candidates.[16] Clear winners were rare; the victors got 40% of the vote, and one-third won with less than 30%.

The degree of support for Hu Nim and Hou Yuon in 1966 was therefore unusual, as was the fact that it was obtained without significant economic influence in their districts and in the face of considerable pressure from Prince Sihanouk, who campaigned actively and specifically against them.[17] These two, representatives of the previous assembly, and Monh Moeung, a railways union activist, had incurred the Prince's wrath as early as 1963, when a student demonstration and police riot in Siem Reap had developed into a small rebellion, leading to the resignation of the Cabinet. All three men were named by Sihanouk in a list of 34 leading 'subversive leftists'. And, soon after, when the now rightist-dominated Cabinet resumed office, Hou Yuon and Khieu Samphan, State Secretaries of Economic Planning and of Commerce, were the sole omissions. Fearing repression, any of the leftists on Sihanouk's list, fled into the countryside. Hou Yuon, for his part, though out of the Cabinet, retained his Saukong seat in the National Assembly.

Michael Vickery saw the strong showing by the Left in Kompong Cham in 1966 as 'one of the first indications that Sihanouk was losing his magic. . . clearcut cases of popular support in the face of official opposition'.[18] It is ironic that, four years later, the protest demonstrations against Sihanouk's overthrow were the largest in the country. But it would be misleading to characterize these uprisings as simply peasant outrage at the overthrow of the Prince; since the local peasants had so resoundingly rejected Sihanouk's political approaches in 1966.

Hou Yuon and Hu Nim were not to last very long in the National Assembly. 2 April 1967 saw the beginning of the Samlaut rebellion, soon laid at the door of the leftist politicians (see Chapter Nine). Lon Nol prepared to call them before a military tribunal. Hou Yuon and Khieu Samphan disappeared in late April to join the revolution in the countryside. It was widely believed that they had been killed by the secret police, and 15,000 of their supporters demonstrated in Phnom Penh and nearby villages; protesters elsewhere included 80 process workers from the Kompong Cham textile factory. With banners and loudspeakers, they marched for four hours through the town on 5 May 1967, and tried in vain to present a petition to the Provincial Governor. The crowd condemned the then Prime Minister Lon Nol and held his Government responsible for 'the disappearance of the two heroes'.[19] In October 1967, Hu Nim went underground in Kompong Cham Province, following a speech in which Sihanouk advised them to 'go over to the other side, as Khieu Samphan and Hou Yuon had done'.[20] In December the by-elections held to replace Hou Yuon were boycotted by most Saukong voters. The winner received only 2,481 votes, compared to Hou Yuon's 12,477 the year before.[21]

Hou Yuon kept his local political organization intact, even strengthened it, after he went underground, although his presence was sometimes reported in other parts of Kampuchea over the next three years. The protest meetings of March 1970 in Peam Chikang were, it seems, repeated in other subdistricts of Saukong. Lach Soeum, who had replaced Hou Yuon as the local representative, was attacked by a crowd of about 50 at his house in the west of the district.[22]

Hu Nim's district was also difficult to win over. His replacement was In Tam, a well-known Government figure evidently selected as candidate for his prestige. In Tam resigned his own seat in Poes electoral district of

Kompong Cham in August 1968 in order to stand in Chrey Vien, thus dashing the election hopes of Sos Saoun, who had stood against Hu Nim in 1966 but had only received 11% of the vote. The new representative in Poes was Kim Phon, well known to be a fervent admirer of Sihanouk[23] and who had been unsuccessful against In Tam (in third place, with 11% of the vote to Tam's 55%). The March 1970 assassination by local peasants of Sos Saoun and Kim Phon, both of whom had been so soundly defeated at the polls in 1966, one by Hu Nim and the other, in spite of his support for Sihanouk, again points to more than mere outrage at the demise of the Prince.

What social and economic conditions prevailed in Kompong Cham? In the 1950s, Jean Delvert made detailed studies of two subdistricts not far to the north and west of the provincial capital.[24] In the rice-growing subdistrict of Krala, landholdings were inequitably divided among the 168 families surveyed. The richest 20% of the population owned 64% of the land (the richest 5% owned 28% of the land, of which they rented out 19%). On the other hand, the poorest 80% of the population owned only 36% of the land; including a huge group (44%) who owned only 2% of the land.

As a result, only 125 families made a living from farming. Of these, 24% were very small landowners (with less than one hectare) and another 14% were small landowners (with from 1-2 hectares). A further 18% were sharecroppers, tenants or partial tenants, and 43% were middle peasants (with 2-5 hectares). In addition, 12% of these 125 farming families possessed no beasts of burden, and those owned by another 5% were inadequate; 25% were without a plough and 49% had no ox-cart (rent or purchase of these was expensive).

Of the 43 families who did not make a living from farming, three large landlords lived from rents. A few were widows who rented out small parcels of land left them by their husbands. The rest were 'petty merchants' or labourers, most of whom only eked out a bare subsistence. One 'miserable man' did not even own a house and for seven months of the year performed the 'considerable' feat of climbing 57 sugar palms twice a day to collect their juice to sell.

In Roang, Delvert studied 399 families and found that river-bank land was also divided up inequitably. The poorest 52% of the population possessed only 6% of the land; the next 14% owned 8%. The very richest 6%, however, owned 39% of the land; there was also a large rich peasant class, 28% of the population, who owned 47% of the land. Many were landless, 22% owning 'nothing'. Only a quarter of these were able to make a living from agriculture even by renting land. 18% of the population were small 'merchants', mostly selling firewood; one-sixth of these even had to rent the land on which their house was built. Another 14% were 'poor people . . . mostly miserable', who worked as coolies. Two-thirds of Roang's families farmed: 61% of these worked 31% of the land, and nearly half of them had no beasts of burden. The top 19% worked 49% of the land. Yet these figures still disguise 6% who were tenants and 11% who were partial tenants.

It is worth noting that Delvert's enquiry covered 75% of Roang's population but only 54% of its land; it therefore includes 'a large proportion of poor people'. Still, the fact that the remaining 46% of the land was owned by 25% of the population serves to underline the social inequality. Delvert also provides more scattered data for the right-bank districts where peasant unrest was reported in 1970 – Kang Meas (Saukong), Prey Chhor (Chrey Vien), Chamcar Loeu (Speu) and Choeung Prey.

In Roca Koy, one of 10 subdistricts of Saukong, landlordism was of some importance; 12 landowners possessed over 10 hectares; and a 'rather extensive' tract of land was owned by the Mission Apostolique. But because land was 'rather abundant' there and because geographical conditions prevented the usual river-bank practice of doublecropping, the average *property* in Roca Koy was 2.5 hectares, 'which is exceptionally large for the river-banks' (the overall average including the rest of Saukong was less than one hectare).[25] Delvert does not give the average *farm* size in Roca Koy; however, if we apply his general comment that 'he who possesses more than one hectare [of river-bank land] can live without working'[26] to the specific conditions obtaining in Roca Koy, we may conclude that it was something less than 2.5 hectares. This indicates some degree of partial tenancy. It does seem, though, that the availability of land in Roca Koy meant that few there were so poor as to be landless labourers or full tenants. Delvert mentions none of the latter and only a dozen wage labourers (there were 700 farmers). Perhaps this (relative) prosperity in Roca Koy subdistrict helps explain why Hou Yuon received only 55% of the vote there in 1966.

He averaged 81% in the other nine subdistricts of Saukong, which were economically more akin to other river-bank districts: very small property ownership, 'most of the small landowners are at the same time tenants. The rent is high . . .'[27] For instance, in Peam Chikang, five Chinese merchants alone owned more than 30 hectares of land each, amounting to well over 10% of the land there. The annual rents they charged were 'high, up to 10% of the land value'. Another 42 hectares were owned in 1956 by the company Manufacture Cambodgienne de Cigarettes, and rented out to about 80 peasant tenants. By 1959, the figure had doubled.[28]

In Hu Nim's Chrey Vien area, Delvert noted that a single landlord in the Lovea subdistrict owned 52 hectares and in Prey Chhor district four landlords owned more than 10 hectares each.[29] Sharecropping, the mode of cultivation used by big '*concessionaires*', was practised in Prey Chhor, according to Delvert. However, some landlords, 'disheartened' by several years of drought in the 1950s, left their lands fallow.[30] (The situation by 1970 is unknown.) Many peasants had to survive on small farms: 53% of the landowners in Prey Chhor subdistrict owned less than one hectare each,[31] totalling at the very most 32% of the cultivated land. The richest

20% of the landowners owned over 44% of the land (with two hectares or more each), but even some of these were in dire economic straits. Delvert studied a household in Khvet, Prey Chhor, with two hectares of land which had an annual deficit of 1,000 riels, and was forced to borrow this sum each year at 80% interest.[32] And this was described by Delvert as a 'rich rice-growing region'.[33] The population of Prey Chhor subdistrict had increased by 12% by 1966 over that reported by Delvert; by 1970, continued population pressure can only have increased the supply of labour and decreased the availability of land, weakening further the economic position of the poor.

People from the nearby districts of Chamcar Loeu and Choeung Prey also took part in the 1970 protests. In Chamcar Loeu, peasant tenants farmed 6,000 hectares of land belonging to rubber estates, 2,500 of which were in Chamcar Andong subdistrict,[34] where leftist Monh Moeung received 44% of the local vote – easily his best subdistrict. The rest of the land in Chamcar Loeu belonged 'in the greatest majority of cases to rich Sino-Khmers who were illegally accorded concessions through corruption or who rented land from the plantations'. This, says Delvert, was a source of 'easy profits' for these merchants and officials who were 'in frequent cases' accorded 30 hectares of land.[35] It was also a real means of exploiting the peasantry who were often *sub*-tenants.

This did not mean that the peasantry of Chamcar Loue were uniformly submissive to authority. Some had established themselves without authorization on conceded land and the rubber estate was 'practically obliged to renounce its rights' there; elsewhere they had illegally settled on land belonging to the state. These farmers paid no rent but nor did they possess any security of tenure. Further south, 'nearly all' the families who had established the village of Chamcha in 1948 were landless peasants and in the 1950s were threatened with expulsion by the Administration.[36] Of the peasants in the rest of the subdistrict, Chamcar Krauch, 'the majority rented land', according to Delvert. 'They live miserably, tenants and coolies at the same time.'[37] During the 1960s, tenants seem to have become landless labourers. In late 1966, an American journalist reported on the impact of the 'green revolution' in Chamcar Krauch: the average farm was now over six hectares, too large for a family farm. One landlord, owning 12 hectares, employed six permanent and 24 seasonal labourers.[38]

Even at Speu, with its black soils – 'the best rice field soils in Cambodia'[39] – Delvert found that 20% of the peasants were tenants, another 10% partial tenants, and that there was a 'significant number' of landless labourers.[40] According to Liv Khun Leng, a participant in the 1970 demonstrations, the largest single group of peasant protestors came from Speu; he says they were landowners sympathetic to Sihanouk. Delvert, however, concluded a discussion of the Chamcar Loeu area:

> The society is very hierarchical: small landowners.... miserable peasants renting *chamcar* and either working as coolies on the

> plantations or for rich *concessionaires* or leaseholders. Moreover the conflicts between the peasants, the planters and the Administration, which is anxious to keep its reserves intact, are incessant.[41]

In the west of Kompong Cham Province is the Choeung Prey district, a 'rather mediocre' area, according to Delvert, with sandy soil, 'suffering from drought in the dry season and flooding in the rainy season'. Delvert's study of two subdistricts, Batheay and Pha Ao, revealed that over 25% of the peasants in each were landless. Neighbouring subdistricts appear to have been even harder pressed: 'A third of the population of Sandek and Trap temporarily emigrate to Batheay and Pha Ao as coolie-planters or as coolies for the Public Works', and in Sampong Chey 'very poor people' were 'common'.[42] In 1958, Choeung Prey was one of 39 of Kampuchea's 90-odd districts described by Sihanouk as 'red' or 'pink'.[43] (Interestingly, Kang Meas, Prey Chhor and Chamcar Loeu were not then regarded as red or pink.) Son Phuoc Tho, who in the late 1950s was an associate of Hou Yuon, was elected to represent the Choeung Prey district in the National Assembly in 1962. He fell out with Sihanouk and did not stand for re-election in 1966 (his successor won 34% of the vote, and two runners up 30% and 26%). It was here, at Skoun, that troops opened fire on protestors in 1970.

Large numbers of the workers at Kampuchea's only rubber plantations in Kompong Cham also took part in the 1970 protests. The biggest plantations are on the east bank of the Mekong. Here, Vietnamese labourers are said to have founded Kampuchea's first Communist cell. But Kampuchean poor or landless peasants, who now formed a majority of the plantation workers, soon became known for their political involvement. In 1955, the Pracheachon received 24% of the vote in the Krek electoral district (their national average was 42%)

> despite harassment by the police at their meetings and the banning of their press, as well as the handicap of a candidate who spent most, – if not all – the period of the campaign in goal.[44] In 1958, Sihanouk had described all three districts of Kompong Cham east of the Mekong as 'red' or 'pink'. [5]

After demonstrators from the Chup plantation had assassinated Lon Nol's brother, the plantations were closed down as the workers went on an indefinite strike from 28 March 1970 and staged more rallies near Tonle Bet. The next day, the Government reacted by instructing naval patrol boats on the Mekong to direct artillery fire into the rubber plantations. It was clear that the authorities were losing control of the area, and attempts to force the workers to return to work were unsuccessful.[46] In the easternmost part of Kompong Cham Province, demonstrations were also reported in the rubber plantation towns of Snuol and Mimot, and protesters were reported to have been fired upon by troops.[47]

In fact, the Kompong Cham protests were as much a result of the local numerical strength (linked to significant peasant grievances) and organizational capacity of the revolutionary movement as of loyalty to Prince Sihanouk. Speaking of the development of the revolutionary forces from 1968 to 1970, Pol Pot in 1977 singled out Kompong Cham Province for special mention, even claiming that: 'At night, our army controlled all of National Highway 7.' Highway 7 runs only through Kompong Cham Province, between Skoun and Snuol, precisely the area of the main 1970 uprisings.[48] It was here, in particular, near the rubber plantations in the eastern part of the province, at Damber that the local population later that year called for the return of the revolutionary Khmer Issarak leader Son Ngoc Minh, who had been in Hanoi since 1954.[49] Moreover, according to Charles Meyer, two revolutionary bases were at that time situated very close to the protest area, one on each side of Highway 7, on each side of the Mekong.[50] Officials in the late 1960s did not venture without military escorts into the Baray district adjoining Choeung Prey and Chamcar Loeu districts, nor into Damber.[51] The Lon Nol Government betrayed its own bankruptcy in the face of the growing political crisis in the Province: 'The salvation government regrets these events in Kompong Cham, which the entire Kampuchean nation had considered was fully populated by citizens of the highest consciousness.'[52]

The other major centre of anti-government activity was Ang Tasom district in Takeo Province in the south-west; there, troops killed about 100 peasants and wounded 100 more in two days.

By 27 March, tension seems to have been mounting in Takeo, when In Tam, at the invitation of the Provincial Governor, attended a rally 'to explain the coup to the people'. The next day, 300 peasants near Ang Tasom, 12 kilometres west of Takeo City, overturned two cars belonging to the local Buddhist hierarchy and burnt the files in a local government office.[53] Policemen only 50 feet away did not interfere. The next day, Sunday 29th, a crowd of 2,000 invaded the local offices at Ang Tasom, broke up furniture and destroyed government records. About 50 police and soldiers opened fire, leaving 66 dead and 78 wounded.[54] That same afternoon, 500 peasants massed at Kong Pisei, 15 kilometres to the north, and began to march on Takeo. Tanks forced them to turn back.[55]

The next morning, a crowd of 200 assembled in the market place of Prey Sandek, about 15 kilometres south-east of Ang Tasom. Armed with machetes, clubs and axes, and calling out 'Long live Sihanouk', they forced the townspeople to hang pictures of the Prince outside their homes. When they began to build barricades outside the government offices, the army opened fire, killing 48 and wounding 33. A comment by a local official once again exposed the inadequacy of the Lon Nol Government's explanation of the unrest: 'We are looking for the leaders. In my district, moreover, there are very few Vietnamese, and they are taking care not to put a foot wrong.'[56]

Fighting that took place at nearby Kori that weekend between government troops and what were officially described as 'poorly armed Vietcong' seems to indicate local guerrilla activity. When U.S. and Saigon troops invaded Kampuchea in early May 1970, some of the toughest resistance they encountered was in the Ang Tasom area.

As in Kompong Cham, it was the strength of the local revolutionary movement, as well as loyalty to Prince Sihanouk, which was at the root of these outbreaks; indeed they seem to have been co-ordinated to paralyse government operations in a specific locality (Ang Tasom) in a short period of time.

In the early 1950s, the French colonial authorities had rounded up 282,000 people from these western districts of Takeo Province, as well as another 30,000 from adjacent districts of Kampot, and resettled them in large villages on main roads.[57] Intended to remove the people from the influence of the revolutionaries, it was not completely successful. Sihanouk in 1958 still included the districts where Ang Tasom and Prey Sandek are located, as well as Kong Pisei district and Chhouk in Kampot, on his list of 'red' and 'pink' districts.[58]

In the 1955 elections, the Pracheachon received 34% of the vote in Chhouk electoral district; in 1962, they were outlawed, and in 1966, the winning Sangkum candidate received 29%. In the neighbouring electoral district, which includes Ang Tasom and the area of major 1970 unrest, the Pracheachon got 11% in 1955. The Party's average vote in these and three other districts in the Takeo-Kampot area was 16%, four times its national average. In the 1966 elections, no clear winners emerged in any of the districts where the 1970 uprisings took place; in fact, the average winning vote was 28%, compared with 40% nationally. But the representative elected by the Kong Pisei area in 1966 was Im Phon, a leader of the radical wing of the 1955 Democratic Party who had in 1963 been included on Sihanouk's list of 'subversive leftists'. He was the brother of Mey Pho, a leading Khmer Communist based in Hanoi since 1954.

The Elephant Mountains, which run through the region, were a major base area of the revolutionary Khmer Issarak in the early 1950s, who were apparently succeeded in the late 1960s by the guerrilla movement, and Khieu Samphan was reported to be based there. The revolutionaries enjoyed considerable mobility in the area. According to local accounts, in 1969 Samphan openly passed a day with monks in Tani pagoda, not far from Prey Sandek.

In early 1968, 3,000 local people fled army repression and joined the rebels in the forests and hills. Fierce fighting took place, especially in Chhouk. Prince Sihanouk himself visited Kong Pisei district on 10 February 1968, in an attempt to calm the unrest there, but was unsuccessful. In March, Prime Minister Lon Nol called in the air force to bombard revolutionary positions in Kong Pisei.[59] It is clear in this case too that it would be an oversimplification to regard the protests that broke out in the same area two years later as demonstrations of peasant support for Prince Sihanouk.

Further south, in the coastal area near the Vietnamese border, more unrest was reported. There, also, the strength of the revolutionary movement ment as well as loyalty to the Prince was manifested. In the town of Kampot 'more than 300 persons joined the struggle movement and broadcast aloud the statement of Samdech Norodom Sihanouk'.[60] In Kep, a number of government cars were burnt during pro-Sihanouk demonstrations; according to the *New York Times,* a coconut plantation just outside that town was 'reported occupied by 100 Vietcong and 300 Cambodian rebels, commonly known as Khmer Rouge'.[61]

A third area of unrest was the south-east, centred east of Neak Luong. On 26 and 27 March, meetings were held at various points along Highway 1. A column of trucks, motorcycles and bicycles, including 'thousands of demonstrators' from Prey Veng, and more from Neak Luong,[62] approached the capital from Svay Rieng; it was stopped by troops at Koki, 20 kilometres east of Phnom Penh on the Mekong. Soldiers began another manhunt, and, aided by artillery from gunboats in the river, killed at least 12 demonstrators; the rest retreated. Two more representatives from the National Assembly were apparently attacked by the crowd.[63]

More protests were reported at Kompong Trabek in Prey Veng. On 29 March 'according to Associated Press, hundreds of demonstrators, many carrying Sihanouk's picture, machetes and sharpened bamboo poles, surged through the streets' of the town, urging the Prince's return.[64] The next day, their attempts to march on Phnom Penh were obstructed by barricades hastily thrown up by troops.[65] A few days later, on 4 April, Kampuchean revolutionaries seized the Krasang military post about 20 kilometres north of Kompong Trabek, and took control of that area.[66]

In this region also, the Pracheachon had enjoyed well above average support. In 1955, the Party had received 16% of the vote in the region, including 22% in the district near Kompong Trabek. In 1962, a wealthy Sino-Khmer businessman from Phnom Penh gained influence in his electoral district by bribing the local official, and in the contested elections of 1966 managed to secure re-election by paying all his voters 40 riels each.[67] Even so, this only won him 49% of the vote. Results in surrounding electoral districts also saw narrow pluralities of about 40%, with no clear winners.

There were other developments in this eastern area, closer to the Vietnamese border. For several years, Kampuchean guerrillas had been active along the eastern edge of Svay Rieng Province. When under pressure, these revolutionaries had enjoyed the use of Vietnamese liberated zones in Tay Ninh Province across the border. In October 1968, the Phnom Penh Minister for National Security claimed that the 'Revolutionary Front of the Khmer People' consisted of about 100 guerrillas in that area.[68] A year later, Lon Nol estimated that their number had doubled.[69] On 5 April 1970, soon after the March uprisings, they took the important township of Kompong Trach, situated in an area where the Pracheachon had won 24%

of the 1955 vote – more than that won by the victorious legal candidates in 1966.

The role of the peasants' loyalty to Prince Sihanouk in these demonstrations can perhaps be best assessed by a comparison with other pro-Sihanouk demonstrations when the Prince was under similar, but not such immediate, political pressure.

Early in 1968, the revolutionaries had staged co-ordinated attacks on army posts in the north-east, north-west and south-west of Kampuchea, with 10,000 peasants swelling their ranks. Sihanouk called for his supporters to stand up and be counted, and, in the first week of March 1968, demonstrations in favour of his 'Buddhist Socialist regime' accordingly took place in the towns of Kompong Thom, Kratie, Kompong Speu, Kampot, Kompong Chhnang, Battambang and Kompong Cham. On 4 March, 70,000 'volunteers', according to Phnom Penh radio, were presented to Prince Sihanouk and expressed their determination to suppress the revolutionaries 'and their subversive activities'.[70]

Why did such widespread loyalty to the Prince not manifest itself again in 1970, when he was actually overthrown? Why, in 1970, were there pro-Sihanouk demonstrations *only* in Kompong Cham and Takeo Kampot, areas where the revolutionaries themselves were strong?[71] A close look at the 1968 demonstrations shows that they were quite different from those of 1970.

> On 3rd March 1968, between 08.00 and 09.00 in Kompong Speu and Kratie provinces, the bonzes [monks], military and civil authorities of all levels, members of the Sangkum at both the regional and provincial levels, young men and women, students, and Khmer and Chinese inhabitants of the provinces of Kompong Speu and Kratie numbering in the tens of thousands demonstrated against the Khmer Reds and Blues. They carried side arms, axes, clubs, bows and rifles, and formed a procession which made for the office of the province chief, where one of the demonstrators read a motion of support for the Throne, Samdech Euv, and the Buddhist Socialist regime. The motion also condemned the Khmer Reds and Blues in a variety of terms. After they had read the motions, the demonstrators dispersed and returned to their homes in silence and in orderly fashion.[72]

Subsequent reports by Phnom Penh radio list similar expressions of support from the Public Health Department, the Interior Ministry, the Education Ministry and various other official organizations and higher strata of society, such as the Venerable Chief of the Mohanikay Order and other clergy.

Obviously, these were not 'peasant protests'. In fact, they were organized by the various government departments. The support that the Prince enjoyed among peasants seems to have been rather passive. The absence of the word 'peasant' or 'farmer' in the radio report seems significant. Without either the official government apparatus, as in 1968, or, as in 1970, an underground movement with specific appeal to peasants on a political and economic basis, the Prince simply did not have the independent capacity to mobilize them.

But there is no doubt that Sihanouk did have some sway over peasants. The 1970 demonstrations crystallized around him; his portrait was carried at most of them. One commentator has written:

> It is almost as if Sihanouk's portraits were more important than the man himself, suggesting that these people demonstrated their loyalty to a traditional source of power rather than a political figure. One is reminded of the tenacity with which Javanese peasants, after the re-occupation of Java by the Dutch in 1947-48, insisted on receiving payment in Indonesian Republican currency, which carried the portrait of the man – Sukarno – who had convinced the Javanese that power resided in him and emanated from him.[73]

On the other hand, the *political* limitations of this quasi-religious nature of Sihanouk's appeal are manifested in the demands of the peasant demonstrators from Kampong Reap on 25 March 1970, 'that Prince Sihanouk be allowed to return to Kampuchea to have it out with the Government'. According to Laura Summers, these demands 'embodied the subtle but real suggestion that things were not exactly all right under Sihanouk but that things would certainly be wrong without him.'[74]

Sihanouk's traditional, almost messianic, and personal appeal to the peasantry was only one of the factors motivating the 1970 protests. While many peasants were devoted to the Prince, and many others simply indifferent, such loyalties could easily co-exist with peasant support for the political and economic goals of a strong revolutionary organization, or could even be secondary or irrelevant to that support – they were, in one sense, of another world.

The demonstrations appear to have been well-organized. In Kompong Cham, they were led by recognizable leaders and spokesmen, and raised specific demands. In Ang Tasom, they were geographically intense and closely co-ordinated. The organizers of both these protests seemed to have planned the expansion of the revolutionary movement outwards from the areas it already dominated into a specific locality, taking advantage of a period of political crisis. The association with Sihanouk while it involved little back-pedalling on their part, intensified the crisis for the Lon Nol Government by a show of concerted opposition. The simultaneous columns approaching Phnom Penh from Siem Reap, Kompong Cham and Prey Veng kept the Lon Nol forces occupied, thus giving a space for the revolutionary movement to assume control over some rural localities, in particular Kompong Cham and Ang Tasom.

The timing of public statements also indicates closer involvement by the revolutionaries than by the Prince. From Peking, Sihanouk broadcast a call for resistance on 23 March; the largest demonstration took place on 26 March and others quickly followed. A statement of support for Sihanouk's call, dated 26 March and signed by Khieu Samphan, Hou Yuon and Hu Nim, was later published in the Chinese press.[75] The last major demonstration took place on 30 March; it was not until 4 April, however, that Sihanouk broadcast an appeal stating that 300 lives had been lost and urging his supporters to join guerrilla units instead of attempting further demonstrations.[76]

The rapid expansion of the Kampuchean revolutionary movement to a force of 200,000 by 1973[77] clearly had a sound base, and was not solely a result of Vietnamese Communist assistance. The demonstrations I have examined were organized by Kampuchean revolutionaries independent of the Vietnamese, whose attacks on the Phnom Penh Government forces from April 1970 are politically distinct and need separate treatment.[78] Nor was the growth of the revolutionary movement so dependent on Sihanouk's support. On the contrary, since the only protests after his overthrow were those organized by the revolutionaries, it appears that the Prince was dependent on the revolutionaries. It was only through their appeal to the peasants on socio-economic grounds and their organizational capacities that he was enabled on this occasion to translate his personal popularity into concrete political action.

References

1. Laura Summers, 'The Cambodian Civil War', *Current History*, December 1972, p.261.
2. Hanoi Radio, 1 April 1970, quoting a U.P.I. dispatch. F.B.I.S.; *Daily Report,* 1 April 1970, p.K3.
3. Summers, op. cit., p.262.
4. Interview with Ung Bunhuor, 21 November 1977, Sydney. This seems to be the incident referred to by Francois Ponchaud, in which he says 60 people were killed by troops. *Cambodia Year Zero* (London 1977) p.187.
5. Jean-Claude Pomonti and Serge Thion, *Des Courtesans aux Partisans,* (Paris, 1971) p.178.
6. Phnom Penh Radio, 27 March 1970 (F.B.I.S.).
7. Charles Meyer, *Derriere le sourire Khmer* (Paris, 1971) p.38.
8. Summers, op. cit., p. 262.
9. *New York Times,* 29 March 1970.
10. See for instance Ponchaud, op. cit., p.187.

11. Pomonti and Thion, op. cit. p.178
12. The most detailed analysis of the 1955 Kampuchean elections so far published is contained in 'Looking Back at Cambodia', by Michael Vickery, *Westerly* (University of Western Australia), No. 4, December 1976, pp. 14-28, a longer version printed as Chapter Three of the present volume. Vickery examines the general conditions in which the elections were held and documents particular examples of repression of the Democratic and Pracheachon parties.
13. Statistics for the 1955 election results were published in issues of the government *Journal Officiel*. I am grateful to Michael Vickery for making them available to me.
14. The 1966 election statistics are from the records of the Bureau des Elections, Ministere de l'Interior, Royaume du Cambodge. Copies in possession of the author.
15. Vickery, op. cit. p. 109. in this volume.
16. The influence of local elites in the 1966 election in Kampuchea was strikingly illustrated in the rural electorate of Prek Sdei in the Koh Thom region south of Phnom Penh. The winning candidate received 26% of the vote, a low figure for which the explanation is simple. Prek Sdei was in effect divided up into six distinct territorial fiefs, each dominated by a particular candidate. Out of a total of 18 subdistricts, the winner headed the list in only six, which are contiguous. The runner-up got 49% in a single subdistrict, even though his average vote was only 19% and his next best subdistrict, 31%. The third place-getter similarly won 64% in a single subdistrict, although his average was 18% and his next best, 23%. The fourth place-getter headed the list in five subdistricts, all contiguous, in which he averaged 51% (including a 78%); his total average was only 16%. The fifth place-getter actually obtained a majority in two contiguous subdistricts, although his total average was only 13%. Even the sixth place-getter headed the list in two contiguous subdistricts, in which he quadrupled his total average vote of 9%.

    The contrast with the neighbouring electorate of Prek Ambel is remarkable. There, the revolutionary Khieu Samphan received 74% of the total vote, consistently averaging 77% in 11 out of 12 subdistricts. Samphan wielded no significant economic power in the district. There was one similarity with Prek Sdei, though. In the 12th subdistrict a local figure, whose next best subdistrict gave him only 7% of their votes, actually outpolled Samphan by 47% to 44%.
17. One method used in these mini-campaigns was the publication of articles attacking these men in the official press. Vickery comments: 'In earlier years this would have resulted in "spontaneous" demonstrations or petitions against these men. Surprisingly, nothing happened. . . .' op. cit., p. 109. Another method was to fund candidates to stand against the revolutionaries. The provincial Governor of Kompong Cham paid for the campaign of a local ferry-owner who stood against Hou Youn, but received only 5% of the vote.
18. Vickery, op. cit., p. 109.
19. *Realites Cambodgiennes,* 19 May 1967, p.3 and 11 August 1967, p.4.

See 'The Samlaut Rebellion, 1967-68' by Ben Kiernan, Working Papers Nos. 4,5; Monash University Centre of Southeast Asian Studies, 1975, reprinted in the present volume. Also, the 'local news' section of a contemporary Phnom Penh Newspaper, in possession of the author.

20. B.B.C. *Summary of World Broadcasts,* FE/2600/A3/3.
21. *Le Monde,* 2 February 1968.
22. Interview with Ung Bunhouar, op. cit.
23. *New York Times,* 28 March 1970.
24. The information that follows is drawn from Jean Delvert, *Le Paysan Cambodgien* (Paris, 1961), Ch. XV.
25. Ibid., pp. 496, 499, 558-9.
26. Ibid., p.552.
27. Ibid., p.606.
28. Ibid., p.497, 506-7, 409.
29. Ibid., pp.497-8.
30. Ibid., pp.505-6.
31. Ibid., p.684.
32. Ibid., p.529-30.
33. Ibid., p.293.
34. Ibid., p.592. This high concentration of tenants in Chamcar Andong was complemented by a high percentage of ethnic Khmer among local rubber plantation workers (74%), compared to a general figure of 28% for all the rubber plantations (1956 figures). Delvert, ibid., p.591.
35. Ibid., p.593.
36. Ibid., pp.593, 597.
37. Ibid., p.599.
38. Don O. Noel, 'Cambodia: Up by the Bootstraps', Alicia Patterson Fund, New York, 29 November 1966, pp.10-11.
39. Delvert, op. cit., p.599.
40. Ibid., pp.601-2.
41. Ibid., p.594.
42. Ibid., p.345.
43. 'Le Communisme au Cambodge', *France-Asie,* Vol. 15, No. 144, (1958) p.201.
44. Vickery, op. cit.
45. 'Le communisme au Cambodge', op. cit.
46. *Le Monde,* 31 March 1970 and 1 April 1970.
47. Pomonti and Thion, op. cit., p.178.
48. Speech in Phnom Penh, 27 September 1977.
49. Meyer, op. cit., p.389.

50. See the map at rear of Meyer, op. cit.
51. Ibid., p.200.
52. Phnom Penh Radio, 27 March 1970, F.B.I.S.
53. *Le Monde,* 31 March 1970.
54. Ibid ,1 April 1970.
55. Ibid., 31 March 1970.
56. Ibid.
57. Delvert, op.cit., p.208.
58. 'Le Communisme au Cambodge', op. cit.
59. *Realites Cambodgiennes,* 22 March 1968, p.25. See Kiernan, op. cit. Part 2, pp.14, 22.
60. F.B.I.S. 30 March 1970, p.K7, quoting Hanoi Radio of 29 March 1970.
61. Ibid., 31 March 1970, p. 6.
62. F.B.I.S., 30 March 1970, p. H1, quoting Phnom Penh Radio of 27 March 1970.
63. *Le Monde*, 31 March 1970 and Pomonti and Thion, op. cit., p.178.
64. F.B.I.S., 1 April 1970, p.K3, Hanoi International Service, 1 April 1970.
65. Ibid., p.A1, Peking International Service, 1 April 1970. For corroboration of this see *Le Monde,* 1 April 1970.
66. Ibid., p.A4.
67. Jerome and Jocelyne Steinbach, *Phnom Penh Liberee: Cambodge l'Autre Sourire,* (Paris, 1976), p. 36. The businessman's name was Eap Lean Hoat.
68. *Le Monde,* 20 November 1969.
69. See the map published in *Sangkum,* October 1969, p.97.
70. BBC *Summary of World Broadcasts*, Phnom Penh Radio, FE/2716/A3/12.
71. According to one report, troops fired on a column of demonstrators heading towards Phnom Penh from Siem Reap at the town of Kompong Thom, and some soldiers and police in Siemreap killed their officers and deserted. I have not been able to find out any more details about protests in the north-west of Kampuchea in 1970. It may be relevant that, according to reliable sources, in the late 1960s a revolutionary guerrilla base was established to the north of Siem Reap, and that government officials did not venture into the Kompong Svay area near Kompong Thom City without armed escorts. Meyer, op. cit., p.200.
72. B.B.C. *Summary,* op. cit., FE/2716/A3/12.
73. Fritz Buchler, 'The God-King in Peking', unpublished B.A. thesis, University of New South Wales, School of History, 1974, p.44.
74. Summers, op. cit., Also the *New York Times,* 28 March 1970, reported demonstrators' demands that Sihanouk return to Kampu-

chea 'to be judged by the people'.

75. On 10 April 1970. See *Survey of China Mainland Press,* United States Consulate-General, Hong Kong, 4638, 10 April 1970, p.190.

76. *Le Monde,* 19 April 1970.

77. *U.S. Policy and Programs in Cambodia,* Hearings before the Subcommittee on Asian and Pacific Affairs of the Committee on Foreign Affairs, House of Representatives (U.S.A.) May-June 1973, p.89, intelligence estimate. A similar figure is given by Sam Adams, former Cambodia analyst for the United States C.I.A. Personal communication, 26 September 1976.

78. The distinction is often blurred, of course. In their attacks on Lon Nol positions at Saang, for instance, in the Prek Ambel electoral district where Khieu Samphan gained 74% of the vote in 1966, Vietnamese Communist troops were assisted by 'local Khmer and Cham villagers, who had joined the Communist forces'. *(Washington Post* 22 April 1970). In early May 1970, a French rubber plantation manager from Kompong Cham told the *New York Times* that 'the North Vietnamese had armed most of his 1,600 workers and had taken them along as they fled from U.S. tank and air attacks. 'They gave guns to the people and now they are fighting with the VC,' said Jacques Louat de Bort' (7 May 1970, p.3.)

PART III

9. Pol Pot and the Kampuchean Communist Movement by Ben Kiernan

Between April 1975 and December 1978, a series of massive purges took place in Kampuchea's ruling Communist Party. During that time, top members of the government disappeared, were executed or killed in the nine or more attempted *coups d'etat*, including the Minister of the Interior, the Minister of the Economy and Finance, the Minister of Agriculture, the Minister of Public Works, the Minister of Information, the second Vice-President of the State Praesidium, the first Vice-President of the State Praesidium, the Ministers of Communications, Trade, Industry and Rubber Plantations, and the Deputy Prime Minister in charge of the Economy.[1] By 1979, a group led by Pol Pot and including Ieng Sary, Son Sen and their wives, as well as Nuon Chea, held unchallenged power in the severely weakened and politically isolated Party. (Yugoslav journalists who visited Kampuchea in March 1978 reported that, even three years after victory, Party membership remained secret and the rural population were generally unaware of who among them were members)[2] Although these leaders together form a clique, in what follows I have identified them with an individual by referring to them as 'the Pol Pot group'.

The party was torn apart by real divisions. It is a grotesque distortion to see these merely as the conflicts of a united party cherishing its independence with 'agents' infiltrated from outside. I think the bitterness of these internal struggles stems from a small but highly-placed group's attempt to impose a policy of nationalist revivalism on a socialist organization.

Ideological Conflicts

In my view there were three major political tendencies in the Kampuchean Communist movement in the 1960s and 1970s. The first was a national chauvinist group led by Pol Pot. Its major concern was to build Kampuchea rapidly into a 'developed industrial country with great strength for national defence',[3] by means of a 'super great leap forward' *(moha loot phloh moha ochar)*.[4] Its central, most repeated slogan was 'build and defend' Kampuchea[5] and, at least as its movement became increasingly militarized, the group seems to have worked towards what might be called a millennial corporate state. The new state drew its strength from agriculture, from the furious labour of a mobilized peasantry and the militant and selfless patriotism of peasant youth cut off from previous debilitating influences and psychologically remade by its new leadership; there was no longer any need to bow to foreigners, for now Kampuchea could inspire fear in its neighbours and back demands for territorial concessions with force.

During the 1960s the Pol Pot group was based in the rugged North-east of Kampuchea. In the early 1970s it extended its influence in the Northern Zone (Kompong Thom and Siemreap Provinces) and by 1975 had gained control of the South-West Zone (Takeo, Kampot, Kompong Speu) through the zone military commander, Ta Mok. From 1977 to 1970, it had full control over the national government.

The second tendency was exemplified by Phouk Chhay and Hu Nim, leaders of the Khmer-Chinese Friendship Association in 1966-67. Also attracted by the 'mass democracy' ideology of China's Cultural Revolution were many of the over 2,000 students and teachers[6] who joined the guerrilla movement in various parts of the country in 1967-68. Other leaders, like Tiv Ol, were closely associated but also concerned with reinvigorating Khmer culture. This tendency was not an organized faction, its members tended to be well-educated, and they might well be called revolutionary 'independents'. During the 1970-75 war, they seem to have been most active in the South-west Zone. In 1977, Phouk Chhay, Hu Nim and Tiv Ol were executed, as were nearly all revolutionary intellectuals outside the Pol Pot regime. But a careful reading of the 200 pages of Hu Nim's 'confessions', extracted under torture before his execution, yields considerable information about the political positions of these three men.[7]

However different their visions of Kampuchea's future, people of both these tendencies were committed to rapid and radical social change, with an overwhelming emphasis on the rural areas. But admirers of the Cultural Revolution, while tending to regard Vietnam as 'revisionist', nevertheless clearly saw themselves as part of an international revolutionary movement. The Pol Pot group did not; in June 1976, its internal party magazine claimed that the Vietnam-Kampuchea conflict exemplified 'the continuous non-stop struggle between revolution and counter-revolution'.[8] The following year, at a political education session in Kompong Cham Province, foreign-educated intellectuals were told by a Pol Pot cadre: 'We cannot trust any foreign countries, including China.' The cadre went on to say that foreign countries were all 'enemies' of Kampuchea.[9]

The remnants of the third group were now led in Phnom Penh by Heng Samrin and Pen Sovan. These people were attracted directly by the Vietnamese socialist model. Many of them were trained by Vietnamese Communists, in the Khmer Issarak movement in Kampuchea in the 1950s, or in Vietnam from 1954 to 1970, or in Kampuchea in the early 1970s. The best-known members of this third group were Keo Moni, So Phim, Chou Chet and Non Suon, all of whom were executed between 1976 and 1978. The Eastern Zone (Prey Veng, Kompong Cham and Svay Rieng Provinces), of which So Phim was Party Secretary until 1978, was the centre of activity of this Vietnam-influenced tendency, but it was also prominent in the South-west until 1975 (through Chou Chet) and in Kandal Province (under Non Suon), and retained some influence in Battambang from the Khmer Issarak period. Most of these people were party veterans who shared a long revolutionary experience, and came from more modest backgrounds, than the first two groups, although like the second they saw the Kampuchean struggle as part of an international one. Their contacts and superior numbers also gave them a kind of semi-organized political cohesion, despite the fact that the degree of Vietnamese influence on them varied. Many – the first to be eliminated, mostly between 1971 and 1975 – shared Hanoi's view of the need for a co-ordinated Indochina-wide struggle for independence and socialism, while others were more inclined to implement orthodox Vietnamese-style Marxism in Kampuchea independent of any direct Vietnamese involvement. Unlike Pol Pot's group they were in principle not at all hostile to Vietnam, but in the case of many the degree to which they could be called 'pro-Vietnamese' depended on the degree of real aggressiveness (and on the degree of real assistance) in Hanoi's policy towards Kampuchea.

Although the ideological, if not organizational, lines separating these three tendencies seem clear, some leaders managed to transcend them: and of course, as people reacted to various events, their views were subject to changes. For instance, before 1975 Khieu Samphan seems to have shared perspectives with both the Pol Pot group and the Cultural Revolution supporters, and Hou Yuon drew on both the latter and the third, Vietnam-influenced tendency. In each case, however, this finally worked to their political disadvantage: Khieu Samphan moved closer to the Pol Pot group and survived as little more than their mouthpiece, while Hou Yuon moved closer to the third group and was eliminated with them (see glossary of names).

In the rest of this section, the differing ideologies of these three tendencies within the Kampuchean Communist movement will be examined, mainly by comparing material from the Pol Pot *Black Book* of September

1978 and from a 1975 issue of the Pol Pot-controlled internal magazine of the Communist Party, *Tung Padevat* (Revolutionary Flags), with a 1973 *Summary of Annotated Party History* prepared by the military and political service of So Phim's Vietnam-influenced Eastern Zone.

Nation, Race and History

For many Kampucheans, particularly the educated, their country is a nation constantly shrinking in size and threatened with extinction. Hundreds of years ago, the kingdom of Champa was wiped off the map by Vietnamese southward expansion, leaving the Cham people stateless. In the 19th Century, it was only French domination which stopped Kampuchea being overrun by Thailand from the west and Vietnam from the east. Kampuchea's diminution on the map continued less dramatically into the 20th Century.[10] Foreign patronage – Thai, Vietnamese, French and American – far from resolving this national problem, in fact has contributed to it, making many Kampuchean nationalists fear and distrust all foreign powers. And, reinforcing this in a very particular way is the historical enmity felt by many members of the ethnic Khmer middle class towards culturally alien Vietnamese who, under the French colonial system were able to monopolize any bureaucratic posts open to Asiatics.

Dreams of recovering the glory of the Angkor period (9th to 15th Centuries) thus led to the issue of regaining the long-lost territories. Surin and Buriram Provinces of Thailand have long been inhabited by ethnic Khmers, numbering possibly half a million in 1979. The more than one million ethnic Khmer residents of Vietnam's Mekong Delta are known to Kampucheans as 'Khmers from Lower Kampuchea' (Kampuchea Krom). There is also a tradition of cultural and racial affinity with smaller ethnic groups of the region. Lon Nol, President of the U.S.-backed Khmer Republic from 1970 to 1975, spelled out his hopes of 'reuniting' the Khmers in Kampuchea, Thailand and Vietnam, the Chams in Kampuchea and Vietnam, the hill-tribes in Kampuchea and Southern Vietnam, and even the Mons in Thailand and Burma. That such an idea (and under Lon Nol it was largely an idea)[11] could seriously be raised at that political level itself demonstrates the tenacity of racial/cultural sentiments in Kampuchean nationalist politics. I believe Pol Pot's nationalist perspective is also a traditionalist one comparable to Lon Nol's,[12] and I will return later to the question of the Pol Pot group's possible expansionist designs, but it appears that its racial perspective is more limited (and thus perhaps more insecure and prone to violence) than Lon Nol's. According to one observer:

> the officials of the [Pol Pot] regime affirm that their country is 99% populated by Khmers, thus ruling out with the stroke of a pen the very existence of the Cham population, hundreds of thousands of Chinese and Sino-Khmers, small groups of Burmese and Lao, mountain dwellers and other more or less Khmerized minorities [Kuy, Pear, etc]. Here we have a lucky country which is not

> troubled by the problem of 'national minorities'.[13]

There are confirmed reports from refugees in Thailand and Vietnam that entire villages of Chams were wiped out, by armed forces of the Pol Pot regime after 1975.[14]

But the Pol Pot regime echoed Lon Nol in directing its racism primarily at the Vietnamese. The 100-page *Black Book,*[15] proudly tells us that Kampucheans do not often use the words 'Vietnam' and 'Vietnamese' to describe their neighbours, preferring the term *'Yuon'*, the 'name given by the Kampuchea's people to the Vietnamese since the epoch of Angkor'. Its meaning, the *Black Book* incorrectly claims, is 'savage'.

Clearly, the regime made no attempt to discourage racial prejudice, to say the least. In the 1970s, for instance: 'The population of Kampuchea seethed with deep hatred towards the Vietnamese so that it was not necessary to conduct campaigns for arousing it.' And in 1973, the *Black Book* continues,

> the representative of the Communist Party of Kampuchea told the Chinese comrades that the Kampuchean revolution is independent and sovereign, but if the Kampuchean revolution had bound itself with Vietnam, it would not be able to wage the struggle, because even in the bosom of the Party, there would not be unanimity.

Passing over this thunderbolt of irony, we read: 'All the more among the people who hated the Vietnamese!' Clearly, 'the bosom of the Party', whoever that may be, links their attitude to Vietnamese with the historical basis of popular sentiments:

> The acts of aggression and annexation of territory perpetrated by the Vietnamese, in the past as well as at present, have clearly shown the true nature of the Vietnamese and Vietnam; that is, a nature of aggressor, annexationist and swallower of other countries' territories. The annexations of Champa (A.D. 1471-1693) and Kampuchea Krom (A.D. 1623-1939) have demonstrated it.

And even: 'The Cham race was totally exterminated by the Vietnamese . . . .' Because 'the Vietnamese have not changed their true nature', the Vietnamese *race* must be regarded as the enemy. If Vietnam's December 1977 invasion of Kampuchea had succeeded, 'everyone would have been satisfied at home [in Vietnam], for in Loc Ninh and Tay Ninh, for example, tens of thousands of Vietnamese people were getting ready to come and install themselves in Kampuchea'.

The Pol Pot regime, during two years of conflict with Vietnam, was never to adopt an ethnic Vietnamese group as their favoured 'liberation movement' there. Rather, they maintained very close links with the hill-tribe dissidents of the anti-Hanoi section of the FULRO organization,[16] one of whose members in 1978 declared on Radio Phnom Penh that 'Ho Chi Minh was a fascist'.

About 200,000 ethnic Vietnamese residents of Kampuchea were expelled by the Pol Pot regime in 1975. Ethnic Khmers sympathetic to the Vietnamese Communists were invariably described as Vietnamese 'agents'. According to Serge Thion, this was 'as if it is impossible for a Khmer militant to believe that the general line of the Vietnamese revolution is good, or even that it is the best in contemporary Indochina.'[17] On 10 May 1978, Radio Phnom Penh announced: 'So far, we have attained our target: 30 Vietnamese killed for every fallen Kampuchea .... So we could sacrifice two million Kampucheans in order to exterminate the 50 million Vietnamese – and we shall still be 6 million ....'[18] This statement preceded a central government attack on the Eastern Zone, whose leaders and population were accused of having 'Khmer bodies with Vietnamese minds'.

National Chauvinism: Kampuchea's historical predicament has also provoked intense nationalist fervour in certain circles, evident in the speech by Pol Pot made on the occasion of the founding of the Revolutionary Army of Kampuchea on 22 July 1975, printed in *Tung Padevat* (August 1975).[19] The recent victory over Lon Nol's regime was described as a 'great success unknown before in the whole world ... the world's first ever great victory', with the enemy defeated 'in a record time'. Most significantly, Pol Pot ended his marathon speech with the following qualification: 'Let me stress that whatever I have just said is not a boastful glorification of our Party, Revolutionary Army, people and country at all .... Our possibilities and conditions for building our country are second to none. That is our firm belief.' This raises the issue, in a Marxist-Leninist framework, of the significance of the world revolution for Kampuchea and the links between the Kampuchean Party and foreign Communists.

The authors of the 1973 Party history[20] took an orthodox view, similar to that of the Vietnamese Communist leadership:

> The conditions for the formation of the Party in our country were not different in principle from those of the revolutions which formed the world's Marxist-Leninist parties. To the best of our knowledge of France, England, the U.S.S.R., China, Vietnam, etc., all followed the same principle of revolution, that is, the people's revolutionary movement; and the people are the workers (in the industrial countries) or farmers (in the underdeveloped agricultural countries).
>
> The formation of the Party was certainly according to Marx and Engels' 'Declaration of the Communist Party', Lenin's disciples' party, the Great October Socialist Revolution, China's people's democratic revolution, and revolution throughout the world.

In stark contrast, Pol Pot's 22 July 1975 speech addressed to 'about 3,000 revolutionary army unit representatives of the Central Committee' of the Party, asserted:

> We have won total, definitive, and *clean* victory, meaning that we have won it without any foreign connection or involvement. [sic]
>
> We dared to wage a struggle on a stand completely different from that of the world revolution. The world revolution carries out the struggle with all kinds of massive support – material, economic and financial – from the world's people. As for us, we have waged our revolutionary struggle basically on the principles of independence, sovereignty and self-reliance . . . In the whole world, since the advent of the revolutionary war and since the birth of U.S. imperialism, no country, no people, and no army has been able to drive the imperialists out to the last man and score total victory over them [the way we have]. Nobody could.

The speech is curiously devoid of technical Communist terminology unlike the 1973 history, which explains the ideological origins of the Marxist movement in Kampuchea as follows:

> Proletarian class Marxism-Leninism was injected into our revolutionary movement by the international Communist movement and the Vietnamese Communists. It is certain that our Communist combatants were a number of Kampucheans who were trained in the Indochinese Communist Party, about 40 men in 1951; in the French Communist Party, 10 men in 1951; and in the Thai Communist Party, 3-4 men in 1951.
>
> These Kampuchean Communists took the following path in forming the proletarian class Marxist-Leninist Party in Kampuchea . . . with the firm support of the Indochinese Communist Party (new name: Vietnam Lao Dong Party), we held a Conference in 1951.

Pol Pot's major public speech, two years later, in September 1977, also dealt with the history of the Party, yet made no mention of any foreign assistance at any stage, thus ignoring the advantageous effects of Vietnamese military action against the Lon Nol regime in the 1970-73 period and the significant Chinese aid projects after 1975.[21] To the extent that in his earlier (July 1975) speech Pol Pot recognized *any* connection between the Kampuchean Revolution and the outside world, it was the benefits the latter had received from Kampuchea's liberation.

> If my memory serves me well, on 12 April 1975, U.S. imperialism sent 50 helicopters to evacuate its men. The U.S. imperialist retreat in panic from Kampuchea was filmed and shown to the whole world. . . .

> The world's people knew about it and saw it the same evening. . . . Never before had there been such an event in the annals of the world's revolutionary wars.
>
> In one word, the great victory won by our people and revolutionary army under the leadership of the Communist Party of Kampuchea has become a precious model for the world's people, the world's revolutionary movement and the international Communist movement.

After the victory of April 1975, the Pol Pot group revealed their millennial xenophobia in their reply to Japan's almost immediate request for diplomatic relations: Kampuchea would not be interested in establishing relations with Japan 'for the next 200 years'.[22]

Views of the Revolutionary Past: The historical perspectives of the Pol Pot group also differ from those of cadres of the group attracted to the Vietnamese model of socialism. According to the 1973 history:

> In the French colonialist period, our people, especially the farmers, arose continually and everywhere against the French imperialists and their lackeys . . . For example, the Pou Kombo, Achar Sva and Visses Nhov movements; the Rolea and Phea Ear inhabitants' movements; the Kompong Speu, Kampot, Ba Phnom, Kompong Svay and Kraing Leav farmers; the 'En Chey' farmers' anti-tax movements; the Kratie and Stung Treng people's movements, etc.

None of these, or any other anti-colonial predecessors of the Communist movement, was ever publicly referred to by representatives of Pol Pot's Democratic Kampuchea between 1975 and 1979. On the other hand, with the displacement of Pol Pot in favour of the pro-Vietnam faction, the new Heng Samrin Government in April 1979 re-named certain Phnom Penh streets after Pou Kombo and Achar Sva and two other 19th Century anti-colonial rebel leaders.[23] Such recognition of nationalist heroes of Kampuchea's past by the pro-Vietnamese Government is an acknowledgement of and identification with a genuine tradition of independence: it is nevertheless quite distinct from a vision which sees Kampuchea's entire past as consisting of foreign domination, whose lessons for the present are only negative. The millenarian character of Pol Pot's nationalism – after 'two thousand years of exploitation', history effectively begins with the Party and the building of a new era 'more glorious than Angkor'[24] – springs from its very extremism.

It might be argued that anti-colonial rebel leaders were simply not *named* by the Pol Pot regime, and that this is due to a rejection of personality cults in line with a policy of 'collective anonymity' in government. But it was not just the leaders but the specific rebellions themselves that were ignored. Secondly, the celebrated 'anonymity' of leadership was in fact not the product of collective decision-making but of its opposite, disunity and, until 1977-78, reflected serious internal political challenges to the Pol Pot group.

Indeed, once Pol Pot was in complete control in 1978, portraits, busts and statues of him began to be produced.[25]

The Pol Pot group and the authors of the 1973 history also gave divergent accounts of the impact of the 1954 Geneva Conference on Kampuchea's Revolution. In 1977, Pol Pot described the Conference as a sell-out in which all the gains of the Communists 'vanished into thin air'[26] with Prince Sihanouk's assumption of power. According to the 1973 history, however, the Conference was a 'victory over the French imperialists and their lackeys . . . . [won] with the Party and people of Vietnam, Laos, and the entire world', as a result of which, the Kampuchean Party was able to 'force the feudal, bourgeois and reactionary class, the landowners, to follow the policy of neutrality'.

Another, more middle-of-the-road and 'independent' view, was expressed by Hou Yuon at a meeting in May 1972:

> The socialist powers of Europe, bloodied by the Second World War, and the Asian socialists, much weakened by the Chinese and Korean wars, overestimated the strength of the imperialists at that moment and pressured the all-consuming Indochinese revolutionary forces to end the fighting and accept the peace treaty with the imperialist forces.

According to a witness, Hou Yuon 'saw in this a calculated tactical manoeuvre by the socialists'.[27] He clearly recognized that the Vietnamese revolutionaries suffered as much from it as the Kampucheans.

Expansionism: A lesser-known element of the Pol Pot programme, but one that affected all Kampuchea's neighbours, is the racially-based expansionism we have already mentioned. On 5 January 1979, Pol Pot described the Vietnamese as Kampuchea's 'hereditary enemy'. This was the first public hint of a policy that had been propagated in villages in widely dispersed parts of Kampuchea since 1977.

Mrs Lang Sim, a Khmer refugee now in France, was in Snuor district of Battambang Province in mid-1977 when new cadres arrived from the South-west Zone. She attended a meeting, about 30-strong, in her village of Lopeak at the end of that year where they said that 'Kampuchea aimed to fight to recover Kampuchea Krom from Vietnam, as well as Surin and other provinces from Thailand'.

Bopha, a Phnom Penh woman who lived in the Saang district of Kandal Province after the 1975 evacuation, said that the Khmer Rouge there were 'all right' until April 1977 (we know from other sources that the Province Party Secretary had been arrested on 15 March); then, brutality against the population became a hallmark of government control of Saang. In 1978, Bopha went on, the Khmer Rouge cadres told villagers, including herself, that the Government of Kampuchea 'aimed to fight to get back Kampuchea Krom'.

Nguon Son, a worker in a large Phnom Penh 'mineral factory' under the Pol Pot regime, recalls that around November 1978, Ta Khon, the Director of the factory, said in a meeting that 'we aim to liberate the people of Kampuchea Krom and have already liberated 10,000-20,000 of them'.

A former Khmer interpreter for North Korean advisers in the Pol Pot period, who had an opportunity to travel widely in Kampuchea, said that the policy to reconquer Kampuchea Krom from Vietnam was 'not official', in that it was not mentioned in official statements and publications. Nevertheless, 'right through 1978, from the beginning of the year until the end, everybody I met in the army was talking in those terms'.

In 1979, Prince Sihanouk provided some of the background in his book, *Chroniques de guerre . . . et d'espoir:*

> In September 1975, I was indeed surprised to hear Khieu Samphan, Son Sen and company say, smiling and very pleased with themselves, that their soldiers were 'displeased' with 'the Party', because the latter did not give them the green light to go and take back Kampuchea Krom as well as the border districts of Thailand which belonged to Kampuchea in the past (Aranya, Surin, etc.).[28]

Later Sihanouk provided more detail about this conversation:

> In the past, they said, our leaders sold out Kampuchea Krom, sold out South Vietnam to the Vietnamese. Our armies can't accept the status quo. We must make war against Vietnam to get back Kampuchea Krom. As the first step, if there are [sugar] palm trees, the soil is Khmer. In Chaudoc and Ha Tien, there are still palm trees. We must occupy.[29]

Sihanouk's book explains that after the 1975 Khmer Rouge victory, they

> . . . tried to conquer a part of Kampuchea Krom and committed horrible atrocities on a large number of Vietnamese male and female civilians (including old people, women and children).
>
> The Pol Pot Government rejected all the proposals for a peaceful solution presented on several occasions (in particular 5 February 1978) by the Hanoi Government. . . .
>
> In 1978 Khieu Samphan confided to me, concerning the Kampuchean-Vietnam war, that his soldiers [Khmer Rouge] were 'unstoppable'; whenever they saw sugar palms in the territory of Kampuchea Krom, these patriotic soldiers could not prevent themselves from crossing the frontier and advancing 'until they came to the last Khmer sugar palm'. . . . According to Son Sen, Deputy Prime Minister in charge of National Defence, his glorious 'revolutionary army of Kampuchea' considered itself capable of dealing very easily with Giap's [Vietnamese] army, and with the much more puny one of Kukrit Pramoj and Kriangsak Chamanond [Thailand]![30]

Although Sihanouk's account is possibly sensationalized, it is not unlikely that the Pol Pot group outlined such a policy to the Prince as early as 1975. But, apart from a number of clashes in May-June of that year, extensive forays into Vietnamese territory did not begin until 1977. Around the same time, serious incidents along the border between north-east Thailand and Kampuchea began, just when Pol Pot's group was successfully consolidating its power within the Party. Unlike the Communists in other parts of Thailand at that time, Pol Pot's Khmer Rouge and joint Khmer Rouge-Thai Communist forces used brutal militarism, rather than political persuasion to win the support of the population.

According to the left-wing Bangkok journal *Thai Nikorn,* around December 1977 representatives of the Communist Party of Thailand (C.P.T.) North-eastern Committee reached a secret agreement with the Kampuchean Party Secretary of Oddar Meanchey Province (adjacent to Surin), representing Pol Pot's Communist Party of Kampuchea (C.P.K.). The meeting agreed:

> To set up a mixed force of C.P.T. and C.P.K. in order to act in the southern part of North-east Thailand . . . It was agreed that the Kampucheans would send one unit of forces to join the C.P.T. movement, in order that the mixed force should use Pol Pot's lessons on how to seize power, i.e. wherever the conditions are ripe for striking against the stable underpinnings of Thai civil servants, an effort should be made to strike, and every day and every night, in order to terrorize Thai officials. Wherever conditions are not ripe, a report should be made to the central unit of the Kampuchean side. If it should be thought appropriate, *the Kampuchean base unit will enter Thailand and strike against the base without the mixed force having to become involved*[31] (emphasis–B.K.)

The Thai Communist guerrillas in this southern part of north-east Thailand (mostly Surin, Buriram and Sisaket Provinces) were nearly all local ethnic Khmers and enjoyed the use of about a dozen base-camps inside Northern Kampuchea (formalized in the December 1977 agreement); it was internally known as Angkar Siem[32] or 'the Thai Angkar' *(angkar,* the Khmer term meaning 'the organization', was used by the Communist Party of Kampuchea to describe itself. It is curious that a Thai group would explicitly describe itself as virtually the Thai branch, as the word 'Siem' implies, of a characteristically-named Kampuchean movement – unless, of course, certain 'Thai military strategists' are correct in thinking 'that Phnom Penh increased its support for the Thai Communist insurgency along the Northern Cambodian border to back irredentist claims on a wide swathe of Thai provinces settled by a mixed Khmer-descended population'.[33] A similar evaluation of Pol Pot's designs by the C.P.T. leadership, together with a realization of the political disaster of using coercion against the Thai border population, plus Chinese pressure on Pol Pot to stabilize the Thai front in order to concentrate his forces against Vietnam, may have been the reason for the C.P.T's crack-down on the activities of Angkar Siem around mid-1978.

In this connection, one may legitimately ask what non-military purpose could have been served by the construction of a long road through the forest of Northern Kampuchea, parallel with the Thai frontier? Work began on this road in early 1977, according to someone who had participated in several work-teams composed of teenage Khmer peasant boys.[34]

Early 1977 saw many changes in village leadership and policy in various parts of Kampuchea, as cadres selected by the Pol Pot group from the South-west Zone started to arrive in the villages. In the case of the Saut Nikom district of Siemreap Province, cadres from Kampot arrived in March 1978. Sovannareth, aged 19, was at that time working in a bean-growing production unit in the district. He recalls the anti-Vietnamese and anti-Thai line:

> They arrested the previous local leaders, and made us suffer more than those cadres had. They said they were 'real, strong socialists' and that their predecessors were 'traitors'.
>
> At a meeting of 1,000 people in the village where I worked, the south-western cadres put up banners denouncing the 'Vietnamese aggressors of our land who are trying to form an Indochina Federation'. Another banner asked the Vietnamese a question: 'You want us to join a Federation: do you know how to manufacture guns?' Another said: 'I am a Kampuchean, and I resolve to fight the Vietnamese', and others 'Long live the great and strong Kampuchean revolution'. There were many other banners as well.
>
> We sat on the ground during the meeting, which lasted from 6 p.m. to 10 p.m. The village chief talked about how the people resolved to work hard so that guns and ammunition could be bought to defend the country. Fifteen village chiefs from the district also talked for about 10 minutes each, telling us to 'destroy all bad habits and oppressive acts'.
>
> Then, the big leader spoke. His name was Ta Meng; he was about 50 years old, and killed people like anything, right in front of others. He talked about how the country had developed, showing photographs, and about the war between the Revolutionary Army and the Vietnamese. He said they had killed 30,000 Vietnamese in Svay Rieng Province, destroyed 50 tanks and shot down four Russian-made planes. In order not to waste anything, he said, the bodies of the tanks had been used to make plates for the people to eat on. . . .
>
> Their plan was to take back Kampuchea Krom. He said that the Vietnamese were swallowers of Khmer land and that 'the Khmer people resolve to liberate again the Khmer land in Kampuchea Krom'. He talked all about 'Moat Chrouk' [Chaudoc Province of Vietnam] and 'Prey Nokor' [Ho Chi Minh City] and so on. He called for the recruitment of 10 youths from each village to join the army . . . .
>
> He also said that Thai planes had attacked Kampuchea's Oddar Meanchey Province, and that 'we are preparing to attack the Thai in order to take back the Khmer land in Thailand'. Later he said: 'We will have to fight Thailand in 1979, and we will certainly win. The

> Thais do not know how to fight because they have never fought before. For example, we went into their villages and killed them and burned their houses, and there was nothing they could do.' He said they aimed to get back the provinces of Surin and Sisaket and so on from Thailand. This was in June 1978, in Koh Kong village.[35]

Social Policy

How does one set about analysing the social programme of the Pol Pot group? Perhaps the most notorious aspect of life in Democratic Kampuchea from 1975 to 1978 was its militarism: the forced evacuation of the cities, the coercion of the population into economic programmes organized with military discipline, the heavy reliance on the armed forces rather than civilian cadres for administration, and the almost total absence of political education or attempts to explain administrative decisions in a way that would win the psychological acceptance of the people affected by them. There was also the *huge* number of summary arrests and executions of unorganized civilian recalcitrants (which increased in frequency from 1975 to 1978) and the *huge* number of civilian deaths from starvation and related diseases. Because the Government collected most of the rice crop from the villages, exporting some of it and storing more in the hills, the number of deaths from starvation certainly did not decrease in 1977-78, when the harvests were large from the position in 1975, when the rural economy was still shattered by the disastrous effects of blanket bombing by U.S. B-52s.[36]

What is the connection between the nation and the people in this version of nation-building? Evidently the effort to create 'a developed industrial country with great strength for national defence' licensed all manner of impositions on the people. As Pol Pot stated in 1975: 'We made the war and won the victory rapidly. We must thus build the country rapidly too. . . .'[37]

Communalism: The three elements of militarism, racism and expansionism certainly make up a strong dose of good old-fashioned chauvinism. But the ideology of the Pol Pot group drew upon Marxism-Leninism, too. There is no evidence that any of its top spokespeople ever publicly displayed enthusiasm for the ideology of the Cultural Revolution; but signs of this influence can be found in the fierce advocacy of egalitarianism, manual work participation by cadres and communalism during their years in power. This extract from another article in the August 1975 issue of *Tung Padevat* is particularly enlightening:

> . . . in the recent past a number of untoward events have been observed. These events call for immediate attention and timely correction if the Party's wish is to be fulfilled. They are as follows: after liberating various cities and Phnom Penh a number of cadres and Party men, combatants and revolutionary people were assigned to various duties in the provincial capitals and Phnom Penh. Later on, these comrades brought their wives and children, some even bringing their parents and relatives, from the rear areas to live with

> them in the offices. As the office work is limited, when these people arrived there was no office work left for them. Still, these people received the same daily food ration as office workers. In order to ease the atmosphere, these people have joined in production work, such as planting vegetables, in the office compounds. They have taken these offices as bases to build themselves and fulfil revolutionary missions. Some of them have managed to make a good life, having so far avoided contradictions. But others are less fortunate, as they have no office work to perform and no production tasks to fulfil, and there are thus contradictions. How do they solve these contradictions? Many have sent their wives, children and families to stay with friends in different offices, pretending to solicit the help of these 'masters' and 'mistresses' in teaching their dependents about revolutionary stands. This is tantamount to the old society's practice of sending the children to live in the monasteries.
>
> Our comrades may wonder if levelling land, planting bananas, cabbages and morning glories in the office compounds is not fighting in the concrete movement, what is it? Let it be known that working for production in the office compounds is good, but it is only used to improve the livelihood to a certain degree; it is not part of the militant movement to transform and build the society at all.
>
> If this is so, where should you go and fight to temper yourselves in the concrete movement? According to the new positive conditions, the best areas where you should do this are: 1) the co-operatives, and 2) various state-owned factories and state-owned work-sites.
>
> These are where the struggle is being waged to transform and build the society. The party's view, stand, and political, ideological and organizational lines are gathered and concretely implemented there. The good virtues of the masses of workers, poor peasants and lower middle-class peasants are gathered there. It is in these places that private, individual ownership is being eliminated and the public, collective ownership set up and strengthened.

From this article we might think that revolutionary cadres in Phnom Penh in August 1975 enjoyed considerable freedom of movement and could participate in a wide range of activities; after all, this article is merely giving cadres some sound advice and pointing out several ways in which they could help the movement. However, it is also possible that this particular article (only five pages out of 80 in the Party's internal monthly magazine) was written by an admirer of the Cultural Revolution, who had to be content with a mere cautionary note about the psychological chasm developing between cadres and people under Pol Pot – probably a matter of considerable concern to him or her (and to others) in the Party – because he or she was not in a position to push the full Cultural Revolution line. From this perspective, the limited suggestions that cadres should be persuaded to take up any of several alternative future activities indicates that control of the

Party's ideological machinery (such as the political education of *new* cadres) lay elsewhere. Significantly, the major political struggle is still identified – in the article's title and content as the elimination of private individual *ownership* –the target apparently being social attitudes and expressions as much as social structures. Further, it is not the Cultural Revolution slogan 'serve the people' that is stressed, but political development of cadres. This was important to the Pol Pot group, though not necessarily to benefit the people by improving their living standards and increasing their access to the decision-making process. Rather it would prevent the formation of a *materially* privileged social elite. Of course, these issues may be linked, but this author did not (or could not) attempt to do so.

Perhaps there is one aspect of the Cultural Revolution ideology acceptable to the Pol Pot group: it was concerned (for different reasons) to prevent the development of 'a new bourgeoisie'. The Pol Pot group did not want Kampuchea's future to allow a materially rapacious social elite like the one that *sold the country to foreigners* in the past. While this article does not contradict that aim, another 'patriotic', social elite was clearly developing, and the revolutionary opposition to the Pol Pot group seems to have been unable to do more than protest.

The significance of the emphasis on communalism at the popular level during the 1975-78 period is more difficult to pin down ideologically. Communal labour, with the whole country 'a vast work-site', was one of the hallmarks the Pol Pot regime presented to the world. However, according to many refugees from different parts of Kampuchea, in 1977-78 labour targets, in what a socialist system would term the more 'advanced' work teams, the youth groups and the mobile task forces, were set up on an individual basis. Each worker was allocated a particular area of earth (usually three cubic metres) to move each day for the raising of irrigation works,[38] or a particular area (usually one-sixth of a hectare) of forest to clear.[39] If this target was completed, the individual concerned would sometimes receive a higher ration of rice or rice porridge that day; sometimes, the worker would only receive his normal ration, if and when the target was fulfilled. This confirms Francois Ponchaud's description of 'the daily norms demanded from the workers', as reported to him by refugees during 1978: 'for example in Preah Net Preah, "4 to 5 cubic metres of earth to dig each day for a man, 2.5 to 3.5 for women, 2 cubic metres for adolescents, or even 5 cubic metres for 2 adolescents. At night we had to dig another cubic metre." Those who did not manage to fulfil these norms had their food reduced or even withheld'.[40]

In Sang Nokor village, in Kompong Svay district of Kompong Thom, labour had been communal at least since the arrival of evacuees from Phnom Penh in May 1975. Local peasants and former urban dwellers worked together in the fields and on irrigation projects in work teams with specialized tasks and group targets. Then, in mid-1977, cadres from the South-west Zone arrived to replace all the district leaders, who were 'soft'. The newcomers were 'very tough', and 'killed many people in the second half of 1977'. Food intake was reduced, since people were no longer allowed to find their own supplementary rations and could eat only what was served to them in the communal dining halls established at the beginning of the year. The system of labour also changed. For transplanting and harvesting, every day each person had to work an area 10 metres by 100 metres. Individuals could stop work whenever their daily target was fulfilled, but they had to fulfil it personally even if they were sick. On irrigation works built by the population of Sang Nokor, each worker had to shift five cubic metres of earth per day, a heavy task according to informants.[41]

According to another refugee interviewed in Australia in 1976, cadres of the regime explicitly stressed not only *national* economic self-reliance (like the Chinese Cultural Revolution) but also, in speeches to Battambang people in 1975, *individual* self-reliance in relation to other workers.[42] More systematic inquiry is necessary but it seems likely that the communal ideology of the Cultural Revolution was not faithfully implemented in Kampuchean villages, especially in 1977-78.

The communal dining halls, established throughout Kampuchea by mid-1977, may have owed something to the 'ultra-leftist' early stages of the Cultural Revolution and to the Great Leap Forward in China. However, they also strengthened state control of the administration and population, and prevented any storing of food for escape attempts or planned uprisings, and provided the authorities with a *daily* method of 'reward and punishment' at the most basic human level.

Self-Reliance: One of the clearest outlines of economic policy by the Pol Pot regime appeared in a discussion of the situation in the South-West Zone, in *Tung Padevat* of June 1976.

> We rely on agriculture in order to expand other fields such as industry, factories, minerals, oil, etc. The basic key is agriculture. Self-reliance means capital from agriculture. From 1977, the state will have nothing more to give to the Zone(s) because there are no longer any resources. So we must acquire them by exchange, by taking rice from the Zone(s) to make purchases. Health services and social action also rely on agriculture. Doctors are to cure the sick. The important medicine to cure sickness is food. If there was enough to eat there would also be little sickness. It is the same for culture. Once we have the capital we can expand scientific culture. But now we must produce rice first. Producing rice is a very great lesson. City people do not know what farming is, do not know what a cow is, do not know what harvesting is. Now they know and understand, they are no longer scared of cows and buffaloes. Our lesson's subject is real work. Real work provides experience; if we have the experience, with additional measures it would become scientific. The important point is to solve the food problem first. When we have the food, we will expand simultaneously into the learning of reading, writing and arithmetic.

This policy of heavy reliance on agriculture was shared by all Communist tendencies in the 1975-76 period. However, differences existed over the degree of self-reliance to be pursued, in particular whether available (let alone imported) machinery should be used. The Pol Pot group's view was clearly expressed in the same issue of *Tung Padevat:*

> In district 'E', with a land area of 4,000 hectares, we have every possibility. By taking care of rice seedlings, preparing the seed neatly, transplanting correctly, taking care of water and fertilizer, we would certainly get eight tonnes per hectare over the 4,000 hectares. In the years 1978-79, we could expand the land area up to the 7,000 hectares that the district possesses. With this, using just enough fertilizer and no machinery, we have already marched into modern agriculture.

Communists attracted to the Vietnamese socialist model, on the other hand, favoured the use of machinery in the development of modern agriculture (see Chapter 9 in this volume). The conflict apparently did not come into the open until 1977. In his prison 'confessions', Hu Nim, the Minister of Information and a supporter of the Cultural Revolution, describes a 1976 conversation (later branded a 'K.G.B. agent' by the regime) with Moul Sambath (Nhim), Party Secretary of the North-west Zone (where foreign visitors could observe tractors ploughing the land). He says Nhim favoured such use of machinery and opposed the austerity of 'the party's self-reliance policy'. In January 1977, however:

> Brother No. 1 requested a new orientation in radio broadcasts. He encouraged me to emphasize as models any district or region which possesses the firm collectivist standpoint of the Party and mainly uses labour and not too much machinery. Brother No. 1 suggested examples, poor regions where the land is dry and infertile. . . . where they use no machinery at all, only labour. This made me realize that brother Nhim's stand, for a system of plenty, was a great deal different from the Party line.

Why this debate remained submerged until 1977 is unclear. Probably the continuing power struggle throughout 1976 was a contributing factor. The policy statement in *Tung Padevat* in June of that year that 'from 1977 the state will have nothing more to give to the Zone(s)' and must extract rice from them may also be relevant.

Patriotism and Materialism

The Pol Pot group seems to have been aiming at a kind of moral, as much as material, independence. Discussing the situation in the liberated zones during the 1970-75 War, *Tung Padevat* of August 1975 noted:

> Even sometimes our people had to show gratitude to the traders because they gave them rice in hard times. It was this which hurt our Party most. We had our own revolution, our own state power and our own land; still we were not our own masters. . . .
>
> When [the traders] gave the revolution 100 or 200 riels, 10,000 or 20,000 riels, *they made us feel* that they were so generous towards us. So, they did not serve the national liberation war, nor the people's livelihood at all. . . . They went where they wanted (my emphasis–B.K.)

The millennial concern with *symbols* was later manifested in the dynamiting of Phnom Penh's National Bank, the levelling of the Catholic Cathedral, and avoidance of terms like 'Khmer' and 'Republic', simply because they were stressed by the Lon Nol regime (until 1978, by which time a decent interval had elapsed). But this concern actually pre-dates victory. The magazine states that in 1973:

> Our state was their satellite . . . the Kratie township showed the same signs as in the old society. Honda motorcycles were speeding up and down the streets like before, while our ragged guerrillas walked in the dust. *This showed* that they were still the masters while we remained the gendarmes [sic] like in the time of Norodom Sihanouk, the time of Lon Nol . . . (my emphasis – B.K.)

It is not surprising to find the group emphasizing motivations of either patriotism or treason rather than material interest: 'We allowed them to make profits, reasonable profits . . . The ordinary merchants did this, but the other ones did not. We were not corrupt. They could . . . sell goods as dearly as they wanted to make exorbitant profits . . . under us, but they did not want to do it.' And, as far as 'handicrafts and industry', were concerned, 'Our policy was to allow the private sector to function in this field. But, the capitalists refused to comply. Only our state was active.' In the same view of the world, property relations are also seen as independent of material forces in society. Discussing the year 1975, the magazine says: 'Our present system has surpassed the popular-democratic system. As far as economic production is concerned, this is not yet a socialist system. But concerning the system of property, it is already socialist.' In fact, it is specifically private property as an expression of economic power that is seen as a great danger.

> Private property . . . has no power to oppose us. Because we do not allow it time to strengthen and expand its forces it will collapse and disappear without fail. If we had kept Phnom Penh, it would have had much strength. It was true that we were stronger, and had more influence than the private sector when we were in the countryside. But in Phnom Penh we would have become their satellite. However, we did not keep them in Phnom Penh. Thus, private property has no power.

After this 1975 evacuation, the nation's entire population (not just Party members) was divided into three categories: 'depositees', 'candidates' and 'full rights' *(penh sith).* These terms clearly indicate a policy of transforming not just the material forces in society but the people themselves. Even more significantly, the terms imply that huge numbers of people were still not ready for the revolution, not just the 'depositees' from the towns but also many peasants or former peasants. What may turn out to have been the greatest slaughter of all in Pol Pot's Kampuchea – the 1978 massacre and evacuation of the inhabitants of the Eastern Zone and its aftermath – was, significantly, preceded by a radio broadcast on 10 May outlining the need to 'purify the masses of the people'. The people in this instance were *overwhelmingly* peasants, whose 'impurity' stemmed from their years of living under the control of the Eastern Zone opposition and consequent government suspicion that they would welcome a Vietnamese invasion to overthrow Pol Pot.

In the December 1977 secret meeting with the Thai Communist Party representatives on the border, the Pol Pot group reportedly proposed that the Thai revolutionaries should take heed of 'Comrade Pol Pot's lesson' that 'people are the strength of those they support', that is, 'those who support the government are that government's strength, those who support the Communist Party are that Party's strength'.[43] The logical conclusion of such a view is that, where popular discontent undermines the government, the offending population should be removed.

Tactics and Organization

A political tactic, the evacuation of the cities, was a means of dealing with an enemy of little perceived socio-economic substance. By the same token, political means of dealing with the enemy must be followed through unsparingly. Despite the elimination of their socio-economic base, the bourgeoisie are still considered a constant and severe threat, for the almost moral reasons we have already encountered.

> The bourgeoisie have nowhere to go. They have become satellite to the worker-peasant power. They have been forced to carry out manual labour like the peasants. These people are new peasants coming from the bourgeoisie. . . . Their economic foundation has already collapsed, but *their views still remain, their aspirations still remain.* Therefore, they continue to contradict with the Revolution. Whether they can carry out activities against us is the concrete condition which prompts us to continue the revolution (emphasis original).

Because of the political and moral, rather than socio-economic or historical, nature of the enemy and the struggle against them, they can thus be defeated by primarily tactical methods. Objective conditions become almost irrelevant. Pol Pot's July 1975 speech noted:

'Our victory . . . . has not been won by chance, nor has it been possible through the help of any factual conditions. It has been possible because we made perfect preparations in an all-round manner . . . .' He then gives four reasons for the 1975 victory, clearly regarding tactical/organizational factors as outweighing the struggle between social classes: 1) 'the efficient and correct leadership of the C.P.K.'; 2) 'our people are very courageous . . . and especially, they have been organized into co-operatives . . . since 1973'; 3) 'of secondary significance [was] increased production and supply of food to the rear areas'; 4) 'not to be forgotten though it is only of secondary significance [is] the support we received from the world'.

The primacy of tactics and administrative organization over social questions is also spelt out in another *Tung Padevat* article:

> Land reform is not a phase. We have already done it. Some of us do not even know that we have implemented it. This means that there have been no major obstacles. This is because land reform means taking land from the owners and giving it back to individual peasants. Now, land is the property of the collective. . . . We have traversed the period of land reform with ease.

Administrative measures are seen as capable of totally transforming the entire society in a very short period of time, on condition that they are backed by the construction of a new moral/political universe. There is no better example of the prominent place of 'moral independence' in the ideology of the Pol Pot group than the following passage from the *Black Book.* By mid-1972, we are told,

> The Vietnamese were driven into a situation where they thought they had to snap up the bait launched by the U.S. imperialists, that is: 1) cease-fire and elections; 2) U.S. aid of more than 3,000 million dollars. . . . The Vietnamese agreed to negotiate with the U.S imperialists and to cease-fire, for they could no longer carry on the war and were enticed by the U.S. bait.

To the Pol Pot group, the material and social significance of this 'bait' counts for little (as does the fact that to squeeze even some of it out of the U.S.A. would have been, and was, a *victory* for Vietnam). Much more significant is the fact that 'bait' issuing from foreigners is not 'clean'.

Revolutionary Classes and the Class Struggle

The authors of the 1973 Party history, on the other hand, while agreeing that 'the factor leading to victory [is] the Marxist-Leninist Party', clearly take a historical and materialist view. They emphasize the 'proletarian class' nature of this Party and stress the importance of getting 'firm control of the struggle between the social classes'. Discussing the colonial period in detail, they write:

> If we speak of strength, we see that our people, especially the farmers, are a very powerful force, the backbone. However, this force did not win victory over the enemy because it did not receive direction from the Party and did not have a proletarian class army, proletarian class policy, and proletarian class strategy in the struggle against the enemy.
>
> Based on these experiences, we continue to wage our people's and democratic revolution by uniting the strength of the people, especially the farmers, with the Marxist-Leninist Party and the proletarian class.
>
> What qualities were necessary to form the Party at that time? There were then few proletarians in our country. So, their struggle was weak . . . So, we were not able to form it in our Kampuchea because the number of proletarians and their qualities were insufficient to direct the revolution at that time. Meanwhile, we based ourselves on our concept of our national society to form it in our country. This concept was as follows: Our country is an underdeveloped agricultural country. It was under the French imperialist colonial yoke. . . . The basic contradiction was between the farmers and the French imperialists, and between the farmers and the feudal lords. From this was born a very powerful proletarian class revolutionary movement.

Victory is seen as historically inevitable, so setbacks encountered by the Party are against the mainstream of social development. But the Party must nevertheless adapt itself to such development. The 'Marxist-Leninist class leaning and devotion to the class struggle' must be 'retained always to win power by annihilating the enemy regime and setting up a workers' and farmers' regime, and to create class ardour and fury. This ardour and fury must be aroused according to the contradiction of the day, whether it be large or small.' But this is difficult to achieve:

> Take care to include working-class ideology and organization in the composition of the Party ranks. Our Party was formed in an underdeveloped agricultural country. The Party was thus born out of a basically agricultural movement. Our country's farmers are greatly oppressed by the imperialists, the feudalists and the bourgeoisie. The revolution's structure is thus well founded. However, our farmers still do not have a working-class nature; they still have a special farmers' agricultural nature. The Party is composed of elements from the middle class and intellectuals, a large number of which still retain the structure and nature of their origins
>
> Thus, to make the Party more working class in nature, it is necessary to concentrate to the maximum degree on the working class spirit and on establishing the Marxist-Leninist ideology within the ranks of our Party . . . . the Party's ruling ranks must have a majority working-class composition.

There is no corresponding concern with working-class roots in the Pol Pot group, nearly all of whom, like Pol Pot himself, came from the elite and were educated.

Not a single text of Marxist-Leninist proletarian ideology was translated into Khmer and made available for study by the Pol Pot regime. The only complete work from the Communist world to be translated was *Who's Who in the C.I.A.;* its list of names was used for interrogation purposes in the regime's central political prison. For them, the peasantry, and particularly poor peasant youth, were the core of the revolution. In September 1977, Pol Pot said that pre-revolutionary Kampuchean society had been divided into the following five classes: 'the working class, the peasant class, the bourgeoisie, the capitalist class and the feudal class . . . . Among all the conflicts, the most outstanding was the one between the peasants and the landowners.' Significantly, Pol Pot claimed that 'the peasants suffered oppression by all other classes', obviously including the working class.[44]

This was not always the Party's analysis. In his 1964 book *The Co-operative Question* (reproduced in Part II of the present volume), written when he was a leading member of the Party, Hou Yuon had said that 'the cities do not support the rural areas, they ride on their shoulders'. He then added that this does not mean that 'city workers ride on the shoulders of the poor peasants in the rural areas'. On May Day 1971, a revolutionary radio broadcast had noted: 'In Kampuchea's history of struggle . . . Kampuchea's workers and peasants constituted a basic force in which Kampuchean workers were always the most advanced, the most valiant and the most active vanguard.'[45]

The gulf separating the two political world-views was clearly illustrated after 1975 by the replacement of urban factory workers with young military personnel, mostly from poor peasant backgrounds.

Political Control

Perhaps the most significant area of Marxist-Leninist influence upon the Pol Pot group was in its use of organizational tactics and control techniques very similar to those of Stalinist Russia. (In Pol Pot's case, however, it is difficult to see a strict Stalinist influence in terms of *ideology*. He participated in a youth brigade in Yugoslavia in 1950, two years after the bitter rift between Stalin and Tito.[46] This was unprecedented for an associate, as Pol Pot was, of the then pro-Stalin French Communist Party.) Among these tactics were the aspiration to quasi-absolute power through control of the military and Party apparatus at the highest level. Since at least 1973 Pol Pot has held the two posts of Party Secretary and Chairman of the Party Military Committee. Control of the lower levels, including even the Party Central Committee, was left for later.

From 1973, a series of 'concentric' purges of cadres in regions, provinces, districts and villages followed a recognizable pattern. Training programmes, organized by the highest level of the Party, and often only known about at that level, produced waves of progressively tougher and tougher cadres as far as population control was concerned. Each wave of cadres was in turn replaced and usually executed by the next. Local administration was thereby gradually brought under closer and closer central control, with increasingly restricted manoeuvrability for local cadres all too aware of the fate of their predecessors and the gathering momentum of the wheel of history. It is indicative of the scale of the human tragedy of Democratic Kampuchea that, as this bloody process went on, for instance by 1977-78, training programmes were increasingly filled by very young people.[47]

The elimination of key Party leaders at various points in the 1960s and 1970s, in circumstances for which the victims appear to have been totally unprepared, also was a means of advancing the position of the Pol Pot group. The secrecy of the group's operations is illustrated by the fact that Ieng Sary, in a private 1973 discussion with Kampuchean cadres and representatives of the revolution based in Europe, said that there was no Communist Party active in Kampuchea. (This may also be related to the group's failure, up to that point, to win full control of the Party, which undoubtedly existed.)

On a much wider scale, it is difficult to make sense of the ruthless brutality of the Pol Pot armed forces without supposing that this is how they had been trained to establish their authority and that it was the only way to implement their programmes.

The Common Ground

It is clear that there were significant strains within the Communist Party of Kampuchea as early as the mid-1960s, and that vast gulfs of ideology and tactics separated many of its leaders. But then, how did they manage to work together for so long, as part of the same movement?

Part of the answer is that to a large extent they did not. The Party was small (particularly in the 1960s) and many of its members were in North Vietnam or China, while others were members of autonomous guerrilla groups scattered throughout the countryside. From 1970, the different tendencies seem to have crystallized into geographical regions: the Pol Pot group in the north-east and north, the Vietnam-influenced tendency in the east, and the Cultural Revolution supporters group in the south-west. According to the *Black Book,* only in June 1975 did 'each Zone hand over their armed forces to the Central Committee', at the 'ceremony of the founding of the Revolutionary Army of Kampuchea throughout the country' to which Central Committee leader Pol Pot made his long speech.

Some were prepared to compromise more than others for the sake of internal unity, probably to their own eventful detriment. The following sad passage is one of the great ironies in the Party history, written in 1973, the year in which the internal purges by the Pol Pot group began in earnest, directed against the tendency which included the document's authors:

> disunity on the political point of view, with the personnel divided

> into partisan groups, should be a cause for alarm, and is a danger for the Party. These problems cause anxiety and suffering, because instead of attacking the enemy outside, we are offering our own flesh as prey for the enemy. . . .
>
> During the period from 1960 to 1967 in its history, the Party successfully confronted numerous and serious obstacles to building internal unity in all areas. Doing so is one of the Party's principal achievements.

This was the period in which Pol Pot achieved the position of Party leader.

There *was* ideological common ground: for example, a concern to prevent the rise of a materially privileged class of cadres seem to have united the Pol Pot group and Cultural Revolution supporters. And all groups placed a strong emphasis on mobilizing the peasantry: Kampuchean socialists might have seen this as a means for the peasants as a whole to enhance their social rights and play a political role in accordance with their material interests. In 1970, official reference was made to a Kampuchean Peasants' Association led by Chou Chet,[48] and even in 1975, a Khmer Rouge document captured in fighting near Phnom Penh referred to a Farmers' Association. The Pol Pot group's heavy reliance on the peasantry was differently nuanced, with its stress on the poorest 30%, carefully distinguishing in practice from the 40% or so who were middle peasants. This 30% was indeed the most dynamic social force whose dire poverty left them with everything to gain and nothing to lose in *any* kind of social revolution. But, even so, the Pol Pot group relied on *members* of this group rather than the poor peasants as a whole: Chou Chet's Peasants' Association disappeared without trace after 1975. Although the Pol Pot regime sponsored Womens', Workers' and Youths' Associations on a national scale, no official sanction was ever bestowed on a Peasants' Association. Certainly none existed in practice.

The extent of the Pol Pot dependence on youth and on marginal social groups such as the hill-tribes indicates their failure (or their lack of any intention) to mobilize the peasantry *as a class.* The *Black Book* makes a clear political distinction between the hill-tribe people and the Khmer peasantry of the plains (as well as between Party leaders and cadres).

> In the north-eastern part of Kampuchea, the Vietnamese had difficulties in carrying out their strategy because of the presence of the leadership of the Communist Party of Kampuchea. They tried to get support from the population, but they failed. The north-eastern population are scarce (30,000 to 40,000 inhabitants), but the Vietnamese feared them very much for this population are very faithful to the Kampuchean revolution.

On the other hand, the *Black Book* goes on: 'In the flat open regions, the Vietnamese succeeded in duping some elements among the population and cadres'.

In 1963, Pol Pot and Ieng Sary had secretly fled Phnom Penh for the tribal north-east,[49] and probably spent much of the next five years there. As well as being National Secretary of the C.P.K., Pol Pot was also Party Secretary of the North-east Zone from 1968 to 1970,[50] during a period when some of the Zone's tribes rose up in rebellion against the Sihanouk regime. At least during May 1970, at a time when Pol Pot was abroad, both Ieng Sary and Son Sen were 'responsible for the North-east Zone'.[51] In July 1975, Pol Pot said that his movement 'came out of the jungle' in the remote areas. In 1978, he told Yugoslav journalists that he knew 'perfectly well these national minorities' and regarded them as among his 'backing base'. During 1977-78 more than 200 educated Khmers, who had returned from France in 1976, were put to work in the fields in northern Kompong Cham Province. They were supervised by 30 soldiers led by a 24-year-old north-eastern tribesman named Kan. According to one of them, Pol Pot employs many hill-tribe people because they are faithful.'[52] The latter statement is borne out by other sources which indicate that a disproportionately large number of members of the Jarai, Brou, Tampuon and Stieng tribes joined the Pol Pot forces in 1968-76. Significantly, the Lao national minority in the north-east (and some other minorities elsewhere) seems to have been the exception to this.

So it appears that, despite general unity on the principle of mobilizing the peasantry, serious differences of political practice divided Kampuchean Communists, with the Pol Pot group tending to recruit on an individual basis, from numerically small social groups, the poorest peasants, the hill-tribes and the young.

A more important source of unity was the great stress all three factions placed on nationalism, no doubt partly because of the real experiences of the Kampuchean revolution. Even the staunchly internationalist authors of the 1973 history moved some way towards the perspective of the Pol Pot group when they advised cadres to:

> learn from the experience of foreign parties in order to perfect our own Party, building it according to the real situation of the Kampuchean revolution. In learning from the experiences of foreign parties and the international Communist and workers' movement, we must also take into account the complex present-day problem, the principles of independence and the spirit of being master of events, and also remember the idea of studying good as well as bad cases and considering whether or not they could be utilized, according to the real state of our party and country . . . .
>
> In parallel, however, the Party also has numerous bad experiences resulting from the learning and copying of foreign experiences. On the other hand, it made us completely ignorant; on the other hand, it hindered and even sometimes destroyed the revolutionary movement and progress in organizing the Party. In this case, it is better to

> learn nothing from foreign experience.

This is unlikely to be a reference to the 1954 Geneva Conference, and is probably an allusion to the late 1950s when, the document says, 'the influence of revisionism abroad . . . gave rise to confusion of political ideas and weakened the revolution's situation'. The Kampuchean Party seems to have reacted similarly to the Vietnamese when Khruschev took the Soviet Union into a period of 'peaceful co-existence' with the U.S. and reduced support for struggling revolutionary movements. After a brief tilt towards Chinese anti-revisionism and support for armed struggles, Vietnam was apparently attracted back towards the Soviet Union by Brezhnev's increased support for Vietnamese liberation after 1964. But for the Kampuchean Party it was already too late. 'It was the period of revisionism which destroyed our Party.' And the critical effect was to fuel the xenophobic and chauvinist elements in Kampuchean revolutionary nationalism.

The Rise of the Pol Pot Group, 1960-75

Decimated by police repression, particularly in 1959, the Kampuchean Communists called a Party Congress in 1960. Pol Pot was to claim in 1977 that the Party had been 'really born' at that 'First Congress', which, he said, adopted a political line independent of the Vietnamese Party.[53] By contrast, the 1973 history, which refers to the meeting as 'the second general assembly', describes it as an important organizational breakthrough in a period of 'straightening out activities' after a series of setbacks, and says it made the decision to 'form the Marxist-Leninist Party in Kampuchea'. Whatever political line was adopted, it does not seem to have been a great victory for the Pol Pot group. The Party elected Tou Samouth as its leader.

To my knowledge the Pol Pot group has made only one public reference to Tou Samouth: in the first edition of the *Black Book* in September 1978. There we read that in 1946, Tou Samouth was working in the south-west and in contact with the Vietnamese. Interestingly, a 1953 booklet issued by the Kampuchean Communist movement had recognized Tou Samouth as its leader, describing him as 'an authoritative priest who has built up the south-west liberated zone'.[54] The *Black Book* of 1978 then goes on to say that Samouth and others

> were under the total leadership of the Vietnamese and relied entirely on them. They could do nothing and understood nothing by themselves. The Vietnamese decided and ordered everything in their place. That is why when they were foresaken by the Vietnamese after the Geneva Agreements, they could do nothing. As they were puppets, they knew nothing about politics, they were incompetent to do anything

> and had no revolutionary position. After the Geneva Agreements, when the mission of leading the revolution fell on them, they were not able to assume it. At that time, the Vietnamese set up a provisional committee of leadership. But it was only in 1957 that some revolutionaries were informed of it. In this committee were Sieu Heng, Son Ngoc Minh, Tou Samouth and two or three others less well known.
>
> After Geneva, left alone, this provisional committee of leadership collapsed by itself, like a house of cards at the slightest puff of air, without being touched by anybody.
>
> But there were real Kampuchean revolutionaries who faced the situation. They went on accomplishing their revolutionary tasks . . . .

In the period after the 1960 Congress, Sihanouk publicly announced that Tou Samouth was active underground in Kampuchea, describing him as 'the famous Setha'.[55]

Pol Pot told Yugoslav journalists in March 1978 that he had become acting Party Secretary after 20 July 1962, when the unnamed previous Party Secretary was 'kidnapped by the enemy'. Interestingly, the authors of the 1973 history confirm that the man who disappeared on that date was Party Secretary Tou Samouth: 'on 20 July 1962, comrade T.S.M., Secretary of the Party was kidnapped by the enemy, leaving no trace. This was great grief for the Party which had just been reorganized.' It is clear that the Pol Pot group felt no such grief at the disappearance of a Vietnamese 'puppet'. Vietnamese allegations that Pol Pot himself was 'no stranger to this elimination' may well be correct.[56] It is interesting that in the second, more considered and most widely distributed version of the *Black Book,* the references to Tou Samouth were surgically deleted from the passages quoted above, possibly with an eye on this controversy.

Pol Pot was to be confirmed as Party Secretary in 1963, the year when he and many others fled to the jungle from Phnom Penh and thus put the Party on a war footing. Further Party meetings, like that of 1960, were very difficult, if not impossible, to organize. Although the secrecy surrounding the Party's activities at that time, as well as the massive neutralization of its cadres in the late 1950s, give the impression that only a very small number of people were still involved, rank-and-file followers were not lacking. In 1976, a former Kampuchean student in Australia, Lay Roget, told me of a visit he had made in 1963 to a village in Pursat Province, during his youth. Villagers travelling down from the upland locality of Leach spoke of a caravan of 'two or three hundred ox-carts', which had just arrived in the area from Takeo Province, having secretly trekked through the rugged Elephant Mountains of the south-west and deep into the Cardamomes of the west. It is known that these people were not led by any of Pol Pot's immediate group,[57] although Ta Mok was probably closely involved.

China and Vietnam

During 1965, Pol Pot left Kampuchea to spend several months in Hanoi and in China. Deng Xiaoping and Liu Shaoqi at that time held appropriate Party positions in China for them to have received the Kampuchean delegation.[58] The *Black Book* throws some light on what happened next. At the very end of a chapter entitled 'The Strategy of "Indochina Federation" of the Indochinese Communist Party of Ho Chi Minh', discussion of events in 1955 finishes curiously on the following note: 'In 1966, the Communist Party of Kampuchea consolidated and strengthened its position of independence, sovereignty and self-reliance, and clearly discerned the true nature of the Vietnamese.' And at another point, we read, 'As early as 1966, the Communist Party of Kampuchea has judged that it could have only state relations and other official relations with Vietnam, for there was a fundamental contradiction between the Kampuchean revolution and the Vietnamese revolution. The Vietnamese wanted to put the Kampuchean revolution under their thumb.'

Had Pol Pot found encouragement for this view whilst in China the year before? Impossible to know for certain. But important developments were taking place in Indochina. Huge numbers of American troops began arriving in Vietnam from 1965, and the benign neutrality of the Sihanouk Government was increasingly valued by the Vietnamese Communists, along with their ability to use parts of Kampuchea's border areas for sanctuary and shipment of supplies. According to a writer who was then sympathetic to Pol Pot's regime:

> Sihanouk's anti-Americanism became most precious to the Vietnamese. . . . The contradiction between the Vietnam Workers' Party's needs in terms of liberating the south and the C.P.K's needs in terms of revolutionizing Kampuchea became most acute. The V.W.P. probably believed that the C.P.K. could resolve this contradiction by some variation on united front tactics. The C.P.K. probably believed that such tactics just could not work. Each Party saw the other as thinking only in terms of its own interests.[59]

This is scarcely evidence of any long-standing desire of the Vietnamese 'to put the Kampuchean revolution under their thumb' and eventually coerce it into an 'Indochina Federation'. Nor is it evidence for what is claimed in another part of the *Black Book:* 'For the Vietnamese leaders, the problem of the liberation of South Vietnam was not their big concern. For them, the problem of Kampuchea was far more important.'

Interestingly, it is not at all certain that 'the C.P.K., at that stage believed that 'some variation on united front tactics . . . just could not work'. According to the 1973 Party history: 'as of 1964, the Party had a great deal of influence . . . . At the same time, the organization of our Party contributed its part to the international revolution in the resolute struggle against the imperialists, especially the American imperialists and their lackeys, in defence of world peace.' This is almost certainly a reference to Party attempts to strengthen and capitalize upon the neutrality of the Sihanouk regime in order to aid the Vietnamese Communists, not the policy of the Pol Pot group who were preparing for war against Sihanouk. Hou Yuon, a member of the Party and a legal parliamentary representative, in November 1964 published a book in which he clearly called for heightened class struggle *within the framework* of the 'patriotic' regime, in order to improve the living conditions of the peasantry and bolster Sihanouk's anti-U.S. position.[60]

The Party history of 1973, also includes in its list of important victories of the 1960s the rejection of American aid by Sihanouk in 1963, the cutting of diplomatic relations with the U.S. by Sihanouk in 1965 and the resignation of the first Lon Nol Government in 1967. This mid-1960s analysis is clearly different from the position of the Pol Pot group, as later stated in the *Black Book.*

Whatever the agreed policy of the C.P.K. at the time, it is beyond doubt that the conflict of interests between the Kampuchean and Vietnamese revolutions in the mid-1960s was a product of American imperialism, and not of Vietnamese territorial ambitions in Kampuchea. Therefore, interests were bound to coincide again sooner or later, especially once the thrust of the American aggression had been blunted. Recognizing this, and contradicting its previous assessment of the 'true nature' of the Vietnamese Communists, the *Black Book* says that in 1970, 'the leaders of the Communist Party of Kampuchea made constant recommendations to preserve the solidarity with the Vietnamese'. And that as late as 1975, 'the Central Committee of the Communist Party of Kampuchea still regarded Vietnam as a friendly country with which Kampuchea had differences'.

The Samlaut Rebellion

Not long after the international contacts and events of 1965-66, the Kampuchean revolution took up arms. On whose orders? According to Pol Pot's July 1975 internal speech: 'In Battambang Province in March-April 1967 an armed uprising took place . . . . However, at that time our Party asked that this be postponed for a while in order to examine and sum up the state of the contradictions and the possibility of the use of arms.'[61] And in a public speech in 1977, Pol Pot said that the 1967 uprising against Lon Nol 'was started by the people themselves. At that time the Party Central Committee had not yet decided on a nationwide armed insurrection. The people in Battambang did it first, since the movement of the peasants' struggle was indefensibly fluid.'[62]

'The Party' launched its armed struggle only in 1968, according to Pol Pot.[63] In another 1977 official speech, Nuon Chea concurred, saying that the struggle began on 18 January 1968, when the Revolutionary Army of Kampuchea was formed and engaged in its first attack on government forces stationed at the post of Bay Damram in southern Battambang. But Reim, a refugee who lived and worked in the village of Bay Damram in 1976, was told by the local subdistrict chief that the Party had launched armed struggle in Battambang in May 1967. The conversation between Hu Nim and Nhim recorded in Hu Nim's 'confessions' also points to an earlier date:

> Brother Nhim described the history of his struggle. . . . He recalled the period of the combined political and armed struggle '1968-70'. Brother Nhim paid a lot of attention to the struggle under his leadership on Phnom Veay Chap, which he regarded as an important period. However, the Party was not interested and did not mention this in its history. Brother Nhim said: 'I regard Phnom Veay Chap as a mountain of heroes, because the people and troops who fought on that mountain were very patriotic. They fought the enemy, who had plenty of weapons such as tanks and airplanes. Then we broke out of the enemy's encirclement and victoriously withdrew from the mountain. Even though a number of troops and people sacrificed their lives, their sacrifices were very valuable because they provided important experience in armed struggle. It was as a result of this experience that our village guerrillas attacked Bay Damram post on 18 January 1968, and were crowned with victory', he concluded.

Nhim was clearly referring to a period of armed struggle led by him and other Party members in 1967, *before* the Pol Pot group's official date for its launching. Further, in early 1972 in the South-West Zone (where Phouk Chhay was political commissar), an official Party history distributed by the Central Committee noted that 'from 1967, the Party resumed the armed struggle. The events at Samlaut were prepared in advance . . . .'[64] It is possible that it was Kampucheans inspired by the Cultural Revolution, then in full swing in China, rather than the Pol Pot group, who were involved in the 1967 Samlaut uprising. (They also carried more weight in the Party Central Committee in early 1972 than the Pol Pot group.) Certainly, an important demonstration in Phnom Penh on 11 March, 1967, calling for withdrawal of government troops from southern Battambang,[65] was organized by Cultural Revolution supporters and leftist 'independents'. And later that month, leading revolutionary Tiv Ol took to the jungle after Sihanouk was enraged by his presentation of Chinese revolutionary songs at a university New Year celebration. The first clash at Samlaut took place on 2 April.

As for the third Communist tendency, the authors of the 1973 Party history are curiously ambiguous on this issue. 'Our Party played the role of leader in the revolutionary struggle movement, that is to say, conducting politics with the support of arms, as it has solemnly proclaimed since 1968 (?).[sic]' At several points the document takes the year 1967 as the beginning of a new stage in the Party's development, but does not say whether this was because of the commencement of the armed struggle. Its authors also hint that they were not intimately involved in the Pol Pot group's 1968 decision to take up arms either: 'Our Zone [the Eastern Zone] *worked to co-operate* with this political movement supported by arms in the country from 1968 to 1970.' (my emphasis–B.K.) It is clear that by 1970, at the latest, Pol Pot's group held the highest authority in the Party. But imposing their plans at other levels and elsewhere remained a problem. And not a small one.

Foreign Intervention

On 18 March 1970, Prince Sihanouk was overthrown and replaced by General Lon Nol, who proclaimed the Khmer Republic. Lon Nol quickly became involved in the war in neighbouring Vietnam by attempting to remove Vietnamese Communist troops from largely uninhabited areas along a narrow stretch[66] inside the Kampuchean border, where they were seeking sanctuary from American ground attack. As U.S. bombing and Saigon ground attacks across the border were stepped up, the Vietnamese pushed further into the interior, soon to be followed by a large-scale combined U.S. Saigon-force.

There was thus a common interest between Sihanouk – now in exile in Peking and calling for an uprising against those who had overthrown him – the Kampuchean revolutionaries and the Vietnamese Communists, who were penetrating deep into the country in the name of the newly-formed National United Front of Kampuchea (FUNK).

A number of documents captured by the U.S. army from Vietnamese Communist troops during 1970 reveal in detail the motivations and style of this Vietnamese move.[67] A member of a security unit stationed in Kampuchea in late April summed up a long series of notes, 'Our prime mission is to fight the U.S. in South Vietnam. Our mission in Kampuchea is an emergency mission . . . . We must co-operate with our friends in areas where they are present. In areas where they are not present, we must still carry out the tasks, then turn over [the results] to our friends.' Who were 'our friends'? Evidently not just those Kampuchean revolutionaries who had long-standing links with Vietnam, most of whom were still in Hanoi.

> Forces are available but the ideology and sense of organization of our friends are poor. Therefore, we must be patient in providing help for their movement (because their capability of learning is slow we must use explanations that suit their level of understanding when we request their help, they request us to provide them with weapons, medicine, food, provisions, etc.).
>
> Our request for the friendly side to indoctrinate and motivate their people cannot be immediately implemented, therefore, we should be patient. . . . Assistance to this movement requires our efforts and enthusiasm. We must consider our friends' revolution as our own. Only in this way can we achieve great victories. . . . our relations with our friends are the ties between comrades, based on love, equality, mutual respect.

> Eliminate the thought that we are a 'big country' and that the friendly country is poor and weak. We must be patient and must sympathize with our friends (sometimes the capability of a district military commander of the friendly country is only as good as a soldier of our army).
>
> (A number of our friends joined the revolution only since the last demonstration.)
>
> Provide mutual support and share difficulties with our friends, our friends do not have a regime yet. (After we attacked the enemy posts our friends seized all the war booty.) We have to understand them because actually they are short of many things.
>
> We should share with them what we have.[68]

One senses in these writings *both* the traditional paternalistic Vietnamese view of Kampuchea and a genuine attempt to break down that attitude.

A circular from the 'Command Committee of Group 180' (evidently an armed security regiment), dated 16 April 1970, dealt with 'Guidance for Tasks in Kampuchea'. It warned Vietnamese soldiers that:

> When the government and associations are set up, we must improve their capability, so that they can do their jobs themselves.
>
> We must avoid the impression that such organizations are initiated by the South Vietnam Liberation Army or the 'Viet Cong'. We must make them realize that they are masters.
>
> Moreover, we must make them (especially Buddhist monks and intellectuals) understand that the leaders of the present Kampuchean revolution are Sihanouk and the Front [FUNK] and that the revolutionary force belongs to the Kampuchean patriots (It is advisable to tell the working-class people that the Kampuchean Revolution is led by the People's Revolutionary Party of Kampuchea [P.R.P.].
>
> We must also tell them that we are their friends, opposing the same common enemy, and that we will always wholeheartedly support them. We must explain to them that their co-operation with us does not mean that they serve us. (The explanations must be made in a careful and tactful manner in order to avoid misunderstanding.)[69]

Despite their common interests with Sihanouk, the Vietnamese were still apparently prepared to foster social revolution in Kampuchea. In January 1970, when Sihanouk was still in power, a resolution of the J-12 section, presumably a border area office, noted its inability to help Kampuchean Communists as much as it would have liked: 'Kampuchea always uses the assistance given us in the matters of messing, billeting, travelling, and especially transportation as a lever to put pressure on us concerning the Red Kampucheans by restricting our own messing and billeting activities [sic] . . . .[70]

And in April 1970, after the Vietnamese troops moved in, the Group 180 circular pointed out:

> Concerning the selection of members for the governmental committees, [they] must be true patriots who love the people [Kampucheans]. They must profoundly hate the U.S. imperialists and their henchmen, Lon Nol and Sirik Matak, and be determined to overthrow them.
>
> We must make sure that the majority of members in the governmental committees belongs to the worker-peasant class. It is possible to include one or two members of Sihanouk's former government or monks, provided that they enjoy the confidence of the people and enthusiastically resist the U.S. and its henchmen. However, they must not be given important positions such as the chairmanship of [the Committee] or the direction of military and security affairs.[71]

The Vietnamese also demanded a high standard of conduct from their troops in Kampuchea. As early as mid-1969, a J-12 section cadre noted:

> After we win victory, Kampuchea will live side by side with our country, a peaceful country with a correct policy . For this reason, Kampuchea cannot fail to support us . . . *Our required attitude:*
> 1) We should firmly maintain the attitude of a man who is fighting for a just cause, and who is winning; 2) We should treat the Kampucheans as our equals; we should be friendly but constantly vigilant;
> 3) In trying to win Kampuchea to our side, we should consider the Kampuchean population as our main objective and try to win their support . . . .
> *Review of our past attitude:* We did not respect the territorial integrity of Kampuchea and looked down on the Kampuchean people. For instance, our messing, billeting and movement have had adverse effects on the Kampuchean people's standard of living.[72]

The January 1970 J-12 resolution says:

> Efforts should be made to obtain support from the Kampuchean people. We should give them adequate assistance in matters concerning public health and social welfare. We should encourage them to work on production and provide them with favourable conditions for earning their living. We should indemnify the people for any damages or losses caused by our troops, settle all misunderstandings and troubles, and strengthen solidarity and friendship between the people and us . . .[73]

According to captured handwritten notes of a Vietnamese unit's plan of action between 15 and 29 April, 1970, the troops

> should absolutely avoid manifesting pride of being from a larger country. They should not be too enterprising and do everything

> by themselves instead of giving advice and letting the Kampuchean revolutionaries do their job. They should not infringe on the Kampucheans' customs, disturb their way of living, or violate their property. They should strictly practise the Party's principle of wholehearted devotion to the cause of the masses, the principle of equality, and the maintenance of mutual respect between the two brotherly peoples. . . .[74]

A report of a 'base area meeting' on 19 April noted:

> In the establishment of a relationship with the [Kampuchean] people, cadre and members should display a correct attitude, respect their habits and traditions, and absolutely not touch their property, because they treated us as their liberators. We should tactfully refuse what they offer us. Everybody should work to help both the South Vietnamese and Kampuchean revolutionary movements develop, properly fulfil our responsibility, and do production work in accordance with the prescribed criteria.[75]

On 29 April 1970, a cable from the Communist High Command of South Vietnam spelled out to Group 180 its concern that Vietnamese troops develop good relations with the Kampuchean people.

> Recently, many armed action units, cadre, and soldiers have, by their correct attitude, won the confidence of the people, positively contributed to the rapid establishment of the Front Committees, and created a good influence.
>
> However, in many places, some cadres and soldiers are still violating discipline, which is adversely influencing the morale and thinking of the people and harming the good nature of the revolutionary army. Following are the most common undisciplined actions:
>
> Our cadres and soldiers have often shot at random. Some of them have stood in the middle of a Kampuchean village and shot at high-flying enemy aircraft with an A.K. assault rifle.
>
> They did not follow our movement regulations and went anywhere they wanted. Some went close to and some went through Kampuchean villages. Some of them went to the villages to purchase goods, some entered villages to request food, and others organized parties.
>
> They have also violated the customs and habits of the Kampuchean people. . . . All measures taken against the people, including the accusation of bad people, the punishment of the 'Kampuchean' traitors, the punishment through economic measures, etc., must be carried out by the Front Committees and [local] people and not by the action teams. Instead of simply killing them, appropriate punishment, ranging from warnings and house arrests up to the death penalty, should be applied against the 'Kampuchean' reactionary traitors.

> If the confiscation of private property of reactionary individuals is necessary, we should motivate the people to do it themselves and share the property among themselves. In this way, the people are only recovering what they have lost and are not receiving a donation from us. . . .
>
> Unit commanders should indoctrinate all of their cadre and soldiers and help them to fully understand the political significance of the 10-point code of conduct in the establishment of relations with the local people. . . .
>
> *The 10 Point Code of Conduct*
>
> 1. Absolutely do not enter pagodas or violate their environment.
> 2. Secure the people's assistance in all matters dealing with the pagodas.
> 3. Take off your hat and do not make noise while passing or approaching pagodas or Buddhist monks.
> 4. Do not threaten or disturb the people. Respect the elders and adopt a correct attitude towards women, youths and children.
> 5. Do not take anything from the people, either from their homes or from their fields.
> 6. Do not enter into private business with the people or accept anything from them. The unit representative should explain this policy to the people and solve all problems arising from it.
> 7. Return to the people what has been borrowed in serviceable condition and pay for that which is damaged.
> 8. Do not station troops in the people's homes or do kitchen work in the *Phum* [hamlet].
> 9. In combat or in case of danger, sacrifice yourselves to save the people's lives and property.
> 10. Every request for the people's help should be made through the local Front Committees, local cadre and action teams.[76]

This policy succeeded in winning some support from Kampuchean villagers. In Kandal Province, in April 1970, Vietnamese troops recruited 20 'Khmer sympathizers' and five youths of Sino-Vietnamese extraction in the Prek Ambel area, according to an eyewitness,[77] and in the Saang area they were supported by 'local Khmer and Cham villagers, who had joined the Communist forces'.[78]

By September 1970, U.S. intelligence estimated that Khmer Communist forces now numbered 20 'Khmer V.C.' battalions and five 'mixed' Khmer-Vietnamese battalions, while there were 80 battalions of Vietnamese Communist troops in Kampuchea. The same intelligence report continued:

> Vietnamese advisers are instructed to keep a low profile; only two may be present at any NUFK [FUNK] meeting and they are caution-

> ed repeatedly to 'strive to avoid bad attitudes before the committees under all circumstances' . . . [Vietnamese Communist] advisory teams are present also in the northern provinces; the government commander at besieged Kompong Thom has reported that enemy forces are receiving substantial support from Khmer villages north of the town. . . . Whether the Vietnamese advisors have been able to maintain an attractive or even low profile is open to some question; there have been reports of undisciplined acts by V.C./N.V.A. troops.

As for the troops of America's Saigon allies, the report went on:

> A.R.V.N's misconduct, however, appears to be more flagrant and widespread, and the Communists have apparently manipulated Cambodian anger with A.R.V.N. excesses to draw villagers into pro-NUFK (FUNK) activities in a number of areas.
>
> Despite these and other difficulties, the NUFK appears to be making headway. Although there has been some refugee movement out of Communist-occupied areas and a few reports of village-level resistance, the rural population in areas of Communist activity seems largely to have acquiesced to Communist control. While much of this acquiescence may merely reflect peasant passivity in the face of superior military force, there are some indications of political success. The most dramatic is a recent report, based on POW and refugee interrogations, from the FANK G-2 to Lon Nol. It concludes that 'the enemy has devoted its time to organizing the conquered areas', that 'the results have been positive', and that 'the population has been largely taken in hand by the enemy and could become in a relatively short time a trump for him'. The reasons for this are described as follows: 'initially reticent, sometimes hostile, the population seems to be turning in favour of the enemy for two reasons: (a) they have appreciated not being submitted to taxation and excesses by the invaders who, for propaganda purposes, are well-behaved and respectful of the needs and cares of the population. In some cases they have been supported by the Buddhist monks because they have always avoided attacking religion; (b) aerial bombardments against the villagers have caused civilian loss on a large scale . . . .'[79]

In July 1971, a U.S. Defense Intelligence Agency appraisal[80] estimated that Khmer Communist organizational strength at 40,000 to 60,000 people, including main force units of 5,000 to 10,000 organized into 18 battalions. 'The Communists have found some backing among the Khmer peasantry, and the Chinese and Vietnamese minorities . . . . It is estimated that the Communists control some two to three million people in Cambodia out of a total of about seven million . . . . For the most part, however, the Vietnamese Communists have apparently acceded to Khmer demands for autonomy . . . .' In the north and north-east of Kampuchea, where the Pol Pot group was then most active, the appraisal pointed out: 'On occasion, after withdrawal of V.C./N.V.A. forces, the local populace has refused to co-operate with the Khmer Communists . . . In many areas, especially the north-east, the populace is dissatisfied under the Vietnamese occupation . . . . The Vietnamese answer has generally been to make his presence as inconspicuous as possible while turning routine administrative details over to Cambodians.' In the south-west, on the other hand, a 1971 C.I.A. report[81] on Takeo Province noted that the Khmer Communists

> take great care not to antagonize the peasantry. They help them with the harvest, offer to pay a reasonable sum for the supplies they need, treat the women with respect and refrain from abusive language or behaviour. . . . They have gained considerable sympathy from the local peasantry, who support them. . . . and warn them of the arrival of [Lon Nol] troops. The only people in this area who do not actively support the V.C./N.V.A. and Khmer Communists are the wealthy merchants, local functionaries and professors.

And in nearby Kompong Speu Province, according to another C.I.A. report: 'By maintaining tight discipline and carefully avoiding actions which might antagonize the local population the V.C./N.V.A. have been able to convey the impression that they have the true interests of the peasants in mind.' William Shawcross takes the example of one village outside Kompong Speu town, which had been pillaged by Saigon troops in June and July 1970. 'When the North Vietnamese won control of it in September, they reminded the villagers that they had never had to worry about South Vietnamese looting before Sihanouk's removal and promised to help them defend themselves in the future. Communist efforts, according to the [C.I.A. Phnom Penh] station, had already won at least a hundred recruits in this one village alone.'[82] This village, Chbal Mon, later became the headquarters of Khmer Communist leader Chou Chet, who was killed by Pol Pot in 1978.

Describing the general situation throughout Kampuchea, the July 1971 D.I.A. appraisal concluded:

> Khmer Communist cadres have resorted where necessary to coercion, intimidation and assassination. Some have used their new positions to settle old scores with government officials who formerly opposed them when they were 'bandits' under the Sihanouk regime. On the whole, however, they have attempted to avoid acts which might alienate the population, and the behaviour of Vietnamese Communist soldiers has generally been exemplary when compared with the South Vietnamese.'

Obviously, the *10 Point Code of Conduct* had had its impact.

A Khmer peasant interviewed in Thailand in 1979 recalled regular visits to his locality in northern Kompong Cham Province by Vietnamese Communist units during 1970-73. A former village schoolteacher recalls: 'The people didn't reflect on whether the Vietnamese were taking over their land; they liked them because they paid for everything they needed, from oxen or buffaloes even down to a chili pepper. They did not steal from the people – they paid for everything, those North Vietnamese. They never killed any local people. In 1971-72 the Khmer Rouge started to kill captured Lon Nol soldiers, but the Vietnamese never did.'[83]

The authors of the *Black Book* see the Vietnamese attitude to Norodom Sihanouk as too positive. In 1967, they say, under the Prince's regime: 'when Comrade Khieu Samphan joined the *maquis*, the Vietnamese reproached the Communist Party of Kampuchea for making an erroneous decision.' But elsewhere in the *Book*, it is pointed out that in 1969, 'the Central Committee of the Communist Party of Kampuchea criticized the statements of the intellectuals who had joined the *maquis* and attacked Samdech Norodom Sihanouk. It considered that those statements ran counter to the Party's line.'

There is a real contradiction here. While uncompromisingly opposed to Sihanouk, his regime and his followers of all kinds, the Pol Pot group nevertheless wished to harness his following to their own organization. But the *Book* also (retrospectively?) distinguishes between Khieu Samphan, President of the State Praesidium of Democratic Kampuchea from 1976, and others like Hu Nim who joined the *maquis* at the same time, during the Samlaut rebellion. Greatly influenced by the Cultural Revolution, these *maquisands* were also anti-Sihanouk and apparently prepared to follow such a policy publicly. Perhaps it was this 'independent' group which, in March 1967, sponsored a revolutionary organization among villagers of Krava and nearby areas in the Baray area of Kompong Thom Province. Their leaflets protested the official collection of rice from the farmers at low prices; they also described both Lon Nol *and* Sihanouk as 'men of straw' who had 'sold out their country to the United States'.[84] The leaflets appealed to villagers to join their struggle, promising to distribute to them important administrative positions and end all state taxation when final victory was achieved. Judging from a number of common family names among many of the 21 members of this organization named by *Phnom Penh Presse* (12 April 1967), the group seems to have successfully recruited village people in the area. The group's President and Vice-president were said to be called Mak Sean and Net Pon; to my knowledge these names have never re-appeared in Kampuchean Communism.

The third, Vietnam-influenced, Communist tendency was prepared to work closely with Sihanouk and his supporters in a more genuine United Front than Pol Pot, for his part, had in mind. This is why one account, in stating that the revolution in rural Prey Veng, the major province of this group's Eastern Zone, was still in the hands of those opposed to Pol Pot, described them as 'Sihanoukists'.[85]

The Return of the Exiled Issaraks

In mid-1970, 1,500 or so Kampuchean Communist Party members and hundreds of others began the long trip home from Hanoi along the Ho Chi Minh trail. At a time when Party control was expanding rapidly and cadres were in critically short supply, the returned Communist cadres were to work with the Pol Pot group and about 300 Communist cadres who had remained in Kampuchea since 1954 and were in co-operation with the Vietnamese Communists. Hanoi-based Party leader Son Ngoc Minh had informed the returnees before they left Hanoi that tasks would be assigned to them on their arrival by the Party in Kampuchea, i.e., by Pol Pot's C.P.K. Certainly rifts had developed among these people during their long exile,[86] although the political significance of these divisions is unclear. But the ramifications of the rift between the Pol Pot group and *all* the returnees are clear. Pol Pot's view has been expressed by Steve Heder:

> instead of tying the C.P.K. to the Vietnam Workers' Party, these Kampucheans only generated worse conflicts and suspicions. At one point they might have been welcomed or they might have overwhelmed the 'anti-Vietnamese' elements of the C.P.K. Now they were, at best, a tolerated minority, and at worst seen as infilitrators and enemies. For the C.P.K. leadership, it seemed they had come not to help, but to replace or destroy.[87]

Why did it seem this way? According to Prince Sihanouk:

> During the year 1978 Khieu Samphan told me quite clearly that even throughout the anti-American war [1970-75] the Communist Party and revolutionary army of Kampuchea never ceased to consider North Vietnam and its army as the enemy number one, American imperialism only occupying second place as far as enemies of Kampuchea were concerned. Last year [1978] . . . Khieu Samphan declared to my wife and myself that these cadres and officers had 'neither the minds nor the hearts of Khmers', that they had become spies of the 'Vietminh', and consequently (I quote), 'we were obliged to rid ourselves of them'. This meant quite simply that this Khmer Vietminh 'reinforcement' committed by Hanoi in 1970 to support our anti-American struggle had ended up being (physically) liquidated by the Khmer Rouge.[88]

Chauvinist paranoia, racism and the asphyxiating desperation with which another tolerated minority bearhugged revolutionary power to themselves surely played their part in this reception for 1,000 experienced and technically skilled Communists.

In an interview in early 1978, Li Yang Duc, a Khmer Communist trained in North Vietnam and China and a member of the Party Committee for

Kampot Province until September 1974, said that prior to his flight to Vietnam at that time there had been a violent purge of members of the 'third force'. He went on: 'The third force comprised, in the vocabulary of the Party, Sihanoukists and former members of his administration on the one hand, and Communists who had been regrouped in North Vietnam on the other.'[89] The 1973 Party history confirms this purge: 'The Party took the position of strength, attacking finally and chasing absolutely the third force which was the obstacle.' The history makes it clear immediately, however, that the third force was seen as an 'obstacle' not because it was an enemy of the Communist movement, but rather because it *divided* it: 'This third force tended to split our country's political forces in three or four directions.'

However one interprets the term 'our country's political forces', this statement is an indication of significant support for the Vietnamese Communist line in the Kampuchean Communist movement. If the phrase means 'the revolutionary forces', this is already clear. If it means the entire national body politic, it must be a reference to the difficulty of attracting to the cause people from the Lon Nol side while Hanoi-trained cadres (and Sihanoukists) were participating in the revolutionary side. In that case, the 'split' over the issue would have been between potential Lon Nol defectors and the Communist Party itself.

Outside the country, according to informed sources, the Hanoi Government was told by the C.P.K. that the treatment being accorded an ailing Son Ngoc Minh was 'inadequate' and a request was made for his transfer to Peking. This request was granted, and in 1972 Minh, leader of the anti-French revolutionary movement from 1946-54, died or was killed in China.

The Kampuchean returnees from Hanoi were, according to one of them, Ieng Lim, assigned 'the combat positions', whereas 'only the local Khmer Rouge held political positions within the local organizations'.[90] In late 1971, underground Party spokesmen in Phnom Penh noted that of the 1,500 who had returned only 8 months previously, half of them were already dead; the cause of death was 'uncertain'. They also noted that Party leaders had rebuffed attempts by the Vietnamese Communist troops (then their major military force) to get co-operation in the form of a joint command.

Ieng Lim defected to the Lon Nol regime in late 1971 because he claimed, 'it was evident that the war was for the benefit of North Vietnam and not the Khmer revolution'. He also said that in the rural areas 'Sihanouk is not popular, and only Khmer fillers in Vietnamese units wear Sihanouk badges' – perhaps he thought the Vietnamese were giving in too much to Sihanoukists in the united front. Interestingly, however, he compared the relations with the people enjoyed by the Lon Nol army (FANK), the Kampuchean revolutionary Khmer Rouge as a whole, and the *local* Khmer Rouge in particular: 'Ieng Lim also observed that FANK troops were not 'close to the people'. He said that Khmer Rouge cadres were able to win the allegiance of the villagers [but that] the *local* Khmer Rouge had arbitrarily executed peasants for minor infractions, and that he himself had stopped the killing of civilians at Baray in Kompong Thom.' (my emphasis – B.K.)

If the Pol Pot group can be compared to a double-ended hammer beating the peasantry into a keen blade to wreak history's vengeance on their neighbours then its full force was first manifested in Kompong Thom Province in the Southern Zone.

There, in September 1970, local Khmer Rouge troops fired on Vietnamese communist forces from behind while the latter were attacking a Lon Nol unit.[91] And it was in this Province which, curiously, had been a seat of unrest in *1967,* that the massacring of peasants by Pol Pot forces in 1973 was to drive tens of thousands of people into the Lon Nol zone.

Other reports confirm the destructive effects of early Pol Pot chauvinism in the area. Pon, a Khmer student from Kompong Cham Province, joined the Communist forces after the 1970 Lon Nol coup. He and nine other Khmer youths were trained by Vietnamese revolutionaries in Kompong Thom for a year or so after which eight of the others asked to go and work with the Khmer Communists instead. The Vietnamese agreed, and they departed. Not long after, two veteran Khmer cadres trained in Vietnam arrived and reported that people were being killed by the Khmer Rouge on account of their Vietnamese training. Pon also recalled that, in 1972, Vietnamese troops were quartered briefly in the village of Baray, staying in the houses of peasants and generally enjoyed good relations with them. Soon after they moved on, Khmer Rouge units entered the village and threw grenades into the houses of the peasants who had hosted Vietnamese soldiers, killing a number of entire families. In 1972, Pon decided that he no longer wanted to work with the revolution, and asked the Vietnamese Communists with whom he was working for permission to go home. They agreed and took him most of the way back to his native village by truck.

The Struggle in the South-West Zone

In the meantime, however, events in other provinces coming under the rapidly expanding control of the revolutionary movement as a whole were evolving differently. The movement gained significant popular support in the South-West Zone from 1970-72. Genuinely democratic elections were held in the villages and hamlets under revolutionary control in 1970, according to an official U.S. observer, Kenneth Quinn, in a detailed 1974 report on Kampuchea's southern border area.[92] In a discussion of border areas of the South-West Zone, he says:

> in Kompong Trach, where the [land redistribution] was carried out in all villages in 1972, no person was allowed to retain over five hectares of rice land or one hectare of garden land or orchard. Rice land over that limit was given to people with fewer than five

> hectares or to people's associations in the village. Orchards and garden land were not redistributed but kept under district government control.

And in the Special Zone, nearby Kandal Province 'where rice land is less abundant, all land was confiscated and then parcelled out, with each family getting one hectare'.[93] It should be noted that the amount of land retained or gained by each family in these cases was not particularly low by the pre-war Kampuchean average for landholdings. As a result of this, Quinn noted, in these two zones, 'many poorer people supported the early programme such as land redistribution because they received benefits'.[94]

Sihanoukists or Communists? These reforms were largely carried out by 'Sihanoukist royalists', according to Quinn, as distinct from their opponents in the united front [FUNK] , the 'Communists'. It is clear, however, from the nature of these reforms, and from Quinn's definitions of the two groups, that there was a much more significant distinction to be made between the Pol Pot group ('the Communists') and *the alliance between Sihanoukists and the pro-Vietnamese Kampuchean Communists.* For instance, the 'Communists', according to Quinn, aimed to repress the Buddhist religion, whereas the opposition wished to retain it. It was indeed repressed during the Pol Pot regime, but was 'reintroduced' by the pro-Vietnamese Communists in 1979. Also, Quinn's 'Communists' were 'strongly anti-Vietnamese', whereas their opponents 'were in favour of full co-operation with the Vietcong and North Vietnamese'. And the 'Communists' favoured strict control over travel and trade and harsh penalties for breaking them, while the opposition did not: such controls and penalties were implemented by Pol Pot during 1975-78, and revoked in 1979 with the change of Communist government. According to Quinn, 'the Communists planned to collectivize agriculture' (which they did from 1975) whereas their opponents wished 'to retain the status quo'. The latter is simply not true in the light of the land reforms from which 'many poorer people' benefited.

According to the C.I.A.'s former Kampuchea analyst, Sam Adams, during the 1970-73 period the Khmer Communist leader 'Pol' regarded the revolutionary organization in the Kandal area as challenging his control.[95] We now know, from Ith Sarin's account, that the Kandal area was led *not* by Sihanoukists, but by Sok Thuok, a high-ranking member of the Central Committee of the Communist Party. Thouk's deputies were 'comrade Hang' and Ros Cheatho, also a member of the Party, according to Sarin.[96] In the large Saang-Koh Thom sector of Kandal Province, the political commissar was Non Suon,[97] leader of the socialist Pracheachon Group *(Krom Pracheachon).* The Pracheachon had operated legally in Kampuchea until Suon, Chou Cheat and others were jailed by Sihanouk from 1962-1970 on a charge of pro-Vietnamese subversion. Non Suon, also known as Chey Suon, was described by a long-standing Communist Party member who defected to the Lon Nol regime in 1971 as 'one of the most important Communist cadre in the country'.[98] Intriguingly, in the Kandal area, according to Quinn,

> in December 1973, the Khmer Communists in Kandal dropped the masquerade of supporting Sihanouk and publicly identified themselves as members of the Communist Party led by Khieu Samphan. In late December, they staged rallies in populated areas which affirmed the anti-Vietnamese and anti-Sihanouk character of their policy . . . Samphan is believed to have served originally as Party chairman for Kandal Province, which is especially interesting since it is only from Kandal that we have had reports of propaganda cadre referring to him as head of the Khmer Communists. This could possibly indicate some intra-Party struggle for power.[99]

This may, in fact, be a description of a setback for Non Suon. But, although 'comrade Hang' and Ros Cheatho disappeared without trace after 1972, both Non Suon and Sok Thuok were still politically prominent in 1976, probably indicating the continuing precarious rise of the balance of power in Kandal.[100] In fact, Non Suon was active in Kandal as late as September 1976.[101] By 1978, when the Pol Pot group was undoubtedly in full control, its *Black Book* attacked his Pracheachon as having been 'placed in position' by Vietnam.

> Some elements of this group openly attacked the Communist Party of Kampuchea, when the others carried out manoeuvres of seduction. And they launched continuous attacks at the time when our Party had not yet achieved its unity in the whole country. Such was the activity organized by the Vietnamese against the Communist Party of Kampuchea inside the Party itself.

It is clearly an oversimplification, then, to divide the anti-Lon Nol forces merely into 'Communists' and 'Sihanoukists'. Sihanouk supporters in the countryside had no independent national organization; their reliance on the revolutionary groups for leadership was evident in the 'pro-Sihanouk' demonstrations that broke out following the Prince's overthrow in 1970. The differences in policy and style described by Quinn are basically the differences between the Pol Pot forces and the pro-Vietnamese Kampuchean Communists, who were much less anti-Sihanouk.

Interestingly, Quinn did not notice or mention any identifiable independent group. It is possible that in the southern border areas, any such people formed part of the 'Communist' faction described by Quinn; they may have formed an alliance with the Pol Pot forces based on opposition to Sihanouk and local experiences with the Vietnamese troops. (This may explain how Khieu Samphan could be both anti-Vietnamese and lay claim to the post of

Party leader held by Pol Pot.) In the Saang-Koh Thom districts of southern Kampuchea, for instance, clashes apparently took place in 1970-71 between Vietnamese troops and Khmer Communists; their immediate cause is unknown but they may have led to more support for an anti-Vietnam policy. While these clashes were mentioned by Hou Yuon at a meeting in the *north* of the South-west Zone in May 1972, the general policy he advocated then was still 'unity with the Lao and Vietnamese people to drive the American imperialists out of Indochina'.[102] This is quite a different line from that being implemented by the Pol Pot group.

When Did Pol Pot Gain Control of the South-West? While Pol Pot evidently found some allies among Communist 'independents' or Cultural Revolution supporters, in most of the South-West Zone, there seems to have been co-operation between the latter and pro-Vietnamese revolutionaries and members of the Pracheachon Group. In May 1970 the Zone had been represented at a resistance congress by Hu Nim. In 1972 the zone's Chairman was Chou Chet, a member of the C.P.K. Central Committee, the best known Pracheachon figure after Non Suon; he had also been jailed by Sihanou. According to Ith Sarin, Chet had 'heavy influence' in his zone (political, administration, economic, military, social responsibility was in the hands of the Chairman of each zone). Phouk Chhay was political commissar of the South-west Zone's armed forces and with Hu Nim was perhaps the most influential Kampuchean admirer of the Chinese Cultural Revolution. Ta Mok was military commander, another important figure in the zone was Hou Yuon, revolutionary Minister of the Interior.[103] All but Ta Mok, a close ally of Pol Pot were later purged. Cadres in this zone were reported by Ith Sarin to connect directly to the C.P. with the former people's Party (*Kanapak Pracheachon*) founded in 1951.[104] According to the *Black Book,* this party was 'secretly organized' by the Vietnamese unknown to Kampuchean revolutionaries; it 'existed only in name'.

Further, an official Party history distributed by the C.P.K. Central Committee in early 1972 to South-west Zone cadres noted that the period from *1954* to *1967* was one of 'political struggle'.[105] It made no mention of what Pol Pot later called the founding 'First National Congress' in 1960, officially a key date and an anti-Vietnamese turning point in his 1977-78 version of C.P.K. history. (In August 1973, the inaugural issue of the Party magazine *Revolutionary Young Men and Women* also referred to the 'political struggle from 1954 to 1967' and made no mention of 1960,[106] and in his July 1975 speech even Pol Pot said that 'in fact our Party was founded in 1951'.) Perhaps the Pol Pot group's 1977-78 version is a revision *even of their own* political experiences. The only other possibility is that the South-west Zone in 1972 was still largely uninfluenced by the politics of the Pol Pot group, and that the groups then administering the Zone *also* wielded much influence in the C.P.K. Central Committee at that time. Clearly the Pol Pot group were facing an uphill battle.

Ith Sarin, who spent a year in the northern part of the South-West Zone (the region west of Phnom Penh), provides a rare insight into the political programme being implemented there in 1972-73.

> Each administrator must have righteous precepts for living and righteous, clean politics; that is: 1)Love, respect and serve the pepple-workers-peasants with the whole heart and soul; not be dictatorial towards the people, not intimidate the people. Must always be modest and simple towards the people; 2) Along with always protecting the interests of the people, do nothing to disturb the goods of the people, even a single pepper or a can of rice.May not extort goods of the people either by 'hot' or 'cold' means. May not take bribes from the people.[107]

Sarin also noted, however, a degree of continuing peasant support for Prince Sihanouk, especially among elderly villagers; this seems to contradict Ieng Lim and underline the wisdom of the pro-Vietnamese group's policy of fostering a genuine socialist-Sihanoukist alliance. This policy was not totally implemented. In Sarin's opinion, the 'Sihanouk-Khmer Rouge coalition is clearly a fraud'.[108] But Quinn reported that the Khmer Rouge Chairman of the Zone, was maintaining 'pro-Vietnamese and pro-Sihanouk stands'.[109] He was probably under pressure from strongly anti-Sihanouk pro-Cultural Revolutionists such as Phouk Chhay, *as well as* (later) from the Pol Pot forces who were both anti-Sihanouk *and* anti-Vietnamese. Still, some sort of alliance was hammered out. Sihanouk himself reports Khieu Samphan as claiming after 1976 that the Sihanoukist forces (as well as the pro-Vietnamese Communists) were 'sold body and soul to the Vietnamese', who had trained them.[110]

Ith Sarin also made it clear, however, that the socialists had developed their own base of popular support, independent of Prince Sihanouk, in the South-West Zone. He also described cadre-training programmes that seem strongly influenced by the ideology of the Cultural Revolution:

> Each Khmer Rouge had to be absorbed in the 'philosophy of the people', had to join with the people. Helping out in the problems of the people, especially the people of the base areas, is the primary matter the higher levels of the Organization [Party] paid attention to. When the people raised a dam or dug a pond or a dike or built a house, the Khmer Rouge teams nearest the hamlet took turns together to go help and paid attention to what they were doing, too. At the time of transplanting, harvesting, threshing, they also took turns to give punctual assistance. The Organization helped with the affairs of the poorest farmers most of all . . . The Khmer Rouge Organization strongly forbids disturbing the produce or goods of the people. Making free with or violating peasants' girls is a matter for heavy punishment. According to continuous observations, these

> disciplines are fully and effectively respected and complied with. Another effective point in Khmer Rouge 'Psychological Activity' towards peasants is help during troubles. If a peasant in a hamlet is sick, the Khmer Rouge will often go to the house to give an injection or leave medicine even at night or during a storm. In ploughing, transplanting, harvesting or threshing seasons, each bureau must send out its members to help. This being 'together with the people' in order to 'serve the people' is the implementation of one of the Khmer Rouge theories in educating Khmer Rouge cadres.
>
> These kinds of psychological activities were really successful and deeply affected the people more than the instruction in theory did. The farming people of the base areas who knew nothing of socialist revolution quickly began to love and support the Organization because of its sentiments of openness and friendliness.[111]

Ith Sarin wrote this after defecting to the Lon Nol regime.

There is no doubt of the contrast between this situation and that in Pol Pot's Democratic Kampuchea, especially in 1977-78 (and in the areas controlled by the Pol Pot group during the 1970-76 period). Ith Sarin also wrote that cadres were instructed to be completely devoted to the people but 'not to always let the people lead them around by the nose'. According to Timothy Carney, who translated Ith Sarin's 1973 book, this was 'a hint of things to come'.[112] However, I find it difficult to see a close connection between the Pol Pot regime and a movement which considers its cadres need to be reminded not to let the people lead them around by the nose. Compare Ith Sarin's description of the relationship the revolutionary authorities enjoyed with the people in the South-west Zone in 1972, with the following instructions issued to people of Battambang by the authorities of Democratic Kampuchea in 1976-77: 1) Soldarity and independence; 2) Adhere to the political line [set]; 3) Adhere to the established order; 4) Adhere to the rules and regulations of the organization; 5) Carry out the plans set by the organization.[113]

To a large extent the change came from 1973 as the Pol Pot group got their first significant foothold in some Zones. It is interesting to watch their technique. Quinn noted in 1974 that the Chairman of the South-West Zone, Chou Chet,

> has had his authority and his influence over the Khmer Communists in southern Kampot and Takeo reduced because of his pro-Vietnamese and pro-Sihanouk stands and, in fact, was even ambushed and slightly wounded by the Khmer Communists in late November while travelling with some North Vietnamese soldiers on Route 16.[114]

Summing up the struggle between factions, Quinn said that the chief of the South-west Zone had

> attempted to reconcile the two factions, indicating central support for unity rather than division. This suggests that the split may be merely a local aberration occurring only in the [southern] border areas and not a national policy.
> Another, and more likely possibility is that, in addition to the combined Front military chain of command, there is a separate command structure of the Khmer Communists which is issuing orders independently of the Front. . . . In other words, while the Front may be issuing orders trying to unify the organization, separate orders may be emanating from Khmer Communist central headquarters telling their province chairmen to disregard the Front at the local level. This could explain their continued co-operation in attacking Phnom Penh, while at province level and below they are at each other's throats.[115]

One probable reason for Party leader Pol Pot's refusal to establish a mixed command with the Vietnamese troops is that a separate Kampuchean command would prove much easier to undermine.

As a result of the Pol Pot group's success in this struggle in the south of the South-west Zone, 'In early 1973 when the Khmer Communists entered the new harsh phase of their campaign, in which all rules were strictly enforced and unpopular programmes carried out, with stiff penalties for non-compliance, almost all popular feeling turned against them.[116]

The Pol Pot group's account of events in the south-west at this point can be found in the 1978 *Black Book:*

> In July 1973, in the South-west Zone, the Vietnamese behaved barbarously in a former revolutionary base of Kampuchea, in Sre Khnong Village . . . . *In that Zone, the Communist Party of Kampuchea did not have important armed forces.* On the contrary, the Vietnamese had two regiments . . . . Their headquarters were at Amleang, where their liaison committee with the committee of the South-west Zone of Kampuchea was. (my emphasis–B.K.)

We know from Ith Sarin that in May 1972, political commissar Phok Chhay reported that the South-West Zone's armed forces *already* numbered 15,000 paid Kampuchean regular troops and cadres. (Ith Sarin also noted that the 'South-west Region is the biggest, has the greatest troop strength and the most important leadership "cadre" '.)[117] Undoubtedly these were 'important armed forces'; well over a third of the Khmer Rouge regular army.[118] The real point the *Black Book* is making is that they, and their political leaders, did not belong any more to 'the Communist Party of Kampuchea'. Like the Eastern Zone, the south-west had long been a target of 'Vietnamese subversion'.

As early as 1966, the *Book* informs us,

> In the East and South-west Revolutionary bases, the Vietnamese carried out activities aiming at creating confusion and division in the ranks of the Kampuchean revolution. They acted by themselves and made also act the Khmer elements they had organized for a long time and infiltrated into the ranks of the Communist Party of Kampuchea.

And later, after 1970,

> The Communist Party of Kampuchea has never received a single rifle of the promised 5,000 ones from the Vietnamese. The latter used those rifles to arm venturers, bandits, delinquents, former soldiers or policemen dismissed by the Lon Nol regime. The Vietnamese gathered those men and organized them in battalions, companies, platoons, etc. . . to set up a parallel army in which soldiers were Kampuchea nationals and cadres were Vietnamese. In the Eastern Zone, they succeeded in setting up two battalions, that is about 600 men. It was the same in the South-west Zone.

Well, Ith Sarin did not get the impression of significant Vietnamese political control during the time he spent in the South-west Zone. He wrote: 'Vis-a-vis North Vietnam, the C.P.K. is in close co-operation, but less favourable than with Red China . . . . The C.P.K. seems to have control over all activities in its Zones. The Vietcong/North Vietnamese are far from being the masters.'[119] The South-west Zone troops suffered extremely badly in the attack on Phnom Penh in July 1973 when, apparently because of poor co-ordination between Khmer Rouge contingents, the south-western army alone was left exposed to the full might of American B-52 bombing.

A Local View: Tan Hao, a 23-year-old ethnic Chinese woman from a poor family, lived under Khmer Rouge administration from 1972 to 1979 in the South-west Zone, in the remote coastal province of Koh Kong. Her view of the struggle within the Kampuchean revolutionary movement there is worth quoting in detail, with my comments in square brackets

'In 1972 the Khmer Rouge liberated Sre Umbel in Kompong Seila Province [Khmer Rouge Region No. 37]. A number of people ran away to Phnom Penh and to Kompong Som [under the control of the Lon Nol Government], but many others fled to Koh Kong Province [Khmer Rouge Region No. II – both regions formed part of the South-West Zone]. To get free, our family fled to Thmar Sar village in Koh Kong, three hours by boat from Sre Umbel. We became fishermen there.

'Thmar Sar was in the hands of the free Khmer Rouge – in 1972 there were different Khmer Rouge groups. We had to find our own place to live there, but there were shops, and we could sell the prawns we caught, and people went in and out of Vietnam and Thailand. In 1972 it wasn't hard. We were our own masters; we could travel, we had food and money and we could buy what we wanted and do what we wanted.

'The Khmer Rouge there would ask the people to support them and give them chickens, ducks, fish, rice, and money. If we had anything we gave it to them; they didn't force us. They cleared and worked their own land, and in their free time they helped people in the fields. If any work needed to be done they did it.

'The leader of the Khmer Rouge in Koh Kong was Ta [grandfather] Prachha, who was an ethnic Thai. There was another leader called Prasith, who was also ethnic Thai and had struggled since the 1960s. Prasith had come to live in Thmar Sar in 1970. [In Koh Kong Province, but apparently not in Thmar Sar, ethnic Thais formed a significant proportion of the population.]

'Vietnamese Communist troops lived in Thmar Sar in 1973. They said they were there to help the Khmer fight Lon Nol. The Khmer Rouge and the Vietnamese co-operated with each other. Some of the local people liked the Vietnamese a lot, because they did many good things in Thmar Sar; they visited from house to house, and occasionally called the people to meetings and taught them about the use of medicine and how to do injections. They didn't kill anybody; they liked the Khmer people like their own people. They liked the ethnic Chinese, too.

'In 1973 there were ethnic Vietnamese, Khmer, and Chinese' 'armed forces' in Thmar Sar. They came and asked everybody what nationality they were; we replied, 'Chinese'. We were called to different meetings from the Vietnamese and the Khmer, and were addressed by ethnic Chinese revolutionary cadres. This was so that everybody could understand what was being said at the meetings. The different forces didn't do much; they just talked about struggle and Communism, and about the benefits the poor people could gain once they were released from oppression by the rich people. It was appealing; they were trying to change our way of thinking. Some people who had come from China ran away, because, they said, the Communist system is hard, but most people went to work with the revolutionaries.

'Meanwhile, in Kompong Seila there were different Khmer Rouge who were very strict; life was hard for people who lived there. They weren't allowed to buy and sell and exchange, and had to ask permission from the Khmer Rouge in order to go anywhere.

'Then, in late 1973, the Vietnamese in Thmar Sar were told to go back to their country and we saw no more of them. In October or November, the ethnic Chinese revolutionary cadres all disappeared as well, and the Chinese force was dissolved. Only the Khmer force remained.

'In 1974, hard times began. Zone and Regional armed forces from Kompong Seila arrived in Koh Kong; they included many women. Ta Prachha was arrested and taken away. They said he was going to study, but actually they killed him. Everybody in Koh Kong was afraid, because their leader had been taken away. Prasith disappeared about the same time. Many people fled to Kompong Som, and many others like us wanted to flee but couldn't.

'From now on, everyone in the village had to go and work together *(krom pravas dai),* and it got harder and harder. The Khmer Rouge began killing people; people who did anything wrong were taken away and shot. In 1974 they recruited every youth of 16 years old or more into the army. If you didn't go they asked you why you didn't love your country and fight for it. Some who didn't go were killed. They were hard.

'In 1975, when they won, they communalized everything: pots, pans, tomahawks, axes . . . .'[120]

It is vital to stress again that the losers in this political struggle were not 'Sihanoukists'. Prachha had been a guerrilla leader in Koh Kong since at least 1968. And the Heng Samrin Governments 1979 account of the disappearance of Prasith is consistent with Hao's account: 'In 1973 [the Pol Pot forces] liquidated many authentic revolutionaries in the province of Koh Kong, including comrade Prasith, deputy secretary of the Party regional committee. They pronounced the dissolution of a certain number of units of the resistance army which they suspected of not being faithful to their political line.'[121]

Some sections of the South-west Zone were able to resist for a time encroachments of the Pol Pot group. From Quinn's account it appears that the revolutionary opposition won two large battles against the Pol Pot forces in the south-west in November and December 1973.[122] In late January 1974, a large 'pro-Sihanouk' force was reported 'manouevring to gain control of all Route 16 from Tani to Tuk Meas, as well as part of Route 205 east of Tani'.[123] In mid-year, journalist James Fenton recalls visiting a revolutionary zone 10 kilometres north of Takeo which had been temporarily re-occupied by the Lon Nol army. Local residents pointed out some villages which had been held by the *Khmas Krohom* (or 'Red Khmer', the term also used by Quinn for what were clearly the Pol Pot forces), and others that had been in the hands of the 'Khmer liberators' (*Khmae rumdoh,* the group Quinn described as 'Sihanoukist royalists'). Fenton was told that the 'Red Khmer' distinguished themselves by the harshness they employed in their dealings with villagers. He gained the impression of a 'leopard-spot' pattern of control within the revolutionary zones.[124]

This may explain the testimony of a Kampuchean refugee who spent nearly a year in Takeo Province in 1975. Hong Var reported hard working conditions there, but little use of violence against the population. In her village she said three-quarters of the peasants 'really liked' the local Khmer Rouge cadres (one of whom was a woman said to have been trained in Hanoi); the rest, however, who were older peasants, resented the fact that Sihanouk had not returned to power after the victory of April 1975.[125] Was this then a *Khmae rumdoh* village whose population were led to anticipate the Prince's reinstatement as well as a socialist revolution?

Meanwhile, the purges by the Pol Pot group, factional violence and U.S.

bombs decimated revolutionary cadres and troops, leaving a political vacuum in certain localities which was filled by the various small groupings of revolutionaries. In 1974, near Takeo city, a group local peasants took to be Khmer Rouge began to terrorize the population and force them to begin building a 'new capital', declaring that the 'old one, Phnom Penh, would be destroyed.[126] However, building a new capital is not known to have been a policy of the Pol Pot group, or indeed, its revolutionary opponents: it is possible that those involved were actually members of the *Khmae khieu* ('Blue Khmer'), a local group which had spontaneously sprung up in the very unstable social environment, and was reported to have been active in rural areas near Takeo in 1974.[127] An autonomous group of *Khmae rumdoh* claimed in 1974 to muster as many as 10,000 men in the far west of the South-west Zone, 100 miles from Phnom Penh.[128]

At any rate, by 1975, the South-west Zone had become a stronghold of the Pol Pot group. Phouk Chhay, Hou Yuon and Chou Chet were all removed from the positions of authority they held there, and military commander Ta Mok became the dominant figure in the Zone.[129]

The North-west, North and East

Less is known of developments in other zones during the 1970-75 war. As late as November 1972, Hanoi-trained Issarak Leav Keo Moni was reported to be commanding troops in the North-west Zone's Battambang Province.[130] In other parts of the north-west at that point, insurgent leaders 'seemed to have no programme beyond loyalty to Sihanouk'.[131] Here things also appear to have changed as from 1973: late in that year delegations from north-western insurgent units, probably under strong attack from Pol Pot forces, were sent to Phnom Penh for talks with the Lon Nol regime and even met with Americans.[132] In the south-west of Battambang and the north of Pursat Province, an area of longstanding revolutionary influence, reports of massacres of villagers, almost certainly carried out by Pol Pot forces, circulated from 1974.[133] But 'a friend of Keo Moni' named Khek Penn[134] managed to hold on as revolutionary leader in Battambang until 1976.[135]

Other areas to feel the weight of the Pol Pot programme at an early stage were Kralanh district of western Siemreap (1974)[136] and the Baray district of Kompong Thom (1971 and particularly from 1973). These provinces both form part of the Northern Zone. Kompong Thom is the native province of Pol Pot himself,[137] and it appears from several sources that for most of the 1970-75 period he made his headquarters there.[138] Very little is known about political developments in the remote North-east Zone during the war, although unconfirmed reports of violence against the population there apparently emerged in mid-1974 and were published in a Lao newspaper.[139]

In discussions with a number of Khmer refugees in South Vietnam in late 1974, James Fenton was told of a dissent Communist force operating in Kompong Cham Province. These were revolutionaries who had refused to go along with the Pol Pot group's anti-Sihanouk policy. Fenton wrote in the *Washington Post,* 'A group called the *Khmae saor,* or 'White Khmer', had broken away from the Khmer Rouge and taken to the forests. The White Khmers, whose leaders are former Communist officials, are mostly Cham Moslems. They support Sihanouk and oppose collectivization of property. They believe simply in the abolition of middlemen.'[140] This last statement suggests the cautious, more reformist attitude to revolution characteristic of Vietnamese-style Communism; it also indicates that while the dissident insurgents were Sihanouk supporters, this did not mean that they were fighting simply to return to maintain the status quo of the Prince's regime (recall Quinn's description of 'Sihanoukists' in these terms). The abolition of middlemen would have involved much more than minor changes to the traditional social structure, and is reminiscent of the policies advocated by Hou Yuon in *The Co-operative Question* in 1964.

According to Quinn, in the Eastern Zone, the revolutionary opposition to Pol Pot's group still controlled Prey Veng Province in 1974.[141] Although only a few accounts by refugees from Prey Veng are as yet available, it is unlikely that Pol Pot forces took the province before 1977. After that, there were popular and military rebellions in Prey Veng and elsewhere in the Eastern Zone.[142] As a result the entire administration and military apparatus of the Zone, right down to the village level, was purged. (The victims were, once again, certainly not just 'Sihanoukists'. The *Black Book* described 'the Eastern Zone army' as an 'agent of the Vietnamese'). But still, the Zone's *population* proved resilient to the Pol Pot forces' political control. Thus, according to the Heng Samrin Government: 'In the province of Pursat in the Western Zone, they concentrated 40,000 inhabitants from the Eastern Zone and exterminated them in three stages from June 1978.'[143] Tragically, this accusation is supported by six former inhabitants of different villages in northern as well as western Kampuchea. Each reports the arrival in 1978 of thousands of villagers from the Eastern Zone and their subsequent *selective* extermination by executions on a mass scale and by starvation.[144]

Kampuchean refugees who fled to Vietnam from the Eastern Zone in 1977-78 told Wilfred Burchett that the population had not been harassed by the regular armed forces (in many cases these troops had secretly assisted people to flee, they said) but lived in terror of a young, ruthless militia group which they called 'the blackshirts'.[145]

Evacuation of Villages

Thus we find a situation with deep divisions in the revolutionary ranks, one of constant battering at the fabric of the society *and* at the revolutionary movement by an alien youthful militia. It is reminiscent of the activities of what Quinn called 'tough young militant cadre who had never been seen before' in some southern parts of the South-west Zone in 1973.[146] There, the most significant shockwave administered to the villages was their forced relocation in formerly uninhabited forest land which was to be owned and worked in common. Quinn says:

> This programme was carried out *extensively* in Kampot, Takeo and

> Kandal Provinces, beginning as early as *1972* in Kompong Trach district of Kampot. Initial relocations were small and it was not until mid-1973 that the programme was carried out on a large scale. This was preceded by a purge of low-level cadre. In parts of Takeo and Kampot, the Khmer Communists brought in a large number of new cadres to implement this programme, having lost faith in many older cadre whom they considered to be either pro-North Vietnamese or not tough enough to carry it out.
>
> This large-scale relocation process, which lasted from July to December 1973, had extremely harsh results, was bitterly opposed by most people and caused many to flee to South Vietnam.[147] (my emphasis—B.K.)

It is worth noting that by *1974*, the relocations were still limited to districts of Kampot Province long associated with the revolutionary movement: Quinn says that by then 20,000 people had been relocated in Kompong Trach and Banteay Meas. But for Takeo and Kandal Provinces he mentions only 'several thousand' people in Kandal,[148] relocations which can hardly be described as 'extensive'. The Pol Pot group, Quinn reports, also attacked religion and drafted monks into the army or forced them to leave the pagodas to work in the rice fields. But even in those 'revolutionary' parts of Kampot noted above, his study shows large numbers of monks still in the local pagodas until July 1973.[149]

So it appears that the Pol Pot group's position of strength at the centre of the revolutionary movement, though manifested in Kompong Trach in Kampot as early as 1972, was slow to take hold in extensive sections of the revolution and rural areas under its control.

What was the point of these relocations, which were to become a hallmark of Pol Pot's regime once it had gained power? A belief in egalitarianism certainly inspired economic levelling, even though its actual effect was to introduce shared poverty. (Most relocated villagers were not permitted to bring many belongings with them.) And the revolutionary state obtained much greater control over the activities of its citizens, for instance by confiscation of the 'communal' harvest and the rationing of food.

There was also a rational project to increase rice production by opening up forest land, whose virgin soil is extremely productive, at least for the first few harvests. (Its exhaustion after that may explain some cases of subsequent further relocations of village communities between 1975-78.) One Kampuchean refugee, who was in Kompong Thom Province in 1971-72, says that rice yields from jungle plots were twice as high as from the soils of the recently abandoned village land.[150] Jungle rice is also faster ripening, a sensible resort in case of food shortages; and since it is planted without ploughing the land, the need for water buffaloes, whose numbers are inevitably reduced in time of war by hungry armies (and bombardments) is largely eliminated. So, when Quinn notes that in the relocated villages of the south in 1973, 'production outstripped previous individual efforts',[151] this is not entirely attributable to the efficiency of co-operative production.

But, as later became common in Democratic Kampuchea, the villagers obtained little material benefit from their increased output. The bulk of the harvest was taken away to unknown destinations, not without dispute and in some cases violence.[152]

Finally, it should not be forgotten that many of the relocated villages had already been destroyed by American bombing.

The U.S. Bombardment

In 1973 the Pol Pot group gained the decisive – but not necessarily irreversible – upper hand. What were the events behind this? From February to August of that year, 257,465 tons of bombs fell on Kampuchea, 50% more than the total tonnage dropped on Japan throughout the Second World War. According to William Shawcross in *Sideshow: Kissinger, Nixon and the Destruction of Cambodia,* 'the immediate and lasting effects of that massive, concentrated bombardment will probably never be accurately known'. But it certainly made its mark.

Under the Freedom of Information Act, Shawcross was able to obtain a map of the U.S. bombing targets between January and August 1973; it reveals extremely intense bombardment of the heavily-populated areas of Kampuchea. In March 1973, Associated Press reported 'complaints among the people about the bombings by U.S. B-52's and jet fighters, with increasing reports of bombs killing civilians and destroying villages'.[153] A later Associated Press report by Richard Blystone noted:

> Among dozens of refugees interviewed, many said fear of U.S. bombing was one of their reasons for fleeing, but few told of actually being bombed. At a pagoda outside of Phnom Penh one woman said her 13-year-old son and two cousins died two weeks ago when a bomb hit a jungle bunker in which the family had taken shelter.
>
> Asked whether they wanted the bombing stopped whatever the consequences for the Phnom Penh Government, her neighbours grew enthusiastic. They said 'yes'.[154]

Only one month later, the impact was already recognized as dramatic.

> Wells Klein, Executive Director of the American Council for Nationalities Service and a consultant to the Congressional Judiciary Committee on Refugees . . . said that at least half of the [Kampuchean] population under non-government control [which he estimated as 2 million] must be classified as refugees or displaced persons [partly because of] the resumption of U.S. bombing. . . . He called U.S bombing the main reason for refugee movement.[155]

Shawcross reports the reaction of one U.S. embassy official to all this:

> Inside the embassy, Harben was appalled and now did what others might have done. He cut out, to scale, the 'box' made by a B-52 strike and placed it on his own map. He found that virtually nowhere in central Cambodia could it be placed without 'boxing' a village. 'I began to get reports of wholesale carnage,' he says. 'One night a mass of peasants from a village near Saang went out on a funeral procession. They walked straight into a 'box'. Hundreds were slaughtered.'[156]

In 1971, by comparison, even under very much less intense American bombardment of Kampuchea, 60% of refugees surveyed at the time gave bombing as the main reason for their displacement.[157] And earlier, in September 1970, U.S. intelligence reported: 'It was recently discovered that many of the 66 'training camps' on which FANK [Lon Nol's military wing] had requested air strikes by early September were in fact merely political indoctrination sessions held in village halls and pagodas.'[158]

The statements of the relatively small number of Kampuchean refugees whom I have questioned about the bombing are revealing. A peasant named Thuon Cheng (see 'Life under the Khmer Rouge' in this volume) vividly recalled the bombardment of his village, Banteay Chrey, in northern Kompong Cham Province.

> In 1973, the Vietnamese stopped coming; in the same year, the village had to endure three months of intense bombardment by American B-52 planes. Bombs fell on Banteay Chrey three to six times per day, killing over one thousand people, or nearly a third of the village population, in the three months.

Several of Cheng's family were injured. After that 'there were few people left to be seen around the village, and it was quiet'. No Communist troops had ever been stationed in Banteay Chrey.

According to the target map, by far the heaviest bombing was in the Southwest Zone, where a huge block of densely-populated territory was carpet-bombed with amazing intensity. Hong Var, interviewed in Thailand in 1979, spent most of 1975 in the village of Sla, in Takeo Province. According to her account:

> The peasants frequently told in detail about their 'horrifying' experiences during the war when Sla was a target of U.S and Lon Nol bombers They told how they had to dig trenches, and be prepared at any time to run from the fields, put out cooking fires, and so on. They hated bomber pilots and would have killed any bomber pilots whom they came across. . . .[159]

Others also have reported refugee accounts of summary executions of hated bomber pilots after the war ended.

Peang Sophi was in Battambang City when it fell to the revolutionaries in 1975. He recalled enraged peasant guerrillas heading straight for the town's airport, where they tore to pieces two bombing aircraft that they found there. 'They would have eaten them if they could', Sophi said in an interview in Australia in 1976.[160]

The number of Kampucheans killed and wounded during the bombardment is in the hundreds of thousands. Economic destruction was immense. According to a U.S. Senate sub-committee, the war created about 3,389,000 refugees out of the Kampuchean population of seven million.[161] At least half of these were displaced during 1973 alone.

Pol Pot already held the top position in the Communist Party and was consolidating his hold over the revolutionary movement in certain zones; but it was the massive suffering of the 1973 bombing, and the outrage it provoked, which undoubtedly gave his group a political leverage within the revolution which it might never have gained otherwise, even at the leadership level. As fierce hatreds were born in thousands of peasant hearts, the shrieking, militaristic slogans of chauvinism and the shrill authoritarianism behind it no longer fell on the deaf ears of peasants living a poor but relatively stable existence on a family farm.

The bombing also transformed the revolutionary army. The U.S. Seventh Air Force Commander estimates that 16,000 insurgents were killed during those six months. Shawcross continues:

> . . . the Khmer Rouge would have lost well over half of its assault force. Even if one spreads this loss across the entire army, this means 25% killed. There is a military rule of thumb, generally accepted by battle commanders, that units cannot sustain losses of more than 10% without suffering often irreversible psychological damage.
>
> That summer's war provides a lasting image of peasant boys and girls, clad in black, moving slowly through the mud, half-crazed with terror, as fighter-bombers tore down at them by day, and night after night whole seas of 750-pound bombs smashed all round. Week after week they edged forward, forever digging in, forever clambering slippery road banks to assault government outposts, forever losing comrades and going on in thinner ranks, through a landscape that would have seemed lunar had it not been under water.[162]

As for unit commanders, 'a hardened group of zealous men who had lived up to ten years in the isolation of the jungles', for them

> . . . 1973 confirmed a historic conviction that survival, let alone victory, could be guaranteed only by absolute independence and an astonishing fixity of purpose. They faced an enemy who at least appeared to have enormous support from his sponsor, while they them-

> selves could not trust even their own leader, let alone their friends. Their attack upon Phnom Penh was a madness born of desperate isolation, which bred a dreadful hatred of their enemy and a contempt for the attitudes of the outside world.[163]

Shawcross attributes this 'contempt for the attitudes of the outside world' in part to the 'indifference of their allies', referring apparently to the reduction in Vietnamese support once the January 1973 Paris Agreement on Vietnam had been signed. He says 'their shortages of munitions', along with the bombing, prevented a 1973 victory for the Kampuchean Communists. In fact, the Pol Pot group at least has never publicly complained about the arms supply from Vietnam – just as it has never acknowledged the receipt of *any* supplies from that source.

Vietnam and the Bombardment: But the *Black Book* does claim that the Vietnamese paid scant attention to Kampuchean independence when they (unsuccessfully) pressured the Kampuchean Communists to negotiate a settlement with Lon Nol's regime. It is difficult to know what to make of this criticism. Clearly, for a settlement to be reached in Vietnam but *not* in Kampuchea necessarily meant that the U.S. would be free for massive deployment of their air power on Kampuchea alone. Kissinger made this clear in negotiations, as the *Black Book* reluctantly admits: Did Kissinger really talk like this? Probably. But anyway the Vietnamese were involved in this affair'. Beyond saying that the Vietnamese twice informed the Kampuchean Party of Kissinger's threatening attitude, the *Book* does not make it clear what sinister motives the Vietnamese might have had. Is there any reason to believe that the bombs would not have fallen on Kampuchea if Vietnam had *not* pressured the Kampucheans to negotiate?

The *Black Book* also recognizes that the Vietnamese gained nothing out of all this. 'So, when the Vietnamese informed the U.S. that they had failed in forcing Kampuchea to negotiate and cease-fire, the U.S. were very mad and decided to send their B-52's to bomb Hanoi in December 1972, until the Vietnamese implored them to stop bombing and to resume the negotiations.' If we take account of the fact that the treaty signed the next month was fundamentally the same as the one drawn up in October 1972, we arrive at the conclusion, not drawn by the *Black Book,* that the Christmas 1972 bombing was the price *Vietnam* paid for Kampuchea's right to refuse negotiations.

Given America's criminal readiness to lay waste a country where it could not achieve 'peace with honour', what alternatives were available to the Kampucheans? Had the Pol Pot group negotiated a political settlement with the Lon Nol regime, then in difficult straits and a weak bargaining position, it is unlikely that the bombs would have fallen on Kampuchea. But it is also unlikely that this would have given the Pol Pot group the time they needed to clinch full control over their own side of the negotiating table. As we have seen, they were at that stage by no means the unchallenged leaders of the revolution, and elections following a political settlement would undoubtedly have brought to power other political forces more popular than the Pol Pot C.P.K. leadership. According to the *Black Book*: 'Would we have to negotiate with the U.S.? *The Kampuchean revolution* did not have to negotiate with them because they were the aggressors of Kampuchea. They had to stop their aggression and withdraw. Besides, the *Communist Party of Kampuchea* did not have anybody to carry out the negotiations.' (my emphasis– B.K.)

Did the *Kampuchean revolution* have anybody to carry out negotiations? Well, at any rate 'The Communist Party of Kampuchea did not know with whom to negotiate, for Lon Nol was already dying . . .' Besides, the *Book* lets on cryptically, 'a ceasefire would spread confusion in the determination of the people and the Revolutionary Army of Kampuchea in waging their struggle'. But this was not all. 'If the Kampuchean revolution failed, the Vietnamese revolution would also fail. It would be the same for the other revolutions in South-East Asian countries. But if the Kampuchean revolution carried on its struggle and its move forward, whatever the situation, it would be able to play its part in developing the revolutionary situation in South East Asia.' And so militant international solidarity informed Kampuchea's refusal to co-ordinate its strategy with that of a neighbouring revolution.

Can we assume that the Pol Pot group wished to avoid the U.S. bombing if possible? If so, the logic of their position (later expressed in the *Black Book*) – a position springing from their inability to impose themselves on the revolution at that point – is as follows: *Vietnam should not have negotiated a settlement with the U.S.*, because that settlement exposed Kampuchea alone to the bombing, unless we in Kampuchea negotiated as well, which we were not prepared to do. But this is not the point of view expressed in the *Black Book:* 'The Communist Party of Kampuchea had adopted such a position of struggle with neither compromise or ceasefire only to defend the interests of the Kampuchean revolution. It did not want to interfere in Vietnam's affairs.'

Whatever the attitude to the U.S. bombing adopted by the Pol Pot group, it is clear that the interests of the people of Kampuchea and Vietnam were closely linked. A desire for 'absolute independence' and a 'contempt for the attitude of the outside world' were not in fact the necessary outcome of the 1973 Kampuchean (and December 1972 Vietnamese) experience. Had Vietnam and Kampuchea co-ordinated a regional strategy, social disaster might well have been avoided. There is no doubt that the Pol Pot group with its ambitions shares the blame, along with U.S. imperialism, for the destruction of Kampuchea. By deliberately, for its own reasons, isolating Kampuchea to face the bombs alone, the Pol Pot group effectively fostered in Kampuchea that critical level of contempt for the outside world that otherwise need never have developed, even allowing for U.S. aggression. Thus the Pol Pot group was to lay the ideological and psychological foundation for even more destruction, in the name of building a state whose independence would be 'total, definitive and clean'.

The Lines Are Drawn

During late 1973 and 1974 the Kampuchean war became a decidedly conventional one. The Lon Nol regime, surrounded in nearly all the provincial towns they held, had a presence in a few rural areas, and survived only on U.S. military and economic aid. Sieges and trench warfare became the norm in most areas. Whereas in 1970-73 the revolution had recruited many local guerrillas who were 'farmers by day, and soldiers by night', these seem to have been replaced by full-time youth militia in the villages. As for the regular army, also increasingly youthful and largely unmarried, it now had very limited contact with village people. It was confined to front lines and, among other things, was trained to produce its own food and to be 'self reliant, clean and honest'. Physically isolated from the peasants (who were often relocated to behind the lines areas), it was being schooled in an entirely new lifestyle independent of the masses. Infrequent contacts with war-torn peasant communities were marked by a degree of scorn; the peasants were increasingly likely to be regarded as pathetic, dependent beings with little sense of patriotism, little discipline, too tied down by immediate material concerns such as providing for their families.

From 1975 to 1978, many Kampuchean refugees reported that troops were stationed not in the villages or co-operatives but in the forest. They nevertheless had access to nearby populated localities and would quickly arrive on the scene in the event of popular unrest. They were capable of the most brutal repression, partly because of their social isolation and partly because of the 'elite' patriotic morality, discipline and pride instilled in them. In one case where hundreds of soldiers were stationed in a village, a peasant refugee recalls that 'they lived separately from the people in a big hall which no one else was allowed to visit'. He never chatted with any of the soldiers in the two and a half years he lived in the village with them. The village was Banteay Chrey in the north of Kompong Cham Province, very close to the Baray district of Kompong Thom, the scene of insurgent violence against the peasantry well before the end of the war. In Banteay Chrey such violence began immediately after the defeat of the Lon Nol regime in April 1975.[164]

It is instructive that the earliest reports of the more or less regular use of violence against the rural population by revolutionary insurgents emanated from old revolutionary base areas in remote regions. Baray is one of these, as is western Siemreap, And the districts of Kompong Trach and Banteay Meas in Kampot and south-west Battambang were all centres of revolution as early as 1950. The emergence of the millennial corporate state in these areas before others indicates that the Pol Pot group certainly had captured the Party apparatus at the highest level, and was able to work outwards from its safest sanctuaries. Still, it had to purge most of the local cadres there first (and repress many of the local peasants), and, as we shall see, the process was far from complete in the rest of Kampuchea by 1975.

Democratic Kampuchea

It is now clear that the evacuation of Phnom Penh was largely motivated not by economic or humanitarian concerns but by political ambitions, an important move in the Pol Pot group's bid for total control of the revolution. (This does not necessarily mean that its effects had to be detrimental to the economy or to the living conditions of the people involved, given the immediately available alternatives.) But, although the orders to carry it out came from the very top, conflicting reports of *the manner of its implementation* (eg. violence against the population in some areas but not in others),[165] indicate continuing political differences in the revolutionary ranks. The capital was taken on 17 April 1975 (and evacuated straight away) by troops of the 'Northern and Eastern Zones',[166] that is by at least some troops of the revolutionary opposition as well as those of Pol Pot. On the very day of victory, there were reports of fighting between soldiers coming from these two areas of the country. Immediately afterwards, Phnom Penh radio announced that the new government was willing to accept foreign aid; the next day, this decision was publicly revoked in another broadcast.

Early Conflicts

The Pol Pot group has claimed that an 'attempted coup d'etat' against the revolutionary leadership took place even before victory in April. Clashes with Vietnam followed quickly in May; it is still impossible to state clearly which side of the border was the source of this aggression, although Vietnam has provided more detail in its version of events. Then, on 28 May 1975, orders went out from Phnom Penh to the provinces to cease the killings (then taking place on a large scale in certain areas) of people connected with the defeated Lon Nol regime.[167] Who was responsible for issuing these orders, which were disobeyed by local units in some areas, and later countermanded from Phnom Penh? And what did Hanoi-trained cadre Khek Penn have in mind when he apologized to 600 peasants and evacuated urban dwellers in Anlong Vil district of Battambang for their diet of rice porridge, promising that city people would be able to return home in eight months' time and that schools and currency would be reintroduced?[168] (This was in August 1975. Khek Penn was responsible for the economic office of the North-west Zone, but disappeared not long afterwards, to be killed by Pol Pot forces in 1977.)

In July 1975, there took place the intriguing 'ceremony of the founding of the Revolutionary Army of Kampuchea *throughout the country*, that is the ceremony when each zone handed over its armed forces to the Central Committee' (my emphasis–B.K.), during which 'the enemy plotted to assassinate the leaders of the Communist Party of Kampuchea', according to the *Black Book.* Did this occasion herald full control of the country by the Pol Pot group? Evidently not, since in September 1975 there was another 'coup attempt' in Phnom Penh, according to a statement by Ieng Sary on

17 March 1978. In the *Black Book* we read: 'In September 1975, the enemy plotted once again to assassinate the leaders of the Communist Party of Kampuchea. They organized 3 to 4 fighters of a unit of the Eastern Zone of Kampuchea to carry out the plot, but these fighters did not know the leaders and consequently did not know whom to fire at.' If this was all that occurred on that occasion, why did Phnom Penh Radio stop broadcasting for two days on 16 September?[169]

The outcome of these struggles is unknown, but it seems that, although in a strong position during the year of 1975, the Pol Pot group was far from holding complete sway. During 1976, its control would be held back to some extent, but these problems were ironed out during 1977 and the Pol Pot group emerged supreme. Ieng Sary later described this process as involving four more illegitimate coup attempts in 1976 and 1977.[170] Although what actually happened on these occasions is unknown, the dates Sary gave mark a series of turning points, as we shall see.

Vietnam and China

But first it is important to place post-1975 Kampuchea in its international context.

Did the political antagonists inside Kampuchea benefit from outside assistance of any material significance? It is unlikely. Vietnamese Communist troops, contrary to what is generally believed, did withdraw from their border sanctuaries in Kampuchea after the victories of April 1975. Chinese Foreign Minister Huang Hua made this point in a speech to cadres of his ministry in 1978. U.S. intelligence reports largely confirm this,[171] although adding that some Vietnamese forces may have remained in north-eastern Kampuchea for an unknown period. The *Black Book* details this:

> In fact, only one part of the Vietnamese withdrew from Kampuchea. Another part remained.... They were however much less numerous than before.... It was in Rattanakiri Province where they were most numerous to remain in Kampuchean territory. There more than 1,000 scattered here and there ... about 20 kilometres from the border.

Not a large group, and in a remote, rugged area where the border is much more difficult to define than elsewhere. Soon after, the *Black Book* says, these Vietnamese threatened and were forced to withdraw from the area.

But the power struggle in China *did* influence relations between Kampuchea and Vietnam during the Pol Pot period. Although the radical Chinese leaders of the Cultural Revolution (and their supporters in Kampuchea) had significant differences with Vietnamese policy, these came largely within a framework of solidarity. The radicals' defeat by the Deng Xiaoping line by 1977, however, directly contributed to the serious escalation of the existing differences between Kampuchea and Vietnam into full-scale fighting. During this same period, in Kampuchea, supporters of China's radicals and supporters of Vietnam were crushed.

The argument is supported by examination of the stand taken by Albania, formerly China's closest ally, and by an analysis of China's 'Three Worlds theory'. Soon after the public break between Vietnam and Kampuchea in January 1978, Albania urged Peking not to 'pour oil on the flames'. When Albania then supported Vietnam in its new dispute with China, China withdrew its aid to Albania as well as to Vietnam. Albania accused China of 'big-country chauvinism' and 'war-mongering', and of 'instigating the bloody conflict between Kampuchea and Vietnam, two fraternal neighbouring countries'.[172]

China's radicals drew upon a similar ideology of promoting co-operation between Vietnam and Kampuchea. While they were at their zenith in Peking, from April to October 1976, Vietnam and Kampuchea enjoyed their best (although 'comradely' rather than 'warm') relations in the whole of the 1975-79 period. During those months, China did nothing to discourage good relations between the two countries. The outbreak of war in early 1977, as well as the continued reluctance of both Kampuchea and China to negotiate solutions to their disputes with Vietnam, can be directly related to the change of leadership in China.

China's Three Worlds theory calls for a united front of third world with second world (advanced capitalist) countries in opposition to the superpowers. Although the policy was actually launched by Deng Xiaoping in March 1974, under the radicals, the idea was given general approval by *Peking Review*, but not as a 'theory'. For the radicals, the enemy was *both* superpowers equally, and they expressed this in articles such as 'U.S.S.R. and U.S.A. Arraigned in the Same Dock'. But the position certainly seems to have different significances for Deng and for the radicals, visible even in Deng's early formulations and certainly clear by the time the radicals were overthrown in 1977-78. Thus in Deng's original April 1974 speech (three months after China's seizure of the Paracel Islands from South Vietnamese forces), he supported 'the struggle of all peoples against imperialism, and in particular against hegemonism'[173] (my emphasis—B.K; under Deng, the term 'hegemonism' refers to the U.S.S.R.). In January 1978, *China Reconstructs* spoke of the need 'to isolate the two superpowers, Soviet Social-Imperialism in particular' and pointed out, ignoring the U.S.A. that the theory is 'a blow to the heart of Soviet Social-Imperialism'. It is absolutely beyond doubt that the thrust of China's foreign policy has changed to an anti-Soviet united front, to include the U.S.A. and its allies. *Peking Review* (21 January 1978) talked of 'the revolutionary policy of forming the broadest united front, *whatever the content* . . . to strike at the main enemy'.

At this point, Albania parted company with China (in January 1977). Albania had possibly already seen this trend emerging in some Chinese circles when it warned China in 1971 against 'relying on one imperialism to oppose the other'. On 5 October 1976, after Mao's death and within days of the arrest of the radicals in Peking, the Three Worlds theory was (to my knowledge) for the first time publicly attributed to Mao.[174] It is since then that it has been termed a 'theory'.

China's changed attitude to Vietnam in 1977-78 corresponds to the changed interpretation and emphasis given to the Three Worlds theory. By contrast, under the radicals, *Peking Review* discussed the Non-Aligned Nations movement without mentioning the theory, and approvingly quoted Sadat of Egypt: 'the initial definition of a non-aligned country as one not adhering to either power bloc should be changed into one with a free will, free from big power pressure.'[175] Within this framework, Vietnam's undoubted 'free will', despite its identification with the Soviet bloc, would have made it China's ally as a non-aligned country, not to say a socialist one. Only in the framework of a united front everywhere aimed at the Soviet Union could Vietnam be regarded as China's enemy.

The year 1976, with its rapid power shifts in the Chinese leadership, was marked by corresponding changes in foreign policy. The period of the radical line, from April to October, was followed by a year of particularly high border tension, according to a recent detailed Vietnamese history of its relations with China.[176] It is important, therefore, to examine the developments of 1976 more closely.

1976 – Division, Deadlock and Darkness

The last Vietnam-Kampuchea clash for some time took place in January 1976. The next month, leading cadres, apparently plotting a coup against Phnom Penh in Siemreap in north-west Kampuchea, were killed by a bomb,[177] perhaps from a foreign plane coming from Thailand. This 'coup attempt' was not mentioned by Ieng Sary in his 17 March 1978 statement.

Then, in March 1976, an anti-Deng campaign gained force in Peking; on 7 April he was sacked and the radicals rose to their zenith. In Phnom Penh, according to Ieng Sary's statement, there was an 'attempted coup' in April by 'Vietnamese and K.G.B. agents'. Was he referring to Prince Sihanouk's resignation as Head of State (4 April), clearly related as it was to the death of the Prince's Chinese supporter Chou En-lai and the impending demise of Chou's *protege* Deng? It is more likely that he meant the rise to the Vice-Presidency of So Phim, a Kampuchean revolutionary leader since the early 1950s and later accused of being a traitor sympathetic to Vietnam.[178] On 14 April, as well as announcing Pol Pot the Prime Minister of Democratic Kampuchea, Phnom Penh Radio introduced seven new State and government leaders, including So Phim, for the first time. Their political paths have since diverged. Six of these seven were later purged or took up guerrilla dissidence; Nhim Ros, named second Vice-President after So Phim, Tang Si (Chou Chet) and Kang Chap were all killed in 1978. So Phim rebelled in May 1978 (and was killed soon after) as did Mat Ly, named with Chou Chet as a member of the Standing Committee of the People's Representative Assembly.[179] Significantly, Mat Ly is a member of the Cham minority nationality: in 1978 he became a Central Committee member of the United Front for National Salvation led by

Heng Samrin. (In mid-1979 Mat Ly was Vice-Minister of the Interior in the People's Republic of Kampuchea.)[180] So Phim, Nhim Ros, and Mat Ly had not been officially mentioned before April 1976, although in early 1975 So Phim was reported to have been in the secret five-person inner leadership of the revolution; it would seem that in his case this 'coup attempt' signified the end of a period on the outer perimeter, and for the others a rise to prominence. The new appointments thus appear as a compromise between the three tendencies in the C.P.K: supporters of Pol Pot, who probably lost a degree of influence, supporters of Vietnam-influenced people like So Phim, and admirers of the Cultural Revolution like Hu Nim, the Minister of Information, who saw their differences with Vietnam within a general framework of solidarity.

Another new name introduced by Radio Phnom Penh on 14 April was Vorn Vet, said to be a former rubber plantation worker and trade union activist [181] in November 1978 Vorn Vet (formerly Sok Thuok) was to lead an unsuccessful coup attempt against the Pol Pot group.[182] The radio announced his appointment as Deputy Prime Minister and Minister of the Economy. Under Vorn Vet were created six economic committees, each headed by a President accorded ministerial rank. These Presidents were not named by the radio on that day, but it was later announced that the Agricultural Committee was headed by Non Suon (Chey Suon); the Communications, Trade, Industry and Rubber Plantations Committee Presidents were to share his eventual fate.

Incidentally, this period saw the earliest official use of the name 'Pol Pot'. A person of that name had been elected in the ballot for seats in the People's Representative Assembly held on 20 March 1976, as a 'representative' of rubber plantation workers.[183] When on 14 April he was proclaimed Prime Minister this caused great surprise among outside observers, none of whom had come across this name before. It seems that it was at this point that Saloth Sar, whose name had not been officially mentioned since April 1975, adopted the name Pol Pot. According to a witness, at the first anniversary of victory celebrations held on 17 April 1976, Saloth Sar as well as Khieu Samphan (the new head of state) made a speech in Phnom Penh; but only Samphan's speech was broadcast on the radio.[184] This was three days after Saloth Sar had become Prime Minister under a name totally unknown to the population of Kampuchea and not linked to any name (Saloth Sar, for instance) that they *might* have known. This secrecy, unprecedented in socialist history, even caught out some high-ranking Kampuchean officials. Thiounn Prasith, Director of the Asian Department of the country's Foreign Ministry, informed members of the Kampuchean Mission in Paris at the time that Pol Pot had fought in the anti-Japanese resistance in the 1940s, and was born along the Kampuchea-Vietnamese border where he had worked in a rubber plantation near Memot.[185] None of these facts is true, nor even corroborated by Pol Pot's official biographies issued in 1977 and 1978. Most likely Thiounn Prasith (unless for some amazing reason he was lying) simply accepted the assertion that Pol Pot was a representative of workers in the rubber plantations, most of which are in the Eastern Zone, and simply made some appropriate political extrapolation. It is indicative of the closeness of the political tussle that such a high-ranking cadre thought it not unreasonable that a member of the Vietnam-influenced constituency in the Party would become Prime Minister.

The Central Committees of the Communist Parties of Kampuchea and Vietnam agreed in April 1976 to sign a border treaty in June. Between 4 and 18 May, preparatory talks were held in Phnom Penh. It was agreed to co-ordinate border liaison committees, but there was little agreement on the maritime frontier, and Kampuchea postponed the June summit indefinitely. Following the February plotting in Siemreap, further plots in the other north-western provinces of Battambang and Oddar Meanchey were reportedly hatched in May, to what effect is unknown.[186] Significantly, though, 'following the meeting' of 4-18 May, according to Vietnam, 'border incidents decreased in number'.[187] Neither side, including Vietnam in its detailed history of border clashes, mentions *any* fighting between the two countries during the rest of 1976. In addition, Deputy Foreign Minister Phan Hien and Vietnamese reporters visited Kampuchea and reported favourably on economic reconstruction; women's delegations from the two countries exchanged visits, and agreement was reached over air links. Interestingly, the *Black Book* neglects to mention the important May 1976 talks, probably because they did indicate some rapprochement with Vietnam.

But the internal C.P.K. magazine *Tung Padevat,* in its June 1976 issue, makes some interesting observations about the situation on the border. 'Within the general framework of the country, the enemy carried out several activities along the land and sea border from the months of November and December [1975] to January and February [1976]. From March onwards, the situation has softened considerably. Along with this we have destroyed the enemies within our country and scattered many of them. They have no strong forces . . .' Interestingly, there is again no mention of the May negotiations. The magazine goes on: 'We want to build socialism quickly, we want to transform our country quickly, we want our people to be glorious quickly. But especially this is to prevent the enemy from harming us. *Even now the enemy cannot persist in trying to have his way with us.* . . . The enemy is hesitant towards us . . . . We believe that we could quickly build up the country. It is impossible for the enemy to attack us . . . .' (my emphasis – B.K.) 1976 was clearly not a year in which Kampucheans saw any serious indication of Vietnamese ambitions on their country, even though Pol Pot's regime had broken off negotiations.

It was not long after the May talks, on 2 June, that Kampuchea made its only significant departure from *established* Chinese foreign policy (the radicals' policy on this issue is unclear to me), by denouncing in extremely strong terms rumours that Kampuchea was about to recognize the Chilean military regime.[188] Such rumours, perhaps quite true originally, had been circulating in Paris for some months, and Kampuchean representative Thiounn Prasith awaited orders from Phnom Penh before replying to them. He did so at a meeting of Non-Aligned Nations in Algiers, by means of a formal intervention devoted specially to the issue, in which he called for the overthrow of the Chilean Government. This is quite distinct from Chinese policy on Chile after 1973, and quite similar to Vietnamese policy on an issue which Vietnam and its supporters consider of great importance.[189]

But perhaps the most interesting developments took place in September 1976. There are many unanswered questions, but it appears that the Pol Pot group was finding itself more and more isolated in Kampuchea. There were definitely moves to publicly identify the Communist Party of Kampuchea, which had been known to the population and most of the outside world only as *angkar,* 'the organization'. Simply because the Pol Pot group, once securely in power, held off this disclosure for another year (when it took place partly as a result of Chinese pressure), these moves do not seem to have come from them.[190] But Pol Pot may have deemed it wise to swim with the tide. On 18 September, he praised Mao Zedong (Mao Tse-tung), who had died on the 9th, as 'the greatest educator of the proletariat after Marx, Engels, Lenin and Stalin . . . Marxism-Leninism-Mao Zedong Thought will shine eternally.'[191] He said *angkar* was a Marxist-Leninist organization.[192]

These and other more confusing developments can probably only be explained by an extremely intense and possibly three-sided conflict within the Party. During these weeks, as leaders struggled frantically for survival as well as dominance, shallow and shifting alliances seem to have formed on specific issues; this may have included some sort of deal between the Pol Pot group and Cultural Revolution 'independents', although some of the latter were not hostile to Vietnam and aligned with the Vietnam-influenced group against Pol Pot. Wavering and lack of organization among the 'independents', however, may have been critical here. Thus, the establishment of a regular air link between Phnom Penh, Vientiane and Hanoi on 20 September was accompanied, on the same day, by the arrest and imprisonment of Keo Meas, a leader of the old Pracheachon group who had in 1975 returned from many years in Hanoi and was at that point in the office of the Party Central Committee. But this particular struggle was by no means over.

On 27 September, Pol Pot was sacked. 'For health reasons', he was replaced as Prime Minister by Nuon Chea, whom sources close to Vietnam called 'correct line' at one time.[193] This was clearly a political dismissal. In March 1978, Ieng Sary revealed that there had been another 'coup attempt' in September 1976 by 'Vietnamese and K.G.B. agents'.[194] In May 1978, he told a visiting American that September 1976 had seen incidents in Phnom Penh (refugee sources tell of a strict curfew there at the time), as well as 'on the border with Vietnamese agents'. More importantly, a veteran Kampuchean Party member, who later escaped to

Vietnam, confirms the fierce struggle inside the C.P.K. in September 1976, and adds:

> In its September 1976 issue, *Red Flag,* organ of the Communist Youth, dealt with the C.P.K.'s history and pointed out that it had been founded in 1951 and had benefited from significant aid on the part of fraternal parties, notably the Vietnamese Party. However, on their side, the 'new forces' affirmed in the *Revolutionary Flag,* organ of the Central Committee of the C.P.K., at the same time, that it had seen the light of day in 1960 and that it had developed along specifically Khmer lines, by relying only on its own forces.[195]

The Pol Pot group clearly lost this battle. According to an October 1976 broadcast of the radio of the Communist Party of Thailand, which officially supported Pol Pot's group, a Kampuchean newspaper, (as distinct from the internal Party organs cited above) had recently given 30 September 1951 as the founding date of the Kampuchean Revolutionary Organization.[196] Three days of celebrations of the Party's *twenty-fifth* anniversary began the day after Pol Pot's dismissal. Three days after that, Kampuchea unprecedentedly attacked Deng-Xiaoping,[197] whose sacking in Peking sick months before had until then drawn no comment from Phnom Penh. The Kampuchean Government was now in the hands of a coalition between the Vietnam-influenced group and the 'independent' supporters of the Chinese Cultural Revolution.

Over the next weeks, Kampuchea made a number of new moves. Rubber was exported to Singapore via Thailand, and a trade delegation led by Non Suon was sent to Albania, Yugoslavia and North Korea. Most significantly, though, contact was made with UNICEF and even with U.S. firms about aid and purchases of drugs and anti-malarial equipment. This was a radical departure from what was by far the most senseless and anti-popular aspect of Democratic Kampuchea's 'self-reliance', the attempt to make do with traditional medicines. Had this unsuccessful experiment in chauvinist regression been abandoned earlier, thousands of lives would have been spared, and without greatly 'smearing' Kampuchean independence. In 1971, the Pol Pot group had ordered the closure of medical schools and military training schools operated by the Vietnamese Communists for Kampuchean students. According to the *Black Book:* 'Indeed the Party had already opened military training and medical training schools for the whole country. These schools spent more time on political education than on technical training.'[198] Rejection of this policy on popular health could only have beneficial effects on the living conditions of the people.

But events in Peking were moving in another direction. On 30 September the Chinese leaders had opened a meeting that was to restructure the world. Within days, the radical figures of the Cultural Revolution were under arrest, and the stage was clear for the return of Deng and vast changes in China's internal and foreign policies. It is difficult to believe that Kampuchea was not affected: within a fortnight, Pol Pot was back as being Prime Minister again.[199] It seems likely that he had actually regained power by 15 October, the date of the arrest of Keo Moni, a very senior Hanoi-trained leader later named as having been working in the office of the Party Central Committee at the time. In characteristically furtive style, Pol Pot's return (unlike his departure, significantly) was never officially announced. On 22 October, he simply signed, as Prime Minister, a Phnom Penh public statement denouncing 'the counter-revolutionary Gang of Four anti-Party clique' who had just been deposed in China, in terms stronger than those of any ruling Communist Party. On 1 November, Non Suon was arrested at the airport on his return from abroad and later executed.

In foreign policy terms, Pol Pot's return to power heralded a decisive setback for the Vietnam-influenced Communists *as well as* the Cultural Revolution supporters: like China, Kampuchea did not attend Vietnam's Fourth Party Congress in December. (Formal congratulations were sent, however, while none were sent to China's Eleventh Party Congress the next August, in which radicals, one-third of the Chinese Central Committee, were sacked. This curious priority probably reflects both the continuing – although rapidly dissipating – strength of the Cultural Revolution supporters in Kampuchea, and perhaps even their determination to preserve relatively close relations with Vietnam.)

But Vietnam had already read the writing on the wall. At the December 1976 Congress, former Vietnamese ambassadors to Peking and others associated in some way with China were dropped from the Vietnamese Party Central Committee. This no doubt also reflected a degree of Soviet influence; but leadership divisions in Vietnam, minimal compared to those of Pol Pot's Kampuchea, provided outside powers with no comparable internal leverage. In fact, at that same Congress, Vietnam was able to rebuff Soviet pressure to join Comecon.

Also in December, Kampuchean Minister of Information Hu Nim was probably expressing serious concern when he stated his confidence that China 'would not allow revisionism and the capitalist classes to rear their heads' after the overthrow of the radicals.

1977 – the Second Revolution

After a year of peace, tension resumed between Kampuchea and Vietnam in January 1977, as Kampuchea began withdrawing from all border liaison committees (a process which, according to Vietnam, was completed by May).[200] That same January, Albania first disputed China's Three Worlds theory, Kampuchean diplomats withdrew from Albania and Hu Nim and Touch Phoeun (Minister of Public Works and a long-standing associate of Hou Yuon) were officially mentioned by Phnom Penh for the last time, at an Albanian Embassy reception on the 17th.

Also in January 1977, tension mounted on Kampuchea's two other national frontiers. On the 27th, Pol Pot armed forces began 18 months of incidents along the Thai border by attacking a village inhabited by Thai citizens near Aranyaprathet. The Pol Pot Government quickly claimed, correctly, that the village was in its territory, but the reason for the death of more than 20 Thai villagers remains unclear. As for the third frontier, after a visit to southern Laos in November 1978, Nayan Chanda concluded: 'It is now clear that the situation on the [Lao-Kampuchean] border has been deteriorating since the end of 1976.'[201]

Significant internal developments in Kampuchea also date from early 1977. Large-scale purges of village, district, province and even zone level cadres and troops are reported from all over Kampuchea, except for some areas identified with the Pol Pot group. Nearly every refugee interviewed mentions such purges in their village, usually carried out by South-West Zone cadres, from the first half of 1977. Kry Beng Hong, a witness at the trial of Pol Pot and Ieng Sary in Phnom Penh in August 1979, pointed out that in Kompong Cham Province, where he lived, 'In 1977, the cliques coming from the south-west rounded up and eliminated all the groups of Hou Yuon and Hu Nim in Prey Chhor district.'[202] Hong, like refugees outside the country, reported mass executions of the population as well as cadres from that point in time. American intelligence reports indicate that at this point Pol Pot was personally touring the north-west and northern regions (where plots had been hatched the previous year) and directing the purges.

There were also new policies. Food rations, already low, were cut significantly, and communal dining halls were introduced in those areas where they had not already been established. In many villages, all children except the very young were taken from their parents and housed in communal halls, either in the village or a long distance away. In either case, they rarely saw their parents again, and were assigned various tasks, some of which, like building roads, were economically important.

Although there were already, in 1975 and 1976, plentiful reports of brutality against the population, there were also a number of equally reliable reports of peasants not being badly treated and of peasant support for the revolutionary movement in that period. While all evacuated urban dwellers suffered to some extent, reliable reports of their treatment by the administration vary significantly, ranging from imposition of the harsh economic measures that one might expect in a period of recovery to mass murder.

For instance, while well-publicized refugee reports tell of large-scale starvation and terror in 1975 and 1976, especially in parts of Kampuchea's north-west and north near Thailand, a number of first-hand reports from the South-west and Eastern Zones and from Kandal Province portray a different situation during the same years. Refugees who lived in villages in Takeo, Kandal, Prey Veng, Kompong Cham and Svay Rieng in 1975, and a smaller number who lived in the east in 1976, report little or no starvation, although food rations were tight in some cases; some, but not all, report executions of members of the defeated army and administration, while others report their arrest, several months' re-education and subsequent release. None report the use of violence against the general population such as that reported in other areas, although newly-arrived urban dwellers were scorned or discriminated against in some villages. Most report good relations between the peasantry and the revolutionary cadres in their localities;[203] one refugee who lived from May to November 1975 in a Kompong Cham village says that the Eastern Zone troops (unlike the Northern Zone troops who were 'ruthless') 'did a lot of good things' to help urban evacuees also. Another, So Davinn, a Phnom Penh resident who lived in a Kandal village in 1975, reports strict discipline and work schedules, but says the work was 'not so hard' and targets 'easy to fulfill'. 'We had freedom: if we needed something we just let the Khmer Rouge know', Davinn says. Phnom Penh evacuees in his village received equal treatment to the local peasantry, who 'liked the Khmer Rouge' and were also hospitable to the new arrivals. According to Davinn, the local revolutionary cadres were 'humane people' and caused him no trouble; he heard no complaints from other urban evacuees either. There were no executions, no deaths from overwork, as the sick were exempt from labour, and no starvation, as there was 'plenty of food'.[204]

On the other side of the country, in Thmar Puok district of Battambang, refugees I have interviewed report considerable peasant support for the Communists in 1975-76. A village schoolteacher said that the local people had supported the revolutionaries during the war, and 'really liked them' until about mid-1976. He said that for himself and the other villagers (there were no city evacuees sent to his village) there were 'no problems' during the first two years after victory. Significantly, the local Communist cadres at that time described the Vietnamese as 'brothers and sisters'. But in 1977, this line changed (the Vietnamese were now 'enemies'), and communal dining halls and strict regimentation were introduced. In 1978, killings began, and he was bound and taken away by soldiers for execution. He managed to get away and escaped to Thailand.

A peasant woman, also from Thmar Puok, said that in 1975-76 the Khmer Rouge 'did good things' in her village, and that she was 'happy' doing the communal labour tasks required of the population. But from 1977, she said, the Khmer Rouge did 'bad things', and individual labour targets now meant that work was no longer 'happy' as well as being more demanding and difficult. Another woman, a Phnom Penh evacuee, reported that in 1976 there was 'plenty of food' in Thmar Puok, but that this changed in 1977, which was also the year that 'the killings began'. Local cadres were executed as well as the villagers.

Several refugees from the neighbouring district of Oddar Meanchey Province confirmed what had been reported to me by a former schoolteacher – that the Khmer Rouge cadres during 1975-76 were 'kind, to tell the truth'. But again, all reported a significant hardening of attitudes towards the population, accompanied by violence and a purge of the former cadres, in 1977.

So it seems that in areas like these, though life was often difficult, there was little sign before 1977 of the widespread tragedy that was to come in the last two years of the regime. And significantly, the difficulties of 1975-76 were more a result of the destruction of Kampuchea's rural economy (primarily by American bombers) during the war, than of policies of the revolutionary movement in these areas. According to the report prepared by the members of the U.S. AID team after they fled Phnom Penh in April 1975:

> . . . without large-scale external food and equipment assistance there will be widespread starvation between now and next February. . . . Slave labour and starvation rations for half the nation's people will be a cruel necessity for this year, and general deprivation and suffering will stretch over the next two to three years before Cambodia can get back to rice self-sufficiency.[205]

There are enough conflicting reports to conclude that the country was still politically divided. But the conflict of evidence disappears from early 1977, when Kampuchea came under the unchallenged control of the Pol Pot group and violence against the people indisputably increased on a nation-wide scale. A former Phnom Penh resident, evacuated in April 1975 to the countryside where he spent the next four years, clearly located the beginnings of *peasant* disaffection with the Government in the year 1977-78: 'They hate them . . . although at first they didn't like them or hate them, but after they had been cheated *for three years* and seeing that their freedom had been reduced, they *began* to hate them.'[206] (my emphasis–B.K.). A refugee who lived in Prey Veng Province from 1975 to 1978 reported tough working conditions for evacuated urban dwellers, but added that the local peasantry 'liked and trusted' the revolutionaries in the area during 1975 and 1976. When these local revolutionaries were systematically arrested and executed in 1977, there was a popular uprising in the province.[207] The veteran Kampuchean Communist cited above described political developments in this way:

> An extremist and chauvinist tendency . . . appeared in the bosom of the Khmer Party, manifesting itself more and more openly after the [April 1975] liberation of Phnom Penh; it was characterized by a tyrannical internal policy and a bellicose and at the same time almost isolationist foreign policy. Nearly all the old members of the Party opposed this in one form or another. *Up until mid-1976, the situation had not yet really deteriorated.* (my emphasis – B.K.)

Asked about the September 1976 dispute over the Party's founding date, he described the Pol Pot group's version: 'Such a falsification of history meant a denial of the role, on the theoretical plane, of the veterans and of former allies, *for purposes that were then still unknown*'.[208] (my emphasis – B.K.).

Pech Lim Kuon, who trained Khmer Rouge pilots in Phnom Penh for a year after April 1975 before fleeing to Thailand, insisted that, although during that period the revolutionary government was not popular, peasants were not being killed and workers in the fields were not being supervised by armed guards.[209] At the Oslo Conference on Human Rights in Kampuchea, he remarked privately to a journalist that had he been a poor peasant he would not have fled.[210]

A Vietnamese refugee who speaks fluent Khmer travelled through Kampuchea for several months in early 1976, stopping in many villages as he worked his way to Thailand. Told in Thailand of reports of mass executions in Kampuchea, he commented: 'I could not believe it. Walking across the country for two months, I saw no sign of killing and nobody I spoke to told me of it. I still don't believe it happened.'[211] It *did* happen in some areas; in particular, executions of Lon Nol military and officials. But in some areas, during 1975-76, it did not.

Things obviously changed from 1977. Hui Pan, a former bicycle repairman from Siem Reap Province, said that from February 1977 all the officials in the province were replaced and executed. The new officials proved harsher than the old. 'Under the old Khmer Rouge, perhaps 30% of the Lon Nol soldiers were killed. The new Khmer Rouge killed all the rest.'[212] 14-year-old Mien, who has brought up in a village which fell under Communist control after 1970, in Preah Vihear province, insists that his peasant parents remained happy, even after 1975 when land was co-operativized, until early 1977. He reported no executions and food was adequate. But in 1977, after 'the revolution began' in 1976, life changed. Food rations were cut and served only in communal dining halls. All children except the very young were progressively taken from their families. An execution of a former urban dweller apparently took place just before Mien's departure from home.[213]

Denise Affonco, a Khmer of French citizenship who spent the 1975-79 period in the Kampuchean countryside, says that in her village in Battambang Province there was starvation throughout. But, 'the terror began in February 1977 when the 'Nirdey' [South-west cadres] arrived in the villages. They replaced the local cadres. Then, we started to see people disappearing. They were taken away at night and never seen again.'[214]

Sarun, who spent the period from April 1975 to mid-1976 in eastern and central Kampuchea before moving to Battambang Province, saw events this way: 'In 1975, there were a lot of executions of former Lon Nol soldiers. In 1976, executions were rare. In 1977, there were many.'[215] Eight Khmer refugees in a camp at Rach Gia in Vietnam wrote a letter to Kurt Waldheim, Secretary-General of the United Nations, dated 25 January 1978. It referred to 'a resurgence of massacres since 1977, after a brief calm in 1976'. The Kampuchean authorities, the letter said, had killed ordinary people regularly during 1977, and 'sometimes massacre entire families'.[216]

After interviewing Khmer refugees to Thailand, Francois Ponchaud painted a similar picture:[217]

> After the large numbers of lives lost in the blood-letting during 1975, the no less severe purges of 1977 are food for thought. The shortage of food and health services continues to cause enormous ravages, over and above executions. It seems that a 'second revolution' took place in 1977, which a refugee was able to read about in a brochure designed for cadres which he got his hands upon by chance.
>
> This revolution was apparently instigated by a secret circular, 'No. 870', emanating from Pol Pot, and distributed to cadres who had made an oath of allegiance. . . . According to the document read by chance, 'even if we must expend a million lives, our party must not regret it; it must be established forcefully!'

Vietnamese sources give the same quotation. A Kampuchean veteran Communist who fled to Vietnam gives further details about circular 'No. 870'. He says that 'not long after' September 1976,

> . . . we received a directive from the Central Committee, headed 'Service 870', which was its code name, dealing with the purging of members alleged to be under Vietnamese influence and in fact not in agreement with the line being applied: those who 'lacked confidence in the Khmer leadership' would be sent to do manual work, under supervision, while 'avowed dissidents' would be expelled from the Party and handed over to the security forces. An immense purge thus began, under the slogan of 'the three eradications': to eradicate the agents of the C.I.A., those of the Soviet K.G.B., and those of the revisionist Vietnamese expansionists hiding in the ranks of the Khmer revolution. Never before had our Party been so decimated and overturned![218]

Although January 1977 was a turning point, the struggle in Kampuchea was not over. The 10 April arrest of Hu Nim was significant: he was not publicly replaced until December 1977,[219] and not for foreign consumption until February 1978. He was then replaced by Yun Yat, the wife of Son Sen. (Touch Phoeun was simply not replaced.) These events were described by Thai intelligence as a February 1977 'coup' in which Pol Pot gained ground at the immediate expense of Nuon Chea. It seems that Kandal Province (called the Special Zone) was even at this stage a serious problem for the Pol Pot group. Vietnamese sources give the following account of the February 'coup': 'In February 1977, 600 men of division 170, in charge of securing the protection of the capital, launched an unsuccessful mutiny; Cha Krey, deputy chief of the general staff and commander of the Phnom Penh Special Zone paid with his life for this aborted attempt; three other leaders were burned alive in the town stadium.'[220] The *Black Book* claims that Cha Krey was a Vietnamese agent 'in charge of assassinating the leaders of the Communist Party of Kampuchea'. Intriguingly, it gives his rank as 'a chief of the units quartered in the south of Prey Veng Province', and dates his unsuccessful coup and arrest from April 1976. Nevertheless, the arrest of the 'Commander of the Battalion for guarding' the Party Central Committee, on 26 February, was followed by that of the Party Secretary for Kandal Province, on 15 March. It is significant that Ieng Sary's 1978 list of 'illegitimate' coup attempts does not mention February 1977. It may have been at that time that Pol Pot's recent political triumphs (including the arrests of Ministers Koy Thuon and Touch Phoeun on 25 and 26 January) were followed up by a successful military offensive.

Kampuchea was clearly in turmoil and the border clashes, later described by Vietnam as 'most serious', which took place in April 1977 can hardly be divorced from the internal situation. Such clashes have been described by a number of Vietnamese and Kampuchean refugee eyewitnesses as outright attacks by the Pol Pot forces on Vietnamese villages;[221] their intensity increased along with Pol Pot's ever-widening purges. Phouk Chhay was arrested on 14 March and Tiv Ol on 6 June.

Even more wide-ranging purges from late August 1977 left Pol Pot supreme (but not unchallenged: Ieng Sary mentions another coup attempt in September). In mid-September, Vietnam claims, Kampuchea mounted 'particularly serious' border attacks, and on the 17th Phnom Penh Radio clearly described Vietnam as an enemy. While Vietnam claims to have suffered Kampuchean attacks since at least April, and it is known from refugee and intelligence sources that fighting was taking place from that point, the Pol Pot regime says the earliest Vietnamese aggression in 1977 was in the month of June. (This was revised to December, in the *Black Book* devoted to this subject which appeared nine months after this statement, in September 1978.) Pol Pot's trip to Peking on 29 September and his public emergence as C.P.K. Secretary-General elicited full Chinese support.

There is no discussion at all of the crucial period from April 1976 to mid-1977, in the Black Book.

Opposition in the Party still remained, however. Vice-President So Phim evidently had enough local backing to weather the purges and was still officially Vice-President and Party Secretary of the Eastern Zone as late as 7 December 1977.[222] Supporters of the Chinese radicals may also not have been totally defeated until 21 December, when Hu Nim's removal was publicly announced. From November the Pol Pot regime named about 30 new leading officials.

As a result of this overturning of the Kampuchean revolutionary movement, visiting Yugoslav journalists in March 1978 reported that the C.P.K. in power 'isn't a part of the National United Front (FUNK), which appears to have been replaced by the emerging new political structure'.[223]

Kampuchea 1978: Exposed to the Sino-Vietnamese Conflict

From December 1977, constant fierce and brutal clashes characterized the Vietnam-Kampuchea war, with the Vietnamese at least suffering large numbers of civilian casualties. Hundreds of thousands of Vietnamese peasants fled to the cities from the border, and the settlement programme in the New Economic Zones was completely disrupted. On 5 February 1978, Vietnam proposed a ceasefire, mutual withdrawal of forces to lines five kilometres each side of the border, international supervision of the area and a negotiated solution to the border dispute. Kampuchea did not reply to this statement, later pointing out that the proposal had not been considered because it involved 'handing over to Vietnam a five kilometre stretch of Kampuchean territory'.

From late February, Vietnam firmly backed attempts to overthrow the Pol Pot regime, such as the unsuccessful rebellion in the Eastern Zone in May, led by So Phim until his death in action. China's developing dispute with Vietnam over the nationality of ethnic Chinese living in Vietnam could not, according to Peking, be resolved by Vietnam's second set of 'proposals for "negotiations" '. When talks did begin, China abandoned them.

The advent of Deng Xiaoping's 20th Century version of Chinese 'self strengthening' in internal policy corresponds to more classically nationalistic foreign policy. Although different from the policies of the Cultural Revolution, there are precedents for these in Chinese Communist history. According to Anthony Barnett:

> Relations between [Vietnam and China] began to deteriorate as long ago as 1954, at the Geneva Conference. It was there that Vietnam was divided and Chou En-lai, as we have since learnt from the *Pentagon Papers,* played a decisive role with the carving knife.
>
> Cho [and Mao] sought three main objectives at Geneva. First, they wanted to neutralize Indochina and rid it of the threat of American troops. Second, they hoped this would enable them to break the military encirclement of China by means of an international treaty, which in turn would also allow them to break out of their diplomatic isolation and forced dependence on the Russians. Finally, if they could achieve this by acting as the guarantor of neutral states such as Sihanouk's Cambodia, while dividing Vietnam, their suzerainty would be complete. Chou secretly informed the French that he recognized the reality of the South Vietnamese government they were attempting to construct.[224]

In the same year, 1954, the Chinese Government had published a map of East Asia which described Kampuchea, Vietnam and the rest of mainland South East Asia, as well as the Sulu islands, Korea and other places, as former 'Chinese territories' which had been lost during the period 1814-1919.[225] This was an early (and for many years lonely) echo of the ludicrous Chinese claims on the South China Sea as far as Indonesia, which were published from 1974.

In 1978, China was less enthusiastic about Kampuchea's internal policy than in 1976, when the political situation in both countries was different, but it provided Kampuchea with economic and very significant military aid throughout 1977-78. Perhaps existing Chinese military supplies assisted Pol Pot's return as Prime Minister in October 1976 (presumably Pol Pot had not lost the post of Chairman of the Party military committee); these and later supplies certainly facilitated the horrifying widespread slaughter that followed. More significant may have been the fact that Pol Pot was probably able to *promise* Chinese aid of all kinds to political waverers while organizing his comeback. It really is still impossible to say exactly how such aid affected Kampuchea, but it is clear that it did and that in the interests of their foreign policy China's leaders favoured the return and subsequent supremacy of Pol Pot's regime.

But what was the *internal* dynamic of Pol Pot's hostility to Vietnam? The Vietnamese proposal for an 'Indochinese Federation' had literally not been mentioned by Hanoi since the dissolution of French Indochina in 1954, and there is absolutely no evidence that Vietnamese leaders harboured such all-consuming ambitions thereafter. The peaceful year 1976 showed that Vietnam was prepared to leave Kampuchea alone, even a staunchly independent and pro-Chinese Kampuchea, so long as there was no military threat to Vietnam. It is clear that responsibility for the fighting that began in early 1977 lies with Kampuchea – or rather, with the Pol Pot group. A Kampuchean document, regarded as authentic by sources sympathetic to the Pol Pot regime, found its way to Vietnam after being addressed to 'Comrade Rin, Committee Chairman of the Fourth Division of the Eastern Zone', i.e. to Heng Samrin. Dated 17 July 1977, before Samrin's defection to Vietnam, the document includes a report of the 'Eastern Region Conference', to which it appears Heng Samrin had not been invited. It reads, in part:

> We must continue to be on guard and be prepared to do battle with and smash the enemy at all times. . . . If the enemy commits agression . . . we must cross into and stop and smash him right on his land. This is intended to further increase his difficulties. . . . He will no longer dare to repeat his aggression against us; rather, it will be his turn to strain to stop us.
>
> However, we will not act upon this guideline precipitously; its implementation must be delayed. Only when the time comes that we must do battle will we bring it up; we must first generalize our unity.
>
> It must not be disseminated among the people or among fighters.

Neither this, nor the *public* official Kampuchean document detailing Vietnam se 'aggression' during the Pol Pot period (the *Black Book*), makes any accusation that Vietnam attacked across the Kampuchean border in July of 1977 or had done so for more than a year beforehand. But the Kampuchean Government was clearly expecting a large-scale conflict, and had already formulated an aim to make Vietnam 'strain to stop us'. The document added: 'We must also be prepared to go into enemy territory to collect intelligence . . . . in order to prepare for victorious attacks.'[226] Vietnamese claims of serious attacks in this same period, which precedes that in which Kampuchea claims to have been seriously attacked, cannot be ignored.

It is perhaps not surprising that, given the chance to negotiate a solution to the fighting in early 1978, the Pol Pot regime refused. Undoubtedly the Pol Pot group intended to use a conflict with Vietnam in order to isolate and accuse of treason the Vietnam-influenced group in the Communist movement. And undoubtedly it expected an increase in the degree of popular support it enjoyed after it had demonstrated that its members were patriots defending the Khmer race from extinction threatened by the 'historic enemy'. By then, the Pol Pot group would probably have been unable to retain power without continuing the thrashing, three-way spiral of massacre of the population, purge of the administration and aggression across the frontiers.

But in my view the anti-Vietnam war was not simply the last tactical refuge of the Pol Pot group. Its deep-rooted chauvinism had combined with the unmeasured effects of years of marked and increasing political isolation, within Kampuchea as well as from the outside world. It apparently expected to defeat Vietnam, perhaps by deliberately provoking what it thought would be an ill-fated Vietnamese offensive: this might even open the way for a victorious counter-attack to seize Kampuchea Krom back from the hands of the disorderly remnants of the retreating army not necessarily an unlikely scenario in the mind of Pol Pot when he predicted 'certain victory' over the Vietnamese invaders (on 5 January 1979) because they are 'the hereditary enemy of the Kampuchean people'. In other words, he was confidently counting on historically-based racism to offset popular reaction to what his own regime had done to ruin millions of lives. A tall order. And, significantly, the vulnerable Vietnam that Pol Pot saw himself fighting was the same mythical country that the U.S.A. had tried for so long to portray to the world. According to Pol Pot's *Black Book:*

> [in the early 1960s] the Vietcongs had no more territory at home, in South Vietnam, because of the Ngo Din Diem policy of strategic hamlets, for Robert Thompson, basing on his acquired experiences in other countries, set up strategic hamlets all over the territory of South Vietnam so that the Vietcongs had neither land nor population . . . .

> When the [1970] coup d'etat broke out in Kampuchea, the Vietnamese had only one card to play; it was to turn towards the Communist Party of Kampuchea and ask for help and assistance from it. . . .

Irrational territorial ambitions, as well as internal instability, are part of the explanation for the tension and conflict created by Democratic Kampuchea with all of its neighbours, especially after 1976. The strength of pro-Vietnamese sentiment amongst the revolutionary opposition to Pol Pot, as well as Chinese encouragement, focused these ambitions on Vietnam. And these ambitions cannot be separated from the millennial corporate state, based on nationalist revivalism, and the tyrannical internal policy it demanded.

References

1. These people were, in order: Hou Yuon, arrested around August 1975; Koy Thuon (January 1977); Non Suon (November 1976); Touch Phoeu (January 1977); Hu Nim (April 1977); Nhim Ros, killed after being accused of working as a 'Vietnamese agent' (March 1978); So Phim, killed at the time of a rebellion in the Eastern Zone in May 1978; Mey Prang, arrested in November 1978; Sua Doeum (February 1977); Cheng An (November 1978); Phuong (June 1978); and Vorn Vet, who, according to Ieng Sary 'committed suicide' after leading an unsuccessful coup i November 1978 *(Le Monde,* 2 June 1979).

   This chapter was written in August 1979 as a discussion paper for the *Journal of Contemporary Asia*, Vol. 10, Nos. 1-2, 1980, and was revised in early 1980.
2. *Asian Wall Street Journal,* 9, 10, 11 March, 1978.
3. These are the concluding words of an article entitled 'Another Importan Success of Our Co-operatives and Revolutionary Movement', the final article in *Tung Padevat* (Revolutionary Flags), 'the monthly internal magazine of the Party', No. 8, August 1975.
4. *Tunc Padevat,* No. 6, June 1976, pp. 51-2.
5. See David P. Chandler, 'The Constitution of Democratic Kampuchea: Th Semantics of Revolutionary Change', *Pacific Affairs,* Vol. 49, No. 3, Fa 1976, p.513.
6. This figure comes from a well-placed confidential source.
7. Details of the arrest (for subsequent execution) of 262 revolutionary lea by the Pol Pot regime from April 1976 to 9 April 1978 can be found in 'Important Culprits', the English translation of a Pol Pot regime docume released by the Heng Samrin Government in August 1979. Unless other cited, such information used below comes from this document, which is often confirmed by other sources. Hu Nim's 'confession' is presented a analysed at length in the *New Stateman,* 2 May 1980.
8. *Tung Padevat,* No. 6, June 1976, p.21.
9. Interview with Hing Sopanya, who returned from Paris to Kampuchea i October 1976, *Creteil,* 14 November 1979. The cadre's name was Soeur

10. Battambang and Siemreap Provinces and other districts of Kampuchea were seized by Thailand between 1940 and 1946.
11. Although one of Lon Nol's staunchest supporters was a Cham colonel, Les Kasem, with a Cham battalion, and Lon Nol maintained very close contacts with the FULRO movement among the hill-tribes of South Vietnam.
12. There is no evidence, however, that Pol Pot shared Lon Nol's reliance on astrology or magic for political purposes. Lon Nol was notorious for his confidence in a young soothsayer named Mam Pro Moni; at one stage, on his advice, Lon Nol had helicopters drop sand over Phnom Penh to protect it from rockets. According to Associated Press, in early 1973, Amnesty International was 'anxious to learn more about 55 astrologers arrested after predicting the overthrow of the Lon Nol government' (W111). In September 1972, Lon Nol had warned 'that the Communists were trying to kill Cambodians with rabbits by attaching explosives to the animals and turning them loose near Cambodian military posts' (W258, by Dennis Neeld).
13. Serge Thion, 'L'ingratitude des crocodiles', *Les Temps Modernes,* January 1980. For the figure of '99% Khmer', see colour magazines such as *Democratic Kampuchea,* produced in Phnom Penh in 1978.
14. See Francois Ponchaud, *Cambodia Year Zero* (Penguin, 1978) and Hanoi's *Kampuchea Dossier,* (Hanoi, 1978). Also *The Vietnam-Kampuchea Conflict: A Historical Record* (Hanoi, 1979) which says 'A mad xenophobia [reigned in Pol Pot's Kampuchea] . . . all non-Khmer people . . . have fallen victim to persecutions'; *Kampuchea* Dossier, Part 1, pp.28-30, deals with the fate of religion and ethnic minorities, including Chams.
15. *Livre Noir: Faits et Preuves des Actes d'Aggression et d'Annexion du Vietnam contre le Kampuchea* (Phnom Penh, Ministry of Foreign Affairs, September 1978). A later version, slightly different in significant parts, is available in English and French. Where there is discrepancy, in what follows I have used the original version.
16. As did the Lon Nol regime. The comparison between Lon Nol and Pol Pot goes further. Consider these statements by the former in 1973, remarkably similar to the way the Pol Pot regime placed *its* interests in a geopolitical context: Communism 'seeks to engulf the Khmer people and nation as a stepping stone to an attack on all South East Asian nations by savage means and with manifold theories and procedures'; the North Vietnamese 'must withdraw their troops out of our territory and put an end to their visions of *hegemony* on all the countries that border the Mekong River' (my emphasis – B.K.) (W258, TO27, AP, Bangkok)
17. Thion, op. cit.
18. For more extensive quotation of this broadcast, see the article by Lowell Finley in *Southeast Asia Chronicle,* No. 64, p.33.
19. The speech is entitled 'Long Live the Great Revolutionary Army of the Communist Party of Kampuchea'.
20. *Summary of Annotated Party History*, by the Eastern Zone military political service. Copies of this and the issue of *Tung Padevat* cited above may be found in the Echols Collection at Cornell University

Olin Library.

21. Phnom Penh Radio, 28 September 1977; see BBC *Summary of World Broadcasts* (SWB), 1 October 1977, FE/5629/C2/1 ff.
22. This information comes from the former Saigon ambassador to Tokyo, and is yet to be confirmed.
23. Phnom Penh Radio, 3 April 1979; see U.S. C.I.A. *Foreign Broadcast Information Service (FBIS)*, Daily Report, Asia and the Pacific, 4 April 1979, p. H4. Further, the former Avenue Charles de Gaulle was fittingly renamed after Achar Hem Chieu, a nationalist monk whose arrest in 1942 led to the first major anti-French demonstration in Phnom Penh. Chieu later died in a French jail on Poulo Condore (later Con Son) island.
24. See the national anthem of Democratic Kampuchea.
25. A number of these have been photographed since January 1979 by visitors to Phnom Penh.
26. *SWB*, 1 October 1977, FE/5629/C2/6.
27. Ith Sarin, 'Nine Months with the Maquis', in Timothy Carney, *Communist Party Power in Kampuchea* (Cornell University Southeast Asia Program, Data Paper No. 106, 1977), p.37. This book contains much rare information about the Kampuchean Communist movement during the 1970-75 war, with a thoughtful introduction.
28. Norodom Sihanouk, *Chroniques de guerre . . . et d'espoir* (Paris, Hachette Stock 1979).
29. Speech to the Asia Society, New York, 22 February 1980.
30. Sihanouk, op. cit. pp.79, 81, 114. See also note 221 below.
31. *Thai Nikorn,* 14 May 1979.
32. See *Far Eastern Economic Review (FEER),* 5 May 1978, 9 June 1978 and 28 July 1978, for information about Angkar Siem. It is inconceivable that the name could be a term spontaneously used by the local peasantry. See also 'Commune Life in Cambodia', *Eastern Star* (Bangkok) 14 March 1979, which transliterates the term straight into Thai as Ongkarn Siem, also an unlikely Thai usage. This article notes that the organization was responsible for all seven provinces of north-east Thailand with Khmer majority or minority populations.
33. FEER, 5 August 1977. Would the Thai Communist Party leadership go along with this? Perhaps, given the fact that it lined up ideologically with Kampuchea and China against Vietnam, and was benefiting from bases in Kampuchea. It is quite possible, though, that the only contacts between the Thai C.P. and Angkar Siem were at the *very* top level; and Angkar Siem, with its Kampuchean advisers, acted pretty much independently of Thai politics.
34. Interview with Sat, aged 13, in Thailand's Surin Province after his escape, 1 March 1979 (published here in Chapter Ten). Sat was told that the road he was helping to build in the forest was to go from Samrong to Preah Vihear.
35. Interview at Rouen, France, 10 October 1979.

36. The preceding information comes from over 100 detailed interviews with refugees carried out by Chanthou Boua and myself between 1975 and 1979.
37. *Tung Padevat,* August 1975.
38. Interviews with Mien, aged 14, on 7 and 19 March 1979 and Hok Sarun, 1 April 1979 (both published here in Chapter Ten). Mien also said that in his work-team of teenage boys in the forest, each boy was allocated a small plot of vegetables to tend in the evenings; they could only go to sleep when this work was done.
39. Interview with Srey Pich Chnay, 5 and 15 March and 19 April 1979 (see Chapter 12).
40. *Bulletin d'Information sur le Cambodge (BISC)* (14 rue Wilhelm, Paris 75016), 5, October-November 1978, p.20.
41. Interview with Te Ean Chhoeng and Tao Sun Hauv, Alencon, France, 2 October 1979.
42. *The Early Phases of Liberation in Northwestern Cambodia: Conversations with Peang Sophi'*, David P. Chandler with Ben Kiernan and Muy Hong Lim, Monash University (Australia) Centre of Southeast Asian Studies, Working Paper No. 10, 1976. According to Sophi, 'Khmer Rouge urge people to be self-reliant, to work harder . . .'; 'what is emphasized over and over is the self-reliance of Cambodians . . . . vis a vis the developing national revolution'. See pp. 11, 13.
43. *Thai Nikorn,* 14 May 1979.
44. *SWB*, 4 October 1977, *FE*/5631/C2/2.
45. Carney, op. cit., pp.5-6.
46. Pol Pot reported this and several other aspects of his personal history, but not the fact that his name was originally Saloth Sar, in an interview with Yugoslav journalists in Phnom Penh in March 1978.
47. This information comes from many refugees. According to William Shawcross, 'One Western doctor who worked in Phnom Penh before April 1975, who at first welcomed the Khmer Rouge victory, and who has worked with refugees since then, points out that in the last four years Khmer Rouge cadres have become younger and more violent'. *Asian Wall Street Journal,* 29 March 1979.
48. At this point Pol Pot, interestingly enough, was outside Kampuchea. Chou Chet had attended a conference of the People's Movement of United Resistance, in a 'liberated area' on 7-8 May 1970; according to the *Black Book*, Pol Pot returned to Kampuchea from China in June.
49. See 'Interview of Comrade Pol Pot . . . to the Delegation of Yugoslav Journalists', mimeograph, March 1978, p. 23; *Nhan Dan* (Hanoi), 28 March 1974, p.1; *JPRS South and East Asia,* No. 471, 10 May 1974, p.5. These sources are cited in S. Heder, 'Kampuchea's Armed Struggle: The Origins of an Independent Revolution', *Bulletin of Concerned Asian Scholars,* Vol. II, No. 1, 1979, p.21. Son Sen, for his part, remained in Phnom Penh for a year after the others' departure;

Carney, op. cit., p.44. Nuon Chea's movements at this point are unknown. Khieu Ponnary and Khieu Thirith, the wives of Pol Pot and Ieng Sary, stayed in Phnom Penh for at least a year after their husbands left.

50. *FBIS,* Daily Report, Asia and the Pacific, Pyongyang Radio, 3 October 1977; see 4 October report, p.H38.
51. *Black Book,* op. cit.
52. Interview with Khuon Thlai Chamnan, Chatenay-Malabry, France, 9 August 1979.
53. *SWB,* 1 October 1977.
54. 'The Anti-Imperialist Struggle in Cambodia: the Early Years', in Gettelman and Kaplan, *Conflict in Indochina* (ed. New York, Random House, 1970), p 59.
55. Norodom Sihanouk, *Le Cambodge et ses relations avec ses voisins,* (Phnom Penh, Ministere de l'Information, 1962), p.59.
56. *FEER,* 21 April 1978. This includes the possibility of the security forces being informed of Samouth's whereabouts by Pol Pot's group.
57. See note 49. Francois Ponchaud also mentions clandestine disappearance in Pursat Province, which in *Cambodia Year Zero* he describes, incorrectl in the light of other evidence, as those of Pol Pot's group.
58. Timothy Carney, 'Cambodia : The Unexpected Victory', forthcoming.
59. Heder, op, cit., p.12.
60. *Pahnyaha Sahakor* (The Co-operative Question) (Phnom Penh, 1964), reprinted in Part II of this volume. For further confirmation of the point made in the next paragraph, see note 106.
61. *Tung Padevat,* August 1975.
62. *SWB*, 5 October 1977, FE/5632/C/3.
63. Ibid, FE/5632/C/4. Nuon Chea made his concurring speech on 17 Januar 1977, to celebrate the 'Ninth Anniversary of the Revolutionary Army of Kampuchea', which he said had been born during an attack on a military post at Bay Damran, in Battambang Province near Samlaut, in January 1968.
64. Carney, op. cit., p.37.
65. See Milton Osborne, *Politics and Power in Cambodia* (Melbourne, 1973), p.101, and M. Leifer, 'Rebellion or Subversion in Cambodia', *Current History,* February 1969, for details about this demonstration. On the Samlaut rebellion, see my 'The Samlaut Rebellion and its Aftermath, 1967-70: The Origins of Cambodia's Liberation Movement', Monash University CSEAS, Working Papers Nos. 4 and 5, 1975, reproduced in Part II of this volume.
66. All Western intelligence agencies agreed on this, saying that these 'sanctua ies' were only a few kilometres inside Kampuchean territory.
67. *The Vietcong March-April 1970 Plans for Expanding Control in Cambodi* U.S. Mission, Saigon, Vietnam Documents and Research Notes, No. 88, January 1971.
68. Ibid, Document 9.

69. Ibid., Document 6. The PRP had (in 1966) become the C.P.K., as Document No. 8 recognized (p.62). See Carney, op. cit., p.56.
70. Ibid., Document 2.
71. Ibid., Document 6.
72. Ibid., Document 1.
73. Ibid., Document 2.
74. Ibid., Document 7.
75. Ibid., Document 8.
76. Ibid., Document 10.
77. *New York Times,* 20 July 1970.
78. *Washington Post,* 22 April 1970.
79. 'Cambodia: Can the Vietnamese Communists Export Insurgency?' *Research Study,* Bureau of Intelligence and Research, State Department, 25 November 1970.
80. 'Communist Infrastructure in Cambodia', D.I.A. Intelligence Appraisal, 8 July 1971.
81. Cited in William Shawcross, *Sideshow: Kissinger, Nixon and the Destruction of Cambodia* (London, Andre Deutsch, 1979).
82. Ibid., pp.248-9.
83. Interview with Veasna, France, 7 October 1979.
84. Judging from Sihanouk's statements at the time, tracts, ditties and even cartoons criticizing and mocking Sihanouk were being distributed in some villages during that period; Thion, op. cit.
85. K.K. Quinn, 'The Khmer Krahom Programme to Create a Communist Society in Southern Cambodia' (1971-4), unclassified Airgram to Department of State from U.S. Consulate, Can Tho, 20 February 1974, p. 8.
86. 'Khmer Rouge Rallier Keoum Kun', unclassified Airgram to Department of State from U.S. Embassy, Phnom Penh, 13 January 1972. Kun told his American interrogators that Kampuchean Communists Chan Samay, Keo Moni, Keo Meas and Rat Samoeun had 'broken with [leading Hanoi-based Khmer Communist] Son Ngoc Minh over the issue of North Vietnamese control of the Khmer Communist movement'. Son Ngoc Minh died in China in 1972, after living in Hanoi for 16 years; he may have been unable to get on with other younger Khmer cadres trained there, who did return to Kampuchea while maintaining close links with Vietnamese Communists. The new pro-Vietnamese government in Phnom Penh on 3 April 1979 renamed city streets after Son Ngoc Minh *and* after Keo Moni. Keo Moni and Keo Meas were killed by the Pol Pot regime: as yet the fate of Chan Samay and Rat Samoeun is unknown (to my knowledge their names were never associated with the Pol Pot regime).
87. Heder, op. cit., p.19.
88. Sihanouk, op. cit., 1979, pp. 44-5, 56; see also p. 52
89. Interview in *Problemes politiques et sociaux* (Paris) No. 373, 1979, pp.5-7.

90. 'Conversations with Khmer Rouge Rallier Ieng Lim', unclassified airgram to U.S. Department of State from U.S. Embassy, Phnom Penh, 30 November 1971.
91. Shawcross, op. cit., 1979, p.250.
92. Quinn, op. cit., p.11; see also Quinn's 'Political Change in Wartime: the Khmer Krahom Revolution in Southern Cambodia, 1970-74', *Naval War College Review,* Spring 1976, p.7.
93. Quinn, op. cit., 1974, p.28.
94. Ibid., p.34.
95. Personal communication, 26 September 1976. With prescience, Adams also noted that in his view the Vietnamese should keep an eye on their south-western border. 'Nothing serious, mind you, but worth putting up a cyclone fence', he wrote.
96. Carney, op.cit., p.43. Kandal Province was called the Special Region.
97. Ibid., p.34.
98. 'Keoum Kun', op. cit., p.6.
99. Quinn, op. cit. , 1974, p.8.
100. Pol Pot's July 1975 speech refers to 'missions that you comrades are fulfilling at present, such as the defence of Phnom Penh . . .' Sok Thuok was cited as a cadre in the Interior Ministry in March 1976, at a point when there was no Minister of the Interior, Hou Yuon having been arrested *(FBIS,* Daily Report, Asia and the Pacific, IV, 22 March 1976, p. H4.)
101. Interview with Chang Sieng, who returned to Kampuchea from France in February 1976, and attended a large meeting opened by Non Suon in Angkor Chey, Kandal Province, around 13 September 1976. See Chapter Twelve for Non Suon's fate.
102. Ith Sarin, *Sranaoh Pralung Khmaer,* Part 1, translated by Chanthou Boua, unpublished. This part of Sarin's book does not appear in Carney, op. cit.
103. Carney, op. cit., p.43.
104. Ibid., p.37.
105. Ibid.
106. Ibid., p.32. The same document's analysis of struggles in the mid-1960s is slightly different from that of the Pol Pot group (outlined above): 'In the cities, especially in Phnom Penh, the force of youth, that is, worker-producer and student youth, became the nucleus, the wick of the struggle in the movement of demonstrations and meetings to oppose American imperialists and the traitorous power-holders' (ibid.). This 'movement of demonstrations and meetings', which largely developed *after* the departure of Pol Pot's group from the cities, is rarely if ever acknowledged by them.
107. Ibid., p.50.
108. Ibid., p.39.

109. Quinn, op.cit., 1974, p.7.
110. Sihanouk, op.cit., 1979, p.52.
111. Carney, op.cit., pp.46, 49.
112. Ibid., p.11; see also Ith Sarin, op.cit., Part I.
113. Interview with Hok Sarun, op.cit.
114. Quinn, op.cit., 1974, p.7. Quinn actually says Ta Mok was the Zone Chairman, but Ith Sarin and other informants contradict this.
115. Ibid., p.9.
116. Ibid , p. 34.
117. Carney, op.cit., p.43. 'According to Phok Chhay's report to a meeting at the end of May 1972, the monthly expenditures in the South-west Zone reach over two million riels for Khmer Rouge military and civilian personnel, who earn 135 riels each per month', Ith Sarin tells us. Simple arithmetic gives a figure of over 14,800 troops and cadres, which does not include unpaid guerrilla forces and, probably, regional troops.
118. An accepted figure for the Khmer Rouge regular army in mid-1972 is 40,000 soldiers. By 1973, this had risen to 60-70,000 and total Khmer Rouge membership (including poorly-armed local guerrillas) in 1973 was 200,000. It is difficult to believe that this figure could have been achieved without a large measure of popular support in those years.
119. Carney, op.cit., p.39.
120. Interview with Tan Hao (pseudonym), 4 October 1979. The translation is from a tape recording of this interview. The interviewee requested anonymity.
121. Tribunal Populaire Revolutionnaire Siegant a Phnom Penh Pour le *Jugement du Crime de Genocide* Commis par la Clique Pol Pot-Ieng Sary, 'Acte d'Accusation', August 1979, Document No. 3.1, p.31.
122. Quinn, op.cit., p.35.
123. Ibid., p.7.
124. Personal communication, 12 May 1980.
125. Interview with Hong Var, 2-3 April 1979. This interview appears here in Chapter 12; also in *Kursbuch,* (Berlin), No.57, 1979, in German.
126. Donald Kirk, 'Communism and Political Violence in Cambodia' in J. Zasloff and A. Goodman (eds.), *Communism in Indochina* (1975).
127. Peter Dalkin, personal communication, 6 February 1976.
128. *Washington Post,* 8 March 1974.
129. *Kampuchea Dossier,* Part 2, has this extract of a Kampuchean soldier's diary: 'In March 1977, Ta Mok, member of the headquarters of the [south-west] military region, accompanied by two burly Chinese with fair skin and talking Pekinese, came to ideologically prepare the troops who were getting ready to attack Vietnam and advance as far as the first sugar palm, Saigon . . .' (see caption for photograph 5 in

Kampuchea Dossier, Part 2). The diary was apparently captured.

130. *Nokor Thom*, 26 November 1972, cited in Carney, op.cit., p.7.
131. Michael Vickery, 'Cambodia 1973: The Present Situation and its Background', unpublished, p.48; a revised version of this appears in Part II of this volume. A shorter version appeared in *Westerly*, (University of Western Australia), No. 4, December 1976, pp.14-28. Henri Becker, personal communication, Bangkok, February 1976, also referred to the concentration of 'Sihanoukists' among insurgents in the north-west during the war.
132. Carney, op.cit., p.9.
133. Some of the villages to suffer were Tahen, Ta Ngen and Maung Russei.
134. 'Keoum Kun', op.cit.
135. Ponchaud, op.cit., Khek Penn was also frequently mentioned by Bangkok newspapers during 1975, but then dropped from sight.
136. One village to suffer was Sdor Sdam, in 1974. See also interview with Sat, op.cit., whose village of Lbaeuk was not far away; when asked to describe the year 1975, when Khmer Rouge troops came to Lbaeuk for the first time, and 1976, Sat said: 'They were killing people every day.'
137. *FBIS*, Daily Report, Asia and the Pacific, Pyongyang Radio, 3 October, 1977. See 4 October, report, p.H38.
138. The *Black Book* tells us: 'In 1969, the struggle between Kampuchea and Vietnam reached its highest pitch. . . . The Communist Party of Kampuchea had never let the Vietnamese know the place where its leaders were living.' But it was clearly in the north of Kampuchea. When Pol Pot went from Rattanakiri to Santuk district of Kompong Thom province in September 1970, the *Black Book* describes this as his going 'down to the south of the country'! Perhaps Pol Pot never had close personal contact with developments in the real southern and central regions in the 1970-75 period, or even before that. Finally, a November 1970 meeting in Kompong Thom was held 'at a bend of the Chinit River, moving from north to west, that is at 30 kilometres from the refuge of Comrade Secretary Pol Pot. . . .' (It is very likely that the *Black Book* is a largely personal account written in the third person: this was at a secret summit with the Vietnamese.)
139. *Xat Lao*, 9 August 1974, cited in Quinn, op.cit., 1976, p.28.
140. 24 November 1974.
141. Quinn, op.cit., 1974, p.8.
142. See *Kampuchea Dossier*, op.cit. Ngoy Taing Heng, who lived in Prey Veng Province from 1975-78, reports a popular uprising in 1977; interview at Caen, France, October 1979.
143. Tribunal Populaire, op.cit., 'Requisitoire', August 1979, p.8.
144. Interviews with Lim Vanny and five others (Paris 18 October 1979.

145. Wilfred Burchett, personal communication.
146. Quinn, op.cit., 1976, p.11.
147. Quinn, op.cit., 1974, p.32.
148. Ibid, p.33.
149. Ibid., pp.25-6.
150. Interview with Prak Nith, Melbourne, July 1978.
151. Quinn, op.cit., 1976, p.17.
152. Quinn, op.cit., 1974, p.35.
153. A.P., Bangkok, TOO9, W453.
154. Ibid, W384-5.
155. Ibid, W193.
156. Shawcross, op.cit. 1979, p.272.
157. George C. Hildebrand and Gareth Porter, *Cambodia: Starvation and Revolution* (New York, Monthly Review Press, 1976), p.109, n 83. They cite interviews conducted with Khmer refugees in 1971 by the General Accounting Office, Congressional Record, 18 April 1973, p.S7812.
158. 'Cambodia: Can the Vietnamese Communists Export Insurgency?' *Research Study,* Bureau of Intelligence and Research, State Department, 25 November 1970.
159. Op.cit., p.149, see also W.J. Sampson, letter to the *Economist*, 24 March 1977 (?).
160. Chandler et al., op.cit., pp.2-3.
161. This figure is given by Slavko Stanic in 'Kampuchea: Path without Model', *Socialist Thought and Practice* (Belgrade), Vol. XVIII, No.10, October 1978, p.76.
162. Shawcross, op.cit., 1979, pp.298-9.
163. Ibid.
164. Thoun Cheng, 'Life under the Khmer Rouge'in this volume, Chapter Ten, p. 283.
165. See Ponchaud, op.cit. and Hildebrand and Porter op.cit., pp.48-50, for divergent but, I think, equally reliable, first-hand reports of the evacuation of Phnom Penh.
166. *FBIS,* Daily Report, Asia and the Pacific, Vol.4, No.75, 17 April 1975.
167. *Bangkok Post,* 25 June 1975, quotes a revolutionary official telling a prospective refugee to Thailand that he was 'lucky' that this order had gone out three days before. See also *Bangkok Post,* 23 July 1975, and *The Early Phases of Liberation*, op.cit., in May 1975 Peang Sophi was told by Khmer Rouge cadre at a meeting in Battambang Province that 'angkar had ordered these killings stopped', although the rank-and-file troops were 'very angry' with those associated with Lon Nol's regime. Sim Savuth, whose husband is a former Lon Nol soldier, also reports that orders came from Phnom

Penh 'in April or May 1975' to stop the killing of members of the defeated Lon Nol army and administration. Her husband was put to work in the fields with over 3,000 other Lon Nol soldiers in a village in Battambang, and she came to live with him there in September before their December escape to Thailand (interview 9 October 1979). In mid-1976, a high-ranking official arrived on the scene of a mass execution, evidently instigated by local Khmer Rouge troops, and put a stop to it just as Srey Pich Chnay was about to be killed (op.cit.). Also in Battambang in 1975, two Khmer Rouge troops who killed and ate the liver of a civilian in Svay Kong village, Anlong Vil district, were led away and executed by a revolutionary cadre named Samuon. Samuon told villagers that the two were 'terrorists' who might do the same thing again, that they were 'superstitious' and 'politically bankrupt', and that the aim of the revolution was not to make people afraid. Thuy Bounsovanny was an eyewitness to the original killing (interview in Paris, 14 October 1979).

For the difficulties faced by the revolutionary movement in administering parts of Kampuchea up to 1976, see my 'Social Cohesion in Revolutionary Cambodia' in *Australian Outlook*, Vol.30, No.3, December 1976, pp.371-86. In analysing the reasons for continuing violence after the war, I failed to identify the deliberate, if hampered, activities of the Pol Pot group (and there is no doubt, in 1979, that they were deliberate), as a contributing factor *as well as* such difficulties.

168. Thuy Bounsovanny, op.cit. Khek Penn's speech took place in Boeng Thom village.

169. Francois Ponchaud, 'Essai d'analyse de Radio Phnom Penh', 1976.

170. Statement of the Ministry of Foreign Affairs of Democratic Kampuchea, 17 March 1978.

171. Thion, op.cit., also personal communication from Gareth Porter, Washington, May 1978.

172. *Chinese Warmongering Policy and Hua Kuo-feng's Visit to the Balkans,* Tirana, July 1978.

173. This speech was reprinted in *Peking Review.*

174. In a speech by Chiao Kuan-hua at the United Nations.

175. 27 August 1976.

176. *Memorandum on Chinese Provocations and Territorial Encroachments,* Hanoi, 15 March 1978. A brief look at this document reveals complaints about Chinese pressure on Vietnam's border 'especially since 1974', the year of China's seizure of the Paracels and of Deng's launching of the Three Worlds theory. A major incident took place in February 1976 and 'in early 1976' Vietnam says China sent armed troops to occupy an area of Vietnamese territory. Statistics are given for the number of yearly incidents from 1974-78, indicating a regular increase in tension, spectacularly in 1978. Unfortunately, figures for the year 1976 are not broken down into months to give any indication of whether the supremacy of the radicals from April to October was

accompanied by any alteration in the trend. But *after* their arrest, according to this document, 'from October 1976 to 1977 alone', the Chinese 'encroached into Vietnamese territory at dozens of points'.

177. *Asiaweek*, 26 January 1979.

178. So Phim, according to Vietnamese sources was known as So Vanna and had fought in the 1946-54 resistance against the French. The 1973 Party history gives the initials S.V. as those of one leader of six who formed a 'temporary central committee' of the Party after the 1954 Geneva Conference.

179. The sixth new name was Nuon Chea.

180. Tribunal Populaire, op.cit., Document No. 2.1.5.05, dated 23 June 1979.

181. Serge Thion, personal communication; he was told this by Sam San, who was ambassador of Democratic Kampuchea in Vientiane, 1977-78.

182. Ieng Sary in *Le Monde,* 2 June 1979.

183. Phnom Penh Radio, 21 March 1976 *FBIS,* Daily Report, Asia and the Pacific, Vol. 4, 22 March 1976, p.H1.

184. Pech Lim Kuon. Part of this refugee's story appears in the *Bangkok Post*, 5 May 1976 as well as in *Far Eastern Economic Review.*

185. *FEER*, 25 June 1976. There is another, remotely possible explanation for all this: that there are, or were, two Pol Pot's, Saloth Sar having assumed the identity of the original one some time in late 1976. It is clear that Saloth Sar's position on his identity caused problems in the party: in late 1975, when at a Bangkok press conference Ieng Sary was asked about the role of Saloth Sar and why his name was not mentioned, according to the *Bangkok Post* he could only limply reply: 'Go ask him, he's in Cambodia'. One of the questions asked by Yugoslav journalists of the Prime Minister of Democratic Kampuchea in March 1978 was: 'Who are you, Comrade Pol Pot?'

186. *FEER*, 19 May 1978.

187. *White Paper,* Hanoi, op.cit., 20 January 1978.

188. 'Intervention de Thiounn Prasith', at a Ministerial Meeting of the Co-ordinating Bureau of the Non-Aligned Nations, Algiers, 2 June 1976, reproduced in *Nouvelles du Kampuchea Democratique* (Embassy of Democratic Kampuchea, Berlin), No.3, 1976, p.3. Thiounn Prasith said 'our people broke off all relations with this traitorous regime the day after its fascist coup d'etat and have never had relations with it since. . . . We renew the constant fraternal solidarity of the people of Democratic Kampuchea with the valiant struggle that the Chilean people are now waging to instal a democratic and progressive regime in Chile. . . .' He denied 'recent information from the press agencies that the Government of Democratic Kampuchea has established diplomatic relations with the present regime in Chile'.

189 Hanoi's *Kampuchea Dossier,* op.cit., Part 2, p.18, notes that on 1 July

1978, Pol Pot's congratulatory telegram to Peking 'neglected to mention the relations between Peking and people like Mobutu and Pinochet' while praising China's support for 'oppressed peoples and nations'.

190. This interpretation is supported by the fact that it was the *Lao* government which first publicly mentioned the C.P.K. in October 1975, and *again* in April 1976 (see Carney, op.cit., p.5). It is unlikely that *both* these disclosures were unintentional.
191. *FEER*, 29 October 1976.
192. *FBIS*, Daily Report, Asia and the Pacific, Vol. IV, No.183, 20 September 1976.
193. *FEER*, 21 October, 1977.
194. Statement of 17 March 1978, op.cit.
195. *Kampuchea Dossier*, op.cit., Part 2, p.37.
196. Carney, op.cit., p.5. He cites *FBIS*, Daily Report, Asia and the Pacific, Vol IV, No. 210, 29 October, 1976.
197. This was on China's National Day, in a congratulatory telegram which also attacked Liu Shao-ch'i, *FEER*, 29 October 1976.
198. Interestingly, the more considered second edition alters this to 'as much time on political education as on technical training'.
199. *FEER*, 5 November 1976.
200. *White Paper*, Hanoi, op.cit., 20 January 1978.
201. *FEER*, 12 December 1978.
202. Tribunal Populaire, op.cit., August 1979, Document No. 2.1.1.09, pp.14-15. Prey Chhor district was Hu Nim's electoral base, 1958-67.
203. This information is drawn from my interviews with six refugees who lived in Kandal in 1975 and one in 1976, one who lived in Svay Rieng in 1975, four who lived in Takeo in 1975, one who lived in Kompong Cham in 1975, and one who lived in Prey Veng from 1975-78.
204. Poeu San Bopha, interview in Paris, 26 October 1979. Bopha lived in Khnyong village east of the Mekong River. Also interview with So Davinn, Paris, 9/8/79; Davinn lived in Prek Touch village, Kandal Province.
205. Cited in Shawcross, op.cit., 1979, pp.374-5.
206. Interview carried out by Chanthou Boua and James Pringle, Aranyaprathet, 22 May 1979.
207. Interview with Ngoy Taing Heng, Caen, France, 6 October 1979.
208. *Kampuchea Dossier*, op.cit., Part 1, p.37.
209. Pech Lim Kuon's interview with Bruce Palling of *Newsweek*, and with the *Bangkok Post*, 5 May 1976.
210. Torben Retboll, personal communication.
211. *The Times*, (London), 30 January 1978.
212. *Wall Street Journal*, 17 October 1977, report by Barry Kramer.
213. Mien, op.cit.

214. *Le Figaro* (Paris), 27 August 1979; interview with A.F.P. correspondent.
215. Interview with Sarun in Surin, May 1979.
216. *Kampuchea Dossier,* op.cit., Part 1, p.25. The eight are named there.
217. *Bulletin d'Information sur le Cambodge*, op.cit., No.2, May 1978, pp.8, 6-7.
218. *Kampuchea Dossier,* op.cit., Part 1, pp.37-8.
219. *FEER,* 30 December 1977, p.5.
220. *Kampuchea Dossier,* op.cit., Part 2, p.68.
221. Eyewitnesses I have personally interviewed include Veasna (France 7 October 1979) and Heng (France 8 October 1979). Veasna fled to Vietnam in December 1975 from Kampot Province of Kampuchea. He lived in the village of Ap Sase (Minit, Ha Tien, Kien Giang Province of Vietnam until November 1977.
He says there was no fighting between Kampuchea and Vietnam in this border area in 1976. In mid-1977, 'the Khmer Rouge started the fighting', Veasna says. 'I saw this in actual fact with my own eyes, since my house was 500 metres from the border. When the Khmer Rouge crossed the border everybody ran and grabbed their children and all ran into their houses. But the Khmer Rouge came into our village and burnt down houses and burnt goods, and killed about 20 people who were not able to run away . . .' Just before that, in nearby Prey Tameang village in Vietnam, the Khmer Rouge had killed 200 civilians, including ethnic Khmers as well as Vietnamese, he adds. 'The population asked the Vietnamese military to fight back against the Khmer Rouge, but they replied that they didn't have orders from above to do so. In 1977 the Vietnamese did not go into Kampuchean territory.'
Heng fled to Vietnam in October 1975 from Svay Rieng Province of Kampuchea. He lived in the village of Ke Mea in Tay Ninh province of Vietnam until mid-1978. Heng also notes that there was no fighting along this stretch of border in 1976. In May or June 1977, he says, the Khmer Rouge shelled Ke Mea from positions across the nearby border, killing 'hundreds' of people; he says many of them were ethnic Khmers as well as Vietnamese. Despite this the Vietnamese authorities still insisted that the Khmer Rouge were their 'friends'. Only in early 1978, Heng says, did they mount loud-speakers in the villages 'telling their people what the Khmer had done'.
222. This was announced on Phnom Penh Radio on both 6 and 7 December 1977.
223. *Asian Wall Street Journal,* 9, 10, 11 March 1978.
224. *New Statesman,* (London), 23 February 1979, p.241.
225. This map is reprinted in *Kampuchea Dossier,* op.cit., Part 2, photo 6.
226. Ibid., photo 1, reproduces some of the text of this Khmer document; the translation I have used is that of S. Heder, who regards the document as an authentic Pol Pot regime internal document (see *The Call* (Chicago), 5 March 1979, where Heder interprets it as saying that 'Cambodia would not attack Vietnam'.) I am grateful to David Chandler for passing Heder's translation on to me.

10. Testimonies: Life Under the Khmer Rouge

The Early Phases of Liberation: Peang Sophi*

This paper is drawn from nine hours of recorded conversation between Muy Hong Lim and Peang Sophi, a 32-year-old Cambodian who arrived in Australia from Thailand in April 1976. The interviews took place on 29 April, 5 July, 10 July and 24 July 1976; several details were verified in more informal sessions in August and September. Muy Hong Lim and Ben Kiernan, who attended two of the sessions, have checked the draft and translations, but I am responsible for the inferences drawn and the language used. When Sophi was told about the use to which the conversations would be put, he urged us to use his name, rather than a pseudonym, so as to give what he said 'more force'.

His account of life under the revolutionary regime differs in two important ways from others readily available in the West in 1976. Firstly, he spent over six months working actively – and rather happily – under revolutionary guidance: unlike many refugees, he was not punished by the regime for having roots in the 'old society'. Secondly, from about September 1975 onwards, he enjoyed considerable responsibility as the 'economic foreman' of an 800-person rural work team. For these reasons, his account is useful in gaining insights into the style and ideology of the revolution.

To a purist, of course, his eventual escape may show that he was still part of the 'old society' after all. He fled because conditions were hard and because he thought, mistakenly as things turned out, that his best friend had done so. (November 1976).

Peang Sophi was born in Phnom Penh in 1944, the third of six children. His father was a clerk – in 1953, at least – at a French-sponsored High School. In the mid-1950s, the family moved to Stung Treng in northern Cambodia where Sophi completed his education, failing the examination that would have admitted him to a *lycee.* It is ironic that he took these examinations in the hope of attending the Teachers' Training College at Kampong Kantuot, near

* Translated and presented by David P. Chandler with Ben Kiernan and Muy Hong Lim.

Phnom Penh – a spawning ground in the Sihanouk era for Khmer Rouge cadres. To compound the irony, it was financed until 1964 by the United States.

After a stretch of casual employment around Phnom Penh, Sophi moved to Battambang, where his 'adopted older brother' owned a bar. In 1966, he took a job at the textile factory then being built with Chinese economic aid. He started as a construction worker, and was later taught by Chinese Technicians how to operate machines.[1] Over the next nine years (Chinese technicians left in 1967), he became familiar with most of the equipment in the plant. Because of this, he asserts, and because he was 'poor', he was kept at the plant for three months by the Khmer Rouge – i.e. until July 1975.

Aside from an affection for Prince Sihanouk, Sophi was apathetic politically, at least until liberation. He didn't vote in the National Assembly elections of 1966, and in 1972, unimpressed by Lon Nol (whom he refers to as *a khamau,* or 'blackie'), Sophi voted for a rightist anti-government candidate, Im Tam.[2] 'Only high officials,' he asserts, voted for the Marshall [Lon Nol], even though 'We knew, without him, the political situation would become impossible.'

Before liberation, Sophi supplemented his wages (which rose slowly to the equivalent, in 1975, of A$35 a month) by working in his adopted brother's bar. At one point, also, he spent two weeks digging for sapphires in Pailin, west of Battambang. Finding nothing, he returned to his factory job.

On 18 April 1975, the day after Phnom Penh fell to the Khmer Rouge, Battambang was liberated without a shot. Top government officials had fled in helicopters the day before, and the city was in a holiday mood. 'We thought the war was over,' Sophi remarks, 'and that we could work normally again and go about our business with a less corrupt regime.' With hundreds of others Sophi went to the outskirts of town to greet 'our friends', the Khmer Rouge, about whom – in spite or perhaps because of five years' hostile propaganda – he knew very little. Like most of his friends, Sophi welcomed liberation without realizing what it meant: 'The Khmer Rouge had won; fair enough, the war was over.'

In this context, the solemnity of the Khmer Rouge themselves probably came as a surprise. The first ones Sophi saw were heavily armed, 'very young' and dressed in black like peasants, although their trousers, Sino-Vietnamese style, were held up by elastic bands. They were 'unmistakably' Cambodian, and Sophi noticed that they were 'thin and pale; none of them was fat'. They were also contemptuous, and aloof, 'looking us over, distrustfully, from head to toe'. Khmer Rouge cadres later admitted to Sophi that in the early days of liberation they were subject to 'uncontrollable hatred'. It was in this mood that the Khmer Rouge executed Lon Nol officials – and dismantled two T-28 aircraft they found at Battambang airport with their bare hands. 'They would have eaten them if they could,' Sophi remarked.

Battambang was not evacuated at once. After about a week, the Khmer Rouge told its people – but not the workers at the textile factory – to disperse to the countryside, because 'American B-52s' were soon to bomb the city. Although Sophi knew nothing of this exodus at firsthand, it seems likely that local Khmer Rouge spent the first few days after liberation organizing themselves for the move and preparing work-sites near the city to receive evacuees.[3]

During this week, the Khmer Rouge forced the rapid deflation of prices in the city, confiscated radios and gradually phased out the use of money.

At first, Sophi was not impressed by the newcomers. 'We didn't take them seriously,' he says. 'We sat and listened to them, but paid no attention to what they said.' Snobbery, perhaps, played a part in his indifference. According to Sophi, most of the Khmer Rouge were 'real country people, from *far* away' – illiterate, out of touch and ill at ease. For example,

> They were scared of anything in a bottle or a tin. Something in a tin [perhaps insecticide] had made one of them sick, so they mistook a can of sardines, with a picture of a fish on it, for fish poison, and one of them asked a friend of mine to throw it out. I saw them eating toothpaste once, and as for reading, I remember them looking at documents upside down.

After the evacuation, 'about 80' Khmer Rouge, including 20 women, arrived at the textile plant to study work techniques. Most of them came from Samlaut, 50 kilometres to the south-west. At this stage, also, the three ranking executives of the plant (in charge of personnel, administration and technology) were taken off to 'study'. Khmer Rouge cadres later told Sophi, whom they befriended, that the men had been shot because they were 'corrupt' – a charge which Sophi believes was true in two cases, but false in the third.[4]

In May and June 1975, conditions at the plant began to harden. For one thing, workers were made to wear black peasant costumes, with cuffless trousers reaching half-way down the calf. Sophi, who dyed a pair of 'old society' trousers black, was once humiliated at the gate by Khmer Rouge soldiers who cut off the bottoms to the requisite length and ordered him to sew up the pockets. On a more serious level, pay was halted altogether and the Khmer Rouge took political control of the factory, working through two former employees who had been jailed by the Lon Nol regime and who now 'talked politics all the time, and were pure red'. In this period unco-operative workers would disappear to 'study'. Sophi attended several meetings which denounced the 'old society', and others which discussed methods of increasing productivity at the plant. Partly because shortages of fuel meant that the factory could only run two shifts a day, rather than three, and partly because of the arrival of the new politicized workers, the Khmer Rouge seem to have intended all along to phase out the 1,000-odd workers who had been at the plant before liberation. Sophi himself was dismissed in July 1975, charged with eating an extra bowl of rice. From then on, whether tactically or from conviction, or both – Sophi's narrative is not clear on this point – he co-operated with the Khmer Rouge and was rewarded with increased responsibility and power.[5]

From July 1975 until January 1976, he worked on a co-operative farm *(sahakar)* at Wat Rokar some five kilometres south of Battambang.[6] In September and October, he was detailed along with 'seven thousand' people from different worksites, to work on a canal at Snoeung, 20 kilometres south-west of Battambang. He came back to Wat Rokar for the harvest at the end of 1975, and escaped to Thailand in January 1976.

Several aspects of his narrative are worth discussing in detail. These include what he saw of the reorganization of Khmer society: working conditions; the style and content of political meetings; and changes in vocabulary, life-style and culture sponsored by the regime. Although he remained unconvinced by the totality of Khmer Rouge teaching, Sophi was impressed by the integrity and morale of many cadres, and by the ideology embodied in official directives and revolutionary songs. At several points in the interviews, he said, 'The (Khmer Rouge) theory is good.'

Reorganization of Khmer Society

In the summer of 1975, Cambodian rural society, in Battambang at least, was reorganized, first on the basis of 10-family units, and later into work-teams. These numbered from 30 to over 1,000 persons, organized on a task basis, with a module of three 10-man groups. Each of these was organized at the work-sites by three leaders, in charge respectively of 'action' *(sakam),* 'politics', *(niyobay)* and 'economy' *(setekec).* The 'action' leader was in charge of organizing the work force and arranging its day-to-day programme; the 'politics' leader dealt with 'keeping everyone happy', i.e. with morale and cultural affairs; and the leader connected with 'economics' obtained supplies for the work-team, including tools, food and medicine. He also arranged, at harvest time, for the day's harvest to be brought to a central granary controlled by the Khmer Rouge.

The Khmer Rouge chose these leaders, Sophi said, on the basis of skill, class background and effectiveness within a given group. They enjoyed no special privileges, aside from some freedom of movement from site to site, if they were in charge of a large group. In the words of a revolutionary slogan, they were expected to 'join enthusiastically' *(sosrak sosram)* in work which their groups performed. The 33-man groups *(kong)*, in turn, were organized in three groups (i.e. to a total of 99 people) with an additional three-man cadre. The 102-man groups could then be organized; if necessary, into larger bodies; Sophi cited examples of groups numbering 300-, 800- and 1,200 odd workers. The mechanics of reorganization, which Sophi first noted at the canal site, went fairly smoothly, indicating considerable skill on the part of the Khmer Rouge in recruiting supervisory personnel. According to Sophi, the goal of the regime was to set up self-reliant 1,000-worker groups throughout Cambodia 'within the next five years' to produce clothing and tools, while bartering surpluses with other groups producing different commodities or crops. Groups of this kind were to be formed in Battambang in early 1976. Another aspect of reorganization was that at harvest time a special 800-worker harvesting team, composed of young people selected for the purpose, moved from work-site to work-site aiding local workers in bringing in the rice. The group was known as a 'shock troop' *(top sruoch),* and its members were supposed to set an example to others by 'enthusiastically joining the momentum' of everyone's work *(choh cho'p chol'na),* sleeping in the open if there were no accommodation for them

Working Conditions

Working conditions at Wat Rokar, for one with Sophi's strength (he was known as 'friend stocky' [*mit map*] to the Khmer Rouge), were less severe than in the Melbourne factory where he now works. People rose at 5 a.m.. Work began in the fields about an hour later, and lasted until noon. After an hour for lunch, work resumed from 1 p.m. to 5 p.m. The hours were flexible, however, for one Khmer Rouge innovation – linked, perhaps, to the movements' preoccupations with indigenous culture, asceticism and self-reliance – was to work 'according to the sun', following a shared rhythm of work rather than the mechanical rhythm of a clock. At first, the 10-family units, although removed in most cases from their original homes, retained identity by cooking and eating together at the work-sites. This practice was altered in August 1975, when food was cooked in common for work-teams, whose members contributed their personal rations (given them by their 'economic' leaders) to a communal kitchen. In another context, Sophi quotes a Cambodian proverb ('Food from a large pot is never tasty') to criticize the regimentation of the new order. However, rations were usually sufficient, varying from one Nestle's condensed milk can of uncooked rice a day, at the beginning of liberation, to three cans per person ('too much', according to Sophi) during the time spent digging the canal. Sophi stressed that workers on the job were fed more rations than their 'unproductive' dependants, probably as part of *angkar's* programme of stressing the moral value of collective labour,[7] and of punishing those who 'exploited others' work' *(chih ch'oan polikam).* In Sophi's opinion, Khmer Rouge control over rations was a way of controlling the people: 'With enough to eat, we might get lazy; by economizing with us, they kept their strength.'

Sophi took some interest in the work on the canal at Snoeung. He described, by means of a diagram, the dimensions of the canal, its walls and the road being constructed alongside it. He also noted that coconut palms were planted at five-metre intervals beside the canal.

On the whole, then, Sophi found conditions fairly hard, but the administration reasonably just. He brushes aside other refugees' assertions of brutality by saying that many of these people, who lived only two or three months under the Khmer Rouge, had no understanding of the directives that governed working conditions.[8] These came into effect towards the end of 1975. According to Sophi, the seven which he remembered were: 1) Respect the discipline imposed by the organization *(angkar);* 2) Respect the directives of the organization; 3) Pursue solidarity and unity of action; 4) Don't squander common property; 5) Struggle to work hard; struggle to be humble; struggle to be clean and honest; 6) Report daily on work accomplished; 7) Plan the work to be done on the following day.

In speaking of organization and control Sophi stressed that Khmer Rouge cadres as such were not involved at the work-sites themselves. At Wat Rokar in fact there were only three cadres in residence. Each *sahakar* had a 'president', or *protean,* who was a local man, chosen by the Khmer Rouge, and then 'elected' by the *sahakar.* The first of these at Wat Rokar was executed by the Khmer Rouge for listening to 'Voice of America' radio broadcasts and, more generally, for losing enthusiasm for the revolution. He was replaced by a more dedicated figure. The Khmer Rouge cadres themselves, in these early stages, were not identified by personal names, and kept to themselves (at Wat Rokar, the Khmer Rouge soldiers had their own separate field of *padi*), although they had no special privileges or badges of rank, and were friendly enough in their relations with villagers and workers.[9]

In Sophi's opinion, the Khmer Rouge were able to retain control over large groups of people in four ways: by the threat and collective memory of force; by controlling movement in and out of the work-sites; by monopolizing the distribution of food; and by locating the work-sites at considerable distances from roads and other population centres. From time to time, unco-operative villagers disappeared, allegedly to 'study'; a macabre jingle: 'the Khmer Rouge kill, but never explain' *(Khmaer krohom somlap, min del prap)* circulated at the factory.

Two other reasons for Khmer Rouge success – aside from the attractiveness of their programme – seem to have been their special appeal to youth, especially those between 13 and 16 (a neglected group in pre-revolutionary Cambodia) – who were organized into their own work-teams – and their giving power and responsibility to people with what they called 'poor peasant' backgrounds.

Political Meetings

In the early stages of liberation, Khmer Rouge speakers publicly admitted they had been fired by 'uncontrollable hatred' for members of the 'old society'. 'We were so angry when we came out of the forest,' one speaker allegedly said, 'that we didn't want to spare even a baby in its cradle.' At meetings at Wat Rokar and Snoeung, Khmer Rouge admitted executions of 'old society' people, but added that *angkar* had ordered these executions stopped. One reason for this, according to a speaker at Wat Rokar, was that *angkar* wanted Cambodia's population, depleted by at least a million people during the five-year war, to reach 20 million by 1990.[10] Sophi says the figure was 'made up' and adds that everyone was 'much too tired to reproduce' (he uses polite language here) at the end of the day.

Sophi's comments about political meetings at Wat Rokar and at the canal-digging site are interesting. Ironically, for a regime that has ruthlessly pruned foreign words from its vocabulary, the assemblies themselves are known as 'miting'.[11] There were 'miting' of one sort or another every night. Those at Wat Rokar opened with singing 'The Red Flag' (see p.330), a song written in 1970 and more popular, it seems, than the national anthem ('The Victory of

17 March [1975]') promulgated in 1976. Sophi reports, incidentally, that the only flags he saw were merely red, without markings of any kind. As in China, these were flown at work-sites, to raise morale. He never saw the national flag, adopted officially in early 1976, which bears a stylized image of a three-towered Cambodian temple, in yellow, on a red field.

While smaller meetings, limited to work-team leaders, were held two or three nights a week, larger ones, involving entire work-site populations, occurred about once a week. At these, men and women were separated from each other, and grouped according to marital status. In the speeches and discussion that ensued, everyone enjoyed equal status as 'friends'. Subjects for discussion did not include 'individualistic' complaints, however, but were geared to improving work and morale in the collectivity as a whole.

Indoctrination at 'miting' included explanations of the 10 directives, already mentioned, and the memorizing of revolutionary songs. 'Cultural groups', usually formed locally, also performed at 'miting' in song and mime, dramatizing the revolution with prepared, rather than improvised texts; at Snoeung, there were cultural performances every night. Khmer Rouge speakers urged people to be self-reliant, to work harder and to be humble, and belaboured the Americans, as well as 'everyone with a white skin and a sharp nose', according to Sophi. Two sentences he remembers are: 'We have only ourselves; we must offer our work to *angkar*' and 'Robbery only satisfies one person'. His favourite speaker, Ta Mih (a revolutionary pseudonym), spoke in such a way 'that nobody ever got tired'. Mih was the leader of Khmer Rouge militia attached to Wat Rokar and the canal-building site. One of his most effective speeches, as recalled by Sophi, ran something like this:

> In the old days, the big people *[nak thom]* told us we had independence. What kind of independence was that? What had we built. Well, *they* built an Independence Monument. Where did they build it? They built it in the capital. Who saw the thing. The *nak thom's* children. Did country people see it? No, they didn't; they only saw photos. The *nak thom's* children went in and out [of Cambodia], going to this country, that country, and then they came back, to control our kind of people [literally 'our group']. And now what do we do, in contrast? We don't build Independence Monuments like that. Instead, by lifting up embankments, digging irrigation canals, and so on, the children of Cambodians can see what they have done, and country people will see that in the time of their grandfather, the time of their father, and their uncles, they *built* their own independence. . . .

Speeches like this convinced Sophi that 'no one can beat the Khmer Rouge at talking', but he adds that 'When you asked them, "Why do you say one thing and do another?" the answer was that "the organization moves by leaps and bounds" ' – that is, it followed tactics and strategy known in detail only to itself. In this context, also, it is interesting that the Khmer Rouge, in the early stages of liberation, made almost no specific pledges about popular welfare in the future (e.g. when and if schools would be reopened, or currency reintroduced), preferring to stress the dynamic interplay of agricultural prosperity and self-reliance.

These aims and achievements were also treated by a semi-monthly newspaper, *Revolution,* which circulated at Wat Rokar. According to Sophi, the editors of the paper – which emanated from Phnom Penh – were not named, nor did it single out government leaders for special attention, reflecting the anonymity of collective leaders. 'I didn't believe what it said,' Sophi asserts, without mentioning any reasons for his distrust.

Cultural Changes

The changes in rural life-style that were introduced into Battambang in 1975 had been in effect in liberated areas for several years. Uniformity of costume and hair style, enforced in these areas since 1973, were perhaps the most obvious: women's hair was bobbed rather severely, and Maoist peaked caps – unknown in pre-revolutionary Cambodia – were widely worn. Similarly, the formal structure of Buddhism was dismantled and, although some monks appear to have been allowed to stay in their monasteries, most were ordered out of the *sangha* to assist the revolution. Broadcasts from Phnom Penh never mentioned Buddhism, incidentally, even as a shortcoming of the 'old society'. A puritanical strain in Khmer Rouge behaviour can be seen in regulations, such as those cited by Sophi, forbidding women from unbuttoning the top button of their tunics or enforcing the separation of workers by sex when work was done; personal ornaments, including jewellery, were discouraged.

The keynote of linguistic reforms was being 'humble inside the revolution' *(reaka knung pattavot).* Differences in status no longer existed; begging and arrogance, respectively, were not allowed. The Khmer Rouge emphasized that relations between husband and wife and between parents and children should be marked by cordiality, and the use of crude expressions was discouraged. Foreign words, especially French ones, were no longer permitted; what used to be 'commands' were now 'suggestions' and what was emphasized over and over was the self-reliance of Cambodians, and by implication of the Cambodian language, in relation to the developing national revolution.[12]

The details of Sophi's escape in January 1976 are of interest. A band of seven men from Thailand arrived at Wat Rokar and offered to guide Sophi's adopted brother, among others, to the frontier. Sophi's brother refused, unwilling to escape without Sophi, absent that day at a work-site. The band then contacted Sophi, who arranged a *rendez-vous* with them, on the understanding that his brother would join him in the escape. His brother, however, at the last moment changed his mind, convinced that Sophi, by now 'heart and soul' with the Khmer Rouge, would prefer to stay in Cambodia.

In a twist of plot worthy of the *Ramayana,* Sophi, unknown to his brother, had actually planned to escape for some time, and had squirrelled away some extra clothes and rice for the journey. He fully expected to encounter his brother on his escape, but he didn't, and his brother – much more a part of the 'old society' than Sophi, in the eyes of the Khmer Rouge – remains behind as a participant in one sort of new society – the one envisaged by the new regime – just as Sophi, by escaping to Australia, has chosen to participate in another.

Six Revolutionary Songs

These songs were memorized by Sophi during his time at Wat Rokar and Snoeung. The first of them, 'The Red Flag', is sung at the beginning of every 'miting'. Some of the others use existing folk-tunes and traditional rhythms, but the main difference between them and pre-revolutionary songs, aside from such obvious ones as the choice of subject matter, is that the songs are sung in unison rather than by individuals – a trend reflected in the words as well, which praise collective efforts at the expense of individual ones. As far as I know, none of the songs has been printed in the West, even though they – and hundreds like them – were used intensively by the regime of Democratic Kampuchea, as part of its programme of 'national culture' and as weapons in the revolution. David P. Chandler.

The Red Flag

Glittering red blood blankets the earth – blood given up to liberate the people: blood of workers, peasants and intellectuals; blood of young men, Buddhist monks and girls.
The blood swirls away, and flows upward, gently, into the sky, turning into a red, revolutionary flag.

Red flag! red flag! flying now! flying now! O beloved friends, pursue, strike and hit the enemy.
Red flag! red flag! flying now! flying now!
Don't spare a single reactionary imperialist: drive them from Kampuchea.
Strive and strike, strive and strike, and win the victory, win the victory.

Solidarity Group

Dear brothers and sisters in the solidarity group, happy and self-assured: let us celebrate Kampuchea, recently set free, by striking out and leaping forward to construct new rural areas.

We raise embankments, and these form a network, like spider-webs, everywhere. We dig canals, small and large, long and short, bringing water and loam to pour on to our fields.

We use fertilizer now; and now we raise embankments, high and low. We choose the seed we want. We wipe out peats. We build fences to protect our plots from beasts.

And we are very happy because we are the masters to a great degree. Problems of water no longer worry us. Even with the floods and droughts, we can grow rice.

O solidarity group, working in unison, happy and self-assured! Dry-season rice, wet-season rice, light and heavy varieties of rice: our husbandry is successful everywhere.

O solidarity group, you are a new kind of family, special, beautiful and unique. Our happiness is enormous, and we struggle to expand and solidify it, even more.

The new nation of Kampuchea is a glittering, glowing, sparkling kind of light. We strive to work harder and harder, to expand and complete the revolution.

The Beauty of Kampuchea

O beautiful, beloved Kampuchea, our destiny has joined us together, uniting our forces so as not to disagree. Even young girls get up and join in the struggle.

Pity our friends who shoulder arms. Thorns pierce their feet; they do not complain; this is an accomplishment of Khmer children struggling until blood flows out to cover the ground.

They sacrifice themselves without regret, they chase the Lon Nol bandits, with swords and knives hacking at them, killing them, until the Lon Nol bandits are destroyed.

Cultural Group

We press our palms together, and bow our heads, respecting all of you, our friends, who have come together for this evening meeting.

We have come tonight to show our talents, and our popular, revolutionary culture – to entertain you, our young friends.

In the cause of cultural struggle, and in the name of the beautiful art of the ancient Khmer, please correct and improve our performance. Please help us to root out corrupt and rotten culture.

If what we do is right or wrong, please, friends, correct and refine the detail helping us, constructively, to fit in with old traditions, and to achieve a revolutionary culture.

The Summer Wind

As the summer wind blows, the sun shines on the rice fields, where workers and peasants move together. Some have sickles in their hands, and some carry pots of water on their heads.

Look at the ripe rice, as the wind moves it in waves; the workers are happy in their hearts, working nights and mornings, with no fear of getting tired.

We are overjoyed to be increasing the output of village and district. Our economy has made great steps forward, now we have surplusses to put into granaries and to supply the revolution.

Rainfall in Pisakh (April-May)

The rain falls in *pisakh.* There's a cool breeze. Dear friends, the rain falls now and then. We hear roosters crowing everywhere, and our brothers the peasants join together to increase production.

This is the sowing season: we toss corn and beans in front of us. We strive to work, so as to supply the army, holding on and struggling at the front.

The Khmer are happy now, no longer feeling tired, striving to clear the road to peace. All the Khmer children are happy, for the revolution guides Khmer and Khmer towards solidarity.

Intertwined, as one, our anger shoots out at the imperialists – the Americans, and their reactionary lackies, killing them until they disappear.

References

1. Sophi remembers that in setting up the plant, the Chinese planted vegetables and fruit-trees around the factory, to provide food for the workers. The Cambodians neglected these plants, and they died off, only to be reintroduced by the Khmer Rouge after liberation.
2. In 1966, Sophi remembers that the candidate in his district of Phnom Penh, Cheng Heng (later Chief of State in the Khmer Republic), spent huge sums of money purchasing support.
3. These tactics also applied in the Pailin region. See Kunara Sam, 'Quand les armes se sont tues', *Sereika,* No. 1, August 1976, pp.8-10.
4. Sophi admits that the two top executives at the factory were corrupt, but adds that the technical director, a young man, was not.

5. His enthusiasm for the Khmer Rouge – whether genuine or feigned – made his friends suspicious, and he had to go out of his way, *sub rosa,* to show that he was loyal to his adopted brother.

6. Although the word translates as 'co-operative', the *sahakar* of the Khmer Rouge clearly have more in common with Chinese communes or Russian collective farms than with Vietnamese co-operative ones. It is uncertain if parts of Cambodia liberated before 1975, however, underwent as much dislocation as Battambang.

7. The virtues of collective behaviour with respect to individualism were stressed repeatedly by the Khmer Rouge, in radio broadcasts and in the Constitution of 1976.

8. It is possible that in the early stages of liberation, these directives were not widely circulated, but were memorized only by work-team leaders.

9. Sophi noticed, however, that a few symbols of status persist. The highest-ranking cadre he saw, for example, carried pistols, and travelled with two 'runners' *(niressa),* teenage messengers with high status in the revolution. Cadre with lower status carried rifles.

10. See also Foreign Broadcast Information Service (FBIS) Daily Report, Asia and the Pacific, 26 April 1976, which reports a Cambodian official's statement, at an international conference: 'Cambodia has more than 7.7 million people at present. We want more people; we do not want to kill them.'

11. The word in Vietnamese is *mit-tinh;* see Alexander Woodside, *Community and Revolution in Modern Vietnam,* (Boston, 1976), p.267.

12. For more information about linguistic changes, see David P. Chandler, 'The Constitution of Democratic Kampuchea (Cambodia): The Semantics of Revolutionary Change', *Pacific Affairs,* Fall 1976.

The Fate of the Khmer Issarak: Krot Theam

We now take up again the story of Krot Theam, whose experiences in the Khmer Issarak movement were recounted in Part II. What follows is taken from the same interviews with him.

In 1969, Theam left the Buddhist monastery at Thvak in southern Battambang, and became a trader in precious stones in the nearby gem-mining town of Pailin. During the 1970-75 war, he learned of the renewed activities of his former revolutionary teachers Achar Leak and Achar Pres. From other sources we know that at that time Moul Sambath also resumed his old position as Communist commander in Battambang. When the victorious revolutionaries finally entered Pailin in April 1975, they were led by Theam's relatives Sieu Samreth, Sou (a revolutionary pseudonym meaning 'endurance') and Bey. All of them had joined the Khmer Issarak in the mid-1940s along with Theam, but they had remained in the jungle throughout and he had not set eyes on them since 1952.

Theam draws several significant distinctions between his experiences of the revolution from 1949-52 and those of 1975.

First, the victors in 1975 made no mention of either 'communism' or 'socialism'. Secondly, they were not assisted by any Vietnamese revolutionaries. Thirdly, there was little if any mention of Achar Hem Chieu, Pou Kombo, or any of the other historical anti-colonial figures used to inspire the Issarak revolutionaries 20 years before.

Finally, most of the revolutionary soldiers who entered Pailin in 1975 (and evacuated its population to the countryside) were not well-trained. Theam maintains. 'The Khmer Rouge are not good soldiers. We Issaraks were far better than them in the field. They won the war by accident.' Nor did they keep to the rules of revolutionary conduct to which Theam had once been expected to adhere – many were even domineering and violent in their relations with the inhabitants of Pailin, a number of whom were, according to Theam, executed quite arbitrarily. Theam was 'morally shattered' by this experience, and fled to Thailand, in July 1975.

While he found the conduct of the victorious troops 'impossible to understand', Theam did suggest that most of them were illiterate peasants who had to rely on what they could remember. Among the Khmer Rouge in Pailin, his relatives included, he did not meet a single one who was well-trained or 'intelligent'. Also, they had suffered considerably, and over a long period, in the jungle. They had very little to eat, and had had to dig tubers from deep in the ground. Because of bombing raids, they had had to keep constantly on the move. Now, the Khmer Rouge said, 'people in the towns would learn what their life had been like.'

Everybody was put to work growing rice. Monks had to work like the others – raising cattle, slaughtering pigs and chickens and doing other tasks which Theam complained were against the monks' traditional code of behaviour. Some who objected to this were killed; sometimes there was a token attempt at political re-education first. Theam says he had not been hostile to the revolution beforehand, and even afterwards was extremely reluctant to leave his native region whatever the situation there; however, the apparently gratuitous violence of the Khmer Rouge in Pailin was just 'too much'. One of those who fled with him to Thailand was his uncle Yot, who had once been the Khmer Issarak mayor of Theam's village.

In a separate interview in France in 1979, another refugee named Reim recalled that in August 1975 he saw the '60-year-old' Khmer Issarak veteran Achar Leak in the town of Maung in southern Battambang. Reim said that Achar Leak was being held by a Khmer Rouge officer and a group of soldiers, and was being given only rice porridge to eat.

'They Did Nothing At All For The Peasants: Thoun Cheng

Thoun Cheng, a Kampuchean refugee who left his country in June 1977, was interviewed by Chanthou Boua and Ben Kiernan at the Lao refugee camp at

Ubon Ratchathani, north-east Thailand, on 13 and 14 March 1979.

Cheng was born in 1957 in the village of Banteay Chrey, in Chamcar Loeu district, Kompong Cham Province. His father was a carpenter but also, with the help of just his family, worked his six hectares of *chamcar,* or garden farmland, growing pineapples and bananas. Cheng's mother died when he was small; he had three older brothers.

During the 1960s, Banteay Chrey was populated by about 3,200 ethnic Khmers, who mostly worked *chamcar,* and about 400 Chams, who grew rice. There were four Buddhist *wats* and one Muslim mosque. Land was unevenly distributed: an elderly landlord owned 30 hectares in the village and an unusually large holding of 770 hectares in other parts of the district, including one large pineapple plantation. Poor farmers usually owned from one to three hectares.

Cheng studied in primary school in the village; his education was interrupted, though, by a three-year stay with relatives in the town of Kompong Cham, and six months in Phnom Penh.

The overthrow of Prince Norodom Sihanouk in 1970 was greeted with some disappointment by the villagers of Banteay Chrey. Cheng remembers some of them travelling to Kompong Cham to take part in protest demonstrations. Soon after, fighting took place in the area between troops of the new Lon Nol Government and revolutionary Khmer Rouge claiming loyalty to the Prince. The Lon Nol troops retreated and were not seen in the area again.

As Banteay Chrey itself was free of fighting, Cheng's relatives from Kompong Cham, a bus driver and his family, came to live in the village in 1970.

The war put an end to supplies of medicine to the village. Schools were closed, too, and Cheng never got the opportunity of a secondary education. So from 1970, he made furniture and tilled the soil with his father.

Vietnamese Communist troops began making frequent visits to Banteay Chrey. They paid for supplies that they needed and did not mistreat villagers. Indigenous Khmer Rouge troops (who spoke 'like people from Kompong Cham') were first sighted when they entered the village in 1972 and left again without causing upset. They lived in the forest and visited the village frequently over the next three years; life went on as before. The Khmer Rouge never stayed in or recruited from Banteay Chrey and were 'busy fighting the Lon Nol troops all the time'.

In 1973, the Vietnamese stopped coming; in the same year, the village had to withstand three months of intense bombardment by American B-52s. Bombs fell on Banteay Chrey three to six times a day, killing over 1,000 people, or nearly a third of the village population. Several of Cheng's family were injured. After that, 'there were few people left to be seen around the village, and it was quiet'. Food supplies, however, remained adequate. Later, in 1973, the Khmer Rouge temporarily occupied most of Kompong Cham City and evacuated its population to the countryside. 74 people from the town came to Banteay Chrey and 'took up a normal life there'. Some of the evacuees had died of starvation and bombardment by Lon Nol planes along the way.

The Khmer Rouge victory in April 1975 and their evacuation of Phnom Penh city brought 600 more people to Banteay Chrey. The newcomers were billeted with village families. Relatives of Cheng, a couple and their three children, and one single man, stayed in Cheng's father's house. They had set out on foot from Phnom Penh 15 days earlier and arrived tired and hungry, although unlike some others they had not lost any of their family members along the way. (The single man, Kang Houath, was eventually to escape from Kampuchea with Cheng. Houath took part in one of the interviews with Cheng in Ubon. He said that some village people along the way had given the evacuees food, and others had exchanged food for clothes and other goods offered by the Phnom Penh people. The bulk of the people travelling the roads at the time, however, were former peasants who had taken refuge in Phnom Penh during the war and had been instructed or allowed to return to their villages by the Khmer Rouge, Houath added.) In return for food and shelter, the new arrivals in Banteay Chrey helped the locals in their work in the fields.

Also in April 1975, Khmer Rouge troops came to live in the village. It was not long before they began imposing a very harsh life-style on the villagers. Everybody was now obliged to work in the fields or dig reservoirs from 3 or 4 a.m. until 10 p.m. The only breaks were from noon till 1 p.m. and from 5 to 6 p.m. (This compared to an average 8-hour day worked by the *chamcar* farmers in preceding years.) One day in 10 was a rest day, as well as three days each year at the Khmer New Year festival. Land became communal.

Also from 1975, money was abolished and big houses were either demolished and the materials used for smaller ones, or used for administration or to house troops. The banana trees in the *chamcar* were all uprooted on the orders of the Khmer Rouge and rice planted in their place. Production was high, although some land was left fallow and rations usually just consisted of rice porridge with very little meat. After the harvest each year, trucks would come at night to take away the village's rice stores to an unknown destination.

In 1975, the Khmer Rouge also began executing rich people (although they spared the elderly owner of 800 hectares), college students and former government officials, soldiers and police. Cheng says he saw the bodies of many such people not far from the village. Hundreds of people also died of starvation and disease in the year after April 1975 Cheng says. (After the war ended there was no resumption of medical supplies.)

At this time the Khmer Rouge, led by 'friend Sang', claimed that they were 'building Communism'; they occasionally mentioned a Communist Party, although its local (and national) members were unknown to the villagers. The soldiers did not work in the fields but mounted an armed supervision over those who did; people designated non-military members of the Khmer Rouge worked unarmed alongside the villagers. There were no peasant organizations formed or meetings held about work; every decision concerning the work to be done and how to do it was made by the supervisors with no participation on the part of the workers.

There was a large number of Khmer Rouge troops in the village, in the hundreds; they lived separately from the people in a big hall which no one else was allowed to visit. Cheng never chatted with any of the soldiers in the two and a half years he lived with them in Banteay Chrey.

According to Cheng, everyone, including his father, disliked the Khmer Rouge in Banteay Chrey – the work was simply too hard, the life-style too rigid and the food too inadequate. The Khmer Rouge occasionally claimed to be on the side of the poor, the peasants, but 'they did nothing at all for them'. On the contrary, sometimes they said: 'You were happy during the war, now is the time for you to sacrifice. Whether you live or die is not of great significance.'

Cheng managed to hide two radios buried in the ground. The batteries were precious so he listened to them only once or twice a month. Traditional village music was banned; the Khmer Rouge theatre troupes that visited the village about once in three months were the only form of entertainment.

In the April 1976 elections, only the 'very big people' voted in Banteay Chrey. Also, by that stage, the *wats* and the mosque in Banteay Chrey were empty. Saffron-robed Buddhist monks were nowhere to be seen. The Muslim Chams were obliged to eat pork on the occasions it was available; some adamantly refused, and were shot.

During 1976-77 most of the Khmer Rouge leaders in the village changed six times. More than 50 Khmer Rouge were executed in these purges. Sang's position was finally assumed by Friend Son.

Then, from January 1977, all children over about eight years of age, including people of Cheng's age (20), were separated from their parents, whom they were no longer allowed to see although they remained in the same village. They were divided into groups consisting of young men, young women and young children, each group nominally 300-strong. Their food, mostly rice and salt, was pooled and served communally (sometimes there was *samlor,* or Khmer-style soup).

The Khmer Rouge soon began attacking the Vietnamese Communists in speeches to these youth groups. Although like most Kampucheans Cheng is extremely suspicious of Vietnamese, he regarded these speeches as 'propaganda'.

Also in early 1977, 'collective marriages', involving hundreds of mostly unwilling couples, took place for the first time. All personal property was confiscated. A new round of executions, more wide-ranging than that of 1975 and involving anyone who could not or would not carry out work directions, began. Food rations were cut significantly, leading to many more deaths from starvation, as were clothing allowances (three sets of clothes per person per year was now the rule). Groups of more than two people were forbidden to assemble.

1977 was easily the worst year of all, Cheng says. Many people now wanted to escape, although they knew it was very dangerous. Cheng's mind was made up when it became clear that he would remain unable to see his father and brothers. It was June 1977.

Cheng, Houath, a neighbour and one other man took three baskets of dry rice (Cheng did not say how this was acquired), and, avoiding everyone along the way, headed north and east for Thailand. Laos was closer but Cheng had heard on the radio that Laos was 'building communism' too and didn't want to go there. As it turned out, however, the four men lost their way in Preah Vihear Province and hit the Lao border at Kompong Sralao. Although Khmer Rouge troops were thinned out because of the conflict with Vietnam, the refugees were spotted by soldiers who fired immediately, killing two of Cheng's companions. Cheng and Houath were separated but arrived safely in Laos, where they met up again in a local jail on the banks of the Mekong.

Cheng noticed that the Lao soldiers behaved differently from the Khmer Rouge he knew. They 'asked questions first', before apprehending people they suspected, whereas the Khmer Rouge were much more inclined to shoot suspects on the spot. Cheng also gained the impression that living conditions in Laos were considerably better than in Kampuchea.

Cheng (and Houath) spent a total of 37 days in two Lao jails. He was given rice to eat, much more than he had had for a long time in Banteay Chrey. He was not ill-treated, but when he was told that Vientiane was being asked for instructions whether to send him back to Kampuchea, he escaped with Houath and fled to Thailand on 8 September 1977.

An illegal immigrant once more, he spent another 10 months in a Thai jail, before being transferred to the Ubon refugee camp.

Democratic Kampuchea: Sat and Mien

What follow are accounts of the personal experiences of two teenage Kampuchean peasant boys during 1975-78. We interviewed them in a wat (a Buddhist temple) near where they were tending their new master's horses, in a district of Thailand's Surin province; Sat on 12 March 1979 and Mien on 7 and 19 March 1979. We came across the boys while inquiring at the wat about local historical materials. As far as we know, no journalist had ever visited the wat, let alone interviewed Sat or Mien.

A lack of detail is apparent in the boys' recollections (for instance, they were usually sure of the year in which an event occurred, but could rarely give the month) which is quite probably explained by their youth. Still, it is rewarding not only to compare and contrast the two accounts, but also to appreciate the personal impressions the boys formed of the events that went on around them. While these impressions may be judged as hazy, even incorrect in parts, some are worth recording simply as what Democratic Kampuchea meant to someone their age.

The text includes every detail recounted by the boys, arranged in sequence by us. Occasional points we have added appear in square brackets.

'They Were Killing People Every Day'

Sat was born in 1966 in the village of Lbaeuk, Kralanh district, Siemreap Province, Kampuchea. The village is a long way from Siemreap town and Sat has never been there. His father, Kaet, was a rice farmer who had married again after Sat's mother died. Sat had five brothers and sisters; he was the third oldest.

In April 1975, the Khmer Rouge took control of all Kampuchea. When asked if he recalled what happened in his village in the years 1975 and 1976, Sat said, 'They were killing people every day.' Killings took place at some distance from the village, he said, without claiming to have witnessed any executions himself. He heard that victims were bound and then beaten to death. They were usually people found to be fishing illegally or who had failed to inform the Khmer Rouge of all their activities, according to Sat. Also during 1975-76, food was scarce in the village; rice porridge with banana stalks was the usual meal.

Sat can't remember the date of the first appearance of the Khmer Rouge. They came from Oddar Meanchey Province and took rice from the people of Lbaeuk. They soon began ordering the demolition of half a dozen big houses in the village, and the building of a large number of smaller ones to house the villagers. The new houses, many of which became flooded in the subsequent rainy season, were built in a circle around the outskirts of the village; a large 'economics hall' *(kleang setakec)*, one of the functions of which was to provide communal dining facilities, was constructed in the now vacant centre of the village.

The Khmer Rouge recruited a large number of volunteers in Lbaeuk, mostly youths about 20 years old. They were attracted, according to Sat, by the much larger food rations that Khmer Rouge received, and by the fact that they 'did not have to work, and could kill people'. He added, however, that on some occasions Khmer Rouge members who had committed some transgression were executed by their fellows.

The village *wat* was also demolished; several people were killed in an accident that occurred in the process. The large statue of Buddha from inside was thrown in a nearby stream. The local Khmer Rouge leader had given orders for this to be done, without specifying a reason to the villagers; he was obeyed out of fear, Sat says. From that time on, saffron-robed monks were no longer seen around the village.

The year 1976, Sat said, was worse than 1975. By now, no one in Lbaeuk dared complain or question the regime. Sat's father was temporarily jailed by the Khmer Rouge; Sat doesn't know the reason.

In 1977, all young children no longer breastfeeding were taken from their parents and cared for permanently by female members of the Khmer Rouge. The reason given was to enable the mothers to work more effectively. Boys of Sat's age (11) and older were taken *en masse* to a forest locality called Lbaeuk Prey. There were over 100 boys in all. Their task was to plant rice, supervised by about 20 armed Khmer Rouge in their early twenties. They worked there for five months, during which time more than 20 of the teenagers were taken away to a nearby mountain top. Sat did not claim to have seen them killed, but believes they were.

Sat says those taken away, none of whom he saw again, were boys who had not worked hard or had missed work or played games, and had ignored three warnings to this effect. [More minor infringements of the rules, Sat says, were punished with a spell breaking rocks to make roads.] Or, they were people who didn't reply when asked what was their parents' occupations.

Predictably, morale was low among the young workers. Although 'laughing was permitted', there was no singing while they worked and no dancing or other entertainment afterwards. Every night there were meetings, in which the children were urged to work harder; there were no political speeches or discussion at these meetings, and nationalism was mentioned only in the context of the Vietnamese 'attempt to take over our land'. There were no references to China.

Other tasks the boys performed were removing weeds from the rice fields and making fertilizer. The job Sat preferred was tending crops such as watermelons, cucumbers, and other vegetables. He was able to spend a lot of time doing this because he was so ordered. Khmer Rouge leaders on bicycles and with guns [both possessions were a sign of office] occasionally inspected Sat's work. He was never allowed to eat any of the fruits of his labour, all of which were carted away by truck; Sat doesn't know where. The food rations he did receive varied from rice porridge with salt to rice porridge with fish.

At some time in late 1977, there was a one-day rest. Sat is not sure whether this was to celebrate the official proclamation of the Communist Party of Kampuchea led by Pol Pot [28 September 1977].

At night the boys were obliged to mount guard duty. Sat was taught how to use a gun but never considered becoming a Khmer Rouge soldier when he was older.

Many of the boys, including Sat, missed their parents badly. Some of them cried with grief at times; the Khmer Rouge would then beat them with sticks until they stopped crying, Sat recalls. One month after commencing work at Lbaeuk Prey, Sat and other boys were permitted to visit their parents in Lbaeuk. Some of the parents broke into tears on seeing their sons. Sat's father told him he had now been assigned the task of catching fish for the village communal dining hall; he was forbidden to use any of his catch for his or his wife's consumption. Sat's other brothers and sisters had all been taken elsewhere and were not at home. After this visit, which lasted several hours, Sat returned to Lbaeuk Prey and never saw his family again.

In late 1977, all the boys from Lbaeuk Prey were taken in trucks to Samrong in Oddar Meanchey Province. As before, the workers there were all teenage boys. Sat does not know where the teenage girls from his village had been taken.

In Samrong they began building a road that was to go to Preah Vihear [through hundreds of kilometres of uninhabited forest]. The boys were told that the road would be used to transport food and supplies. They all worked at the rate of two or three metres of road per day, using locally-made buckets to shift the earth; some boys threw up the soil, while others packed it down into a road surface. By the time Sat left this site five months later, no vehicles had yet been seen on the road.

There was nothing that Sat enjoyed about this experience. The boys were not taught to read or write or to sing any songs; they were never shown any radios, books or magazines, although Sat noticed that some of the Khmer Rouge had such things.

Later the boys were taken to a place in the forest called Ken, also in Oddar Meanchey Province. They were again put to work building a road. They worked from 6 a.m. to 10.30 a.m., had a short lunch break and then worked until 6 p.m., when they had another short break and a wash and then worked until 10 p.m. There were no rest days. Sat says the work was so exhausting that some of the boys fell down unconscious at the work-site.

Then, early in 1979, a Khmer Rouge leader arrived on a bicycle and announced that the Vietnamese were in Kralanh. The boys were told to walk to nearby Paong; when they arrived they were led towards the Thai border on foot for three or four days, carrying their own food and sleeping when tired.

Sat crossed into Thailand. However, one groups of boys came across some Thai tanks; never having seen such things, they ran frightened back into the jungle, where, Sat says, they were killed by Khmer Rouge soldiers.

Now an unpaid servant for a senior Thai official, Sat is happy enough. His food is sufficient, but he is 'not allowed to walk around or talk to people'.

When he becomes an adult, he wants 'to live with other people'.

'The Khmer Rouge Leader Was A Kind, Easygoing Person'

Mien was born in 1965 in the village of Samlaeng, Roang subdistrict, Preah Vihear Province, Kampuchea. His parents, who were rice farmers, called him Daung.

[In early 1970, troops of the new Lon Nol regime retreated from Preah Vihear and from that point the province was under undisputed Communist control.] During the next few years, Mien recalls, Vietnamese Communist troops passed through Samlaeng on one occasion, provoking a lot of interest but no hostility. They didn't steal anything from or harm the villagers, he says; after paying for what they wanted, they moved on.

Also during the war, Samlaeng was bombed 'many times' over a long period. Mien doesn't know if any of the people were killed.

In 1975 [after the Khmer Rouge captured and evacuated Phnom Penh], a number of people arrived in Samlaeng on foot after walking from Phnom Penh. Some people had died along the way; the villagers helped the new-comers settle in to their new environment, Mien says.

During 1975-76, life went on as before. Mien's parents were 'happy' during this period, he stated on two separate occasions. Khmer Rouge troops lived in the village but did not cause any upset; Mien never heard any mention at all of any actual or suspected executions. Food supplies were adequate.

Then, at some point in 1976, 'the revolution began'. Its purpose was 'to build up the country', Mien was told. The entire village was now obliged to eat in a communal dining hall. Rations were tight – usually only rice porridge. In late 1976, Mien heard that a Phnom Penh evacuee had disappeared from the village and was thought to have been executed. This was the only such case he was aware of while living in Samlaeng.

In 1977, Mien and three other village boys of his age were taken away from their parents. The Khmer Rouge who escorted them away said that they would come back later to take away the other boys in the village, in groups of four at a time. Mien was taken to Samrong in Oddar Meanchey Province, joining a work group of about 30 boys, the oldest of whom was 17. Their job was to clear the forest for *chamcar,* or garden farmland. Each morning they got up at 4 a.m. and worked around the house they lived in, tending fruit and vegetable crops, until 6 a.m. Then they would go into the forest and work there until 10 a.m. when they ate their lunch. This consisted of a carefully rationed bowl of rice porridge, sometimes with salt, sometimes with *samlor,* Khmer-style soup. It was not tasty but Mien was always hungry and would eat it all. At 6 p.m. they would stop working in the forest and return to their houses. Every night the boys were assigned a small plot of land to tend near the houses they lived in. When they finished this task to the satisfaction of their overseers they were allowed to go to sleep.

While still living with his parents, Mien had only been accustomed to doing household chores, and he says he found it difficult to adjust to the new lifestyle. The work was not enjoyable, he says; each boy was allocated an area of forest to clear and they worked some distance from each other. They were not taught to sing songs or dance, or to read or write. He was never allowed to visit his parents again.

Nevertheless, the leader of the Khmer Rouge where Mien worked was a 'kind, easygoing' person who 'never got angry' and did not physically mistreat the children. The Khmer Rouge leader was about 30 years old.

After many months at Samrong, all the boys were sent to a place called Phnom Phtol, or Phnom Seksor. There they spent a few months looking after herds of water buffaloes. In early 1979, with Vietnamese troops approaching the area, they were told to go to Paong; they crossed the border into Thailand, followed by a large number of Khmer Rouge soldiers and children, not long after.

'Your Hands Are Not Used To Hard Work': Hong Var

Hong Var, a Kampuchean refugee in Aranyaprathet camp, Prachinburi, Thailand, was interviewed by Chanthou Boua and Ben Kiernan on 2 and 3 April 1979.

Hong Var crossed the border from Kampuchea into Thailand with her two daughters, Sokmalee, 11, and Panita, 7, on 12 March 1979. They had lived through almost four years of Khmer Rouge rule, and four days of the new Heng Samrin Government presence in their village in Battambang Province. Hong Var told us what had happened during that time; what follows is exactly as she told it, although we have arranged events into sequence.

Var was born in Takeo city but moved to Phnom Penh in the 1960s where she took up a job as a teacher of Khmer language and literature at the Indra Devi High School near her home in the suburb of Tgul Kauk. In April 1975, the final month of the Kampuchean war, Khmer Rouge rockets were falling 'like rain' in Tgul Kauk, so Var took her children to stay with relatives in the suburb of Phsar Thmey. Her husband was studying in France.

When the Khmer Rouge took the capital on 17 April, they ordered everyone to evacuate it. Some people, Var says, were told they could return after three hours, others were told three days. The reason given was that the U.S. might bomb the city, and that in any case the Khmer Rouge wanted to 'clean up' the city.

Few people who left Phnom Penh took anything substantial with them; at the most, food for three days. Var, however, decided not to go at all. She hid with her children and relatives on the fourth floor of a building in Phsar Thmey, but after a week they were discovered by Khmer Rouge soldiers and forced out of the city. Var says she was lucky not to have been killed; some people who refused to leave had been shot, she says. The Khmer Rouge unconvincingly insisted that they would be able to return in three days.

They were given a choice whether to go west to Kompong Speu, south to Takeo or east to Neak Leung, because of the sector of the city they were in. Var decided to head for her birthplace in Takeo, and set out on 24 April with her daughters and two other families of relatives. They packed a jeep with belongings and five or six bags of rice, but it was not long before they had to abandon it and start walking.

Var saw many people she knew along the way; they were very unhappy, she says. They were all moving very slowly and stopping for long periods. Some people, who may have realized after three days that they wouldn't be allowed to return to Phnom Penh, committed suicide by driving their cars headlong into the Mekong River or jumping from a bridge.

While walking, Var also met a number of her former students who had joined the Khmer Rouge movement after 1970. They approached her respectfully, and were quite kind to her, providing her with a pair of rubber sandals. Var was scared of the Khmer Rouge in general and considers herself quite lucky to have met these boys and girls.

Many of the evacuees had not brought food with them, but there was some available, in exchange for goods, from peasants who lived along the road. In abandoned townships or suburbs of Phnom Penh, Var was able to get hold of some food; also she picked fruit and vegetables from *chamcar,* or gardens, along the roadside. She heard that the Khmer Rouge were distributing food at some points but never came across any of these.

It was very hot and tiring walking. People died of exhaustion; Var saw perhaps 100 or so bodies by the wayside in the 50 kilometres she travelled. After two weeks walking, she and her children and relatives arrived in Phnom Chiso district of Takeo Province; it was about 30 kilometres from their destination. Although they wanted to go on, the local Khmer Rouge ordered them to stay and work in the fields. Two weeks later, Var was again disappointed – other people in the area were allowed to return to their villages of origin, but she and her relatives were obliged to stay where they were.

Var spent the next seven months in the village of Sla, in Phnom Chiso. There were 120 families of peasants in Sla, and 70 families of newcomers from Phnom Penh. The peasants sheltered the city people in and under their houses (although the local Khmer Rouge claimed that *angkar padevat* ('the revolutionary organization') was supplying the accommodation). In some houses, three or four families lived together. This led to quarrels, so the Khmer Rouge built some small thatch huts, four metres square, for the families who were unable to live harmoniously with others. These were called *phum thmey* ('new habitations'), whereas the older homes were called *pteah moultanh* or houses belonging to the 'base' people. Var and her children lived in one of the latter.

Working hours in Sla were irregular but usually long. On some days, Var was woken up at 1 a.m., worked till 7 a.m., had half an hour for breakfast and then continued working in the fields until 11.30 or 12. A short break for lunch was then followed by more work, until 5 or 5.30 p.m. and sometimes it was dark again by the time she returned to her house.

Var had never planted rice before and was unhappy to have to do it; the locals taught her well enough, but usually mocked and insulted her while doing so. The Khmer Rouge cadres would say, 'Look at your hands, they are used to holding a pen, and not to hard work'. The peasants, too, when they were uprooting rice seedlings, had a habit of tapping them against their feet to shake off the soil. Var says they were very adept at making sure the soil went all over her, even from metres away. (She says she often tried to do this back to them, but without success.)

Everybody in the village worked as hard as the next person, Var says. However, the peasants definitely got more attention and more food than the city people. When the peasants received rice, Var often ate only rice porridge. At other times, when the peasants received meat, Var got only rice with salt. 'If a pig was killed only the peasants could eat pork,' she says, noting that this was 'contrary to the socialist theory of equality'. It was the same, she says, with the peasants' willingness to exchange food or fish with those who could offer them 'gold'.

Most peasants frequently told Var in detail about their 'horrifying' experiences during the war when Sla was a target of U.S. and Lon Nol bombers. They told how they had to dig trenches, and be prepared at any time to run from the fields, put out cooking fires, and so on. They hated bomber pilots and would have killed any bomber pilot whom they came across, Var says.

The peasants in Sla 'really liked' the Khmer Rouge. Whereas the Lon Nol

Government had neglected them, the Khmer Rouge did help them to harvest and transplant rice. The peasants also had high hopes of the revolution as far as their living standards were concerned, hopes that Var thinks would have been discarded over the ensuing years, along with an erosion of support for the Khmer Rouge.

However, there were a number of peasants in Sla, about one-quarter of them, according to Var, who unlike the others were hostile towards the Khmer Rouge in 1975. These were older peasants who supported Prince Sihanouk and were disappointed that he had not been reinstated after the April 1975 victory. They kept the Prince's portrait in their homes.

The Khmer Rouge leader in Sla was a 27-year-old woman cadre named 'friend Ying', a native of the village who had joined the movement in 1970 and was said to have been trained in Hanoi during the war, after which she took up her post in Sla. Var says she was very tough, very strict and very efficient. Towards the end of 1975, she volunteered to join the army in response to a recruitment drive.

When Var arrived in Phnom Chiso in May 1975, there was only one functioning Buddhist *wat* in the entire district. It was inhabited by only three monks, who spent a lot of their time raising pigs, tending cattle and working in the fields. They also presided at traditional village *bon,* or festivals, some of which were held during Var's time in Sla. By the end of 1975, however, the monks had been obliged to leave the monastery and become laymen.

Although food was short and the regime strict, Var did not mention any deaths from starvation or execution while she lived in Sla.

In December 1975, Var and her daughters, along with hundreds of thousands of people, including all of the 70 Phnom Penh families from Sla, were taken by train to Phnom Srok district, in distant Battambang Province on the Thai border. They lived in Phnom Srok for four months, working in the fields, until rice supplies became very low. As rice was 'abundant' in nearby Thmar Puok district, the Khmer Rouge transferred 2,000 families of Phnom Penh people there from Phnom Srok.

Var found herself in the village of Andaung Klong, in Thmar Puok. There were 354 families in the village, over 1,000 people in all, many of them originating from Phnom Penh. Again she worked in the fields, although she was several times asked if she preferred to spin, sew or raise pigs. After a year she said that she would like to sew, and spent most of 1977-78 making black clothes for the local inhabitants on a sewing-machine.

She noticed a difference between the Khmer Rouge in Thmar Puok and those in Phnom Chiso. The ones she now lived under were much more cruel. A 'small number' of people were executed in 1976, the year in which she says the 'killings began'.

There was no shortage of food in Thmar Puok in 1976, although there had been more in 1975, she heard. The locals told her that the year before they had had 'plenty' of food, more than under the Lon Nol regime.

However, the situation deteriorated steadily. Movement was restricted – a permit was needed to travel even five kilometres, although Var often visited the nearby village of Srae Memai, two kilometres away. At some point in 1976, children were taken from their parents and assigned communal tasks. Sokmalee and Panita were put to work making natural fertilizer. Then in late 1976, all family meals came to an end and everybody in Andaung Klong was obliged to eat in a communal dining hall. Food rations became tight from 1977. In June, July and August 1977, the local Khmer Rouge leadership changed several times. Also during 1977, there were about 100 deaths in the village, from executions and from starvation and disease. But the year 1978 and the early part of 1979 were by far the worst. About 500 people, Var estimates, about half of the village population, died or were killed during that period. People who were caught simply complaining were executed; if a person accidentally broke a ploughshare while working in the fields, he would be accused of being negligent with the property of *angkar* and would be shot, Var says.

It was considerably worse for the Phnom Penh people in Andaung Klong than for the local peasants. Mistakes made by the city people would lead to their certain execution, and they all lived in constant dread. The same offence by a peasant would often be overlooked; still, Var is quite sure that in Thmar Puok in 1978-79, unlike in Takeo in 1975, every single person in her village hated the Khmer Rouge bitterly.

Var managed to survive through the worst period mainly through cunning. In fact, exceptionally, she considers 1978 the easiest year for her, because she had by then begun to benefit from the close relations she had cultivated with some of the Khmer Rouge. From the beginning Var had studied the characteristics and mannerisms of the Khmer Rouge, and had come to know their 'weak points', as she calls them. She maintains that it was 'quite easy' for someone who is reasonably clever to live under the Khmer Rouge.

They liked people who worked very hard. Var would get up early each morning and go to work before most of the others, and finish work later. She thus found herself eating late at night with Khmer Rouge, even the village and district chiefs; she was allowed to wait on them and share their food. They had better food than the ordinary people, Var says, and they would talk about work during the entire meal. Unlike the other Phnom Penh people, then, Var managed to remain healthy. Also, her children were allowed to live with her.

Var notes that the Khmer Rouge, despite their many drawbacks, had very good discipline and never molested women. They also liked people who were lowly and humble, and not proud or ostentatious. When they asked her to do something, Var would reply: 'I don't know how to do it but I will try my best', which always made a good impression. She also flattered them to some extent, and asked them to teach her the political vocabulary they used. She would address them as *'bang'* ('older brother') and not by the term usually favoured by the Khmer Rouge, *'mit'* ('friend'), which denotes equality.

Although her identity was known to the Khmer Rouge in Takeo, once she arrived in Battambang Var never admitted that she had been a schoolteacher in Phnom Penh. Had she done so, she would certainly have been executed, she says. She pretended that she could write only in a very clumsy style. Sometimes she would claim, when asked her profession under the old regime, that she had sold fried bananas in Phnom Penh. The Khmer Rouge would usually express surprise at this, noting that her skin was not as dark as that of Khmer workers and peasants. She then would reply glibly that she had sold the fried bananas in a stall in the shade. Sometimes she was believed; if she was not, she thought she might be suspected of being an ethnic Chinese, therefore a capitalist trader. She would then add that she had been a maid-servant to a Chinese family in Phnom Penh. On another occasion, when a Khmer Rouge noted her skill at sewing, she told him that she had been a dressmaker in Phnom Penh.

Day and night Var would study the behaviour of the Khmer Rouge. Copying them, she ate her food with her hands. Some of the Phnom Penh people in Andaung Klong continued to eat with a fork and spoon, which Var thought was ill-advised. Others, especially former soldiers or officers, would continue to behave in a superior fashion, or simply swagger or boast of their skills. She doesn't know if there were many people like her who managed to keep their identity secret.

In February 1979, news reached the village that Vietnamese troops were approaching. All the cadres and soldiers of the Khmer Rouge fled the area. Not long after, over 100 Vietnamese soldiers arrived in Andaung Klong, with eight tanks. 'They didn't do anything,' Var says; they just established a camp and guarded it. Then they went around to the villagers in their homes, tending the sick, handing out medicine to those who needed it, and fetching water for some of the people. Some of the people were particularly undernourished; the Vietnamese killed a buffalo and gave them the meat. Finally, they opened up the 'economics hall' *(kleang setakec)* which had been established by the Khmer Rouge and took out rice and salt, distributing it to the villagers. Inside there was also a large store of silverware, pots and possessions that had been taken from the people by the Khmer Rouge. The Vietnamese invited the villagers to go and take what they needed from it. Var says the people liked the Vietnamese soldiers, even though they could hardly speak Khmer and were not accompanied by any Kampuchean officials.

Var says she became friendly with a Vietnamese officer with a star on his hat. When Var didn't go to the *kleang setakec,* he came to her house and said that she could go in and take what she wanted just like the others. Var replied that she didn't want much because she intended to return to Phnom Penh as soon as possible, since the Vietnamese had given people permission to do so. (At this point, Var says, she was not even considering escaping to Thailand.) The officer invited Var to return with the Vietnamese soldiers when they left. Nevertheless, Var went to the *kleang setakec* and took some sugar, rice and meat for herself and her children.

When Var pointed out that the people were worried that if the Vietnamese left, the Khmer Rouge soldiers would return and harm them, the officer replied that there was little danger of that since the Vietnamese troops were all over the place.

After only four days, during which no work was done in the village at all and there was a large feast, the Vietnamese troops headed back towards Battambang. 50 or 60 families of Phnom Penh people followed them at a distance. (Var pointed out that, of these families, only two out of 10 had not lost their fathers.) Var's brother was sick at the time, so she decided to wait until he recovered before going back to Phnom Penh. About eight kilometres from the village, the returnees stumbled upon mines laid by Khmer Rouge soldiers, and many of them were killed. 16 kilometres further on, the survivors camped for the night, some distance from the Vietnamese troops. They were attacked by Khmer Rouge soldiers who threw grenades among them. Nearly all of them died in the attack, Var heard. Apparently the Vietnamese camp nearby was not attacked.

Back in Andaung Klong, Khmer Rouge soldiers returned. They only stayed in the village during the day, and were 'calmer' than before. They asked who had collaborated with the Vietnamese, and who had allowed the Vietnamese to kill the buffalo and open up the *kleang setakec.* The terrified peasants replied that the Phnom Penh people had done this, although in fact everyone had, Var says. While this was happening Var was hiding in the house; the peasants told the Khmer Rouge that she had gone with the other Phnom Penh people and had probably been killed by the mines.

In the nearby village of Srae Memai, the returning Khmer Rouge executed 17 men whom they accused of co-operating with the Khmer Serei (or 'Free Khmer', a right-wing guerrilla group).

People in Andaung Klong had asked Var if she wanted to escape with them to Thailand on many occasions, but she had never dared. Then, at the end of the first week in March, there was a big meeting called of all the Khmer Rouge cadres and soldiers in Thmar Puok. Many of them went there. Var told those passing through the village that she was going fishing, and walked to Srae Memai. There she met up with people whom she had known for the past two years, and soon after they all set off for Thailand. Nearly the whole village of Srae Memai left; Var was the only person from Phnom Penh in the group of 207 which arrived in Thailand on 12 March 1979.

'You Used To Be Happy and Prosperous, Now It's Our Turn: Srey Pich Chnay

Interview with Srey Pich Chnay, *by Ben Kiernan and Chanthou Boua, in the Surin refugee camp in Thailand on 5 March 1979, and at Ban Phluang, Surin, on 15 March and 19 April 1979. What follows is an exact rendition of what he told us, except that we have ordered the events in sequence. Comments or statements not made by Chnay himself appear in square brackets.*

Chnay was born in 1955. By the time the 1970-75 Kampuchean war was ending, he was a student of fine arts at the University of Phnom Penh. He says he and nearly all his friends wanted the revolutionary Khmer Rouge to win the war. Some of them in fact tried to persuade soldiers of the Lon Nol army whom they knew to abandon their posts. When the war did end they were jubilant; Chnay had no ideas about how things might turn out, but he didn't expect any hard times.

When the Khmer Rouge ordered the evacuation of the city, Chnay complied, leaving Phnom Penh on 19 April 1975 in a group of seven families, most of which, like his own, included a large number of children. The reason they heard for the evacuation was the the U.S. might be about to bomb the capital. People were told that they would be able to return after three days and to take nothing with them. 'Everyone' believed this, Chnay says. The atmosphere of danger was heightened by helicopters hovering overhead and airplanes dropping food on the roads.

While marching through the city, Chnay saw the bodies of soldiers near the stadium who had been expelled from a nearby hospital and then executed. Some ethnic Chinese citizens gathered on rooftops lining the streets to hail the victorious army; the Khmer Rouge troops fired at them. Also killed were some people who refused to leave the city, and several high-ranking people of the defeated regime who argued with the conquerors for some reason. The Khmer Rouge soldiers were all under 20 years of age.

Ten days out of Phnom Penh, people on the roads were told they could now head for their families' villages of origin. However, within a specified time, if they had not arrived there, they had to remain in the village nearest where they were. There was some food available for the evacuees along the way, but it was not provided by the Khmer Rouge themselves. People who had brought money with them could buy food from the villagers in places they passed through; some items such as pork were very expensive. Exhaustion may have taken a greater toll than hunger; Chnay says he saw between 1,000 and 2,000 bodies of people who had died on the road before him, during the two weeks that he spent walking.

Of the group of seven families Chnay was travelling with, one person had died by the time they arrived in Takeo City, about 60 kilometres from Phnom Penh. From the city they were assigned to different villages in Takeo Province. Chnay and his family ended up in a village near Prey Lovea called Samor Khmae, where they were to spend the next eight months.

The 200 families of peasants in Samor Khmae were now joined by 500 families of former Phnom Penh people. A number of the latter, including several schoolteachers, were sons and daughters or close relatives of the locals. Three or four or even six families of evacuees were put up in each peasant's house, or under the house, or under nearby trees, sleeping in hammocks. The Khmer Rouge in the village began distributing food to the new arrivals.

According to Chnay, the local villagers were 'supporters of the Khmer Rouge'; they had been through the war with them and had been 'taught' to hate city dwellers whom they regarded as 'oppressive'. The Khmer Rouge treated the peasants as a separate group, distributing more food to them than to the city people, and assigning them easier tasks (usually around the village), whereas the city people almost always worked in the fields. Sometimes the peasants as well as the Khmer Rouge themselves, would say to the newcomers, 'You used to be happy and prosperous. Now it's our turn.'

If a pig was slaughtered for a festival or for another reason, the peasants invariably got more pork to eat than the city people. Also, there were occasional fraternal gatherings of Khmer Rouge members and about 50 or 60 peasants from Samor Khmae and three nearby villages. Plenty of food was consumed on these occasions, which took place in the 'economic warehouse' *(kleang setakec)* built by the Khmer Rouge, access to which was completely forbidden to everyone else. Some peasants 'spied' on city people for the Khmer Rouge.

The Khmer Rouge made frequent summary confiscations of possessions from the city people. On the grounds that *'angkar'* [the organization] needs it', people that Chnay knew of lost jewellery, cars and in fact any possessions that were obvious and desired by the soldiers. Not all of this was for the personal use of the soldiers: one Mercedes 220 that had brought an urban family to Samor Khmae was, like most other cars from Phnom Penh in the village, cut in two across the middle. The metal from the rear of the car was melted down to make ploughshares; the motor was adapted to drive a water pump (it didn't always work and there was a shortage of fuel) and the wheels were attached to ox-carts.

Sometimes the Khmer Rouge confiscated possessions like ox carts from the peasants as well. Chnay says that half of the locals were rich and the other half poor peasants; they sometimes quarrelled among themselves. The poor regarded the rich peasants as 'bloodsuckers' who had 'taken from the poor' their large plots of land, their oxen or their buffaloes. Such disagreements would be taken to *angkar,* who would resolve them by confiscating the excess wealth of the rich, or by sending the rich peasants elsewhere.

Despite discrimination against them, the city people generally received sufficient food. During Chnay's eight months in Samor Khmae, not more than 20 people died of disease and hunger there. Those who died were ethnic Chinese who were very unused to hard labour and the difficulties of rural life. A further 15 people, rich or high-ranking officials and soldiers from the Lon Nol regime (including four women), were executed in Samor Khmae during the same period.

The labour *was* hard: everyone, including children, worked the same long hours set by the Khmer Rouge in the village. People rose at 3.30 or 4 a.m.; city people worked in the fields until 11.30 or 12 noon, when they were brought rice porridge which they ate during a break of less than one hour. Work continued until about 5.30 or 6 p.m. In addition they would work about six nights each month for several hours, usually when a particular job needed doing, such as thatching the roofs of houses. Occasionally, there were meetings at night during which people were lectured on the Khmer Rouge ideology.

The Khmer Rouge leader in Samor Khmae was known as Ta ('grandfather') Chaem. Another official, known as the *protean anoukana,* was called Srouy.

He was a former schoolteacher, about 32 years old. Occasionally, high-ranking Khmer Rouge leaders passed through the village; when they did the people were temporarily moved elsewhere.

On 29 December 1975, all 500 families of Phnom Penh people were obliged by the Khmer Rouge to set out on foot for Takeo City, from where they were to go by train to Battambang Province, in the far north-west of Kampuchea. They walked for two hard days and nights; some of the oxen they brought with them died of exhaustion and they had to haul the ox carts themselves. Before they left Samor Khmae, the poorer peasants there had 'advised' the city people to leave behind things like bicycles that they still had in their possession. The peasants told them that *angkar* needed these things and wanted the people to abandon them. But Chnay thinks the peasants intended to keep them for themselves. Some of the city people, nevertheless, managed to retain things like rings and watches that could be hidden.

It was a month before the entire group had completed their journey on foot and by train. The train was crowded; some people, sitting on top of the carriages, fell off and were killed. Others died of disease in the cramped conditions. Chnay made the journey on the train with a group of 20 families. During it, two or three of the people died and many others were sick.

Chnay and his family arrived in the town of Sisophon in late January 1976. Loudspeakers greeted them with instructions for single people over 15 years of age, of both sexes, to assemble and join the *chalat,* or mobile work groups. The purpose of the *chalat* was described as 'to build up the country'; those who joined were promised a good life and adequate food rations. For the next four days, a large amount of food was provided for the potential *chalat* members.

After 10 days in Sisophon, the new *chalat* members were all taken to a locality in nearby Preah Net Preah to harvest rice. There was a total of 2,400 men and 3,000 women, nearly all from Phnom Penh, organized into groups of 100, with three or four groups in each locality. Within these were small groups of 10, each led by three people, all of whom were local villagers. Chnay's parents and young brothers and sisters were also taken to Preah Net Preah, but not to Ampil village, where Chnay ended up. Chnay was told that he could rejoin his family once he had done a certain amount of work harvesting, raising dykes and digging canals, etc.

Although food rations were sufficient, at one and a half cans of rice per person per day in Ampil, disease was more prevalent in the Sisophon area than it had been in Takeo. Security was much tighter, too; Chnay says this was because of the proximity of the Thai border. Movement was restricted (Chnay needed permission in order to visit the local peasants) and assemblies were forbidden. Many of the local people had sons who had been in the Lon Nol army; at that stage these had not been arrested by the Khmer Rouge.

From February 1976 until August 1978, Chnay's *chalat* worked in nine different villages all over northern Battambang Province. Chnay thus obtained a reasonably broad view of what took place there.

After about a month in Ampil, Chnay and his *chalat* were taken to a village called O Rumchek, to build irrigation dykes. For the first few weeks there, the work was hard but the food was adequate. The youths talked, laughed and sang songs while they worked. Two of them manned each *banki*, or bucket, for moving earth.

But after two or three weeks, things became tougher. Singing and laughing were frowned upon: 'finishing your job is the only task to think about' was one order the youths received. Each person now had to carry two *banki* on a shoulder pole, and move three cubic metres of earth per day. Sometimes, if a worker did not accomplish this, he might receive no food for that day. Normal food rations were cut, and working hours lengthened. At night there were frequent meetings in which the old regime was criticized and the value of the new for the country was explained by Khmer Rouge speakers.

The next village Chnay worked in was called Phnom Kombao and was in Preah Net Preah district. Here, food rations consisted of only rice porridge; still, there were no deaths from starvation. The *chalat's* job was to build a 13 kilometre long canal, apparently not for irrigation purposes but for the transportation of rice.

On 20 March 1976, Chnay went to vote in the national elections. The polls were heavily guarded and there were red flags everywhere. On the ballot paper, there was only one name, which Chnay had never heard before; he was instructed to place it in a box, and did so. Chnay points out that only people who had neat clothes were allowed to vote. The rest stayed behind and worked 'as punishment', he says. [Perhaps the polling was filmed for propaganda purposes, although Chnay did not make this point – BK.]

Early in April 1976, at Phnom Kombao, three members of Chnay's *chalat* attempted to escape to Thailand. They were captured; one of them had a gun. Under questioning, this man revealed his association with some other members of the *chalat.* The Khmer Rouge sent the would-be escapees to Sisophon. Then, they asked the rest of the *chalat* if they had any general complaints; if they did, 'schools' would be set up to re-educate them, the Khmer Rouge said. Nobody who had any complaints raised them.

Next, *angkar* asked everyone to disclose their personal history. Saying that Phnom Penh would be opened up again and developed, they offered people the chance to go back there if they disclosed their former occupations. Many teachers and former army officers registered their names and gave their personal histories. Several friendly Khmer Rouge members had advised a few people not to apply to take up their old occupations; Chnay, knowing this, didn't believe that *angkar's* offer was genuine. So he went off for a swim. But while he was away, one of his friends, a former student at Phnom Penh's *lycee* Sisowath, registered Chnay's name as well as his own. One afternoon, four trucks arrived and took away 250-300 people who had registered, including Chnay. Before leaving, they were all given plenty of food to eat and told they were going to Sisophon.

Five hours later, after dark, the trucks reached Sisophon and stopped outside a rice mill. As people got off the trucks their hands were bound and they were tied together with rope in groups of 10. The terrified prisoners asked what was happening to them, but were told only to wait and see. They were all marched a long distance through rice fields; escape was impossible. They spent that night in a large brick building.

The next morning interrogations began. They were all asked: 'What section of the Lon Nol army did you work in ?', as if it was beyond doubt that every one of them was a former military. Some of the prisoners were beaten, and others 'confessed' a false military background out of fear. Chnay says this was the first time he had received brutal treatment at the hands of the Khmer Rouge.

The next three months Chnay spent imprisoned, along with 78 other men (he never saw the other 150 or so again). The inmates were in adjacent rooms; in Chnay's room there were 32 men, all in chains. They received only rice porridge to eat, but according to their guards this was better than the rations received by the rest of the population at that time.

In June, Chnay and some of the men in his room managed to remove their chains. Four of them ran for it; there were gunshots outside. The next morning Chnay, who had decided not to run with the others because his feet were too sore, and the rest of the men in the room were taken to a place called Svay, near Ampil. There they were blindfolded with black cotton and separated into three groups. The first two groups, of 10 men each, were all executed in front of Chnay's eyes. Just as his own group of eight stepped forward to be shot, a big car pulled up at the site. A high-ranking cadre, who spoke with a Phnom Penh accent, got out and ordered that the shootings cease since the prisoners had done nothing seriously wrong. Chnay was saved.

The cadre, whom Chnay thinks was probably a former schoolteacher, then left. [Presumably he had come specifically to try to prevent the executions.] Chnay expressed the view that the cruel jail attendants, acting without orders, initiated the killings themselves.

A week later, Chnay was released from jail. But his hands were still bound, and groups of 10 people were tied together with long ropes. Each person could only move 10 metres independently. Chnay worked in the fields this way for another six weeks, returning to sleep in the prison each night. Then for a time he worked in the fields without bonds, still returning to the jail at night. During this period one Khmer Rouge soldier who felt sorry for him used to give Chnay cigarettes and small amounts of extra food.

Finally Chnay was told to rejoin his *chalat,* at a village called O Rumduol. When he arrived there he found that the jail attendants had indeed been right about the meagre food rations received by the general population. *Chalat* workers were existing on half the rice ration they had been receiving in February and March. The work was harder and rests extremely rare; only occasionally were *chalat* members allowed to go fishing after work in order to supplement their diet. Some women, old people and ethnic Chinese began to die of starvation and diseases like dysentery. Traditional medicines such as roots were encouraged by the Khmer Rouge, but were only effective against certain diseases. Quinine and tetracyclin were available in small quantities, but were usually reserved for use by the Khmer Rouge themselves. Some women workers stopped menstruating.

Chalat members were generally not allowed into villages to mingle with the other inhabitants. Some, however, managed to sneak to see their parents or for other reasons (a few of them were caught and tortured by the Khmer Rouge troops). Although there were a number of hungry children with distended stomachs in the villages, the *chalat* members got the impression that the people there ate better than themselves. They had banana and coconut trees, cows and chickens, etc. Khmer Rouge in the villages attempted to count all these assets and prevent the people from eating them, but they were not always successful. Young children would watch out for approaching Khmer Rouge while their parents killed a chicken. If they were discovered, they would be reprimanded.

Based on his experience of hunger in a number of places between April 1976 and August 1978, Chnay estimates that of a group of 1,000 people in northern Battambang, 500 may well have died during that time (mostly of starvation but also including those executed), the bulk of them during 1977-78 Chnay points out that those who died were mostly former urban dwellers.

During the rest of 1976 and 1977, Chnay worked in the following villages: Wat Smach, Trapeang Thmar, Nam Tau and Phnom Koun Khlaeng. Although they worked according to plans drawn up by the Khmer Rouge, the *chalat* members did have meetings in which they decided how best to do the job. Occasionally their work was inspected by high-ranking Khmer Rouge members who arrived in motor vehicles; the workers were ordered not to look at these people. Sometimes eight or nine workers would pull a plough. Daily supervision of Chnay's *kong* (a group of 100 *chalat* workers) was carried out by Ta Val, who was in charge of four or five *kong* in all. A former teacher at Wat Chumpu school in Pochentong, Phnom Penh, Val was said to have studied in Hanoi after becoming a revolutionary.

Chnay did not like Val, who sometimes said that anyone who tried to escape to Thailand would be shot. According to Khmer Rouge books and newspapers which Chnay saw, people were not meant to address others by the derogatory term 'A' or 'Aing'. Val took no notice of this instruction. He always carried a pistol, and food for him and his four subordinates (who were of local peasant origin) was prepared by as many as ten people. Chnay thinks that if only some of the socialist theory he knew beforehand and had heard the Khmer Rouge express lip service to had been implemented, life would not have been bad. But he says none of it was. At least by late 1976, youth in the *chalat* were quite sure that 'everything was going wrong'.

Early in 1977, a group of female Khmer Rouge (many of them only 17 or 18 years old) from the South-west Zone mainly from Takeo and Kandal Provinces, arrived in the area. They were led by Me ('mother') Chaem, who was about 40 years old. Chnay heard she was married to a drunkard. She took up administrative work in Preah Net Preah district.

In Chnay's *chalat,* the women who arrived were led by Neary Kom, a former teacher whom Chnay had met once before in Preah Net Preah. She was about 35 and very 'sweet' to the people, in Chnay's opinion. Her followers were not always genial, however.

In April 1977, Chnay heard, Ta Val was executed one day as he was returning from the reservoir whose construction he was supervising. His crime was to have 'co-operated with reactionaries'. In June, Ta At, the chief *(Kana damban)* of Battambang's No. 5 region and Val's former superior, was arrested. A new group of officials from Phnom Penh had arrived in helicopters, striking fear into every single Khmer Rouge in the area. Ta At and all his cadres were then executed, and publicly criticized.

In the meantime, the female cadres from the south-west had been very active among the people, asking them about their problems, and distributing medicine and clothes. Food was the people's biggest problem, however. While there was a considerable improvement for one month during which the women distributed rations of rice to the people, rice porridge rations were resumed after that and hunger set in again.

The women from the south-west also enquired at length about people's personal histories. Chnay thinks the women were allied to the new local leaders to whom they were passing on such information. At any rate, during 1977, many people disappeared after being led away by soldiers. Chnay believes that former city dwellers were undoubtedly killed, while peasants were simply moved to another locality.

Sexual relations were forbidden. Even to visit his sister, Chnay needed permission from cadre, who first had to be satisfied that the girl was in fact Chnay's sister. Marriages became collective affairs; parents (and on occasions the bride as well) were allowed no say in the matter.

At the end of 1977, Chnay and a number of others were sent to a place called Phnom Kong Var for 'training'. He spent three months there, clearing forest during the day and attending political meetings designed to 'change attitudes' during the evenings. Each worker had to clear one *rai* (one-sixth of a hectare) per day; or rather, if they achieved this, their rations would be increased. At the meetings they were told that if they worked hard and spent a sufficient period 'helping everyone' in this way, they would be able to go back to Phnom Penh and resume their former occupations. They all worked hard in expectation of this; many of them were former Lon Nol military, who had borne one or two stripes.

Then, early in 1978, Chnay rejoined the larger *chalat* group at a village called Phum Daun Chraeng. He found that people were now being led away by soldiers every day and every night, at least after April. In that month, yet another group of officials arrived and arrested their predecessors. This group came from the Western Zone, in particular Kompong Chhnang Province. Saying they were out to demolish the previous 'regime' and to 'get the Khmer Krohom' (Khmer Reds), they encouraged people to air their grievances and at the same time made every effort to discover people's personal backgrounds. They spoke reassuringly and many people were honest with them about their backgrounds.

In fact, however, during the next four months they arrested and led away more people than any previous group had. On several occasions when they approached Chnay, he thought they were coming to get him and made himself scarce for a couple of hours. Out of 100 people arrested and taken away, Chnay thinks 95 would have been former urban dwellers.

The women from the south-west remained in place and in good relations with the people.

In mid-1978, the *chalat* was transferred to the village of Kouk Tayou in Preah Net Preah, where they set to work planting rice. The village was not far from that where Chnay's parents now lived; one day Chnay was ordered to carry out an errand in the village where he had last heard of his father and mother two years or more earlier. Taking two cans of rice which he had managed to hide away over previous months, Chnay managed to find his father and give him the rice. His father asked him to return the next day, and Chnay did. His father knew that he was about to be arrested, Chnay says, but nevertheless he advised Chnay to stay where he was and not try to escape, because things might improve after a while, he said. His father was 68 years old.

Not long after, Chnay heard that his father had indeed been taken away and presumably killed, along with Chnay's younger brother and sister. Three weeks later, Chnay escaped, along with two brothers, a brother-in-law and their wives. Near the Thai border they reached Phum Being, where they had to cross deep water. All the girls drowned while swimming across; after a 17-day journey, Chnay, his two brothers and his brother-in-law arrived in Thailand on 13 September 1978.

'We Just Had To Work Like Animals': Hok Sarun

Interview by Ben Kiernan and Chanthou Boua with Hok Sarun, *a Kampuchean peasant refugee in the Aranyaprathet refugee camp in Thailand, 1 April 1979. What follows is exactly what Sarun told us, although we have arranged events in sequence. Statements not made by Sarun himself appear in square brackets.*

Sarun's story is of particular interest, partly because it is that of a poor peasant, a member of the group upon whom the Pol Pot regime claims to have based its support. Also, Sarun was a member of the chalat *work group in Region No. 5 in Battambang Province, as was Srey Pich Chnay whose account Sarun's corroborates in important respects. Sarun and Chnay were unknown to each other, both in Kampuchea and in Thailand, and were interviewed in separate refugee camps.*

Sarun was born in 1954, in the village of Kencho, Preah Net Preah district, Battambang Province, Kampuchea. He had five sisters, three of whom were married by 1975. His parents were among the very poorest in the village, he says, owning two hectares of rice land. [This is a higher than average farm for most of Kampuchea, apart from Battambang Province where rice was generally sown by broadcasting and family farms tended to be larger than elsewhere.] By the late 1960s, Sarun's father was already an old man and Sarun spent his days helping him in the fields.

About 2,500 people lived in the village during the 1970-75 war. The richest farmers among them owned one or two ox carts, two oxen and 20 or 30 *rai* of rice land, or about three to five hectares. The poorest owned only 10 *rai* and were sometimes without livestock. [Such class distinctions are muted compared to the average for Battambang Province.] Sarun says Kencho wasn't a rich village at all; life was tough and there was just enough food to eat.

At some point during the war, many of the villagers were drafted into the Lon Nol government local militia. The only way this could be avoided was for an able-bodied man to take his family elsewhere, which many did. Once, in 1974, members of the Khmer Rouge army attacked the village militia post and then withdrew.

When the war ended in April 1975, those who had moved elsewhere returned home. Also, the victorious Khmer Rouge took control of Kencho. They immediately called a meeting and took down everyone's names; they drew up three separate lists of wealthy people and government officials, rich or middle peasants and workers, and poor peasants and workers. To find out everyone's full biography and social position, they double checked: Sarun's neighbours were asked about his parents' social standing, past activities, the number of children they had and what they did, and so on.

Two weeks after their arrival, the Khmer Rouge executed four entire families of farming people whom they described as 'rich'; Sarun says they had owned two ox carts or two ploughs. The troops also executed the abbot of the local Buddhist monastery at Cha Loeu, publicly hanging his robes on a tree afterwards. All other monks were obliged to become laymen.

All land, tools and livestock in the village were communalized. Rice was from that point rationed out by the Khmer Rouge in small but adequate daily quantities (although less than the average daily intake for 1974). Work groups were organized both to till the land and to gather various edible materials from the countryside.

The Khmer Rouge told people that they had to co-operate in working hard to build up the country. They didn't try to recruit many followers in Kencho but did appoint three locals as village officials. Their names were Chom, Kun and Chhet. Sarun says these three were 'not rich and not poor' and that they 'had been able to get by in the past'. One of them was a former barber. The privileges that went with their new positions included larger food rations than the rest of the people; they also had the right to kill livestock for their food, whereas the villagers usually made do with rice porridge.

In August 1975, male and female unmarried youths were drafted into the *chalat,* or mobile work group. Sarun and one unmarried sister joined, and the other, youngest, sister was obliged to join a 'children's group'. His parents cried 'like rain' as their children departed.

Before the Prochum Ben festival, many families of townspeople arrived in

Kencho and neighbouring Prasath areas. The unmarried youths among them were also drafted into work groups and many of them joined Sarun's *chalat* at a place called Ta Dek. The Kencho area was now organized into four co-operatives, numbered one to four, each with about 2,000 families including the new arrivals. [Given Sarun's estimate of the pre-1975 population as 2,500, the influx of urban people into the area appears to have numbered more than 7,000 families.] Each co-operative had its children's group, whose task was to make natural fertilizer from manure they collected and plants they cut down.

Northern Battambang was now known as Region No. 5, and was composed of four districts – Preah Net Preah, Sisophon, Phnom Srok and Thmar Puok. The Region *chalat* numbered 5,000 youths. They were divided into groups, or *kong,* of 100 workers, each with its own communal kitchen. Rice was delivered to these kitchens by the Khmer Rouge, and the *chalat* members then cooked their own meals. These consisted of one can of rice per person per day, which made up one bowl per meal, sometimes with salt and the Kampuchean dish *prahoc* as well. Every two weeks or so they ate fresh or smoked fish.

The first major task for Sarun's *chalat* was to build a reservoir *(tanub)* at a place called O Runteah Bainh. A retaining wall was built seven kilometres long; it was 10 metres wide at the base, and six at the top. Sarun says no water was or could easily have been introduced into it as there was no water source in the area; he says it was 'not built to help the farmers'. He was not told what its purpose was. Of Khmer Rouge labour management he says: 'If they want something done somewhere, they just take people there and get them to do it; they never explain why. We just had to work like animals.' During four to six weeks in this place there were many deaths among the workers from overwork and lack of food. Some who protested these conditions were executed.

From there Sarun's *chalat* group and others, totalling 5,000 workers, were sent to clear the forest at Phnom Kong Var, near Sisophon district, for four months. During that time, while labouring to uproot a tree, Sarun began coughing blood and was sent to recuperate in a hospital *(paet)* in Svay Sisophon. He rested there for 28 days, without being able to inform his parents. Medicines in the hospital were traditional, as Western medicine was reserved for officials of the Khmer Rouge.

By now between 400 and 500 of the 5,000 *chalat* workers were dead, mostly those who had never experienced hard work before. Even in the hospital, rations consisted of only salt and rice porridge. Patients cut human flesh from the corpses of those who died beside them, and barbecued and ate it. 'That is a true story', Sarun says.

From the hospital Sarun returned to work at Phnom Kong Var for a brief period. The youths worked in the rain and sun, and members of all social groups, urban and rural, complained bitterly. Sarun says any such person who complained and didn't 'struggle in their work' was executed by the Khmer Rouge. The workers were not supervised by armed soldiers, however. Troops visited the site Sarun worked at once every two or three weeks. Work was supervised by unarmed Khmer Rouge members who did not work themselves.

In early 1976, Sarun and part of his *chalat* were transferred to Trapeang Thmar to help build a reservoir there. Some of the 5,000 workers remained behind to tend crops now being grown at Phnom Kong Var.

10,000-15,000 workers assembled at Trapeang Thmar, including regional and district level *chalat* and rural and urban youths. Rainwater was intended to flow down from a hill to one side and fill the reservoir. The work began early in the year, at harvest time, and continued for two months, until late March, During this period, they ate rice.

[On 20 March 1976, according to the Khmer Rouge Government in international statements, elections were held throughout the country.] At Trapeang Thmar, according to Sarun, the population didn't vote in the elections and did not know who the candidates were. Only the Khmer Rouge soldiers voted.

Not long after, although the reservoir was not yet finished, Sarun and 10,000 of the other workers were transferred to the Prey Moan (Kouk Rumchek) area in Preah Net Preah district. Here their task was also to build a reservoir *(ang tik),* this one 500 metres square. Rations were reduced and the meals reverted to simple rice porridge.

Sarun worked at Prey Moan for 20 days. Shortly before a visit to the work-site by some high-ranking officials, the youths worked through one entire night. Then, at Buddhist New Year, Sarun was allowed to return home to visit his parents for three days. Among other things, his mother told him of some village people who had been killed by the Khmer Rouge in his absence.

At this point, members of the various district-level *chalat* returned to work in their districts. The regional *chalat* was disbanded; some of its members were sent to work at Phnom Kong Var, while others, including Sarun, went to Trapeang Thmar with the Preah Net Preah district *chalat.* There they were assigned the tasks of maintaining the reservoir [the construction of which was now apparently complete], building further irrigation works and growing dry season rice using the water now available. Sarun was to remain at Trapeang Thmar for over two years. His sister worked with another *chalat* group just over a kilometre away.

Sarun's main work now involved adjusting and maintaining the level of water in the rice fields. He rose each morning at 3 or 4 a.m., depending on when they were ordered to start work. Sometimes a bell would ring, while at other times the *protean krom,* or group leader, woke people up. Work lasted until 11 a.m. or 12 noon when they ate rice porridge and took a break. The length of the break depended on the tasks at hand; it was short when there was a lot of work to do, for example at transplanting time. They worked again until 5 or 6 p.m. and then rested.

Meetings were held at night once or twice a week, or often one night in three. The group leader, returning from a briefing by *neak thom* (literally, 'big people'), would call a meeting to repeat the message to the workers.

Usually the meetings lasted one hour to one hour and a half. Sometimes the theme was 'livelihood' *(prochum chivapeap)* or the raising of morals. But mostly the meetings were about 'struggle in work'. A set of five instructions was stressed at every meeting: 1) Solidarity and independence; 2) Adhere to the political (set); 3) Adhere to the established order *(ka cat tang).* (Sarun defined this concept with the following example, 'If they want you to go to Trapeang Thmar at night, go.') 4) Adhere to the rules and regulations of the organization *(angkar).* ('If you are sick and can't work, you must inform the superiors, not just be an absentee.') 5) Carry out the plans set by *angkar.*

Beginning in early 1977, food rations were reduced 'even more' than before. There were now only eight cans of rice for 10 people each day. To make it last the day, it invariably had to be mixed with water and made even thinner rice porridge than before. At harvest time, early in 1977 and early in 1978, higher rations briefly applied.

Sarun recalls that four or five of the *chalat* workers 'digging the earth with me' were defrocked monks who had been obliged to merge with the population. Women *chalat* members worked and lived separately from the men. Everyone worked very hard; there was no laughter or singing while working. When earthworks were being raised, each worker was assigned three cubic metres of earth to shift each day. A worker received no food until he had completed his daily assignment. Sometimes workers kept going until midnight to do so, and often friends came to help those whose progress was slower.

In his movements around northern Battambang, Sarun says he came across no villages in which the people were not mistreated. The Khmer Rouge claim to help the peasant classes was just propaganda *(khoosena),* he says, noting that he never saw any sign of assistance for the rural people. Instead, the Khmer Rouge were merely destructive; for instance, they destroyed Buddhist pagodas. They built no houses for the people; rather they simply rebuilt small houses out of the materials taken from large houses which they had demolished. Sarun's general impression of Khmer Rouge officials was that they were 'never skinny', unlike most of the general population.

However, having worked in the *chalat* from August 1975 until his escape to Thailand in August 1978, Sarun is not sure whether conditions in the village co-operatives were better or worse than those he faced. But he thinks they were much the same. His three married sisters stayed in Kencho with his parents and he is ignorant of their present fate. Although he says former city people suffered a lot more and died in much greater numbers than peasants, food rations were the same for both groups who lived and worked side by side in the co-operatives as well as in the *chalat.* There was no attempt to recruit peasants or *chalat* members into the Communist Party of Kampuchea led by Pol Pot, which Sarun says only accepted members of the administration.

During 1975-76, the overall leader of the *chalat* in Region No. 5 was a man called Val. He was an 'old cadre' who had been an active 'red' for a long time, Sarun says. He never met Val personally and didn't see him often or know anything much about his past, such as where he might have received his training. Other cadres under Val were all from Battambang, Pailin and many other places in the North-west Zone.

Early in 1977, a new group of male and female cadres from the South-west Zone arrived in Preah Net Preah. They were very tough, and began a largescale series of arrests and executions. Anyone who had been in any way connected with the Lon Nol Government disappeared, including former village chiefs and schoolteachers and people who had been Lon Nol soldiers even just for one day. Sarun's boyhood friend from Kencho, Keo Liem, was arrested and killed. Others disappeared at night. *Chalat* leader Val himself and all his cadres were also arrested and killed, Sarun heard, and replaced by newcomers from Takeo or Kampot.

The new administrators established a strict regime of food and work. People who were too sick to work were in some cases fed, in others not.

Then, in June or July 1978, a new group of male and female cadres arrived, from the Western Zone. They arrested all the cadres from the south-west. Stepping up repression even further, the new rulers were 'so tough that they even arrested members of the *chalat*' and killed them; examples he gives were sons of rich people or of former Lon Nol militiamen, or people who complained about conditions. There were huge numbers of deaths; even at the work site Sarun saw people being bashed to death by the cadres from the Western Zone.

One evening, five of Sarun's friends, three young men and two women, were arrested and killed. Their parents had not been poor before 1975. Sarun anticipated that, because he had been friendly with the five, the Khmer Rouge might come after him as well. The next night he deliberately slept some distance from his mosquito net; soldiers did in fact come but could not find him. He left the area alone on 29 July 1978, and arrived in Thailand six days and five nights later, at Kok Khyung near Wat Thmey, after travelling through the jungle.

Some time later he heard from more recent refugees that his sister in the *chalat* had been executed following his escape.

Sarun says he will only return home if he is sure that Pol Pot is dead and there are no Khmer Rouge left, and 'freedom is restored', by any leader. As for the new government of Heng Samrin, Sarun says: 'The reds always kill people . . . and Heng Samrin is a socialist, too.' Uncertain whether the new government is the same as the old, he doesn't want to return to Kampuchea, although he says there are a number in the Aranyaprathet refugee camp who do. [By late May 1979, about 2,000 refugees who arrived in Thailand before 7 January had returned to Heng Samrin's Kampuchea.]

'We Weren't Even Allowed To Speak Chinese': Tae Hui Lang

Interview with ethnic Chinese refugee from Kampuchea. Tae Hui Lang. The recorded interview took place at Chatenay-Malabry, France, on 10 August 1979, about two months after she had left Kampuchea. What follows is exactly as she told us, although we have recorded events in sequence.

Tae Hui Lang was born in the Cardomom mountains of Kampuchea's Pursat Province, of ethnic Chinese parents. After she had grown up, her family left the village and went to Pursat city where she opened a store. She married Tiv Chhim Huot.

Lang was in Pursat in April 1975, with her husband and father, when Khmer Rouge troops entered the town. On the 17th they came to the market, overturned the stalls and drove vehicles around with speakers blaring, telling those who had taken refuge in the town from the fighting in the countryside to go back to their native villages. Shopkeepers were ordered to stay for a while and 'assist' the victorious army.

Then, on 24 April the market was fired upon from the other side of the river near the provincial office; people were ordered to leave the city immediately, without being allowed to get ready or pack. The market was in chaos as people were screaming and running in all directions amidst the sound of gunfire. Lang's father asked permission from the Khmer Rouge soldiers to go into his house and pick up a few small cooking pots; he was allowed to do this but was watched by armed troops who made sure he took nothing else. Then they and two other families set out from Pursat in a car, heading north-west towards Battambang Province. Lang decided not to go to her home village in the Cardamoms, because she says that some of the people there liked her but others didn't, and she was afraid that the latter would get the Khmer Rouge to make trouble for her. At any rate, the Khmer Rouge troops in Pursat told her family to head for Battambang.

Some of the troops who had taken Pursat were ethnic Khmer villagers from the Cardamoms. They came from places like Leach and Telo and other 'nests' of the Khmer Rouge movement, as well as from most rural districts of the province. Lang knew some of them from her village, where some of them had worked for her father. They had been rice farmers, but had changed a lot since those days. 'Before, they weren't cruel, and we could understand each other. Now, we couldn't understand each other. They had power.' Most of these people had been landless labourers or farmers who could not pay their debts and had run away from their village to join the Khmer Rouge. They used to drink a lot, gamble and 'steal other people's wives'. When they now came back to their villages, they were looking for those people who had been their enemies before, in order to settle old scores. Lang knew a lot of people like this, most of whom had left their villages in 1967-69. She saw others in the Khmer Rouge units who used to live in Pursat city. Like the others, these were drinkers and gamblers, none were ex-schoolteachers. There were also some Khmer Rouge from Takeo Province who had to come to Pursat at some stage.

Lang got the impression that the Khmer Rouge were different from one place to another: 'In some places they were nice, in others bad, in some places cruel, in others not very cruel.'

There were large numbers of people walking along Highway 5 from Pursat towards Battambang. There were also many bodies by the roadside; mostly corpses of Lon Nol soldiers, Lang said. After two days travelling, they met a large crowd of people coming the other way from Battambang City. They had been given three days' notice of the evacuation, and so had brought food and clothes, etc., with them, whereas the people from Pursat had nothing. The two groups met at Maung, and from there were sent off the highway into the countryside to settle down. (At Trapeang Chong along the way, a number of marchers had been sent off the highway towards Bak Enchien, Leach, Kilo 57 and other 'nests' of the Khmer Rouge, Lang said.)

On 26 April 1975, Lang's family were ordered to settle down in the village of Kach Rotes, along with about 200 other families. There were many other small villages nearby, such as Thmey and Samrong Russei; these had all been evacuated during a big battle in the area before the end of the war. Some of the inhabitants had gone into the forest, while others had fled to Battambang; some of the latter had recently returned home, but very few, and most of these had been killed by the Khmer Rouge soon after, according to Lang. When Lang arrived, Kach Rotes was deserted and the houses were all in ruins. Nearly all the new arrivals were from Battambang City.

The Khmer Rouge told everyone to build their own houses, but to do so at least one or two kilometres from Highway 5. Once accommodation was assured, work in the fields began. At first the people survived on whatever food they had managed to bring with them or could find for themselves, but soon the Khmer Rouge cadres arranged for rice to be brought to Kach Rotes. Although this rice was old and of poor quality and there was some hunger in the ensuing months, Lang says that in general the year 1975 was 'not tough'.

After the harvest in late 1975, the entire village was put to work building dams and canals. Those who had families worked on sites near the village, while single people were taken to more distant places. Urban evacuees were treated differently from what were called 'the people of the bases' or the 'old people'; the latter were villagers who had been taken away by the Khmer Rouge during battles for the local villages, and had been 'trained' by the Khmer Rouge in their liberated zones and been through bad times with them during the war. Lang said the Khmer Rouge had helped these people work the land in the liberated zones and had also assisted them in other ways. The 'old people' had got used to a meagre diet during the war, and were all very thin although tough. She says they didn't like the Khmer Rouge; nobody did. In fact most people were scared of them, and the 'old people' yearned for freedom just like the urban evacuees. But in 1975-76 the 'old people' lived in different villages and were given higher rations of food than the urban dwellers. As a result, they had enough to eat whereas the city people were always hungry.

Kach Rotes was situated 24 kilometres from Battambang City, in Maung District of Battambang Province. The district chief was called Sou; he had been a schoolteacher before joining the revolution. The village itself was run by a committee of three people whose names were Yin, Tit and Ngor, as well as half a dozen other minor officials. They had to report any problems to the district level. Most of these people were from Takeo Province and had left their villages a long time ago to work with the Khmer Rouge; the rest were locals. In either case, Lang was told by villagers that they had been social outcasts before, people who couldn't pay their debts and had run into the forest in the year 1970. Those from Takeo had lived in villages in Pursat, such as Sala Trau and Prey Touch, for many years before 1975. The Khmer Rouge also established militia *(chhlop)* and troops called *yuthea* and *mekang.* According to Lang, the *yuthea* were in charge of 'killing anyone who did anything wrong'. A few months after arriving in the village, Lang's uncle, who had been a two-stripe officer in the Lon Nol army, was taken away and killed, without his wife being notified. He was a native of the district. Lang said ordinary soldiers, who had been commandos 'even just for a day', were executed as well.

The *yuthea,* of whom there were hundreds in the locality, had their headquarters in a pagoda. (All pagodas had been emptied and the monks forced to become civilians.) As for the *mekang,* they were recruited from the 'old people' who always had enough to eat. 'We ate only rice porridge, while they ate rice cooked in large pots.'

One Khmer Rouge cadre in Kach Rotes boasted that 'we defeated the American imperialists, now we can also defeat Thailand and Vietnam and regain the territory from them that belonged to Kampuchea historically.

After the annual harvests people were able to eat their fill for two to three months, but then the rations were always reduced again. The reason given for this was that other villages had not produced very much rice, and that the people of Kach Rotes should be charitable and help them. Trucks came and took 300-400 sacks of rice from the village to feed people in other villages. The ration became one can of rice per day for three to four people, and then less and less until, in the two or three months before the harvest, one can of rice for 10 people. People at that stage were eating leaves and gathering *trokuon* vegetables from the forest. The work was not so strenuous at that time of year, except for single people who worked hard in every season.

In late 1975, after the first harvest, communal dining was introduced. Thirty families ate together in one hall from then on. Any vegetables that were grown around people's houses were used for communal meals. But these were not of any great quantity, since there was no rest from work, and many of the workers were constantly being moved to different sites. Lang and her husband, when they were not ploughing or harrowing local rice fields, were sent to work in distant fields as far as Maung, up to 30 kilometres away, since they had no children to look after. This was despite the fact there there was much arable land around Kach Rotes which was not being used by local villagers, but by people from other areas brought there by the Khmer Rouge temporarily. Lang doesn't know the reason for this 'stupid' policy; she was simply told to go. Sometimes she and her husband had to get up at 2 or 3 a.m., take tools and draft animals and walk long distances to work. There they had to build temporary housing and would not return to Kach Rotes for several months.

At some point in 1976, about six months after the local Khmer Rouge cadre had referred to the reconquest of Kampuchean territories occupied by Thailand and Vietnam, the chief of Region No. 4 came to Kach Rotes. At a meeting he told people that Kampuchea simply wanted to defend what is now its own territory and live in peace, and that there should be no talk of fighting Thailand or Vietnam to win back lost territory.

Towards the end of 1976, the local leaders of the Khmer Rouge were replaced, including a number of people who had once been schoolteachers. They were accused of being traitors and disappeared, sent to co-operatives to do manual labour like the people. From the end of 1976, the 'old people' and the urban dwellers began to be treated equally. From then on, everyone received the same low ration of food, and the 'old people' became very hostile to the Khmer Rouge. Nevertheless, they continued to do what they were told out of fear.

After the harvest was complete, the people of Kach Rotes were put to work clearing the forest to plant corn. While doing this the branch of a tree fell on Lang, causing an injury that still hurts today. Her younger brother had a similar accident, and is now unable to walk properly; this occurred while he was digging earth to build a reservoir in the rain. He slipped and fell, and as he lay there a Khmer Rouge member accused him of being a malingerer, and refused to help him. Around the same time, Lang's uncle broke his leg while working.

Production of food was in fact rather high, according to Lang, with harvests of both heavy and light rice. Workers complained that from what they produced there should be plenty to eat. They were told to dig small canals in the area, but there was no local source of water, although there was in the Maung area. So, because of the dry season, the canals around Kach Rotes were empty five months of the year. Production could have been even higher if this labour had not been wasted. But Lang thinks the Khmer Rouge just wanted to keep people busy working. Workers were told to go and tend fields in areas they knew were unsuitable for rice-growing, but they didn't dare point this out. At other sites people had to work all year round, to little productive effect, even though they knew that the soil there could produce only one reasonable crop per year.

In 1977, Lang gave birth to a baby boy. No medical assistance was provided, but local midwives were present.

In 1977, executions of workers by the Khmer Rouge increased in number. More people were killed in 1977-78 than in 1975-76. The victims were ordinary people who had committed some minor infraction and were accused of being traitors to *angkar* (the revolutionary organization).

There was another change in the local leadership during 1977, and in the second half of 1978 a serious rift developed between Khmer Rouge members in the area. Those involved were divided into the North-western cadres and those who had recently arrived from the South-west, mostly Takeo and Kampot Provinces, but also from Kompong Chhnang. The Nirdey leaders all brought their families with them although in the militia groups accompanying them were many single people. The newcomers accused the North-western cadres of being traitors, and of 'taking rice from the people to feed the Vietnamese'. Throughout the area they gradually disarmed and arrested most of the North-west group, including the *mekang.* They accused them of having 'old ideas' *(kbal cah),* and executed them. Although some people told Lang that they had simply been sent off for re-education *(lot dam),* Lang thinks that cadres dismissed in 1978 were all killed, unlike those dismissed in 1976 and 1977.

Conditions immediately improved, but only for a short time. People were allowed to eat their fill for one or two months, but then rations were cut back drastically, to previous levels. The reason given by the new cadres was that the people were not working hard enough. 'There was not enough to eat or drink, and we were working the whole time, just like under the North-westerners. The South-west people said the North-westerners had killed many people, but in fact they were just the same and had only said this to get into power. None of those reds were any good,' Lang added.

Thus by late 1978, although the North-West group remained in control of some localities, the cadres in the area had been decimated. 'Not long after, the Vietnamese entered the area with ease,' according to Lang, pointing out that this would not have happened if the two factions had maintained their unity. Those who remained to run the Khmer Rouge administration were mostly South-west people, who were small in numbers.

11. Kampuchea Stumbles to its Feet by Ben Kiernan

In July 1978, a youth named Korb, bound hand and foot, arrived at a Pol Pot regime extermination camp. The local security chief, 'Comrade Uncle An', was handed the following note:

> Formerly this person was normal in character. Then, over about ten days, he went crazy. He was taken to be cured in the subdistrict hospital. When he is alone he is quiet, and doesn't say a word; if many people come in, first he begins to whistle, and then he sings the following rhyme out loud:
>
> O! Khmers with black blood
> Now the eight-year Buddhist prophecy is being fulfilled.
>
> Vietnam is the elder brother
> Kampuchea is the younger.
> If we do not follow the Vietnamese as our elder brothers
> There will be nothing left of the Khmer this time but ashes.
>
> O! Khmers with black blood
> Servants of the Chinese
> Killing your own nation.
>
> Now you Americans have the upper hand,
> You must repay the Khmer quickly.
>
> Because the Khmer have strived and struggled for a long time.
> Don't bring the wicked B-52s to pay us back. That's not enough.
> Bring atomic bombs. That is the repayment needed.
> Because the Khmers are building one hundred houses at a time.
>
> O! Khmers with black blood.
> There will be nothing left of the Khmer this time but ashes.
>
> O! Damrey Romeas mountains
> The timber is all gone now.
> No forest, no rocks any more.
> Because the Americans are paying Kampuchea back with blood.
> Only garlic remains.

It would be hard to find a more apt depiction of Kampuchea's tragic recent history than this troubled representation by the unknown youth Korb. It is all there: the crazed anguish of people living in the national concentration camp that was Pol Pot's Democratic Kampuchea; the brief flat statement on Pol Pot's relationship with China, not entirely accurate but closely echoing popular belief in Kampuchea today; the agonized resignation to personal and national destruction; the bitterness engendered by past American actions (such as the 1973 bombing) in Kampuchea, as well as the mysterious comment about more recent U.S. policies (were the roots of America's support for Democratic Kampuchea against Vietnam already evident to Korb in 1978?); and finally the forced dependence of the Khmers on Vietnam as their 'elder brother', without whose patronage, difficult as it may be to accept, the other factors determine 'there will be nothing left of the Khmer this time but ashes'.

I arrived in Kampuchea on 1 July 1980, and spent the next four months there. I travelled over 6,000 kilometres through most of the country's nineteen provinces. After a year-long series of applications to Heng Samrin's People's Republic of Kampuchea (P.R.K.) authorities, I was finally admitted, with the aim of gathering material to write a history of modern Kampuchea. I interviewed over 500 people, mostly peasants, in Khmer, and was thus able to get a fair idea of recent social and political events and the way people saw them. (I was able to check what people told me, more often than not in the presence of a young government-appointed guide, against what one hundred Khmer refugees had told me in unsupervised interviews in 1979 about their experiences under the Pol Pot and Heng Samrin regimes before they left Kampuchea for France. There were no great inconsistencies.)

Eighteen months after the 'elder brothers' moved in, I found near universal relief that Pol Pot's regime had come to an end. Despite the continued presence of 35,000 Democratic Kampuchea troops on the Thai border and several pockets of resistance inside the country, people's confidence in their ability to build a relatively stable and unharassed life for themselves was noticeable. Two political factors mitigate this confidence – uncertainties about the future generated by the presence of the Vietnamese, and the potential threat of a Democratic Kampuchea revival with Chinese, Thai and Western backing. Of these two evils, there is no doubt that the Vietnamese are regarded as the lesser. And in the meantime, the Kampuchean Phoenix is rising from the ashes in a way that Korb might not have believed possible.

The most important thing was the successful December rice harvest. 1980 was an extremely tough year: although I heard very few reports of actual starvation, peasants usually told me they were hungry. Partly because of tremendous transportation problems, an inexperienced administration, sporadic and possibly insufficient delivery of international aid rice to Kampuchea, as well as local corruption, rice rations distributed to peasants by the P.R.K. government averaged only one to two kilograms (varying from one-quarter of a kilogram to seven) per person per month. Peasants survived largely by living off the rich Kampuchean countryside, eating fruit, vegetables, secondary crops such as corn and potatoes, crabs and fish. But the government effectively prioritized the delivery of tens of thousands of tons of seed rice, aid from both Western and Vietnamese sources, into the hands of the newly-established 'production solidarity groups' of about fifteen peasant families each; this meant that the harvest must have been at least twice as big as the poor one of 1979. The P.R.K. has announced that, like the previous crop, the 1980 harvest will not be taxed. Although its revenues are almost non-existent, the government has so far managed to avoid taxation of the peasants by using international aid to feed the urban population, the administration and the workers. (The Ministry of Health, for instance, has a staff of 10,000, from doctors to cleaners and carpenters, and the Ministry of Agriculture employs 15,000.) In general, the international aid programme has proved to be reasonably successful, and the food situation should be much improved in 1981.

Another reason for the general recovery is the fact that the Vietnamese Communists occupying the country are not behaving in the way the Khmers' traditional enemy has behaved in the past. In Kampuchea there are very long memories of 19th Century Vietnamese invasions, with their massacres of Khmer leaders and peasants, damage to their distinct local culture, and Vietnamese settler colonization on Kampuchean land. There is no evidence that any of these things are occurring in Kampuchea today, despite the enormous influence Vietnam has had in the establishment and functioning of the P.R.K. administration, and the fears of a loss of independence this has generated.

Culture

One of the most striking features of Kampuchea in 1980 was the reappearance and increasingly wide diffusion of traditional Khmer culture, suppressed and largely destroyed by the Democratic Kampuchea regime from 1975 to 1979.

At the National Theatre in Phnom Penh, for example, performances are of a high artistic standard. They cover quite a range: classical royal ballet, usually based on the Khmer version of the Ramayana, and performed in elaborate, colourful silk costumes, masks and head-dress; folk dances, such as the Khmer *angre* and *rook trei,* performed with bamboo sticks and fishing baskets, again with costumes and traditional masks; the favourite Cham Muslim dance 'The Love Handkerchief', with its magical rhythm and theme of romantic enchantment; and a hill-tribe minority ceremonial dance called 'Kill the buffalo/Drink the wine'.

The theatre also performs overtly political scenes, such as Kampuchea-Vietnam-Laos solidarity dances, and one called 'Peace in Indochina' which s is more like a war dance, however defensive. And there is a shocking re-enactment of the final stages of the Pol Pot period massacre: the semi-darkness and slow motion are punctuated by a woman's voice singing a very moving lament of the suffering with tremendous sadness and beauty. In the end Heng Samrin's

Salvation Front troops arrive and apprehend the Pol Pot killers. Their victims wake up and stand in a chorus as fists go up, all eyes turn to the massive P.R.K. flag suddenly projected at the back of the stage, and then hands are religiously outstretched towards it. The scene ends with the singing of a eulogy of the new revolution. Despite its violence and the insufferable memories that recalls (recent versions have emphasized the agony rather than the violence) and the ceremonial ending, 'Blood and Tears', as it is called, is a popular scene in Phnom Penh today, no doubt because of its realism. The Kampuchean tragedy has not lacked melodrama. One thing is missing, however – the overwhelming role played by Vietnamese in abolishing the killer regime.

Comedy scenes include 'The Shameless Enemy', a hilarious half-hour in which three clowns jump around the stage in and out of each other's arms, terrified out of their wits by the ghost of a man who has just died. At the very end the inevitable Front troops burst in, unmasking the ghost who just as inevitably turns out to be a Pol Potist. As he is led away, the leading clown, an experienced actor who is now the political cadre of the threatre group, explains to the audience that they should not allow the enemy who seems to have disappeared to keep manipulating and haunting them. It is a thoughtful scene, of social relevance in Kampuchea today, and its cathartic impact is effected with some subtlety.

An important event in Phnom Penh was the traditional Khmer music festival in early July 1980. Elderly singers and musicians had been brought to Phnom Penh from villages all over the country, to pass on their nearly extinct skills to younger people. As the curtain rose, a dozen old men and women were asked to step forward from the vast traditional orchestra on the stage, and were introduced one by one. The audience was told their ages, the names of their villages, and their musical skills and repertoires. Tragically, only two weeks later one of these precious people, forty-eight year-old Mme. Bou Chhon, was killed in Battambang Province, when her car hit a mine laid by guerrillas on a back road, on the way to a country performance. She was reported to have known over 400 traditional Khmer songs.

But the cultural revival goes one. From 10-16 July, a conference was held at the Fine Arts Museum in Phnom Penh to prepare the recording of traditional songs and the transcription of music to be distributed all over the country. During a visit to the National Palace on 20 August, I stumbled on a meeting of 200 songwriters and poets from many different provinces. It was being addressed by its convener, Information and Culture Minister Keo Chanda. In October, the P.R.K. State Publishing House was officially opened, and its first volume of Khmer literature is expected to appear soon.

What is more interesting and significant than these events in the capital is the extent to which the revival of Khmer culture is penetrating to the rural districts and villages. As always, the classical royal ballet is not found in the countryside, but everything else is, in particular folk dancing. Every province now has its professional theatre and performing groups, and the P.R.K. is well on the way to achieving its aim of a cultural group for each of the country's 100-odd districts, as well as the children's theatre groups which have been set up in many urban and rural orphanages.

Takeo province has a professional theatre of about thirty people, who perform every Saturday night in the provincial capital, and in various districts on other days. On 27 August, during my stay in Kampot Province, there were two local public performances, one by the orphans and one by the provincial drama troupe. The latter have been trained by an extremely talented English-speaking young man, who in 1979 had built up a provincial troupe in Kompong Thom (which I was to see also) and was then sent to Kampot to do the same.

This young man produced an uproarious comedy entitled 'Pol Pot Runs out of Food'. Ravenous guerrillas in black pyjamas hide behind bushes and lick their chops frenetically as a peasant laden with all the goodies of the Kampuchean countryside (rice and bean cakes wrapped in banana leaves, rice wine, sugar palm juice in bamboo cylinders, fruit, and a stick of sugar cane) proceeds to spend a leisurely afternoon getting drunk and fishing in a pond, oblivious of the suffering antics of his former oppressors. There was also a long skit on the dangers of illiteracy for the poor, performed in the framework of the *yike,* a traditional Khmer dramatic form. Again the comedy was great. Another scene of the agony of the Pol Pot period, in which the stage was littered with skulls, was followed by Khmer-Laos-Vietnamese solidarity dances as well as hill-tribe dances, magic shows, male-female comedy exchanges known as *ayai,* and folk dancing.

An hour out of Kompong Thom city I came across the newly-formed Santuk district orchestra in the middle of a rehearsal. The female singer, the six old men playing traditional instruments, and the two boys on drums and guitar informed me they were all supported by a government salary of 90 riels per month, about the same as that of a junior official. They told me that Staung district had a cultural group of fifty people, and Baray a much smaller one.

But the cultural revival goes on beyond government-sponsored theatre groups and orchestras. One evening in the hostel in Konpong Chhang Province, I chatted to two young women employed there as cleaners and, although they were at first reluctant, I convinced them both to sing a song. As they did so, other hostel workers, cooks, mechanics and sentries drifted in. Everyone knew and sang at least one song; there were love songs, folk songs, and laments, including one about Phnom Penh written by the Information and Culture Minister. There were also two or three with overt political messages about socialism and Vietnam-Kampuchea Friendship. I recorded ninety minutes of songs; what was most interesting was that all but two or three of them had been composed in the eighteen months or so since Pol Pot's overthrow.

The man most responsible for all this is Keo Chanda, the P.R.K.'s Minister of Information and Culture. Chanda is a veteran of Kampuchea's independence struggle against the French in the early 1950s, after that he sent secretly to Hanoi and studied economics, Returning to his country in 1970 to take part in the movement against the U.S. and the Lon Nol government, he broke with the Pol Pot group in January 1973 and retreated to Vietnam. 'The Vietnamese didn't trust me at first.' he told me. 'Pol Pot thought I was a Vietnamese agent, and the Vietnamese thought I was a Pol Pot agent.' Chanda claims that with Pen Sovan (the P.R.K.'s Vice-President, Defence Minister and Communist Party Leader) and two others, he formed 'a new party' in Vietnam in 1973, which was not recognized by the Vietnamese Communists until 1978. In that year Chanda played a leading role in the establishment of the Salvation Front in preparation for the overthrow of Pol Pot.

Chanda's long years in Vietnam did not result in his losing touch with his native culture. He showed me his 1974 diary, which is filled with verses of Khmer poetry, much of it with a strong anti-Pol Pot political message. In 1979, he wrote the words to the P.R.K.'s national anthem.

Similarly, the fact that Chanda is married to a Vietnamese didn't prevent him from sacking the first Vietnamese adviser to his Ministry, in 1979. 'He wanted us to do Chinese revolutionary dances,' Chanda claimed, which is interesting in the light of the China-Vietnam conflict. 'So I sent him back to Ho Chi Minh City, and now I have an adviser who does what he is told.'

In Hanoi in November 1980, Vietnam's Deputy Foreign Minister Vo Dong Giang told me, 'Yes, the Information and Culture Ministry in Phonm Penh is a very independent Ministry, and is making great progress'.

Religion

The restoration of national culture has been accompanied by the return of organized religion, which was abolished under Democratic Kampuchea. Nearly all Khmers are at least nominal Buddhists. Monks in their saffron robes can now be seen in every district, although they are fewer than their pre-1975 numbers. Many monks were executed by the Pol Pot regime, but it would also seem that the country is not yet productive enough to support large numbers of monks living from alms donated by the population, as 70-100,000 of them did in former years. Also, the socialist P.R.K. regime would be likely to keep a close watch on religion and probably intends to limit the monks to smaller numbers than before. An unconfirmed report has it that since some months ago no-one under fifty years old has been allowed to enter a monastery; although one often sees small saffron-clad boys who presumably entered during 1979; in a Kompong Cham street I met two Buddhist nuns. Three of the thirty-odd members of the Salvation Front's Central Committee are Buddhist monks.

In November 1980 a festival known as *kathen,* held in Kompong Speu Province raised 2,500 riels ($600 or more) for the rebuilding of a rural monastery demolished by the Pol Pot regime. On 27 July, on a trip through the countryside of Kompong Cham, I saw three different groups of about 100 people, mainly women, on roads heading towards local monasteries with offerings for the monks to celebrate one of the four holy days each month. On 7 October I travelled by small boat across the flooded plains of Prey Veng and up a river to a district I had asked permission to visit the night before. We arrived in Prek Chrey village, where no Westerners had been for at least 10 years. The Pchum Ben fifteen-day religious festival was in progress there, featuring daily feasts and gatherings at the monastery, built on stilts above the water. The one local monk who had survived the Pol Pot period was presiding. The next day I travelled fifty miles by car and then for three hours down another river to a village I had named, and came across the same festival there. We took part in furious, drenching river-boat races in a picnic atmosphere.

In most re-opened monasteries there were three to six monks, and in Phnom Penh's Unnalom monastery I was told there were twenty. These numbers are still low, but the re-appearance and daily activities of monks in the towns and villages gives the population a good deal of confidence that the assault on their lifestyle launched by the Pol Pot regime is not about to be repeated.

The other major organized religions in Kampuchea are Islam and Christianity. The Muslims, a race known as the Chams, were decimated by executions, starvation and disease in the Pol Pot period. My impression is that, proportionately, they suffered even more than the Khmers, largely because of Pol Pot's racialist policies. Their numbers seem to have fallen from as many as 200,000 to as few as 50,000. But wherever there are Cham communities in Kampuchea today, there are newly re-opened mosques, with turbanned holy men in checked sarongs (skirts) and serious young boys studying the Koran and even Arabic, as well as the Khmer script.

Ibrahim, a Muslim dignitary, who studied ten years in Cairo and is now one of the seventy-odd members of the P.R.K.'s Ministry of Religious Affairs in Phnom Penh, insists that the Chams once again have the freedom to organize their religious activities and that the former Muslim 'networks' throughout the country have been re-established. Communications, he said, were facilitated by government assistance: Yos Po, Secretary-General of the Salvation Front and currently in charge of the Ministry, was at that time leading a delegation of Muslims to visit Cham communities in Kampot Province. There are now six mosques open in the Phnom Penh area, and a good number in the provinces, but Muslim dignitaries are thinly stretched: only twenty of the previous 113 in Kampuchea survived the Pol Pot period.

Kampuchean Christians are very few in number (perhaps several thousand) and are therefore less politically significant and more vulnerable. They are also seen by some, probably incorrectly, as less 'national' than other religious groups. They do not seem to be receiving the same treatment from the P.R.K. regime as the Buddhists and the Muslims. Until June 1980 there were five weekly Protestant services being performed again in Phnom Penh, by a Khmer pastor, but at that point several Protestants were arrested and interrogated by the police; others then became afraid to go to the services, and now there is only one each week. Little information is available about Kampuchea's remaining Catholics.

Education

The P.R.K. has made significant progress in the educational field, after the closure of schools during the Democratic Kampuchea period. By the end of 1979 there were nearly one million children (half of whom were in Kampuchea's eastern and south-western provinces) attending daily primary school in makeshift buildings or under trees. The majority of experienced teachers perished in the Pol Pot period; only 4,500 of today's 20,000 schoolteachers are qualified. The rest are simply high-school graduates or less, given rough training courses before and after they commence teaching. In Sa'ang district of Kandal Province, for example, I saw such a course involving the district's 480 teachers. Lessons included politics, teaching techniques, and psychology. Further south, in Koh Thom district, was one of the country's dozen or so junior high schools, recently opened. (There are two or three of these in Phnom Penh, and many others are scheduled to open during 1981).

Four days later I went to Kompong Cham and met the province's education director, a former philosophy professor. He has a staff of 34 ('I need 50') responsible for the 700 primary schools in the province. When the provincial high school opens in 1981, he said, English, French, Russian and Vietnamese will be taught. Foreign languages, including French, will apparently also be taught in Takeo Province. UNICEF officials in Phnom Penh were pleasantly surprised to hear the provincial governor, a former Khmer Rouge defector, direct the new high school there to teach whatever foreign languages it has the resources to teach. An alternative proposal, now apparently under review, is to establish a National Foreign Languages School which would cater for those interested outside of school hours. If this is adopted, then the education system would be entirely Khmer.

The first school textbooks, in Khmer, have now been printed. There is one for each of about a dozen subjects so far, including History, Literature, Folk Tales, Mathematics, and Morality. The national weekly newspaper, *Kampuchea* is also apparently distributed to schools for use in reading and probably political lessons.

The Kompong Cham education director believes that the new system of schooling 'will be a good one . . . because it will be free', and the students will not have to depend on the poorly-stocked libraries if they cannot afford the expensive textbooks imported from France, as in the past. Books will be written in Khmer, and distributed free, he said.

At the tertiary level, the Faculty of Agricultural Science and the Faculty of Medicine in Phnom Penh have been operating again for some time. In September 1980, two young doctors graduated after completing their final year of studies, which had been interupted by Pol Pot's 1975 victory.

The Khmers and the Vietnamese

As Kampuchean society slowly comes to look like a normal society in a developing country, and the P.R.K. administration becomes increasingly stable and runs the country's affairs with some degree of efficiency (as is now the case), the question of the Vietnamese presence in Kampuchea is raised more and more frequently. How do the Khmer people see the Vietnamese in their country, and the government that they effectively established there?

Phnom Penh

The day after our arrival in Phnom Penh my wife and I had some long unsupervised conversations with people in the streets, and heard a range of views.

A group of women selling steamed corn on a footpath told us that the Vietnamese troops had saved their lives by defeating Pol Pot, and had been behaving themselves rather well since. One woman lived very near a Vietnamese military camp; she said the troops helped her fetch water and had also given her some medicine. 'They grow their own vegetables, and bring the rest of their food from Vietnam' she noted. 'I have never seen them do anything wrong, and have never heard of them molesting Khmer women.' Another woman agreed. A third had just come into town on a Vietnamese truck: when I asked how much the trip cost she replied: 'They don't charge anything, out of solidarity. Kampuchea is poor.'

The first woman stressed that if the Vietnamese hadn't come things would be very grim indeed, and the crowd which had by now gathered around murmured agreement. The food situation, for instance, was better now than under Pol Pot, because 'we are allowed to go looking for food ourselves', a practice banned in many areas of Democratic Kampuchea. The woman had received only two and a half kilograms of rice from the authorities since January 1979, but still said she was able to get enough to eat.

About 200 metres away two more women were sitting by the roadside, selling rubber sandals which they fetched by train from the Thai border. As we came up to talk to them, others gathered around, and in response to questions about the Pol Pot period, everyone emphasized the mass killings of 1977-78.

One woman volunteered the view that she was alive today only because the Vietnamese had come in. The others agreed: 'Pol Pot would have killed us all.' She went on to say that the Vietnamese had brought rice to Kampuchea for its people, and that although there was not yet enough to eat there was little starvation. They all expressed enthusiasm for the P.R.K. regime (one woman pointed out that there were 'schools everywhere' now) and confidence that 1981 would be a 'plentiful year'.

At this point, a young man peered above the crowd and asked me in English: 'Do you want to know the real events in Kampuchea?' I said yes, and asked him to sit next to me on the roadside, where he went on, still in English: 'The real events are that the Vietnamese have saved us. But they have forced our President to sign a treaty allowing them to stay in Kampuchea for twenty years. They give us only small arms, no heavy weapons.' The others were all looking on, unable to understand the English. I asked him to talk in Khmer but he declined. Then I said I had studied the

Kampuchea-Vietnam conflict and it was clear that Pol Pot's forces had begun the war by attacking Vietnam, and that Vietnam had then responded. He was aware of this and agreed that the Vietnamese would not be in Kampuchea had it not been for Pol Pot's attacks on them. He said: 'Yes, it's Pol Pot's fault. . . but the Vietnamese take half of Kampuchea's foreign aid back to Vietnam.' I asked if he'd seen evidence of this himself – 'Yes'. When? 'In April 1979.' But, I protested, the only foreign aid that had arrived by that time was Vietnamese aid. 'The Vietnamese took televisions and other goods from Phnom Penh just after they came. I saw them. Pol Pot did *not* destroy those things.' (This Vietnamese looting, or at the very least stockpiling of goods, in the early months of 1979, is also reported from other sources.) When I asked him again, still in English, about the diversion of foreign aid, he didn't answer.

A young man on a bicycle said in Khmer from the edge of the group that he'd been to Thailand to buy goods but that 'our Vietnamese brothers and sisters' (a sarcastic use of the term others had been using) had taken his goods as he crossed back into Kampuchea, leaving him only his bicycle. He said he would never go back to Thailand again.

A woman accompanied by a young child eating a small loaf of bread emphasized to me that things were 'far better now than they were before, under Pol Pot', mentioning the increased availability of food (although there was 'not enough yet') and medicine.

The unwillingness of the first young man to use Khmer to express his discontent with the P.R.K. regime in front of a group of people quite casually expressing views different from his, I found again in the case of two truck drivers a week later sitting near Phnom Penh market. A group of people were telling me that the Vietnamese had saved their lives, and one of the drivers said that life for him was 'normal' now; nevertheless, he replied quietly to my question, 'Kampuchea is not a very happy country'. He was unwilling to elaborate further in front of the others, and had to leave immediately, he said, to bring a load of Soviet corn destined for Kratie Province, from Kompong Som port.

Some time later, another young man asked me was I worried that there might be another war in Kampuchea. I said I didn't think so: Pol Pot seemed very unpopular, while the Vietnamese army were too strong to be threatened. I asked if he was worried that Pol Pot might come back if the Vietnamese army withdrew soon. His reply was: 'We are strong enough to defeat Pol Pot ourselves. We are worried that the Vietnamese want Laos and Kampuchea.'

Yet another young man, who like the previous one was educated and had become a Phnom Penh official, told me he didn't trust the Salvation Front for the first eight months of their rule. For most of 1979 he had remained in a village, concerned that educated people were being called upon to take up government jobs simply in order to kill them off. Pol Pot's regime, he said, had tricked people this way before. But finally, he said, he saw that things were now different, and that the Salvation Front had a 'good policy of building up the country', and he decided to work for them. While the first man may have been a sympathizer of the anti-Communist guerrilla movement, the Khmer Sereikar, which has about 3,000 troops on the Thai border, the second had no time for them at all.

I talked to a young woman about her experiences under Democratic Kampuchea, and she said: 'I am happy with things as they are.' She added that she was so glad to be rid of Pol Pot's regime that she was not asking much of the P.R.K. regime 'which is trying to raise the living standards of the people, but doesn't have many resources. I don't agree with some Phnom Penh people who believe in Sereikar and want capitalism back.' A friend of hers agreed, saying that if Sereikar gain power it would be easy for Pol Pot to defeat them and stage a comeback. She even accused the Sereikar of colluding with Democratic Kampuchea forces.

Close relatives of both these women had escaped death in June, when the train they were travelling on to Battambang was ambushed by Pol Pot guerrillas; 150 had been killed. Later on I was to meet a woman trader who had also been on that train, *and* on another one similarly ambushed in July, resulting in at least forty deaths. (There had been no Vietnamese troops on those trains, all these women insisted.)

On 9 July I met a group of Phnom Penh people in the street selling coconuts. They began telling me about their experiences under Pol Pot, one woman's husband had been killed in August 1978, and the others had all lost family members. They mentioned that things had improved significantly since Pol Pot's overthrow, and then several of them asked: 'What can you do to make sure that Pol Pot never comes back? The Khmer people are very afraid of Pol Pot.' I said I thought Pol Pot's regime had no real future, although they were receiving foreign assistance in Thailand. I mentioned that the conservative Australian government continued to recognize Democratic Kampuchea as the legal government (which at time of writing is still the case), as did Thailand. This caused a bit of a shock. One young man who had ridden up on a bicycle asked me to go back home and 'tell the Australian government not to do that.' He then pointed to his dark skin and said passionately: 'I am a pure Khmer, and I used to hate foreigners, but I changed my mind after I saw what Pol Pot did to his own people. The Vietnamese have come and helped us, and as far as I can see they still haven't killed one single Khmer.'

Although Phnom Penh is near unanimous in its hatred and fear of the Democratic Kampuchea forces, there is still quite a range of views in the city about the Vietnamese presence and the Salvation Front Government. Most of the people I met in Phnom Penh did appear disposed to give the P.R.K. the benefit of the doubt (for the time being at least), if they weren't a little enthusiastic about the future. It is clear to nearly everyone that the Salvation Front, apart from having formed the Khmer force in the very real liberation struggle, is working to rebuild Kampuchea, and no-one I met described them to me as 'traitors'. One older man who had grave doubts about 'the political line of our country' and the intentions of the Vietnamese, even though he was employed as a government official, told me: 'We are all trying very hard in our work, we Khmers. We have to get Kampuchea back on its feet.'

Although this same man was to cast aside many of his doubts and fears about Vietnam in the ensuing months, there are other Phnom Penh officials who wish to live neither in a socialist society nor in one with close links to Vietnam, but will close ranks with the Salvation Front for some limited time in order to play their part in Kampuchea's rebirth. Many others, having already decided to leave, made their way to Thailand in 1979, and small numbers of Phnom Penh people followed them in 1980.

The Countryside

The countryside lacks the range of political attitudes which we found in the capital. Politics, unless it endangers people's existence, is less of an issue, there are fewer middle-class people troubled by the socialist ideology of the P.R.K. regime, and the villages are less secure from guerrilla attacks. It is my impression also, that, among most Khmer peasants, anti-Vietnamese feeling has seldom been as strong as among the urban and educated classes, and in many cases it is non-existent. Finally, the behaviour of Vietnamese Communist troops stationed in rural Kampuchea is usually careful and often exemplary. On 15 July in Sophi village, Takeo Province, I asked peasants if the Vietnamese soldiers bothered them, and received an answer that I had often heard before inside and outside Kampuchea, and would hear again: 'They don't do anything.' Later I had two separate conversations with men from the same village, along the Mekong River east of Phnom Penh. When I asked about the thirty Vietnamese stationed there, the first, a peasant, replied: 'There are no problems. They don't ask for or steal food, or molest women.' What do they do? I asked. 'They guard the roads, ensure security, and fight the Khmer Rouge. Occasionally they come and chat with us in our houses.' The second man, who had recently taken up an official position in Phnom Penh, gave a similar reply but from a different perspective, perhaps: 'It's as if there are no problems.'

In the ferry town of Neak Leung on 14 July, I went off alone behind some shops and started talking to several workers rebuilding one of them. They asked me to help with foreign aid, especially clothes, and pointed at some ragged children who had gathered around. 'We Khmers like the Soviet Union a lot,' they said, presumably thinking I was a Russian. I asked why, and they answered: 'Because of the Soviet aid we have received since liberation.' What kind? 'Medicine, clothes, etc.,' they replied, ticking the items off on their fingers. However, there was not enough rice to eat, and in some remote parts of Kampuchea people were starving to death, they said. But they had 'much more' to eat now than in the Pol Pot period. One man said things were 'happy now, but another interrupted: 'No, just happier than in the Pol Pot period.' All of them wanted more foreign aid, in order to become 'even happier', and they said they were confident that things would be 'plentiful' in 1981, after the rice harvest.

Three of these people had fled Democratic Kampuchea and gone to Vietnam in 1978, and their families had been decimated by executions after they left. They had 'studied' in Vietnam. 'What did you study?' I asked.

'We learnt to decide who were our friends and who were our enemies, and Pol Pot is definitely our enemy.'

On another river ferry, at Kompong Cham in August, I saw a group of six young men poring over a Vietnamese colour propaganda magazine. I asked: 'Are the Khmer people afraid of Pol Pot returning if the Vietnamese withdraw?' The reply was: 'Very much.' 'We'll all be dead if that happens,' interjected an older peasant. But, I said, there is now a Kampuchean army of some strength which can fight Pol Pot. 'Yes', he said, 'but it is very small . . . Pol Pot killed all the men.'

Fear that a Vietnamese withdrawal would open the way for Democratic Kampuchea forces is widespread in the provinces. On my second visit to Neak Leung on 29 July, a furore hit the market as local Khmers caught red-handed two Vietnamese in civilian clothes stealing money from a peasant woman. The two were apprehended, and on their declaring themselves to be 'Vietnamese soldiers', were bound by the woman herself and unceremoniously marched off to the Kampuchean security office. A few minutes later, a young boy of about ten joined a group of children who were peering open-mouthed at one of the few Westerners they had ever seen. Evidently reflecting some of the talk that was going around the crowd at that moment, as he came up the boy said to another child: 'If the Vietnamese all leave, Pol Pot . . . .' I didn't catch the rest, but asked him if he wanted the Vietnamese to go or stay. He replied: 'I want them to stay.' More often, however, Vietnamese discipline ensures that such an uncomfortable choice never arises. At Prek Kdam in Kandal Province, a peasant told me: 'The Vietnamese are good to us. They don't cause any problems.'

In Kompong Chhnang Province in September, on two separate occasions I heard Khmers praising the bravery of Vietnamese soldiers during the fierce fighting against Pol Pot in 1979. They were said to have thrown down their arms and run after their enemies bare-handed; some were killed, but the others took their prisoners alive. The Khmers said this would earn the Vietnamese promotion, but they also approvingly quoted Vietnamese as saying: 'If Khmers keep on getting killed, there won't be any left.' The Vietnamese policy of re-educating rather than executing Pol Pot prisoners, however, was regarded by some as 'too easy', because after re-education and release some of the prisoners had taken to terrorism again. Some Khmers complained to me that the Vietnamese not only spared Pol Pot people but also 'fed them full', and there are a number of authentic accounts from 1979 of Khmer crowds sweeping aside Vietnamese soldiers and tearing apart their prisoners. In Kompong Thom in October 1980, a local Kampuchean militia commander told me he had recently captured a former Democratic Kampuchea deputy district chief. When I asked if the man was undergoing re-education, the reply was: 'No, we killed him for the time being.'

In general, though, the wildness seems to have subsided, and the Vietnamese and Salvation Front policies of re-education and reconciliation seem to have taken root. An official in Kompong Cham, speaking in French, pointed out to me that some Democratic Kampuchea people were now village chiefs in his province. I asked why. 'Because of the government's policy of national reconciliation of all the political parties and forces.' Is that a good idea, even to include some Pol Potists in such reconciliation? 'Yes.'

In summary, it seems that the presence of 150,000 or more Vietnamese troops in Kampuchea had not by, late 1980, provoked any serious reaction among the vast majority of the population who are against the Democratic Kampuchea regime. Peking is far more unpopular among Khmers than Hanoi is. Very few indeed actively want the Vietnamese to stay in the country indefinitely, but very many are well-disposed towards them, and most seem to share the views of the Kompong Cham official quoted above. I had asked him if he was afraid of or concerned about the Vietnamese when they first arrived in Kampuchea. 'I was against Pol Pot, and they were fighting Pol Pot, so there was no problem with them,' was the immediate answer. Are the people worried that the Vietnamese might stay a long time? 'If they leave, Pol Pot will come back. If Pol Pot remains a threat for a long time, the Vietnamese must stay a long time. That is necessary – the people are extremely afraid that Pol Pot might come back.'

The effect of the Pol Pot regime's policies was to provoke a substantial inversion of traditional Khmer perceptions of their relationship to Vietnam. A 19th Century account tells of Vietnamese burying three Khmers up to their necks in a triangle, and using the men's heads as a teapot stand with a fire lit between them. As the Khmers scream in agony, the Vietnamese protest: 'Don't spill the master's tea!' This story has been taken very seriously in Khmer nationalist circles in the 20th Century, and has been used by all previous Kampuchean regimes, in particular those of Lon Nol and Pol Pot. But it doesn't retain its force today.

In a Takeo village in July I met a former Phnom Penh student, who would have been in the thick of the urban-based Lon Nol regime's anti-Vietnamese euphoria in the early 1970s. But, evacuated from the capital by the victorious Pol Pot forces in 1975, he had spent the Democratic Kampuchea period along the Vietnam-Kampuchea border. Apart from his own difficulties, he had seen the Pol Pot attacks on Vietnamese villages in April 1977. He told me the Pol Pot cadres had tried to whip up anti-Vietnamese fervour by relating the tale of 'the master's tea', and his spontaneous comment was: 'They didn't say anything important about Vietnam; they just kept harping on that story all the time.' It is not uncommon now to hear Kampuchean officials remark that traditional antagonism between the two countries is 'out of date'.

Out of date or note, the inability of the Democratic Kampuchea forces to capitalize on it to raise a successful anti-Vietnamese struggle has led them to act out a tragic historical irony. In the Pol Pot period, Khmers judged to be insufficiently hateful towards the Vietnamese were massacred in huge numbers, accused of having 'Khmer bodies with Vietnamese minds'. This raised the same threat of genocide that Democratic Kampuchea claimed was a Vietnamese policy. An unconfirmed on-the-spot account from early 1979, reported to me in France a year later, indicates that Khmer peasants in Siemreap Province, accused of being 'Vietnamese slaves' because they had reclaimed confiscated household utensils, were buried up to their necks by Pol Pot guerrillas. As a fire burned them to death they were told not to spill the master's tea.

Guerrilla War

The initial Vietnamese invasion of December 1978-January 1979 did not decisively crush the Pol Pot regime. Fierce fighting took place in many provinces for the rest of the year – there were even naval battles on the Tonle Sap Lake, between Pol Pot and Salvation Front troops, as late as September 1979. But by early 1980, the war inside the country was over, and remnants of the Democratic Kampuchea army, now numbering about 25,000 troops, had regrouped on the Thai border and in bases inside Thailand.

Since then, supplies of food and medicine mainly from Western sources, and supplies of Chinese arms and ammunition unloaded at Thai ports and carried in Thai military vehicles (there is now much hard evidence for this) to Pol Pot border camps, and further regroupment, as well as time to rest, have all enabled the Democratic Kampuchea forces to increase their strength on the border to just under 40,000.

While these forces represent a military threat, their political potential inside the country is a different matter. A recent in-depth investigation carried out from Thailand by Stephen Heder, a Khmer-speaking specialist under contract to the U.S. State Department, concluded that more than half the peasants in Kampuchea are prepared to and do report on, or hand over, Democratic Kampuchea agents who enter their villages, to the Vietnamese or Salvation Front forces. Among the Khmer middle class, persecuted by the Pol Pot regime more than the peasants were, the proportion of active anti-Democratic Kampuchea people is undoubtedly higher.

Given this situation, it is not difficult to understand why the expected Democratic Kampuchea wet season offensive for 1980 never got off the ground. There were two attacks on Khmer trains in the north-west which caused 200 deaths, and three attacks on rice trains in the south-west (thirteen Khmer workers killed). Two Russian dock-workers were killed near Kompong Som port in November, and occasionally international aid trucks were blown up on major highways. But none of the highways or railway lines were cut (a poor showing considering the ease with which the Khmer Rouge had been able to do this during the 1970-75 war), and even on the Thai border Vietnamese and Salvation Front casualties were not high. In four months of constant travel in the Kampuchean countryside during the 1980 wet season, I never saw any signs of recent fighting and villagers generally reported a stable military situation since the end of 1979. My movements were hampered by bureaucracy and flooding far more than by any guerrilla activity.

Still, I did come across a guerrilla presence in one or two localities.

Ta Mok, the commander of the Democratic Kampuchea army, is perhaps the most feared man in the country today. In 1977-78, the bloodiest years of the Pol Pot regime, his South-west Zone forces left a trail of death as they purged most of the southeast, west, north and north-west of Kampuchea. He is now reported to be based in a camp on Mount Suriya, in the Cardamom ranges along the Thai border, with his veteran South-west Zone lieutenants Phal, Ai and Lovei and a number of elephants. On nearby Mount Aural is another group of 100 Democratic Kampuchea guerrillas led by Yim, a former chief of Kompong Chhnang Province.

Mok's name has not been heard in the South-west for over a year. But his son-in-law, San, a former schoolteacher, was sighted there in mid-August when he unsuccessfully called a meeting of villagers in the forest, only 5 kilometres from Takeo city, Mok's former headquarters. San had been chief of Tram Kak district west of Takeo during 1977-78, and he is now reported to be leading 3-400 guerrillas there, in the Damrey Romeal mountains. I went to within 3 kilometres of these hills on 16 July. I was told that some local villagers had relatives in the hills and were secretly supplying them, although it was clear from talking to a number of peasants that they would never willingly support Democratic Kampuchea in the future, whatever happened. When asked if they were afraid of the guerrillas so close to their village, people told me they would be if there were not Vietnamese encampments at the foot of the hills. Later I met two peasants heading towards these encampments, hoes over their shoulders. When asked they said they were not afraid to go that far. I raised the subject of the Pol Pot period; with passion they said it had been harsh primarily because in 1977-78 they had been forced to work 'night and day'.

The second-in-command of the Pol Pot army is Ke Pauk, former chief of the Democratic Kampuchea Central Zone. In 1977-78, Pauk purged only the north-east of Kampuchea, but with even more brutality than Mok. The attacks on eastern Kompong Cham and Prey Veng Provinces in May 1978, and the massacre of entire villages there and evacuation of many of the survivors (in most cases to be massacred or starved elsewhere later), in my view constituted the greatest single atrocity of the Pol Pot regime, causing quite possibly 100,000 deaths. (This is apart from Pauk's murderous attacks on many Vietnamese villages across the eastern border in 1977-78.)

Pauk is still around. On 15 October 1980, I travelled through rice-fields in a boat along a narrow canal to his native village in Baray district of Kompong Thom Province. People there told me that six days before a group of 100 Pol Pot guerrillas had passed by only 4 kilometres away, led by two of Pauk's lieutenants, Oeun and Huon. In September the sub-district militia had twice confronted Democratic Kampuchea forces, and in one case broke up a meeting of twenty-seven Pol Pot cadres.

In Kompong Cham on 26 July, local officials had told me that three districts and three sub-districts on the Kompong Cham-Kompong Thom border are to some extent 'dangerous' because of Pauk's troops, numbering 'thousands' and operating in groups of up to thirty: 'they live by stealing from the people. Last week they robbed seventeen families of everything they had, in a village opposite here. I had to go there afterwards and distribute blankets an clothes,' one official in Prey Chhor district told me on 4 August. He said Pauk was camped in the Tuk Cha forest on the boundaries of Prey Chhor, Stung Trang, and Chamcar Loeu districts. Four days later, Preap Pichey, the governor of Kompong Cham Province, told me that Pauk had been located on the Chinit river in Stung Trang district, Pol Pot's 1970-75 headquarters. 'We are looking for him, to shoot him, everyday, but so far we haven't been successful,' Pichey said.

More revealing was the account of Nou Vanna, a young woman who now works in Kompong Cham City but sometimes goes back to her native village in Stung Trang. In a private discussion in early August she said two sub-districts there were insecure, and two others were under the control of Democratic Kampuchea forces.

> The Khmer Rouge live with the people, exchanging rubber latex and twine with the people for rice or medicine. They came and robbed people in Prek Sdei village. There they also arrested the president of the Women's Association of Preah Andong sub-district. They tied her to a pole to be eaten by mosquitoes, and sexually mistreated her, for two months. Then they released her, and now she is mentally all confused, cannot pronounce her words, and is always wanting to go to sleep.
>
> No-one can go to Chheu Teu and Veal Bompong subdistricts, and the government has never been able to distribute any rice there at all. The local people eat only corn and potatoes: they swell up and some of them have died.
>
> Some families in the other two subdistricts have sons in the Khmer Rouge; sometimes this is known and sometimes not. They usually give rice to their sons. Sometimes a husband is with the Khmer Rouge and the wife lives in a village. If we don't give her rice she would criticise the Front, saying that the Front does not help the people, and that would lead to conflict.
>
> There are many Khmer Rouge battallions in the forest. In the rainy season when they cannot get anything to eat they go to the islands in the Mekong river, and billet one soldier with every family. The people can't do anything about it. They understand the line of the Front but they say, what can they do in a situation like that. They would be killed by the Khmer Rouge. Sometimes our soldiers there go hungry also, and there is no medicine either.
>
> Everytime I go to Stung Trang I never stay long; the army cannot guarantee security there. While the Vietnamese are here it is still all right, but if the Vietnamese leave there will be problems.

Real power within the Democratic Kampuchea forces is vested in the regional warlords such as Pauk and Mok, and their lieutenants. Changes in the top echelons of the movement would be unlikely to shake the grip of these people, or alter the nature of their army.

The Future

Despite these small areas of internal guerrilla activity and control, Kampuchea is recovering steadily from destruction, war, and decimation of its population. Although in my estimation about one and a half million Kampucheans died in the Pol Pot period (perhaps half a million by execution and a million by starvation or disease), the Khmer race is not about to disappear. The population of the country is now thought to be around six million. Local hospital records in Kirivong district of Takeo Province show that from January to August 1980, births outnumbered deaths by 1,450 to 165. This did not seem to be an unusual phenomenon given the number of pregnant women and young babies to be seen throughout the country, although the background of violence and death has created a situation in which women now make up 54% of the population, and a much higher percentage of the adult population, and this creates serious problems for them.

Extensive travels along the Vietnam-Kampuchea border revealed no evidence whatsoever of Vietnamese coming to settle on Kampuchean land. In both Vietnam and Kampuchea I was informed by people living near the frontier that such settlement is prohibited, even for former Vietnamese inhabitants of Kampuchea expelled to Vietnam by the Lon Nol and Pol Pot regimes.

Likewise, the Kampuchean economy is getting back on its feet. As the December 1980 harvest began, the price of rice in Phnom Penh markets fell from 3 riels per kilogram to 1½ riels. All indications are of a reasonable crop, although some foreign aid will still be necessary in 1981, mainly to feed the city populations and allow the government to keep its word that it would not tax the peasants for this harvest. If this occurs the basis would be laid for further economic recovery, and Kampuchea could expect to begin exporting rice by 1983.

And finally, the revival and reinvigoration of traditional Khmer culture, along with the reappearance of the Buddhist religion and the establishment of a national education system once again should ensure that Kampuchean society retains much of its distinctive character.

What *is* a possible danger for the Kampuchean nation is simply a loss of political independence. The key here is not the Vietnamese military presence (at least while Democratic Kampuchea remains a potential threat), but the Vietnamese advisers in the Kampuchean government ministries. The main contact these advisers have is with Khmer officials, central and provincial, and among such officials opinions about them seem to vary over a range quite similar to the range of political opinions I found in Phnom Penh.

In Svay Rieng Province I met a mixed group of Khmer officials and Vietnamese advisors in the state canteen, dining convivially and speaking mostly in Khmer but sometimes switching to Vietnamese. The advisers were from Long An Province, which is twinned with Svay Rieng and, as is normal under these arrangements, they had brought aid with them: mosquito nets, blankets, clothes, seed rice and, I noticed, even the tables in the canteen. ('Pol Pot destroyed a lot of tables,' I was informed.) On the other hand, in one district of Prey Veng, Khmer officials were clearly reticent in front of an adviser. In Kompong Speu, at least two of the Vietnamese advisers are in fact ethnic Khmers from the Mekong Delta, since Kompong Speu is twinned with the largely Khmer Vietnamese Province of Cuu Long; relations seemed good there. In Kampot Province, an official told me: 'We Khmers really need the Vietnamese advisers, because we are all ignorant. Pol Pot killed all the educated and skilled people. Some of the Vietnamese here know everything; they have even studied in France.'

In Phnom Penh there are more frequent complaints about the powers wielded by 'advisers'; on the other hand, just as many people insist that the advisers *they* have contact with are 'correct' in that they simply give advice and do not make decisions. A third view I heard went as follows: 'There is as much corruption in Phnom Penh now as in 1972 [the middle of the Lon Nol period]. Our Khmer administration is a shambles, and although some of the Vietnamese advisers are no good, but if the Vietnamese were not here the situation would be hopeless.'

There is a real problem here, and that is some of the people who came to power in the wake of the Vietnamese invasion. Some of them are extremely talented (this applies to most of those trained abroad, whether in Hanoi, e.g. Keo Chanda, or in the West, e.g. the U.S.-trained Deputy Minister of Agriculture Kong Samol, as well as to locally-trained officials) and others are simply veteran revolutionaries with no formal training but a wealth of practical experience, eg. Agriculture Minister Men Chhan. But others are simply incompetent or corrupt, by-passed by history in the case of one provincial Governor who spent the years 1954-79 in Vietnam, or making the most of international aid funds in the case of some of the middle-class survivors of the Pol Pot period now in high positions in Phnom Penh, or just fumbling drunkards and timid yes-men in the case of the Kampot Province officials who were most enthusiastic about their Vietnamese advisers 'because we are all ignorant.'

All these people, good and bad, came to power with the assistance of Vietnam, partly because they were trusted by the Vietnamese, and only when the Vietnamese advisory role in the administration is scaled down will there be a full opportunity for all the Khmers to separate the sheep from the goats. Ironically enough, the Vietnamese are unlikely to attempt to do this themselves on any scale for fear of it being regarded as 'interference in Kampuchea's internal affairs'. But such a shake-out is becoming all the more necessary (and the Vietnamese advisers less necessary) now that the Kampuchean administration is relatively well-established and stable. I believe the danger is that some Khmer officials, claiming that 'we are all ignorant', will stick to the easy way out and refuse to accept responsibility for their tasks while competent Vietnamese, upon whom they will become dependent, remain in place and unwilling to replace them by more suitable people, and I believe this danger is greater than the danger of the situation becoming 'hopeless' if the advisers are withdrawn. Despite Pol Pot's decimation of the educated classes, there are still enough educated and capable Khmer in the country (and overseas) who could be called upon to take up more responsibilities in the bureaucracy.

In an important sense, too, the foreign political backing it has received has allowed the perspective of the Salvation Front Government to drift away from that of the Kampuchean people. The main streets of Phnom Penh have been renamed after revolutionary figures of real significance in Kampuchean history but most of the people have never heard of them. The names of 19th Century rebels and underground Communist leaders are not on the tips of the tongues of a people who have lived through a series of dictatorships, ten years of war, and the four years of unprecedented brutality, starvation, hardship, and cultural destruction of the Pol Pot period. One looks at the street signs in vain for the name of Sinn Sisamuth, the now legendary Khmer singer whose reputation extended to Laos and Thailand and who was executed by the Democratic Kampuchea regime in 1975; or even for the names of Hou Yuon and Hu Nim, Communist leaders killed by Pol Pot who were well known and are still respected through the entire spectrum of Kampuchean politics, and recalled with widespread fondness in their home province of Kompong Cham. ('If those two had been in power instead of Pol Pot, everything would not have gone wrong,' one woman told me in a village there.) One might have hoped that, with the Salvation Front's evident attempt at national reconciliation, the factionalism that has always plagued Kampuchean political groups was about to disappear. Not yet, apparently. And not likely, until the Salvation Front is able to stand on its own feet and adapt itself to other Kampuchean perspectives just as current as its own.

Interestingly, it is already clear that a number of Vietnamese advisers are packing their bags. A year ago, Takeo Province had forty Vietnamese advisers, now Khmer officials there say there are none; minor officials in Prey Veng told me privately that their Vietnamese advisers were 'fewer than last year'; two officials in Kompong Cham told me in separate private conversations that the advisers to their province had been reduced in number from twenty to eight; a minor official in Kandal told me his province had had twenty advisers in 1979, but now there were twelve, and only five attached to the administration. In Phnom Penh's Ministry of Foreign Affairs, there were twelve in 1979, two in 1980. All Vietnamese advisers have apparently gone from the Ministry of Education. On 1 November 1980, Vietnam's Deputy Foreign Minister Vo Dong Giang told me in Hanoi: 'If the situation in Kampuchea continues to develop as it is now, we will be able to withdraw all of our advisers soon.'

According to Vietnam's ambassador in Phnom Penh, Ngo Dien, all the advisers at the district level are now being withdrawn. I found this to be largely the case. In Kong Pisei district of Kompong Speu, for instance, all three have gone back to Vietnam, according to local Khmer officials. Ngo Dien told me that the number of Vietnamese advisers in Kampuchea had been reduced by 50%, although this number was increased again by 30% with the arrival of technical and 'more qualified' personnel.

The technical assistance provided by these Vietnamese advisers has in many cases been greatly appreciated. And clearly, an important prerequisite for Kampuchean independence after Pol Pot's destruction is the existence of the infrastructure of a state itself – an administration, a co-ordinated economy, a currency, a communications network, an education system, hospitals, and a national army. Vietnamese advisers have contributed a lot to the building up of this Kampuchean infrastructure, laying at least the groundwork for the existence of an independent Kampuchean state. But, equally clearly, the withdrawal from the administration of those whom the unfortunate Korb would have called the 'elder brothers' must continue steadily, if the political aspirations of a large number of Kampucheans are ever to be fulfilled.

As I have mentioned, the presence of the Vietnamese army in Kampuchea does not raise the same issues (even among those Khmers who would like most of the advisers to leave immediately). Independence is not likely to mean much for the country if the Democratic Kampuchea army is able to seize power again.

On 21 October 1980, I interviewed the Kampuchean Foreign Minister, Hun Sen, and put the following questions to him:

Q: What do Hanoi and Phnom Penh mean when they say, 'the situation in Kampuchea is irreversible'?

A: It means that no outside force can replace our government with another one.

Q: In the West it is often assumed to mean that Vietnamese troops will never leave Kampuchean territory.

A: That is not what it means at all. Those people are seeing more in it than I do.

Q: Does not the Twenty-Five-Year Friendship Treaty between Vietnam and Kampuchea mean that Vietnamese troops will remain in Kampuchea for 25 years?

A: No. There is some confusion about that among young people here, but it does not mean that.

Q: When will the Vietnamese troops leave Kampuchea?

A: When the Pol Pot problem and the problem of other groups trying to overthrow our government is solved, that is, when Thailand stops allowing China, and the U.S. and France, to support Pol Pot, Khieu Samphan, and Son Sann, and when we have negotiated with Thailand a proper solution to the border problem and the refugee problem. Then there will be no external threat to Kampuchea, and the Vietnamese will leave.

The numerous schools for Khmers set up in Kampuchea, and in Vietnam, by the Salvation Front government with Vietnamese assistance, have played an important part in the development of an official class, administrative ability, and the resurgence of a Kampuchean state. Several Khmers I spoke to had significantly revised their previous anti-Vietnamese feelings after a three-month course in Marxism-Leninism in Ho Chi Minh City. The course itself, they thought, was not always useful, but living in Vietnam had shown them a side of that country they had known little about; the lack of violence on the part of the revolutionary authorities there struck them as a stark contrast to the policies of Democratic Kampuchea. They also mentioned the 'correct policy' towards the Khmer minority in the Mekong Delta, and in one man's case, even 'the beauty' of traditional Vietnamese women's costumes, which, like many Khmers, 'I had never thought were beautiful before'.

Large numbers of Khmers are now prepared to accept the Salvation Front's close links with Vietnam. Although almost none would accept an obviously subordinate Kampuchean role in the future, few see the relationship in those terms at the present time. And the alternatives – a Pol Pot comeback, or renewed civil war and destruction – force many to see consolidation of the P.R.K. regime as the only hope for a stable, independent state.

A lot depends on Vietnamese intentions, which have not been clearly demonstrated. Nothing in the history of the Kampuchea-Vietnam conflict in recent years indicates that it was a result of Vietnamese aggression. But it is up to Hanoi to show in its future actions that it is not out to dominate Kampuchea politically. Steady withdrawal of Vietnam's administrative advisers would be a clear signal of this. And it is up to the West to try to ensure that all material support for Democratic Kampuchea from China and Thailand as well as from Western sources, ceases; and to discontinue its own diplomatic (and covert) support for Democratic Kampuchea. Until that happens, withdrawal of the Vietnamese troops is a gamble on the lives of Kampucheans which, in the light of recent Kampuchean history, few should be prepared to take.

Late one night in October, our car approached Neak Leung once more. Knocking on the door of the ferryman's house, we asked him to take us across the Mekong. The man came out into the hot evening from a game of cards, apologizing about his bare chest. He proudly told us he had worked on this ferry continuously since 1954, except for the Pol Pot period.

In 1973, he said, American B52s had bombed Neak Leung, and 700 people had died. He said he had been wounded even though he was sleeping on the ferry that night, and he pointed to a scar on his forehead. In 1975 the victorious Khmer Rouge had evacuated the town, and he was sent to a distant village near Kratie. Two years later, executions began. '1977 was a terrible year,' he recalled. There had been 1,000 people in the village, but by the end of 1978 'there were no men left to plough the land' – they had all been killed or taken away under mysterious circumstances. He lost eighteen members of his family in those years.

Talking quickly and earnestly, he was clearly overwhelmed that Democratic Kampuchea was a thing of the past, and was enthusiastic about 'the Heng Samrin period'. Looking up at myself and British journalist William Shawcross, he said how happy he was that Kampuchea was receiving foreign aid from so many countries.

In Neak Leung in 1979 he had spent ten days in a political school, probably run along Vietnamese lines. Among other subjects he had been taught 'politics, social action, and science'. 'I have some idea about things now,' he said confidently.

As the ferry started up and we crossed the Mekong in the darkness, I wondered whether Korb, if he were alive to hear this story so similar to his own tragic poem, would have been able to recognize the 'younger brothers' he had described in 1978.

Ben Kiernan
December 1980

Glossary of Khmer Terms

Khmer Terms

achar: a former Buddhist monk or a pagoda ceremonial leader, usually a figure of some respect.

chamcar: word for garden farmlands devoted to crops other than rice, such as tobacco or bananas, usually on the river banks.

Cholon: the Chinese and business centre near Saigon in South Vietnam.

Cochinchina: the southernmost of the three French colonial divisions of Vietnam, including Saigon and the Mekong Delta.

Kampuchea: the Khmer-language term for 'Cambodia' and the official name of the country (for instance in the U.N.) since 1976. Originally it was the name of an ancient Khmer dynasty.

Kampuchea Krom: Khmer term for Cochinchina, the southernmost section of Vietnam including the Mekong Delta. The area was once part of the Angkor Empire and was occupied by Vietnam in the 18th Century.

khum: a Khmer sub-district (sometimes the word is translated as 'village'), consisting of several *phum,* or hamlets.

Khmer Krom: an ethnic Khmer inhabitant of Kampuchea Krom. The term means 'lower Khmer', see *Kampuchea Krom* above.

Khmer Loeu: tribal Kampucheans inhabiting the mountainous north-east provinces. The term means 'highland Khmer'.

phum: Khmer village (sometimes the word is translated as 'hamlet'). It literally means simply 'inhabited place', and could refer to any number of houses from two or three to several hundred.

piastre: the currency of French Indochina, usually denoted by a dollar sign.

rai: measurement of land area, used in the north-west provinces: one-sixth of a hectare.

riel: Kampuchean unit of currency. In the 1960s approximately 30 riels equalled one U.S. dollar. Money was abolished by Pol Pot in 1975, and the riel was only reintroduced by the People's Republic of Kampuchea in early 1980.

srok: Khmer district. A number of srok constitute a province *(khet).*

thang: a Khmer measurement of paddy rice quantities, averaging about 25 kilograms.

wat: Buddhist temple or pagoda.

Names and Organizations

Names and Organizations

Champa: The kingdom of the Cham people, which once controlled most of central Vietnam. Champa was destroyed by Vietnamese southward expansion by the 16th Century. Cham minority populations remain in Vietnam and Kampuchea.

Democratic Party: The major nationalist party tolerated by the French colonial regime after 1945. However it was disbanded under French pressure in 1951, re-formed under a more radical leadership after independence, then disbanded again under pressure from the Sihanouk regime in 1957. After 1970 some former members reconstituted the party and participated in the politics of the Khmer Republic, while others joined the guerrillas in the jungle.

FANK: (Forces Armees Nationales Khmeres): The army of the Lon Nol regime.

FUNK: The French-language acronym for the National United Front of Kampuchea, (NUFK), the coalition formed in 1970 between Prince Sihanouk and the Kampuchean revolutionaries to combat the American-backed Lon Nol regime.

Geneva Conference: International conference in Switzerland in 1954, involving France, the U.S.A., Britain, China, the Soviet Union and the Vietnamese Communists. The parties negotiated the French withdrawal from Indochina and stipulated a temporary divison of Vietnam pending nationwide elections which the Saigon Government and its U.S. backers then refused to allow to be held. In Kampuchea, the Conference handed over power to King Sihanouk, without admitting the Kampuchean revolutionaries to the negotiating process. The International Commission for Supervision and Control was set up to monitor subsequent events in Indochina, including the 1955 elections in Kampuchea (see Part II).

Hem Chieu: A Buddhist monk and active nationalist, arrested in 1942 for preaching anti-French sermons to the Khmer militia. His arrest provoked the 'Umbrella War of 1942' (see Part II). Chieu died in prison in 1943.

Hou Yuon: Described by the *Far Eastern Economic Review* as a guerilla leader with a 'giant intellect' (4 August 1969), 'of truly astounding physical and intellectual strength' (15 January 1970), Hou Youn had a long career in the Kampuchean revolutionary movement.

He was born in 1930 in Saukong district of Kompong Cham Province. His father grew rice and tobacco in the village of Antung Saor on the Mekong River. Hou Yuon distinguished himself at school, and in 1949 was awarded a scholarship to go and study at the University of Paris. A member of the 'Marxist Circle' of Khmer students in France in the early 1950s and Chairman of the General Union of Khmer Students there, in January 1953 he signed a telegram to King Sihanouk accusing him of 'strangling democracy'. Other signatories included Pol Pot and Ieng Sary, although one inside source recalls that these two often differed with Hou Yuon in political discussions during those years. In December 1955 Hou Yuon completed a doctorate in law; part of his thesis on the peasantry is included in Part I of this book. Early in 1956 he returned home, and immediately became involved with other radicals in a 'Committee in Defence of Neutrality', to stiffen Sihanouk's anti-imperialist stand. This campaign achieved success the next year when the fourth National Congress in Phnom Penh, which attracted a crowd of 15,000 and which Hou Yuon addressed on the question, voted to adopt neutrality as a major policy platform.

In 1958 he was elected unopposed to the National Assembly, after joining Sihanouk's Sangkum Party, by his home district of Saukong. The people there referred to him as Ta Mau, or 'dark elder', because of his complexion. The next two years Yuon spent in various Cabinet positions, such as Minister of Economic Planning. He was dismissed from the Cabinet in early 1963 after a serious student demonstration set off a chain reaction that led to the total exclusion of left-wing influence from the Government, and the publication by Sihanouk of a list of 34 'subversives', on which Yuon's name appeared.

The next year he wrote *The Co-operative Question,* partly reproduced here in translation from the Khmer. Despite Sihanouk's attempts to prevent him winning, in the 1966 elections Yuon received 78% of the popular vote in Saukong.

However in April 1967 the Samlaut rebellion broke out. Sihanouk accused Hou Yuon, Khieu Samphan and Hu Nim of instigating it, and they were threatened with a military tribunal. Sihanouk noted that to kill Yuon and Samphan would only make them 'martyrs like the Buddha'. They both took to the jungle the next day, leading to the widespread belief that they had been executed. Resulting protest demonstrations involved 15,000 people in and around Phnom Penh and, in Kompong Cham town, a march by 80 local process workers.

Hou Yuon spent the next three years in the jungle, and when the Lon Nol coup took place in March 1970 he was with Hu Nim, who had also fled Phnom Penh, on top of Mount Aural in the south-west of the country. He was named Minister of the Interior, Communal Reforms and Cooperatives in the resistance government nominally headed by Sihanouk in Peking.

On 10 May 1972, Yuon attended a meeting of some 10,000 people in the southwest liberated zone. A defector, Ith Sarin, later recounted:

> They came from all directions in processions, carrying red flags . . .

> There were two banners welcoming Hou Yuon . . . At 8 p.m. the chairman who had organized the meeting shouted out to welcome Hou Yuon, saying, saying, 'Long live friend Hou Yuon, outstanding son of the people of Kampuchea!' Everybody stood up to look, and warmly applauded him. We were very surprised to see him alive, in the flesh. He waved to us in welcome from the front row of the platform of honour. . . . Hou Yuon gave a long unprepared speech for about three hours . . . After Hou Yuon's speech, the Buddhist monks, the local Khmer Rouge administrators, the army commanders, the political commissars, and the representatives of the Chinese and Vietnamese communities applauded and expressed their support for the revolution.

In October 1972, another defector, a former Khmer Rouge district chief from the southwest told *Areyathor* newspaper that he had 'often worked closely with Hou Yuon'. The defector went on:

> Working as the Khmer Rouge leader, Hou Yuon does not talk very much; he always seems to think very hard before talking. This characteristic seems to be different from his Phnom Penh days . . . He is not fussy about what he eats. He eats whatever the people eat . . . He only wears black clothes, made of *padip*. . . Hou Yuon likes to wear old black clothes when he meets the people. The people of the Zone like him a lot. (Sang Hael, *Niw damban khmae krohom,* Phnom Penh, 1974).

Ith Sarin, for his part portrayed Hou Yuon as 'robust, solid, tall, with a copper complexion, jovial in temperament, very open but close and combative, deeply cultured and politicized. A good leader of men, he rejoiced in guerrilla life. His popularity among his comrades and the inhabitants was uncontested.' Sarin listed Hou Yuon as a member of the Communist Party Central Committee, while Sang Hael quoted 'some former Khmer Rouge' who reported that Yuon was a member of its political bureau. The former Khmer Rouge district chief said. 'The South-west Zone is controlled by the Khmer Rouge whose big leader is Ta [elder] Yuon . . . In the Khmer Rouge regions, those who have the title Ta are usually the military chiefs, big leaders, or supervisors.' Although Hou Yuon appears to have enjoyed considerable influence in the revolutionary movement at that stage, he was definitely sharply downgraded at some point. Ith Sarin wrote in May 1973:

> It was to exploit this popularity and his political credit to the maximum that the National United Front of Kampuchea and the Party Central Committee offered him the honorific portfolio of the Interior. Nowadays, Hou Yuon has no real authority within the party. His Party comrades tended to accuse him of revisionism because his materialistic revoluionary concepts were less rigid, more supple, and more liberal.

Hou Yuon disappeared from sight after the 1975 Khmer Rouge victory and was never officially mentioned by the Pol Pot regime. But Hu Nim, who was arrested by Pol Pot in early 1977 and forced to 'confess' a CIA past under torture, described Hou Yuon in these prison writings as follows:

> Hou Yuon was frontally and openly opposed to the party and the party line before and after liberation. He did not respect the party and did not listen to anyone. He was very individualistic. After the coup in 1970, he thought that Vietnam must be asked to help in the offensive to liberate the east bank of the Mekong River. During a 1970 revolutionary livelihood concept study session with the Organisation, Hou Yuon dared to scold the brothers ['Brother no. 1 and Brother no. 2', a reference to Pol Pot, and perhaps Ieng Sary], saying that the party was using his name as a screen by making him a 'puppet Minister'. Hou Yuon wanted the party to contact the Soviet Union during the war. He was always angry, he did not agree with the party on any problem. After liberation, when the party abolished money and wages and evacuated the people from the cities, Hou Yuon again boldly took a stand against the party line.

He seems to have paid for this with his life, but how and when are unknown.

Hu Nim: A supporter of the Democratic Party in the 1955 elections, Hu Nim went to study law in France from 1955-57, then returned to Kampuchea and was elected to the National Assembly in 1958 after joining Prince Sihanouk's Sangkum Party. He briefly became a Cabinet Minister in 1962, and made two official visits to China before being driven underground by Sihanouk's regime in October 1967, in response to his activities inspired by the Chinese Cultural Revolution. A member of the Central Committee of the Communist Party of Kampuchea, from 1970 he was Information Minister in the revolutionary government, and after 1975 held the same post in Democratic Kampuchea. He seems to have finally broken with Pol Pot, however, early in 1977, and he was arrested, tortured, and then killed on 6 July of that year. A lengthy analysis of his life and fate can be found in the *New Statesman,* 2 May 1980; Timothy Carney's *Communist Party Power in Kampuchea* (Cornell University, 1977) contains a biographical sketch.

Ieng Sary: Born in South Vietnam of mixed Khmer and Chinese Parentage, Ieng Sary was a leading figure, along with Rath Samuoeun and Keng Vannsak, in the 'Marxist Circle' of Khmer Students in France in the early 1950s and led the General Union of Khmer students in Paris before his return to Phnom Penh in the late 1950s, where he took up a teaching job. He went underground in 1963 with Pol Pot and surfaced only in 1971, as Special Envoy from the internal wing of the revolution to Prince Sihanouk's headquarters in Peking. He was Foreign Minister of Democratic Kampuchea from 1975, and one of the top three figures of that regime.

Indochina Communist Party (I.C.P.). Founded by Ho Chi Minh in 1930 as the Vietnamese Communist Party, but later that year its name was changed in response to a Comintern directive. In 1951, the I.C.P. was divided into three

national parties for Vietnam, Laos, and Kampuchea, although close links between them were maintained.
Indochinese Union: A colonial term for French Indochina.
Khieu Samphan: A junior member of the 'Marxist Circle' of Khmer students in Paris in the early 1950s. He completed a thesis on the Kampuchean economy in 1959, and then returned to Phnom Penh where he established a leftist French-language newspaper. A Cabinet Minister in 1962, he was a member of the National Assembly from that year until 1967, when he fled to the jungle in fear of government repression. Minister of Defence and then Deputy Prime Minister in the revolutionary government from 1970, and Head of State of Democratic Kampuchea from 1976. In late 1979 he replaced his colleague Pol Pot as Prime Minister of the overthrown Democratic Kampuchea regime, although Pol Pot retained control of what remained of party and military affairs.
Khmer Republic: The state created after the Lon Nol coup against Prince Sihanouk's regime in March 1970. The Republic was defeated by the Khmer Rouge Communists in April 1975. A good outline of its history and relations with its U.S. patrons can be found in William Shawcross's *Sideshow.*
Khmer Rouge (Red Khmers): General term (coined by Prince Sihanouk) for the movement led by the Communists. After 1975 the term referred to the Pol Pot regime and not to the dissident Communists who (with Vietnamese assistance) eventually overthrew it.
Lon Nol: Served in the French colonial forces, then became Minister of Defence under Sihanouk for most of the 1954-70 period; with U.S. backing he led the overthrow of Sihanouk in March 1970 and withdrew to the U.S. in March 1975 on the eve of the defeat of the Republic of which he was Head of State.
N.L.F.: The National Liberation Front of South Vietnam (called the 'Viet Cong' by its opponents), which was formed in 1960 and led the struggle against the Americans.
NUFK: See FUNK.
OROC (Office Royal de Cooperation): The Royal Co-operative Office of the Sihanouk regime, 1954-70.
Pach Chhoeun: A small businessman in Phnom Penh, he edited *Nokor Wat* and was a key figure in resistance to the French in the 1930s. Leader of the 1942 demonstration, he was imprisoned from then until 1945. He worked briefly with the Communist Viet Minh in 1946, then surrendered to the French and became Minister of Information in a Democratic Party government in 1951, before its dissolution by Sihanouk. Strongly anti-monarchist, he became an elder statesman of the Khmer Republic in 1970, and died in Phnom Penh in 1971.
Pathet Lao: The revolutionary united front in Laos which fought the U.S. with the help of the Vietnamese Communists. In 1975 the Pathet Lao assumed control of the country.
Phouk Chhay: Maoist leader of the General Association of Khmer Students in the Sihanouk period. Jailed by Sihanouk in 1967 but released in 1970, he

fled to the jungle and became political commissar of the revolutionary armed forces of the South-west Zone and a member of the party Central Commitee. Never officially mentioned by the Pol Pot regime, he was arrested in 1977 and killed on the same day as Hu Nim.
Pou Kombo: Led a rebellion against the French and King Norodom, 1865-67; he is credited with being Kampuchea's first anti-colonial hero. He was also known as Achar Leak (see General Introduction).
Pracheachon ('Citizens' party). usually known as the Pracheachon Group: A public section of the underground People's Revolutionary Party formed in 1951 by the separation of the Indochina Communist Party into three national Communist parties. The Pracheachon retained strong links with the Vietnamese Communists. It contested the 1955 and 1958 elections, without success (see Part II). Most of its leaders, including Non Suon and Chou Chet, were jailed by Sihanouk in 1962. When released in 1970 they joined the guerrilla movement, but several former party members such as Pol Pot's brother Saloth Chhay formed a new 'Pracheachon' under the auspices of the Khmer Republic of Lon Nol. Non Suon, Chou Chet, and most other Pracheachon figures were executed by the Pol Pot regime between 1976 and 1978.
P.R.G.: The Provisional Revolutionary Government of South Vietnam, established by the N.L.F. and its southern allies in 1969, in the liberated zones of South Vietnam.
Samlaut: Scene of the outbreak of the 1967-8 rebellions, in southern Battambang province of Kampuchea; see Part II.
Sangkum: The Sangkum Reastr Niyum, or Popular Socialist Community, was formed in 1955 by Sihanouk after he abdicated the throne to play a direct role in the political arena. The Sangkum held all the seats in the National Assembly from 1955 to 1970, when Sihanouk was overthrown and it was dissolved.
Sieu Heng: Born in Battambang of a Khmer family from South Vietnam, Heng began resistance activities in 1944 (see Part II). A leading Issarak figure, he visited Vietnam and China during the 1946-54 anti-French struggle, then returned to north-west Kampuchea to take a prominent role in the 'National Liberation Central Committee' based there. After the Geneva Conference, he was evacuated to Hanoi on an International Commission for Supervision and Control plane. However, he separated from Issarak Leaders Son Ngoc Minh and Leav Keo Moni almost immediately and walked back to Kampuchea through the jungle. According to the 1973 Party History, Sieu Heng then became Secretary of the Communist Party 'temporary central Committee', which was set up 'not in conformity with the Party's conditions'. On his own later admission, in a 1970 interview with U.S. State Department Officer Andy Antippus, Heng began working for Lon Nol in 1955. He secretly provided the general with intelligence on party organizations and cadres, many of whom were liquidated during the next few years. He officially defected to the government in 1959, and became a farmer in Battambang. After 1970 he was an officer in the Lon Nol regime's armed forces. The 1973 Party

History records that as temporary Party leader 'Sieu Heng taught the people that there were no social classes in our Kampuchean society . . . They had to follow the ruling class with Sihanouk at the head. . .' However, the document also says Heng was opposed to party struggle against the 'Sam Sary and Dap Chuon groups', establishment cliques which tried to overthrow Sihanouk. Whatever political line Sieu Heng ostensibly advocated within the Communist Party, the fact that while holding the Party's highest post he was working for its enemies facilitated the destruction of its organs and the usurpation of party leadership by the Pol Pot group.

Sihanouk, Norodom: Placed on the throne of Kampuchea in 1941 at the age of 18, Norodom Sihanouk functioned as part of the French (and, for six months in 1945, Japanese) colonial apparatus until 1952. At that point he saw the strength of the nationalist movement and realized that if he did not establish nationalist credentials he would be swept away along with French rule. He began a 'Royal Crusade for Independence' involving overseas travels during which he put strong pressure on France in public statements. He was successful in winning the main trappings of independence during the next two years. He abdicated the throne in 1955 and ruled the country from then until 1970 through his Sangkum Party. His authoritarian, paternalistic style, oscillated between a degree of royal benevolence, neglect, and fierce repression, but in foreign policy he maintained a fairly firm anti-imperialist stand based on neutrality combined with at times important assistance to the struggle of the N.L.F. in south Vietnam. Overthrown by Lon Nol in 1970, he assumed nominal leadership of FUNK from his Peking headquarters, returning to Phnom Penh after victory in 1975. The next year, however, he was put under house arrest by the Pol Pot regime and was replaced by Khieu Samphan as Head of State. He was sent to the United Nations in early 1979 to represent the Pol Pot regime immediately before its overthrow by Vietnamese-backed forces, but has since broken with the Pol Pot group and spent most of 1979 in North Korea.

Si Votha: A prince who led anti-colonial uprisings in Kampuchea in 1861, 1875-6, and 1885-9. He died in the jungle, still unsubdued by the French, in 1892.

So Phim: Leader of the Communist resistance to Pol Pot's group before being killed in May 1978. An Issarak veteran and member of Sieu Heng's temporary Party Central Committee in 1954, Phim appears to have worked underground during the Sihanouk period while maintaining contact with the Vietnamese communists. After 1970 he became Chairman of the Eastern Zone revolutionary forces as well as Party Secretary for the zone, a position which he held until his death. He was also called So Vanna, Muoi Su, Hay So, and Sos Sar Yan or simply Yan.

Son Ngoc Minh: Probably the first Khmer member of a Communist Party, Minh became leader of the first official Kampuchean Communist organization in 1951. His real name was apparently Thach Choeun, and he was born in the Mekong Delta (see Introduction). After Geneva he withdrew to Hanoi, where he lived until 1972. Shortly after being moved to Peking for medical treatment at the request of the leaders of the Communist Party of Kampuchea, he collapsed and died.

Son Ngoc Thanh: Born in south Vietnam of mixed Khmer-Vietnamese parentage, he received a high school education in France, and on his return became a librarian at the Buddhist Institute in Phnom Penh in the 1930s. A leader of the Khmer nationalist movement at that time, he founded *Nokor Wat,* the first Khmer-language newspaper, with Pach Chhoeun in 1936. He played a role in the 1942 demonstration against the French, and after its repression spent the next three years in Japan. After a brief period in office under Japanese auspices in Phnom Penh, he was jailed by returning French forces. Released in 1951, he took to the jungle soon afterwards. He spent the next 20 years engaged in clandestine anti-Sihanouk activity in south Vietnam and Thailand as leader of the Khmer Serei, a movement descended from a Japanese-sponsored force which developed close links with U.S. intelligence and Special Forces. After Sihanouk was overthrown in 1970 he returned to public life in Kampuchea, and in 1971 was named Prime Minister of Lon Nol's Khmer Republic. He soon fell out with Lon Nol, however, and returned to south Vietnam, where he is reported to have died in 1976.

Son Sen: A Khmer born in south Vietnam, Son Sen studied in France in the early 1950s and formed part of the 'Marxist Circle' of Khmer students there. Like Ieng Sary he then returned to a teaching job, in his case at the Kompong Kantuot Training College for Teachers, near Phnom Penh. He also went underground with Pol Pot in 1963. He was Defence Minister of Democratic Kampuchea from 1975, and a leading member of the Pol Pot group.

Theravada Buddhism: The Buddhism of the Lesser Vehicle practised in Kampuchea, Thailand, Laos, Burma and Sri Lanka. Its philosophy is more introspective and less worldly than the Buddhism of the Greater Vehicle (Mahayana), which is practised in China, Japan, Korea, Tibet and Vietnam.

Tou Samouth: A former Khmer Buddhist monk from south Vietnam and a student at the Pali School of Higher Learning in Phnom Penh in the early 1940s. Samouth became deputy leader of the People's Revolutionary Party founded in 1951, and General Secretary of the Communist Party in 1960. He was assassinated in 1962, and Pol Pot took his place.

Tung Padevat (Revolutionary Flags): The internal monthly magazine of the Communist Party of Kampuchea under Pol Pot. Several issues only have become available in the West.

V.C./N.V.A.: The 'Viet Cong/North Vietnam Army', the usual American and Lon Nol regime term for their Vietnamese Communist enemies, southern and northern.

Viet Minh: The Communist-led league for the independence of Vietnam, formed by Ho Chi Minh in 1941.

Bibliography

Boua, C. 'The Situation of Women and Girls in Kampuchea Today', (Bangkok, UNICEF, 1981).

Boua, C., Kiernan, B., and Barnett, A., 'Bureaucracy of Death: Documents from inside Pol Pot's Torture Machine', *New Statesman,* 2 May 1980, pp.669-676.

Burchett, Wilfred, *Mekong Upstream* (Hanoi, 1957).

Burchett, Wilfred, *The Second Indochina War: Cambodia and Laos Today* (London, Lorrimer, 1970).

Caldwell, Malcolm and Lek Hor Tan, *Cambodia in the Southeast Asian War* (New York, Monthly Review Press, 1973).

Carney, Timothy, *Communist Party Power in Kampuchea (Cambodia): Documents and Discussion,* Cornell University Southeast Asia Program Data Paper No. 106, 1977.

Chandler, David P., *The Land and People of Cambodia,* (Philadelphia, Lippincott, 1972).

Chandler, David P., *Cambodia before the French: Politics in a Tributary Kingdom, 1794-1847,* (Ann Arbor, University microfilms, 1974).

Chandler, David P., 'Royally-sponsored Human Sacrifices in Nineteenth Century Cambodia: the Cult of *Nak Ta Me Sa* at Ba Phnom', *Journal of the Siam Society,* July 1974.

Chandler, David P., 'An Anti-Vietnamese Rebellion in Early Nineteenth Century Cambodia: Pre-colonial Imperialism and a Pre-nationalist Response'. *Journal of Southeast Asian Studies,* March 1957.

Chandler, David P., 'The Constitution of Democratic Kampuchea: The Semantics of Revolutionary Change', *Pacific Affairs,* Fall 1976.

Chandler, David P., 'Transformation in Cambodia', *Commonweal,* 1 April 1977.

Chandler, David P., 'The Tragedy of Cambodian History', *Pacific Affairs,* Fall 1979.

Chomsky, Noam and Edward Herman, *The Political Economy of Human Rights,* Vol. 2: *After the Cataclysm: Postwar Indochina and the Reconstruction of Imperial Ideology,* (Boston, Southend Press, 1979).

Debre, Francois, *Cambodge: la revolution de la foret,* (Paris, Flammarion, 1976).

Delvert, Jean, *Le paysan cambodgien,* (Paris, Mouton, 1960).

Forest, Alain, *Histoire d'une colonisation sans heurts: Le Cambodge et la colonisation francaise (1897-1920),* (Paris, Editions l'Harmattan, 1979).

Heder, Stephen, 'Kampuchea's Armed Struggle: The Origins of an Independent Revolution', *Bulletin of Concerned Asian Scholars,* Vol. II, No. 1, 1979.

Heder, Stephen, 'The Kampuchean-Vietnamese Conflict', *Southeast Asian Affairs,* Institute of Southeast Asian Studies, Singapore, 1979.

Hildebrand, George C. and Porter D. Gareth, *Cambodia: Starvation and Revolution,* (New York, Monthly Review Press, 1976).

Kampuchea Dossier (Hanoi, Foreign Languages Publishing House, 1978-9), 3 parts.

Khieu Samphan, *Cambodia's Economy and Industrial Development,* doctoral thesis, Paris, 1959. Translated by Laura Summers, Cornell University Southeast Asia Program Data Paper No. 111, 1979.

Kiernan, Ben, 'Kheiu Samphan: Cambodia's Revolutionary Leader', *Dyason House Papers,* June 1975, pp.5-8.

Kiernan, Ben, 'Social Cohesion in Revolutionary Cambodia', *Australian Outlook,* Vol. 30, No. 3, December 1976, pp.371-386.

Kiernan, Ben, 'Why's Kampuchea Gone to Pot?', *Nation Review* (Melbourne), 17-23 November 1978.

Kiernan, Ben, 'Vietnam and the Governments and People of Kampuchea', *Bulletin of Concerned Asian Scholars,* Vol. II, No. 4, 1979, pp.19-25.

Livre Noir: Faits et preuves des actes d'aggression et d'annexion du Vietnam contre le Kampuchea, Ministry of Foreign Affairs of Democratic Kampuchea, Phnom Penh, September 1978, 2 editions.

Meyer, Charles, *Derriere le sourire khmer* (Paris, Plon, 1971).

Osborne, Milton E., *The French Presence in Cochinchina and Cambodia, 1859-1905; Rule and response,* (Ithaca, Cornell University Press, 1969).

Osborne, Milton E., *Politics and Power in Cambodia,* (Melbourne, Longmans, 1973).

Osborne, Milton E., 'Peasant Politics in Cambodia: the 1916 Affair', *Modern Asian Studies,* Vol. 12, 1978, pp.217-243.

Pin Yatay, *L'Utopie meurtriere; un rescape du genocide cambodgien temoigne,* (Paris, Laffont, 1979).

Ponchard, Francois, *Ca mbodia Year Zero,* (Penguin, London, 1978).

Porter, D. Gareth, 'The Sino-Vietnamese Conflict in Southeast Asia', *Current History,* December 1978.

Prud'homme, Remy, *L'Economie du Cambodge,* (Paris, 1969).

Reddi, V.M.,*A History of the Cambodian Independence Movement, 1863-1953,* (Tirupati, Sri Venkatesvara University, 1973).

Sihanouk, Norodom, with Wilfred Burchett, *My War with the C.I.A.,* (Penguin 1973).

Sihanouk, Norodom, *Chroniques de guerre . . . et d'espoir.* (Paris, Hachette-Stock, 1979).

Summers, Laura, 'Defining the revolutionary state in Cambodia', *Current*

History, Vol. 71, 1976, pp. 213-17, 228.

Summers, Laura, 'Democratic Kampuchea', in B. Szajkowski (ed.), *Marxist Governments: A World Survey,* (London: Macmillan, 1980).

Shawcross, William, *Sideshow: Kissinger, Nixon and the Destruction of Cambodia,* (London, Andre Deutsch, 1979).

Thion, Serge, with Jean-Claude Pomonti, *La crise cambodgienne: des courtisans aux partisans,* (Paris, Gallimard, 1971).

Thion, Serge, 'L'Ingratitude des crocodiles', *Les Temps modernes,* January 1980.

Index

BARNES & NOBLE
NO REFUND W/O LABEL
1-86 $14.95